THE
OLD TESTAMENT GUIDE

For our grandchildren
Daniel and Bethan, Neve, Lily, and Arlo.

THE
OLD TESTAMENT GUIDE

Andrew Knowles

Text copyright © 2001 Andrew Knowles

This edition copyright © 2020 Lion Hudson IP Limited

The right of Andrew Knowles to be identified as the author of this work has been asserted by him in accordance with the Copyright, Designs and Patents Act 1988.

All rights reserved. No part of this publication may be reproduced or transmitted in any form or by any means, electronic or mechanical, including photocopy, recording, or any information storage and retrieval system, without permission in writing from the publisher.

Published by
Lion Hudson Limited
Wilkinson House, Jordan Hill Business Park
Banbury Road, Oxford OX2 8DR, England
www.lionhudson.com

ISBN 978 1 9125 5238 2

e-ISBN 978 1 9125 5239 9

The Bible Guide first edition 2001

Acknowledgments

Unless otherwise stated, scripture quotations are taken from the Holy Bible, New International Version, copyright © 1973, 1978, 1984 International Bible Society. Used by permission of Hodder & Stoughton, a member of the Hodder Headline Group. All rights reserved. 'NIV' is a trademark of International Bible Society. UK trademark number 1448790.

Scripture quotations marked NRSV are from the New Revised Standard Version of the Bible copyright © 1989 by the Division of Christian Education of the National Council of Churches in the USA. Used by permission. All rights reserved worldwide.

Scripture quotations marked KJV are taken from The Authorized (King James) Version. Rights in the Authorized Version are vested in the Crown. Reproduced by permission of the Crown's patentee, Cambridge University Press.

Scripture quotations marked The Message are taken from The Message, copyright © by Eugene H. Peterson 1993, 1994, 1995, 1996, 2000, 2001, 2002. Used by permission of NavPress Publishing Group.

Scripture quotations marked the New Heart English Bible are taken from the New Heart English Bible (NHEB). Public domain.

All maps and diagrams by Tony Cantale Graphics.

Cover image © wjarek@shutterstock.com

A catalogue record for this book is available from the British Library

CONTENTS

Author's Preface 6
What is the Bible? 8
Genesis 21
Exodus 60
Leviticus 95
Numbers 127
Deuteronomy 146
Joshua 165
Judges 181
Ruth 196
1 and 2 Samuel 200
1 and 2 Kings 223
1 and 2 Chronicles 261
Ezra and Nehemiah 303
Esther 327
Job 337
Psalms 355
Proverbs 382
Ecclesiastes 399
Song of Songs 416

Isaiah 423
Jeremiah 460
Lamentations 496
Ezekiel 504
Daniel 536
Hosea 550
Joel 556
Amos 560
Obadiah 568
Jonah 571
Micah 575
Nahum 580
Habakkuk 583
Zephaniah 587
Haggai 592
Zechariah 595
Malachi 604
The Deuterocanonical Books 609
Index 613

AUTHOR'S PREFACE

When I began to write the original single-volume *Bible Guide,* nearly thirty years ago, I resolved that the book should be 'simple'. The result was, I hope, a companion to the Bible that was helpful to those who sought further understanding of the text, as well as those preparing teaching or study courses. It has been most rewarding, from time to time, to receive news that this has been the case. For ease of use, the current Lion Scholar edition of *The Bible Guide* is now in two volumes, *The Old Testament Guide* and *The New Testament Guide.*

The original *Bible Guide* was first published in 2001. Two fine scholars, both friends from student days, gave valuable advice: Dr Chris Wright (now of the Langham Partnership), and Dr Stephen Travis of St John's College Nottingham (now St John's College of Mission). Two experienced tutors, Dr John Bimson, and the Revd Mike Butterworth, gave generous access to their teaching notes. Martin Manser took forensic care with the referencing and indexing, and alerted me to any gaps that needed to be filled. And Canon David Winter reviewed the manuscript with astringency and enthusiasm: a critical friend indeed.

I owe everything to those who have taught and continue to teach me the Bible. I dedicated the original book to my own Bible class leader, Gordon Buchanan, who, on Sunday mornings and as part of a very small group, faithfully taught us the Scriptures. The list of those who have challenged and inspired me since, by the grace and courage of their lively faith, is very long indeed.

I am indebted to Lyn Roberts and her team at Lion Hudson, for their care and encouragement in producing this new edition.

The world has changed since 2001, with climate change, militant Islamism, and the advance of AI presenting challenges and opportunities that will shape humanity for generations to come. How shall we live – as individuals, families, communities, and nations – if wisdom, justice, and peace are to prevail? I know of no greater or more vital resource than the Bible to convey to us the nature, presence, and purpose of the living God. Here is truth to guide, nurture, love, and restore us. God has, through his son Jesus Christ, done all that is necessary to save and renew this world. What remains is for us to become partners in this amazing and privileged task.

Andrew Knowles
Kendal
Epiphany 2020

WHAT IS THE BIBLE?

The Christian Bible (which means book) is a collection of books that has been divided into two parts.

The first part is known as the Old Testament. These are Jewish Scriptures and include ancient stories, histories, laws, poems, prophecies, and wise sayings. The 'testament' of the title refers to a binding covenant (an agreement) between God (Yahweh) and the people of Israel (the Jews). In this covenant God chooses the Jewish people (Israel), blesses them, and blesses the world through them. It was a covenant that was sealed and regularly renewed by the sacrifice of animals. The blood of bulls, yearling lambs, and goats atoned for the sins of individuals and communities through being sacrificed.

The second part of the Bible is known as the New Testament. This 'testament' marks a fresh initiative by God, who sends his Son, Jesus, into the world to complete the mission first entrusted to the Jews. The God who was first revealed to the Jews is the only God, now made fully known through his Son Jesus Christ.

The New Testament begins with four accounts of the life of Jesus (the Gospels), and goes on to cover, in narrative and letters, the early experiences and expansion of the Christian church.

Christians understand that this new covenant commitment by God was most fully expressed in the death of Jesus. The sacrifice of Jesus was a once and for all event that atoned for the sins of all people for all time. His death is commemorated in the Christian church's service of Eucharist or Holy Communion. Bread is broken and shared and wine is poured out and drunk as a sign of the complete self-giving of Jesus for all humankind.

What is the Old Testament?

The Old Testament is a collection of Jewish Scriptures. Through various kinds of literature, from ancient stories of human origins to visions of

Books of the Old Testament	
Law	Genesis
	Exodus
	Leviticus
	Numbers
	Deuteronomy
History	Joshua
	Judges
	Ruth
	1 Samuel
	2 Samuel
	1 Kings
	2 Kings
	1 Chronicles
	2 Chronicles
	Ezra
	Nehemiah
	Esther
Poetry and Wisdom	Job
	Psalms
	Proverbs
	Ecclesiastes
	Song of Songs
Prophecy	Isaiah
	Jeremiah
	Lamentations
	Ezekiel
	Daniel
	Hosea
	Joel
	Amos
	Obadiah
	Jonah
	Micah
	Nahum
	Habakkuk
	Zephaniah
	Haggai
	Malachi
Deuterocanonical books/Apocrypha	

cosmic battle, an adventure of faith unfolds. It is the history of the Jewish people in the light of their experiences of God.

The founding father of the Jewish people is Abraham. Abraham believes God's promise that he will be the precursor of a great nation, and that God will give them a land to call their own: the 'promised land' of Canaan.

Abraham and his wife, Sarah, have only a fleeting glimpse of all that God will do, but the promises are passed on through the generations of their descendants. Along the way, there is slavery in Egypt, from which God rescues his people in the Exodus. And there is defeat and captivity in Babylonia (the 'Exile'), from which the Israelites are delivered and restored to their homeland.

Central to the Old Testament story is the Jewish Law ('torah', or 'yoke'), which God gives to his people through a great leader, Moses. The foundation of the law is the 'Decalogue', or Ten Commandments. The first four commandments outline Israel's duty to God. The last six commandments provide boundaries for behaviour within the community.

The law is Israel's great treasure. When learned and lived, the law enables God's people to be at peace with God and with one another.

The Old Testament teaches us that God speaks with his people to guide, correct, and encourage them. Some individuals, known as prophets, have a responsibility to speak to the people on God's behalf. They warn of dire consequences if God's law is disobeyed, and give inspiring assurances of the blessings of obedience.

There are also writers who compose or collect wise sayings and words of advice. These are distilled into proverbs or developed as reflections on the wonders, ironies, and mysteries of life.

Finally, at the heart of these Jewish Scriptures is a collection of prayers and worship songs, both joyous and soulful. These are the psalms which have resourced God's people, both Jewish and Christian, through all the ages since they were first composed.

The stories that were first passed on by word of mouth are written down. The lessons of history that God both judges his people and saves them are recorded. The collections of proverbs and psalms are gathered and set in order. The messages and visions of the prophets are preserved, either because they have proved to be true, or because they hold deep insights for the future.

These diverse Scriptures, from different authors over many years, become a treasured library of Jewish literature. They are painstakingly written on parchment and stored in rolls or scrolls. When scrolls or their fragments come to light, even though they vary in age by a thousand years, the copying by the scribes is found to be faithful and accurate. These Scriptures speak of a God who is forever present and true. This is the Hebrew Bible, the Christian Old Testament.

The Old Testament story

'In the beginning...'

The earliest stories in the Bible are of Adam and Eve, Cain and Abel, Noah's flood, and the tower of Babel (Genesis 1–11). They have much in common with myths, as they portray the ages before recorded history. They deal with how things began and depict the tension between God's holiness and human sin.

Then comes the story of Abram who became Abraham – the ancestor of the nation of Israel. Abram responds to God's call to leave his home and become a nomadic shepherd. By a solemn covenant, God promises to make Abraham the father of a great nation and to bless the world through his descendants. He also promises to give him the land of Canaan. It is because Abraham believes God against all odds that he is known as 'the father of the faithful'.

The whole Bible story flows from God's covenant with Abraham, to bless him and the whole world through him (Genesis 12–36).

Abraham's son is Isaac and his grandson is Jacob. They are the promise-bearers, the heirs of the covenant, the ancestors of the nation of Israel. It is Jacob who is given the name Israel.

Jacob has twelve sons, who become the patriarchs of the twelve tribes of Israel. One of these sons is Jacob's favourite, Joseph. Joseph becomes a slave and prisoner in Egypt, but rises to become the country's first minister (Genesis 37–50).

'Let my people go!'

In Egypt, the Israelites (Hebrews) sink into slavery. God rescues them through the leadership of Moses, who is a Hebrew brought up as an Egyptian prince. God inflicts a series of plagues on the Egyptians, climaxing in the death of all their first-born sons in a single night. The Hebrews are spared when the angel of death 'passes over' their homes – hence the night and its special meal are called 'Passover'.

Moses leads the Israelites out of Egypt across the Red Sea (or Sea of Reeds). This is the exodus – the dramatic escape from slavery by which God rescues his people and begins to make them a nation (Exodus 1–15).

Moses is to lead the Israelites to their Promised Land of Canaan. It is a short journey, but it takes forty years. God gives the people his law (the Ten Commandments) at Mount Sinai, but they rebel by making and worshipping a golden calf.

An entire generation dies in the wilderness and even Moses himself is not allowed to enter the Promised Land. He does, however, receive God's instructions for the building of the tabernacle. This is a tent where God dwells among his people, surrounded by an enclosure where they offer sacrifices. The tabernacle is a forerunner of the temple (Exodus 16–40).

God's plans for his people

God gives Moses instructions on how to appoint priests, offer sacrifices and celebrate festivals (the book of Leviticus). Israel's experiences in the wilderness and the approach to Canaan are narrated (the book of Numbers). As they are about to enter Canaan, the 'Promised Land', Moses reviews the lessons God has taught them and the law he has given them (the book of Deuteronomy). Moses is not permitted to go into the Promised Land.

The conquest of Canaan

Moses is succeeded by Joshua ('God saves'), who leads the campaign to conquer the land of Canaan (Joshua 1–12). It is a campaign in which God fights for his people, most famously in the collapsing of the walls of Jericho.

At the end of his life, Joshua divides the land between the tribes of Israel. The Israelites are exposed to the customs and religion of the Canaanites, who worship the fertility gods of Baal. Joshua challenges them to be faithful to the Lord their God. The land is never completely conquered until the reign of King David.

The judges

After Joshua there is no clear leader. Israel is ruled by 'judges' who emerge from time to time to tackle a crisis or fight an enemy (the book of Judges). The best-known judge is Samson, to whom God gives great strength to fight the Philistines. The nation disintegrates into social and moral chaos.

The bloodthirsty adventures of the judges are offset by the love story of Ruth and Boaz. They are the ancestors of King David (the book of Ruth).

Prophets and kings

Samuel and David

The last of the judges is Samuel, who is also a prophet. Samuel is brought up at the shrine at Shiloh, where he sees the corruption of the priests. When he is old, the people ask him to appoint a king (1 Samuel).

Samuel believes that only God is Israel's king. He tries to persuade them against having a human king, but the people want to be like the other nations. God guides Samuel to anoint Saul as Israel's first king.

Saul is a man of royal appearance, but he is not completely obedient to God. He suffers from depression and becomes jealous of the young hero, David. It is David who shows true faith in God by slaying the Philistine giant, Goliath. Samuel seeks out David and anoints him to be Israel's next king.

David and Solomon

David is Israel's greatest king, reigning around 1000 BC. He is able to unite the rival tribes of Israel and protect the nation from her enemies. He captures the city of Jebus and makes it Jerusalem, 'city of peace'. He brings the ark of the covenant, the symbol of God's presence, to Jerusalem. He establishes peace and justice for all, and makes preparations to build a temple (2 Samuel).

David is a man who listens to God and obeys God. His many psalms express a wide range of feelings towards God, from high praise to near despair (the book of Psalms). In a tragic error of judgment David has an affair with Bathsheba, the wife of one of his soldiers. He loses his moral authority, fails to govern his sons and suffers the rebellion of one of them, Absalom.

David is succeeded by Solomon, who is his son by Bathsheba. Solomon asks God for wisdom to rule Israel well. His wisdom becomes legendary and he is an author and collector of wise sayings (the book of Proverbs, Song of Songs).

Solomon establishes a wealthy and well-organized kingdom. He builds and dedicates a fine temple for God. However, he contracts many marriages with foreign women, who introduce him to their pagan gods. He also disrupts Israel's rural society. He presses large numbers of people into the army and building projects. He imposes heavy taxation to pay for his lavish lifestyle and grandiose schemes.

The two kingdoms

After the reign of Solomon, the nation of Israel splits into two kingdoms (the books of Kings and Chronicles). The northern kingdom is composed of ten tribes and keeps the name Israel. The southern kingdom retains Jerusalem and the temple and is ruled by the descendants of David and Solomon. It is called Judah.

The northern kingdom of Israel

The first ruler of the northern kingdom is Jeroboam. He prevents his people worshipping in Jerusalem by building rival sanctuaries at Dan (in the north) and Beersheba (in the south). He sets up calf idols and claims that they are Israel's true gods.

Israel has a succession of kings, of whom the greatest is Omri. He establishes Samaria as a strong capital. He also marries his son, Ahab, to a Phoenician princess called Jezebel. Jezebel introduces worship of the Baal-god Melkart as a major religion in Israel and has many of God's prophets killed.

Jezebel is opposed by the prophet Elijah. Elijah predicts a long drought (the Baals are supposed to send rain) and defeats the Baal prophets in a contest at Mount Carmel. Elijah is succeeded by Elisha, whose ministry includes the extraordinary healing of Naaman, an enemy commander, from leprosy. The evil reign of Ahab is ended by Jehu. Jehu establishes Israel's longest dynasty, lasting almost 100 years.

During the 9th century BC, Israel's powerful neighbour is Syria, with her capital Damascus. Syria takes territory from a weak Israel, until she herself is invaded by Assyria (803 BC).

Jehu's grandson is Jeroboam II (about 841–753 BC). He is able to recapture lost ground and restore Israel's borders. During his reign Israel becomes secure and prosperous. There are signs of religious enthusiasm, too, as pilgrims journey to worship at sanctuaries such as Bethel and Gilgal.

A prophet arrives from the south with a revolutionary message. He is Amos, a shepherd, and he condemns both the wealth and the worship of Israel. It is wealth which is made by exploiting the poor. It is worship which makes no difference to an immoral and unjust society.

Another prophet, Hosea, likens Israel to an unfaithful wife. She plays the whore with other gods. Hosea should know, as this is the story of his own marriage. Both Hosea and God long to win back their loved ones.

The last thirty years of the northern kingdom are overshadowed by the threat of the powerful Assyrian empire. Both Ahab and Jehu pay tribute to prevent Assyria invading, as does a later king, Menahem.

In 735 BC Israel forms an alliance with Syria against Assyria. Together, they invade Judah, which in turn calls on Assyria for help. The Assyrian emperor, Tiglath-Pileser, conquers Syria and cripples Israel. Israel's capital, Samaria, attempts a further rebellion and is besieged. After a three-year siege Samaria is captured by the new Assyrian king, Shalmaneser V.

This is the end of the northern kingdom. Amos had predicted such a fate as God's punishment for Israel's unfaithfulness. The people of Israel are deported and replaced by a mixture of Syrians and Babylonians.

This new population, so mixed in race and religion, will become the Samaritans.

The southern kingdom of Judah

When the nation splits, Judah keeps the capital city of Jerusalem, with its temple and priesthood. Judah's kings are the royal line descending from David. These factors give the people of the southern kingdom a great sense of security, because they believe that God will always protect his temple and his king. The truth is that Judah is poor and unattractive to a conqueror.

During the 8th century BC, Judah's most successful king is Uzziah. He reigns for fifty-two years, and is able to strengthen Judah's defences and fortify Jerusalem. Judah gains prosperity and confidence at this time. In the uncertainty which follows Uzziah's death, the prophet Isaiah has a magnificent vision of Judah's true king, the Holy One of Israel (Isaiah 6).

After the fall of the northern kingdom, the southern kingdom continues for 135 years.

Judah is blessed with a good king in Hezekiah. He restores the temple and purges the nation of idols. The leading prophets at this time are Isaiah and Micah, both of whom live in Jerusalem.

Judah is a small country, overshadowed by Assyria to the north and Egypt to the south. Isaiah and Micah advise King Hezekiah to stay neutral and rely on God; but the king pays tribute to appease Assyria and considers a rebellion in alliance with Egypt.

In 701 BC the Assyrian king, Sennacherib, besieges Jerusalem. The city is saved by a miracle when the Assyrian army is stricken by plague. Isaiah's advice was proved to be correct.

Hezekiah is succeeded by his son, Manasseh. He is an evil king who reintroduces the Baal-gods and other occult practices.

Manasseh's grandson is Josiah, who is only eight years old when he becomes king. When he comes of age, Josiah turns his nation to God once again. Zephaniah is prophesying at this time, and in 627 BC the young Jeremiah is also called to be a prophet.

During repairs to the temple, in 622 BC, the Book of the Law is found. This may be a copy of Deuteronomy. Josiah has it read aloud in public. He then leads his people in renewing their covenant with God, destroying pagan idols throughout the land and celebrating the Passover in Jerusalem.

Meanwhile, Jeremiah is certain that Judah is about to fall. This will be God's judgment, despite the reforms of recent years. Another prophet, Habakkuk, receives the astonishing message that God will use the power of Babylon to punish Judah.

To most people the destruction of Jerusalem and the temple is unthinkable. God will never allow it to happen. When King Jehoiakim has a scroll of Jeremiah's prophecies read to him, he shreds it into a fire, piece by piece.

In 616 BC the international scene undergoes a major change. The Babylonians invade Assyria and, in 612 BC, destroy her capital, Nineveh. A story about the prophet Jonah describes Nineveh repenting; but another prophet, Nahum, rejoices at her downfall.

In 609 BC Pharaoh Neco of Egypt tries to assist Assyria against the Babylonians. He is defeated and killed at the Battle of Carchemish on the River Euphrates. So Babylon becomes the reigning superpower in the region.

The book of Daniel describes how Daniel, an exiled Jew who remains faithful to God, becomes a valued adviser to successive pagan kings. His bravery and wisdom make him a role model for all persecuted Jews in future generations.

In 597 BC, on the orders of King Nebuchadnezzar, the Babylonian armies capture Jerusalem. They take King Jehoiachin (Jehoiakim's son) and 3,000 of the leading citizens as prisoners into exile. Among the captives is a young priest who will also become a prophet. His name is Ezekiel.

Ezekiel shares the years of exile with God's people, confronting them with the reality of God's holiness and judgment. He has a vision that the Lord, the God of Israel, is with them even in Babylon. He also sees God's glory depart from the temple and the total destruction of Jerusalem. This comes about in 587 BC.

Once the worst has happened, Ezekiel begins to deliver prophecies of renewal and hope. One day God will give his people new, obedient hearts. They will be restored to a new covenant relationship, a new Jerusalem and a perfect temple.

Jeremiah, in Jerusalem, preaches the unpopular message that this disaster is God's judgment. He also predicts a return from exile one day, and buys a plot of land in Jerusalem as a sign of hope for the future. He writes to the exiles to warn them that they will be in Babylon for some time. They are to settle down and seek to be a blessing to their oppressors.

When Jerusalem is destroyed and its population deported, Jeremiah stays behind with the survivors. They even seek refuge in Egypt, which is the last place someone like Jeremiah would ever want to go. His 'Lamentations' describe his grief at the destruction of Jerusalem.

The return from exile

The exiles are held captive in Babylon for fifty years. At the end of this time a new power arises: that of Persia. In 559 BC a brilliant military leader becomes king. He is Cyrus II. In 550 BC he conquers the armies of Media, and becomes emperor of the Medes and Persians.

God uses Cyrus to defeat the Babylonians and release the Jews. Isaiah calls Cyrus the Lord's 'anointed' – the word which signifies a chosen ruler or 'christ' (Isaiah 42:1).

In 539 BC the Persians take King Belshazzar by surprise and capture Babylon. Cyrus is quick to issue decrees of liberation for the Jews and other subject nations. He believes in and encourages religious freedom. The Jews are free to return to Jerusalem and rebuild the temple.

The Jews return to Jerusalem in stages and over a number of years. The precise sequence is not entirely clear.

The first and main group is led by Zerubbabel, who is the grandson of King Jehoiachin. He leaves Babylon in 537 BC. With him is Joshua, the high priest.

The returnees start to rebuild the temple, but progress is slow. Resources are slender, opposition from the Samaritans is fierce and morale is low. The work comes to a standstill until 520 BC, when the prophets Haggai and Zechariah encourage a fresh start. The new temple (a poor replacement for the first) is completed by 515 BC – seventy years after Solomon's temple was destroyed.

The little community continues to struggle until further help arrives. In 445 BC Nehemiah comes to Jerusalem with the permission of King Artaxerxes to rebuild the walls. Nehemiah is an excellent organizer and the task is completed in fifty-two days, despite some very unpleasant opposition. After nearly 150 years, Jerusalem becomes a fortified city once again.

At some other point (perhaps 458 BC) Ezra brings another group of returning exiles. Ezra is both a priest and a scribe. He is also an expert in the law of Moses.

Ezra leads the Jerusalem community in an act of repentance and renewal of the covenant. He teaches God's law and establishes a regime of strict obedience to it. A particular concern is the forbidding of marriage to people outside the Jewish community.

The prophecy of Malachi may belong to this time. He too is concerned with mixed marriages, as well as the payment of tithes and the offering of worthy sacrifices.

At this point the Old Testament history ends. There is a silence of 400 years until the New Testament begins.

God's story

The Old Testament is more than a history of Israel. It is the story of God's revelation of himself.

Far off and close

God is the supreme creator. He is holy, 'above' and separate from his creation. And yet he is most intimately aware of, and concerned about, every detail of life. He loves genuine worship. He is angered by injustice and corruption. He looks for faithful relationships, honest trading, protection for the weak and generosity to the poor.

Seen in action

God cares deeply about how a nation and its individuals behave. He holds people responsible for their actions. He promises to bless obedience and punish wickedness. The Old Testament stories show God in action: in compassion and rescue, anger and punishment, judgment, mercy and renewal. God is ultimately committed to forgiving, restoring and recreating all things.

Reigning supreme

The Lord reigns over all. He is the creator of the universe and the Lord of history. Even Israel's formidable enemies and conquerors, the tyrants of Egypt, Assyria, Babylon and Persia, are God's subjects. He uses them to fulfil his great purposes.

Faithful with the faithful

God loves to work with humble and responsive people. Abraham, Moses and David are the great examples.

Abraham dies without seeing the multitude of his descendants or possessing his land. Moses is not allowed to enter the Promised Land, nor David to build the temple. All leave 'unfinished business', yet their lives are completed by faith. God treated them as friends and gave them honoured places in his plan.

And the story continues. The Old Testament promises that Abraham's 'seed' will bless the world; a prophet 'like Moses' will appear one day; and a king 'like David' will rule over everything in the end.

GENESIS

Genesis starts at the very beginning: how things began and the way things are. It is an epic of God's creation and our place within it. In a series of ancient stories, we have teaching about God's power and love, our own nature and roots, and the shape and direction of human life. We are given a scenario of the world God intended – and what it has become.

Genesis begins with a bang – nothing less than the big bang of creation and the eternal God who causes it.

We follow the story of creation to its climax in the making of the human race. We hear how life on earth is fatally damaged by the rebellion of people against their creator. We meet the judgment and mercy of God as he seeks to purge the world with a flood, but saves Noah with his family and ark full of animals. We see how God deals with the proud and self-centred people who build a tower to reach the heavens...

And we meet Abram. God calls Abram to trust him by living a homeless, nomadic and apparently hopeless life. Through Abram (or 'Abraham' as he becomes) God founds a family which will become the nation of Israel, and whose destiny is nothing less than the new creation.

Genesis is a book of enormous power and breadth. It lays the foundations for our knowledge of God and our understanding of his purpose. It explains to us our own nature and situation – why it is that we are at odds with God, each other and the world around. But Genesis doesn't abandon us to our fate, because it shows us a God who doesn't give up. In Genesis, God embarks on the long and painstaking task of winning people back to the loving, joyful, eternal life he always intended.

OUTLINE

Ancient stories from the mists of time (1:1–11:32)
  The story of creation (1:1–2:3)
  Adam and Eve (2:4–25)

The fall (3:1-24)
Cain and Abel (4:1-26)
From Adam to Noah (5:1-6:8)
Noah and the flood (6:9-9:17)
The spread of nations (10:1-32)
The tower of Babel (11:1-32)
The stories of the patriarchs (12:1-50:26)
Abraham (12:1-25:11)
The descendants of Ishmael (25:12-18)
Isaac (Abraham's son) (25:19-26:35)
Jacob (Abraham's grandson) (27:1-35:29)
The descendants of Esau (36:1-43)
Joseph (Abraham's great-grandson) (37:1-50:26)

Introduction

Genesis means 'origin'. It is the glorious account of how things began.

Genesis wasn't the first book ever written – nor is it the oldest part of the Bible. But when the Bible was put together, this book had an obvious claim to come first.

The book of Genesis is in two parts: ancient stories from the mists of time (1:1-11:32) and the stories of the patriarchs (12:1-50:26).

Ancient stories from the mists of time

These stories are beautiful in their telling and simple in their teaching. They cover the creation of the world and early human history – but with a difference. They tell the tale from God's point of view.

Genesis is a book about God. It tells us something we can never guess: that there is only one God. He has personality, power and opinion – and he creates to perfection.

The first story tells how God created the universe, stage by stage. He made something from nothing, and brought order out of chaos. Although the story doesn't give scientific details, it describes creation being shaped in a purposeful way. In other words, we're living in a designer universe and not a chance accident.

The universe is not an accident. It was conceived, wanted and brought into existence by God. He originated the design, generated the power and executed the production. And he worked it all from nothing.

As the story of Genesis unfolds, we see God's heartfelt love for the people he has made. Human beings are the crown of his creation. We are made to show the world what God is like: God said, 'Let us make humankind in our image, according to our likeness; and let them have dominion… over all the earth' (1:26 NRSV).

So the story of creation leads into the story of the first humans: Adam and Eve. The couple are made for each other and can commune with God. They are set in a perfect environment, the Garden of Eden. They are different from the rest of creation, because they alone are 'the image' of God. They can influence the world around them, and are given the mandate to govern it.

God's intention is that human beings should enjoy his creation and care for it, wisely managing its resources and tending its species. God gives men and women, uniquely in all creation, a mind and will of their own. But Adam and Eve use their free will to defy God. Human beings have independence of choice, and the freedom even to reject God's love. When Adam and Eve, the first couple, disobey God's instruction, the entire creation is tragically spoiled. This moment is called 'the fall'. They are expelled from the Garden. Their life becomes one of hard work, sorrow, discomfort, conflict and death. Because they disobey God, they lose their hope of eternal life.

From humanity's fall onwards, Genesis is the story of a dreadful falling-out. All the relationships are damaged and distorted – between God and humanity, between humanity and creation, between partners, siblings, families, communities and nations. God intervenes to punish people and correct situations. His love, justice and desire to help are always evident. He makes himself known, guides those who turn to him and shapes the course of history. But, by the end of the book, the situation is in no way resolved. Already the world needs a Saviour.

The story of the first human beings is followed by that of the first murder. Adam and Eve have two sons, Cain and Abel. Cain is jealous of Abel and kills him – only to be challenged and condemned by God. Cain becomes an outcast, bearing for ever his burden of guilt. This story shows how easily jealousy leads to murder. But human life is precious to God – and he holds us responsible for our actions.

Then comes the longer story of Noah and the flood. God decides to drown the corrupt and sinful world and start again. He warns Noah of a coming flood, and commands him to build a huge wooden vessel – the ark. Noah builds the ark with the help of his sons, and they take refuge from the flood. With them are their wives, and a large assortment of animals in breeding pairs. This story describes how God passes judgment on the corruption of the world, but spares just one faithful man and his family. It closes with God promising a safe and reliable world in the future, and signing his word with a rainbow.

The last of these ancient tales is of the tower of Babel. It dates from the founding of communities and the development of building skills. One such community attempts to build a tower to reach the heavens, to establish its prestige and permanence. But God judges their pride, confuses their language and scatters them far and wide. It's a story against the Jews' old enemy, Babylon ('babble town'!). It reminds us of our human littleness and futility. And it tells, in a quaint but astute way, how different nations and languages came to be.

Genesis contains a sparkling collection of stories. These stories teach us that God loves us as children but treats us as adults. Our disobedience hurts him and provokes his anger. But, even as he judges us, he softens his sentence with mercy. But Genesis is more than just stories. Here is

Favourite stories

In the Bible's top-ten stories, Genesis must supply half the favourites. The creation, Adam and Eve, Noah's ark, the tower of Babel, Jacob's ladder and Joseph's coat all jostle for attention. This one book has inspired the imagination of painters, poets, playwrights and producers in every age. Milton's epic poem 'Paradise Lost', Michelangelo's majestic portrayal of 'The Creation of Adam' on the ceiling of the Sistine Chapel, and the fun-filled productions of 'Joseph and the Amazing Technicolor Dreamcoat' in theatres around the world bear witness to the power and fascination of these ancient tales. And what children's store is complete without a whole range of posters, toys and story books depicting Noah's ark?

food for thought to engage the finest minds. How did the universe come to exist? Was it by accident or design? And how can we understand ourselves within it? Are we up-market apes or low-grade angels?

Genesis answers questions like this with a bold presentation of God, in all his power and holiness, justice and love. It holds up God's world like a mirror, so we can see ourselves in all our dignity and deviousness.

The stories of Adam and Eve and Cain and Abel probe the deepest recesses of our nature. They expose the shabbiness of our motives and the poverty of our love. Greed and jealousy, anger and guilt are the driving forces of our lives. The account of creation, with God commissioning humanity to care for planet earth, takes us to the heart of the debate about conservation and our present ecological crisis. It is only for love of God – and with his help – that we can change our ways and reverse the exploitation and pollution which is plunging us towards extinction.

The stories of the patriarchs

The patriarchs are the founding fathers – the ancestors of the Jewish race and the pioneers of their faith.

The first of them is Abram, who becomes Abraham, 'the Father of Nations'. God calls one man, Abram, to live a life of faith. God promises him a multitude of descendants and a land of his own. The idea of a chosen race (Israel) in a Promised Land (Canaan) is born.

Genesis is a source book for three of the world's great religions. Jews, Muslims and Christians all look back to Abraham as their ancestor.

With Abraham a tender seed of faith is planted. From this seed will grow a family and a nation to which God will always be committed. Eventually, and despite many failures, setbacks and betrayals, this nation will be the people who receive God's Son, the Messiah.

After Abraham come his sons Isaac and Ishmael. Some people trace the hostility between Israeli and Arab to the rivalry between Isaac and Ishmael. Today's bloody disputes over territory spring from God's promise of a land for his people.

Then come Abraham's grandsons Esau and Jacob. Esau and Jacob are twins, with Esau the elder. In theory, it is Esau who should inherit the special relationship with God, but in fact this falls to the devious and self-seeking Jacob. After many adventures, Jacob becomes 'Israel' – a name of strenuous defiance meaning 'He Struggles with God'. With the help of two wives and two maidservants, Jacob has twelve sons. They are the forefathers of the twelve tribes which later make up the nation of Israel.

Jacob's favourite son is Joseph. Joseph is a spoilt brat who dreams of lording it over his family. Sold into slavery by his jealous brothers, he ends up in prison in Egypt. But, thanks to his gift for interpreting dreams, he emerges to become Egypt's prime minister.

Not only does Joseph correctly forecast years of famine, but he takes charge of the operation to store and ration food. When his brothers come from Canaan to get grain, Joseph is in the very position of dominance he had predicted! But Joseph's pride has been softened through his sufferings, and he greets his brothers with tears – and a gracious explanation of events.

The story of Genesis draws to a close with Jacob and his family moving to Egypt. They survive the famine, but are a long way from the Promised Land. Rather eerily, the book ends with the death of Joseph and the closing of his coffin – as if the promises of God have gone to ground and passed from sight.

Who wrote the book of Genesis?

For many centuries it was assumed that Moses wrote the book of Genesis. He is the main character in four of the first five books of the Bible, which are known as the 'books of Moses'. He also has the Hebrew background and Egyptian education to enable him to write them. We read of Moses writing down God's laws and keeping a record of Israel's journey from Egypt to Canaan.

Some of the stories in Genesis are very old, and must have been passed from parents to children for many generations before they were collected or written down. Again, Moses was the sort of person who could have gathered and edited them. If it wasn't Moses, then we don't know who shaped and organized this material. Whoever it was, the result is a flowing story of God's people and a clear picture of God's purpose for them.

The story of Joseph helps us prepare for the story of Jesus. Jesus, too, was rejected by his own people and put to death. But God raised him to glory, to bring deliverance and forgiveness to all.

Discovering Genesis

Ancient stories from the mists of time

The story of creation (1:1–2:3)

The Bible, and the story of creation, begins with God.

We cannot see God, for he is spirit. But we can *know* God by his actions – just as our own character is revealed by our behaviour.

The words 'in the beginning' (1:1) tell us straight away that God is embarking on a project which he will develop, sustain and bring to completion. It is a vast project – nothing less than the creation of 'the heavens and the earth', the universe.

The earth is 'formless' (1:2) and God gives it shape and meaning. It is 'empty' and he starts to fill it. It is dark and he commands light.

As we wonder whether it is right to call God 'he', the writer introduces the Spirit of God. The Spirit hovers over the waters, attentive, thoughtful and poised for action. The picture is more like a mother bird tending her chicks than an old man in the sky.

There is nothing remote or detached about the way God works. He is a 'hands-on' creator, keenly committed to this marvellous work, absorbed in concentration and fizzing with enthusiasm. His Spirit moves to shape the chaos, fill the void, lighten the darkness and bring a universe to life.

'Let there be light,' says God (1:3), and his words have power to bring light into existence. As the story unfolds, we see that God's word is his deed. When God speaks, it happens.

Centuries later, the Gospel of John begins with an echo of Genesis. Speaking about Jesus Christ, the Gospel introduces him as 'the Word' of God: 'In the beginning was the Word, and the Word was with God, and the Word was God... Through him all things were made...' (John 1:1–3).

In a few sentences, we are introduced to God, his Spirit and his word. We have a matter-of-fact statement that the universe was made by God, with the kind of power that turns nothing to something, and darkness to light. As the Bible story unfolds, we will discover God as the one who makes everything new, even forgiving sins, healing sickness and bringing the dead to life.

What a difference a 'Day' makes!

Science has revealed that the universe was formed over a period of billions of years. The book of Genesis seems to simplify the entire process into a single week! However, there's no need to dismiss the creation story just because it is told in 'days'. It is the shrinking of the timescales

> ### Did God make the universe in six days?
>
> Some people say that the story of creation is scientifically true, and that God really did create the universe in six days. Others dismiss both the story and God as flights of fancy. This is an argument that should never have happened!
>
> We must be careful not to make the Genesis story something it isn't. It isn't a scientific account of physics, cosmology and biology. It is a statement that 'God did it all – and it was very good'.
>
> The simplicity and sequence of the creation story is impressive. The bursting forth of light is followed by water and space, land and seas. Then come plants, animals and humans. The cosmos emerges from chaos in an ordered way. The text provides an excellent screenplay. Through the eye of an earthbound camera we watch the panorama of events – including the realistic detail of the sun, moon and stars appearing through water vapour and smoke on the 'fourth day'.
>
> The modern physicist sees more clearly than anyone that the universe is positively designed for living. If gravity were stronger, stars would burn out too quickly for life to evolve on their planets. If protons and neutrons were different by even a fraction, there could be no hydrogen, no stars – and you would not be reading this. It takes a lot of faith to say that all this is a meaningless accident.

that enables our limited minds to handle the immense scope of God's achievement.

Genesis gives us the big picture of God and his creation – without losing us in the infinities of light years and the abstractions of particle physics. Science can stun us with statistics, or bury us in facts, but leave us no wiser about God.

It's good to have the Bible's unique perspective on the universe – that it is God-made and God-given. Genesis deals with the mighty process in a single chapter – and gets on to the main business of God's purpose for humankind.

In recent years it has been popular to compare the history of the world to an hour, with human life occurring only in the closing seconds. Such a timescale puts us in our place as a brief and finite species.

The Bible's view is quite the opposite. The book of Genesis gives just a few seconds to the countless aeons of prehistory, and devotes the rest of its pages to God and us. We learn that human beings are not a chance and feeble speck, but the summit of God's creation and the key to his purpose.

Then God said, 'Let us make humankind in our image...'

Our modern knowledge provides us with many images of primitive people. We discover them as ape-like creatures which gradually become more resourceful, sociable and physically upright. Increasingly, like ourselves, they hunt, live in caves, make tools, paint walls, erect landmarks and bury their dead.

Genesis describes God creating human beings 'in his own image'. The emphasis is not on men and women being ape-like, but how they are. Humankind, in mint condition, is a divine hologram. Because of sin, the image of God is now spoilt. But we can still detect traces of God's likeness – in our creativity, decision-making, compassion, love of company and sense of humour.

'Male and Female he created them'

The division into 'male and female' comes after the basic creation of 'humankind'. God makes human beings for 'one-anotherness' – and this, too, is a glimpse of God himself. There is a one-anotherness in

God, when he says 'Let us make...' God, his Spirit and his Word are all introduced in the opening sentences of Genesis.

As the Bible's teaching unfolds, we will see the emergence of the three-in-one description of God. He is 'Father, Son and Holy Spirit'. We will hear of the love God, and the longing of Jesus that human beings should share it: 'That all of them may be one, Father, just as you are in me and I am in you. May they also be in us...' (John 17:21).

'God blessed them...'

God gives human beings the unique responsibility of ruling the earth and its creatures. Everything is given for discovery, enjoyment and satisfaction – although it seems, at this stage, that the menu is strictly vegetarian!

As God completes the heavens and the earth, his verdict is that it is 'very good' (1:31). And if God is perfect and his judgment true, it must have been very good indeed.

'On the seventh day [God] rested from all his work'

God stops work, not because he is tired, but because he has finished (2:2). The result is a universe full of infinite variety and yet completely integrated. 'God blessed the seventh day and made it holy, because on it he rested...' (2:3). The seventh day becomes the 'sabbath', from the Hebrew word for 'ceased'. In years to come a commandment will declare it a day of rest for men and women, families, households and animals. By blessing the day, God invites the whole of creation to share his satisfaction and enjoy his peace.

Jews keep Saturday as their day of rest, their sabbath, while Christians have merged it with Sunday – the day of Christ's resurrection. Taken seriously, with joy and imagination, it is the perfect antidote to the stress and demands of modern life.

Of course, God's work of maintaining and renewing the creation continues, irrespective of the sabbath. 'My Father is always at his work to this very day,' says Jesus, when criticized for healing an invalid on that day (John 5:17). Without God's authority, attention and sustaining love, the universe would revert to chaos.

Adam and Eve (2:4–25)

The Lord God forms human beings from the dust of the ground – the same material he has used for the plants and animals. But to humanity he gives the special dimension of relationship. From the beginning humankind is 'a living being' – a seamless body–soul. A person, wanted and loved.

God sets man in the Garden of Eden. Eden means 'delight', and 'Garden' has a sense of spaciousness, pleasure and peace. Rivers flow from Eden to water the world around. This lovely place is somewhere north of today's Persian Gulf, in an area known as the 'Fertile Crescent'.

At the centre of the Garden are two trees – one the tree of life and the other the tree of the knowledge of good and evil. God allows the human beings to eat the fruit of all the trees, except these two. If they take fruit from the forbidden trees, they will forfeit the life-sustaining love of God. They will die.

Why does God forbid human beings the fruit of the trees of life, and the knowledge of good and evil? Is he afraid that they will get above themselves and start to experiment with test-tube babies and deep-frozen corpses? Is he worried that they will see through God, call his bluff and hijack his world?

Although human beings have conquered the world, split the atom and landed on the moon, we have only the merest glimmer of God's creativity and wisdom. The 'trees' in this story are a test of whether we will accept God's authority. Will we accept that God's boundaries are for our good?

'The Lord God formed man…'

The more we discover and understand about the human body, the more amazing it seems. Eye and foot, tongue and brain, fingerprint and eardrum are all uniquely formed and coordinated. And what about imagination, reason, passion, laughter and self-awareness? 'I am fearfully and wonderfully made,' says the writer of one of the psalms.

As Genesis tells the story, the first man gives names to all his fellow creatures. He has the care of them; but none of them is his equal. So God makes a woman for the man as he sleeps. When he wakes, the man recognizes his 'other half'. At last he can name someone after himself:

This is now bone of my bones and flesh of my flesh; she shall be called 'woman', for she was taken out of man. (2:23)

'For this reason...'

The partnership of a man and his wife is not to be split by any other loyalty – not even to parents. Father and mother are excluded as a new creation takes place: husband and wife become 'one flesh', one new 'self' in marriage.

The man and the woman belong together and complete each other. They're different, but they match. Their bodies fit. Heart to heart, they correspond. They are at ease with each other. They aren't embarrassed or self-conscious about their bodies. They are comfortable in their one-anotherness. Sadly, it is not to last.

The fall (3:1–24)

Enter the serpent – crafty and critical. He is a picture of the devil, Satan, who seeks to spoil God's relationship with humankind. He raises questions in the woman's mind. What did God say? And to what extent did he really mean it? Surely God is keeping a few privileges for himself! He doesn't want human beings becoming too enlightened. And so the most damaging idea is born: that God is somehow against humanity. He doesn't want any competition.

The woman's eyes and imagination (and hands and mouth) do the rest. She eats the fruit and shares it with her husband. As the serpent promised, their eyes are opened – to see each other naked and ashamed. Their security vanishes; so does their trust in each other. They try to cover up with leaves. When God comes calling, they hide from him. They lie to him. They blame each other – and the serpent.

God deals with each in turn. He questions the man first and then the woman. The man is defiant. As far as he's concerned, it was God who gave him the woman and the woman who gave him the fruit. His only fault had been to eat what was put in front of him. The woman blames the serpent. She explains she's been cunningly tricked.

The tragedy of sin

In the New Testament, Paul points out that 'it was the woman who was deceived' – as though the man, left to himself, would have known better. If he did know better, then his disobedience was all the more wilful. He defied God with the full intent of a clear head and a rebellious heart.

Jesus takes this story to be about the reason we die. We are all sinful, because we share Adam's rebellious nature. It is a story about the tragedy of sin – and the spiritual deadness which results from it. It was this kind of death (a complete inability to respond to God) that Jesus Christ came to defeat.

Think of a deadly virus, easily caught and incurable. Originally it came from just one person, Adam, but it has spread throughout the world.

The Bible sees sin in a similar way. It came from a single act of disobedience and has contaminated the entire human race. Paul says there are no exceptions, for 'All have sinned and fall short of the glory of God' (Romans 3:23).

Jesus came to deal with the deadly virus of sin, and restore us to spiritual life. From one person, Jesus Christ, eternal life is spreading to the whole of creation. For this reason Jesus is sometimes called 'the Second Adam'. While the first Adam was the cause of death, Jesus Christ is the source of life: 'For as in Adam all die, so in Christ all will be made alive' (1 Corinthians 15:22).

God curses the serpent. From now on his place will be in the dust. He will be for ever at odds with humankind. God forecasts that the woman's offspring will crush his head – a prediction that will be fulfilled when Christ inflicts crushing defeat on Satan.

To the woman, God says that childbirth will be painful and marriage will become a power struggle. She will need her husband, and he will rule her.

The fall of humanity spoils the relationship with the rest of creation as well. God says that the very ground is cursed by their disobedience. The easy, gentle partnership of human beings and the world of nature is gone. From now on, if people want to eat, they must scratch a living from the earth, until they die and become part of that earth themselves.

Cain and Abel (4:1-26)

When Adam and Eve disobey God, they are banished from the Garden of Eden. They become farmers.

Their first son, Cain, is also a farmer. Their second son, Abel, is a shepherd. We may detect some rivalry between their two ways of life in their choices of sacrifice. Cain brings a cereal offering, but Abel brings meat. We learn that God prefers Abel's gift.

It isn't that God likes meat rather than grain. The point is that he prefers a cheerful offering to a grudging one. A sacrifice is only pleasing to God if it comes with love.

Abel brings select portions of the first young animals from his flocks – and finds joy in doing so. Cain brings some grain, but his heart is hostile. He is the first person in the Bible to pretend religion – but it gives him no pleasure.

When the phoney sacrifice is rejected, Cain is angry and jealous. God warns him that evil is waiting to invade him. Cain can let jealousy take

The first people

Adam and Eve are presented as the first man and woman to be conscious of God and responsive to him. They are the crown of God's creation, and their fall into sin is a tragedy.

But clearly there are other humans around, as the wider world is already populated. Cain in his wanderings finds a wife and founds a city. Soon we read of generations that have the skills to make music and work with bronze and iron.

Putting these clues together, we can date the people of these stories as living between the Neolithic and Bronze Ages – from 6000 to 2500 BC.

It may seem an anticlimax to think of Adam and Eve in a world in which there are already other people. But this doesn't prevent us taking the main point – that God made human beings with individual personalities and sensitive consciences. These people are 'new' in their awareness of themselves, in their responsibility for their actions and in their relationship with God.

control and become a murderer, or he can resist it. Either way, God will hold him responsible for his action, and his brother's welfare.

Cain yields to anger and kills Abel. When God asks him where his brother is, Cain snubs him. But God knows what has happened, and is deeply outraged. Not only has the first murder occurred between brothers, but lifeblood has been shed on God's earth. God declares Cain guilty, and curses him with a hard and homeless life. But Cain isn't to be killed in turn. God's way is not to recycle evil, but to contain it, and, whenever he is asked, to forgive.

From Adam to Noah (5:1–6:8)

Genesis lists the ancestors from Adam to Noah, including some remarkably long-lived people:

When Enoch had lived 65 years, he became the father of Methuselah. And after he became the father of Methuselah, Enoch walked with God 300 years and had other sons and daughters. Altogether, Enoch lived 365 years. Enoch walked with God; then he was no more, because God took him away. (5:21–24)

These astonishing ages (of which Methuselah holds the record at 969) provide plenty of scope for discussion. In those days, great ages were attributed to great people as a mark of honour. It may be that entire branches of a family tree were named after one person. Or perhaps their lifestyle was healthy, their environment unpolluted and their family free of disease. We don't know.

The memory that Enoch didn't die (but 'God took him') reminds us that God never intended death to touch us.

Heart trouble

Humankind is the pits! As God surveys the human race, he finds everyone planning evil all the time (6:5–8). But, while human hearts are full of wickedness, God's heart is full of pain. He alone knows our true glory and the paradise we have lost.

It is because God's heart aches for lost humanity that he will one day send his Son to be our Saviour. Jesus will show, by his suffering and death, exactly what our sin costs God.

Noah and the flood (6:9–9:17)

Noah is a good man in a wicked world. While other people are violent and corrupt, Noah keeps company with God and shares his thoughts. When God resolves to destroy all life with a flood, he makes an exception of Noah. He tells him to make an ark – a giant coffin-like structure, the length of a football field and three storeys high. This is to be a refuge for Noah and his family when the flood of God's judgment comes.

Noah and his three sons build the ark from wood plastered with reeds and waterproofed with tar. It's a magnificent act of faith in a region of little rain and far from the sea. They believe that God will do as he says and spare their family. They hope that life on earth and the knowledge of God will survive through them and be re-established in a clean new world.

When the ark is completed, they stock it with a huge selection of animals and birds and a supply of food. Like Adam before him, Noah seems to have a special affinity with God's creatures, tending animals and handling birds. They come in pairs and board the ark as the storm clouds gather. The story records that the flood begins when Noah is 600 years, two months and seventeen days old. An unforgettable day.

Soon the ark is engulfed in a deluge of water – as though God is throwing creation into reverse, drowning all in a soup of ocean and vapour. Inside the ark, people and animals are buried alive, but safe – a model of God's saving power for every generation to come.

The ark rides the flood for five months, until the waters begin to subside. It finally comes to rest on Mount Ararat. Noah sends first a raven and then a dove to search for land. The raven doesn't return – probably because it finds plenty of floating corpses to live on. But the dove comes back with a freshly picked olive leaf – the very first sign that life will continue and all will be well.

Months later, the land is dry enough for the company to leave the ark. Noah makes sacrifices to God even from among the few animals they have. He is determined to put God first in this brave new world.

And God in turn makes a vow:

I will never again curse the ground because of
humankind, for the inclination of the human heart is

evil from youth; nor will I ever again destroy every living creature as I have done. (8:21 NRSV)

God promises Noah:

*As long as the earth endures,
seedtime and harvest,
cold and heat,
summer and winter,
day and night
will never cease.* (8:22 NRSV)

What about other flood stories?

The early chapters of Genesis are about the people of Mesopotamia – a fertile area where early humans settle and build communities. Mesopotamia means 'between rivers'. It is the fertile land which lies between the great rivers, the Tigris and the Euphrates. To the south is Babylonia, to be known in the future for its power, wealth and pagan pride. Both regions have folk memories of great floods, and stories of the heroes who built vessels and survived. Traces of these floods have been found in the ruins of some of the ancient cities, but nothing as vast and totally devastating as Noah's flood.

In one famous flood story from Babylonia, the hero is a man called Atrahasis. He is at the mercy of a multitude of petty and quarrelsome gods. The gods regard humans as unpleasant and noisy neighbours, and resolve to wipe them out. But then they miss the delicious smell of burnt offerings!

This and other pagan stories, dating from around 3000 BC, show a very different understanding of 'god' and the reasons for flooding. There is nothing about awesome judgment, life-saving faith or the merciful promise that it won't happen again.

The Genesis story tells of one creator-God, who is holy and just. He is determined to save the righteous and punish the wicked. There are various simple details (such as the actual date of the downpour) which a family could have remembered and handed down. It is possible that Noah's story is told to put the record straight about the flood and why it happened.

The story of the flood leaves us with many questions. If God wanted to wipe out all corruption, he clearly didn't succeed. But the story conveys the seriousness of sin, the reality of God's judgment and the certainty of his power to save.

In centuries to come, the ark will be a picture of the church. It is a place of safety and deliverance in the midst of a wicked world.

God blesses Noah and his family. They are to repopulate the earth. Sadly, humans and animals will now be afraid of each other. Humans will be meat-eaters, but they must respect blood. Blood is the liquid of life and belongs to God. Human blood is doubly sacred, because humankind is the image of God.

Of course, the people who boarded the ark took with them their old human nature. Noah's sons and their wives aren't perfect and their experience doesn't change them. Soon the world will be seeded again with selfishness and pride. But God's word stands. All disasters of flood, fire, famine or disease will now be restricted. God will never again destroy the whole world.

The rainbow covenant

God gives his word that all natural disasters will now be local and limited (9:1–17). He will never again destroy the whole world. It is a promise to every creature on earth in every place and for all time. This is God's free and generous assurance, which he signs as only he can – with a rainbow.

The spread of nations (10:1–32)

After the great flood, the world is populated by Noah's sons, Shem, Ham and Japheth. Japheth is the eldest, but Shem is the most important to the Bible story.

Japheth

Japheth's descendants spread north of the Fertile Crescent, to the Caspian Sea in the east and the Aegean Sea in the west (10:2–4). They become several nations, some of which will be a threat to Israel in the future. Gomer, Magog, Tubal and Meschech are described by the prophet Ezekiel as warlike nations to the far north (Ezekiel 38:1–6). The Madai are probably the Medes living south of the Caspian Sea. Javan refers to a Greek people beyond the Aegean, and Tiras may be the Etruscans. The names of individual people can become the name of a clan, nation, race or place. It is thought that Ashkenaz becomes the Scythians, the Kittim inhabit Cyprus and the Rodanim live on the island of Rhodes.

Ham

Ham's descendants occupy Canaan and the territories to the south, including parts of Africa and Arabia (10:5-20). They develop as four main groups – Cush, Mizraim, Put and Canaan. The 'sons of Cush' are Ethiopians in Africa, to the west of the Red Sea. Another segment of Cush becomes the Kassite people who (perhaps led by Nimrod) settle far away, east of Assyria beyond the Fertile Crescent. Seba and Sheba are similar peoples who settle on the eastern shore of the Red Sea. With Havilah and Dedan, they occupy part of Arabia. Mizraim is a plural word which may refer to Upper and Lower Egypt. The Philistines are listed as coming from Egypt, although it is from Crete that they will later invade Palestine (and give it their name). The Caphtorites also come from Crete.

Shem

Shem's descendants are the Semites or Semitic peoples (10:21-32). Although Japheth is the eldest son, it is Shem who receives a special blessing from Noah (9:26); and it is through Shem that the line of God's promise passes from Adam to Abraham.

It is Shem's son Eber who is the ancestor of Abraham. Abraham is called 'the Hebrew' (14:13) – a name which might come from 'eber' (meaning 'passing through'), or from the word 'habiru' (meaning 'a wandering, insignificant people'). The Bible story now concentrates on these descendants of Shem. They will be the Hebrews who are rescued by God from landless slavery in Egypt, to become his 'chosen race' of Israel, living in the 'Promised Land' of Canaan. Another of Shem's sons is Joktan, who is the ancestor of many Arab races.

Seventy nations spring from the sons of Noah – or seventy-two in the Septuagint (Greek) version of the Old Testament. Although God has special dealings with the descendants of Shem, he has an ultimate purpose for all the nations. His plan is to draw the whole earth into his perfect kingdom and saving love. Jesus echoes God's mission to all nations when he sends out seventy (or seventy-two) disciples to announce that God's kingdom is coming (Luke 10:1).

The tower of Babel (11:1–32)

This is the last of the ancient folk tales of 'how things began'. It tells of the founding of Babylon, not as a 'gate of heaven', but as a proud and misguided folly.

The story tells of an ambitious community which tries its strength against God. The people want to build a city which will be the centre of the world and a stairway to the sky. Using the very latest construction materials (bricks and tar), they set about building a tower.

God, 'coming down' to investigate, is hardly afraid of their competition. But he is greatly concerned by the emergence of a united, godless society. To confound the project, God confuses the people's language so that they can no longer work together. They are scattered far and wide, leaving the tower half-built.

The name 'Babylon' means 'gate of God'. In the story of the tower, the name is changed to 'Babel', which sounds like the Hebrew word for 'confusion' or 'mixing'.

A tale of two cities

Throughout the Bible, Babylon is the capital of all that is anti-God. It is a centre of ruthless power and gross immorality. In every way it is the opposite of Jerusalem – the city of God whose name means 'peace'.

At the end of the Bible, God utterly destroys Babylon and gives humankind a 'new Jerusalem'. It is the perfect city, not built by human effort (like Babel), but given by God. Instead of human beings trying to get to God, God comes to live with them. Instead of confusion and scattering, this city gives light and unity to the nations:

I saw the holy city, the new Jerusalem, coming down out of heaven from God... And I heard a loud voice from the throne saying, 'See, the home of God is among mortals. He will dwell with them... The nations will walk by its light, and the kings of the earth will bring their glory into it'. (Revelation 21:2–3, 24 NRSV)

The ruins of sacred towers have been discovered throughout the area of Mesopotamia. These multi-storey landmarks are called 'ziggurats', and were built more than 2,000 years BC. They have ramps or stairways to enable people to climb to the top and talk with the gods.

The stories of the patriarchs

Abraham (12:1–25:11)

The scene and the tone change. We leave the mists of prehistory to arrive at a particular time and place. We focus on a particular man. His name is Abram.

God's call to Abram

Abram lives in a well-established city called Ur. God calls him to leave this comfortable home and venture out on a life of faith (12:1–9). Abram is to receive a new land and found a great nation.

It is to Abram that God makes the keynote promise that will shape the whole story of God's people. God declares his covenant plan to bless Abram and his descendants. All other nations will be blessed through this nation and judged by their response to its people. Already God has a plan to bless and reunite the races he has scattered from the tower of Babel (11:1–9). Here we glimpse for the first time the good news that God will one day restore the world and bless its peoples.

Abram becomes a nomadic shepherd, seeking to discover God through his experiences. With his wife Sarai and nephew Lot, he travels from Mesopotamia down through Canaan to the Negev desert. At Shechem, the heart of the future 'Promised Land', Abram builds an altar to the Lord, much as astronauts might plant their national flag on the moon.

Shechem is at the crossroads of Palestine. At Shechem the main roads meet – between north and south, east and west. Here stands the great tree of Moreh – perhaps the site of a pagan shrine. And here Abram builds an altar to the Lord. God's people will return to this place in centuries to come. Joshua will summon the twelve tribes – six to one side of him on Mount Ebal; six to the other side on Mount Gerizim. Here they must choose between obeying God or serving idols, between blessing and curse, between life and death. Shechem is a place of decision; a place to make up your mind.

An embarrassing episode

When famine causes Abram and Sarai to move to Egypt, Abram pretends Sarai is his sister (12:10-20). Pharaoh, the king of Egypt, takes her into his household, and finds himself punished by God for doing so.

Pharaoh reproaches Abram for not being honest with him, but sends them away with generous gifts of servants and cattle. There is a similar episode some years later, with a king named Abimelech.

The parting with lot

As their herds increase, Abram and Lot have to split and go separate ways (13:1-18). Abram gives Lot first choice of the land. Lot chooses the fertile plain of the River Jordan, with its infamously wicked cities of Sodom and Gomorrah.

Does Abram feel dispirited when Lot takes the best land, camps near Sodom, and then returns to city life? Not at all! Abram doesn't pilot his life by human bearings. He moves in God's magnetic field (although not without mistakes – as we have already seen).

Abram has learned the great lesson of 'letting go'. He settles at the oak of Mamre – about twenty miles south of Bethlehem.

Victory and blessing

When the cities of the plain are ransacked by rival kings, Abram becomes a military leader. He raises an army and rescues Lot (14:1-24).

There are many alliances and power struggles between the city states of Middle Bronze Age Palestine, about 2000 BC. Genesis describes the Valley of Siddim as 'full of tar pits' (14:10). That valley was to disappear under the Dead Sea, which the Romans later called 'Asphaltites', because of the lumps of tar they found floating in the salty water.

On his triumphant return from battle, Abram is given bread and wine and blessed by Melchizedek, the priest-king of Salem. Abram gives him a tenth of the wealth he has won in the fighting. But when the king of Sodom tries to strike a deal, Abram will have none of it. He wants only the wealth God gives.

Salem will become Jerusalem in the future. Melchizedek appears from nowhere. His name means 'King of Righteousness'. The New Testament describes him as, 'Without father or mother, without genealogy, without beginning of days or end of life, like the Son of God, he remains a priest for ever' (Hebrews 7:3). This unique blend of priest and king will be fully revealed in Jesus Christ.

God's covenant with Abram

God speaks to Abram in a vision (15:1–21). He promises to protect Abram and to reward him for his faith. But Abram is consumed with the fact that he is childless. How can he have any sense of completeness without a son to succeed him?

Justification by faith

Abram is the first to trust God's promises against all the odds. From now on, faith means believing what God says. This simple trust in God's word counts as 'righteousness' – being right with God.

The apostle Paul looks back to Abram as the father of all who have faith. Abram wasn't at peace with God because he was circumcised or had kept God's law. These developments came later. Abram was right with God because he believed God's promises.

He was old and his wife was past childbearing, but he believed God would give him an heir. He was homeless and a nomad, but he believed God would give him a land:

He did not waver through unbelief regarding the promise of God, but was strengthened in his faith and gave glory to God, being fully persuaded that God had power to do what he had promised. (Romans 4:20–21)

In the time of the Reformation, this important truth of 'justification by faith' was rediscovered by Martin Luther and others. It became a crucial weapon in the fight against fanciful traditions and superstitious practices in the church.

We are justified (made right with God) by faith alone – not by good deeds, religious devotion or the prayers of others. Such actions may be important ways of expressing our faith; but faith itself is trusting only in what God has done for us, not what we have done for him.

An heir

God promises Abram that he will have an heir – not just a faithful servant inheriting his estate, but his very own son (15:1-6). He shows Abram the myriad stars in the night sky, and promises that his descendants will be too numerous to count. And Abram believes what God says.

A land

The conversation turns to the land God has promised to give Abram (15:7-21). Abram asks how he can be sure he will take possession of it. For answer, God tells Abram to bring animals and birds for sacrifice. Abram kills them and cuts the animals in half. He arranges them and stands guard to prevent them being disturbed.

At sunset, Abram falls asleep and is enveloped in deep darkness. God tells him of things that are to come – the slavery of the Hebrews in Egypt and their great escape; the return of Abram's descendants (in the time of Joshua) to deliver God's judgment on the wickedness of Canaan.

After nightfall, a smoking brazier and a blazing torch pass between the pieces of the sacrifices. This is the awesome presence of God in smoke and fire and deep darkness. These conditions will appear again in the future, when God descends on Mount Sinai to give Moses the Ten Commandments (Exodus 19:18).

God solemnly promises Abram that he will give his descendants the land on which he is lying, from Egypt in the south to the great River Euphrates in the east. This will be the extent of Israel's empire when David is king.

The covenant

God makes a covenant with Abram. This is a binding contract by which God and his people are for ever united. The ceremony of God's holy fire passing between the divided sacrifices symbolizes that this bonding will never be broken. In future, a covenant between two people may be expressed by sharing a meal or exchanging a handshake. The 'new covenant', which God makes with his people through the sacrifice of Jesus on the cross, will be remembered in the fellowship meal of Holy Communion.

Hagar and Ishmael

Abram is now very prosperous, but has neither the land nor the children God promised him. In desperation, Abram and Sarai agree that he should sleep with their Egyptian maidservant, Hagar. Hagar becomes pregnant with Ishmael and has to flee from Sarai's jealousy (16:1–16).

The covenant of circumcision

Now God confirms his covenant with Abram (17:1–27). God changes Abram's name to 'Abraham', and promises that he will become what the name means – the 'Father of Many Nations'.

To mark the covenant, Abraham and all the men and boys of his household are circumcised. In the future, all baby boys are to be circumcised when they are eight days old. Sarai is also given a new name. She is to be 'Sarah', meaning 'princess'. God promises she will give birth to a son, Isaac, despite the fact that she is ninety! Ishmael (now thirteen) is circumcised along with Abraham. He will also become the ancestor of a great nation (the Arabs); but he is not to inherit the covenant and the land.

Three visitors

One day Abraham entertains three strangers (18:1–15). In some mysterious way this is an encounter with God – or with the Lord and two angels. The Lord promises Abraham that Sarah will bear a son. Sarah overhears – and bursts out laughing, much to her own embarrassment! When the baby is born, he will be called Isaac, which means 'He Laughs'.

It's hard to imagine Sarah at antenatal class when she should be in the old folks' home. We can try dividing her age by two – making her attractive to Pharaoh at thirty-five and the happy mother of Isaac in her forties. Or we can accept that Abraham and Sarah have exceptionally long lives, and that Isaac's birth is a miracle. The emphasis of the story is on the helplessness of Sarah in her barren old age. Why else would Abraham's divine visitor say, 'Is anything too hard for the Lord?' (18:14).

The destruction of Sodom and Gomorrah

The three strangers are on their way to judge the wickedness of Sodom and Gomorrah (18:16–19:29). Abraham begs that Sodom may be spared, for the sake of any good people there (such as Lot). The Lord agrees that if there are even as few as ten good men in Sodom he will not destroy it.

The strangers (now 'angels') stay with Lot in Sodom, where a mob threatens to rape them that night. With the angels' help, Lot and his daughters manage to escape to the small town of Zoar. But Lot's wife, pausing to look back, is caught in the terrible volcanic disaster that engulfs the cities. She becomes a pillar of salt.

Lot and his daughters

The end of Lot's story is pathetic and degrading (19:30-38). He is afraid to settle in Zoar and takes his daughters to live in a cave in the mountains. After his ambition for security and prosperity in the wicked cities of the plain, this is a terrible humiliation. We can't help but compare his miserable fate with the outcome of Abraham's humble faith.

Without husbands, Lot's daughters decide to make their father drunk and have sex with him. In this way they become pregnant. Their descendants will be the peoples of Moab and Ammon, who will bring shame and disgrace on Israel in the future. Moabite women will seduce God's people into immorality and idolatry (Numbers 25:1-3). The Ammonites will sacrifice their children to the pagan god Molech (Leviticus 18:21).

Abraham and Abimelech

Lot is not perfect, but neither is Abraham.

Abraham settles in Gerar, where he becomes afraid that the local king, Abimelech, will kill him for his wife (20:1-18). Sarah is very beautiful, and Abraham has long ago decided to avoid trouble by saying she is his sister; which is partly true, as they have the same father (20:12).

There has already been a similar episode with the king of Egypt (Genesis 12:10-20). On both occasions, the sin of taking another man's wife brings suffering on the ruler's people. On both occasions, the ruler reproaches Abraham and Abraham apologizes and explains his lie. Some scholars believe that these two stories are in fact the same; but it's quite possible (and very human) that Abraham hasn't learned from his first mistake. His old fear has led to his old deceit. He is saved by the forgiveness of God and the generous understanding of a pagan ruler.

The birth of Isaac

At last, and despite her old age, Sarah gives birth to Isaac (21:1-21). Sarah puts pressure on Abraham to get rid of Hagar and Ishmael. He sends them away with great sadness. But God is with them, and they survive their desert journey to start a new life.

The treaty at Beersheba

Abraham now makes a treaty with Abimelech, who is a powerful neighbour – perhaps one of the early Philistine immigrants into the south of Canaan (21:22–34). As we have already seen (20:1–18), Abimelech is an open and honest man who respects Abraham's faith and has given him permission to live in this area of the Negev. Now they come to an agreement over the use of a well, which Abraham has dug, but Abimelech's servants have seized. The treaty is probably marked by sacrifices of animals, but also by Abraham giving seven ewe lambs to Abimelech and the two men swearing an oath.

The place is called Beersheba, which means 'well of seven' or 'well of the oath'. Abraham plants a tamarisk tree as a landmark and worships God there. Beersheba will be an important base for both Abraham and his son Isaac, and mark the southern boundary of the Promised Land.

Abraham is tested

Some time later, when Isaac is an older child or teenager, God tells Abraham to take him to Mount Moriah (22:1–24). There he is to offer him as a sacrifice. Child sacrifice is practised by some pagan religions, and Abraham might well think it is the ultimate sign of commitment. Isaac is his dearest possession. However, with the fire laid, Isaac bound and the knife raised, God calls to Abraham to stop. Nearby is a ram, caught by its horns in a thicket. The Lord has provided a sacrifice, and Abraham's faith in God has passed its greatest test.

In the future, Solomon will build his great temple on the site of Mount Moriah. Today Abraham's rock is covered by the 'Dome of the Rock' Mosque in Jerusalem. It is near here, also, that God will offer his only son, Jesus, as a sacrifice for the sins of the world. Jesus will be described by John the Baptist as 'the Lamb of God' (John 1:29).

The death of Sarah

Sarah dies and Abraham buries her in the land of Canaan (23:1–20). He negotiates a burial plot at Hebron, and insists on paying the Hittites the proper (perhaps even a high) price for it. It is a cave in a field, and by purchasing it Abraham becomes a landowner.

Abraham – father of the faithful

As we follow Abraham's story, we become aware that the supreme quality of his life is his faith. He has wandered in an unknown land, worshipped an invisible God and believed in an unfulfilled promise. By the time he dies, Abraham owns no more of the Promised Land than a cave in a field, which he has bought for Sarah's grave. For descendants he has just two sons, of whom one has been sent away. But God is committed to Abraham. His plan is to bless him and make a nation out of him. This nation is to be a blessing to the whole world.

God is showing in Abraham's life what he can do in every life. But he can only work where there is faith. Abraham is the spiritual father of all who have faith in God.

The apostle Paul writes of Abraham:

He is our father in the sight of God, in whom he believed – the God who gives life to the dead and calls things that are not as though they were. (Romans 4:17)

This is the only piece of the Promised Land that Abraham will possess in his lifetime; but it is a marker, by faith, of all that God has vowed to give him and his descendants. The place is called Machpelah. Abraham will also be buried here, as will Isaac and his wife Rebekah, and Jacob and his first wife Leah (49:29–32).

Isaac and Rebekah

Isaac is the promise-bearer. He is the link between Abraham and the future. It is crucial that he should marry within the family of faith, and have a son.

Abraham sends his most trusted servant to find a wife for Isaac from among his relatives (24:1–67). We might think Isaac is weak, to let someone else do his courting. But Abraham is taking no risks. It would be dangerous for Isaac to be attracted to Canaanite women or distracted by their pagan religion. He remembers what happened to Lot.

The servant (perhaps Eliezer) asks God to guide him to the right woman. His prayer is wonderfully answered. He meets the beautiful, youthful Rebekah at a well outside Nahor. She gives him a drink, carries water to his camels – and turns out to be the daughter of Abraham's nephew.

Rebekah's father is Nahor, and her brother is Laban. They try to delay the proposed marriage, but the servant handles the situation faithfully and well. Soon he is taking Rebekah home to Isaac, who happily marries her.

Abraham's last days

Abraham has another wife besides Sarah. Her name is Keturah and she bears him six sons. The family tree will list Abraham's sons by three women: Sarah, Hagar and Keturah, who is called a concubine or secondary wife (1 Chronicles 1:28–34). Through Keturah, Abraham is the ancestor of many Arab peoples, of whom the most famous mentioned here is Midian.

Of all Abraham's sons, Isaac is the one who is to inherit God's promise – to bless the world through him, make him a great nation and give him a land. Before he dies, Abraham is careful to give a fair inheritance to each of his other sons, and to send them away from the region which is to be occupied by Isaac (25:1–11). When Abraham dies, Isaac and Ishmael (his half-brother and rival) are united in burying him at Mechpelah, in the cave he had purchased as a tomb for Sarah (23:19).

The descendants of Ishmael (25:12–18)

Ishmael is Abraham's son by Hagar, who was Sarah's Egyptian maidservant. He in turn has twelve sons who become the rulers of tribes. The Arab nations today trace their ancestry to him.

Isaac (Abraham's son) (25:19–26:35)

Isaac's sons: Jacob and Esau

At first it seems that Rebekah is unable to have children. Then God gives her twin boys. They start fighting even before they are born! God explains to Rebekah: 'Two nations are in your womb' (25:23). These two nations will always be at odds with each other. When the twins are born, the first is called Esau, which means 'Hairy', and the second is named Jacob, which means 'Cheat'. This is because Jacob is born clinging to Esau's heel, as though trying to overtake him to be born first.

The twins grow up. Esau becomes a man of the great outdoors. He brings home wild game from his hunting trips. This pleases Isaac, who loves his food. Jacob is a mother's boy. He stays home and helps with the cooking.

One day, when Esau returns hungry, Jacob has some delicious stew prepared. Before he lets Esau taste any, he makes him resign his rights as the elder son. Esau, faced with the choice of food or future, takes the food without a second thought.

The full meaning of 'Jacob' is 'Took by the Heel'. It has the sense of 'coming from behind, catching, spoiling, being determined to get what isn't his'. In later life, God will name Jacob 'Israel' – which means 'Wrestled'. Jacob is a man who will never give up, and nor will the people who descend from him.

Isaac prospers

Like his father Abraham, Isaac lives as a herdsman. God renews the promise to give him the land of Canaan, and descendants 'as numerous as the stars in the sky'.

They live among the Philistines – a vigorous, pagan people. Like Abraham before him, Isaac is afraid he might be killed by someone who wants to take his beautiful wife. For a long time he pretends that Rebekah is his sister. He is challenged by the Philistine king, Abimelech, who sees Isaac being more than brotherly to Rebekah.

Isaac is prosperous and has large herds, but no land. He has a constant problem getting water for his people and animals. He digs wells, but then has to move on.

Something about Isaac's wealth and peaceableness impresses his neighbours. 'We saw clearly that the Lord was with you' (26:28), they say when they come to make a treaty. They agree to give Isaac some land at Beersheba.

Meanwhile, Esau grows to manhood and marries pagan women. This distresses his parents, whose own marriage was so clearly guided by God. Isaac expects Esau to inherit the promise, and his choice of wife will be important. But Esau doesn't care about such things.

Jacob (Abraham's grandson) (27:1–35:29)

Jacob is cunning and hard-working; the underdog who somehow comes out on top. He is an unpleasant and selfish young man, but God blesses him. In due course he will become 'Israel' and give his name to a nation.

Jacob steals his brother's blessing

When Isaac is old and blind, the time comes for him to bless his successor (27:1–40). He sends Esau to catch something tasty for a meal. After he has eaten, he will give him the special blessing which passes the promises of God from father to first-born son.

Rebekah has other ideas. While Esau is away, she dresses Jacob in Esau's clothes, disguises his arms and neck with goatskin, and sends him to Isaac with a tasty dish. Isaac is suspicious, but accepts the food and drink. By the time Esau returns, Jacob has received the blessing.

The blessing is unique and non-transferable. There is no question of Isaac taking it back. All he can promise Esau is a life of conflict and discontent. Esau resolves to murder Jacob as soon as he gets the chance.

Jacob's dream at Bethel

Jacob has to run for his life. Isaac and Rebekah send him north to marry one of his uncle Laban's daughters. He goes with the promise ringing in his ears: 'May God Almighty bless you and make you fruitful and increase in numbers until you become a community of peoples.' The word 'community' will become the Old Testament's word for 'church'.

Travelling up through the hills, Jacob stops for the night. Lonely and homeless, he lies down with his head on a stone. As he sleeps, he

Bethel – 'house of God'

Jacob calls the place of his dream 'Bethel'. It had also been known as Luz. Most scholars think this is at or near Tell Beitin, eleven miles north of Jerusalem, where there are remains of an Early Bronze Age city.

Abraham had visited Bethel, and Jacob will return here. In future years, when the land is conquered by Joshua, it will be captured by Ephraim, one of the Joseph tribes. The ark of the covenant will be kept here for a while, and it will become a sanctuary and place of pilgrimage. Samuel will include it in his annual judge's tour.

When the northern kingdom of Israel is formed, King Jeroboam will make Bethel his religious centre. He will build a shrine to rival the temple in Jerusalem, and create his own priests. The prophet Amos will arrive to condemn the practices there. The worship may be impressive, but the worshippers are wicked (Amos 5:5–13).

dreams (28:10-22). He sees a stairway, reaching all the way from earth to heaven – with angels coming and going on God's business. The Lord speaks to him.

Young Jacob is stopped in his tracks. God is real. God is here. God knows all about him, and has a plan for his life. In the morning, Jacob takes the stone he used as a pillow and stands it as a landmark. He strikes a bargain with God. In return for food, clothes and safe travel, he will worship God, make this place a shrine and give God a tenth of his wealth. It's a shrewd deal. This is Jacob, after all!

Jacob and Rachel

Jacob continues his journey and arrives in Haran. There he asks for his uncle Laban, and meets Laban's daughter Rachel. We have encountered Laban once before – in the negotiation for his sister Rebekah to marry Isaac. In those days he drove a hard bargain and tried to play for time. We find he hasn't changed.

Laban welcomes Jacob with open arms. He has two daughters he wishes to marry off. Leah is the elder. She has a problem with her eyes. Rachel is the younger. She is shapely and beautiful. Jacob agrees to work for Laban for seven years in return for marrying Rachel.

But uncle Laban is too sharp to be left with an elder, unmarried daughter on his hands. When Jacob wakes up after a wedding feast and a rather dimly lit marriage ceremony, he finds Leah lying beside him! Laban explains that it's their custom to marry the older daughter first – and signs up Jacob to work *another* seven years for Rachel. In uncle Laban, the crafty Jacob has met his match.

In later years the Jewish law forbids the marrying of sisters while both are alive. It can only result in jealousy, rejection and hurt. But God has a purpose for Leah. While Rachel struggles to get pregnant, Leah gives birth to six sons and a daughter. Half the tribes of Israel, including the royal tribe of Judah and the priestly tribe of Levi, will honour Leah as their mother.

Jacob also has four sons through his wives' maids, Bilhah and Zilpah. Only after many years of barrenness does Rachel give birth to Joseph and Benjamin.

Jacob proves to be a good and businesslike shepherd. Under his management, Laban's flocks increase. When Jacob has completed the fourteen years of service for his wives, Laban persuades him to stay on. His payment is to keep any speckled or spotted sheep that are born in the flock; Laban immediately withdraws the goats that might father such offspring. Jacob breeds them anyway. He gets the animals to mate while looking at branches he has speckled – a doubtful but God-blessed technique. Over a period of six years Jacob becomes very rich.

Jacob and Laban have now lost all respect for each other. The Lord tells Jacob it is time to return home. Without telling Laban, Jacob gathers his wives and children and flocks – and leaves. For extra protection, Rachel steals her father's gods.

It takes Laban a week to catch up with them. When he does, he makes a tear-jerking speech about wanting to kiss his grandchildren goodbye. He also wants his gods back. Laban is allowed to search for the gods, but doesn't find them because Rachel is sitting on them. Jacob doesn't know that the gods are in Rachel's baggage, and makes a speech of fiery indignation. How can Laban possibly accuse him of theft?

Eventually Laban and Jacob agree to live separate lives, and mark the boundary between them. They call the place 'Mizpah', which means 'watchtower'. God will watch over them when they're apart.

Jacob and Esau are reunited

Jacob has left Laban behind, but Esau lies ahead. He sends news of himself to Esau, and asks for a kindly welcome home. The message comes back that Esau is heading towards them with a small army (32:1–33:20).

With a breaking heart, Jacob divides up his family and flocks – so that some may escape the coming massacre. He begs God to keep his promise and protect them. The following day he sends animals and servants ahead in groups. Each is briefed to say they are a gift to Esau from Jacob; and that Jacob himself is following. In this way Jacob hopes to buy enough goodwill for Esau to spare them. Finally, he sends his family on ahead.

Jacob is in torment. There is nothing more he can do. He doesn't know which way to turn for escape. All night he wrestles with someone – a dark angel, or his fear of death, or his uneasy conscience.

As dawn breaks, the strange opponent dislocates Jacob's hip. Jacob clings on, refusing to admit defeat. He won't let go without a blessing to resolve this terrible conflict.

The One wrestling with Jacob gives him a new name: 'Israel', meaning 'He Struggles with God'. Then he blesses him.

Only then does Jacob realize he has been fighting God. It wasn't a dream. He has a permanent limp to prove it.

So Jacob comes of age. This is the supreme crisis of his life, as he struggles with Esau and God, past and future, fear and faith. He wins through to a new identity and peace.

In the morning Esau appears, galloping towards them with 400 men. As Jacob prepares for death, Esau runs forward – and hugs him! Jacob is overwhelmed. His new-found peace with God is echoed in his reconciliation with his brother.

Jacob and his family settle at Shechem in Canaan – a day's journey from Bethel, where his long journey of faith began.

Dinah

God's chosen family are living among pagans. Jacob's daughter, Dinah, is raped by a man called Shechem, a Hivite, who wants to marry her (34:1–31). Hiding their rage, Dinah's brothers pretend friendship and agree to the marriage. In fact they hold out hope of many marriages between the two peoples in years to come. All they ask is that the Hivite men should be circumcised.

The Hivites agree. While they are still sore, Simeon and Levi (Dinah's actual brothers) attack the city and kill Shechem and his father. Jacob's other sons join in, seizing cattle, carrying off women and children and looting houses. So rape is avenged by deceit and cruelty, to everyone's discredit.

Jacob's return to Bethel

It is time to get right with God. The Lord calls Jacob back to Bethel, the place of his first commitment (35:1–29). The family purges itself of all superstition by burying its foreign gods and lucky charms. For his part, God renews his promise that Jacob will become a great nation and receive the land of Canaan. Jacob sets up a stone and pours out an offering – just as he did twenty years before. In those days God's blessings were just a dream. Now they are his daily experience.

God and 'brother or sister'

There is a close relationship between God and 'brother or sister'. Jacob discovers that to be at odds with one is to be out of sorts with the other. Jesus teaches that we must make peace with a brother or sister before bringing a gift to God:

Leave your gift there before the altar and go; first be reconciled to your brother or sister, and then come and offer your gift. (Matthew 5:24 NRSV)

One of the letters of John makes a similar point:

Those who say, 'I love God', and hate their brothers or sisters, are liars; for those who do not love a brother or sister whom they have seen, cannot love God whom they have not seen. (1 John 4:20 NRSV)

On the way south towards Ephrath, Rachel dies while struggling to give birth. The baby survives and is called Benjamin, which means 'Son of My Right Hand'. Rachel is buried about twelve miles north of Ephrath (Bethlehem). So Jacob comes home to his father Isaac in Mamre. When Isaac dies at a great age, Esau and Jacob bury him there. It's the end of an era.

The descendants of Esau (36:1–43)

The writer narrates the wives and children of Esau and the generations of Edom that flowed from them.

'Edom' is Esau's nickname. It means 'red' – the colour of the stew that Jacob traded for the birthright. It is also the name of Esau's descendants, the Edomites, and their land – which stretches south from the Dead Sea to the Red Sea.

The story of the Edomites runs parallel to that of the Israelites throughout the Old Testament. When the Israelites are on the move from Egypt, Edom refuses to allow them to pass along its border. In later centuries, David conquers Edom, and Solomon builds a port and exports its copper. There is suspicion and hatred between the two nations. The psalmist says that Edom cheered when Jerusalem was destroyed.

Joseph (Abraham's great-grandson) (37:1–50:26)

Joseph is Jacob's favourite son. He shows his favouritism by making Joseph a princely robe. When Joseph dreams, he sees himself as superior to the rest of his family, and that they bow down before him. The other brothers are angered by Jacob's bias and Joseph's boastings.

One day, far from home, the brothers seize Joseph. They strip him of his precious robe and sell him as a slave to some Midianite merchants. Brutally, they stain the costly coat with goat's blood and show it to Jacob. Jacob is heartbroken at the evidence that Joseph is dead.

Meanwhile, Joseph is very much alive. He is taken to market in Egypt and sold to Potiphar, who works for Pharaoh. Pharaoh is the king of Egypt and Potiphar is captain of the king's guard. Between 1720 and 1550 BC Egypt is ruled by the Hyksos pharaohs who, like Joseph, have come from Canaan. They favour servants and administrators from Semitic (that is, Asiatic or 'foreign') backgrounds.

The Lord blesses Joseph, and soon the young man is trusted to manage Potiphar's entire household. Everything goes terribly wrong when Potiphar's wife tries to seduce him. Joseph refuses her, explaining that this would be a betrayal of his master, and a sin against God.

Potiphar's wife is obsessed with Joseph, and her lust turns to rage. She snatches his cloak and later tells her husband that she obtained it when Joseph tried to force himself on her. Joseph is thrown into prison.

In prison, the Lord's favour (and Joseph's charm and competence) work wonders. He runs the place for the warder and interprets dreams for his fellow prisoners. The king's chief cupbearer and the royal baker both have their curious dreams explained. Two years later, when Pharaoh himself is troubled by nightmares, the cupbearer remembers Joseph and recommends him to his master.

Pharaoh's dreams are of thin corn consuming full corn and lean cows devouring fat cows. Everything comes in sevens! Joseph explains that the two dreams carry the same message, and that God is showing Pharaoh the future. Seven years of plenty will be followed by seven years of famine.

Joseph goes on to suggest how Pharaoh might meet the crisis. He should appoint a suitable person to prepare for the famine and administer the relief supplies. With the help of area commissioners, this man will ensure that surplus food is stored during the good years and distributed during the bad years.

Not surprisingly, Joseph gets the job. Pharaoh makes him his chief minister. At the age of thirty, Joseph is in charge of all Egypt. He marries and has two children – Manasseh (meaning 'Forget') and Ephraim (meaning 'Twice Fruitful'). He feels that God has helped him forget his troubles and flourish in spite of them. During the years of plenty, Joseph organizes the storage of vast quantities of grain. Then the years of famine bite – just as Joseph had predicted.

Joseph's family come to Egypt

Among those who travel to Egypt to buy grain are Joseph's brothers. Joseph is now completely Egyptian in appearance and manner. He stands before them dressed in fine linen, wearing his gold chain of office and the Pharaoh's ring. The brothers have changed very little and Joseph recognizes them immediately. They bow before him with their faces to the ground – and Joseph remembers his boyhood dream.

Speaking through an interpreter, Joseph accuses his brothers of being spies. He gets them to admit that their youngest brother is still at home, and another is dead. He orders them to go and bring Benjamin to prove their story, while he holds Simeon as a hostage.

Although it is twenty years since the brothers sold Joseph, he is still on their consciences. As soon as they get into trouble, they guess they are being punished for what they did.

Meanwhile Joseph isn't the spoilt and bossy brat of years ago. His own sufferings have changed him. He is deeply moved to see his brothers, and has to turn away to weep even while he cross-questions them. Without revealing his true identity, he has their bags filled with grain, puts their money back in their sacks and supplies them with food for their journey.

As they return home, the brothers discover their money has been returned to their sacks. Their hearts sink. God is doing something very strange here. When Jacob hears their story, he is panic-stricken and refuses to let Benjamin go with them to Egypt. But the family faces starvation, and he is forced to agree.

When the brothers arrive back in Egypt, Joseph has them shown to his house for lunch. They fear they are under arrest and explain to Joseph's steward that there has been some misunderstanding. When Joseph arrives he continues to astonish them by asking after their father – and sitting them at table in order of age! When he sees his young brother Benjamin, he has to hurry out to weep.

The following morning the brothers are sent on their way – but not before Joseph has supplied them with grain, returned their money and had his own silver cup planted in Benjamin's sack. Joseph orders his steward to catch them up and charge them with theft. Sure enough, the cup is found hidden in Benjamin's grain.

Back at Joseph's house, Judah makes an impassioned appeal for Benjamin to be spared. If anything happens to Benjamin, their father will die. Judah offers to take Benjamin's punishment and become Joseph's slave. Finally Joseph relents. He clears the room of attendants, and makes himself known to his brothers. He explains that God has been at work throughout this long adventure:

I am your brother Joseph, the one you sold into Egypt!
And now, do not be distressed and do not be angry
with yourselves for selling me here, because it was to
save lives that God sent me ahead of you... to save
your lives by a great deliverance... it was not you
who sent me here, but God. (45:4–5, 7–8)

Joseph has it all worked out. They must fetch their father and bring their families and flocks to Egypt. Pharaoh sends wagons for them and promises that 'the best of all Egypt' will be theirs. They are settled in the fertile land of Goshen.

The last days of Jacob and Joseph

As Jacob prepares to die, he makes Joseph promise that his body will be taken from Egypt and buried with Abraham and Sarah in the Promised Land. He blesses Joseph's sons, Ephraim and Manasseh. Jacob crosses his hands to give priority to Ephraim, the younger of the two – just as Jacob had himself been given the first-born's blessing instead of Esau. The God of Jacob is One who makes the first last and the last first.

Jacob blesses each of his sons. He has great insight into their character and destiny. He has particular condemnation for Reuben, and blessings for the royal line of Judah and the godliness of Joseph. When Jacob dies, Joseph has his body embalmed and carried in solemn state to Canaan for burial.

Genesis closes with Joseph's own death and the placing of his body in an Egyptian coffin. In due course this coffin, too, will be taken to the Promised Land.

EXODUS

The book of Exodus describes how God rescues his people, the Israelites, from slavery in Egypt. The climax of their escape comes when God causes a wind to part the waters of the Red Sea. The Israelites cross in safety, but the Egyptian army is drowned. This is the defining moment of the 'Exodus' which means 'way out'. (The same idea is in our word 'exit'.)

God leads his people through the desert to Mount Sinai, where he gives them his law and prepares them for their new life in Canaan, the Promised Land.

The Israelite leader is Moses. He is born a Hebrew, raised as an Egyptian prince and works as a shepherd on the slopes of Sinai. He is assisted by his brother Aaron, who acts as spokesman and later becomes Israel's first high priest.

OUTLINE

The slavery of the Israelites and the birth of Moses (1:1–2:25)
God calls Moses (3:1–4:31)
The great escape (5:1–15:21)
The desert journey (15:22–18:27)
The giving of the law (19:1–24:18)
The tabernacle and the priests (25:1–31:18)
Rebellion and judgment (32:1–34:35)
The climax of Exodus (35:1–40:38)

Introduction

The story so far

The family of Jacob (also known as 'Israel') has migrated to Egypt to escape a famine in their homeland, Canaan. One of Jacob's sons, Joseph, was already in Egypt – serving as the minister in charge of famine relief.

Out of gratitude to Joseph, the king of Egypt ('Pharaoh'), invited Jacob and his other sons to settle with their families and herds in the fertile district of Goshen.

Now times have changed. Jacob and Joseph have been dead for many years and their memory forgotten. Meanwhile, the Egyptians have become anxious at the large number of Israelites in their country. They fear that this powerful minority will cause trouble.

The exodus

The book of Exodus continues the story which began in Genesis. It tells how God's people, the Israelites, are trapped in Egypt where they work as slaves. But God calls Moses, who is Hebrew by birth and Egyptian by upbringing, to lead Israel out of slavery. He reveals himself to Moses by telling him his name, 'Yahweh', which means 'I Am Who I Am', or 'I Will Be Who I Will Be'. The Israelites are to leave Egypt and move to Canaan, the land God promised to Abraham. In all this, Moses is to be assisted by his brother Aaron.

God works wonderful signs through Moses, and inflicts terrible plagues on Egypt. In the end, God kills all Egypt's eldest sons in a single night, but 'passes over' the Israelites. This becomes the Passover, which is remembered for all time as the moment Israel became a nation.

The Egyptian king, Pharaoh, has no choice but to allow the Israelites to leave. But then he changes his mind and pursues them with his army. In a dramatic intervention, God parts the waters of the Red Sea, so that the Israelites can escape, but the Egyptians are drowned. This is the exodus.

As the Israelites journey through the desert, the joy of freedom evaporates and they start to grumble. God provides them with water, and the strange 'manna' – their daily bread. After three months they come to Mount Sinai. This is where Moses had worked as a shepherd and first met God. Now God gives Moses the Ten Commandments and the other laws by which Israel is to live.

The people swear that they will obey God's commands. In return, God makes a covenant with them. They are to be a holy nation, with God as their king. Their way of life will set them apart from all other nations.

But while Moses is away on the mountain, receiving further laws from God, the people rebel. They persuade Aaron to make a golden calf – a god they can see. Moses returns to find the Israelites engaged in a wild pagan orgy. He calls the tribe of Levi to use force to bring the people under control. Then he begs God to forgive them.

God gives Moses detailed instructions for the building of a special tent. This is the tabernacle where God will live among his people. The tabernacle is to house an ark or box containing God's law. Outside the tabernacle, in a screened compound, will be an altar for sacrifices. Aaron and his sons are to be set apart, robed and consecrated as priests.

The book of Exodus closes with the tabernacle being completed with its furniture, its fittings and its priesthood. All is consecrated to the Lord, who dwells there in a cloud of glory.

God's power to rescue his people

Exodus shows God in control of history and of the whole world. He is not just a family god, the focus of superstition and nostalgia. He is the One and Only – the Lord.

God has chosen Israel to be his people. He breaks the power of a cruel tyrant, Pharaoh, to set them free. He leads the Israelites through the desert, gives them his law and instructs them in worship. The climax of the exodus is the building and dedication of the tabernacle, the tented enclosure where God dwells among his people.

Exodus is a book about God's power to rescue his people however desperate their situation. Many oppressed groups have taken courage from this story. God hears the cry of the poor and weak. Freedom fighters in South America and civil rights leaders in the United States have alike echoed Moses' mighty command to Pharaoh: 'Let my people go!'

The exodus is a very human story. We follow the career of Moses, who is called to challenge Pharaoh and lead the people. He feels totally inadequate for the task. The people themselves are first fearful, then fickle. Their slavery has seeped into their souls, making them coarse, suspicious and angry.

But Moses is not the hero of the story. The vision and the end result are God's. Moses is in fact a reluctant leader and an unimpressive speaker. It is only his trust in God that makes him great.

Exodus is a story of God's goodwill and power; the story of how he rescues his people against all odds and gives them freedom and dignity. It is the story of Israel becoming a nation for God.

Israel, too, has many failures. The people are often ungrateful and rebellious. Nevertheless, it is with them that God makes a covenant, and to them he commits his law. They have been rescued from slavery. Now the law will teach them how to be truly free. The appalling lapse when they abandon God and worship a golden calf is a solemn reminder of the weakness of human nature. Moses' prayer for the people in their disgrace, and their developing friendship with God, are among the Bible's greatest treasures.

The final part of the book is about the building of the tabernacle – the mobile sanctuary where God will dwell. The special nature of God is expressed in the detailed and orderly structure, the choice of materials and the skill of the craftspeople. The people are given ways of expressing God's holiness and sharing it. Their worship is focused in sacrifices and offerings. The book ends on a high note, with the tabernacle being dedicated by Moses and filled with the cloud of God's glory.

The heart of the Old Testament

The book of Exodus gives the Jewish people their roots. God rescued them when they were down and out. To this day they celebrate the Passover with the sense and thrill of their God-given freedom.

The exodus became Israel's prime example of God's overwhelming power and perfect timing. The great moment when the Red Sea parted for the Israelites and then engulfed their enemies reverberates throughout the Bible. Centuries later, when the Jews return from exile in Babylon, they see their deliverance as a new exodus.

And then there is the law. At Sinai, God gives guidelines for the good life. The Ten Commandments put God first and others next. They tackle human behaviour at source – in the mind and imagination.

In the building of the tabernacle, Exodus provides a model for every holy place. Here is an attempt to use design and space, materials and skills, to speak of God. Every detail of the tabernacle points to God. All subsequent temples and churches owe something to the tabernacle as their prototype.

For Christians, Exodus marks the beginning of many exciting trails. Luke's Gospel says that when Jesus prayed about his approaching death, he was joined by Moses and Elijah. They talked about his departure ('exodus') and so looked forward to God's mighty rescue beyond the suffering of the cross (Luke 9:31).

There are unmistakable links between Passover and the death of Jesus. Jesus shared the Last Supper with his disciples at Passover time. John's Gospel actually has Jesus dying on the cross while the Passover lambs are being sacrificed in the temple. Certainly Paul makes the connection when he writes, 'Christ, our Passover lamb, has been sacrificed.' Jesus was remembered as saying, as he passed the wine at the Last Supper, 'This cup is the new covenant in my blood.'

Matthew's Gospel tells us that when Jesus died, the curtain of the temple – like the tabernacle curtain hiding the Most Holy Place – 'was torn in two from top to bottom'. So, through the sacrifice of Jesus, people are no longer excluded from God's holy presence.

The letter to the Hebrews explains that, through his death, Jesus offered himself as the perfect sacrifice and acted as the perfect high priest (Hebrews 9:11–12).

Paul teaches that every Christian is like a tabernacle – a place where the Holy Spirit dwells, and where others may meet with God. Our body is a temporary tent, which looks forward to eternal life with God (2 Corinthians 5:1–5).

Who wrote Exodus?

The book of Exodus is the second of five books, which together are called 'the Pentateuch'. They are also known as the 'books of Moses', because Moses is the main character in four of them (Exodus, Leviticus, Numbers and Deuteronomy).

The old Jewish tradition is that Moses actually wrote these books, apart from the description of his own death (the end of Deuteronomy) and the events which took place afterwards. Sometimes it has even been said that he wrote these passages too, as he was a very great prophet. However, there is nothing in the books themselves to say that Moses wrote them. They contain stories, poetry and laws which are extremely old. They might have been passed on by word of mouth for several generations, before being written down in (say) the early years of David's reign.

Many scholars believe that the final versions of these books were put together from several different sources. Two major strands have been identified by the different names used for God: 'J' material calls God 'Yahweh' (the Lord), and 'E' material refers to God as 'Elohim'. In fact, 'Yahweh' is a verb meaning 'I AM' – expressing the ever-present reality of the living God. Another kind of material is information and regulations for priests, and is known as 'P'. More recently, there has been attention to the people who might have preserved these stories – and so 'J' has stood for Judah and 'E' for Ephraim.

Of these five books, Exodus contains the greatest mixture of contents. It includes the story of Moses in Egypt as well as the desert journey to Canaan, the giving of the Ten Commandments and the construction of the tabernacle. The exultant song of Miriam after the crossing of the Red Sea is particularly old, while some of the laws are not about desert life so much as the society of towns and farms which lies in the future.

However the material has come to take its present form, the story is the same. Moses is the central character and he is the most likely person to have written the basic, original material. He had a sophisticated Egyptian education as well as a deep understanding of Hebrew culture and origins; and he was an eyewitness. There is reference to him keeping a written record of events (Exodus 17:14), and writing God's law in a book for the Levites to keep in the covenant box (Deuteronomy 31:24).

The revelation that there is one holy, personal, covenanting God must have come through a very great mind. We know of no one greater than Moses, and Exodus is very much his story.

DISCOVERING EXODUS

The slavery of the Israelites and the birth of Moses

The book of Exodus continues the story which began in Genesis. It begins by listing the twelve sons of Jacob. These are the men who will give their names to the twelve tribes of Israel. The Israelites are also known by a gypsy-like name for wandering Semites: the 'Hebrews'.

The Israelites become slaves (1:1–22)

The Israelites have multiplied in the generations since Joseph. The Egyptians are alarmed at their growing numbers and decide to suppress them. They force them to become slaves and put them to work building store cities for Pharaoh. When this makes no impression on this sturdy race, the king embarks on a programme of ethnic cleansing. All Hebrew boys are to be killed at birth, or thrown in the river.

The store cities (1:11) of Pithom and Rameses were built to house the treasures of Pharaoh Rameses II, in the 13th century BC. This suggests a date for the exodus at about 1250 BC, although some scholars date it to the 15th century BC.

Moses is born – and hidden (2:1–10)

In this desperate situation, one baby boy survives. His parents are from the tribe of Levi, which will one day become the priestly tribe. The baby is placed in a mini-ark and hidden in the reeds by the River Nile. There his loud cries, which had made it impossible to hide him at home, become an asset. He is found and adopted by none other then Pharaoh's daughter. She asks his own mother to care for him through babyhood, and then adopts him. She names him 'Moses', which means 'Draw Out', because she drew him out of the water. Moses is brought up in the royal household, with the double advantages of an Egyptian education and his mother's love.

Moses murders an Egyptian (2:11–25)

As a young man, Moses is moved by the terrible hardship of his people. One day he loses his temper and kills an Egyptian who is beating a Hebrew. As a result, he has to flee the country. He goes to live in Midian where he marries a priest's daughter, Zipporah. They start a family and for many years Moses works as a shepherd for his father-in-law.

Moses is passionately concerned for justice, but he is impetuous. In his years as a shepherd he learns patience, discovers the ways of the desert – and meets with God.

God calls Moses

The burning bush (3:1–12)

One day, Moses is feeding his flock on the slopes of Horeb, 'the mountain of God'. Mount Horeb is also called Mount Sinai. Both names are used in Exodus. Horeb may come from a Hebrew word for 'desert', and Sinai may be linked with the desert of Sin. Although it is clearly to the south of Canaan (and Elijah went there in later years), the actual mountain is not known. It wasn't a holy mountain in terms of God living there. It was simply the place where Moses met with God.

On Mount Horeb Moses catches sight of a bush which is on fire but not burning up. When he goes over to look more closely, God calls him by name.

God warns Moses not to come any closer and to take off his sandals. The very ground is 'holy', because God is present. The book of Exodus will teach us much about holiness. Holiness is always to do with God. Only God is holy and to be in his presence is an overwhelming experience. A sinful person can no more approach a holy God than a tissue can survive in a furnace.

The God who had been missing, presumed dead, now makes himself known to Moses. 'I am the God of your father, the God of Abraham, the God of Isaac and the God of Jacob' (3:6). After the years of silence and the hardship endured by the Israelites, this is a stunning revelation.

God tells Moses that he, too, is moved by the plight of his people. He intends to rescue them and bring them out of Egypt to Canaan – 'a good and spacious land, a land flowing with milk and honey' (3:9). And the leader of this epic adventure is to be – Moses!

God's name (3:13–22)

When asked his name, God replies, 'I Am Who I Am.' The Hebrew YHWH (pronounced 'Yahweh') means 'I Will Be What I Will Be'.

God is alive, immediate, and present. In the past he was known by what he did for the patriarchs: Abraham, Isaac, Jacob and Joseph. Now he will be known by what he does for the Israelites. The proof will be that his people will be rescued from slavery – and worship him on this mountain.

'The LORD' is the English translation of Yahweh or 'Jehovah'. It comes from the days when strict Jews would not pronounce God's name, because their lips were unholy. Instead, they took the letters of YHWH and the vowels from 'Adonai' ('my Lord') to make 'Jehovah'.

Signs for Moses – and Aaron (4:1–31)

Moses asks for more definite signs that the Lord is at work. God turns Moses' shepherd staff into a snake and makes his hand leprous. If the people don't believe Moses, he is to pour Nile water on the ground and it will become blood. Such Bible miracles are always grouped around special events. They are the pointers to some mighty work of God.

Desperately, Moses pleads that he isn't a good speaker. But this is no problem to God. The Lord of creation, who gave people their mouths and all their senses, is well able to help Moses speak. So in the end Moses has to tell the truth. He simply doesn't want to go. He isn't good at leadership. No one will believe him. He is happy where he is. He's a coward.

God agrees that Moses' brother Aaron will assist him and speak for him. Reluctantly, Moses returns to Egypt. On the way he has a fierce struggle with God, which is resolved when Zipporah circumcises their son. Perhaps Moses is bringing his covenant commitment up to date, before calling on others to do the same.

The great escape

'Let my people go!' (5:1–21)

Moses and Aaron go to Pharaoh with the reasonable request that the Hebrews should be allowed a three-day pilgrimage into the desert. They have their own God, who is calling them to hold a festival.

But Pharaoh does not acknowledge this Lord, the God of Israel. His answer is to make life even harder for the slaves. From now on, they will have to find the straw for making bricks, while still producing the same number. The Hebrews obviously have too much time on their hands if they're planning a pilgrimage!

And so the Israelites make bricks with a mixture of mud, sand and straw. This is shaped in wooden moulds and dried by the sun. The straw is vital for bonding the mud, as it decays in the clay and improves the plasticity of the brick.

'I will free you' (5:22–6:27)

The Israelites blame Moses and Aaron for getting them into deeper trouble. Moses (for the first time, but not the last) turns his discouragement into prayer.

The Lord reassures Moses of his overwhelming commitment to rescue the Israelites from Egypt. He states again that he is the very same God who made covenant promises to Abraham, Isaac and Jacob. Now he has 'remembered' his covenant. He is Israel's next of kin, and can be relied on to 'redeem' her – to rescue her from trouble.

Moses faithfully relays God's message to the Israelites – but they are too angry and disillusioned to take it in.

'I will harden Pharaoh's heart' (6:28–7:13)

Moses is feeling totally inadequate. He is also tongue-tied. But God tells him to challenge Pharaoh with complete confidence. God is in control. He is even going to 'harden Pharaoh's heart' so that Pharaoh will become set in his resistance. Then, when the climax comes, the full contrast between Israel's God and the gods of Egypt will be clearly seen.

Moses is now eighty. He was forty when he killed the Egyptian, and he has been a further forty years working as a shepherd. Forty years is 'a generation' – the time it takes to grow up and have children. When Moses dies at the age of 120 his life will have spanned three generations.

Despite their sense of utter weakness, Moses and Aaron obey God. When Pharaoh demands some proof that God is on their side, Aaron throws down his staff and it turns into a snake. Pharaoh is unimpressed. He gets his own people to do the same. Even when Aaron's snake eats the rest, Pharaoh won't change his mind.

The plagues (7:14–11:10)

The River Nile is worshipped as a god in Egypt. It is the country's lifeline. Without its waters, Egypt would die. Now Moses commands Aaron to strike the water and it turns to blood. It becomes thick, red and undrinkable. Pharaoh's magicians can conjure the same effect, but they can't produce a cure.

This is the first of ten plagues which God inflicts on Egypt. The Nile and all water flowing from it are turned 'to blood'. Thousands of fish die – and rot. Multitudes of frogs leave their swamps and take to the houses. Pharaoh promises to let the Israelites go, if only Moses will ask the Lord to get rid of the frogs. But once they're dead and heaped in piles, he changes his mind.

The frogs are followed by plagues of gnats and flies, animal sickness, and boils on humans and cattle. There is a storm of thunder and hail in which branches are stripped from trees and the crops are ruined. But the storm doesn't hit Goshen, where the Israelites live, and it stops when Moses prays. Meanwhile, Pharaoh's magicians manage to conjure up some frogs, but admit defeat with the gnats. When it comes to boils, they themselves can hardly walk!

After the hail, a strong east wind brings clouds of locusts. They eat all that's left after the storm. Moses had warned Pharaoh that the Lord would do this and the wind had risen when Moses raised his staff.

When Pharaoh asks forgiveness, Moses prays to the Lord and a west wind drives the locusts away.

The plagues

The plagues seem to have occurred over a period of several months, from the flooding of the Nile in July to the Israelites' departure from Egypt in the following spring.

The Nile rises each year in July and August, reaching its high point in September and subsiding in October and November. When the waters are particularly high, they bring down red clay from Ethiopia. Sometimes the plankton and bacteria multiply, to give a dramatic reddish effect.

Decomposing fish could have driven the frogs inshore – where they might have died of anthrax, which would also kill the cattle. Swarms of mosquitoes would breed on the stagnant water, while flies would incubate in the piles of rotting frogs. Together they would carry disease from animals to humans, causing bites and skin sores.

Storms that flattened barley and flax (but not wheat and spelt) would have come in January or February. Such weather was more likely in Upper Egypt than in Goshen, which is near the sea. Locusts come in dense clouds in March, blown on the east wind up the Nile Valley. It was wind, too, which would complete the drying of the red clay and whip it into a dust storm. The resulting dense darkness could last for several days.

The plagues can all be explained by natural events, but God's mighty power is evident in their intensity and timing.

Finally there is total darkness throughout the land – except, of course, where the Israelites live. It's a darkness that can be felt and it lasts for three days.

Each of the plagues can be explained by natural causes, but it is the fact that they happened when they did – and on such a scale – that indicates God at work.

The tenth and final plague is truly terrible. The eldest sons of all Egyptian families – humans and animals – are to die in a single night. But the Lord will 'pass over' the families of the Israelites and spare them.

The Passover (12:1–30)

Moses tells the Israelites to prepare for this 'Passover'. Every family is to kill a lamb and daub its blood on the outside door. This is a sign for the

Lord to 'pass over' the home. The people are to pack their possessions, get dressed for a journey and eat a hasty meal.

At midnight the first-born of the Egyptians start to die, from Pharaoh's son to the child of the lowest slave. While desolate cries are heard from the Egyptian houses, the Israelite homes are secure and calm. Nobody stirs, not even the dogs.

At midnight, a new age begins for the Israelites. Passover is to be their New Year's Day; their birth as a nation.

The first month of the year has the Canaanite name 'Abib', which means 'ripening corn'. Later the Jews will call it 'Nisan', a name from Babylonia. In Western months, it comes towards the end of March and the beginning of April. The Jewish Passover sometimes coincides with the Christian Maundy Thursday.

Moses tells the whole community of Israel what to do. This 'gathering for God' is our first glimpse of a word which will later be used for 'church'. Such a 'community' or 'church' is a group of people who are 'called together' to hear the word of God.

On the tenth day of the first month, each household is to take a lamb. It must be a year-old male and can be a sheep or a goat. On the fourteenth day the animal is to be killed. This is halfway through the month, when the moon is full. The Passover is a festival timed by the new moon, but not in honour of it. In later years, the Passover date will be announced when the new moon is seen in the sky above Jerusalem.

The blood of the lamb is a sign rather than a sacrifice. The animal's life is paid by a family so that the first-born son will be spared. But this isn't a payment for any sin. There is no priest, no ceremony and no confession. The lamb is simply killed and its blood painted on the sides and tops of the Hebrew door frames.

A bunch of 'hyssop' is used for painting the lamb's blood on the doorposts. This isn't the plant we call hyssop today. It may be a common shrub or herb, such as Syrian marjoram.

The lamb is roasted whole on a spit over an open fire. It is eaten with bitter herbs and bread made without yeast. Everything is to be eaten up. Nothing of this holy meal is to be left as if it doesn't matter, or taken away for use in magic. And all is to be done in a hurry, because God's time for action has come.

When the Passover is eaten in Jewish homes today there is no lamb, because there is no temple in Jerusalem and therefore no sacrifices. Instead, there is the shank bone of a sheep as a token. The bitter herbs have become a reminder of the bitterness of slavery.

The Feast of Unleavened Bread includes Passover and lasts for a week. Perhaps Moses orders bread without yeast because there is no time for the dough to rise. If some is for the journey, it will pack flat and last well.

The exodus (12:31–14:31)

Pharaoh commands Moses and Aaron to leave Egypt. The Israelites ask the Egyptians for silver, gold and clothing. No doubt some gifts are made with goodwill, and others given just to get rid of the terror. In any case, the Israelites leave Egypt laden with treasure just as God had promised.

The departure is so sudden that the Israelites travel with unleavened bread still in their kneading bowls. The Lord goes ahead of them in a pillar of cloud. At night the cloud moves behind them, to shield them from the Egyptians.

The quickest route, along the coast, is also the most dangerous. Instead, God leads the Israelites inland on a desert road to the Red Sea, or 'Sea of Reeds'. This is not the 'Red Sea' of the Persian Gulf, but a marshy area of papyrus or other reedy plants.

The exact place of the exodus and the route through the wilderness is not known. It isn't even certain which mountain is Sinai. One theory has the Israelites travelling a long way south to Mount Horeb, and then up to Kadesh Barnea. Another takes a more direct route across to Kadesh, with Jebel Helal as the holy mountain.

Once the Israelites have left, Pharaoh changes his mind. But God is at work in Pharaoh's defiance. He is hardening Pharaoh's attitudes and preparing him for total defeat.

Pharaoh pursues the Hebrews with horses and chariots. He catches up with them as they camp by the Red Sea. The Israelites fear that all is lost, but Moses speaks to them with authority and confidence. They must stand firm in their faith in God and watch what he will do to deliver them once and for all.

The Lord tells Moses to stretch out his hand over the sea. Then, throughout the night, the Lord causes a strong east wind to divide the water and create a dry path for the people to cross.

It is unlikely that the waters are stacked up each side of the fleeing Israelites, as in a Hollywood epic. This great deliverance is more in the timing than the special effects. But the water to either side certainly protects the Israelites from being outflanked by the Egyptian forces. When the chariots use the same route in the early hours of the morning, they are doomed.

As Pharaoh's finest battalion charges, the God of Israel intervenes. In fire and cloud he throws them into muddy, panic-stricken chaos. The chariot wheels stick, the horses rear, the drivers fight for control and then turn back. As they do so, the Lord tells Moses to stretch out his hand again. The first rays of daylight reveal the waters flooding back to drown the pride of Egypt. Israel's awesome and pitiless enemy is routed, without a blow being struck. This is God's mighty act of deliverance.

The song of Moses and Miriam (15:1–21)

Moses and the Israelites sing a song which tells the story of God's thrilling victory. It has strong rhythms and uses ancient words and phrases. There is a great sense of God surging up powerfully like a wave, to toss Pharaoh's soldiers and swallow the chariots. The Lord is supreme as both God and king. The exodus is his sovereign act to rescue his people from tyranny and slavery. He is Israel's redeemer.

Miriam, Moses' sister or half-sister, leads the women in a song and dance of victory. The words are particularly old:

I will sing to the Lord,
for he is highly exalted.
The horse and its rider
he has hurled into the sea. (15:1)

The exodus becomes an important image in later psalms and prophecies, for example Psalm 106:9–12:

He rebuked the Red Sea, and it dried up;
he led them through the depths as through a desert.
He saved them from the hand of the foe;
from the hand of the enemy he redeemed them.
The waters covered their adversaries;
not one of them survived.
Then they believed his promises and sang his praise.

The desert journey

Once in the desert, the Israelites have to learn to trust God. The route and pace of their journey depend on finding pasture and water for their flocks and herds.

The waters of Marah and Elim (15:22–27)

The Desert of Shur is barren and sandy. When they get to Marah (meaning 'bitter' – like myrrh), they find the water unpleasant. Marah may have been today's Ain Hawarah, which has an artesian well tainted by mineral salts.

The people grumble. The joy of freedom evaporates in the heat of hardship. This is the first of many occasions when they blame Moses for their troubles. Moses, in despair, cries out to God.

The Lord 'shows' Moses a piece of wood. Moses throws the wood in the water and it becomes sweet. The Hebrew word for 'show' is 'torah'. It means 'instruction' – the way to something good. It will be used for the 'Torah', the law of God, which the psalmist will describe as 'sweeter than honey' (Psalm 119:103).

The wood may have been a shrub such as a barberry bush, which would have a strong enough flavour to make the water drinkable. The Lord reveals himself as One who can give his people a healthy life, if they follow his way.

The Israelites move on some seven miles to Elim, which means 'terebinths' or 'oak trees'. This could have been the modern Wadi Gharandel, which is a more comfortable oasis. These places are hard to trace, because the names have been changed so often by nomads passing through.

Quail and manna (16:1–36)

The grumbling goes on. The people wish they were back in Egypt, sitting round pots of stew. But the Lord is going to provide them with daily bread.

That evening, fresh meat arrives, in the form of a flock of quail. Quails are small game birds, like partridges, which fly low and roost on the ground. They migrate north across the Sinai peninsular between March and April, on their way from Arabia to southern Europe. And they are tasty to eat.

The following morning, when the dew has dried, the Israelites find the ground covered with thin flakes, like frost. They say in Hebrew, 'Manna?' ('What's-its-name?') – and the phrase sticks.

Manna is to be the Israelites' basic food for the next forty years. It is 'white like coriander seeds and tastes like wafers made with honey' (16:31). Moses tells the people to collect an omer (probably about four

What is manna?

There are various theories about manna, but in the end it remains a mystery and a miracle. Certain insects in the Sinai peninsular secrete drops of honeydew on tamarisk bushes overnight. The drops melt in the sunshine and fall to the ground, where they are carried off by ants. The substance sounds like manna, but is only produced for a few weeks of the year, round about June. Only by a miracle could food be provided on the scale and with the regularity required to feed the Israelites. Relying on manna is a major step in Israel's learning to trust in God and his promises (Deuteronomy 8:3).

Manna is God's food supply: 'bread from heaven'. It is a daily proof to the Israelites that God cares for them and will provide for their needs as each day comes. This theme is found in the Lord's Prayer, when Jesus teaches his disciples to pray, 'Give us today our daily bread' (Matthew 6:11).

When Jesus feeds a multitude by blessing and breaking five small barley loaves, the people are excited that a new Moses has appeared to lead them. Jesus explains that he isn't like Moses, whose manna lasted only a day. The Israelites who ate that manna died in the desert. Jesus declares himself as God, the provider and life-giver, when he says, 'I am the bread of life... the bread that comes down from heaven, so that one may eat of it and not die' (John 6:47–50 NRSV).

pints) per person every morning, except the sabbath. On the day before the sabbath they must collect enough for two days and cook or bake it to make it last.

Water from the rock (17:1–7)

When the Israelites camp at Rephidim, they are again short of water. Rephidim is today's Wadi Feiran, the principal oasis in southern Sinai. It may be that the Israelites were prevented from getting to water by the Amalekites.

Moses feels that his life is in danger, because the people are so angry with him. The Lord leads Moses to a rock at Horeb, and tells him to strike it. Water gushes out, as it does when the smooth surface of limestone is split. Moses may have been familiar with this extraordinary method of finding water, as he had been a shepherd for forty years in a nearby region.

The place is given two names: Massah ('testing'), because the people doubt whether the Lord is with them, and Meribah ('quarrelling'), because the Israelites quarrel with Moses. In a similar episode, Moses is commanded simply to speak to the rock. In the event he strikes it twice with his rod, and God is angry with him. Again, the place is called Meribah (Numbers 20:9–12).

Prayer battle (17:8–16)

The Amalekites attack the Israelites. They are probably anxious to keep Rephidim for themselves. It is known by Arabs today as the 'Pearl of Sinai', a mini-paradise of palm trees and pasture.

At this point we meet Joshua. He is later described as Moses' assistant. Here he is commanding a contingent fighting the Amalekites. The Israelites must learn to rely on God in battle just as they have done for food and water. Moses prays from a vantage point overlooking the conflict, with Aaron and Hur either side to support his hands as they are raised in prayer.

When the enemy is defeated, the Lord tells Moses to declare a lasting ban on the Amalekites. This is to be both in writing on a scroll and by word of mouth to Joshua. In years to come, the Amalekites will be defeated and destroyed by Saul (1 Samuel 15:7–8).

Jethro visits Moses (18:1-27)

Moses' father-in-law, Jethro, arrives with Moses' wife and sons. He sees how overburdened Moses is with the care of so many people and offers him sound advice on how to share the load. Jethro's principles of selection and delegation have never been surpassed and are valued and applied to this day.

The giving of the law
Mount Sinai (19:1-25)

The Israelites arrive at the Desert of Sinai and camp near God's holy mountain. Moses goes up to speak with God and God gives him a solemn message for the people.

Israel has been given her freedom to become a nation. Now she receives her calling to belong to God. She is singled out from all the nations of the world to be God's priests: his pure, distinct, holy representatives. The Israelites will represent God to the nations and bring the nations to God. God's reputation is to depend on Israel's example.

It is a solemn moment. The people are to focus on God's holiness by washing their clothes and abstaining from sex. Sex is not dirty, but it is engrossing. The Israelites are to devote themselves entirely to the task in hand. Even so, they must keep their distance from the holy mountain.

The presence of God is awesome. The Lord descends on the mountain with fire, smoke billows up, the landscape shudders, a ram's horn trumpet sounds a crescendo... and God speaks.

It is tempting to think that Mount Sinai is an active volcano, but it may not be so. There are volcanoes to the east of the gulf of Aqaba, but the traditional Mount Sinai is today's Gebel Mosa, one of three fine peaks near modern Feiran (Rephidim). It isn't volcanic.

The Ten Commandments (20:1-17)

The keynote of Israel's relationship with God is to be obedience. The people's commitment to God is to be shown by keeping his laws. The Lord reveals these laws to Moses, beginning with the Ten

Commandments. They are firm, clear and concise. Although several begin with the words 'You shall not...' their effect is very positive and liberating. In their simplicity and directness they apply to everyone, without exception, for all time.

The first commandments deal with respect for God:

'I am the Lord your God, who brought you out of Egypt... You shall have no other gods before me' (20:2-3). The Lord is identified as the One who alone rescued his people from Egypt. The Israelites are not to worship any other god. To take another god is idolatry, just as to take another sexual partner outside marriage is adultery.

'You shall not make for yourself an idol' (20:4 NRSV). The Israelites are not to make images of any god, nor even to attempt to portray the true One. Any carving or painting, however sincere, can only have the effect of shrinking the concept of God and misleading his worshippers. God is invisible.

'You shall not misuse the name of the Lord your God' (20:7). God's people are not to abuse or misuse God's name. They must not empty it of meaning by using it lightly, or by making vows which they then break.

'Remember the Sabbath day by keeping it holy' (20:8). The sabbath, every seventh day, is to be kept for rest and enjoyment of God's blessing. It is to be a day of freedom and fresh perspective.

The last remaining commandments have to do with people's behaviour towards each other. Every person's life is to be respected. So are marriages, possessions and reputations.

'Honour your father and your mother' (20:12 NRSV). Parents are to be honoured. This is God's social structure, which will enable the nation to survive. The word 'honour' means more than just respect for parents. It implies giving money or an allowance to provide for your parents in their old age. Jesus rebukes some Pharisees for breaking this commandment. They have set aside for 'religious' use the money which should be maintaining their parents (Matthew 15:1-6).

'You shall not murder' (20:13 NRSV). This is just two words in Hebrew: 'No killing!' It means that there is to be no violent murder of a personal enemy. Later laws understand that death is sometimes

> **Jesus and the law**
>
> Jesus teaches that obedience to God starts with our thoughts. This is already at the heart of the law, as the tenth commandment shows, but Jesus makes it particularly clear.
>
> In the Sermon on the Mount, Jesus says of murder, 'Don't even nurse anger' (Matthew 5:22–23). On adultery, he says, 'Don't even give her that "look"' (Matthew 5:28). This is a fascinating glimpse of Jesus' own self-discovery and self-control, as well as being essential guidance for our own thoughts.

accidental. The death penalty, as well as killing enemies in battle, are an accepted part of Jewish life.

'*You shall not commit adultery*' (20:14 NRSV). A man is not to have sex with another man's wife. It is the worst kind of stealing, short of murder.

'*You shall not steal*' (20:15 NRSV). A person has a right to life, freedom and property. These rights are respected and protected by the commandment not to steal. No society can establish trust when theft and burglary are rife. Terrible pain and disruption come from such crimes as kidnapping and slavery. Death itself can result from the theft of someone's livelihood or savings.

'*You shall not give false testimony against your neighbour*' (20:16). This is again about stealing. This time the theft is of someone's reputation. With so many laws carrying the death penalty, a lie may cause a person to be executed for something they didn't do. Even gossip can be lethal and result in a living death for someone who can't prove the truth.

'*You shall not covet*' (20:17 NRSV). God forbids jealousy of someone else's possessions. This is a law against mental theft and a warning against being discontented. It is also a 'threshold' commandment. To cross it may lead to breaking one of the other commandments as well.

Other laws (20:18–23:13)

After the Ten Commandments, God gives Moses a variety of laws. Here, and in the books of Leviticus, Numbers and Deuteronomy, there are as many as seven groups of laws. They are collections of rules and detailed procedures.

Here we find guidance for owning servants and settling quarrels. There is compensation for injuries to people or damage to property. The weaker members of society – orphans, widows, the poor and the stranger – are given special protection. And just as people are to rest on every seventh day, so cultivated land is to rest every seventh year.

'Eye for Eye, Tooth for Tooth'

This regulation sounds brutal and vindictive (21:24). In fact it is simply an attempt to be fair. Someone who inflicts hurt is to receive an equal hurt as his penalty. Nothing more and nothing less. *Only* an eye for an eye, and *only* a tooth for a tooth. It is a restriction on unlimited vengeance.

In the Sermon on the Mount, Jesus teaches a better way, which is forgiveness: 'Do not resist an evildoer. If anyone strikes you on the right cheek, turn the other also' (Matthew 5:39 NRSV). In forgiving, hurt is absorbed by the wronged person, and not recycled in revenge. This is what Jesus himself did on the cross.

Three annual festivals

Three times a year there are to be festivals. So God declares three weeks of official holiday every year.

The Feast of Unleavened Bread falls at the beginning of the barley harvest. It is a week in which the Israelites eat bread made without yeast. It celebrates the Passover, when they remember their escape from Egypt. The Feast of Harvest (or 'Weeks') comes seven weeks later, while the wheat harvest is being gathered. The Feast of Ingathering is in the autumn when the last crops, including the grapes and olives, are safely stored.

'Do not cook a young goat in its mother's milk' (23:18–19)

To those who love pets, this command goes without saying. We may think it's a ban on a tasteless and cruel act, but it probably refers to a pagan ritual or fertility spell.

Covenant

A covenant is made when God commits himself to bless and protect his people. He does so of his own free will and keeps his promise despite his people's failures and rebellions. By the time of this covenant at Sinai, God has already made binding promises to Noah and Abraham. In the future he will also make a solemn commitment to preserve the royal line of David.

'If...' (23:20-33)

The laws which begin with the Ten Commandments are rounded off with a wonderful promise. Chapters 21 to 23 form a mini-book, dealing with the terms, conditions and benefits of the covenant.

If the Israelites will honour God in every aspect of their life, he will give them health and security. He will also go ahead of them into Canaan, to drive out their enemies and give them the land.

The covenant confirmed (24:1-12)

The covenant is the agreement by which the Lord becomes Israel's God, and Israel commits herself to be God's people and keep his law. The Lord calls Moses and Aaron, together with Aaron's sons Nadab and Abihu, and seventy elders. They are to worship God at a distance, while Moses alone approaches the Lord.

Moses tells the people God's laws and writes them down as a permanent record. The Israelites promise obedience and Moses builds an altar at the foot of the mountain. They offer sacrifices and Moses reads them the book of the covenant. This book may be the same three chapters we have just read.

The people swear: 'Everything the Lord has said we will do.' The rest of the Old Testament will be the story of their failure to keep this promise.

Moses sprinkles the people with blood from the sacrifices. Then the select group, Moses and the elders, share a meal in God's presence. It is a time-honoured way of marking an agreement.

Moses on the mountain (24:13-18)

Moses spends forty days and nights alone on the mountain top, enveloped in the cloud of God's presence and glory. The glory of the Lord 'settles' on Mount Sinai – a word which has the sense of pitching a tent, or staying for a while.

God's glory is his 'weight' or worth. The signs of his presence are dense cloud and raging fire.

Moses is one of the Old Testament's 'mountain men'. Both he and Elijah have awesome encounters with God at Sinai. One day Jesus will meet with them in the cloud of God's glory on the Mount of Transfiguration. He will talk with them about his own 'exodus' or departure (Luke 9:30). Unlike Elijah, there will be no fiery chariot for Jesus. His path to glory must pass through death on a cross.

The tabernacle and the priests

Offerings for the tabernacle (25:1-9)

The Lord asks that the Israelites, of their own free will, may give the materials for building a tabernacle. This is to be God's own tent, so that he can live among his people. It is to be made with extraordinary care and attention to detail. In the tent there will be special furniture: an ark, a table and a lampstand.

The ark (25:10-22)

The ark is a wooden chest, about a yard long and two feet in width and height. It is overlaid with gold and topped with cherubim. This is the ark of the testimony, where the stone tablets containing the Ten Commandments will be kept. Although Noah's boat and Moses' basket are both called arks, a different word is used here.

The table (25:23-30)

The table is for 'the bread of the Presence'. These are twelve loaves (one for each tribe), freshly baked and placed in the presence of God.

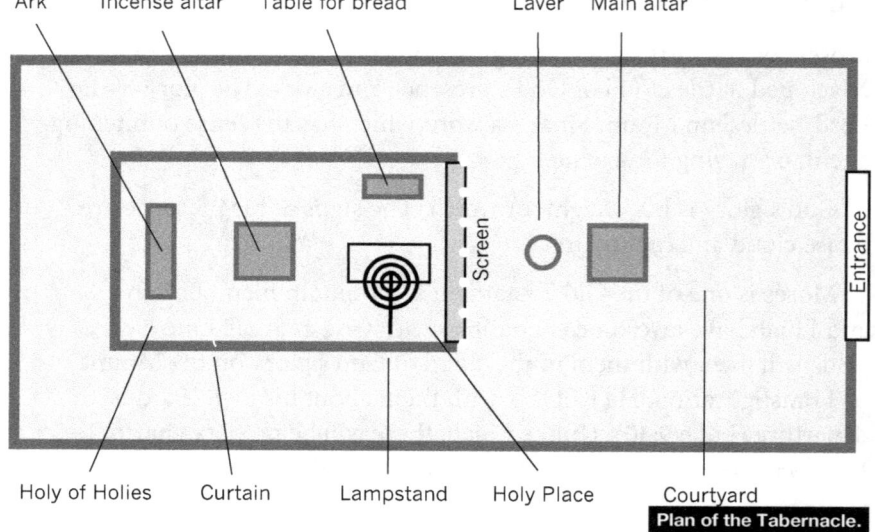

Plan of the Tabernacle.

The lampstand (25:31-40)

There is to be a six-branched lampstand which, with its centre stem, will provide seven lamps. It is to be decorated with almond buds and blossoms in gold.

The tabernacle (26:1-37)

The first tabernacle is a 'tent of meeting' which Moses pitches outside the camp. Anyone can seek God there. Moses himself speaks with God 'face to face, as one speaks to a friend'.

Now the tabernacle is to be a curtained sanctuary *within* the camp. It can be assembled and dismantled to travel with the Israelites on their journey, as God himself does.

There is considerable detail about how the tabernacle is to be made and furnished. Mobile meeting tents and pavilions were well known in Egypt long before the time of Moses. Incense altars, too, have been discovered from various Canaanite sites dating from the 10th century BC.

The basic structure of the tabernacle is a wooden frame, about 45 feet long by 15 feet wide. It is covered with ten linen curtains. The material is

'The Lord is here'

The tabernacle is the prototype of all later temples and churches. It is a place to meet with God.

When Jesus is born, John's Gospel says, 'The Word became flesh and lived ['tabernacled'] for a while among us.' Paul teaches that every Christian is a tabernacle of the Holy Spirit.

The tabernacle has many links with the New Testament and what Jesus comes to do. The letter to the Hebrews says that Jesus, in offering his life as a sacrifice for the sin of the world, 'entered heaven itself, now to appear for us in God's presence' (Hebrews 9:24).

---

gorgeously embroidered with blue, purple and scarlet thread. It is then protected from the weather by eleven goat-hair curtains and layers of animal skins.

Inside the tabernacle it is cool, dark and airless. There are two sections or compartments. The first is the heart of the tabernacle, the 'Most Holy Place'. Here stands the ark of the covenant. The ark has an 'atonement cover' of pure gold, on which blood from the sacrifices is sprinkled. This is a sign that sin has been covered and cancelled.

The second compartment is the 'Holy Place'. It is separated from the Most Holy Place by a curtain. This is the curtain which, in Herod's temple, will be torn from top to bottom when Jesus dies (Matthew 27:51).

In front of the curtain is the altar of incense, covered with gold and with horns projecting at the four corners. The altar stands directly opposite the ark.

On the north side of the altar is the table for the 'bread of the Presence'. On it are twelve loaves, specially baked from fine flour and arranged in the presence of God. They remind the twelve tribes that they are always living in God's sight.

Every sabbath, the priests place fresh bread on the table and eat the old bread in the Holy Place. One day the young hero David will, rather shockingly, ask for the bread of the Presence to feed his men (1 Samuel 21:2–6). A thousand years later, Jesus will approve what David did. He lets his own men pick ears of corn on the sabbath, because he puts people before protocol (Mark 2:23-28).

On the south side of the altar is the lampstand.

The courtyard (27:1-21)

The tabernacle is set in a courtyard, about 50 yards long and 25 yards wide. The area is marked out by a high linen screen, hung on posts and held by guy ropes and pegs. This is where the people can assemble when sacrifices are offered or for other special occasions.

In the eastern half of the courtyard stands the altar of burnt offering. It has no top, but is hollow to form an incinerator. It is covered in copper and, like the altar of incense, has horns at the corners. The burnt offering from the main sacrifice is offered here. The horns can be for tying animals, or for a person to cling to when making a request.

Between the altar and the door of the tabernacle stands a bronze 'laver', or basin. This is for Aaron and his sons to wash their hands and feet, before entering the tabernacle or approaching the altar. God's work is holy and must be done with clean bodies and pure hearts.

The priestly garments (28:1-43)

Aaron and his sons are to have special robes. Aaron, as high priest, is to be magnificently dressed in breastplate, ephod, robe, tunic, turban and sash. The instructions are full of symbolic detail, although the meaning isn't always clear to us today.

Like the linen drapes of the tabernacle, the garments are to be finely embroidered – this time with the addition of gold thread. Gold is the colour of God's glory.

The consecration of the priests (29:1-46)

Aaron and his sons are to be consecrated – set apart from everyone else to serve God as priests. They must be made clean, by washing and sacrifice, before they can take on their holy work.

Moses washes the priests and dresses them in their robes. He anoints Aaron with holy oil, pouring it over his head. This is the sign of the outpouring of God's spirit for a special task. Then Moses makes a sacrifice for their sins.

The priests lay their hands on a bull. In this way they identify themselves with the animal that is to be killed on their behalf. The bull is then slaughtered in God's presence, at the entrance to the tabernacle. The bull's blood is smeared on the horns of the altar and poured out at the base. Some of its fat, liver and kidneys are burned on the altar. The bulk of the carcass is burned outside the camp. It is an awesome symbol of the damage and cost of sin.

Next a ram is chosen. Aaron and his sons lay their hands on its head. It is slaughtered, cut up and the pieces washed. This time the whole animal is burned on the altar. This means that the priests are wholly acceptable, no longer torn apart by sin. Now they are pleasing to God.

Another ram is killed. Some of its blood is smeared on the priests – on their right ear lobes, right thumbs and right big toes. Some is sprinkled on the altar and some over the priests and their robes. Now they are entirely embraced in the life and work of God at the altar.

Parts of the ram – the breast and thigh – are waved before the Lord, together with the sacred bread. The meat is cooked for the priests to eat. This, with the sacred bread, is their ordination meal.

For a week, Aaron and his sons offer sacrifices to consecrate the altar. When these are completed, the routine of morning and evening sacrifice begins. Each day, at dawn and dusk, a year-old lamb is offered, with flour, oil and wine.

The sequence of washing and bloodshed is complete. Each sacrifice and ceremony has played a part in opening the way to God. Now a holy bridgehead has been established between God and his people. The poured out blood is the focus. The priests are the living links. The purpose is that the Israelites will enjoy communion with God for ever.

The altar of incense (30:1–10)

Inside the tabernacle there is a small altar. It stands in front of the curtain in the Holy Place and is used only for burning incense. The incense itself is made to a unique recipe. Aaron burns it twice a day as he tends the lamps. Once a year he cleanses and rededicates the altar, with blood from the annual Day of Atonement sacrifice.

A holy poll tax (30:11–16)

Every man over twenty years old is to pay half a shekel for 'atonement money'. Although the rescue from Egypt is God's free gift, this holy tax acknowledges what God has done for each person. The amount is the same for rich and poor alike and the money is used to maintain the tabernacle. Centuries later, this becomes the two-drachma temple tax collected from Jesus and Peter in Capernaum (Matthew 17:24–27).

The 'laver' or basin (30:17–21)

There is a bronze basin for the priests to wash their hands and feet. They must do this before entering the tent of meeting or approaching the altar for sacrifice. Their hands and feet will often be spattered with blood. But, more importantly, the washing will help them focus their minds and hearts on the seriousness of approaching God.

The anointing oil (30:22–33)

Moses is told to make the anointing oil. The base is olive oil and the spices are rare and expensive. This oil could have many uses, such as treating wounds or sunburn, or perfuming hair and skin. The Lord tells Moses that this particular formula is to be kept exclusively for the priests.

Incense (30:34–38)

The incense, too, is made to a special recipe. It contains rare and expensive spices, together with salt to preserve it and help it burn.

Incense is burned as a sign of prayer. It gives a fragrant smell and clouds of smoke. With so many other strong smells around (animal dung, burning fat, hot blood and crowds of humans in desert heat) the incense will soothe the senses and condition the air.

The skilled workers (31:1–11)

God is providing a gifted worker to head up the design and manufacture of all the sacred furniture, fittings and robes. His name is Bezalel, which means 'Overshadowed by God'. His skills are inspired by God.

The sabbath (31:12–18)

The Lord reminds Moses of the importance of keeping the sabbath. By setting aside every seventh day, Israel acknowledges God as Lord over work and time.

Although work is necessary and even exciting, it must never become an end in itself. It must not come between the Israelites and their God. To observe the sabbath as a holy day of rest must be for ever a distinctive aspect of Jewish life.

The Lord concludes his instructions to Moses by giving him the two 'tablets of the testimony'. These are stone plaques on which God has written the law, probably in the form of the Ten Commandments.

Rebellion and judgment

The golden calf (32:1–33:6)

Moses has been away from the camp for more than a month. The Israelites begin to assume that he has had an accident, or simply gone away and left them. They were never very impressed with him anyway.

The people put pressure on Aaron. Sullen, impatient and boorish, they want a god they can see. Aaron gives in to their demands. He collects all the gold earrings, melts them down and fashions a golden calf. Then he builds an altar for the worship of the calf-idol and announces a festival.

This a tragic lapse, but it is very true to human nature and our own experience. The high points of commitment are often followed by shameful failure. This is why Jesus is so impressive in resisting the devil's temptations just after his baptism.

The calf is a young bull. The bull is a favourite with all fertility cults, because of its strength and power to reproduce. Baal, chief of the many gods of Canaan, is sometimes depicted as a bull. The Israelites feel defenceless and rather inferior without something similar. And pagan rites are great fun. Let the party begin!

The Lord is seething with anger at this terrible betrayal. He tells Moses to stand aside so that he can destroy the people and start again. But Moses pleads with God. He appeals to God's promises, his name and his reputation. He argues that the Egyptians will say that God has rescued his people only to kill them in the desert. He reminds God of his promise to multiply the descendants of Abraham, Isaac and Jacob.

For his part, God seems almost to want Moses to pray in this way. He agrees to spare the people and decides on a different course of action.

Long before he arrives at the camp, Moses hears the shouting and singing. Joshua, who is with him, thinks there must be a battle going on. Moses knows it's the sound of a drunken celebration.

Seeing the calf and the dancing, Moses flares with anger. He smashes the tablets of the law. He destroys the calf. He grinds the gold to powder, scatters it on water and makes the people drink it. This is like the later punishment for adultery. Israel has betrayed God, her husband, and must drink 'the waters of bitterness'.

Moses turns to Aaron for an explanation. Aaron pleads that the people have bullied him. All he did was throw their gold jewellery in the fire and there was a miracle. The calf made itself!

Moses calls on his own tribe, the Levites, to arm themselves and bring the people under control. Their faithfulness in this crisis will lead to them becoming the priestly tribe.

Moses tries to repair the damage with God. Unlike Aaron, he takes full responsibility for what has happened. He offers himself as a sacrifice for the people's sin, even if it means that he must be blotted out of God's book of life.

The Lord answers that each person will be responsible for his or her own sin. But, in any case, they must now travel on without him. The land of the Canaanites awaits them but the special relationship with God is over. The covenant is cancelled.

The people are chastened and go into mourning. Once and for all they discard their ornaments as a sign of repentance.

The tent of meeting (33:7–11)

Moses has a tent outside the camp. It is known as the 'tent of meeting' and is a forerunner of the larger tabernacle which is to be built inside the camp. The people stand in their tent doors as Moses goes to pray for them. When they see the cloud of God's presence, they worship from a distance.

Moses has a direct experience of talking with God. He doesn't rely on visions, dreams or inspired guesses. 'The Lord used to speak to Moses face to face, as one speaks to a friend' (33:11 NRSV).

Moses begs to know God more closely. He puts it to the Lord: 'If your Presence does not go with us, do not send us up from here' (33:15). The Lord is pleased with his prayer and agrees to continue with the people.

Moses asks if he may be allowed actually to see God. The request is impossible, because the force of God's glory would destroy Moses instantly. But the Lord hides him in the cleft of a rock and passes by. Moses is allowed to catch a glimpse of God's 'back'.

'When my glory passes by' (33:12–23)

God is to be known by his name and his word.

Moses can only see God's 'back'. He can only know God through what has just happened – by what God has *done*. An example from the world around us is that we can only see the wind by what it has just done.

When Jesus comes, he will be the perfect image of God in human life. All of God's nature and personality will be seen in him. But the full, revealed, unleashed glory of God? We would be safer standing beside an atomic explosion.

The new stone tablets (34:1–28)

The Lord instructs Moses to cut new tablets of stone. Moses returns to the mountain and receives the law afresh.

God describes himself to Moses as:

The Lord, the Lord,
a God merciful and gracious,
slow to anger,
and abounding in steadfast love and faithfulness,
keeping steadfast love for the thousandth generation,
forgiving iniquity and transgression and sin,
yet by no means clearing the guilty,
but visiting the iniquity of the parents
upon the children
and the children's children,
to the third and fourth generation
(34:6–7 NRSV)

This is a glorious definition of God, which is often repeated in the Old Testament (Psalm 103:6–8; Jonah 4:2).

Moses begs God's forgiveness for the people and asks that they might go on to their Promised Land. The Lord makes a covenant with him and promises to do great deeds through the people. They are to advance on the Promised Land and drive out all the pagan tribes, smashing their idols, altars and fertility poles. There is to be no compromise with pagan religion or intermarriage with pagan people.

The radiant face of Moses (34:29–35)

Moses returns to the people with the new tablets of the law. His face is so radiant with the afterglow of God's glory that for a while he has to wear a veil.

The climax of Exodus

The climax of the book of Exodus is not the escape from Egypt or the giving of the law at Sinai. It is the construction and dedication of the tabernacle, where God will dwell among his people in the beauty of holiness.

Moses calls the people together. He reminds them again not to work on the sabbath – not even to labour in lighting a fire. It is the keeping of sabbath which will mark out Israel as different from other nations.

Materials for the tabernacle (35:1–29)

Now Moses invites the people to bring materials for the building of the tabernacle. They come with precious metals, coloured yarn, fine linen, goat hair, rams' skins, acacia wood, olive oil and spices. There are even precious stones for the high priest's garments, the ephod and breastpiece.

The tabernacle is constructed (35:30–40:33)

The skilled worker Bezalel and his assistant Oholiab embark on the great project.

Bezalel has the power of God's Spirit upon him to do this sacred work. In the New Testament, too, spiritual gifts will enable very practical ministries. The skilled workers, designers, embroiderers and weavers are all worshipping God with their skills, just as the people are with their overflowing generosity.

The ark, the table and the lampstand are each made as the Lord instructed Moses. So, too, the altar of incense, the anointing oil and the fragrant incense. Everything is assembled for the glory of God.

The altar of burnt offering is built of acacia wood, with horns on the corners, and overlaid with bronze. There are bronze utensils to match: pots, shovels, sprinkling bowls, meat forks and firepans. And there is the bronze basin on its stand.

The priestly garments are made with the greatest care and attention to detail; the ephod of gold, with blue, purple and scarlet yarn and fine twisted linen. Precious stones are mounted in gold settings. Nothing but the best is good enough for God.

Moses inspects the work and sees that all has been done to the Lord's specification. So he blesses the Israelites.

The Lord tells Moses to set up the tabernacle, the tent of meeting, and bring in the ark of the testimony, the table and the lampstand. The altar of incense is to be placed in front of the ark and the entrance is to be covered with the curtain.

The altar of burnt offering is to be placed in front of the entrance of the tabernacle, and the courtyard area screened off around it. All the items are to be anointed. The tabernacle and all its furnishings are to be holy.

Aaron and his sons are brought to the entrance of the tabernacle. They are washed and clothed. Aaron is robed in his sacred garments, anointed and consecrated to serve the Lord as priest. His sons are also robed and anointed for priesthood.

The glory of the Lord (40:34–38)

When all is finished, the Lord comes to hallow the place. The cloud of his presence covers the tabernacle, and the glory of the Lord fills it. Now whenever the cloud lifts, the Israelites will know it is time to move on. And wherever they go, the Lord will be with his people in cloud and fire.

LEVITICUS

The book of Leviticus gives detailed instructions for carrying out sacrifices and other religious ceremonies in ancient Israel.

God is holy, and every aspect of the life of his people must reflect his holiness. By sacrifice, sin can be cleansed or covered. Through the other regulations, the whole of life can be related to the holiness of God.

The name 'Leviticus' comes from the first word of this book in the Hebrew Bible. It means 'and he called' and refers to the Lord calling Moses to give him these instructions. Inevitably, the name 'Leviticus' has a strong association with 'Levi' – the name of the tribe set apart to be priests.

The best-known words from the book, found in 19:18, are those which Jesus calls the second great commandment: 'Love your neighbour as you love yourself.'

OUTLINE

Instructions for priests (1:1–16:34)
Everyday holiness (17:1–27:34)

Introduction

The story so far

The people of Israel, Jacob's descendants, have been rescued from slavery in Egypt. Led by Moses, they have journeyed across the desert to Mount Sinai, where God has made a covenant with them and given them his law. Now Moses is given further instruction on how the people can maintain their special relationship with God.

Leviticus – a well-planned book

At Mount Sinai, God gave Israel a unique identity and role in the world. They are to be a priestly people and a holy nation (Exodus 19:6). The book of Leviticus falls into two halves reflecting each of these.

Chapters 1 to 17 are mainly to do with the priestly tasks of sacrifice and getting right with God. 'Love the Lord your God with all your heart, soul, mind and strength.'

Chapters 18 to 27 are a call to Israel to be holy in every practical area of life. 'Love your neighbour as yourself.' These chapters are sometimes known as the 'holiness code'.

The first half of the book leads up to the great climax of the Day of Atonement in chapter 16, when a right relationship is restored between the nation and God. The second half reaches its high point with the Jubilee in chapter 25, when right relationships are restored in the community and nation.

God rescued his people from Egypt by a mighty act of grace. They didn't earn, deserve or (at times) even want their freedom. Now God's goodness to them is to be fully shared – and shown to the world. It is to fill every part of their lives.

Living with a holy God

Leviticus begins with 'how to make sacrifices'. It provides a manual for all kinds of ritual for the time when the Jews will have a temple in Jerusalem. The slaying of large numbers of animals is alien and disgusting to many people today. Such bloodshed is an awesome image of the seriousness of sin and the cost of salvation.

When the last temple is destroyed, in AD 70, all sacrifices cease. But Jews and Christians continue to read Leviticus because of its teaching about the holiness of God and the everyday life of the believer. For Christians, Leviticus also gives many pointers to Jesus, who is the perfect high priest and sacrifice. The letter to the Hebrews, towards the end of the New Testament, gives a Christian interpretation of the themes we first meet here.

Leviticus goes on to teach 'holiness for everyone'. It covers all the many-sidedness of human life, from sabbath to sex and from murder to menstruation. Holiness extends to all God's people – not just the priests; and to every place – not just the tabernacle or temple. Everyone who belongs to God is called to be holy in every way.

To this end, the law and the sacrifices are major ways of staying in tune with God. The rules of diet, health and hygiene are a guide to living life in his honour.

Who wrote Leviticus?

Leviticus is the third of the five books of the 'Pentateuch' (the 'Five Scrolls') which are also known as the 'books of Moses'.

The original instructions for priests come from Moses himself, but in his day there is no temple. Moses' instructions are for the worship at the 'tent of meeting', where God meets with him in the years of travelling through the wilderness from Egypt to Canaan (1:1). Other priestly authors have added their insights and regulations in later years, to provide the more elaborate rituals of Solomon's temple and the second temple which was built after Israel's return from exile in Babylon. The leading priest at the time of the return is Ezra. It may be during his time, around 400 BC, that Leviticus reaches its final version.

The importance of sacrifice

'At-onement'

Sacrifice is a way of approaching God, to mark an occasion, thank him for a blessing, or ask his protection or forgiveness. Because God is holy, anyone approaching him must first be cleansed from their sin. Sacrifice is the way God provides for a person or group to receive forgiveness. This process is called 'atonement' or covering, from the idea that the blood hides sin by covering it and so enables God and sinners to be 'at one' again.

Is sacrifice pagan?

The sacrificing of animals is common to many religions. It is only when we look at the reasons for Israel's sacrifices that we see a clear difference from pagan practices.

In Israel, the sacrifice is for the benefit of the ordinary person who brings it. It is he who places his hand on the sacrifice, kills it and receives the words of forgiveness. There are no sex acts or fertility rites, and no attempts to contact the dead or pray to ancestors. There is no casting of spells, studying of entrails or fortune-telling. There are no self-inflicted wounds to prove sorrow to God, and there is no sacrificing of children.

In Jewish sacrifice there is no attempt to bribe God or manipulate his favours. People can't impress God with a large sacrifice, because they aren't graded according to wealth and power. There is no special offering required of a king, for example. Every person or family is expected simply to bring the best sacrifice they can manage, without reducing themselves to poverty. If a family is poor, then a pigeon or a cup of flour is enough.

Where there is a larger sacrifice, it is to indicate a greater responsibility for sin. The high priest offers the largest, because of everyone he has sinned most knowingly! In all this, the only purpose is to be made right with God and receive his forgiveness.

How does the theme of sacrifice develop?

In Isaiah 53, the prophet describes the innocent suffering and death of the 'servant of the Lord'. This servant dies, not for his own sin, but for the sin of others. In other words, he is a sacrifice – 'led like a lamb to the slaughter'. His death is a 'guilt offering' to cover the wrongs of others, so that they may become right with God.

When Jesus comes, he is this 'suffering servant'. Matthew's Gospel says that Jesus fulfils Isaiah's words: 'He took up our infirmities and carried our sorrows' (Isaiah 53:4 NIV). Peter writes in his first letter: 'He himself bore our sins in his body on the tree, so that we might die to sins and live for righteousness; by his wounds you have been healed' (1 Peter 2:24). This understanding comes from Jesus himself.

In Luke's account of the Last Supper, Jesus warns his friends that he will be 'numbered with the transgressors'. After his resurrection, he explains everything to the two people he meets on the road to Emmaus:

Beginning with Moses and all the Prophets, he explained to them what was said in all the scriptures concerning himself. (Luke 24:25–27)

The death of Jesus includes every aspect of sacrifice. He is a ransom for our guilt. He cleanses our sinful lives. He pays the debt we owe for our wrongdoing. In Mark's Gospel Jesus says he must give his life 'as a ransom for many'. This is the function of the burnt offering in Leviticus – to provide atonement for sin and deal with guilt.

The fullest explanation of the death of Jesus is found in the letter to the Hebrews. The writer tells us that Jesus' death on the cross is the supreme sacrifice of all time – a sacrifice to end all sacrifices.

The sacrifices described in Leviticus are solemn, costly and moving. But they are never enough. They are for ever being repeated, because sin is never fully dealt with. The letter to the Hebrews describes this weary and repetitive process:

Day after day every priest stands and performs his religious duties; again and again he offers the same sacrifices, which can never take away sins. (Hebrews 10:11)

The writer expresses the painful knowledge that all the sacrificing of animals has never really dealt with sin. Jesus, on the cross, at last makes a sacrifice which works for everyone for all time. He dies shouting triumphantly, 'It is finished!' As the letter to the Hebrews explains:

When this priest [Christ] had offered for all time one sacrifice for sins, he sat down at the right hand of God. (Hebrews 10:12)

Like the 'sin offering', the blood of Christ has power to cleanse. It not only removes the guilt of sin, but also purges away its pollution. When we accept the death of Jesus for us, we can approach God with confidence. Our sins are forgiven. Our consciences are clear:

Therefore... since we have confidence to enter the Most Holy Place by the blood of Jesus, by a new and living way opened for us through the curtain, that is, his body... let us draw near to God with a sincere heart in full assurance of faith, having our hearts sprinkled to cleanse us from a guilty conscience and having our bodies washed with pure water. (Hebrews 10:19–22)

The 'fellowship offering' of Leviticus is a sacrifice which becomes a shared meal. It expresses a joyful unity of life, between God and people and between the worshippers themselves. In the New Testament this becomes the agape, Eucharist or Lord's Supper. By breaking bread and sharing it, believers give thanks for the sacrifice of Jesus, broken for them. By pouring wine and drinking it, they remember his blood shed for the sins of the world.

The New Testament writers encourage believers to care for one another because of their fellowship with Christ. Paul warns the

Christians at Corinth that if they don't share their meal (if the wealthy eat while the poor go hungry), then it isn't the Lord's Supper.

When you come to eat together, it is not the Lord's supper you eat, for as you eat, each of you goes ahead without waiting for anybody else. One remains hungry, another gets drunk. (1 Corinthians 11:20–21)

'Living' sacrifices

The most exciting development in the New Testament is that we ourselves are now temples, priests and offerings. Peter writes, 'You… like living stones, are being built into a spiritual house to be a holy priesthood, offering spiritual sacrifices acceptable to God through Jesus Christ' (1 Peter 2:5 NIV). Paul encourages Christians at Rome to offer themselves 'as living sacrifices, holy and pleasing to God' (Romans 12:1).

Our offering of ourselves is not to pay for our sin. Only the death of Jesus can do that. But we can become 'living sacrifices' – offering our bodies and minds, time, gifts and daily life to God. What a glorious development, from the dead animals in Leviticus to our own total commitment today! Jesus looked forward to the time when 'true worshippers will worship the Father in spirit and truth' (John 4:23 NRSV).

A fair share

The New Testament writers don't forget that the old system of sacrifice supported God's priests. Grain, meat and bread from offerings went to feed the priestly tribe of Levi, which had no land or income.

In the New Testament, the ministers of Christ are to be provided for in a comparable way. Paul was prepared to support himself by his tentmaking, but he still insisted that 'those who preach the gospel should receive their living from the gospel' (1 Corinthians 9:13–14).

DISCOVERING LEVITICUS

Instructions for priests

How to make offerings and sacrifices (1:1–7:38)

In the opening chapters of Leviticus, God provides a range of sacrifices and offerings. Animals and birds, grain and fruit can all be used, each with their proper occasion and meaning.

Sacrifice is a way of approaching God by making a costly gift. We first meet it when Cain brings his produce and Abel offers an animal. Later, Noah burns a whole animal on an altar. Abraham makes burnt offerings, but also uses sacrificed animals for special meals – to express a friendship or seal an agreement. When Moses introduces the Passover, it is both a sacrifice and a meal.

What makes a suitable sacrifice?

A sacrifice has to be a person's own property – not a wild animal, and not stolen. It must be something the person has cared for or cultivated – and so is a part of him in some way. And it must be the best – healthy, mature and valuable. But if the person is poor, then even a cup of flour will be acceptable, and the resulting forgiveness will be as complete as if the finest bullock has been offered.

When are the sacrifices made?

Sacrifices are made by the priests every day at dawn and dusk, with a special emphasis on the sabbath. There are also monthly (new moon) and yearly sacrifices. The natural points of celebration are the changing seasons and the harvest festivals, when the firstfruits are offered to God, and the rest released for human consumption. The harvest offerings are used afterwards to feed the priests. But the most important religious festival isn't agricultural at all. It is the annual Day of Atonement – a day of national repentance with fasting and prayer.

At Passover, lambs are sacrificed for each family, and shared at home. Other sacrifices are more personal still – to mark a vow, to thank God for healing, or to purify a mother after childbirth. At the other extreme, there will be sacrifices on a grand scale for the dedication of a temple or the coronation of a king.

How is a sacrifice offered?

Making a sacrifice involves both the priest and the worshipper. The worshipper brings his sacrifice to the altar in front of the tent of meeting. He connects with the animal or bird by laying his hand on it. This offering is his, and is to die on his behalf. He then kills the creature himself. After this the priest takes over to deal with the blood, and to butcher and burn the body. If the sacrifice is for a dreadful and wilful sin, the carcass is burnt completely, away from the altar.

> **Holy Communion**
>
> The sacrifices of the Old Testament are the background to the cross of Christ in the New Testament. Jesus is the perfect offering, provided by God to bear the guilt of the entire human race. Jesus takes upon himself the sin of the world and the punishment it deserves. His sacrifice is accepted. As Jesus dies, the temple curtain is torn apart to show an open door to God. Afterwards, God raises his Son to new life – to declare the forgiveness of sins and the defeat of death.
>
> The sacrifice of Jesus is celebrated in a fellowship meal – called the agape, Eucharist, Lord's Supper or Holy Communion. Here bread and wine are offered in memory of what Jesus did. The bread is broken, just as Jesus' body was broken. The wine is poured out, just as his blood was shed. The bread and wine are then shared by all, to identify each person with the death and life of Jesus. For Christians this is the central act of worship – a shared and uniting experience, with all realizing God's forgiveness, enjoying fellowship with each other and expressing love.

In animal sacrifice, the fat of the kidneys, liver and intestines is burnt for God, while the rest of the meat is eaten by the priests and worshippers. Some food, such as the showbread, may only be eaten by the priests within the Holy Place.

The 'burnt offering' (1:1–17; 6:8–13) is a bullock, sheep or goat, and must be a perfect male animal. Poorer people may offer a dove or young pigeon. Sacrifice is costly, solemn and serious. The life of an innocent creature is being paid for human sin. The commitment is total – the blood poured out and the body completely burnt up.

The 'grain offering' (2:1–16; 6:14–23) is fine flour, made into a cake with oil and incense. These ingredients help it burn and give off a fragrant smell. The smell of sacrifices is thought of as reaching God and pleasing him. It is a reminder that God's anger with sin is being taken out on the sacrifice.

The grain offering is to be mixed with salt – a preservative which is a token of friendship. Yeast or honey are not allowed, because they ferment and are symbols of spreading sin. Part of the grain offering is burnt as a 'memorial portion', to remind God of his promise to protect his people. The rest of the offering is kept by the priest for his wages and livelihood.

The 'fellowship offering' (3:1–17; 7:11–34) is for making peace. It is like a burnt offering, but part of the sacrifice is eaten by the worshipper. It is a meal shared with God, as an expression of harmony.

It's the heart that counts

It must have been a dreadful experience to watch a fellow creature die on your behalf. Even so, sacrifices could become mechanical and thoughtless. In later years the prophet Isaiah will warn against 'meaningless' sacrifices – that is, offerings which are made without any commitment to lead a better life.

The 'sin offering' (4:1–5:13; 6:24–30) provides for unintentional wrongdoing. Some sins are committed through ignorance (and sometimes damage is done to people or property by accident), but there is still guilt. This kind of sin is described in a word which means 'missing the mark'. The examples given are both sacred and secular (the Jews make no distinction). They range from withholding information to touching something unclean.

The 'guilt offering' (5:14–6:7; 7:1–6) has a strong sense of repairing damage between God and people. It is a substantial, expensive sacrifice to emphasize the person's fault for what has happened. The offence has hurt both God and a fellow human being, so the sacrifice is designed to 'mend' holiness and make good the relationships.

How to ordain priests (8:1–10:20)

The Lord said to Moses, 'Bring Aaron and his sons, their garments, the anointing oil, the bull for the sin offering, the two rams, and the basket containing bread without yeast, and gather the entire assembly at the entrance to the Tent of Meeting' (8:2–4).

God chooses Aaron and his sons to be his priests. They are to be responsible for the tent of meeting and the sacrifices – to ensure that everything is done decently and with reverence. They are to be both teachers and living examples of God's holy ways.

In a series of sacrifices and ceremonies, Moses clothes the priests and consecrates them for their special task.

Aaron's high priestly robes

Aaron wears a tunic as an undergarment. It is long and full, tied with a sash. Over this he wears a bright blue robe and an 'ephod', secured by a woven waistband. We have to guess at the appearance of the ephod, which may have been a kind of apron. Over this is worn a breastpiece with a pocket for the 'Urim and Thummim'. The exact description of these has been lost; but they are a kind of holy dice. They are thrown after prayer for guidance, and give God's 'yes' or 'no'. Finally, Aaron wears a turban, with a gold plate on the front of it. This is to honour his head and holy leadership. Moses pours oil over Aaron's head to consecrate him – that is, to set him apart for his sacred role.

Holiness – you put your whole self in!

Aaron and his sons are washed, clothed in their priestly robes and marked with sacrificial blood on their right ears, hands and toes. They are sprinkled, robes and all, with oil and blood. They remain at the door of the tent of meeting for seven days – the timescale of God's creation. After this, Aaron carries out the sacrifices – a calf for his own sins, followed by a goat for the sins of the people. Finally a cow and a ram are killed as a fellowship offering, to celebrate peace between God and Israel. The Lord glorifies the occasion with his presence and consuming fire.

The death of Nadab and Abihu

Aaron's sons Nadab and Abihu took their censers, put fire in them and added incense; and they offered unauthorised fire before the Lord, contrary to his command (10:1).

The holiness which consecrates can also destroy. When two of Aaron's sons produce their own flame for the burning of incense, holy fire flares up to consume them. They have wilfully breached God's command to keep every detail of sacrifice separate from everyday use – and they pay with their lives.

The holy and the common

Aaron's sons should have known better than to confuse the 'holy' and the 'common'. Something is 'holy' when it is associated with God. Everything else is 'common' – that is, a part of everyday life. 'Common' things are clean, unless something has happened to spoil or pollute them. In this case they have become 'unclean', but can be restored through an appropriate sacrifice.

The priests are supposed to prevent the 'common' coming into contact with the 'holy'. Such an event produces a spiritual short circuit and a fatal shock. When Aaron's sons introduce common fire, they are themselves consumed.

Tough love

Israel is to be holy. Holiness is to be the lifestyle of God's people, in sanctuary and sacrifice, marriage and money, food and sex.

This holiness isn't voluntary – it's a command. It is enforced in the sudden death of Aaron's sons when they casually break God's rule. It is spelt out in the many regulations – straightforward in their wording and stark in their consequences.

God's love is tough. If Israel is to continue in freedom, she must beware of the reality and danger of sin. Anything that undermines her relationship with God must be rigorously dealt with.

For the Christian, the teaching of Leviticus is fulfilled in Jesus Christ. He is the perfect, once-for-all sacrifice who brings forgiveness of sin and peace with God. It is through him and for him that we seek to live a life of purity, love and service.

Jesus, too, is tough on sin and tough on the causes of sin. He develops the laws of Leviticus in the Sermon on the Mount. He holds us personally responsible for our thoughts and actions: 'You have heard that it was said to those of ancient times, "You shall not murder"; and "whoever murders shall be liable to judgment." But I say to you that if you are angry with a brother or sister, you will be liable to judgment' (Matthew 5:21–22 NRSV).

How to deal with dirt and disease (11:1–15:33)

Clean and unclean food

The Lord said to Moses and Aaron, 'Say to the Israelites: "Of all the animals that live on the land, these are the ones you may eat: You may eat any animal that has a split hoof completely divided and that chews the cud."' (11:2–3)

Here is guidance as to which animals are wholesome to eat. The distinctions are very simple, and generally follow lines of safety and good taste. Usually there is a health hazard or an instinctive shudder behind these food laws. Animals and birds which have themselves fed on dead meat will almost certainly carry infection. Pork harbours tapeworm and is dangerous when undercooked. Shellfish can cause food poisoning. All eating of blood is forbidden, because it is the very liquid of life and belongs to God.

God's people are to reflect his holiness. What they do with their bodies will influence their minds and spirits. What they believe in their hearts will affect their actions. So, in matters of food and diet, they are to live clean and well-ordered lives.

The overall purpose of the rules is that Israel shall be distinctive and disciplined – living in God's world, God's way. God's own summary of the situation is this: 'I... brought you up out of Egypt to be your God; therefore be holy, because I am holy' (11:45).

'Holy' and 'common'

You must distinguish between the holy and the common, between the unclean and the clean. (10:10)

The Israelites are to make a clear distinction between things that are 'holy' and things that are 'common'. Then again, a common article can be either 'clean' or 'unclean'.

God is holy, and any person or thing associated with him is also holy. The opposite of holy is 'common', or 'profane'. This doesn't necessarily mean 'dirty' or 'sinful'. It simply means 'ordinary, normal and everyday'.

When ordinary people or things become polluted, they are 'unclean'. Certain animals – and death itself – are permanently unclean. But most other conditions can be restored to normality ('made clean') through the appropriate sacrifice. The main task of a blood sacrifice is to make holy something which is common, or cleanse something which is polluted.

It was the priest's task to teach people these distinctions, so that they could lead a clean life in the everyday circumstances of family, home and farm. The laws in Leviticus are the means to this end. Their purpose is to enable God to dwell with his people.

Health regulations

The Lord said to Moses, 'Say to the Israelites: "A woman who becomes pregnant and gives birth to a son will be ceremonially unclean for seven days, just as she is unclean during her monthly period."' (12:1-2)

A woman's monthly period and the act of giving birth are bloody and harrowing experiences. Women are to be treated as 'unclean' at these times, although 'unclean' doesn't mean immoral or sinful. They are to be left alone, to allow body and mind to recover. One day Jesus will heal a woman whose life has been ruined by constant menstrual bleeding. In a desperate gesture of faith, she who is 'unclean' dares to reach out to touch him – to catch his holiness and healing (Luke 8:43-48).

While sex is exciting, the actual business of reproduction is messy and even repulsive. The law provides for the trauma of childbirth to be followed by rest – and completed with a simple offering to God. So a woman can be assured of God's love, cleansing and peace.

The Lord said to Moses and Aaron, 'If some of the people notice a swelling or a rash or a shiny patch on their skin that develops into a contagious skin disease, they must be brought to Aaron the priest or to one of his sons.' (13:1-2)

The priests are also the doctors. By observation and experience, they build up their knowledge of a whole variety of rashes and skin disorders. Some of these can be passed on by touch, so the sufferer must be isolated to protect the rest of the community.

The most dreadful of the skin diseases is leprosy. It begins with loss of feeling, which means that a person can be cut or burnt without noticing. It develops to deform and rot whole areas of the body and is easily passed on to other people.

The law provides ways of diagnosing and isolating these diseases. There are routines of washing and shaving and recommended periods of quarantine. With these rules it is clear when someone is infectious – and when they have recovered.

Sickness, sin and sacrifice

The priest offers the same sacrifices for both healing and forgiveness. This highlights the likeness between sickness and sin.

Because a human being is a harmony of body, mind and spirit, Leviticus assumes that disease is a symptom of sin. Later, in the book of Job, we will read that the two are not necessarily connected, and that sometimes suffering is completely undeserved.

Leprosy is contagious, crippling and (in Bible times) incurable. Jesus is unusual in his readiness to touch lepers and counter their disease with God's health. While Jesus never assumes that sickness is a person's own fault, he sometimes makes the connection. On one occasion, he discerns the guilt behind a man's paralysis (Mark 2:3–5). And he often declares forgiveness of sin as well as physical healing.

Cleanliness and godliness
The Lord said to Moses and Aaron, 'Speak to the Israelites and say to them: "When any man has a bodily discharge, the discharge is unclean."' (15:1–2)

God's law is for the whole of life, and here it deals with some very intimate details. When a man ejects semen or discharges any other body fluid, there are regulations for his cleansing and precautions against any infection. Similarly, a woman is to cope with her period bleeding by keeping away from other people, being careful to wash herself and the everyday things she touches. There is equality here in the way men and women are treated.

All this is practical holiness – the good life. Human beings are made in the image of God and are not to live at the level of squalor and basic instinct. As Paul says, 'Your body is a temple of the Holy Spirit, who is in you' (1 Corinthians 6:19).

The Day of Atonement (16:1–34)

The most important sacrifice is to take place on the Day of Atonement. It falls on the tenth day of the seventh month, towards the end of September. On this day Aaron, the high priest, makes sacrifices for all the sins of all the people. It is also a ceremony by which the tent of meeting itself and the altar outside are made holy again.

This is the only day of the year that Aaron may enter the Most Holy Place. He goes behind the curtain which divides the tent of meeting and separates off the presence of God. This is where God dwells in deep holiness, and where the covenant box (the ark of the covenant) is kept.

The covenant box is called the 'testimony'. It contains the stone tablets which are engraved with the Ten Commandments. Its lid is the atonement cover: the place where atonement is made. Martin Luther called it the 'mercy seat', the earthly throne of God.

Aaron is not to come thoughtlessly or casually into God's holy presence. He is to lay aside his ornate high-priestly robes, wash himself and dress in linen – the garment of an ordinary priest. It is a sign of humility and purity.

He is to select three animals for sacrifice. One is a bull, which he is to kill for his own sin and the sins of his family. The other animals are goats. He is to cast lots, so that God will decide which goat is to be killed and which is to be sent away into the desert. The goat that is to be killed is a sacrifice for the sins of the people. The goat that is sent away into the desert is the 'scapegoat', carrying off the people's sins so that they are separated from them for ever.

Aaron is to sacrifice the bull and take some of its blood into the Most Holy Place. He is to burn a large amount of fine incense, so that the smoke will protect him from seeing God and being killed by the power of his holiness.

Aaron splashes the bull's blood on the front of the covenant box and on the ground in front of it – sprinkling it with his finger, so that he doesn't actually touch the holy box. He does the same with the blood of the goat, making a 'cover' of blood between the holy God and his sinful people. All their sins are 'covered' or painted out by the blood of the lives which have been paid in sacrifice.

Next Aaron comes out of the tent of meeting to sprinkle blood on the altar. This cleanses and consecrates it afresh for holy use. He also lays his hands on the scapegoat, to heap all the people's sins on its head, and then banishes it to wander in the desert. Finally, he takes off his linen clothes, washes himself again and puts on his fine high-priestly robes. He completes the sacrifices by offering the bodies of the bull and the goat on the altar, burning them up completely, because they are sin offerings.

The Day of Atonement is to be kept every year. It is a day of rest, like the sabbath, and the people are to deny themselves. This means that they are to fast, to show their sorrow for their sins. It is the most solemn of festivals, and very different from the Feast of Tabernacles, when there is joyful dancing.

The Day of Atonement isn't mentioned again in the Old Testament, but by the time of the New Testament it has become known as 'the Fast' (Acts 27:9). Today it is Yom Kippur, which strict Jews keep as one of the holiest days in the year. They no longer have the temple or the covenant box, but they keep the day with prayers and tears, and prepare for it with ten days of careful self-examination.

For Christians, the Day of Atonement is fulfilled in the death of Jesus. He went into the holy presence of God with his own blood – not needing to make sacrifice for his own sins, but offering his life for the sins of all people (Hebrews 9). Jesus is both the perfect high priest *and* the perfect sacrifice.

Everyday holiness

The Day of Atonement is a high point and halfway mark in the book of Leviticus. The chapters which follow are sometimes called the 'holiness code'. They contain the laws which express God's holiness in the details of everyday life. Holiness is to be the distinguishing mark of God's people.

The importance of blood (17:1–16)

Blood is sacred to the Jews, because it is the essence of an animal's life. It is also the means that God has given for paying for sin.

From now on the Israelites must bring their animals to the priests to be killed. Even providing meat for the family is an act of worship, because it involves the shedding of a life which belongs to God. The animals are to be brought to the door of the tent of meeting as a peace offering between God and his people.

The Israelites are forbidden to make random killings out in the fields, like pagans making sacrifices to their goat idols, the demon spirits of nature worship. This law is relaxed in Deuteronomy, where it is accepted that people needing meat may live too far from an official place of sacrifice. Even so, the eating of blood is forbidden (Deuteronomy 12:20–25). To this day, Jews will only eat meat which is 'kosher' – that is, carefully drained of blood and reverently prepared for the table.

Safeguarding sex (18:1–30)

Among the Egyptians, when the Israelites were slaves, sex was a family affair. The Pharaohs often married their close relatives, and suffered the dreadful effects of inbreeding.

Among the Canaanites, where the Israelites are heading, sex is a free-for-all. There is sex between family members, sex between people of the same sex, and sex between people and animals. Sex is also involved in the worship of pagan gods, which are themselves sexually permissive and perverted.

God tells his people that they are to be very different. They are to be holy, with their holiness rooted in God's own holiness.

Moses teaches that sex between parents and children, and between brothers and sisters, is wrong. The whole family is to be a network of honour, decency and mutual respect – not spoilt and destroyed by sexual scheming and abuse. These rules are not because sex is dirty, but because it is such a vital and powerful part of our nature. Wrong sex unleashes enormous forces of guilt, depression, jealousy and hatred. We do well to believe God's warnings and accept his boundaries.

These sex regulations will be adopted in Christian cultures as 'prohibited relationships'. It is strange to think that Abraham would not have been allowed to marry his sister Sarah, and Jacob would have been unable to marry the sisters Leah and Rachel. God blessed and used those relationships; but we see in their stories the pain, suspicion and anger that flares up in such marriages.

Child sacrifice

Moses forbids the sacrifice of children (18:21). This was practised by the Ammonites, who worshipped the god Molech. His name is a mixture of the words for 'king' and 'shame'.

For some, to offer up a child must have seemed like the ultimate act of commitment – costly and heartbreaking. Thank God it is so clearly forbidden!

Wrong sex

Moses forbids unnatural and perverted sex (18:22–30). Men are not to have sex with other men, or with animals. It is because of such confused behaviour that God is judging the Canaanites and driving them out of their land. The land itself is ejecting them like vomit. God warns the Israelites that he will expel them, too, if they sin in the same way. God's standards do not vary and he makes no exceptions for the Israelites.

How to live wisely and well (19:1–37)

Here is a fascinating selection of laws. They are listed almost at random, although all their roots can be traced to the Ten Commandments. The common link is that they are all grounded in the holiness of God. 'I am the Lord' is repeated, as God endorses each regulation with his own character and authority. We see, too, that holiness is not just about religion. It is deeply practical, affecting every area of life.

Some of these commands echo the Ten Commandments quite directly: respect your father and mother, observe the sabbath and do not make or worship idols.

Others are practical ways to provide for the needy: leave some gleanings behind when you harvest your grain or grapes, so that poor people and strangers may gather some food. Pay your workers on the day of their labour, so that they can provide for themselves and their families.

The deaf and the blind are to be protected; you are not to take advantage by abusing them or playing tricks.

Some commands deal with the motives that guide our actions: do not be swayed by self-interest when you judge between rich and poor; do not hate your brother or sister in your heart.

There are laws against causing confusion in the world of nature: do not mate different kinds of animals, or mix the crops in a field, or weave clothes from different materials. These laws commend practical purity and holiness – a reminder not to mix the worship of God with pagan practices.

And what about the owner who sleeps with his slave girl, despite the fact that she is promised to another man? This is not counted as serious as adultery, but it is wrong nevertheless. A woman is not to be treated as a prostitute, just because she is unfortunate enough to be a slave. A way is provided for the man to atone for his sin and deal with his guilt.

The godly way of life is described in dozens of fascinating and inspiring examples – about fruit trees and fortune-tellers, mediums and migrant-workers, tattoos and traders…

The secret of understanding a law is to ask which commandment it follows, what principle it upholds or what kind of person it protects. The keynote is found at the heart of this chapter: 'Love your neighbour as yourself' (19:18). This will become known as the Golden Rule, and Jesus will rate it as the second of the great commandments (Matthew 22:39). The first is 'Love the Lord your God with all your heart and with all your soul and with all your strength' (Deuteronomy 6:5) – to which Jesus adds 'and with all your mind' (Mark 12:30 NRSV).

The Israelites come to regard their neighbour as anyone who is a fellow Jew (as opposed to a pagan or foreigner). Jesus will show, in his parable of the Good Samaritan, that our neighbour is anyone we have the chance to help – irrespective of race, religion or convenience (Luke 10:25–37). Leviticus anticipates this attitude with the command: 'Love the alien as yourself' (Leviticus 19:34).

Controls and consequences (20:1–27)

God speaks to Moses not only of laws but also of punishments. When people are responsible for their sin, they must bear the consequence. Sometimes the punishment must be death – as when an Israelite sacrifices his child to Molech, or consults mediums, or curses his parents.

Sexual sins such as adultery, incest, homosexuality and bestiality all carry the death penalty. Such behaviour must be cut like a cancer from the body of God's people. Some of the laws actually speak of being 'cut off' – the guilty person being expelled or excommunicated, to prevent infecting others.

Why is God so strict? Because he wants Israel to model true worship, justice and holy living to the world. To do this she must be a dedicated and disciplined nation – devoted to God's law in heart and home, in dress and diet, in relationships and responses.

Many of these laws are warnings against the cruelty and moral chaos of the Canaanites. Israel is to be different, set apart for God, and holy for him.

The purity of priests (21:1–22:33)

From speaking to the people, God now tells Moses to speak to the priests. The prime function of the priest is to perform his holy duties. For this he must be clean and ready in body and spirit. He is to avoid touching a corpse, unless it is that of a close relative, because death is linked with sin.

Priests must not shave their heads (a sign of mourning), nor trim their beards, nor cut themselves (as pagans do). They must honour God in their speech. They must be devoted and fit for their privileged task of offering food to God.

Priests are to be holy in their family relationships, too. They must not marry prostitutes or divorcees (people who have already been sexually united with someone else), and their daughters must not sink into prostitution. If this should happen, the punishment (for the daughter) is death.

There are similar, but stricter, rules for a high priest. He has been set apart from his priestly colleagues by anointing with oil and clothing with special robes. He is also to be distinguished by his extra degree of holiness.

The high priest must avoid touching the dead bodies of even his nearest and dearest relatives. Nor must he leave the sanctuary to pay his respects to the dead, in case he defiles it on his return. His whole orientation is to purity and life. He may get married, of course, but only to a virgin from a priestly family, so that his children will be born with an unblemished moral pedigree.

Physical deformity

Priests are to be perfect, not only in their choice of wife and way of life, but in their physical well-being (21:16–24). Just as the sacrifices are to be perfect specimens, so must the priests be who are offering them. Priests who are disabled, deformed, diseased or mutilated are excluded from the work of the sanctuary, although they may still eat the holy food. The idea is not to discriminate against the disfigured, but to reflect the perfection of God.

How to treat holy offerings

The priests may eat food which has been sacrificed, and so may their families, but the food is to be treated with respect, and eaten only by those who realize its worth (22:1–16).

There will be times when the priest himself is unfit to touch the offerings, because he is suffering from a disease or has become unclean. He must be very careful not to treat the sacred offerings casually or with contempt.

The priest's family may eat food that has been offered in sacrifice, but a guest or occasional worker may not. A slave may eat, because he or she is a permanent member of the household and is treated as part of the family.

These regulations are to ensure that gifts to God are not misused or discarded behind the scenes once the worshipper has gone home. Those who live off the faith of others must be mindful that they enjoy a very special privilege.

Quality control

What kind of sacrifice is acceptable? God tells Moses that the animals must be perfect (22:17–33).

It might be tempting to offer as a sacrifice an animal that is diseased or deformed. After all, it's only going to be destroyed. But only the best is good enough for God. If the sacrifice is a freewill offering, over and above a necessary sacrifice, then an inferior animal is acceptable – but not if it's an attempt to cheat on a vow.

God shows his concern for all his creatures. A newborn animal is not to be taken straight from its mother and offered as a sacrifice. Nor are a mother and her young to be slaughtered on the same day. As with the law forbidding the boiling of a kid in its mother's milk, this command respects the right and dignity of animals.

A thank-offering is to be eaten on the same day. Once something has been offered in sacrifice, it becomes holy. It is important to treat it with reverence and put it to its proper use. If offerings are treated carelessly, then the worshippers lose their sense of reverence. When something is offered to the Lord, it becomes associated with his holiness – and must be treated accordingly.

Festivals and assemblies (23:1–24:9)

God appoints a series of festivals. They are God's own festivals on which the Israelites are to gather for worship – summoned by the blowing of silver trumpets.

Most of the festivals mark a particular day in the farming year, but they also celebrate great events in Israel's history. They each have their spiritual meaning. They celebrate some aspect of God's greatness and goodness and enable his people to respond to him in celebration and sacrifice.

The feasts are listed in the order in which they occur during the year.

The sabbath

The sabbath is the first festival to be mentioned (23:3). It is unique among the feasts, in that it occurs every week, while the other festivals come only once a year. Sabbath is the most important of the feasts, and the other festivals tend to include it.

The word 'sabbath' means 'stop'. The sabbath is a day of rest as well as a day of assembly and sacrifice.

The sabbath falls on the seventh day of the week. This is the day on which God rested after his work of creation (Genesis 2:2), and the day on which the Israelites rested during their journey through the wilderness from Egypt to Canaan. God provided for their rest by giving a double measure of manna on the previous day, so that no one needed to work.

The Passover and Feast of Unleavened Bread

The Passover is the most important of the annual feasts (23:5). It celebrates the rescue of the Israelites from slavery in Egypt, when God caused the angel of death to 'pass over' the homes of the Hebrews and spare the lives of their first-born sons.

Passover falls on the fourteenth day of the month of Abib – later called Nisan. It marks the birth of the nation of Israel and the Jewish New Year. Once Jerusalem and the temple are established, the Passover becomes an occasion of pilgrimage; but it is always a festival to be celebrated at home and in a family group.

The first Passover is described in Exodus 12. The special sacrifices are described in Numbers 28:16–25.

The Passover is closely linked with the Feast of Unleavened Bread, which takes place the following day (23:6). It celebrates the escape of the Israelites from Egypt, when God commanded the people to make bread without leaven (yeast). Such bread was made quickly, as it needed no time for the dough to rise – and became a symbol of the haste with which the Israelites made their escape.

The Feast of Unleavened Bread lasts a whole week, starting on 15th Abib (Nisan). It begins and ends with a day of rest and solemn assembly, and during it the people bake their bread without yeast.

Jesus, Paul – and yeast

For Jesus, yeast is an image of something that spreads very slowly, but affects a huge area of life. He warns his disciples against 'the leaven' of the Pharisees and Sadducees – the legalism and unbelief which cramps faith and denies God's grace (Matthew 16:6–12). But he also describes the kingdom of God as like yeast 'mixed into a large amount of flour' which slowly and surely spreads until the whole mass is transformed. His kingdom will win (Matthew 13:33)!

Paul understands that Jesus Christ is the true Passover lamb – and, for him, yeast is a picture of sin. Christians are to clear the sin out of their lives and be like unleavened bread, sincere and truthful (1 Corinthians 5:7–8).

The firstfruits

This festival looks forward to the Israelites settling in their own land and producing harvests. The first sheaf of the harvest is to be brought to the priest, who will wave it before God on the sabbath day (23:9–14).

The sheaf is probably barley, which ripens two or three weeks before wheat. Waving it before God means that the whole harvest is offered to him. Only after this is done are the people allowed to enjoy the produce themselves. Special sacrifices are made of lamb and grain – and for the first time in Leviticus a drink offering is mentioned. This is probably wine poured out on the ground in front of the altar.

By the time of Jesus, Firstfruits is celebrated on 16th Nisan – two days after Passover. This is the day of Christ's resurrection. Paul describes Jesus as 'the firstfruits of those who have fallen asleep' – the prototype of all who, by God's mighty power, will be harvested from the grave (1 Corinthians 15:20–23).

The Feast of Weeks

The Feast of Weeks is a harvest festival, marking the end of the wheat harvest (23:15–22). Two loaves are baked from fine flour and leaven, and waved before the Lord. This is an offering of the 'finished product' of the harvest – the daily food of the people of God.

The Feast of Weeks gets its name from coming seven 'full weeks' (fifty days) after the offering of the firstfruits. Because the fifty days could

---

Christians and the Jewish festivals

After the time of Jesus, many of the Jewish festivals take on a new meaning for Christians. The Passover is the day of the Last Supper and the eve of Jesus' death on the cross. 'Firstfruits' is the day of his resurrection. Pentecost is the day on which the Holy Spirit is poured out on his apostles.

The Christian church is a mixture of Jews and Gentiles, so there is not much emphasis on keeping the Jewish feasts. By the end of the 1st century, the first day of the week (the day of the resurrection of Jesus) has taken over from the sabbath as the focal day of worship.

be counted from either a normal sabbath or a special one, the calculation was a matter of great debate!

In later centuries, the Greek for 'fifty' gives this festival the name 'Pentecost'. It falls in the third month, Sivan. This is the time of year when the Israelites received God's law at Sinai, and the day of Pentecost becomes a joyful celebration of that great event.

As well as the harvest offering, there are sacrifices for sin and to express fellowship. As the grain harvest comes to an end, God reminds the reapers to leave some gleanings for the poor.

The Feast of Trumpets

The number seven has special significance for Israel, and the seventh month is marked by three special occasions: the Feast of Trumpets, the Day of Atonement and the Feast of Tabernacles.

The Feast of Trumpets falls on the first day of the seventh month (23:23–25). It comes at the end of the grape harvest – the close of the old farming year and the beginning of the new.

This is a special sabbath, heralded by the blowing of trumpets. The Jewish tradition is that these trumpets are the rams' horns – the ones which are used to announce the Year of Jubilee. They sound a more solemn note than the usual silver trumpets.

This feast is a landmark day of rest, sacred assembly and sacrifice. It is a day to pause and prepare for the great festivals which are approaching.

The Day of Atonement

This is the most important of all the festivals described in Leviticus, and is a fast rather than a feast (23:26–32).

The Day of Atonement falls on the tenth day of the seventh month. On this day the high priest makes sacrifice for his own sin and the sins of the people. He re-consecrates the entire tent of meeting and its surrounds for the worship and service of God.

This is the only day of the year that the high priest is allowed to enter the Most Holy Place and sprinkle blood for the atonement of sin. The ceremony is described in chapter 16.

God's repeated instruction to the people is that they are to deny themselves. They must abstain from food and other pleasures, to fast in sorrow for their sins. This is not a time for joyful celebration, but for deep repentance and solemn sacrifice.

The Feast of Tabernacles

On the fifteenth day of the seventh month, the Feast of Tabernacles begins (23:33-44). This feast lasts for eight days, beginning and ending with a day of rest. It is party time, with feasting and dancing to celebrate the 'ingathering' - the completion of all the harvests.

During this festival, the Israelites remember how their ancestors lived in tents in the wilderness. They build shelters or booths with palm fronds and leafy branches, and live in them for the week.

A great number of sacrifices are offered in careful sequence. Each day, two rams and fourteen lambs are sacrificed as burnt offerings, and a single goat is sacrificed as a sin offering. Bulls are also sacrificed as burnt offerings - beginning with thirteen on the first day and reducing to seven on the seventh. On the eighth day just one bull is offered, to bring the total to seventy (Numbers 28:12-28).

In the time of Jesus, the climax of the Feast of Tabernacles comes on its closing day. The high priest brings a golden pitcher of water in procession from the Pool of Siloam, and pours it out in front of the altar in the temple. He asks God to give rain for the coming growing season - and prays that he will pour out his Spirit on his people. It is a dramatic moment when Jesus stands forward and cries, 'Let anyone who is thirsty come to me, and... drink' (John 7:37-38 NRSV)!

Oil and bread

In the tent of meeting stands a pure gold lampstand, with seven branches bearing seven oil lamps. The oil is clear, made from pressed olives (24:1-9). It is brought by the people to provide light for God's sanctuary. The lamps are tended and their wicks trimmed by Aaron and his sons. The flames burn continually, day and night, as a symbol of God's constant presence among his people.

God commands that twelve large loaves are to be baked from fine flour. The flour, like the oil, is the very best that can be produced. The loaves are to be placed on the gold table in the tent of meeting, arranged in two rows of six. They represent the twelve tribes of Israel, and are known as the bread of the Presence (Exodus 25:23-30).

The loaves are an offering to the Lord and are accompanied by incense in bowls or spoons. After the loaves have been on display for seven days, they are eaten by Aaron and his sons. This is the most holy portion of all the food which they are allowed to consume from the people's offerings.

The custom for providing bread for the gods was practised by the Babylonians. They liked their gods to eat the same food as they did – although their priests had to consume the bread in secret to make sure it disappeared! Israel's custom is different. God doesn't need human food. Rather, the loaves are offered as a sign that he provides his people with their daily bread.

The death penalty for blasphemy (24:10-23)

Moses has to decide a difficult case. A man who is only half-Israelite (his mother is an Israelite but his father an Egyptian) has blasphemed the name of God with a curse. One of the commandments forbids such blasphemy but doesn't prescribe a punishment (Exodus 20:7). Should the man be excused altogether, as he is not a full Israelite?

God's command is that the man shall be taken outside the camp and stoned to death. It is no excuse that he is only half-Israelite. He has blasphemed God's name, which is an act of violence against God and a denial of his presence and purpose in the world. It makes no difference whether he is a native Israelite or a foreigner; he is responsible for his outburst and must bear the penalty.

God also gives Moses directions on how to deal with other violent crimes. Anyone who murders a fellow human being must be put to death. Anyone who kills an animal must replace it in kind. Anyone who inflicts an injury must have a similar injury inflicted in return.

These penalties are intended to be exactly fair, and apply to Israelites and foreigners alike. The victims of crime won't need to take personal revenge, but can rely on the law to give them justice. It also ensures that the punishment fits the crime, and doesn't become an excuse for excessive violence or cruelty. Despite the fairness of 'eye for eye, tooth for tooth', it seems likely that fines and compensations were soon allowed as an alternative.

Sabbaths and Jubilees (25:1–55)

The sabbath year

During their years in the wilderness, the Israelites have become used to 'keeping the sabbath' – that is, resting on the seventh (and last) day of the week.

Sabbath means 'cease' or 'stop'. The sabbath is a day of rest for everyone, when work stops for both people and animals. To enable this absolute rest, God provides a double amount of manna on the previous day (Exodus 16:22–26).

The sabbath rest echoes the story of creation, when God rested from all his work on the seventh day (Genesis 2:2). It was revealed as one of God's laws, when it was given as the fourth commandment (Exodus 20:8–11).

Moses tells the Israelites that, when they have their own land, they are to give the land itself a sabbath rest (25:1–7). Every seventh year, the farmers are to leave the fields unploughed and the vines untended. God promises that the crops which grow naturally, without human labour, will be enough for everyone to eat.

The sabbath year makes good sense from a farming point of view. It allows the land to recover and so renew its fertility. But a far more important point is being made – that God is the real owner of the land and his people are only tenants.

It is God who provides the needs of his people. He has already shown his power and rewarded the people's trust by providing them with daily manna. Now the 'manna principle' is to be applied to a whole year!

The year of jubilee

If every seventh year is a sabbath, then seven times seven (forty-nine) years must herald a very special celebration. The fiftieth year is to be a Jubilee (25:8–55).

The word 'jubilee' comes from the Hebrew for 'ram', because the Jubilee Year is announced by the blowing of rams' horn trumpets. They are sounded across the country on the Day of Atonement. The Day of

Atonement restores harmony between God and his people. Now, through the Jubilee, the peace of God is to enfold the natural world as well.

The Year of Jubilee is the time for rest, restoration and return. As with the forty-ninth year (a sabbath) there is to be no hard labour on the land. Those who have lost their land through debt or bad luck will now have their inheritance restored to them. Families will be relieved of all their usual duties, so that they can be reunited and spend time together.

The land belongs to God, and is only leased by its human owners as their God-given inheritance. Because the land will revert to these original owners (or their families) every fifty years, its price must be adjusted as the Jubilee approaches. It is the number of harvests that give the land its value. The land is most valuable when there are still many years to go until the Jubilee.

Laws for redeeeming property

Various laws are provided for redeeming property (25:25-34).

Sometimes the land that has been lost can be redeemed by the nearest relative (the next of kin), who will step in to rescue the person who has fallen into poverty. Boaz was the next of kin to his relative Ruth, who was both a foreigner and a widow. As her 'redeemer', he first helped her to survive and later married her (Ruth 4:1-4).

The Jubilee laws are clearly for a rural community. They are not expected to work in a town. If someone is forced to sell his town house, then he has only a year to reclaim it. After that it belongs to the new owner.

The Levites (the priestly tribe) can buy and sell houses in their own towns, but the properties will revert to their original owners at Jubilee. Levites are not to sell their pastureland, because God has given it to them for ever.

Special treatment for the poor

Israel's care for the poor and the stranger is based on the fact that the whole nation was once rescued from slavery by God (25:35-55).

Israelites who become poor are to be lent money without being charged interest, and are to be sold food at cost price. This enables them and their families to continue to live in the same community. Israelites

> ### Jesus and the Jubilee
>
> The prophet Isaiah proclaims rescue and release for God's people (Isaiah 60:1–3). This is to be a glorious Jubilee. God will do this great work through his servant, who will be the redeemer of his poor, broken and enslaved people.
>
> When Jesus begins his public ministry, he teaches in the synagogue at Nazareth. He takes this scripture from Isaiah for his text, and astounds his hearers by proclaiming that the prophet's words have now come true.
>
> Jesus claims that he is the servant described in Isaiah's prophecy, whose mission is to proclaim and demonstrate God's Jubilee (Luke 4:16–30). His hearers in Nazareth are outraged by what seems to them a blasphemy. They try to kill him.

are never to become slaves to other Israelites. If they are forced to become servants, then they must be released at the Jubilee.

Foreigners and immigrants may be bought by Israelites as slaves. There is no law that such slaves must be released at the Jubilee. They and their children are the property of their Israelite owners, and can be handed on to the next generation.

If Israelites become the slaves of wealthy foreigners, they have the right to be redeemed from slavery at a later date. Near relatives may act as their redeemer and buy them back, or they may earn enough to purchase their own freedom. Failing this, the Jubilee will release the Israelite slaves and their families when it comes round.

Israelite slaves are to be released at the Jubilee, but foreign slaves are not. This is because the Israelites belong to God, who redeemed them from slavery in Egypt.

Blessings and curses (26:1–46)

God promises great blessings if his people keep his commands, and terrible punishments if they reject them. These rewards and penalties are the consequences of the covenant – like the outcomes of a treaty. It is the stark choice between a way of life or a way of death (Deuteronomy 30:15).

The blessings of obedience

The Israelites are not to carve images of God, or set up sacred stones as pillars. Jacob did this with his stone pillow after his dream of God (Genesis 28:18) – but the Canaanites do the same for their pagan rites.

The Israelites are to keep the sabbath rests and reverence God's sanctuary (the tent of meeting and, later, the temple). These are the special ways by which they will honour God in time and place.

God describes the life he will give his people if they keep his commands. They will live in perfect harmony with nature, with times of harvest so long and full that they will overlap each other. God will also protect them from wild beasts and give them victory over their enemies (26:1–13).

God will bless the Israelites with growing numbers. He will walk among them, as he once did with Adam and Eve in the Garden of Eden (Genesis 3:8). They will be his own free people, secure and confident in his purpose and love.

The penalties for disobedience

If the Israelites disobey God, they will face disease, defeat and death (26:14–45). The climate and the land will be hostile to them, and their enemies will overwhelm them. God himself will be against them, punishing them with sevenfold intensity.

Instead of protecting and strengthening his people, God will attack and scatter them. This prediction will come true when they are divided and defeated, dispersed and exiled. Without the burden of farming, the land will at last be able to take its sabbath rest!

But with the warning of judgment comes the promise of mercy. If the Israelites will turn to God again and confess their sin, then he will honour his covenant and restore them.

The price of keeping faith (27:1–34)

The people of Israel express their commitment to God through vows and gifts. Such a gift may be a person, an animal, a house or a field. If the offerers change their mind, then the gifts can be bought back (redeemed) with a sum of money.

God gives Moses a way of valuing gifts in terms of money. People who have been dedicated to God are valued according to their age and gender. This is a measure of the work they will be able to do. Men are worth more than women. The very young and the very old are worth less than those in their prime. If the price of redeeming a person is too high, then the priest will help to work out an amount that is reasonable.

The priest also helps in valuing houses. A field is valued by the amount of seed it takes to sow it, or the number of harvests it will yield before the next Jubilee. If worshippers want to repossess their houses or fields, they must pay an extra 20 per cent for them. All land reverts to its original owner at the Jubilee.

First-born animals already belong to the Lord, so they can't be offered twice (Exodus 13:2, 12). If the animal is 'clean' (a cow or sheep suitable for sacrifice), it can never be repossessed by the worshipper. If it is an 'unclean' animal, the worshipper may buy it back for 20 per cent extra, or it can be sold to someone else.

A tithe (tenth) of all produce belongs to God, and is to be offered to him. Again, the worshipper can buy it back for its value, plus a fifth.

One in ten of the animals in every herd and flock belongs to the Lord and is to be offered to him. When selecting these animals, the worshippers must not pick out the best or worst, or seek to substitute one for another. And, unlike the crops, they can't buy them back.

These rules show the importance of keeping a vow to God. A gift must be of real value and express a real commitment.

Behind all sacrifice is the seriousness of sin. Sin is so dreadful that it can only be paid for with a pure life, completely offered. So Leviticus points us to the perfect, once-for-all sacrifice of Jesus on the cross.

NUMBERS

The book of Numbers describes the years that the Israelites spend in the Sinai Desert. Between leaving Mount Sinai with the tabernacle and embarking on the conquest of Canaan, an entire generation lives and dies in the wilderness. The book of Numbers counts them, tells us how they are organized, records their laws and narrates their adventures.

The wilderness years have been hard. The people have grumbled against God and rebelled against Moses – and there have been some devastating setbacks. An entire generation has forfeited the right to enter the Promised Land. But through this great shared adventure, the Israelites have experienced for themselves the power and love and mercy of God. They have realized the force of his holiness. They have learned obedience. They are ready for victory.

OUTLINE

The tribes at Mount Sinai (1:1–9:23)
The journey from Sinai to Moab (10:1–21:35)
Events in Moab (22:1–32:42)
A log of the journey (33:1–56)
Preparing for settlement (34:1–36:13)

Introduction

Numbers is one of the five 'books of Moses'. Moses is the central character, leading the Israelites throughout this period. 'Numbers' is almost a nickname, referring to the fact that people are counted both at the beginning and towards the end of the book.

The wilderness years are tough. The Israelites are often hungry and thirsty. At times they wish they were back in Egypt. There are frequent complaints about Moses' leadership and even some attempts to overthrow him. In it all, God is faithful to his promise to protect and preserve his people. It is an aspect of his love for them that, on occasions, he disciplines his people severely.

When was Numbers written?

Numbers is about Moses rather than by him. Although he was in a position to record all this information (33:2 has Moses noting the stages of the desert journey), he would hardly describe himself as 'more humble than anyone else on the face of the earth' (12:3 NRSV)! The book contains some very old poetry, especially in the story of Balaam. The details of history and geography are true to the 13th century BC.

The book of Numbers may not have been written in its final form until some 200 years later, perhaps during the reign of Saul or David. By then there may have been some 'tidying up' of the organization and rules of the wilderness years, as well as some interpretation of what God was doing with his people at this earlier time.

DISCOVERING NUMBERS

The tribes at Mount Sinai

The first census (1:1–54)

It is just over a year since the Israelites escaped from Egypt. That great event is narrated in the book of Exodus. Moses has a tent of meeting where he speaks with God. It is during one of these times of prayer and listening that God tells Moses to take a census of all the men who are aged twenty or over. The aim is to register everyone who can serve in the army. The people are counted by tribes; each tribe is named after one of the sons of Jacob.

The resulting total is astonishing: 603,550! This number has been eagerly discussed by scholars because it is so large as to be almost unbelievable. The Hebrew word for 'thousand' can also mean simply 'a clan of families' or even 'a company of soldiers'. It may be that a translator confused the terms and came up with a rather large estimate of the numbers involved.

The Levites are treated as a special case. They aren't counted, as they are to be excused military service. Their sacred responsibility is to assemble and dismantle the tabernacle and to care for its furnishings. They are even to pitch their tents round the tabernacle to provide a protective screen between the Israelites and the wrath of God. The tabernacle is called the tabernacle of the testimony, because it contains the ark in which are kept the Ten Commandments.

A fighting force (2:1–34)

The Israelites are now an effective force. The panic-stricken and argumentative rabble that scrambled out of Egypt has become a disciplined and well-organized army.

The Levites (3:1–51)

Aaron, the brother of Moses, serves as high priest. In this he is assisted by his sons. They in turn are served by the Levites. Instead of taking the first-born son from every Israelite family, God chooses the Levites as his dedicated tribe. As there aren't enough Levites to account for all the Israelites' first-born, a sum of five shekels per head is collected to cover the rest.

Special responsibilities (4:1–49)

Within the tribe of Levi, different families and clans are responsible for caring for different parts of the tabernacle. The Kohathite clans have the care of the sanctuary. The Gershonites are responsible for the tenting, curtains and ropes. The Merarites look after frames, posts and pegs.

Although the Kohathites are responsible for the furniture of the sanctuary, only Aaron and his sons are allowed to dismantle the shielding curtain and pack the sacred furnishings. If the Kohathites touch the holy articles, they will die. They are, however, allowed to carry them once they are reverently packed.

A holy place (5:1–31)

The Israelite camp is a holy place. Everything is to be kept clean. Every person is to be pure in body and mind. God tells Moses how to keep the camp free of disease by putting certain people in quarantine. People with infectious skin diseases (such as lepers), together with those suffering from discharges, or who have been in contact with a dead body, are to be excluded from the camp. This includes women during the time of their period and men after they have ejaculated semen.

There are regulations for compensating someone who has been wronged. Any offence must be put right, not just between the people concerned, but also with God. There is a special test for a woman whose husband suspects her of being unfaithful to him. She is to swallow bitter water in the presence of the priest. If she is guilty, she will take ill and become barren. This is a very humane law which protects women from quick-tempered or jealous husbands.

The Nazirite (6:1–21)

A man or woman wishing to be dedicated to God for a particular time or task can become a Nazirite. 'Nazirite' simply means 'one who has taken a vow'. It means that the person concerned is set apart from ordinary life for a while.

The Nazirite is not to drink alcohol, have a haircut or touch a dead body while the vow is in force. When we come to the story of Samson in the book of Judges, we will see how he wilfully breaks all these conditions. Here, in Numbers, the ceremony for becoming a Nazirite brings to mind the words of Paul to the Christians at Rome: 'Offer your bodies as living sacrifices, holy and pleasing to God – this is your spiritual act of worship' (Romans 12:1).

The priestly blessing (6:22–27)

God gives Moses a form of words by which the priests may bless people. The blessing has an overwhelming sense of God's goodwill:

The Lord bless you and keep you;
The Lord make his face to shine upon you and be gracious to you;
The Lord turn his face towards you and give you peace. (6:24–26)

This beautiful blessing is echoed in Psalm 67, where it becomes a prayer that God will bless all the nations through Israel.

Offerings for the tabernacle (7:1–89)

As Moses completes the work on the tabernacle, the tribal leaders bring their offerings. They come one at a time, on successive days, with an abundance of costly gifts. These include silver and gold plates and bowls, grain, flour and oil, bulls, rams, lambs, oxen and goats. Everything is weighed, measured, counted and recorded. The heads of families lead by example in their generosity to God. Their gifts will be used to equip the tabernacle for its ceremonies and supply its sacrifices.

At the heart of the tabernacle is the tent of meeting. Here is the ark of the testimony. It is a box containing the two stone slabs which are engraved with the Ten Commandments. On top of the box, at each end, are two cherubim. Between them is the 'atonement cover', where the blood of the sacrifice is to be poured once a year on the Day of Atonement. This is the place where Moses hears God speak – and speaks with him.

Setting apart the Levites (8:1–26)

The Levites are commissioned with a special ceremony. After they have been sprinkled with water, they shave themselves all over and wash their clothes and bodies. This is a systematic 'de-sinning'! They offer special sacrifices. In particular, they have hands laid on them. This is to identify them as representing the whole Israelite community. The Levites in turn lay their hands on the animals that are to be offered in sacrifice for them. The Levites are dedicated to God as substitutes for the first-born sons of every family. There is a contrast here with the first-born sons of Egypt, who died when Israel was rescued from slavery at the first Passover.

The Passover (9:1–14)

People who miss the Passover because they are away on a journey, or ceremonially unclean, are allowed to celebrate it a month later. However, it is regarded as a very serious matter if someone is able to celebrate the Passover at the proper time but fails to do so. There is a generous rule that non-Israelites can join in the Passover celebration on the same terms as everyone else. Israelites may be exclusive but they are not to be racist.

The cloud above the tabernacle (9:15–23)

A cloud covers the tent of testimony. It shrouds it during the day and glows like fire at night. This is the symbol of the Lord's presence. In later years it will be called the 'Shekinah'. The Israelites live in such harmony with the will of God that when the cloud lifts they strike camp and move on; where the cloud next settles, they will pitch camp again.

The journey from Sinai to Moab

The silver trumpets (10:1–10)

God instructs Moses to make two silver trumpets. They are to be used to call people to assembly, to declare war and to proclaim feasts. They are a different kind of trumpet from the rams' horns which are blown to announce the Year of Jubilee.

The Israelites leave Sinai (10:11–36)

At last the Israelites move on from Sinai. They travel in good order, in their tribal and family groups. From here on, the story looks forward to the Promised Land.

Moses' father-in-law is thinking of returning home, but Moses persuades him to continue with them. There is a puzzle about his name. Here he is called Hobab, but elsewhere his name is Jethro. He is a much-valued counsellor to Moses, with an unrivalled knowledge of the area and an instinct for good management.

Fire from the Lord (11:1–3)

Journeying through the desert, the stresses start to show. The people complain about their hardships – and God scorches them for their ingratitude.

Complaints (11:4–23)

There are complaints about the manna – and dreams of the cool salads of Egypt. No one is sure what 'manna' is, but there is a tamarisk plant which produces sweet sticky globules overnight. These fall to the ground and are melted by the morning sun. This could be the substance that the Israelites collected day by day and prepared as food in a variety of ways.

Moses is exasperated by the people's complaints. They are clamouring for meat and Moses feels unable to endure their grumbling any longer. He wishes he could die.

Seventy elders (11:24–35)

God guides Moses to appoint seventy elders to share in the tasks of leadership. God will give them a share of his Spirit to enable them to do the work. God also promises to give the people meat until they are sick of it!

When the elders are gathered and commissioned, they receive God's Spirit and prophesy. Two of those chosen are still in the camp, some distance from the tent of meeting. They also prophesy, to the delight of Moses (and the jealousy of Joshua). Moses is not protective of his own status, but only of God's authority.

The Lord raises a wind which blows in from the Gulf of Aqabah, bringing flocks of quail from the sea. They arrive in astonishing numbers, flying low or falling exhausted. The Israelites gather and eat them, only to be struck down by illness. This is God's punishment on them for their discontent. As many people die and are buried, the place is named Kibroth Hattaavah, which means 'graves of craving'. They have gorged themselves to death.

Opposition (12:1–16)

For some reason Miriam and Aaron are jealous of Moses. They criticize him for marrying a Cushite. They also doubt whether he is really that special. Doesn't God also work through them, his brother and sister? This is a crisis brought on by Moses' low-key style of leadership. So far his troubles have included organizational difficulties, food shortages, outbreaks of spiritual gifts, family jealousies and marriage problems.

God takes Aaron and Miriam to task for daring to speak against Moses. Moses does in fact have a unique relationship with God: one that is an open friendship, 'face to face', without deception or defence.

Miriam is punished with an outbreak of skin disease. She has to spend a week in isolation outside the camp.

Exploring Canaan (13:1–33)

The Israelites have now arrived in the Desert of Paran. They are just a few days' march from Canaan and God tells Moses to send spies on ahead. They are to assess the landscape, the local people and the strength of the defences. The group is made up from a member of each tribe. The significant members are Joshua, son of Nun, and Caleb, son of Jephunneh. In the Valley of Eshcol the spies find such a huge cluster of grapes that it takes two of them to carry it on a pole between them. The name Eshcol means 'cluster'.

After forty days, the twelve spies return. They report to Moses at Kadesh. They give an exciting account of the land and its resources, but feel there is no chance of dislodging its powerful people. Strong tribes occupy the hills and the Canaanites occupy the land between the River Jordan and the sea.

Caleb disagrees with the rest. In his opinion the Israelites are well able to capture the land. The others begin to exaggerate their case – claiming that the land is occupied by giants ('descendants of Anak', 13:33). The Israelites are like 'grasshoppers' compared to them.

The people rebel (14:1–45)

The spies' report plunges the community into crisis. No one gets any sleep that night as the Israelites bewail their fate. They complain to Moses that they were better off in Egypt. If they go forward from here, they are certain to walk into the jaws of death.

Joshua and Caleb speak to the people. They emphasize again that the land is good and that the Lord will give it to them if they obey him. With God on their side, there is no need to be afraid of any enemy, however tall or strong.

The people are about to stone Joshua and Caleb, when the Lord himself appears at the tent of meeting. He is angry and threatens to destroy the people and make a new nation from Moses. This must have been a very great temptation for Moses, but he rejects it – and even rebukes God for suggesting it. Moses begs God not to destroy his people, because the Egyptians will think that the Lord has failed to rescue them. He pleads that God will forgive the Israelites as he has done before. He describes God in an unforgettable way:

'The Lord is slow to anger, abounding in love and forgiving sin and rebellion. Yet he does not leave the guilty unpunished.' (14:18)

God agrees to forgive. But there is a penalty. Of all those who left Egypt, only two will survive to enter the Promised Land. They are the faithful spies, Caleb and Joshua. The Israelites must turn back and wander through the desert until an entire generation has died.

Further offerings (15:1–21)

God gives Moses some further details about life in the Promised Land. When animals are offered in sacrifice, they are to be accompanied by offerings of grain and wine. The grain will probably take the form of fine flour mixed with oil. The point is not that God needs food, but that flour and oil and wine make a wonderful smell when they burn on the altar. The smell pleases the Lord. As a smell is invisible, it is thought of as reaching God, who is invisible.

Israel's law is God's teaching. It is revealed to Israel by God, not devised by the people themselves. A statute is a lasting rule. It comes from the word 'to engrave'. An ordinance (15:15) is a detail of God's law, applied in a particular situation.

Accidental sins (15:22–31)

God deals with the difference between sins which are committed on purpose and sins which are done by accident. There are sacrifices that can be made when a group or individual causes damage or loss of life by accident. It is far more serious when someone sins on purpose.

A sabbath-breaker is put to death (15:32–36)

An example is given of a man who is found gathering wood on the sabbath. This is a wilful breach of God's commandment not to do any work on the sabbath day. The Lord tells Moses that the man must be put to death. The whole community takes part in the execution, which is done by stoning outside the camp. This punishment is extreme because the law it enforces is so crucial for the health of society.

Tassels (15:37–41)

God tells Moses that the Israelites are to wear tassels on the corners of their clothes. These will be a visible reminder of God's law in years to come – and catch the eye when temptations loom!

Rebels (16:1–50)

Two rebellions flare up against Moses and Aaron. Korah, who is a Levite, challenges the fact that only Aaron and his sons are allowed to be priests. Surely the whole people of God are holy! Korah has a large following. Moses suggests that they each bring a censer (incense burner) and try acting as priests the following day.

Meanwhile, Dathan and Abiram start to disobey Moses. They are Reubenites. In their opinion, Moses has brought them out of a land of plenty and stranded them in a desert. By what right does he give them orders?

The following morning, Korah and his followers waft incense to the Lord. Moses warns everyone else to stand well back from the tents of the rebels. The ground splits open to swallow Korah and everyone who belongs to him, their families and possessions. The Lord sends fire to consume the 250 men who are presuming to offer incense. When the horrifying act of judgment is over, the bronze censers are retrieved from the ashes and beaten into the overlay of the altar. As God's holy anger continues to break out, Aaron offers incense to stem the tide of a plague. Even so, 14,700 people die that day.

The budding of Aaron's staff (17:1–13)

The challenge to Aaron's status continues and God tells Moses how to handle it. The leader of each of the twelve tribes is to write his name on a staff and place it in the tent of meeting. God will prove to everyone that Aaron is his chosen priest by causing Aaron's staff to send out shoots. The following morning, Aaron's staff has not only sprouted, but budded, blossomed – and produced almonds!

The duties of priests and Levites (18:1–7)

God tells Aaron that he and his family are to have the care of the sanctuary. The Levites – the wider tribe to which Aaron belongs – are to look after the tent of meeting. After the recent rebellions and testing of authority, the priesthood is to be exclusive to Aaron and his sons.

Offerings for priests and Levites (18:8–32)

The priests and their families will be provided for from the offerings brought by the people. The same will be done for the Levites. When the tribes arrive in Canaan and the territory is divided up, there will be no allocation of land for priests and Levites. God explains to Aaron: 'I am your share.'

The uniqueness of Aaron and his special status is emphasized again. God tells Moses that the Levites must offer a tenth of all that they receive to the Lord, with the best of all (the Lord's portion) given to Aaron.

The water of cleansing (19:1–22)

God tells Moses and Aaron to prepare 'water of cleansing'. This is to be done by sacrificing and burning a heifer and making a solution of the ashes by mixing them with water. This water is to be sprinkled on anyone who has contact with a dead body or a grave. This gives the Israelites a clear procedure for dealing with death and the risk of infection.

Water from the rock (20:1–13)

The Israelites arrive at the Desert of Zin and camp at Kadesh. They will settle here for nearly forty years. The people complain at the lack of water and reproach Moses for stranding them in the desert. Egypt now seems to them a place of pleasure and plenty.

God tells Moses to take his staff, gather the people and call water out of the rock. Moses vents some of his anger by striking the rock twice with the rod. Water gushes out in plenty, but God is angry with Moses and Aaron. The spirit and manner in which Moses has worked the miracle have dishonoured God. In a devastating judgment, God declares that Moses and Aaron will not be allowed to lead the Israelites into the new land. The place is named Meribah, which means 'quarrelling'.

Edom bars the way (20:14-21)

Moses sends messengers to the king of Edom. The Edomites are descended from Esau, just as the Israelites are descended from Jacob. Moses asks permission for the Israelites to use the 'King's Highway' – the caravan track which provides their most direct route to Canaan. The Edomites refuse permission – a snub which Israel will remember for many generations to come.

The death of Aaron (20:22-29)

The Lord tells Moses and Aaron that the time has come for Aaron to die. With Aaron's son Eleazar, they climb Mount Hor. At the summit, Moses transfers Aaron's garments to Eleazar; and Aaron dies.

The destruction of Arad (21:1-3)

The nations and tribes of the area are now on guard against Israel's advance. The king of Arad attacks them – and is completely destroyed.

The bronze snake (21:4-9)

Taking the long route round Edom, the Israelites continue to complain about God's plan and Moses' leadership. God punishes them with an infestation of venomous snakes. When they beg for forgiveness and Moses prays for them, God instructs him to make a snake and put it on a pole.

Moses makes the snake of bronze and hangs it high on a pole. Anyone suffering from snake-bites can look at it and be healed. One day Jesus will take this as an image of himself – nailed to the cross in the sight of, and for the sake of, the whole world (John 3:14-15).

The journey from Kadesh to Pisgah (21:10-20)

The Israelites are now nearing the end of the journey. After a lengthy stay at Kadesh, they move their camp to Oboth and then on to Iye-abarim (the 'ruins of Abarim'). At this point they are about fifteen miles south of the Dead Sea and journeying east. When they come to the arid valley of the Arabah, they join a trade route which takes them north, along the western boundary of Edom. Reaching the Zered Valley, they follow it east through Edom, and then travel north again along Edom's western boundary. Arriving at the River Arnon, which runs swiftly westward to the Dead Sea, the Israelites cross from Moab into the territory of the Amorites and the kingdom of Sihon. The journey is simply summarized in Judges 11:16–18.

We hear snatches of two songs which survive in an ancient saga called *The Book of the Wars of the Lord*. They speak of the slopes and wadis (river beds) encountered on the desert journey, and recall the official opening of a well at a place called Beer! In later years, this 'Song of Israel' was sung every third sabbath, along with Moses' great 'Song of the Sea' (Exodus 15:1–19).

The Israelites travel on through places whose names are unknown today, until they come to the heights of Pisgah in Moab, with a

Balaam's donkey

The wonderful, hilarious story of Balaam is a treasure of wit and wisdom – and features some of the oldest poetry in the Bible. It is written by someone who knows all about donkeys – although not many of us have met one that talks!

Balaam delivers four oracles about Israel, but is completely unable to curse them – much to Balak's annoyance. Balaam is a genuine prophet, who can only say the words God gives him. He proclaims the mystery of Israel:

I see people who live apart
and do not consider themselves one of the nations. (23:9)

Balaam's fourth oracle attains the very heights of prophecy. As he declares the future victories of Israel, we have a tingling recognition of the coming Messiah:

I see him, but not now;
  I behold him, but not near.
A star will come out of Jacob;
  A sceptre will rise out of Israel. (24:17)

panoramic view of Canaan to the west. This is their first sight of the Promised Land.

The defeat of Sihon and Og (21:21-35)

Continuing their journey, the Israelites again ask permission to use the King's Highway. This time it is Sihon, king of the Amorites, who obstructs them. The Israelites defeat him in pitched battle and capture his capital, Heshbon. The mention of various towns and settlements at this point in the journey helps us to date the time of the exodus. Permanent settlements only began in this area after 1350 BC. By the time Israel encounters them, they are already well established – leading us to a date around 1250 BC for Israel's desert journey.

Having conquered the Amorites, the Israelites take the main road towards Bashan. Here they defeat King Og and his army and capture the land. So Israel makes her first gains in the area we now know as Trans-Jordan.

Events in Moab

The story of Balaam (22:1-24:25)

The Israelites arrive in the plains of Moab and camp along the banks of the River Jordan, opposite Jericho. At last they are out of the desert, in a kinder landscape of woods and water, north of the Dead Sea. The king of Moab, Balak, is so alarmed that he sends all the way to the Euphrates for a prophet. So we meet Balaam, who is hired to curse the Israelites and prevent any further advance.

Balaam consults God and discovers that the Israelites are his chosen people. He refuses to curse them. God allows Balaam to return with the messengers (now augmented by a delegation of princes), but proceeds to give him a very rough time with his donkey. With Balaam, God uses a foreigner to bless Israel, although it is Israel who is to bless the nations.

Trouble with Moabite women (25:1-18)

Some Israelite men get involved with Moabite women. Soon the potent mixture of sex and paganism is compromising Israel's holiness. God tells

Moses to stop the rot by executing the leaders and hanging their bodies. This will avert God's anger.

One particular Israelite, Zimri, takes a Midianite woman to his tent in full view of everyone. Aaron's son, Phinehas, follows them and runs them both through with a spear. This puts a stop to a plague which has already claimed 24,000 lives. One day the priestly line of Zadok will trace its descent from the zealous Phinehas, who acted out of a passion for God's holiness. But a young Midianite widow, Ruth, will become an ancestor of King David – and Jesus.

The second census (26:1–65)

As the Israelites approach the end of their journey, God tells Moses to take another census. Moses and Eleazar are to count the men over twenty years of age, to assess the military strength of Israel and prepare for the dividing up of Canaan. As we found with the first census, it is difficult to be sure of these figures. The Hebrew term for a thousand can also be used for a much smaller group, such as a company of soldiers, an extended family or a clan. Certainly the numbers as they stand are huge.

God tells Moses to allocate the new land according to the size of the tribes. Larger groups will have more territory than others, but the actual decisions are to be made by lottery. The Levites are also counted, but they will not receive a share of land, because they are a tribe set aside for the service of God.

None of the people counted by Moses and Aaron in the first census have survived to be counted by Moses and Eleazar in the second. Only Caleb and Joshua remain of the generation that grumbled its way across the desert from Egypt to the borders of Canaan.

Equal rights for women (27:12–23)

From now on, the ownership of land will become an issue. An important legal point is raised with Moses. The daughters of Zelophehad want to know if they can inherit property, because their father had no sons. God tells Moses that they must certainly be allowed their father's inheritance.

Joshua to succeed Moses (27:12-23)

God tells Moses that the time is approaching for him to die. Moses asks God to appoint a faithful leader in his place. The Lord tells Moses to choose Joshua, a man God has already blessed with his Spirit. Joshua is commissioned by Moses in the presence of Eleazar the priest and the whole community. From now on Joshua is recognized as Moses' successor.

Offerings and festivals (28:1-31)

God gives Moses detailed instructions about sacrifices and festivals. All this is important information for the priests, as they lead and regulate the life of the community.

These chapters in the book of Numbers show us the holiness of God and the seriousness of sin. They warn against half-hearted or casual worship. They encourage us to come to God for forgiveness and cleansing. Although we live in a different time, place and culture, the principle of reverence is still all-important.

Sacrifices are offered every day at morning and evening. In addition, there are special sacrifices on the sabbath day and on the first day of every month. Regulations are given here for the Passover, when the Israelites celebrate their deliverance from Egypt, and the Feast of Weeks, which is a harvest festival. Jews no longer offer sacrifices, because they have no temple in Jerusalem. Christians believe that the death of Jesus put an end to the sacrificing of animals, because he was the all-sufficient sacrifice for all time.

Three great feasts (29:1-40)

God gives Moses details of the sacrifices and offerings to be made at the Feast of Trumpets, the Day of Atonement and the Feast of Tabernacles. While the Feast of Trumpets is a time of celebration, the Day of Atonement is one of fasting, reflection and repentance. The Feast of Tabernacles lasts for a whole week and includes an extensive pattern of sacrifices. In centuries to come it will be celebrated by families camping out, to recall the tents and shelters of those wilderness years.

Vows (30:1–16)

When making vows, the word of an Israelite man is to be his bond. A young Israelite woman is entitled to make a vow, but her father may veto it. When she is married, her husband can disallow her pledges. In both cases, the vow must be cancelled promptly, as soon as the father or husband first hears of it.

A holy war (31:1–54)

God commissions Moses for a last campaign. Israel is to destroy the Midianites, who are immoral and pagan. Moses stops his officers sparing the Midianite women.

This is a holy war. God has commanded it, and it is fought in his strength. There are strict rules whereby the soldiers must clean up afterwards. If they have killed anyone or touched a dead body, they must stay outside the camp for a week. They must scrupulously wash themselves and their clothes – and clean their equipment. Even the plunder must be thoroughly cleansed: the precious metals through fire, and the other goods with water. Everything belongs to the Lord and is either carefully saved or completely destroyed.

The Trans-Jordan tribes (32:1–42)

Two of the tribes, the Reubenites and the Gadites, ask if they can settle in the land already captured, on the east side of the Jordan. At first Moses thinks they are backing out of the campaign. The two tribes assure him that they will actually lead the advance and not rest until all the land is conquered. Moses agrees to their proposal and grants these two tribes, together with the half-tribe of Manasseh (one of Joseph's sons), the land captured from Sihon and Og. This great desire for unity among the tribes does not last long after the conquest of Canaan.

A log of the journey

Moses has been keeping a record of all the stages and stopping places of the journey. We get some idea of his sophisticated Egyptian education as we read the entries made over many years. There is a vivid note of the day they left Egypt – marching out boldly while the Egyptians were burying their first-born. There is a postcard view of Elim, with its twelve springs and seventy palm trees. There is the bitter memory that there was no water to drink at Rephidim. The day and place of Aaron's death are recorded, together with his age. But this is mainly a list of places. While we can trace the broad outline of the route – from Rameses to Mount Sinai, and from Sinai to Ezion Geber on the coast of the Gulf of Aqaba; from there to the oasis of Kadesh in the Desert of Zin, and then on to the Plains of Moab – it is impossible to pinpoint the places today. Place names change frequently, especially in the desert.

God gives Moses a summary of his instructions. When the Israelites enter Canaan, they must expel its inhabitants and destroy their pagan gods and hilltop shrines. The land is to be divided among the Israelite tribes by size and by lot. It is not to be owned by a wealthy few, but by everyone as equally as possible. Moses must warn the people that if they fail to purge the land of its old inhabitants, they will bring pain and judgment on themselves in the future.

Preparing for settlement

The boundaries of Canaan (34:1–29)

God gives Moses the boundaries of Canaan, the Promised Land. The boundary runs from the southern end of the Dead Sea, takes in Edom and Kadesh Barnea, and stretches to the Mediterranean coastline. The sea then forms the western boundary. In the north, the limit of the Israelite territory is marked by Hazar Enan. From there the boundary runs south where it joins the River Jordan. The river forms the eastern boundary. These are the ideal dimensions of Israel and will only be achieved in the reigns of David and Solomon.

Towns for the Levites (35:1–5)

The Levites are to be a tribe devoted to the Lord, and won't have a tribal land of their own. Instead, they are to be given forty-eight cities, scattered around the country, each with some pasture for their cattle and flocks.

Israel is not to be ruled by powerful religious leaders who control most of the wealth.

Cities of refuge (35:6–34)

Six of the Levites' towns are to be 'cities of refuge'. Anyone accused of murder can claim sanctuary in one of these places until their case is brought to trial. When there has been a violent death, it is important to establish whether it was a murder or an accident. A high value is set on human life and great care is to be taken to ensure that judgments are true and penalties fair. An 'avenger of blood' is the next of kin of someone who has been killed. The avenger of blood makes sure that justice is done.

Land for everyone (36:1–13)

It is intended that the tribal lands will be permanent. They are not to be fragmented by trade or marriage. This means that the daughters of Zelophehad must marry within their tribe, to keep the land for the clans of Manasseh. The Promised Land is not for the profit of great landowners but for the benefit and survival of all Israel's families.

DEUTERONOMY

The Israelites have completed their journey from Egypt. They stand on the threshold of the Promised Land. For Moses this is a poignant moment, for he himself is about to die.

The book of Deuteronomy is Moses' farewell to the people. He encourages them to go on and occupy the land which God promised to their ancestors long ago. He reviews their journey together and spells out in simple language the terms of their covenant with God. A 'covenant' is a formal agreement, like a treaty.

Much of Deuteronomy is made out like an agreement between God and Israel. If they keep God's law, he will continue to bless them with peace and prosperity as he has promised. If not, they will fall under his curse.

Deuteronomy is a warm-hearted, forward-looking book. It contains brilliant rules for a full and happy life – a life based on a total commitment to God. At its heart are the words which Jesus himself took as the finest summary of the law:

Love the Lord your God with all your heart and with all your soul and with all your strength. (6:5; Mark 12:30)

OUTLINE

The wilderness years (1:1–4:49)
God's law and other instructions (5:1–26:19)
Blessings and curses (27:1–28:68)
Israel renews the covenant (29:1–30:20)
Farewell, Moses (31:1–34:12)

Introduction

Deuteronomy is the fifth of the 'books of Moses' at the beginning of the Bible. The title 'Deuteronomy' means 'a copy of this law' and comes from the Greek translation of a phrase in 17:18. Much of Deuteronomy can be found in parts of Exodus, Leviticus and Numbers, but this is far more than just an extra copy. Deuteronomy is laid out like one of the treaties of those days. It sets out, in everyday language, the terms and conditions of Israel's relationship with God. While Exodus and Leviticus provide information for the priests, Deuteronomy gives instruction and inspiration for everyone else.

Almost the whole of the book is presented in Moses' own words. This is the teaching he gave the new generation of the Israelites as they camped in the Plains of Moab and prepared to invade and capture the Promised Land of Canaan.

Moses has kept notes during the journey through the desert. He has thought deeply about God's dealings with them. Now he recalls and relates and interprets all that God has done.

The Israelites are God's own people. God has rescued Israel from Egypt and given her his law. She is the only nation in the world who has first-hand experience of the one and only God as her Saviour and king. With these great privileges comes the solemn responsibility to love and honour God in return.

Israel is to be a holy nation. This theme will be of enormous importance to the Christian church in centuries to come. Peter will write:

You are a chosen people, a royal priesthood, a holy nation, a people belonging to God, that you may declare the praises of him who has called you out of darkness into his wonderful light. Once you were not a people, but now you are the people of God; once you had not received mercy, but now you have received mercy. (1 Peter 2:9–10)

There are over eighty quotations from the book of Deuteronomy in the New Testament.

In many ways, Deuteronomy is a handbook to go with the covenant of Sinai. It gives detailed examples of how the Ten Commandments are to be lived out in everyday life. It warns of the deadly dangers of getting involved in the paganism of nearby nations. It teaches that obedience to God is good, wise, safe, liberating – and joyful. It deals in detail with right relationships – how people can live at peace with one another and care for the poor. It makes goodness attractive. When we are right with God, then we can get right with one another. When we are right with one another, then the whole world – earth, sky, people, plants and animals – will enjoy peace and plenty, harmony and happiness. In all this, the blessings of God depend on, but are not deserved by, the people's obedience to God.

DISCOVERING DEUTERONOMY

The wilderness years

It is forty years since the exodus. Only Moses, Caleb and Joshua remember the great day when Israel escaped from slavery in Egypt. Now Moses tells the story again for the next generation. He remembers how God called them at Horeb (Mount Sinai) to cross the desert, challenge and defeat the tribes of Canaan and occupy the land between the Mediterranean Sea and the River Euphrates. This is the Promised Land that God swore to give their ancestor Abraham, and which they are now about to possess.

The delay of disobedience (1:1–46)

Moses recalls the terrible burden of trying to care for so many people, and how the problem was resolved by sharing leadership. He describes how the spies were sent ahead and how they brought back reports of a good land but a powerful enemy. It was when the Israelites refused to trust God and go on to victory that they were sentenced to spend the rest of their lives in the desert. A journey that should have taken eleven days in fact lasted forty years. Moses was included in this failure and it is Joshua who will now lead the invasion of Canaan.

Learning to trust God (2:1–3:29)

Moses tells how the extra time in the desert has been used to build up Israel's trust in God. The people have discovered how God guides and provides. He gave them resounding victories over Sihon and the daunting Amorites, and over Og, the giant king of Bashan. Og's bed (made of iron) was thirteen feet long and six feet wide! All this is important experience for the campaign ahead. If God could defeat Sihon and Og, then he can give victory over the strongholds of Canaan.

'The Lord is God' (4:1–49)

Moses tells Israel that her strength lies in obedience to God. She must never forget the darkness and fire of Mount Sinai, when God gave her the Ten Commandments. The law is Israel's greatest treasure. It is to be learned, digested, lived – and taught to the children of every future generation. God is invisible and not to be imaged or modelled as an idol. It will be Israel's privileged task, by her obedience, to show the reality of God to the nations of the world. Moses warns the Israelites that if they turn to idol-worship they will lose their land and not regain it until they repent.

God's law and other instructions

The Ten Commandments (5:1–33)

Moses recites the Ten Commandments. These laws are for the people here and now. They are not to be dismissed as applying only to the old days.

God identifies himself by what he has done. He brought his people out of Egypt. They are to have no other gods. He is invisible. They must not try to make an image of God or express him in terms of heavenly bodies or earthly creatures. Any idol of God would be pitifully inadequate and dangerously misleading. Instead, God wishes to be known by his passion for his people: his jealousy for their love, his hatred of their wickedness and his lasting commitment to their well-being.

God's name is holy. It sums up his personality and purpose. It is a serious thing to abuse God's name, by taking it lightly or using it to endorse empty promises.

The sabbath day is to be kept holy. It is a day when the whole community – including servants, animals, visitors and strangers – has time and space to rest and reflect.

Children are to honour their parents. Families are to be bonded by obedience as well as affection. Elderly parents are to be provided for by their children. Soundly built families make a strong and stable society.

Human life, marriage, possessions and reputations are all to be respected. In particular, jealousy is to be tackled at source – in the heart. A neighbour is any fellow human being – not just a person who lives nearby. Another person's partner and possessions are not negotiable. Don't even think it!

'Love the Lord your God' (6:1–25)

God's law is a guide for living in total commitment to God. God's law is to be Israel's delight and magnificent obsession:

Love the Lord your God with all your heart and with all your soul and with all your strength. These commandments that I give you today are to be upon your hearts. Impress them upon your children. Talk about them when you sit at home and when you walk along the road, when you lie down and when you get up. Tie them as symbols on your hands and bind them on your foreheads. Write them on the door-frames of your houses and on your gates. (6:5–9)

These verses are the Hebrew 'Shema', which pious Jews recite twice a day.

'Tie them as symbols on your hands and bind them on your foreheads.' Orthodox Jews take these words literally and have copies of the law in containers (phylacteries), tied to their wrists and foreheads. God's law is to govern their personal, family and public life.

In later centuries there will be much debate about which is the most important law. Many people choose this verse as their summary: 'Love the Lord your God with all your heart and with all your soul and with all your strength.' Jesus agrees, adding the phrase, 'with all your mind'. In Hebrew, the 'heart' is the centre of the mind and will – not just the emotions. For Jesus this is 'the most important' commandment (Mark 12:28–34).

Destroying pagan nations (7:1–26)

The Israelites are told to destroy the pagan tribes of Canaan. They are to break down their altars, cut down their Asherah poles (fertility symbols) and burn their idols. All temptations to compromise with paganism by preserving idols, intermarrying with the people or even sparing their lives is strictly forbidden. This is not an ethnic cleansing as much as a spiritual purge. It is vital that God's holy people have a new start in a clean land. Even things as neutral as silver and gold are to be rejected, in case Israel relies on them instead of God. All their attitudes, standards and dealings are to reflect the holiness of God, because he has saved and loved them – and because that's what he is like.

'Do not forget...' (8:1–20)

Moses warns the Israelites not to forget the lessons of the desert. It was here that they learned that the Lord provides – and that there is more to life than filling your stomach. Jesus quotes this chapter when the devil tempts him to turn stones into bread: 'One does not live by bread alone, but by every word that comes from the mouth of God' (Matthew 4:4, quoting Deuteronomy 8:3 NRSV).

Moses is here a superb teacher and pastor. He is interpreting the hard lessons of the desert as examples of God's love. He also sees that when life gets easier, faith in God will become harder. It will seem to the Israelites that they have deserved their good life, by luck, prowess or hard work. In fact it is God's gift to them. The earth's natural resources and human ability to produce wealth are both aspects of God's covenant care. They should be grateful rather than proud.

'Not because of your righteousness' (9:1–29)

When the Israelites enter Canaan, God will enable them to defeat even the legendary Anakites, who are like giants. They will be able to do this,

---

Staying loyal to God

Moses warns the people not to forget God when they come into the wealth and comfort of the new land. They are to depend on God just as much as they did in the desert, when they relied on him for every crumb of food and every sip of water. In the future Jesus will quote these verses to counter the temptations of the devil (Matthew 4:1–11). When challenged to throw himself from the highest point of the temple, Jesus answers, 'Do not put the Lord your God to the test' (Matthew 4:7, quoting Deuteronomy 6:16 NRSV). When invited to worship the devil in return for a world empire, Jesus replies, 'Worship the Lord your God, and serve him only' (Matthew 4:10, quoting Deuteronomy 6:13 NRSV). These commandments are not only to do with trusting and obeying God, but also about being loyal to him.

not because they themselves are powerful or good, but because God is with them. They will conquer Canaan because they are executing God's judgment on the Canaanites' wickedness, not because the Israelites are righteous. The Israelites are 'stiff-necked' – resistant to guidance and almost impossible to train. They made and worshipped an idol, a golden calf, even while Moses was on Sinai receiving God's law. The Israelites smashed the Ten Commandments from the start. It was only Moses' earnest prayer that dissuaded God from destroying them there and then.

'Fear the Lord your God' (10:1–22)

Moses recalls how he cut two new stone tablets for the law and made a wooden chest, the ark of the covenant, for their safe keeping. There is a note in brackets that Aaron died and Eleazar became high priest, and that the tribe of Levi was given the task of carrying the ark and pronouncing blessings. Perhaps this was added in later years by an editor who was himself a priest.

Moses comes to one of the great conclusions of his story:

And now, O Israel, what does the Lord your God ask of you but to fear the Lord your God, to walk in all his ways, to love him, to serve the Lord your God with all your heart and with all your soul, and to observe the Lord's commands and decrees that I am giving you today? (10:12–13)

God is supreme over his creation, and greater than all he has made. By an almost incredible act of grace, he has set his heart on this little, obstinate people of Israel. The Israelites must 'circumcise their hearts' – change their minds about God and cut away their resistance to him. They must realize that God is absolutely fair in all his dealings, protecting the weak and providing for the outsider. The Israelites should always remember what it was like to be helpless, when they were slaves in Egypt.

The blessings of obedience (11:1–32)

The land of Canaan is fertile and watered by rains and rivers – unlike Egypt, which was laboriously irrigated by channels from the Nile.

Moses warns the Israelites that if they lapse into paganism, then God will punish them with drought and dearth. The Israelites have a choice. If they keep God's commands, he will continue to bless them. If they disobey God's commands, he will curse them. When they come into the land they will hold a ceremony on the twin mountains of Gerizim and Ebal, proclaiming God's blessings from one and his curses from the other.

One place of worship (12:1–32)

Now Moses gives more detailed rules for life in Canaan. Every sign of paganism is to be destroyed – especially the altars on the summits of mountains, on the tops of hills and under trees. God will show the Israelites one central place of worship, where they are to offer sacrifices and bring gifts to the one and only God. As time goes by, there will be a number of major shrines. An altar will be built on Mount Ebal. Shiloh and Shechem will both become places of pilgrimage. Finally, Jerusalem will be the spiritual centre, established by King David and with the temple built by his son Solomon.

Even so, what matters is not where 'the place' is, but whose name is worshipped there. Moses warns the Israelites that they must have nothing to do with the pagan practices of other nations – not even be curious to know what they do. Pagan worship is savage and senseless, including the killing and burning of children.

Warnings against other gods (13:1–18)

Purity of faith is crucial. Anyone who preaches lies about God is to be put to death even if that person is your own wife. Any town which switches its allegiance to other gods is to be destroyed and left as a ruin. These drastic rules show the seriousness with which God takes false belief and misguided religion.

Clean and unclean food (14:1–21)

Moses repeats the laws of diet and hygiene which are also found in the book of Leviticus. He gives again the guidelines for knowing which animals, birds and fish are 'clean' and which are 'unclean'.

These food laws show that Israel is distinct from other nations in her belief and behaviour. One day this distinctiveness will be based on Christ, and food laws will no longer matter (Mark 7:18-19; Acts 10:11-16).

Tithes (14:22-29)

A tenth of the harvest each year is to be taken to God's centre (a shrine, or the temple) and used for a festival in his presence. The Levites and all who have no means of support, such as foreigners, orphans and widows, are to enjoy a share of the produce.

Every three years, the tithe is to be stored and used to feed those who are destitute. Providing for the poor is an important aspect of Israel's economy.

Cancelling debts and freeing slaves (15:1-23)

Once every seven years, all debts are to be cancelled. Ideally, there will be no poor people at all. If God provides and his people are generous, the causes of poverty will be removed. However, God is also a realist. He knows that there will always be those who are poor, and so he commands his people to be generous to them (15:11).

In the same way as debts are cancelled, so is slavery. A slave must be released after six years of service, unless he or she wishes to stay in the owner's employment. These laws reflect the forgiveness and generosity which are at the heart of God. He will bless those who treat others in this way.

Celebrating the feasts (16:1-17)

The rules for calculating and keeping the main festivals are repeated from the books of Exodus, Leviticus and Numbers: the Feast of Unleavened Bread (Passover), the Feast of Weeks and the Feast of Tabernacles.

Appointing judges (16:18-20)

Judges are to be appointed who will make decisions fairly, and not be influenced by favouritism or bribes.

Fair trial (16:21–17:13)

It will be important to stamp out paganism, but there are to be no hysterical witch-hunts. If anyone is suspected of occult practice, he or she may only be found guilty after proper investigation and the evidence of more than one witness. Any difficult cases may be taken to the priests, whose decisions will be binding. To deny or ignore their ruling is a capital offence.

A king who is under the law (17:14–20)

Moses anticipates that one day the Israelites will want a king. When this happens, they must choose a fellow Israelite who will himself be under God's law. He mustn't build up a large personal army or allow himself to be distracted by acquiring wives or wealth. The first thing he must do is sit down and write out his own copy of the law. This scroll is to be his constant companion. These rules about kingship are so appropriate to Solomon that many scholars have wondered whether they were added as a result of his reign. They would, in fact, apply to any oriental king, even long before Solomon's time.

Offerings for priests and Levites (18:1–8)

Just as the king is to be regulated in the liberties and privileges of his office, so are the priests. The priests belong to the tribe of Levi. Their special work is to offer sacrifices and to teach God's law.

Unlike the other tribes of Israel, the Levites have no area of the Promised Land to call their own. Instead, they have forty-eight cities in the territories of the other tribes, together with some pastureland for cattle or crops. They are set aside for God's work and must depend on the other tribes for their food and drink. This comes from the offerings and sacrifices of the people, to which the priests have the right to a portion or share. So God himself is the inheritance of the Levites. They live by faith and blessing rather than land and livelihood.

The rights of a Levite are not restricted to his home town. If he moves to serve God in a sanctuary, he is to receive his share of food there, along with the other priests.

Warning against pagan practices (18:9-13)

Moses issues another stern warning against paganism. This time he is quite specific about child sacrifice and all aspects of the occult. Israel is to be a no-go area for the black arts of witchcraft and spiritism. On the contrary, the whole nation is to live in the light of God's word.

A prophet like Moses (18:14-22)

One day God will raise up another prophet like Moses, who will stand between God and the people to reveal his truth. The apostle Peter will quote these words in his Pentecost sermon, showing that Jesus Christ fulfils this ancient promise (Acts 3:22). Stephen, in a brilliant speech to the Jewish Council, will make the same point (Acts 7:37).

Moses gives a simple test to tell if a prophet is genuine. If things turn out as a prophet has said, then his message was from the Lord. There is no need to take a prophet seriously if he might be an impostor. Time will tell. Jesus warns that many false prophets will appear towards the end of the age (Matthew 24:11).

Cities of refuge (19:1-14)

Three cities are to be set aside as 'cities of refuge'. Anyone who kills another person by accident can run to one of these centres for sanctuary. If Israel's territory increases, then three more cities are to be set aside for this purpose. There is always to be one within easy reach, so that the next of kin doesn't add to tragic accidents by murdering innocent people. If the death was intentional, then the murderer is to be handed over for trial and execution.

Witnesses (19:15-21)

A person can only be convicted of a crime if there is evidence from more than one witness. Such witnesses are to be carefully cross-examined. A false witness is to be given whatever punishment he was trying to inflict on another. 'Eye for eye, tooth for tooth' is known as the 'lex talionis' – the law by which a penalty is absolutely fair: no more and no less. Jesus quotes these words in the Sermon on the Mount. Instead of precise penalty or fair compensation, he teaches non-retaliation and generous forgiveness: giving grace rather than taking revenge (Matthew 5:38–42).

Going to war (20:1–20)

There are special guidelines for going to war. The priests are to tell the soldiers not to be afraid, because God will be fighting for them. Anyone who is worried or scared can go home! Before an enemy city is attacked, its people are to be invited to surrender. If they do so, they are to be spared and taken as slaves. However, if the captured people have vile pagan practices, they are to be completely destroyed before they infect Israel. When laying siege to a city and destroying the surrounding woodland, the fruit trees are to be spared. They have offended no one and they produce food. The natural world is often the first victim of war.

Dealing with bloodshed (21:1–9)

Blood is always important. Blood is the essence of life – and life is God's creation and gift. If someone is found murdered in open country and no one knows who did it, then the people in the nearest town are to make an atoning sacrifice. This doesn't cover the guilt of the murderer, but it protects the innocent people nearby.

Marrying a captive woman (21:10–14)

If a soldier is attracted to a woman who has been captured, he is to treat her with all respect. He may take her to his home, where she must shave her head, trim her nails and change her clothes. This reminds us of the ceremony for becoming a priest. She must be allowed a month to grieve for her loved ones and the passing of her old life. After this, the soldier may marry her. If he later changes his mind, he must set his wife free – not simply make her a slave. These guidelines have a respect for women which was unheard of in other cultures – and is rare in war even today.

Justice for sons (21:15–21)

A first-born son is to have special honour and a double share of his father's property. This is his right by birth and does not depend on

> **Ours to reason 'why?'**
>
> These laws come to us from a different time and culture. They often seem primitive and out of date. To understand them, we need to look for their underlying purpose.
>
> Behind every law is the desire to reflect and express God's justice and generosity.
>
> It may help to ask such questions as: 'Who will benefit from this law?' 'Whose interest is being protected?' 'Whose power is being restricted?' and 'What is this law trying to promote – or prevent?'

whether he is the favourite son. A delinquent son is to be presented to the elders of the town, publicly accused and sentenced to death by stoning. A father does not have power of life and death over his children. Such cases are to be referred to the civil authorities. If a criminal is executed by hanging, his body must be buried at nightfall. There is to be dignity, not savagery, in applying God's law.

God in the detail (21:22–22:30)

Here is a cluster of rules to encourage kindness and holiness. People are to respect one another's possessions – returning stray animals or lost property. Some actions are forbidden because they are a confusion of God's created order. For example, men and women must not wear each other's clothes. A mother bird is not to be taken from her nest. There is to be no mixing of seeds, crops or animals – nor of the fabrics used in making clothes. All these are little practical details which together express a wholeness of heart and life.

Sex and marriage are also holy. A woman is to remain a virgin until she is married. If it turns out that she is not a virgin, then she is to be executed by stoning. Sex before or outside marriage carries the death penalty. Promiscuous behaviour is a confusion of God's order. Being engaged ('betrothed') is just as binding as marriage. We see this in Joseph's dilemma when Mary is found to be pregnant (Matthew 1:19). Those who commit adultery are to be put to death. There is no such thing as sex without responsibility. Rape is as serious as murder. A man who rapes a woman who is neither married nor engaged is to pay a fine to her father and marry her. Sex between parents and children, or between close relatives, is expressly forbidden.

Staying clear and keeping clean (23:1–14)

Certain people are to be excluded from Israel's assembly. There is a ban on men with damaged testicles, illegitimate children and foreign enemies. These laws prevent confusions and highlight consequences. God's holiness extends to the whole of life, and there are simple guidelines for such normal functions as having wet dreams or going to the bathroom.

Finding the right balance (23:15–25:19)

Some of these laws find a precise balance between severity and generosity. Divorce is allowed to resolve ruined marriages, but not to license promiscuity. Newly-weds are excused all other duties, so that they can establish their marriage. Taking security for a loan must not wreck another person's business or deprive them of their only clothes. Some of the harvest is to be left in the fields and on the trees, so that the poor can find food. Israelites are never to forget what it is like to be helpless and in trouble – as they were themselves, when they were slaves in Egypt.

Legal punishments are to be administered with dignity, under proper supervision and within maximum limitations. They are penalties, not humiliations.

An ox is to be allowed to eat while it is working. This is a principle Paul applies to Christian ministers and missionaries (1 Corinthians 9:3–12). If possible, a widow is to be married to one of her husband's brothers, and have a son to continue the dead man's name. This is sometimes known as Levirate marriage. There is a public non-marriage ceremony if the brother-in-law refuses to do his duty! (See also Ruth 4:7.)

Firstfruits and family roots (26:1–19)

The Promised Land is God's gift to Israel. At harvest time, the first basket of produce is to be taken to the priest and presented as a thank-offering to God. The person bringing the gift is to recite a brief history of Israel, from the time God called Abraham ('a wandering Aramean'), to the present day. In this way, individual Israelites take their very own place in the story and life of God's people.

Every third year, a tithe (10 per cent) of the harvest is to be given to the Levites and to the poor. Israel is to remember that obedience and blessing go together. Responsibility to God is fulfilled through practical care for the poor.

Blessings and curses

The altar on Mount Ebal (27:1-8)

In the centre of Canaan there are two prominent hills – Mount Ebal and Mount Gerizim. Moses gives instructions that large stones are to be coated with plaster and inscribed with God's law. The stones are to be set up on Mount Ebal, and sacrifices are to be offered on an altar there.

Curses for disobedience (27:9-26)

Half the tribes (or perhaps their representatives) are to stand on Mount Gerizim, and half on Mount Ebal. Those on Mount Gerizim are to pronounce the blessings. They are all the tribes which have descended from Jacob's wives, Leah and Rachel. Those on Mount Ebal are to pronounce curses. They are (apart from Reuben) the tribes which have descended from Jacob's maidservants, Bilhah and Zilpah. The curses are for those who break God's commands, by making idols, harming defenceless people or having forbidden sex.

Blessings for obedience (28:1-14)

For those who obey the Lord fully, there are many wonderful blessings. God's love will be experienced in the quiet enjoyment of everyday life – families, farms, shopping and housework, comings and goings. A basket is used for carrying produce, and is the symbol of harvest. A kneading trough is used for working dough – and is a symbol of daily bread. God will protect his people from their enemies, provide rain for their crops and promote their businesses. The fear and frenzy of fertility rites are not for Israel! All this is conditional on Israel's faithful obedience to God's commands.

Further curses (28:15–68)

Disobedience will trigger distress, disease, disaster, drought, darkness, destruction and despair. Moses outlines the tragedy that awaits a faithless Israel:

In hunger and thirst, in nakedness and dire poverty, you will serve the enemies the Lord sends against you. (28:48)

Such curses were a standard feature of ancient treaties.

Israel renews the covenant

When God first made a covenant with Israel at Mount Sinai, it was broken immediately. Even as God was giving Moses the Ten Commandments, the Israelites were making and worshipping a golden calf-idol. Now the next generation is to renew its commitment to the living God.

'Carefully follow the terms of this covenant' (29:1–29)

Moses calls the whole community together. He reminds them of the great things God has done for them. He has rescued, guided and protected them – and supplied all their needs for forty years. They have experienced God's power and discovered that his ways are true. The alternative is terrible. Disobedience provokes God's anger and brings destruction.

'The Lord is your life' (30:1–20)

Moses knows that one day Israel will abandon God's way and be defeated and dispersed. But there is no place or situation from which God is unable to bring them back and restore them. Despair and desolation will be followed by delight. Now Moses delivers his final challenge – and gives the people full responsibility for their choice:

I call heaven and earth as witnesses against you that I have set before you life and death, blessings and curses. Now choose life, so that you and your children may live, and that you may love the Lord your God, listen to his voice, and hold fast to him. (30:19–20)

Farewell, Moses

Joshua to succeed Moses (31:1–8)

Moses knows that he is about to die. He puts his affairs in order. He exhorts the Israelites to take possession of Canaan. He encourages Joshua to take on the leadership with the strength that God will give him.

The reading of the law (31:9–13)

Moses writes out a copy of the law and commits it to the care of the priests. It is to be kept beside the ark of the covenant. He knows in his heart that the agreement will soon be broken. Nevertheless, he commands that it be read every seven years, during the week when Israel gathers for the Feast of Tabernacles.

Scholars have discovered many ancient agreements – known as 'Suzerainty treaties' – which date from the Near East at this time. They list the terms and conditions, benefits and penalties which govern the relationships between masters and servants, lords and slaves. Such agreements were to be kept safely and read in public from time to time.

A song of judgment (31:14–32:47)

Moses writes a song and recites it to the people so that they can learn it by heart. He begins with words of praise:

I will proclaim the name of the Lord.
Oh, praise the greatness of our God!
He is the Rock, his works are perfect,
and all his ways are just.

A faithful God who does no wrong,
upright and just is he. (32:3–4)

The song goes on to describe Israel's behaviour in the most unflattering terms. They are 'a warped and crooked generation... a nation without sense' (32:5, 28). But God has chosen them, loved them, and treated them with both severity and compassion.

Moses knows that betrayals, disasters and difficulties lie ahead for his people. The song is a means of lodging God's truth in their hearts for generations to come.

God tells Moses that he is to die on Mount Nebo – a part of the Abarim Range in north-west Moab, overlooking Canaan. Moses is not to enter the Promised Land, because of what happened when he struck the rock at Meribah Kadesh. Moses and Aaron failed God that day, with their anger and lack of faith.

Moses blesses the tribes (32:48–33:29)

Moses blesses each of the tribes in turn – as Jacob had done before his death. For each tribe, Moses has words of praise and encouragement. Some of his words to 'Jeshurun' (an old, poetic name for Israel) have provided comfort for every generation of believers:

The eternal God is your refuge,
and underneath are the everlasting arms. (33:27)

The tribe of Simeon isn't mentioned. It may have become part of the tribe of Judah.

The death of Moses (34:1–12)

Moses climbs Mount Nebo and surveys the Promised Land. His prayer to see it is granted. He can die content that his mission is accomplished.

Muslims identify Mount Nebo with Jebel Osha.

Moses dies at the age of 120. In Egypt, such an age would be attributed to a person of great distinction. In the Bible, his epitaph is even finer: 'Moses, whom the Lord knew face to face' (34:10 NRSV).

Moses was the greatest leader Israel ever had. Despite his sense of inadequacy, he accepted God's call to confront Pharaoh and head up the exodus. In a quiet, self-effacing way, he discerned God's will and made it known to others. He encountered all kinds of difficulty and discouragement during the trek across the desert – but met every crisis with honest passion and unfailing prayer. His enduring achievement was that he received the revelation of God's law, and made every effort to record it, teach it and establish it for future generations.

JOSHUA

The book of Joshua tells how the Israelites capture the rest of the land of Canaan – the land God had promised to their ancestor Abraham.

Joshua succeeds Moses as the leader of Israel. Like Moses, he tells the people what God wants them to do. In the course of the military campaign, the Israelites discover that victory depends on obeying God. When they obey God, they are successful. When they try to fight in their own strength, they fail.

At the end of his life, Joshua commits himself and his family to obey God – and challenges all the tribes of Israel to do the same.

OUTLINE

Israel prepares to invade Canaan (1:1–5:12)
The conquest of Canaan (5:13–13:7)
The land is divided (13:8–22:34)
Epilogue (23:1–24:33)

Introduction

Joshua is the sixth book of the Bible. It links the first five books ('the Pentateuch'), which narrate the beginning of the nation of Israel, with the later books, which tell of Israel's longing for a king.

The hero of the book is Joshua, whose name means 'The Lord Saves'! This is the same name as 'Jesus' in the New Testament. Joshua is a worthy successor to Moses, listening to God and leading the people in much the same way. He has a difficult task, because the land of Canaan cannot be conquered by military might. It can only be captured through a venture of faith. The disobedience of even a single person can lead to disaster for everyone. Above all, there is to be no compromise with the pagan nations who live in Canaan, or their gross fertility gods.

Who wrote Joshua – and when?

We aren't told who wrote this book, but parts of it are very personal to Joshua himself. The story of the conquest is told by someone who was clearly there to see it – and some of the people involved (such as Rahab) are still alive at the time of writing. The practice of making a pile of stones – to mark the crossing of the River Jordan, or the site of an important grave – is typical of this time in history. An important clue to the date is to be found in a reference to three Canaanite towns: Gaza, Gad and Ashdod. Their inhabitants are called Anakites. This could mean that the events described took place before 1200 BC, because after that time Philistines settled in these towns. Some scholars believe that the Philistines arrived some 200 years earlier.

Have historians found any signs of ancient battles? Those who have dug in the foundations of the old Canaanite cities have discovered that many of them were destroyed towards the end of the 13th century BC. In some places a thick layer of ash is a sign that the whole community was wiped out. This may have been the work of the invading Israelites, or the debris of later battles. We must remember that the conquest of Canaan took a long time. Jerusalem isn't captured until the days of David, around 1000 BC.

The campaign to capture Canaan

Joshua begins his campaign in the south of Canaan by laying siege to Jericho, which lies in the Jordan Valley. Once Jericho is captured, he attacks Ai, which sits high in the hills about fifteen miles to the west of Jericho. The next obvious target would have been Gibeon, but the Gibeonites trick Israel into a peace treaty. This treaty commits Israel to fight for Gibeon against an alliance of five Amorite kings. Joshua surprises the Amorites by marching through the night to attack them – and God gives an extra-long day for their destruction. In the following months, Israel captures and destroys all the major cities in the southern part of Canaan.

In the north, the king of Hazor unites several Canaanite tribes to resist Israel's advance. But they are no match for Joshua, who destroys both them and their cities. (In fact, chapter 12 lists thirty-one defeated kings and their towns.) It is typical of the writer to note that all this is in accordance with God's plan. 'It was the Lord himself who hardened their hearts to wage war against Israel, so that he might destroy them totally, exterminating them without mercy, as the Lord had commanded Moses' (11:20). For us, such a view of God's will is very unsatisfactory. His people still have a long way to go before they discover the true balance of God's justice and mercy.

As Joshua comes to the end of his active life, it is clear that there is still much land to be conquered. However, God instructs him to allocate a territory to each tribe, even if they do not yet possess the areas concerned. So Joshua divides the land, in faith that one day Israel's victory will be complete. In fact this won't happen until the heady days of David's reign. It will be David who finally captures Jerusalem, the last stronghold, from the Jebusites.

The importance of obedience

The secret of success is to love God totally. Such love will be shown by obeying God's law. God urges Joshua to obey the law of Moses carefully – like a straight path, from which it is dangerous to stray. The law is to govern his speech, thought and behaviour. If Joshua obeys God's law, then he will be prosperous and successful.

Israel learns that disobedience to God results in failure when her troops are routed at Ai. One of the Israelites, Achan, has disobeyed God and deceived his fellow Israelites by keeping and hiding some of the plunder from the capture of Jericho. The result is an alarming defeat for Israel's army. In his farewell speech at the end of the book, Joshua calls on the people of Israel to make a clear choice for God. Some of them are still harbouring the old household gods from Mesopotamia and Egypt. Many are tempted by the fertility gods of the Amorites. 'But as for me and my household,' says Joshua, 'we will serve the Lord' (24:15 NRSV).

Spiritual lessons

For Christians, the lessons of the book of Joshua are spiritual. Our Joshua (Jesus) has won a great victory over the powers of sin and death. Like the people of Israel, we must live in the light of this victory and allow God to establish his rule in every part of our lives.

Discovering Joshua

Israel prepares to invade Canaan

The Lord commands Joshua to 'be strong' (1:1–18)

God speaks to Joshua. He gives Joshua his own personal call to lead the people after Moses' death. The promise of the land has not died with Moses, nor has the principle of obedience. Joshua is to be strong, courageous – and devoted to God's law. And God makes him this solemn promise: 'As I was with Moses, so I will be with you; I will never leave you nor forsake you' (1:5).

Like Moses, Joshua has the faith to translate his conversation with God into commands to his officers. The people are to strike camp and prepare to cross the Jordan and enter their Promised Land.

Some of the tribes – the Reubenites, the Gadites and the half-tribe of Mannaseh – are allowed to settle their women, children and animals in the land that has already been won. However, their warriors are to continue in the army until the whole country is conquered. They are to lead the advance – perhaps because they will be the keenest to complete the task and return home. It is a sign of the unity and good discipline of the Israelites that they readily agree.

The spies lodge with Rahab (2:1–24)

Joshua sends two spies ahead to reconnoitre Jericho. Jericho is an oasis town, often called the 'city of palms', and has been the site of a settlement from the earliest times. Built on a mound, and defended by walls and towers, it bars Israel's way into the Promised Land. The capture of Jericho must be the first objective of Joshua's campaign.

Cleverly, the spies lodge with a prostitute or innkeeper. Her name is Rahab. She hides them under the flax which she is drying on the flat roof of her house. She tells them she knows that the Lord, the God of Israel, has brought his people from Egypt and is now giving them this land. Rahab begs that she and her family may be spared. The spies agree, and Rahab helps them escape by a rope from her window, which is set in the city wall. They arrange that she will tie a scarlet cord in the window as a sign to the invading army.

When the spies return to Joshua, they are able to report that the walls of Jericho may be high, but the morale of its people is low.

Crossing the River Jordan (3:1–4:18)

This is a holy war. Joshua tells the people that the ark of the covenant – the symbol of God's commitment to them – will lead the way. They are to consecrate themselves, devoting themselves completely to the task ahead. The priests carry the ark into the waters of the Jordan, and immediately the water ceases to flow from upstream.

The same God who brought his people through the Red Sea is now bringing the next generation through the Jordan – despite the fact that the river is normally swollen at this by melted snow time of year. We don't know how the waters were dammed – only that it took place some twenty miles upriver. At the exodus, the drying of the river bed was attributed to the blowing of a strong east wind. Whatever is happening at the Jordan, God is behind it. God's timing is deliberate and precise.

The standing stones at Gilgal (4:19–24)

God speaks to Joshua, and Joshua instructs the people. Joshua is being established as a leader in the style of Moses, a leader whose word proves to be true.

A 'holy war'?

The campaign to capture Canaan is sometimes described as a 'holy war'. The idea of a 'holy war' has been wrongly used to justify many acts of cruelty. It inspired the Crusaders who fought for possession of Jerusalem in the Middle Ages. It was a central theme in the American Civil War, when both sides claimed they were fighting God's cause. It was used by white South Africans to dispossess their black neighbours, and by extreme Zionists to expel Palestinians from modern Israel. This has been a terrible and shameful use of the Bible to justify human self-interest.

A representative from each tribe is chosen to bring a stone from the bed of the River Jordan. The stones are set up at Gilgal, as a sign to future generations of the miraculous crossing. This is a permanent tribute to the power of God and a reminder that all the tribes entered the land together.

Circumcision at Gilgal (5:1–12)

The Israelites are now just sixteen miles from Jericho. The Amorite and Canaanite kings are terrified at their approach. This is the moment for the new generation of fighting men to be circumcised. In circumcision, the foreskin of the penis is cut round in a circle and rolled back. This is a considerable act of faith and courage, as the Israelite soldiers will be unable to fight for several days.

Gilgal means 'circle' or 'rolling'. God says to Joshua that he is now rolling away the reproach of Egypt. The people are no longer being punished for their breach of the covenant at Sinai. They are united with God in purpose and strength.

This is a new beginning. The families of Israel celebrate the Passover with unleavened bread and roasted grain – the produce of Canaan. The next morning, there is no manna on the ground outside the tents. The wilderness journey is over.

The conquest of Canaan

The commander of the Lord's army (5:13–15)

On the approach to Jericho, Joshua has a visible encounter with God. A man stands before him with a drawn sword and announces himself as 'commander of the army of the Lord'. Joshua bows before him. This is the Lord's battle, and Joshua submits to his supreme commander. The tiny nation of Israel will be joining far greater forces: the mighty powers of nature and the angelic hosts of heaven.

Stage one: the capture of Jericho and Ai (6:1–8:35)

The campaign to capture Canaan will be in three stages. In the first phase, the Israelites will cut the land in half from east to west, capturing the strategic towns of Jericho and Ai (6:1-8:35). In the second phase, they will defeat an alliance of Amorite kings in the south and take their cities (9:1-10:43). The third phase will see the capture of the northern part of the country, by defeating an alliance of pagan tribes under the leadership of the king of Hazor (11:1-23).

The fall of Jericho

The strategy for capturing Jericho is unique in the history of warfare (6:1-27). For once, God's will and Israel's obedience are in perfect harmony. God tells Joshua that the Israelites must march around the city, with the ark of the covenant leading the way and the priests blowing trumpets. This march is to take place each day for six days. On the seventh day, the Israelites are to march seven times round the city before giving a sustained blast on the trumpets and a loud shout. The city wall will collapse and the Israelites will be able to march straight in.

This 'perfect plan' is shaped on the number seven. There are to be seven priests with seven trumpets; the people are to march around Jericho on seven days – including seven times on the seventh. The trumpets which the priests blow are rams' horns. They are the same trumpets that are used to announce a Jubilee Year – the fiftieth year when, in the future, debts will be cancelled, slaves and prisoners will be released, and all land is returned to its original family. The number fifty is significant because it marks the completion of seven lots of seven years.

Joshua and the Israelites fulfil God's instructions and the walls of Jericho collapse. Whether this happens because God intervenes with an earth tremor, we don't know. Historians investigating the site of Jericho have not found any particular signs of this great event – but then the destruction was complete. Jericho is not rebuilt until King Ahab restores it 500 years later. In that time, sun and wind may have erased much of the evidence.

Although the population of Jericho is destroyed, Rahab and her family are spared, as the spies had promised. The elderly Rahab is still living at the time this account is written. Is she the same Rahab who becomes an ancestor of David – and Jesus (Matthew 1:5)?

Achan's sin

Israel's next target is Ai. This is a town set in the hills about fifteen miles to the west of Jericho. While Jericho lies below sea level (the lowest town

Does God want to massacre his enemies?

The conquest of Canaan is unique. It does not give permission for any person or race to commit mass murder or ethnic cleansing.

In Canaan there were certainly some dreadful pagan practices to be purged and diseases to be eradicated. And clearly the Israelites believed that God wanted them to exterminate their enemies. But this is not the whole truth.

We see in the Bible that a true picture of God only emerges gradually. At various stages, it was possible for people to be wrong about God – his nature, plan or way of doing things. In particular, the policy of wiping out entire nations in a violent bloodbath is very different from the approach we later see in Jesus.

How can we understand the killing fields of the days of Moses, Joshua, Samuel, Saul and David? Did God really command such bloodshed, or were even these great men affected by the times in which they lived? Did they slay their enemies believing it was God's will – or assume that God approved because he gave them victory?

One thing is certain. Our picture of God gets clearer as the Bible story unfolds. It becomes perfectly clear only when we see the life and example of Jesus. It isn't that God has changed, but our understanding of him has developed.

When Jesus is asked by James and John if they may destroy a Samaritan village, he rebukes them (Luke 9:54–55). God's way is not to destroy but to save; not to take life but to give it; not to wreak vengeance, but to forgive and make peace, even at great cost to himself.

---

in the world), Ai stands nearly 1,000 feet higher. Joshua's spies report that the capture of Ai will be a fairly simple task. They won't require the whole army. It comes as a shock when the Israelite task force is unexpectedly defeated. Suddenly, Israel's confidence vanishes.

God reveals to Joshua that the defeat is because of sin. Someone has taken and hidden some of the plunder from Jericho. God's express command had been that Jericho's treasures were to be either devoted to the Lord or destroyed. The fact that even one person has disobeyed has brought defeat on the whole nation.

The fault is traced to Achan (7:1-26). He has kept a beautiful robe and some silver and gold and buried them in the ground beneath his tent. This is such a serious breach of Israel's obedience to God that Achan and his family are stoned to death. The place of execution is called the Valley of Achor, which means 'trouble' or 'bitterness'.

There is a similar terrible episode in the early days of the church in Jerusalem, when a couple named Ananias and Sapphira are struck dead for deceiving the Apostles over money (Acts 5:1-11). These punishments seem out of all proportion to the crimes. We have to understand that both acts of disobedience are enough to pollute the purity of God's people at a time of great spiritual advance. The offenders must be cut out like a cancer, to prevent the disease of disobedience from spreading.

The destruction of Ai

Joshua now uses his entire army to attack Ai (8:1-29). He sets up camp with 5,000 of his troops across the valley within sight of Ai, but conceals a further 30,000 in the hills. When the king of Ai confidently attacks the smaller force, the Israelites pretend to flee. The army from Ai gives chase, leaving the city defenceless. Joshua turns and signals his men in the hills to come down and destroy the place. This time God allows the Israelites to keep the livestock and plunder.

The covenant is renewed

At Mount Ebal, in the centre of Canaan, Joshua builds an altar. He summons the people to offer sacrifices to God and renew their covenant commitment to him (8:30-35). This great assembly probably takes place at Shechem, between the twin peaks of Gerizim and Ebal. Joshua makes replicas of the tablets of the law by coating large stones with plaster and writing on them the Ten Commandments.

Moses had given instructions for the renewal of the covenant (Deuteronomy 27-28). Half the tribes are to stand on the slopes of Mount Gerizim. These are the tribes descended from Jacob's wives Leah and Rachel. They are to recite the blessings which come from keeping faith with God. The rest of the people – the tribes descended from Jacob's slave girls – are to stand on the slopes of Mount Ebal. They are to pronounce the curses that will befall those who disobey God's commandments.

Stage two: the conquest of the south (9:1–10:43)

A cunning plan

One of the tribes of Canaan, the Gibeonites, develop a plan to avoid being destroyed by Israel (9:1–27). They send a delegation to Joshua at Gilgal, dressed and equipped as though they have travelled a great distance. They explain that they have heard of Israel's victories and have come to make a treaty. Without consulting God, Joshua agrees terms of peace – only to discover that they are a neighbouring tribe! Finding himself bound by his own solemn word, Joshua strikes a compromise. He forces the Gibeonites to become woodcutters and water-carriers in the service of the altar and tabernacle.

We are told that Gibeon is an important city, larger than Ai, and that its men are good fighters. Historians have discovered a large well in the centre of Gibeon. It is 80 feet deep with access by a staircase. How appropriate that the Gibeonites are set to draw water!

The sun stands still

The king of Jerusalem calls on four other Amorite kings to join him in attacking Gibeon. The Gibeonites call for Joshua to rescue them. Joshua marches quickly through the night to take the enemy by surprise. As the Amorites flee, God bombards them with large hailstones, and makes the sun stand still until the victory is complete (10:1–15).

'O sun, stand still over Gibeon...' (10:12) is a quotation from the Book of Jashar – a collection of songs which is now lost to us but tells of the great deeds of Israel's early heroes. Joshua calls on God to hold the sun and moon in the sky, and so extend the daylight for the work of slaughter. Some people think it was the darkness of the hailstorm that merged day with night while the killing went on.

The conquered kings and cities

Joshua assures Israel that God will always give such victories. Joshua now completes the conquest of the southern part of Canaan (10:16–43). He attacks each of the major cities except Jerusalem and destroys them, leaving no survivors. The writer is careful to record that 'all these kings and their lands Joshua conquered in one campaign, because the Lord, the God of Israel, fought for Israel' (10:42). When we consider that the Canaanites were strong and good fighters and that their cities were well fortified, we realize that Israel's success was a God-given miracle. Historians have confirmed that the cities of southern Canaan, Lachish, Eglon and Debir were completely destroyed at about this time.

Stage three: the conquest of the north (11:1-23)

Now the northern kings unite to resist the Israelites. They are led by Jabin, king of Hazor. He masses a considerable force at the waters of Merom, about ten miles west of the Jordan, between two lakes. God tells Joshua not to fear the enemy's superior equipment of chariots and horses. The horses will be hamstrung and the chariots burned. The Israelites won't even need to salvage them, because the only resource they need is the presence of God.

As in the southern campaign, Joshua uses speed of approach and surprise attack. He routs the northern army, pressing home his advantage until every enemy soldier is killed and all the chariots and horses destroyed.

Joshua consolidates the victory by capturing Hazor. This is a large city covering about 200 acres and with about 40,000 inhabitants. In recent years, excavation of Hazor shows that it was destroyed around the middle of the 13th century BC. In its ruins are the remains of Canaanite temples, with signs of the astrology and nature worship which were practised in them.

The power of the north is now broken and the land is at Joshua's mercy. He destroys Hazor and overruns the other centres of population. The writer emphasizes that the destruction is complete and that Joshua is carrying out the commands that God had given to Moses. The Canaanites are being destroyed because of their all pervading paganism. The whole area is being purged of fertility cults and magic. Instead, it is to become God's land and the home of his people.

Last of all, the Anakites are destroyed. They were the race of giants which had so frightened the Israelites and sapped their morale just forty years earlier.

A catalogue of victory (12:1-12)

The writer lists all the kings that Israel has defeated, including Og and Sihon who were defeated by Moses.

He describes the main features of the land west of the Jordan. By the 'hill country' he means the Judean highlands. The 'western foothills' lie between the central highlands and the coastal plain. The Arabah (whose name has a sense of 'burned up') is the dry rift valley which runs south of the Dead Sea to the Gulf of Aqabah. The 'mountain slopes' are probably those which border the Dead Sea. The Negev (which means 'the dry') is the semi-arid land which stretches off to the desert in the south. All this territory is divided between the tribes and given to them as a permanent inheritance.

The land still to be taken (13:1–7)

The years have passed and Joshua is now an old man. Despite his successes, large areas of Canaan are still unconquered. We have the first mention of the Philistines – a seafaring people who have come from the Mediterranean island of Crete and occupied the coastal towns of Canaan. They will have a long-running enmity with Israel, but eventually give Canaan its most enduring name – 'Palestine'.

God promises to drive out the Sidonians. Their land is to be divided between the tribes of Israel and is allocated in faith that it will one day become theirs. The mention of the half-tribes of Manasseh goes back to the days of Joseph. Joseph had two sons – Ephraim and Manasseh, whose descendants are counted as half-tribes. They are the tribe of Joseph by another name (Genesis 48:11–20).

The land is divided

A summary of settlements (13:8–19:51)

The land of Canaan is divided between the tribes of Israel. Their territories and towns are listed here with careful attention to detail. The whole land was not in fact conquered until the time of David, but it is here allocated in faith. The broad picture is that the tribes of Judah and Joseph are given most of the south of Canaan, with Benjamin between them. The tribe of Dan is given the coastal plain, which proves impossible to occupy because of the presence of the powerful Philistines. The remaining tribes are awarded land in the northern area of Canaan which is not yet completely conquered. It will be many years before they enter into all that has been promised.

In detail, the tribes of Reuben and Gad, and the half-tribe of Manasseh, settle in the area that was first conquered, to the east of the River Jordan. The land on the other side of the Jordan is divided between the tribes of Judah and Joseph. Judah is given the southern section – the territory won from the five kings. Caleb, still vigorous at eighty-five, begs for the privilege of driving the Anakites from the hill country and so winning Hebron for his inheritance. Joshua (like Caleb, one of the original spies) is pleased to grant his request. Joseph (the half-tribes of Ephraim and Manasseh) receives the fertile land at the heart of Canaan. North of this, the territory is still unconquered – and guarded by fortresses. Joshua urges the Israelites to clear the forests and press on to complete the conquest.

At the end of chapter 19 we learn that the task of dividing the land was undertaken by Eleazar the priest, Joshua and the heads of the tribal clans. They allocate it by casting lots – perhaps something like throwing dice – at the entrance to the tent of meeting. This is a way of letting God make the decisions. Although he is the leader, Joshua is under the authority of this group and given his share of the land last of all. He asks for the town of Timnath Serah in the hill country of Ephraim.

Cities of refuge (20:1–9)

Certain cities are named 'cities of refuge'. They are to act as a sanctuary for anyone accused of murder. Such people are to be protected from anyone seeking revenge (usually the next of kin) until they can be given a fair trial.

Towns for the Levites (21:1–45)

The priestly tribe of Levi has no land of its own, as a sign that it belongs to the Lord. God himself is Levi's inheritance. Now the other tribes allocate some of their towns and pastures to the Levites to provide them with homes and a livelihood.

The eastern tribes go home (22:1–34)

With the main task of conquest completed, Joshua allows the Reubenites, the Gadites and the half-tribe of Manasseh to go home. They immediately perplex the other tribes by building their own

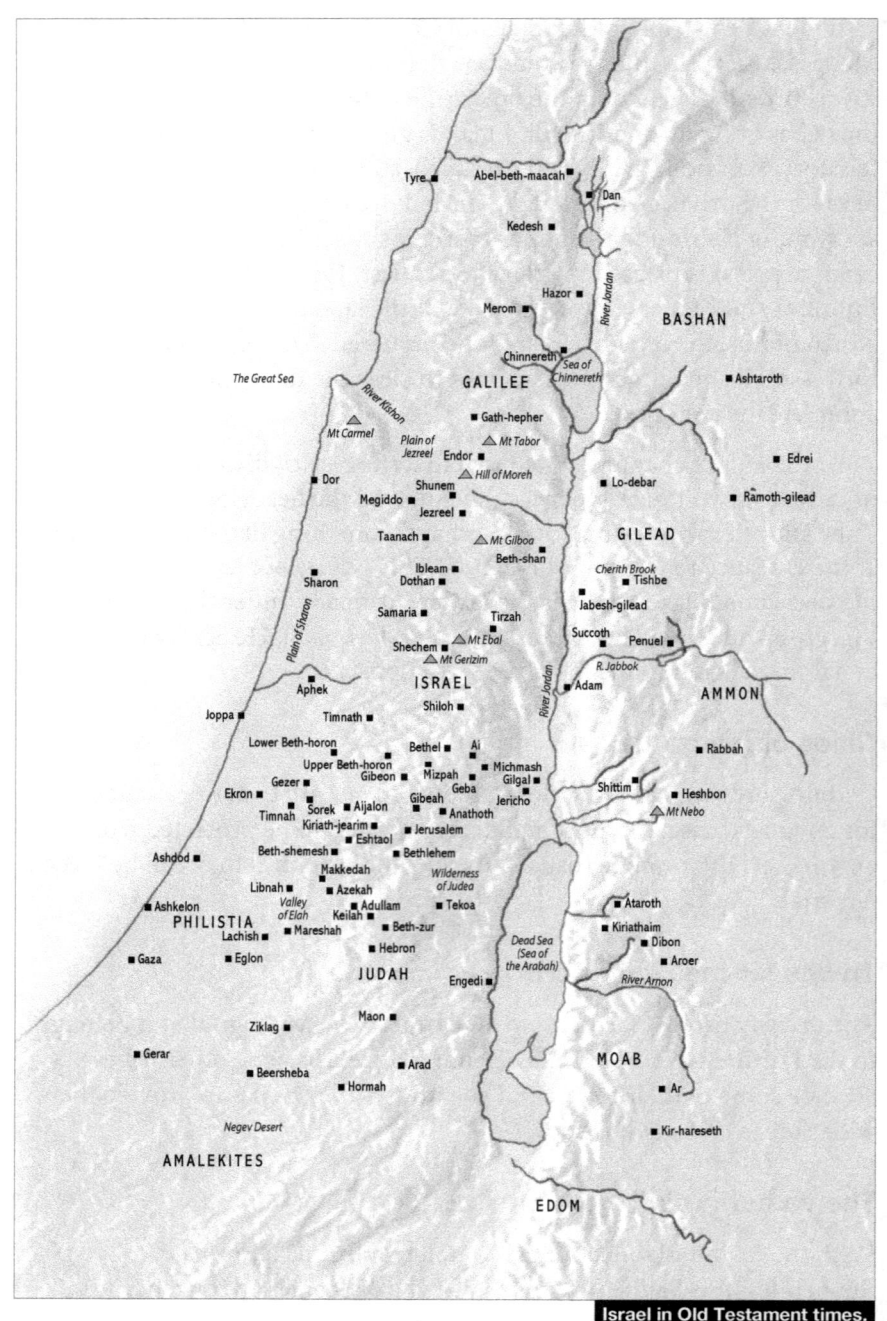

Israel in Old Testament times.

impressive altar on the east side of the Jordan! When challenged about this they explain that the altar is not for sacrifices; nor is it intended as a rival to the central altar of all Israel. They explain it as 'a witness' – a sign of continuing faith in Israel's God, and solidarity with the other tribes, even though the Jordan forms a boundary between them.

Epilogue

Joshua's farewell (23:1–16)

Joshua bids farewell to the people. He urges them to continue to obey God's law and have nothing to do with the pagan peoples who are still living in the land. If the Israelites mix their worship with that of the Canaanites, or marry them, they will perish.

Joshua reviews Israel's history from the time of Abraham. God has given them, by his amazing power, victory over every enemy. Now, in his goodness, he is giving them a land of beauty and plenty, ready cultivated to supply their needs.

Back to basics (24:1–27)

Joshua calls the tribes of Israel to Shechem – the place of decision at the crossroads of Canaan. Here he challenges them to commit themselves afresh to the Lord. He challenges them to renew the covenant that was first made with God and Moses at Mount Sinai. If they decline to do this, they must decide whom they would rather serve – the pagan gods of Egypt, Canaan or Mesopotamia.

Joshua leaves the people in no doubt about his own decision. He boldly declares that he and his family will serve the Lord. The people protest that they will do the same; but Joshua warns them not to take the decision lightly. If they choose the Lord, they must get rid of their idols. If they fail to do so, the consequences will be terrible.

The book of Joshua may have been written at a time when the law of Moses was being rejected and the Israelites were intermarrying with pagans. Some families or clans may have reverted to ancient household gods and superstitions – or taken up with new ones. Joshua's speech is a ringing call to repent and commit themselves to the Lord, the only true God of Israel.

Home at last (24:28–33)

The book of Joshua closes with the burials of three great leaders. Joshua dies and is buried at Timnath Serah – the place he chose for his inheritance. Joseph's coffin, brought all the way from Egypt (Genesis 50:26), is committed to a family grave at Shechem in the heart of the Promised Land. And Eleazar, Israel's second high priest, is laid to rest on his family's land in the hills of Ephraim. All God's promises have been fulfilled. They are home at last.

JUDGES

The book of Judges tells the story of Israel after the tribes have settled in the land of Canaan. During this time they are guided by 'judges', who lead them in battle against their enemies.

In Hebrew, 'to judge' means 'to put things right'. The judges are the leaders of the community. They give legal rulings and take whatever actions are necessary, including going to war. They 'judge' Israel's enemies by overpowering them in the name of God.

This is a dangerous, lawless time, with Israelite society fragmented, her enemies aggressive and her morals in decline. At the beginning of the period there is no clear leader to follow Joshua, and by the end there is no leader at all. The book closes with the grim words: 'In those days there was no king in Israel; all the people did what was right in their own eyes' (21:25 NRSV). But this is also a book about God's readiness to save his people and to forgive them when they repent and turn to him.

OUTLINE

The partial conquest of Canaan and the death of Joshua (1:1–3:6)
The great deeds of the judges (3:7–16:31)
Israel in decline (17:1–21:25)

Introduction

When Joshua dies, there is no clear leader for the people of Israel. The land of Canaan is not completely conquered, so several of the tribes find themselves living among pagan neighbours. After Joshua's death, the people begin to stray from their commitment to the God who brought them out of Egypt. They worship the Baals and the Ashtoreths, the fertility gods of the neighbouring tribes. Because of this disobedience, God stops protecting his people and they suffer defeat and oppression.

However, there are some fine acts of faith and heroism. Gideon wins great victories with God's help. Samson, too, although he is a weak character, is given superhuman strength to overcome the Philistines.

The book of Judges shows us how easily human society can break down without God. The people of Israel are in great danger of collapsing as a nation and culture because of their idolatry. We see how leadership plays an important part in the life of any people, and that Israel needs a strong and godly leader.

At the end of the book, Israel is sinking by spiritual decline into moral chaos. Defenceless people are hurt or killed, and civil war threatens an end to the tribe of Benjamin. Here is a depressing record of human depravity.

Who wrote Judges?

We don't know who wrote the book of Judges. If an editor compiled these stories, then perhaps we hear him speaking in these words:

Then the Lord raised up judges, who delivered them [the Israelites] out of the power of those who plundered them. Yet they did not listen even to their judges; for they lusted after other gods and bowed down to them. They soon turned aside from the way in which their ancestors had walked, who had obeyed the commandments of the Lord; they did not follow their example. (2:16–17 NRSV)

The writer explains that God is angry with the tribes of Israel because they have not pressed on to defeat their enemies and occupy the whole land. In the end God allows the pagan peoples to remain, to be 'thorns in Israel's side' – to test whether the Israelites will be faithful to their God.

We notice a pattern in Israel's behaviour. The people disobey God and fall into the hands of their enemies. They cry out to the Lord for help and he rescues them. Then there are some years of peace before they fall into sin again. In all this, God uses a number of imperfect leaders to rescue his people at times of crisis.

Where does Judges come in the Bible?

In the Bible, the book of Judges is included among the history books. The Hebrew Bible calls these books 'the Former Prophets'. Bible history is about what God is doing in the lives of his people. Judges may be part of a 'deuteronomic history' which includes the books of Deuteronomy, Joshua, Judges, Samuel and Kings. The writers or editors of these books judge everything by the principle set out in the book of Deuteronomy: that God honours those who honour him.

A particular sentence keeps cropping up: 'In those days there was no king in Israel; all the people did what was right in their own eyes.' This is a clue that the writer is looking back from a time when the people of Israel finally have a king, and can see the disasters that befell them when there was no clear, godly, leader.

Discovering Judges

The partial conquest of Canaan and the death of Joshua

'Their gods will be a snare to you' (2:3). God warns the Israelites that the Canaanite gods will tempt and trap them. They will be attracted to the bloody, violent and sexually permissive practices of their pagan neighbours. Like birds winging their way into a trap, they will be captured, hurt and killed.

When Joshua dies, at the age of 110, he is described as 'the servant of the Lord' (2:8). He is buried some ten miles north-west of Bethel, in the land he has won from the Canaanites. He was born into slavery in Egypt, shared in the exodus as a young man, and was one of the brave spies who went ahead into the Promised Land. After the death of Moses, Joshua led the military campaigns which captured much of Canaan. When the push for victory faltered and the people were tempted by paganism, Joshua continued to stand by his faith in the living God.

The unfinished conquest of Canaan (1:1–2:5)

The tribes of Israel have each been allotted an area of Canaan, their Promised Land. Now they must go in and conquer their territories.

The successes of Judah in the south

The tribes of Judah and Simeon fight together, as their ancestors were brothers. Judah is successful in defeating the Canaanites, together with another local people, the Perizzites (1:2–21). They capture and mutilate a local king, Adoni-Bezek. They also burn the ancient city of Jerusalem, but a later note (1:21) has the Benjaminites living there alongside the Jebusites, who are the original inhabitants. Jerusalem lies between the territories of Judah and Benjamin and will become King David's capital for the united tribes.

Judah's forces advance south and west of Jerusalem. To the south is the hill country around Hebron and, beyond, the dry wastes of the Negev. To the west lie the foothills which run between the central mountain range of Canaan and the coastal plain.

Particular stories are recorded of how people receive their share of the land. Caleb gives his daughter in marriage to Othniel; and she asks her father for a water supply in the desert. Caleb himself is given the city of Hebron (which means 'alliance'), which will become Judah's centre and David's first capital. Judah's army also tackles the cities of the coastal plain (Gaza, Ashkelon and Ekron), but is unable to hold them against the iron chariots of their enemies. Israel's weaponry is still in the Bronze Age.

The capture of Bethel

The Joseph tribes (the half-tribes of Ephraim and Manasseh) are successful in taking Bethel (1:22–26). This is where Jacob had his famous dream (Genesis 28:19), and where there will be an important shrine for the northern kingdom in years to come. 'Beth-el' means 'house of God'.

An unfinished task

Despite Judah's successes, there are many failures to note as well (1:27–36). Some tribes are unable to expel the Canaanites and have to live alongside them. This will be a constant tension and source of corruption, as the Israelites feel the attractions of moral compromise, intermarriage and idolatry. It is King Ahab's marriage to Jezebel, a princess from Phoenicia, which plunges Israel into Baal-worship in the time of the prophet Elijah.

Confrontation at Bokim

God confronts his people. They are failing to keep their part of the covenant bargain (2:1–5).

God has been faithful to them in rescuing them from Egypt. He has brought them to the land of Canaan. But Israel should be destroying the pagan religions of the Canaanites, not settling down to live with them. Now the Canaanite idols will be an ongoing problem – like painful thorns and a deadly trap.

When the people hear God's verdict, they weep. The place is called Bokim, which means 'weepers'.

The death of Joshua (2:6–9)

When Joshua dies, at the age of 110, he is described as 'the servant of the Lord' (2:8). He is buried some ten miles north-west of Bethel, in the land he has won from the Canaanites.

Joshua's life has spanned the history of the exodus, the wilderness wanderings and the conquest of Canaan. He was born into slavery in Egypt, took part in the exodus as a young man and was one of the brave spies who went ahead into the Promised Land. After the death of Moses, Joshua led the military campaigns which captured the heart of Canaan. When the push for complete occupation faltered and the people began to compromise with paganism, Joshua continued to stand by his faith in the living God.

The reason for judges (2:10–3:6)

After the death of Joshua, Israel's faith and unity breaks down. The tribes merge with their Canaanite neighbours and accept the local forms of Baal-worship. They no longer live by faith in God, and suffer defeat at the hands of their enemies.

God does not abandon his people, but gives them 'judges' – leaders who are gifted with faith, strength and wisdom. These judges rescue the Israelites from a series of desperate situations, so that they continue to experience God's power to save them. However, they repeatedly lapse back into their old ways. Once a crisis is passed, they forget God again. They return to the attractions of paganism until another defeat brings them to their senses. This pattern is repeated throughout the era of the judges.

The great deeds of the judges

The book of Judges has stories of twelve of Israel's judges or rescuers. The main attention is given to Deborah and her general Barak, as well as to Gideon, Jephthah, and Samson. Their stories are full of energy and interest. A minor judge, Ehud, is left-handed – a gift which he uses to assassinate an enemy king (3:21).

Each of the judges is associated with a particular enemy. Ehud fights for Israel against the Moabites. Deborah and Barak fight the Canaanites. Gideon delivers Israel from the Midianites. Jephthah rescues Israel from the oppression of Ammon. Samson is the Israelites' champion against the Philistines.

Othniel (3:7–11)

For the first time (but not the last) we read the author's refrain: 'The Israelites did evil in the eyes of the Lord' (3:7).

God is angry and jealous (perfectly angry and perfectly jealous) because his people are serving the pagan Baals and Asherahs. These are the male and female fertility gods, through which the Canaanites try to control the natural world of seasons, weather and crops. They are human inventions – idols which have no reality or power in themselves, but the people who believe in them are in bondage to superstition and fear. The stories of these gods are full of violence, cruelty and lust – which are re-enacted by their worshippers in real life.

Asherah, in Canaanite mythology, is the goddess wife of the chief god El. When there are several Asherahs (or Asherim), they are the female gods of the Baals.

Because of their idolatry, Israel's God allows his people to be defeated and oppressed by Cushan-Rishathaim. Cushan is the king of Aram, in north-west Mesopotamia. His added title, 'Rishathaim', means 'doubly wicked'.

After eight years of misery, the Israelites plead with God to rescue them. He empowers Othniel to be their champion. Othniel is a nephew of Caleb, who was the colleague of Joshua in the days of the invasion of Canaan. God's Spirit gives Othniel the inspiration, courage

Who are the Baals?

The Baals are an extensive family of Canaanite gods. They are nature idols, worshipped to bring rain and fertility for crops, cattle and humans.

The leading figure is Baal the son of El, the god of storm and rain. His name can also mean 'husband' or 'Lord' – which makes him sound similar to Israel's God. We can understand Israel's confusion – and the temptation to experiment with paganism.

Baal's wife or partner is Ashtoreth, the goddess of war and fertility. Together, they are a terrifying partnership. The attempts of their worshippers to please them may range from acts of gross indecency to child sacrifice. The degradation and cruelty of Canaanite religion is a major reason for the judgment of God in the conquest by Israel.

and strength he needs to become a successful military leader (or 'judge') and defeat Cushan.

Ehud (3:12–30)

Again the Israelites commit themselves to idol-worship, and God allows them to be defeated. This time their oppressor is Eglon, king of Moab. Moab is to the south of Canaan and east of the Dead Sea. Eglon joins forces with the neighbouring tribes of Ammon and Amalek to attack Israel and capture the city of palms (the ruined site of Jericho).

After eighteen years of oppression, the Israelites cry to God for help. This time God gives them Ehud, who is remarkable in that he is left-handed. He uses his left hand to assassinate Eglon, king of Moab, by thrusting a double-edged sword into him. Ehud hid the sword by strapping it to his thigh when he went to pay tribute to the enemy king.

Shamgar (3:31)

After Ehud, another judge delivers Israel. He is Shamgar, who defeats 600 Philistines by striking them down with an ox-goad (3:31). An ox-goad is sharp, metal-tipped like a spear and up to ten feet long! It seems to be a makeshift instrument at a time when weapons are banned. Samson makes similar use of a donkey's jawbone (15:16).

Deborah and Barak (4:1–5:31)

After the time of Ehud, the Israelites again commit evil. Now God allows Jabin, king of Canaan, to make them his subjects. Jabin's army commander is Sisera, who has a force of 900 iron chariots at his disposal.

After twenty years of oppression, the Israelites cry out to God for help. Their leader ('judge') at this time is Deborah, whose name means 'Bee'. She sends for Barak ('Lightning') and outlines a plan to defeat Sisera by luring his chariots into the River Kishon. The Kishon is a wadi which is flooded by torrential rain at a certain time of year. Barak is reluctant to attempt this battle unless Deborah goes with him. She agrees, but predicts that the fame of slaying Sisera will go to a woman.

Sisera's chariots get bogged down in the Kishon and are overwhelmed by Barak's forces, just as Deborah has planned. Sisera flees on foot, and takes refuge in the tent of a woman called Jael. He assumes she will protect him, but in fact she kills him by driving a tent peg through his temple while he is asleep. This great victory, with its grisly detail, is celebrated in the vivid and rhythmic 'Song of Deborah' (5:1–31). The song is very old and was probably written soon after the great deeds it records.

Gideon (6:1–8:35)

The Israelites have been driven out of their settlements by Midianite raiders. Their animals have been killed and their crops trampled.

Gideon is secretly threshing wheat in an underground cellar when an angel visits him. Gideon finds himself commissioned to be Israel's deliverer – although he explains that he is a very junior member of a very weak clan. Even his tribe, Manasseh, is only a half-tribe!

But in God's sight Gideon is a mighty warrior. In a night raid the reluctant hero pulls down his father's Baal altar and cuts down an Asherah pole – a pagan fertility symbol. In their place he builds an altar to the God of Israel and (using the Asherah pole for firewood) sacrifices a bullock.

Gideon is now to fight the Midianites. He makes doubly sure that this is what God wants by seeking guidance in an unusual way. He asks God for a sign that dew will settle on a fleece overnight, but the surrounding ground will remain dry. Just to make sure, the following night he asks for the opposite to happen.

Then God tests Gideon. He tells him to reduce his fighting force from 32,000 to 300, by sending home those who are afraid and by ruling out those who kneel down to drink. The few who stay on their feet and lap the water are worth all the rest – because they are always ready for battle and on guard against surprise attack.

One night, Gideon spies on the enemy camp. He finds that God is undermining the Midianite morale by sending them dreams of defeat. Encouraged, Gideon splits his force into three groups and gives each man a trumpet – and a flaming torch in an earthenware jar. Normally only an officer would carry a torch – so the Midianites are going to think themselves surrounded by thousands of men.

With the blowing of trumpets, smashing of jars and brandishing of torches, Gideon and his mini-army rout their terrified and demoralized enemy.

Abimelech (9:1–56)

Abimelech is not a judge. He is one of the sons of Gideon ('Jerub-Baal'), whose mother is a Canaanite from Shechem. His story is included as a brief, violent and unsuccessful attempt at kingship.

Shechem is a city at the centre of Palestine. 'Shechem' means 'shoulder', because the town lies on the shoulder of land between two mountains, Ebal and Gerizim. This is where Joshua had called the Israelites to renew their covenant with God (Joshua 8:30–35). It is also the burial place of Joseph, whose coffin was brought from Egypt (Joshua 24:32).

Abimelech is ambitious to rule. He persuades his Canaanite relatives in Shechem to help him murder his seventy brothers who are the other sons of Gideon. Only Jotham, the youngest, escapes the public execution, which is carried out on a particular stone. Abimelech is then crowned king beside the great tree at the sacred pillar in Shechem.

The survivor of the massacre, Jotham, climbs to the top of Gerizim. There he makes an impassioned speech to the people of Shechem, telling them they have made a worthless choice. Abimelech is like a thornbush – useless, treacherous and inflammable.

Abimelech's kingdom is small (about four towns) and his reign short (just three years). In suppressing a rebellion at Shechem he destroys the city and burns down its tower. When he besieges the tower at Thebez, his skull is cracked by an upper millstone dropped on him by a woman, and he dies.

Tola and Jair (10:1–5)

Tola and Jair are both judges who lead Israel for a number of years. Like Shamgar before them (and Ibzan, Elon and Abdon afterwards), we know very little of their lives and achievements. But Jair was clearly prominent and prosperous in his day – with his thirty sons riding thirty donkeys!

Jephthah (10:6–12:7)

The Israelites continue to indulge in Baal-worship, and God punishes them through crushing defeats at the hands of the Philistines and Ammonites. The Ammonites not only dominate the Israelite settlements to the east of the River Jordan, but also cross over to oppress the great tribes to the west.

In this grim situation, Jephthah emerges to lead the fight against the Ammonites. He has been rejected by his family because of his illegitimate birth, but has become the head of a band of dissidents. Now his clan turns to him for help.

Jephthah argues with the Ammonites that the disputed land belongs to Israel. It was given them by God, who helped them drive out the Amorites. However, the matter comes to war.

Jephthah is filled with God's Spirit for the task of leading the military campaign. Rashly and unnecessarily, he vows to sacrifice the first person who greets him on his successful return home. It is strange that Jephthah is both filled with the Spirit of the Lord and yet misguided about the Lord's demands. God is adamantly opposed to human sacrifice.

Tragically, the person who meets Jephthah on his return home is his only daughter. She insists that he fulfil his vow, asking only a delay of two months so that she can spend time in the hills and with her friends. Jephthah's action means that he kills off his own family line.

Men from the tribe of Ephraim ask why Jephthah didn't summon them to the fight against the Ammonites. Jephthah replies that he did, but they didn't respond. An exchange of insults leads to civil war between Gilead and Ephraim. The Ephraimites are defeated and flee for home, but the Gileadites seize them as they try to ford the Jordan. They identify the Ephraimites by their accents, because they can't pronounce the word 'shibboleth', which means 'ear of corn'.

The tribe of Ephraim is permanently weakened by the massacre at the hands of Gilead. Until now they have been the leading group in central and northern Israel. When the tribes of Israel finally choose a king, he will be Saul, from the weak tribe of Benjamin.

Samson (13:1–16:31)

Now the Israelites fall under the power of the Philistines. They are a warlike, seagoing people who have arrived from Crete and settled along the coastal strip of Canaan. They are pressing inland to give trouble to the Israelites. God raises up a champion for Israel in Samson.

Samson is the only son of an elderly, hitherto childless couple. His birth is a miracle. He is brought up as a Nazirite, dedicated to God. He doesn't eat meat or drink wine. He lets his hair grow long. He abstains from sex and avoids touching dead bodies. In other words, Samson is as pure and holy as possible. In addition, he is given a special gift of superhuman strength.

But, for all his physical prowess, Samson is a weak character. He wilfully chooses a Philistine woman for his wife. He flaunts his great strength to tease, taunt and hurt his enemies.

One by one, Samson breaks all his Nazirite vows. On one occasion, he kills a lion with his bare hands – but keeps it a secret. Sometime later he finds that bees have nested in the lion's carcass, so he scoops out and eats the honey. At his wedding feast he turns the episode into a riddle:

Out of the eater, something to eat,
Out of the strong, something sweet. (14:14 NRSV)

The Philistines ask Samson's wife to find out the secret of his great strength. When he realizes that they are trying to trick him, he kills dozens of Philistines and destroys their crops. In the end the Philistines use another woman, Delilah, to coax the truth out of him. He gets closer and closer to telling his secret.

Eventually Delilah wears Samson down with her begging, and he tells her his secret. His strength is in the Lord, and his commitment to the Lord is expressed in his long hair. As soon as she can, Delilah betrays Samson to his enemies and has his hair cut while he sleeps.

Deprived of his strength, Samson is captured, blinded and sentenced to hard labour by the Philistines. But his hair grows – and his relationship with God is restored. One day, when the Philistines make sport of him in their pagan temple, he prays for his strength to return. Hauling at the pillars which support the temple roof, Samson collapses the building, killing thousands of his enemies.

Samson is a mighty, tragic figure. He has abandoned his calling, broken all his vows, made a fool of himself with women and misused his spiritual gift. He reminds us of Esau, who treated holy things lightly because he was so confident of his prowess and privileges (Genesis 25:29–34). Samson's life is a warning against taking God for granted. A holy calling must be matched by a holy life.

Israel in decline

The writer shows us Israel in a state of anarchy. Here is religion corroded by superstition and society corrupted by cruelty. Might is right and the weakest go to the wall. The great sense of Israel being a nation under God has broken down.

Micah's idols (17:1–13)

Micah has stolen some silver from his mother. Not realizing that her son has done this, she utters curses on the thief. When he returns the silver to her, she tries to cancel the curse by offering part of the silver to God.

Micah has the silver made into an idol. This is a curious mixture of true and false religion – offering something precious to God (which is encouraged) and making an idol (which is forbidden).

Micah enjoys being religious. He sets up his own shrine, with an ephod and idols. An ephod was, in Aaron's time, an ornate garment covering the chest and stomach. It may have had a pouch containing the Urim and Thummim which were used to discover God's will. By now the ephod may have become something that could be carried – but still associated with seeking God's guidance and blessing.

Micah appoints one of his sons as the priest. This is the kind of 'do-it-yourself' religion which will be banned in Israel in the future. The worship of God is not to be reduced to an exclusive, private, local action. There is only one God, and he is to be worshipped by everyone in one place – eventually, the temple in Jerusalem. When Micah takes on another priest, who is actually from the priestly tribe of Levi, he feels God will show him special favour. This is also a sign of his superstition.

The Danite migration (18:1–31)

One of the tribes, the descendants of Dan, are still looking for a place to settle. In their search, some of them arrive at the house of Micah and recognize the young Levite who is the priest there. He directs them to Laish, which is a beautiful stretch of country occupied by peaceful and unsuspecting people.

The advance guard returns with the full force of Danites. They take the contents of Micah's shrine, the ephod, the idols and the young Levite, to give them good luck in conquering Laish. Although Micah protests and makes as if to fight, there is nothing he can do. The people of Laish are equally defenceless in the face of the Danite onslaught. So Dan wins some territory in the northernmost part of the land of Canaan, and keeps Micah's idols in the shrine at Shiloh. The young priest is named as Jonathan, a descendant of Moses. But all has been done by deceit, superstition and brute force. No one has tried to discover and do God's will.

A Levite and his concubine (19:1–30)

A Levite (a member of the priestly tribe) is living with his concubine or slave girl. On their way from Bethlehem to Ephraim, they take special care to stay with fellow Israelites – at the town of Gibeah which belongs to the tribe of Benjamin. They expect shelter and hospitality, but receive none.

Eventually an old man takes them into his home. During the evening some local men come pounding on the door, demanding sex with the Levite. The Levite saves himself by sending out his girl to them. They gang-rape her all night, and in the morning she lies dead on the threshold of the house.

The Levite is appalled at what has happened. The security and respect which the tribes of Israel owe each other has been breached. An innocent woman has been unspeakably abused and done to death. To convey the brutality and shame to all Israel, he cuts his slave girl's body into twelve pieces and sends a grisly and stinking segment to every tribe – including Benjamin, which has been responsible for the deed.

This is a sign of the times! This is what Israel has come to! Without God's law, there are no healthy relationships, no safe communities and there is no hope of justice.

The Israelites fight the Benjaminites (20:1–48)

When the tribes of Israel receive the dreadful evidence of the woman's severed corpse, they gather together at Mizpah. 'Mizpah' means 'watchtower', and the place is not far from Jerusalem. The eleven tribes of Israel resolve to raise a united army to discipline the offending tribe of Benjamin.

At first the Israelites demand that the Benjaminites hand over the men who committed the rape and murder, but this request is refused. Instead, the Benjaminites gather an army, which includes 700 formidable slingsmen. A sling is a fearsome weapon, jettisoning a stone of up to a pound in weight at very high speed and with enormous accuracy – as Goliath will find out to his cost when he is confronted by the shepherd-boy David.

The numbers of men gathering for battle are extremely large, and it is uncertain how to translate or interpret this information. Sometimes a number can refer to a clan or family, or to a contingent under the command of an officer.

The Benjaminites are hopelessly outnumbered, but they are great fighters. This is the tribe that produced Ehud – and will produce Saul. For two days they defend Gibeah and inflict death and destruction on the Israelites with their slings. The Israelites seek God's guidance with increasing earnestness – tears of penitence, fasting for grief and sacrifices for forgiveness and peace. They worship God at Bethel, where Phineas is the priest guarding the ark of the covenant. Phineas has been a great man of action himself in the past.

On the third day of the battle, the Israelites adopt a different strategy. They retreat from Gibeah in two directions, drawing out and splitting up the Benjaminites who pursue them. But an extra force of Israelites then emerges from hiding to capture Gibeah and set fire to it. The Benjaminites turn to see their city going up in flames, and are routed. Some escape to the rock of Rimmon, a few miles from Bethel, where they manage to survive, but the rest of the Benjaminite men and their cities are destroyed.

The tribe of Benjamin is spared (21:1–25)

Once the battle is over, the full horror of the situation sinks in. The tribes of Israel have been torn apart by civil war, and one of them, Benjamin, has been brought to the brink of extinction. The Benjaminites will die out because the other tribes have vowed never to let their daughters marry them.

As they weep and worship, the Israelites realize that the men of Jabesh Gilead have failed to help in the crisis. The people of Jabesh Gilead are descended from Joseph, and so have a close relationship with the Benjaminites, who are descended from Joseph's much-loved brother. Nevertheless, they have withheld their support from the common cause of Israel and must be punished.

A force is sent to destroy Jabesh Gilead and to seize its young women to be wives for the surviving Benjaminites. When there is still a shortage of females, the Benjaminites are encouraged to kidnap the girls they need from a festival at Shiloh. This outrage is agreed by all the tribes and any protest will fall on deaf ears. The important thing is that the tribe of Benjamin will continue to exist.

So God's holy people lurch from moral disaster to impetuous bloodshed and high-handed injustice. There is no wisdom, sanity or restraint. The writer explains that the Israelites lack a king – by which he means a powerful and godly leader such as David and Solomon will be. But the first sign of hope in this desperate and divided situation will be Samuel, the last and greatest of the judges.

RUTH

The little book of Ruth is a love story. Ruth is a foreigner to Israel. She comes from Moab. Ruth and her sister were both married to Israelite men, but they are widowed. Ruth shows great love and loyalty to her mother-in-law, Naomi, who is also a widow. Together they travel from Moab to Naomi's home in Bethlehem. There Ruth meets Boaz, her husband's next of kin. Boaz is a good man who deals kindly with them. In due course, Boaz marries Ruth. Their great-grandson will be King David.

OUTLINE

Naomi and Ruth travel to Bethlehem (1:1–22)
Ruth meets Boaz, a local farmer (2:1–3:18)
Boaz and Ruth are married (4:1–22)

Introduction

This gentle story comes from the days of the judges and is a contrast to their bloodthirsty adventures. We see that God cares for strangers and widows – and weaves even our tragedies into his perfect plan.

Throughout the story, Boaz stands out as a man of truth and generosity. He lives out the laws of Moses in their true spirit – which is to show the character of God.

Boaz is kind to a stranger. He has compassion on two widows. He allows his crops to be gleaned by the needy. He respects and protects Ruth when others might abuse her. He makes a wise decision, acts on it promptly and deals openly and fairly with all concerned.

Although Boaz is the saviour who brings about a happy ending, it is Naomi who is the hero and driving force of the story. It is she who has faith, and takes the initiative, to return to Bethlehem – and steer Ruth in Boaz's direction! And when baby Obed is born, he is (as everyone says) really a son for her.

Who wrote the story of Ruth?

We do not know who wrote this story. It is set in the days when the judges were leading Israel, but has a much more peaceful atmosphere than the tales of their exploits. It tells how God can guide and bless people even in the midst of personal tragedy. It shows how a righteous man, Boaz, protects and provides for two widows. It also has a special interest as background to the story of David. It seems to be told as a true story and is therefore one of the Bible's history books.

DISCOVERING RUTH

Naomi and Ruth travel to Bethlehem (1:1–22)

There is a famine in Israel. A man called Elimelech takes his wife, Naomi, and their two sons to find food in Moab.

In the old days, the people of Moab had been hostile to the Israelites on their journey to Canaan. Their women were also blamed for seducing Israelite men and persuading them to worship the Baal-gods (Numbers 25:1–3). As a result, Moabites were banned from marrying Israelites for ten generations (Deuteronomy 23:3)!

After the family have lived in Moab for ten years, Elimelech and his sons die. Naomi and her daughters-in-law, Orpah and Ruth, are left as widows. Naomi feels abandoned by God – without protection or livelihood in a foreign land. Hearing that the famine has ended, she decides to return to her people in Bethlehem.

Naomi realizes that her daughters-in-law will be foreigners in Bethlehem. She tries to persuade them to go back to their own family homes and find husbands there. Orpah agrees, but Ruth insists on staying with Naomi. With moving words she commits herself to her mother-in-law and to Israel's God:

Where you go, I will go...
your people shall be my people,
  and your God my God.
Where you die, I will die –
  there will I be buried. (1:16–17 NRSV)

Ruth's choice is remarkable, because all she has known is tragedy and loss. Yet she, a foreigner to Israel, still puts her trust in the Lord.

When Naomi arrives in Bethlehem, she tells everyone of her loss. When she left she had a family, but now she is alone. Her name means 'Pleasant', but her life has turned bitter. Then a ray of hope breaks into the story. The barley harvest is beginning.

Ruth meets Boaz, a local farmer (2:1–3:18)

Naomi has a relative named Boaz. He is a leading member of the Bethlehem community. When Ruth goes to glean – gathering grain the harvesters have left – she finds herself in one of Boaz's fields. When Boaz comes to visit his workers, he notices Ruth and makes her welcome.

Boaz is a godly man. He shows God's love in his kindness to her, although she is a foreigner. He prays that God will reward her for her loyalty to Naomi. At the meal he shares his food with Ruth – and afterwards he tells his men to leave plenty of stalks in the field for Ruth to glean. She collects and threshes an ephah of barley – about four gallons.

When Ruth arrives home to tell Naomi of her successful day, her mother-in-law explains that Boaz is one of their kinsman-redeemers. In other words, he is a close relative on whom they can rely for help.

One night Naomi sends Ruth to the threshing-floor, where the harvesters are sleeping. She lies at Boaz's feet and wakes him. They talk about her situation and he promises to help. He treats her with the utmost respect – moved that she has come to him and not gone after one of the younger men. But there is a kinsman-redeemer who is a closer relative than Boaz, and he must have first opportunity to look after Naomi and Ruth.

Boaz and Ruth are married (4:1–22)

The following morning, at the town gate, Boaz meets with the other kinsman-redeemer. He invites him to buy Elimelech's land and marry Ruth. There is a law that a man should marry his brother's widow and enable her to have a son to continue the family line (Deuteronomy 25:5–6).

The closer relative declines the offer. Either he doesn't want to marry a foreigner, or he can't afford to buy a field just to leave it to someone else. The way is open for Boaz to purchase the field and marry Ruth.

Boaz marries Ruth and they have a son, Obed. His name means 'Servant'. Proudly Naomi takes her grandson and nurses him. Now *she* has a kinsman! Obed will be the father of Jesse; and he in turn will be father of the great King David.

1 and 2 SAMUEL

The first book of Samuel continues the story of Israel from the time of the judges to the end of the reign of King Saul. At the beginning the Israelites are a loose association of tribes. By the end they are a united nation with their own king.

Samuel is the last judge. He tries to persuade the Israelites not to have a king, but they insist. The first king, Saul, is a disappointment. He disobeys God. He is also jealous of a popular young hero – David. Samuel anoints David as Saul's successor; but for many years David has to flee from Saul for fear of his life. The first book of Samuel ends with Saul's death.

The second book of Samuel continues the story of God's people, Israel. Its main theme is the reign of King David, who is Israel's greatest king.

When David comes to power, he brings unity and peace to a divided nation and a troubled land. He defeats Israel's enemies and establishes Jerusalem as his political and religious centre. He receives God's promise that his descendants will rule for ever.

But David is far from perfect. In mid-life he commits adultery with Bathsheba, the wife of one of his soldiers – and then tries to hide his crime by arranging the man's death. This episode proves to be a turning point in David's fortunes. He loses the respect of his own sons, and they cause both him and the nation great grief.

OUTLINE

Samuel (1 Samuel 1:1–7:17)
Saul (1 Samuel 8:1–15:35)
David (1 Samuel 16:1–31:13)
David becomes king (2 Samuel 1:1–10:19)
David's weaknesses and failures (2 Samuel 11:1–18:33)
The final period of David's reign (2 Samuel 19:1–24:25)

Introduction

In the Hebrew Bible, the two books of Samuel were a single book. When the Septuagint (the Greek version of the Hebrew Bible) was compiled, the books of Samuel and Kings were called the 'books of the kingdoms'. In the famous English 'Authorized (King James) Version' they are numbered as four books of Kings. They tell a continuous history from the time of Samuel (the last of the judges), through the reigns of three great kings (Saul, David and Solomon), to the division of Israel and Judah and their eventual fall.

The books of Joshua, Judges, Samuel and Kings tell the ongoing story of Israel, from the triumphant conquest of Canaan to the bitter exile in Babylon. The writers and editors show how God is at work in the lives of his people. God rewards faithfulness with success – and punishes disobedience with failure.

Samuel

Samuel is the last and greatest of the judges. He is a key figure at a time when Israel's priesthood is corrupt, its enemies are strong and the people are demanding to have a king. Samuel warns Israel of the dangers of having a human king, but follows God's guidance in choosing and anointing two great kings – Saul and David.

Three kings

Saul, David and Solomon are Israel's first three kings. They are each said to reign for forty years – the Bible's clue to a 'complete' period of time. If Saul dies around 1010 BC, we have some possible dates for their reigns:

Saul   1045 to 1010 BC
David   1010 to 970 BC
Solomon   970 to 930 BC

Saul

Saul is Israel's first king. He seems to be the right choice. He is tall, with a striking appearance and a desire to lead well. However, there are occasions when he does the wrong thing – showing that he has no sure sense of God's will. God rejects him as king, and his leadership begins to fail. Saul is a picture of our human impulse to run our lives without God.

David

David is Israel's second and most famous king.

As a boy, he slays a giant Philistine, Goliath. Goliath symbolizes the threat and awesome power of Israel's pagan enemies. But David simply puts his trust in God – and his skill with a shepherd's sling.

As 'king-in-waiting', David gives protection and leadership to poor and disaffected people. He refuses to seize the throne by force, and twice spares King Saul's life.

When he eventually becomes king, David defeats all Israel's enemies and protects her borders. His reign is the only time in Israel's history when she fully occupies all the land which God promised to Abraham.

Solomon

See 1 Kings.

Who wrote the books of Samuel and Kings?

We don't know who wrote these books. Certainly it wasn't Samuel. Although he is a leading character, he dies before the end of the first volume (1 Samuel 25:1)! Most of the material was written by the end of the reign of Solomon, around 900 BC. A tell-tale verse (1 Samuel 27:6) hints that the final editing took place many years later, during or after the exile of Judah in Babylon.

Mixed doubles

Sometimes the author (or editor) tells the same story twice – or even gives two different accounts of the same story. For example, it's hard to tell whether Samuel was the foremost leader of his day or just a local circuit judge. And when exactly did David first meet Saul? Was the young man well known to the king as a musician and armour bearer – or was he a likely lad who suddenly volunteered to fight Goliath? The author gives us the stories and leaves the choice to us.

DISCOVERING 1 AND 2 SAMUEL

Samuel

The birth and call of Samuel (1 Samuel 1:1–3:21)

Samuel is the son of Hannah. Hannah has been childless for many years – feeling abandoned by God and a failure to her husband. At last God gives her a longed-for son. She sings a song of praise – that God can turn despair to hope and failure to triumph. He lifts the lowly and humbles the proud. This song will be echoed, centuries later, by Mary the mother of Jesus (Luke 1:46–55). Out of gratitude, Hannah gives her son Samuel, while he is still a small boy, to serve God at the shrine in Shiloh.

The priest at Shiloh is Eli. He is old and his sons, also priests, are decadent. They feed themselves from the choicest portions of the sacrifices, and sleep around with the women on their staff. Eli is warned by a prophet that God will judge this scandalous situation.

One night, God speaks to Samuel. The voice is so clear that at first Samuel thinks Eli is calling him. God tells Samuel that he is about to judge Eli and his sons – the sons for their wicked behaviour and Eli for not controlling them.

The ark is captured – and returned (1 Samuel 4:1–7:1)

Eli's sons, Hophni and Phinehas, take the ark of the covenant into battle against the Philistines. The ark is captured and they are killed. When Eli

---

A mixed blessing

Sometimes God gives us what we want – but it's not always for the best. The monarchy is a mixed blessing for Israel – a flawed human institution which God can sometimes bless.

Although human kingship is not God's choice, he guides Samuel to anoint Saul – a man with an impressive physique but a weak character. In time, God will bless the monarchy by raising up David – a wise, strong and caring king. David's reign will look forward to the perfect rule of Christ. The security and justice of David's kingdom will foreshadow the kingdom of God.

receives the terrible news, he topples off his chair and dies. The shock also causes Phinehas' wife to go into labour. As she dies giving birth, she calls her baby 'Ichabod', – which means 'No Glory'. The presence of God has departed from Eli and his family.

The Philistines take the ark of the covenant to the temple of Dagon, their pagan idol. Next morning they find the giant statue flat on its face. After that the presence of the ark brings disease and panic to the Philistines – and they resolve to return it to Israel.

Samuel conquers the Philistines (1 Samuel 7:2–17)

The ark of the Lord is returned to Israel. The Philistines have found that its holy presence brings death and destruction; but the Israelites aren't worthy of it either. For twenty years it remains in a kind of quarantine at the house of Abinadab at Kiriath Jearim, the 'city of woods' between the tribes of Benjamin and Judah. The Israelites mourn the loss of the presence of God, and begin to turn to him again.

Eventually, Samuel sends out a message to all Israel. He says that if they are ready to return to the Lord and will reject all foreign gods (especially Astarte, the Baal-goddess of fertility and war) then God will rescue them from the domination of the Philistines.

Samuel calls the tribes of Israel to assemble at Mizpah – west of the River Jordan in the territory of the tribe of Benjamin. There they pour out water in the presence of God, as a sign that he alone can wash away their sins. They fast, confess their guilt and receive God's judgment through Samuel. He is the last and greatest of the judges, ministering to the people as their military leader, prophet and priest.

'Mizpah' means 'watchtower'. It is a small settlement only a few miles north of Jerusalem, whose height above the valleys makes it a good rallying point.

The Philistines hear that the Israelites are massing at Mizpah and assume that they are about to be attacked. They decide to advance their own army, and the Israelites plead with Samuel to secure God's help. This is a very different attitude from the Israel of the past, which assumed that the presence of the ark would give automatic victory.

The Philistines

Israel's chief enemy at this time is Philistia. The Philistines are a seafaring people who have settled in the coastal region between Israel and the Mediterranean Sea. Their technology is more advanced than Israel's, and they make their weapons and armour from iron. Meanwhile, Israel is still in the Bronze Age, and her weapons are less effective.

Rough justice?

It is hard for us to accept that God commands the complete destruction of the Amalekites and their possessions. Is this really the fate he demands for the vile and perverted peoples of Canaan? Certainly he would want Israel to be uncompromising with the beliefs and practices of paganism. Even keeping some plunder from a battle can sow the seeds of greed in God's holy people. Ethnic cleansing may have been the Israelites' best guess at what God wanted them to do. Jesus will show God as merciful towards traditional enemies. On one occasion he forbids James and John to call down fire from heaven on a Samaritan village (Luke 9:54–55).

Samuel offers a sacrifice and prays for God's help in the crisis. As the smoke rises from the burnt offering, the Lord sends a great thunderstorm upon the Philistines, which throws them into confusion and forces them to flee. The Israelites pursue them, having the advantage of chasing them downhill. To mark such a great deliverance, Samuel sets up a memorial stone. He calls it Ebenezer, which means 'stone of help'. It was a place called Ebenezer which had been the site of Israel's last defeat (4:1), but now God has granted repentance and success.

The Philistines cause no further trouble to Israel during Samuel's lifetime. He makes an annual circuit, spending time at Bethel, Gilgal and Mizpah to hear cases and make judgments. By so doing, he restores and sustains the relationship of the people with their God. Each of the places is a sanctuary where God is worshipped; and Samuel builds an altar in his home town of Ramah as well. There is stability and peace throughout Israel under the ministry of Samuel and the government of God. But it isn't to last.

Saul

Israel asks for a king (1 Samuel 8:1–22)

As Samuel grows old, the question arises as to who will succeed him. Other nations have a king to unite and protect them, and the leaders of Israel feel that the time has come for Israel to do the same. Samuel believes that God is the true king of Israel, and the one who appoints leaders and judges for his people. It is also true that no human king is perfect, and some become tyrants who bully and exploit their people. After much heart-searching and debate, Samuel agrees to select and anoint a human king – an impressive young man called Saul. But it is against Samuel's better judgment, and he will live to regret it.

Saul begins his reign well, by leading his people to victory over their enemies. But he is strong-headed and does not always wait for or heed God's advice. He also suffers from periods of black depression and is jealous of the people's hero, David. In the end, he becomes a sad picture – a fine man who has become estranged from God and so is unable to take charge of either himself or his destiny.

Saul becomes king (1 Samuel 9:1–11:15)

We first meet Saul as he searches for his father's donkeys. Saul goes to ask Samuel for help because Samuel is a 'seer' – a holy man who may be able to 'see' where the donkeys are.

But Samuel is interested in Saul for other reasons. He reveals that Saul is to become the king of Israel. Saul is reluctant. He pleads that he and his tribe are very insignificant. Gideon said the same in his day (Judges 6:15).

Samuel anoints Saul and tells him the special signs which will confirm that he is God's choice. One by one they take place – including the outpouring of God's Spirit so that Saul becomes an ecstatic prophet. But when the tribes gather to choose and confirm Saul as their king, he is still unwilling. They find him hiding under a pile of baggage!

Although he is king, Saul has limited power. Samuel writes down certain guidelines and restrictions, which are kept with the ark of the covenant. Saul may be ruler of Israel, but he himself is to be ruled by God.

Samuel's farewell speech (1 Samuel 12:1–25)

Saul is now Israel's king. He is God's anointed leader and the people's united choice. It remains for Samuel to lay down his role as leader. As he does so, he reminds all Israel that he has not burdened or cheated them in any way. He is the last of the judges, who have been God's means of delivering them from powerful and pagan enemies.

Samuel warns the people to be faithful to the Lord – and his solemn words are endorsed by an unseasonal thunderstorm. They have been wrong to demand a king, but God will not abandon them – and nor will Samuel. Samuel will continue to act as God's prophet and fulfil his responsibility to pray for and teach God's people.

The relationship between Samuel and Saul will always be difficult. Samuel has not wanted to anoint a king, and Saul has not wanted to be one. Now Saul must rule Israel with Samuel still around to criticize and correct him. Ideally, Saul should make Samuel his close adviser and friend – but they simply don't get on that well. Saul is proud and increasingly independent. Samuel will never accept anyone between himself and God.

Saul's disobedience (1 Samuel 13:1–15:35)

Saul and his son Jonathan are successful army commanders, driving back Israel's enemies. But there are two occasions when Saul offends God greatly. The first is when he offers a sacrifice without waiting for Samuel. In so doing he usurps the work of a priest and treats the sacrifice as a token of good luck. On another occasion Saul disobeys God by failing to destroy the Amalekites (15:7–9). He makes the excuse that he is saving the Amalekite cattle for sacrifices. But Samuel points out that it is more important to do what God wants (15:22):

Does the Lord delight in burnt offerings and sacrifices as much as in obeying the voice of the Lord?

This is a vital insight into Samuel's understanding of God. In years to come it will be echoed by other prophets and by Jesus himself.

From this point Samuel and Saul part company. They live only ten miles apart, but they never see each other again.

David

Samuel anoints David (1 Samuel 16:1-23)

God sends Samuel to Bethlehem. There he discovers David, the youngest of the sons of Jesse. It doesn't occur to anyone in the family that this shepherd lad might be a future king. But God sees things differently. In another remarkable statement, Samuel shows his deep awareness of the presence and perception of God:

Mortals look on the outward appearance, but the Lord looks on the heart. (16:7)

Samuel anoints David by pouring oil over his head. The young man is filled with God's Spirit for the task of leadership. As the Spirit of the Lord comes upon David, so the Spirit leaves Saul. It is almost as though there is not enough Spirit to go round. But one day there will be. As Joel prophesies:

And afterwards,
  I will pour out my Spirit on all people.
Your sons and daughters will prophesy,
  your old men will dream dreams,
  your young men will see visions.
Even on my servants, both men and women,
  I will pour out my Spirit in those days. (Joel 2:28-29)

Joel looks forward to the era of Jesus. There will come a Day of Pentecost when God's Spirit will no longer be rationed to an occasional priest or prophet or king, but freely given to all God's people (Acts 2:1-11).

From now on Saul is rejected by God. He suffers fits of depression. Young David is summoned to court to play the harp and ease the king's black moods.

David and Goliath (1 Samuel 17:1-58)

A champion is needed to fight a giant Philistine called Goliath. David volunteers. This should be Saul's task, as he is a head taller than any of his men – and has one of the few suits of armour! But David goes out to meet Goliath, armed only with faith in the living God – and his shepherd's sling. This is more than a test of bravery. It is a bold declaration that the God of Israel is greater than all other gods. As David says:

The whole world will know that there is a God in Israel. All those gathered here will know that it is not by sword or spear that the Lord saves; for the battle is the Lord's. (17:46–47)

This is God's war! The lad with faith takes on the giant of fear. Goliath stands for all the pride and power of paganism. David and his sling are so puny that victory can only be an act of God.

David, the king-in-waiting (1 Samuel 18:1–27:12)

David is now married to Saul's daughter Michal, and has Saul's son Jonathan as his closest friend. But the king himself is mad with jealousy. He is determined to take David's life.

David becomes an outlaw. At first he hides out at the cave of Adullam, where he is joined by the outcasts and rebels of Israelite society. Later he makes the town of Ziklag his centre; and on another occasion he takes refuge with the Philistines.

Saul pursues David, killing the priests who have given him sanctuary. On two occasions David actually spares the king's life. He comes close enough to cut a piece from Saul's robe, and take his spear and water jug.

David believes that Saul is God's anointed king. His life and status are sacred, and no one but God may remove him. David himself will not become king before God's time.

David takes refuge with the Philistines

David's life is threatened and he must live by his wits. He goes to Nob, where the ark of the Lord is kept. He asks the priest for bread, but the only food available is the special batch of loaves which are laid out in the presence of God. Only priests are allowed to eat this 'bread of the Presence'. However, David manages to persuade the priest that his mission is very urgent and his men are ritually pure. The priest allows them to eat the loaves.

> ### Understanding leadership
> David has rare insight and understanding. He knows the worlds of politics and of the human heart. Of course, the two go together. Understanding human nature and need is an important part of good government.
>
> Our attitude to monarchy and leadership is still shaped by David's ideals and example. What a shame he was not as skilled at governing his own family!

In the future, Jesus will agree with the priest's decision. Human need is more important than religious formality. Jesus recalls this episode when he confronts the legalistic Pharisees about keeping or breaking the sabbath (Matthew 12:1–8).

After food, David's next need is for a weapon. He persuades the priest to let him take the sword of the giant Goliath – the very sword with which David himself had cut off the great Philistine's head.

To escape Saul, David makes for the very last place he would be expected to go – the Philistine city of Gath. It is an outrageous ploy! Carrying Goliath's sword, he goes to Goliath's home town and becomes a servant of King Achish. Inevitably, the other servants recognize him, but he averts their anger by pretending to be mad. It is a humiliating experience, but later David will look back on it as a God-given means of escape:

I sought the Lord and he answered me;
he delivered me from all my fears. (Psalm 34:4)

Achish takes a look at David and decides he has enough madmen already. So David is able to escape.

Saul and the witch of Endor (1 Samuel 28:1–25)

Samuel dies. Even though they are no longer friends, Saul misses his old adviser. His own relationship with God is dead as well. In terror of the Philistines, Saul decides to consult a medium. She summons the spirit of Samuel. Whether this is really the spirit of Samuel or a demonic impersonation, we don't know. Certainly the message from Samuel in death is the same as it was in life:

The Lord has torn the kingdom out of your hands and given it to one of your neighbours – to David. (28:17)

Grimly, the medium predicts the death of Saul and his sons in battle with the Philistines the following day. Saul has been extremely foolish to seek help by occult means – a form of guidance which God expressly forbids. And no good has come of it.

Achish sends David back to Ziklag (1 Samuel 29:1–11)

The Philistine forces are gathering at Aphek, about thirty miles to the north of Gath. The Israelite army is at Jezreel, on the slopes of Mount Gilboa. David and his men have supported Achish in many military campaigns; but this battle will be different, because it is against Israel and her king. The Philistine commanders don't trust David to be loyal to them. They suspect that he may use the opportunity to change sides and win the battle for Israel – perhaps even seizing Saul's throne. Achish has complete confidence in David, but for his own sake dismisses him from the Philistine force. This is a great mercy, because David is spared having to fight Saul, the Lord's anointed king.

David destroys the Amalekites (1 Samuel 30:1–31)

Meanwhile, an Amalekite raiding party has attacked David's centre at Ziklag, and taken the families, livestock and possessions of all his men. David's reaction is a model of good leadership. He seeks God's guidance, acts wisely and decisively, and secures complete success. In victory he shares the plunder fairly and generously with everyone. We can't help comparing David's confident judgment with Saul's dangerous instability.

The death of Saul (1 Samuel 31:1–13)

Saul and his army are defeated by the Philistines. The royal sons – including David's friend Jonathan – are killed, and Saul takes his own life. It is a degrading death for the king the people demanded, but God rejected.

David becomes king

David's lament for Saul and Jonathan (2 Samuel 1:1–27)

David receives the news that King Saul and his son Jonathan have been killed in battle with the Philistines. He is heartbroken. Although Saul has long treated David as a rival and tried to kill him, David has never wished him harm. When the messenger claims to have helped the stricken Saul to end his life, David has him killed on the spot. Saul was the Lord's anointed king. His life was sacred.

David sings a lament which has been famous ever since. He forbids the news of Saul's death to be published, in case the Philistines celebrate. He curses the mountains of Gilboa where the great men died. He remembers Saul and Jonathan in their prime, as princes, soldiers and friends.

The Book of Jashar ('The Upright') (1:18) seems to have been a collection of well-known poems and songs. No copies have survived but it provides a clue to how the Bible books must have been written, using historical records, songs and stories. The Book of Jashar is also mentioned in the book of Joshua (Joshua 10:13).

The mountains of Gilboa are well known to this day, simply because they are the place where Saul and Jonathan died.

David becomes king of Judah (2 Samuel 2:1–5:5)

Saul has died – and so has his son Jonathan. The way is now open for David to become king – except that there are other contenders. There is sure to be a candidate from among Saul's sons or from his tribe of Benjamin. This could lead to further bloodshed and civil war.

David seeks God's guidance before he takes any step – and then makes the short journey to Hebron. Hebron is where Abraham and the patriarchs are buried, and the place where a king might be anointed, at least over the tribe of Judah.

David is duly anointed as king over Judah, the leading tribe of Israel.

Meanwhile Abner, Saul's general, has made someone else king at Mahanaim. This king is Ish-Bosheth. He is Saul's son, and he reigns over parts of Israel for two years. His name may mean 'Strong Man' – but the real trial of strength is going on between two rival army commanders – Abner (for Ish-Bosheth and the tribe of Benjamin) and Joab (for David and the tribe of Judah).

Joab, David's general, wants revenge on Abner, who has killed his brother Asahel. When Abner holds talks with David to make peace, Joab moves swiftly to seize and murder him. David mourns the death of Abner – a fine leader who was already working to unite the nation. This is just the start of trouble with Joab, who becomes David's hit man whether David likes it or not. Joab is a violent enemy and an unscrupulous friend.

Ish-Bosheth is also murdered, by two of his own supporters who have changed sides. David is appalled at their deed and has them executed.

At last David is anointed king over the united tribes of Israel. He is thirty years old and will reign until he is seventy.

David makes Jerusalem his capital (2 Samuel 5:6–6:23)

David's first action is to capture Jerusalem from the Jebusites. Throughout the years of the Canaan campaign, Jerusalem has resisted all attempts to be captured. Now David makes her his own capital: 'the city of David'. By doing this he gives Israel a centre which has no previous link with any of the tribes.

Next, David defeats the Philistines. Unlike Saul, David only goes to battle if God gives him the command. Like Jesus, he only does what God tells him to do (John 6:38).

David sees life as a whole. The tribes of Israel should be united as the people of God. Politics and religion belong together. He decides to show this by bringing the ark of the covenant (the symbol of God's presence) to Jerusalem (the centre of government).

The ark is carried in procession towards Jerusalem, with great celebration – until Uzzah touches it unthinkingly and is struck dead. The ark is holy and not to be handled roughly – not even touched, except by the appointed priests. David is angry and perplexed by this unexpected tragedy. He leaves the ark in the care of a man called Obed-Edom for three months, until it is clearly safe to proceed.

> **Second best?**
>
> Both the monarchy and the temple are second best. God is the real king of Israel, and he needs no earthly house. But God accepts Israel's need for a king and a temple, to act as a focus for his divine rule and holy presence.

As the ark arrives in Jerusalem, David dances before it, dressed only in an ephod – a kind of priestly apron. He has an enormous sense of joy in the Lord, but his wife, Michal, thinks he looks ridiculous. Her father, Saul, was far more kingly. But David is not ashamed. He is dancing for the Lord, not for anyone else.

God's promise to David (2 Samuel 7:1–29))

David and the prophet Nathan are thinking how strange it is that the king now lives in a palace, but God remains (as it were) in a tent – the old tabernacle shelter of the wilderness years.

Nathan receives a message from the Lord. God doesn't want or need a house. There is even some danger in building a temple, because it will seem to 'fix' God in one place. The Israelites have always experienced God 'on the move', leading them forward on a journey of faith. He does not live in a temple or shrine, but with his people, wherever they are.

Far from David needing to establish God's house, God is going to establish David's 'house' or dynasty. He promises to be a father to David. He will make David very great, and his descendants will reign for ever. One day a son of David (Solomon) will build 'a house for the Lord' – a beautiful temple.

God's promise to David becomes the central pillar of Israel's hope for survival. The people believe that God will never fail them. He has committed himself to preserving David's descendants as kings for ever. This promise echoes God's ancient covenant with Abraham, which included the promise of a land and a great nation of descendants. Now God's promise to Abraham is being fulfilled and continued through the promise to David. God's plan is to bless the whole world through them.

The royal line of David continues to reign in Jerusalem for 400 years – until the destruction of Jerusalem and the exile in Babylon in 586 BC. Even now, the Jews continue to look forward to the coming of their Messiah – a son of David, who will conquer their enemies and establish a universal kingdom of justice and peace.

After the exile, the royal line of David is still carefully traced – until it eventually leads to Jesus. Two Gospel writers, Matthew and Luke, record Jesus' descent from David, through his earthly father, Joseph (Matthew 1:5–6; Luke 3:31).

David's prayer

David expresses his trust in God (7:18–29). He describes himself as God's servant ten times over. It is God who has done everything for him, from

The king and the commandments

In Israel God is king, and everyone is subject to his law. David, God's earthly king, must keep the Ten Commandments along with everyone else.

As David lusts after Bathsheba, commits adultery with her, deceives her husband and has him killed, God's law is tossed aside. In Israel a man may take another wife – but not if she is already married to someone else. Everyone knows this is wrong.

David has wronged God, Bathsheba, Uriah and himself. There will be far-reaching consequences for his family and nation. David sets a bad example for his sons – two of whom, Amnon and Absalom, abuse their royal power to commit sexual outrage.

David is guilty, but he repents. He gives himself totally to prayer and fasting, spending a week without food or sleep, and pleading for the baby's life to be spared.

In his attitude, David is very different from Saul. Where Saul would have blustered excuses and brazened his way out, David completely admits his wrong. He submits to God and asks for forgiveness, cleansing and a new heart. In doing so he pioneers new paths for the human spirit – across deserts of despair to the oases of repentance, and the heights of forgiveness.

After the child dies, David resumes normal life. He has fully expressed his great grief. He has accepted the Lord's judgment.

his days as a shepherd to his anointing as king. Now he begs God to keep the great promises he has made. His prayer is a mixture of humble submission and urgent demand. He prays success for the building of the temple and for all God's work in the world.

David's victories (2 Samuel 8:1–10:19)

David has many years of success. He unites his people, defeats his enemies and secures the borders of Israel. He acts justly, without fear or favour. He is kind to Mephibosheth, the crippled son of his friend Jonathan. He goes out to battle with his soldiers, sharing their hardships and triumphs.

David's weaknesses and failures

David and Bathsheba (2 Samuel 11:1–12:25)

One spring, David decides not to go to war. No doubt he feels that he deserves a rest – a chance to take a well-earned break and leave the fighting to others.

In his idleness, David starts an affair with the beautiful wife of one of his soldiers. Her name is Bathsheba. Her husband, Uriah the Hittite, is one of David's finest men. Her father Eliam is also one of David's famous 'Thirty': mighty warriors. Her grandfather is the wise and subtle counsellor, Ahithophel.

Bathsheba becomes pregnant. David brings Uriah home from battle and encourages him to spend a few nights with his wife. But this man is a professional soldier and he sleeps in the guardhouse. So David tries another plan. He sends a letter to his commander, Joab, with instructions that Uriah be sent where the fighting is fiercest and then left to die.

One thing has led to another. David's lack of self-discipline has resulted in adultery, deceit and murder. At first David thinks he has hidden his crime; but God knows – and so does his prophet Nathan. Sin is always found out.

Nathan rebukes David

David is the most powerful person in the land – and yet Nathan can challenge him in the name of the Lord (2 Samuel 12:1–12). He tells him an innocent little story about a rich man who has flocks of sheep, but stoops to take a poor man's only lamb – to cook for a visitor.

David is furious that such a thing can happen – until Nathan says, 'It's you!' David – a king with wives and mistresses to spare – has stolen a soldier's only wife and taken his life as well.

This is a turning point for David's reign. Until now everything has gone right. After this everything goes wrong. David repents before God with all his heart. We have his words (Psalm 51:1, 4, 10):

Have mercy on me, O God,
    according to your unfailing love...
Against you, you only, have I sinned...
Create in me a pure heart, O God,
    and renew a steadfast spirit within me.

Bathsheba's baby dies; but soon she and David have another son. They name him Solomon.

Solomon will inherit his father's throne and become a king of legendary wealth and wisdom. He will fulfil David's dream of building a temple for the Lord in Jerusalem. We see how God takes even our disobedience and failure and works them into his perfect plan.

Solomon's name comes from the Hebrew word 'Shalom', which means 'Peace'. Nathan arrives with another name as well – 'Jedidiah', which means 'Loved by the Lord'. This baby will not die.

Defeating the Ammonites (2 Samuel 12:26–31)

The conquest of the Ammonites and their capital Rabbah is a considerable success. Joab is a loyal general, and he wants his king to have the honour of capturing the city.

The sins of the father... (2 Samuel 13:1–18:33)

David's adultery with Bathsheba and his murder of Uriah make it very difficult for him to correct his own sons. They know too much about him. We now see how two of David's sons, Amnon and Absalom, also behave disgracefully.

Amnon rapes his half-sister

Amnon is David's eldest son, and heir to the throne. He is infatuated with princess Tamar, but can't marry her because she is his half-sister. A crafty cousin, Jonadab, advises Amnon to pretend to be sick. The king will then send Tamar to look after him!

All goes according to plan – and Tamar finds herself alone in Amnon's bedroom. Despite her pleas, he seizes her, rapes her and throws her out.

Tamar's brother is Absalom. When he finds her in mourning, with ashes on her head and her royal robe torn, he immediately plans revenge. He is a patient man. It takes two years; but eventually Amnon is killed – and Absalom goes into hiding.

Absalom rebels

The king and Absalom don't see each other for three years, until Joab devises a way of bringing them together. He gets a wise old woman to come to King David with a moving story of a son who needs forgiveness. David sees that she is describing Absalom, and allows him to return home. But David ignores his son for another two years – and Absalom grows angry and rebellious.

Absalom is strikingly good-looking. He is especially proud of his long hair. One day he acquires a chariot and fifty men, and starts to pose as king-in-waiting.

Absalom encourages dissatisfied people to turn to him for help. If only he were king, he would give them their rights! He is over-friendly – stopping people bowing to him and shaking their hands or kissing them instead. This continues for four years – and then Absalom declares himself king in Hebron.

Absalom's following is large and growing. As he advances on Jerusalem, David decides to leave. He has no desire for bloodshed or civil war.

Absalom takes control of Jerusalem. He has Ahithophel, one of David's best counsellors, on his side. Ahithophel is Bathsheba's grandfather. He will advise Absalom to sleep with David's concubines. Does he want to humiliate the king for what was done to his granddaughter?

David leaves ten concubines (royal mistresses) in charge of his palace. As he reviews his troops, we notice that the foreign soldiers are loyal to David, although his own son is a rebel. Ittai the Gittite, for example, is a Philistine from Gath, the home town of the giant Goliath.

The people weep as the king crosses the Kidron Valley and journeys towards the desert. David gives instructions for the ark of the covenant to stay in the city. God is in control of everything, and well able to look after himself.

On the brow of the Mount of Olives, with a magnificent view of his royal city, David weeps. Jerusalem is rejecting her king, and no good can come of it. One day Jesus, too, will weep on this spot – and for the same reason (Matthew 23:37–39).

David sends some priests, including Zadok and Abiathar and their two sons, back into Jerusalem to act as informers.

David's behaviour in this crisis is calm and dignified. He has only ever been king by God's authority and the people's assent. If they don't want him any longer, so be it. He does not retaliate when the fiery Shimei curses him and throws stones!

Hushai versus Ahithophel

Meanwhile Absalom and Ahithophel are getting established in Jerusalem. Hushai the Archite appears to join them. Little does Absalom realize that when Hushai says, 'Long live the king!' he means King David.

The two counsellors, Hushai and Ahithophel, give Absalom conflicting advice. Ahithophel encourages Absalom to sleep with the king's concubines. Absalom agrees. He commits this outrage on the roof of the palace, for all to see.

Next Ahithophel advises Absalom to attack David quickly, overtaking his soldiers while they are tired. But Absalom consults Hushai as well.

Hushai points out that David and his men are experienced campaigners. Absalom would do well to marshal all his troops. This will take a while, but they will then surely overwhelm the king by force of numbers. This suggestion appeals to Absalom's pride, and he delays attacking David.

Hushai's advice to Absalom gives David time to organize his forces. He deploys his men in three sections, with Joab, Abishai and Ittai the Gittite as commanders. He gives strict orders to everyone that Absalom is not to be harmed.

In a running battle through the forest of Ephraim, David's units rout Absalom's men. The young prince himself is caught in a tree by his famous hair. Joab, true to form and against David's orders, kills him. When David hears the news, he is broken-hearted.

The final period of David's reign

David returns to Jerusalem; Sheba's rebellion
(2 Samuel 19:1–20:25)

Slowly the country unites again under David's rule. He is forgiving and fair as he deals with those who have rejected him; and those whose loyalty has been suspect.

There is friction between the ten northern tribes of Israel and the southern tribe of Judah. The leaders of Judah take David back to Jerusalem as 'their' king. David is, after all, from the tribe of Judah. The tribes of Israel feel left out, and this flares into a rebellion led by Sheba. The rebellion is crushed when Joab negotiates Sheba's execution in the northern town of Abel Beth Maacah.

Joab is listed as commander 'over Israel's entire army'. He has always been loyal to David – and always beyond his control. David has never checked him for his high-handed murder of rivals – including Absalom, the king's own son. But then, Joab knows how Uriah met his death! In the end, David passes the problem on to Solomon (1 Kings 2:6).

Vengeance for the Gibeonites (2 Samuel 21:1–14)

David accepts that, long ago, Saul wronged the Gibeonites. He hated them as foreigners and put some of them to death. God has sent drought as a result. Now David agrees an 'expiation' – that seven members of Saul's family shall be sacrificed. This act of revenge is requested by the Gibeonites, not commanded by God.

Great deeds (2 Samuel 21:15–22)

The names of great heroes are recorded, and especially those who were 'mentioned in dispatches' during skirmishes with the Philistines. David values the qualities and achievements of his warriors – some of them giant-killers like himself.

David's song of praise (2 Samuel 22:1–51)

David sings of the God who saves. God is a rock, a fortress, a shield and a Saviour. David has found himself protected from so many enemies and rescued from so many dangerous situations. He concludes that the Lord is the living God, with whom he has an ongoing relationship of honour and trust: 'The Lord lives!' (22:47). This psalm appears in a very similar version as Psalm 18 in the book of Psalms.

The last words of David (2 Samuel 23:1–7)

David speaks of the privilege of being the Lord's anointed king. He has found the beauty of reigning with righteousness and in the fear of God. Now he is sure that his royal line will continue after him.

David's mighty warriors (2 Samuel 23:8–39)

Some more of David's mighty warriors are listed, with brief descriptions of their exploits. Three of them stole through Philistine lines to get a drink of water for David from his favourite well at Bethlehem. Kabzeel, 'went down into a pit on a snowy day and killed a lion' (23:20)! But how poignant to see listed last among the 'Thirty' none other than Uriah the Hittite (23:39).

David's folly (2 Samuel 24:1–25)

For some reason David decides to count his armed forces. This is an affront to God, because it implies that David relies on his army for protection, instead of on the living God. Really he knows better, for he writes in a psalm:

Some trust in chariots and some in horses,
but we trust in the name of the Lord our God. (Psalm 20:7)

God punishes David's pride by sending a plague on Israel. The disease cuts down a large part of the population and threatens Jerusalem. David is guided to buy a particular threshing-floor which belongs to Araunah, one of the conquered Jebusites. Here he builds an altar and offers sacrifices to halt the plague, and the danger is averted. Araunah's threshing-floor is high up, overlooking the Kidron Valley. It will become the site of Solomon's temple.

1 and 2 KINGS

The books of Kings continue the story of Israel with the reign of Solomon and the building of the temple in Jerusalem. After Solomon's death the nation divides, with a northern kingdom of Israel and a southern kingdom of Judah.

We follow the parallel stories of both kingdoms, until the northern kingdom is defeated by the Assyrians with the capture of Samaria in 722 BC. After that we follow the history of Judah until Jerusalem is captured and destroyed by the Babylonians in 587 BC. The whole story covers a period of 500 years.

Most of Israel's kings fail her. Even Solomon, who asks God for wisdom and builds the temple, makes foolish compromises with paganism. During this period, the challenge to remain faithful to God is upheld by the prophets – especially Elijah and his younger companion and successor, Elisha.

Outline

The reign of King Solomon (1 Kings 1:1–11:43)
The kingdom is divided (1 Kings 12:1–16:34)
The prophets Elijah and Elisha (1 Kings 17:1–2 Kings 8:15)
The rulers of Judah and Israel (2 Kings 8:16–16:20)
The fall of Israel, the northern kingdom (2 Kings 17:1–41)
Judah, the southern kingdom, until the fall of Jerusalem (2 Kings 18:1–25:30)

Introduction

The books of Kings

The books of Kings follow on from the books of Samuel, and are intended to be read together with them. In the Hebrew Bible, the books of Kings complete a story which began way back in the time of Joshua.

The books of Joshua, Judges, Samuel and Kings are known as 'the Former Prophets'. These are the history books which tell the story of Israel from the arrival of the tribes in the Promised Land to the eventual loss of the land and Judah's exile in Babylon. They may have been written, edited or compiled during the years of exile.

The author has old songs, stories and other documents to hand. He mentions some of them, such as the 'Annals of the Kings of Israel and Judah'. None of them has survived for us to study today. The books we call 1 and 2 Chronicles were written after the Jews returned from exile and are not the same as the 'Chronicles' mentioned in 1 Kings 14.

Running through this history is a strong sense of God's purpose for his people. God has made a covenant with Israel, giving his law and promising his blessing. But, as the book of Deuteronomy points out, obedience and blessing go together. The author of these books is showing us how disobedience and idolatry lead to failure and God's judgment. Some scholars call these books the 'deuteronomic history', because of the strong influence of themes which come from the book of Deuteronomy.

When were the books of Kings written?

The books of Kings were written some time after 561 BC. King Jehoiachin is released from prison about halfway through the time of the Jewish exile in Babylon. This is the last event recorded in the books, which stop short of telling us how the Jewish exiles return to Jerusalem in 538 BC.

All the books from Joshua to 2 Kings may be the work of one author or editor, who is using older writings and records to retell the whole story. If so, he may be one of the people exiled with King Jehoiachin in 597 BC, just ten years before the temple is destroyed.

With their king in exile, their city in ruins and their land taken from them, the Israelites' faith in God has suffered a devastating blow. Perhaps the editor is compiling the work for friends and colleagues in the exiled royal court, to try to make sense of the tragedy which has overtaken them. The prophets had warned that wicked and idolatrous behaviour would bring God's judgment upon them. This is the reason for the present disaster:

The Lord became angry with Solomon because his heart had turned away from the Lord, the God of Israel, who had appeared to him twice. Although he had forbidden Solomon to follow other gods, Solomon did not keep the Lord's command.

So the Lord said to Solomon, 'Since this is your attitude and you have not kept my covenant and my decrees, which I commanded you, I will most certainly tear the kingdom away from you and give it to one of your subordinates. Nevertheless, for the sake of David your father, I will not do it during your lifetime. I will tear it out of the hand of your son. Yet I will not tear the whole kingdom from him, but will give him one tribe for the sake of David my servant and for the sake of Jerusalem, which I have chosen.'
(1 Kings 11:11–13)

The books of Kings give a long account of the reign of Solomon – and then a brief account of the reign of Joash. Yet both kings are said to have reigned for forty years. King Omri is an important figure on the international scene – but his reign is summed up in a few verses: 'Omri did evil in the eyes of the Lord and sinned more than all those before him' (1 Kings 16:25).

Every king in these books is assessed by the same standard: is he faithful to God or not? Does he build pagan altars on the hilltops (the 'high places') or pull them down? The kings that encourage idolatry are leading their people astray, and bringing destruction on their kingdoms.

Two great prophets

The books of Kings also tell the stories of two great prophets, Elijah and Elisha. Elijah dominates 1 Kings 17–19 and 2 Kings 1–2. His successor, Elisha, is the major prophetic figure in 2 Kings 2–8, with further appearances in chapters 9 and 13.

Stories of other prophets are also included in 1 Kings 20 and 22.

DISCOVERING 1 AND 2 KINGS

The reign of King Solomon

Solomon's reign (1 Kings 1:1–4:34)

There is some doubt as to who will succeed David as king. Adonijah puts himself forward, but both Bathsheba and Nathan make sure that Solomon is chosen. Solomon is David's son by Bathsheba. He is anointed by Zadok the priest and Nathan the prophet. David advises him to walk in God's ways, and commissions him to repay favours and settle old scores.

The reigns of David and Solomon are the high point of Israel's history. Solomon asks God for wisdom, and becomes a man of great insight and judgment. He establishes a lavish royal household, supplied by twelve districts. He builds up a large army and, with the help of the seagoing Phoenicians, develops foreign trade. All this is expensive in money and human resources. Samuel had warned that a king would be a burden to his people (1 Samuel 8:10–18).

Solomon's building projects (1 Kings 5:1–9:28)

Building the temple and the palace

Solomon starts to build the temple. Hiram king of Tyre sends cedar and pine from Lebanon, floated on rafts by sea to Joppa. The quarrying and cutting of stone is another major task, involving an army of workers and the advice of foreign experts. All the stone dressing is done at the quarry, so that there is no violent action on the site.

The temple is built on the threshing-floor of Araunah, which David bought to make a sacrifice when Jerusalem was threatened by plague (2 Samuel 24:18–25). Today the Muslim Dome of the Rock stands there – the 'rock' being the place where Abraham was told to sacrifice Isaac (Genesis 22:2). Both Jews and Muslims honour Abraham as a patriarch.

The temple is similar in layout to the old tabernacle, but larger. It has an entrance hall (portico), a sanctuary (the 'Holy Place') and an inner sanctuary (the 'Most Holy Place'). It is in the inner sanctuary that the ark of the covenant will be housed. The ark contains the tablets of stone on which are written the Ten Commandments. The inner sanctuary is shaped like a cube, to provide the 'perfect' space for a holy God.

The writer tells us that it takes seven years to build Solomon's temple. The temple which is built by Herod the Great in Jesus' time takes far longer. It is scarcely completed before it is destroyed by the Romans in AD 70.

Solomon also builds a palace for himself, which is called the 'Palace of the Forest of Lebanon' because of its fine cedar pillars and beams. The throne hall is larger than the temple and provides an impressive court, in which Solomon delivers his famous judgments. It takes thirteen years to build this palace – which is perhaps an indication of Solomon's real priorities.

A skilled worker called Huram

The bronze furnishings for the temple are all the work of Huram, whom Solomon brings from the Phoenician port of Tyre. Two mighty bronze pillars are given the names 'Jakin' ('solid') and 'Boaz' ('strong') – although their exact position is not known.

A great bronze basin, called 'the sea', is the successor to the tabernacle basin. It is used by the priests for washing their hands and feet. It is a superb feat of engineering, measuring fifteen feet across and holding about 10,000 gallons of water.

Solomon doesn't weigh the bronze furnishings, but they are all carefully listed, and their detail lovingly remembered. Tragically, they will one day become plunder for the Babylonians, who will cart them away in triumph (Jeremiah 52:17–23).

The temple is dedicated

The dedication of the temple is the greatest moment of Solomon's reign (8:1–66). The ark of the covenant is carried into the temple by the priests. It is brought from Zion, the southern hill of Jerusalem. The ark unites the days of God's guidance in the wilderness with the grace of his presence now – and the whole city becomes known as 'Zion'. So Jerusalem becomes the centre for both the worship of God and the reign of David's descendants.

The cloud of God's presence fills the temple. This is the cloud which once surrounded the tabernacle. Sometimes it is thick and dark, cloaking God's presence. Sometimes it is dazzlingly bright, denoting his glory. This same cloud will surround Jesus at his transfiguration (Luke 9:34) and receive him at his ascension (Acts 1:9).

Standing before the people, Solomon declares that he has fulfilled the plans of God and his father David. Kneeling before the altar, he prays. He asks that the new building may always be a focal point of God's care, and a place of justice, mercy and new beginnings for his people. He includes a remarkable plea that foreigners will come to this place and receive God's healing and help. Solomon truly shares God's vision that the whole world may find God through the witness of Israel (8:60).

The dedication of the temple is celebrated in a series of offerings and sacrifices, and with a great festival lasting for two weeks.

God appears to Solomon

The writer tells us that God appears to Solomon on two occasions. The first is at Gibeon, where the young king goes to make sacrifices in the early days of his reign. It is at Gibeon that Solomon asks God to give him the wisdom he needs to rule his people well (3:7–12).

Now (again, after a period of commitment and sacrifice), God appears to Solomon a second time (9:1–9). He tells Solomon that the temple is nothing without obedience and faith. He promises Solomon that his royal line will continue. However, he also warns that if Israel worships other gods, disaster will surely follow. The books of Kings are the story of how these words come true.

The queen of Sheba visits Solomon (1 Kings 10:1–13)

Solomon is now internationally famous. His wealth and wisdom make him a living legend. Not only has he built a fine temple and palace, but he has developed trade routes and built a fleet of ships on the Red Sea.

The queen of Sheba comes from Arabia to visit Solomon. Today her country is Yemen. She comes to trade both goods and ideas, and is deeply impressed by all she sees. She praises the God who has done all this for Solomon.

Solomon's downfall (1 Kings 11:1–43)

God has clearly honoured Solomon's request for wisdom and has also given him great wealth. Sadly, the king's confidence now starts to shift from God to his riches. His wisdom also is undermined by his marriages to foreign princesses.

Solomon's problems begin when he uses marriage to make treaties with other nations. This results in him taking wives who bring their pagan gods and practices into his palace and the life of the nation. Although it was usual for kings to have several wives (David had fifteen!), God has expressly forbidden the marrying of foreigners (Deuteronomy 7:1–4) and the taking of many wives (Deuteronomy 17:14–20). Solomon systematically disobeys all these commands, with his wives, weapons and wealth.

Solomon loses his desire to serve God, and becomes a slave to his lust for women. Their gods are the old Canaanite gods. Ashtoreth is the goddess of fertility, who is worshipped in bloodshed and sex. Molech is a god who is worshipped with child sacrifice. Solomon provides places of worship for them, and then joins in himself.

All this makes God angry. For judgment, he resolves that the kingdom will not pass intact to Solomon's descendants. However, because of David's faithfulness (and his promise to him) God grants that one tribe will continue to be ruled by Solomon's line. This will be the southern kingdom of Judah, which includes the capital, Jerusalem, and the temple.

Solomon's problems start to mount up. He has two particular enemies in Hadad and Rezon. Hadad is a survivor of one of Joab's massacres who now has the backing of the king of Egypt. Rezon is a rebel who seizes control of the area around Damascus in the northern part of the kingdom. But the greatest threat to Solomon's reign is much closer. His trusted servant Jeroboam turns traitor.

Jeroboam's ambition to be king is awakened by a prophet, Ahijah. Ahijah dramatically tears his own new cloak into twelve pieces. He predicts that the twelve tribes of Israel will be divided up – ten to Jeroboam and two to the descendants of David and Solomon. It seems that Jeroboam attempts a coup but then flees to Egypt. The king of Egypt, Shishak, is called Sheshonq I in other records. He rules from 945 to 924 BC.

Solomon dies in 932 BC, after a reign of forty years. He is succeeded by his son Rehoboam.

The kingdom is divided

After the reign of Solomon, the kingdom of Israel splits in two. Ten northern tribes, led by Jeroboam, become the nation of Israel. The remaining and largest tribe, Judah-with-Benjamin, is ruled by Solomon's son, Rehoboam.

Israel rebels against King Rehoboam (1 Kings 12:1-24)

Solomon's reign has been harsh on many Israelites. They have become slaves to his building projects, which have taken them away from their families and land. Now the people ask Rehoboam for an easier life – but he refuses. The narrative sounds rather like the story of Exodus, with Rehoboam as Pharaoh and Jeroboam as a new Moses, calling for justice and liberation.

Solomon had asked God for wisdom, but his son takes the advice of hot-headed friends. The result is that Jeroboam wins the support of the northern tribes, while the southern kingdom shrinks to the tribes of Judah and Benjamin. Both stray from God's way. Rehoboam chooses oppression and Jeroboam chooses idolatry.

King Jeroboam worships idols (1 Kings 12:25-33)

Jeroboam begins his reign in the north by making Shechem his capital. Shechem is in Ephraim, which is Jeroboam's home country. It has been a religious site since the days of the Canaanites, and a place of dedication and decision since the time of Abraham.

Jeroboam is insecure. He fears that his people will still be drawn to worship in Jerusalem, and then revert to a king of David's line. To avert this, he sets up a religion of his own, with idols, shrines and priests. He strengthens his control of his people by providing worship centres at Dan in the far north and at Bethel in the south. The shrine at Bethel blocks the way to Jerusalem. The whole state of Israel is idolatrous from the start (Amos 7:13).

The idolatry continues (1 Kings 13:1-14:31)

A 'man of God' arrives at Bethel from Judah. He condemns what Jeroboam is doing. He is a true prophet, and his message is confirmed by the withering of the king's hand and the splitting of the altar. However, he is distracted and misled by a rival prophet, and dies.

From now on, the work of the prophets becomes increasingly important. They take their stand and declare God's word; but they are only proved true if their message is fulfilled. There will be a constant rivalry between true and false prophets – with the added twist that God can even use false prophets to reveal his truth!

Ahijah's prophecy against Jeroboam

When Jeroboam's son falls dangerously ill, he sends his wife to seek advice from the prophet Ahijah. The queen disguises herself in the hope of getting a favourable message, but the prophet knows who she is before she even enters his house. Ahijah delivers a message of judgment which foretells death for her son and disaster for her husband (14:1-20). Jeroboam has failed to be a king like David, and so his line will die out.

Kings of Judah and Israel (1 Kings 15:1-16:34)

The writer now gives a parallel account of the northern and southern kingdoms. He briefly describes each king, giving his name, age, date of succession and length of rule.

The writer always notes whether a king does 'right' or 'evil' in the sight of God, and points out the consequences. David is the standard by which all other kings are judged – although even he failed to keep God's commands, when he committed adultery with Bathsheba (15:5).

The ten kings who do 'right' are all kings of Judah. They continue the line of David and enjoy longer reigns than the kings of Israel. Meanwhile, there are thirty-three kings of Israel who do 'evil'. They follow the idolatrous ways of Jeroboam and cause their people to do the same. There is little continuity of reign from father to son and several meet their deaths by rebellion or assassination.

King Abijah of Judah

Abijah (15:1-8) is the son of Rehoboam and his name means 'My Father is the Lord'. He takes after his father both in idolatry and war-mongering. He continues to promote pagan worship in Judah and also maintains the struggle against Jeroboam in their contest for the kingship of Israel. The royal line of David has fallen on hard times, but God keeps faith with Abijah, for the sake of the good things David did and to honour his promise to bless the heirs to David's throne.

King Asa of Judah

Abijah reigns a mere three years before he dies and is succeeded by Asa (15:9-24). Asa reigns for forty-one years, during which time he tries to purge pagan religions from Jerusalem and Judah. He even cuts down and burns his mother's (or, more likely, grandmother's) Asherah pole, which is a symbol for fertility rites. The historian describes Asa as 'true to the Lord all his days'.

Asa continues the war with Israel, which is now ruled by King Baasha. He bribes the king of Damascus to help him by invading Israel. This attack in the north takes pressure off Judah in the south, and the stronghold which Baasha has been building at Ramah is dismantled. Asa uses the materials of stone and timber to fortify two centres of his own at Geba and Mizpah.

In his old age, Asa suffers from a disease in his feet. This may be gout, or even a sexual disease. 'Feet' can be a polite word for private parts!

Although Asa is recorded as being a good man, he makes a fatal alliance in his dealings with the Arameans of Damascus. It is this kind of reliance upon a foreign power rather than God which will at last result in defeat for both Israel and Judah.

King Nadab of Israel

Nadab is the king of Israel while Asa is king of Judah (15:25-31). He is the son of Jeroboam and his rule is short and wicked. He is killed by Baasha during the siege of a Philistine stronghold. Baasha seizes the throne and eliminates all Nadab's relatives, thus putting an end to the descendants of Jeroboam. This is seen as a judgment on Jeroboam and the fulfilment of a prophecy by Ahijah of Shiloh (not to be confused with Ahijah the father of Baasha!).

King Baasha of Israel

After so violently seizing power, Baasha rules Israel for twenty-four years (15:32-16:7). Although he has overthrown the line of Jeroboam, he continues with the same damaging idolatry. In God's sight he is doubly guilty, because he has destroyed a royal line which God had set up. A prophet called Jehu declares that God's judgment will fall on Baasha and his family.

King Elah of Israel

Baasha is succeeded by his son Elah, whose reign is a mere two years (16:8-14). He is assassinated by one of his senior commanders, Zimri, while he is too drunk to defend himself.

King Zimri of Israel

Zimri (16:15-20) himself takes the throne and makes his first act to kill off all Elah's male relatives and friends. There are to be no reprisals. Jehu's prophecy against Baasha's family has been fulfilled.

Zimri has only been king a week when the troops besieging Gibbethon hear of his rebellion and murder of Elah. They make their commander, Omri, king instead. Omri marches on Zimri's capital at Tirzah; but Zimri takes matters into his own hands and commits suicide by setting fire to his house with himself in it.

King Omri and Samaria

King Omri of Israel (16:21-28) is a powerful figure whose name is mentioned on Assyrian inscriptions. He rules for twelve years, making the hill town of Samaria his capital, and so founding a country which has kept the same name ever since. Our writer says that 'Omri sinned more than all those before him' (16:25) and became the father of another wicked king, Ahab.

Ahab becomes King of Israel

Ahab is a king like Jeroboam (16:29-34). He rules Israel from about 874 to 854 BC. In Samaria he builds a temple to the nature god Baal, whose name means 'Lord' or 'husband'. He also marries a pagan princess of legendary wickedness, called Jezebel.

The prophets Elijah and Elisha

Elijah and King Ahab (1 Kings 17:1-2 Kings 2:18)

Elijah proclaims a drought

One of the greatest prophets in the Old Testament emerges to oppose Ahab. His name is Elijah.

Elijah steps forward to confront Ahab with the word and power of Israel's true God. He declares that the whole land will suffer drought – until Elijah himself gives the word for rain to fall again (17:1-6).

Elijah is challenging the widespread faith in Baal. Baal is the old Canaanite god of rain, whose dying brings drought and whose rising brings new life. Now the Lord, the God of Israel, will be shown to be the true God.

As the drought takes hold, God protects Elijah in hiding by the Kerith Ravine. There the prophet has a steady supply of water, and ravens bring him food.

Elijah and the widow at Zarephath

When the Kerith brook dries up, God guides Elijah to a widow who lives at Zarephath, which today is Sarafand, near Sidon (17:7-24). Sidon is a Phoenician city on the coast – well away from the attentions of Ahab and Jezebel! The widow is foreign, pagan and living in Jezebel's own country; but Elijah has to depend on her for refuge.

When Elijah first meets the widow she is about to prepare a last meal for herself and her son. He tests her faith by asking her first to prepare some food for him. She does so. In the months that follow, her small supply of flour and oil never runs out. The writer tells us that this is to show that Elijah speaks for God and that his word is true.

Elijah is able to help the widow in an even more wonderful way, when her son dies. The woman assumes that she is being punished for some secret sin, and reproaches the prophet for exposing her to God's justice. But Elijah stretches himself on the boy and calls on God to return his life. The child is restored, and his mother declares her faith that Elijah is God's true messenger. The miracle is an encouragement to Elijah, too. His is a lone voice in a hostile situation.

Contest at Carmel

After three years of drought, Elijah presents himself to Ahab again. The king has been sending out search parties for him, while Jezebel has been slaughtering all the prophets she can find. Elijah makes contact with Ahab through a royal servant, Obadiah. This man has remained faithful to God (and protected his prophets) during the dangerous days of Jezebel's persecution.

Elijah challenges Ahab to meet him on the summit of Mount Carmel. He is to bring with him the people of Israel and the prophets of Baal (18:1-46).

Mount Carmel is on the coast, overlooking the sea. Once there, Elijah urges God's people to stop wavering in their faith between God and Baal. There is only one true God, and they must make their choice.

To prove his point, Elijah invites the prophets of Baal to build an altar and prepare a sacrifice. When all is ready, they must call on Baal to light the fire.

The Baal prophets accept the challenge. They cry to their 'Lord' from dawn to dusk – capering round the altar and cutting themselves in frenzy. As they do so, Elijah teases them. Perhaps Baal's attention has wandered? He may be thinking of something else, or locked in the bathroom, or away on business? He's obviously not the kind of god who can handle too much at any one time. Better shout louder!

Then Elijah takes his turn. He repairs the altar of the Lord, which has fallen into disrepair. He uses twelve stones to remind the people that they are the twelve tribes of Israel. He avoids any cheating by digging a trench around the altar and drenching the wood and sacrifice with water – three times over. And then he prays.

God's fire doesn't just lick up from the heart of the wood – it falls from heaven! The people also fall – face down – to acknowledge the true God. Then they round up the Baal prophets and kill them. This is not cruel vengeance, but the punishment laid down for false prophets (Deuteronomy 13:1–5).

Now Elijah takes charge. He tells the king to have a meal, while he himself prays for rain. When a small cloud appears on the horizon, far out to sea, Elijah sends word that Ahab must take shelter. The king drives his chariot seventeen miles – to his summer palace in Jezreel. Elijah – on a spiritual 'high' – runs ahead of him all the way!

Elijah at Horeb

Suddenly, after the triumph of Carmel, Elijah realizes he has Jezebel to reckon with. All his energy drains from him, and terror strikes his heart. He flees for his life – south to Beersheba, where he leaves his servant, and on into the desert (19:1–18).

Exhausted, Elijah sits down under a broom tree and begs to die. Instead, he sleeps; and when he wakes there is hot food and fresh water awaiting him. He eats and sleeps and eats again. Then he travels for forty days and nights – to Horeb, the mountain of God.

The number (forty) and the place (Sinai) show us that Elijah is following in the steps of Moses. Moses led the Israelites for forty years in this wilderness, and met with God at this mountain. Does Elijah spend the night in the same cave in which Moses hid his face while God passed by (Exodus 33:22–23)?

At last, God speaks: 'What are you doing here, Elijah?' (19:9). Is Elijah scared of Jezebel, even though he has so recently seen the far greater power of God? Is he consumed with self-pity, sunk in depression or breaking under stress? Elijah expresses all these conditions as he confesses that he feels persecuted and totally alone.

God invites his prophet to stand outside the cave. He demonstrates the titanic forces of nature in whirlwind, earthquake and fire. But God himself is not in any of these, which are merely his creations. And then there is a gentle whisper. Perhaps even silence.

Again, God asks the question. Again, Elijah pours out his complaint and fear. Then God, clearly and firmly, shows the way ahead. He directs Elijah to anoint two kings, Hazael and Jehu, and to appoint Elisha as his own successor.

Elijah is to take heart. God's purposes will continue to unfold and triumph. He is preparing a new generation of leaders to do his work – and 7,000 faithful Israelites (a perfect number) are praying that it will be accomplished.

The Call of Elisha

As far as we know, Elijah never anoints Hazael or Jehu. Perhaps it is enough that God has revealed them to Elijah as key people for the future. Instead, he journeys back to Judah and to Abel Meholah in the Jordan Valley – the home of Elisha (19:19–21).

The young Elisha is ploughing with oxen when Elijah claims his life by throwing his cloak around him. Elisha begs to say goodbye to his parents, but Elijah is offended by any delay. A backward-looking disciple is useless, as Jesus himself will say one day – and with a ploughing image to match (Luke 9:62).

An age of miracles

The stories of Elijah and Elisha feature several miracles. The coming of drought and the feeding by ravens are the first of many ways in which God honours, protects and vindicates his prophets.

Miracles in the Bible are clustered around the key points of the story. They occur first at the exodus, when God rescues his people from Egypt and provides them with food and water in the desert. Now there is another season of miracles in the time of the prophets. God's people are again in deep trouble, with their faith almost extinguished by a sexually debauched and superstitious pagan culture.

In the event, Elisha *does* delay – but only long enough to chop up his plough for firewood and roast the oxen for a farewell feast.

The first two tasks which God gives to Elijah – the anointing of Hazael (2 Kings 8:15) and of Jehu (2 Kings 9) – are in fact performed by Elisha. Hazael is anointed to be king of Syria in place of Ben-Hadad. Jehu is anointed to be king in Israel in place of Jehoram (Ahab's son).

Ahab's wars

The writer now turns from the story of Elijah and Elisha, and narrates Ahab's military campaigns against Syria (20:1–34). The issue is whether Ahab will now trust God or not.

Ahab's capital, Samaria, is under attack from his northern neighbour, King Ben-Hadad of Aram (Syria). Ben-Hadad's forces are considerably stronger, and he makes oppressive demands on Ahab and the Israelites. However, Ahab takes the advice of a prophet and sends his young officers against the Arameans, ahead of the main Israelite force. The plan meets with unexpected success, as they defeat their enemy in the hills.

The following year, God again gives Ahab victory against huge odds – this time on a plain. Ben-Hadad is trapped in a city called Aphek and forced to beg Ahab for mercy. Ahab agrees, releasing his enemy and making a trading agreement with him.

Ahab, like Saul, has acted without consulting God and obeying him. Through one of his prophets, God tells Ahab that his own life is now forfeit for sparing Ben-Hadad.

It suits Ahab to make an alliance with Ben-Hadad. They need each other against the rising power of Assyria. Israel and the Arameans will join forces to fight Assyria in the battle of Qarqar in 853 BC – the year before Ahab's death. This battle is known from Assyrian records, although it is not mentioned in the Old Testament.

Naboth's vineyard

King Ahab makes Naboth an offer for his vineyard, which is next door to the summer palace in Jezreel. Naboth refuses. He has every right to do so, for this is his family's land for all time (21:1–29).

While Ahab sulks, his wife Jezebel gets to work. She sets up a neighbourhood feast, at which Naboth is accused of blasphemy and stoned to death. Ahab wastes no time in going to take possession of the vacant vineyard, but is confronted on the road by Elijah. Elijah is just as passionate for justice for Naboth as he was for God's reputation at Mount Carmel. He declares that Ahab and Jezebel will die for their sins and their dynasty will end. But Ahab repents and God spares him this immediate disaster.

Micaiah prophesies against Ahab

The king of Judah, Jehoshaphat, makes an alliance with Ahab, the king of Israel. They hope to recapture the city of Ramoth Gilead from Aram (the Syrians). Ramoth Gilead is important for trade, because it protects the caravan route to the east.

The kings agree to seek God's guidance by consulting the prophets (22:1–28). They summon 400 prophets – all of whom predict victory over Aram. But Ahab insists that they consult one last prophet, Micaiah, although he dislikes both the man and his messages.

At first Micaiah, with heavy sarcasm, repeats the assurance of victory. But when Ahab presses him for the truth, Micaiah declares that God has inspired the other prophets with a lie. The allies are heading for disaster and Ahab is being lured to his death.

Micaiah is thrown into prison for his insolence; but events prove him right. The episode is a warning. We cannot lightly discover God's will, without honest listening and wise judgment. Ahab asks for God's guidance and then refuses it. He goes to his death knowing full well that he is rejecting the prophet's message.

The death of Ahab

King Ahab dies in the battle of Ramoth Gilead (22:29–40). In spite of disguising himself, he is mortally wounded by an arrow fired at random. When Ahab's blood is washed out of his chariot, the dogs lick it up – as Elijah had predicted. The writer closes the record of Ahab's reign by noting his various building projects and the style and wealth of his palace. Ahab is succeeded by his son Ahaziah, who reigns for only two years.

King Jehoshaphat

Jehoshaphat's reign in Judah runs parallel to Ahab's reign in Israel (22:41–50). As we know from his desire to seek God's guidance, he is one of the rare kings who tries to do what is right (22:7).

Jehoshaphat clears the country of male shrine-prostitutes, but neither he nor his father removes the 'high places'. These are the hill altars and platforms at which people worship pagan gods.

Elijah and King Ahaziah

Ahaziah is the new king of Samaria (the northern kingdom of Israel) (2 Kings 1:1–8). He takes after his father, Ahab. He and the prophet Elijah quickly fall out.

When Ahaziah is severely injured, he seeks hope for recovery from a pagan idol, Baal-Zebub. Elijah meets the king's messengers on the way to the idol's shrine, and turns them back! Ahaziah should be asking for help from the God of Israel.

The king threatens Elijah by sending two companies of soldiers to arrest him; but the old prophet calls down fire from heaven to consume them. This fierce act of judgment reveals the true struggle between God's prophet and the new king. It is a trial of strength just as serious as the contest on Mount Carmel.

Only when God assures Elijah of his safety does he agree to appear before the king. There he repeats his sentence and the king dies.

Elijah is taken into heaven

Elijah is one of the greatest of the Old Testament prophets. He does not die in the usual way, but is taken into heaven by a whirlwind (2 Kings 2:1–18).

On the day of Elijah's departure, he and his younger companion Elisha visit three groups of prophets. They go to Bethel, Jericho and Gilgal. In each place Elijah urges Elisha to stay – perhaps to make a new home there; but Elisha refuses.

Finally, Elijah strikes the River Jordan with his cloak. The waters part and the two prophets cross the dry river bed together.

In their final conversation, Elisha asks his master if he might inherit 'a double portion' of his spirit. He is asking Elijah to treat him as his eldest son. Elijah has no power to give God's gift to someone else; but he knows that if Elisha is able to see him pass into heaven, then the same spirit is being given to him.

Suddenly a fiery chariot and horses separate the two men, and Elijah is taken up to heaven in a whirlwind. Elisha is left alone – with the cloak which has fallen from Elijah's shoulders. The first sign that he has inherited Elijah's spirit is that he is able to part the River Jordan as his master had done.

Elijah's ascension is a great honour. It was said of Enoch that he 'walked with God; then he was no more, because God took him away' (Genesis 5:24). There is also a legend that Moses didn't die, because his body was never found. It is Moses and Elijah who appear to talk with Jesus at his transfiguration (Mark 9:4). They are with Jesus on that occasion because Moses stands for the Law and Elijah for the Prophets – the two great strands of teaching which lead to Christ.

The stories of Elisha (2 Kings 2:19–8:15)

Elisha's miracles

There are a number of miracles associated with Elisha – some of them quite different from other miracles in the Bible.

He helps a community in Jericho by curing their foul spring water with salt (2:19–22).

He curses young hooligans who insult him. They challenge him to ascend into heaven – and tease him for his baldness; but his curse results in them being mauled by bears (2:23–24)! This is not just a fit of temper on Elisha's part. The youngsters are attacking and mocking the authority of God in him.

He advises the kings of Israel and Judah how to trap rain from a flash flood, and so provide water for their armies (3:14–20).

He helps a prophet's widow pay off her debts by telling her to pour her small amount of oil into her neighbours' empty jars (4:1–7).

He promises a wealthy but childless woman of Shunem that she will have a son in a year's time – and she does (4:8–17).

Some years later, the child dies suddenly. The mother rides to Carmel to find Elisha. For immediate help, the prophet sends his servant Gehazi with his staff to lay on the boy's face. Then he follows, and stretches himself on the child and restores his life (4:18–37).

When a group of prophets fear their stew is poisoned, Elisha tells them how to make it safe (4:38–41).

He assures his servant that twenty loaves of barley bread and some ears of corn will be enough to feed 100 men. It is so – and there is some left over (4:42–44). This miracle is imitated and amplified by Jesus when he feeds a multitude. In John's Gospel they call Jesus 'the Prophet' because of it.

All these miracles demonstrate God's power to heal, help or judge. They are all linked with particular people or places as though they were valued and remembered by these communities for many years.

Some of Elisha's miracles (such as curing a water supply or using a staff for power) echo the great deeds of Moses. Others (like the supply of oil for the widow or raising a child to life) are similar to the works of Elijah. Most of all, they foreshadow some of the miracles of Jesus, who raises Jairus' daughter to life and feeds a large crowd of people from a few barley loaves.

Unlike Elisha, Jesus does not use curses and acts of revenge – except in his condemnation of the Pharisees for their hypocrisy, and the cursing of a fig tree for its lack of fruit. On both occasions he is expressing God's frustration with pretence. When Jesus' disciples want to call down fire from heaven on a Samaritan village, he rebukes them (Luke 9:54–55). While Jesus preaches that God will certainly judge people, his own miracles are acts of mercy. As the Bible record unfolds, people get an ever-clearer concept of what God is really like.

Naaman is healed of leprosy

Naaman (5:1-27) is the supreme commander of the army of Aram – that is, Syria. Syria is Israel's northern neighbour, with whom she has recently been at war. Naaman's fame rests on the fact that God granted him victory. His wife's serving girl is an Israelite who was captured in a raid across the border.

Naaman is his nation's strong man – and yet he is a leper. Leprosy is an incurable skin disease, which will certainly isolate him from other people, and may eventually kill him. But the Israelite serving girl advises her master to seek help from Elisha.

Naaman travels to Israel. He takes with him a large amount of silver and gold, together with valuable clothes or rolls of cloth. He also bears a letter addressed to the king of Israel, requesting a cure.

The king of Israel is dismayed and powerless, but Elisha offers help. When Naaman and his impressive company arrive at Elisha's house, the prophet merely sends out a message. The Syrian commander is to wash himself seven times in Israel's river! Naaman feels grossly insulted and starts for home in a rage, but his servants persuade him to do as the prophet says.

Naaman washes himself in the River Jordan and is healed. He tries to reward Elisha from his treasury of gifts, but the holy man refuses. This is God's work and he wants no payment. Naaman resolves to worship the God of Israel – and takes some local soil to make a place of prayer at home.

Elisha's servant Gehazi can't bear to see so much wealth on offer without taking any of it. He runs after Naaman with a story that some silver and clothes are needed after all – and then lies to Elisha that he hasn't been anywhere.

Elisha confronts Gehazi with the truth. This is a serious abuse of God's grace as well as a breach of trust between them. He condemns Gehazi to contract Naaman's leprosy and dismisses him from his service. A mighty act of God has been spoilt by human sin. A similar greed corrupted

Achan after Israel's conquest of Jericho (Joshua 7:20) – and he was just as severely punished.

Naaman is mentioned by Jesus when he preaches in Nazareth. Naaman's cure is an example of God responding to true faith, wherever he finds it, even if the person is an enemy, a foreigner and a leper. God has the right to bless and heal whoever he chooses, however much popular opinion may disapprove (Luke 4:27)!

More stories about Elisha

The writer gives us many more stories of Elisha's miraculous powers and perceptions.

He retrieves an iron axe-head from a river (6:1–7).

He keeps the king of Israel informed of his enemy's most secret plans (6:8–12).

He trusts absolutely in God's protection, whatever the odds (6:13–18).

He prays that enemy soldiers will be blinded, leads them into captivity and then advises that they be fed and sent home (6:18–23)!

He predicts the precise day when a siege of Samaria will be unexpectedly lifted (6:24–7:20).

He warns the Shunammite woman that a famine is coming, so that she and her family can move to safety. His influence enables her to have her land restored when she returns (8:1–6).

He foresees that Hazael, the king of Aram's trusted servant, will murder his master and become a cruel enemy of Israel (8:7–15).

The rulers of Judah and Israel

Our historian now returns to his account of the rulers of Israel and Judah. There is a strange coincidence in that both nations have kings called Jehoram, although the name of Israel's king is helpfully shortened to 'Joram'.

The writer gives us a history of Judah and Israel in parallel. He tells us the names and ages of kings, the years of their reigns and (in the case of the kings of Judah) the names of their mothers. As before, he is most concerned to record whether or not they do 'right' or 'evil' in the eyes of God.

Jehu, king of Israel (2 Kings 9:1–10:36)

The first mention of Jehu is when God tells Elijah to anoint him as king of Israel (1 Kings 19:16). Elisha sends one of the young prophets to anoint Jehu when the reigning king, Joram, is wounded in battle. Jehu's task is to avenge God's prophets, whom Ahab and Jezebel have killed. Ahab has died, but his queen lives on, and it is their son Joram who is now on the throne of Israel.

Jehu rides with his fellow army officers to Jezreel, where Joram and Jezebel have a summer palace. Next to it is the vineyard for which Jezebel had Naboth murdered.

Jehu ('driving like a madman'!) meets Joram at the vineyard and kills him. He mortally wounds Joram's ally – Ahaziah, king of Judah. Then he rides on to Jezreel, where he calls on Jezebel's attendants to throw her from an upper window. They do so, and she is trampled to death by the horses' hoofs.

Later, when they come to bury Jezebel, they find that dogs have already devoured her corpse – just as Elijah had predicted (1 Kings 21:23).

Jehu's purge

Jehu has killed Ahab's son Joram and widow Jezebel. Now he has seventy other sons of Ahab executed, to prevent any further challenge to the throne (10:1–36). He puts an end to the evil 'house of Omri' which has ruled Israel for three generations.

Jehu also slaughters forty-two relatives of Ahaziah, who is king of Judah and Jezebel's grandson. He summons all the prophets of Baal to their temple in Samaria, leads them in an act of sacrifice and then has them massacred. These bloodthirsty actions are condemned by Hosea. Jehu may be fulfilling prophecy but he incurs God's anger by the way he does it.

Jehu has completed a revolution in Israel and Judah. He has purged two royal families and wiped out Baal-worship. He becomes king

King Hazael of Aram

Hazael has a long and important reign in Aram (Syria), from 843 to 796 BC. He becomes king after suffocating Ben-Hadad II and makes Damascus his capital. He is a tormentor of Israel through three reigns – those of Joram, Jehu and Jehoahaz. He is at various times both a vassal of and a rebel against the mighty empire of Assyria. Assyria at this time is ruled by Shalmaneser III.

himself and reigns for twenty-eight years. His dynasty will last for four generations. Sadly, the historian tells us that Jehu himself worships idols at the shrines of Bethel and Dan. Israel also loses territory to Hazael and the Arameans during his reign.

Queen Athaliah reigns in Judah (2 Kings 11:1–21)

The historian takes up the story of the southern kingdom of Judah. Jehu has killed the king, Ahaziah, but his mother Athaliah now seizes power. She is Jezebel's daughter.

Queen Athaliah tries to destroy Judah's royal family, the line of David. Fortunately, one of her half-sisters resists her, and manages to save Ahaziah's infant son, Joash. He is kept hidden with his nurse in the temple for six years. It is by this slender link that the line of David survives.

King Joash repairs the temple (2 Kings 12:1–21)

When Joash is seven years old, the priest Jehoiada proclaims him king. Athaliah is overthrown and killed. Joash begins a forty-year reign in which the covenant is renewed, Baal-worship is partly suppressed and the temple of Solomon is repaired.

Our historian judges that Joash does 'right' in the eyes of the Lord until Jehoiada dies, although the 'high places' are still left and used for pagan worship. At one point, Joash has to prevent the Aramean king Hazael marching on Jerusalem, by giving him many of the temple treasures. In the end, Joash is murdered by his own officials.

The death of Elisha (2 Kings 13:1-25)

In Israel, Jehu's son becomes king. His name is Jehoahaz, and he is infected by the paganism of Jeroboam. He is under constant pressure from Hazael, the strong king of Aram, but he seeks God's help and is granted some respite. After a reign of seventeen years he is succeeded by his son Jehoash.

It is during Jehoash's reign that Elisha dies. He has been a prophet in Israel for sixty years and has seen the reigns of six kings. When the king visits Elisha on his deathbed, the old prophet promises him some success against the forces of Aram (Syria).

One last miracle is associated with Elisha after he is buried. His bones raise a dead man to life.

King Amaziah versus Jehoash (2 Kings 14:1-22)

Soon after Jehoash becomes king in Israel, Amaziah becomes king in Judah. Amaziah is a good king – though not as good as David. He avenges his father's murder and leads a successful campaign against the Edomites in the desert to the south.

Flushed with success, and with Edomite gods to boost his confidence, Amaziah challenges Jehoash to hold talks. Jehoash refuses – likening himself to a great cedar and Amaziah to a little thistle. To assert his strength, Jehoash attacks Judah. He captures Amaziah, breaks down a section of Jerusalem's defences, ransacks the temple and royal palace, and takes hostages back to Samaria.

At some point in Amaziah's reign there is a rebellion against him. The details are unclear. It seems that his son Azariah is made either regent or king in about 790 BC, while his father is still alive. Azariah is also known as Uzziah, which may be his first name. Azariah may be a 'throne name' given him at his coronation.

Jeroboam II, king of Israel (2 Kings 14:23-29)

Jeroboam's long reign in Israel is mentioned only briefly. He rules for forty years, from 793 to 753 BC. He is the third generation of the line of Jehu and inherits the family's military prowess.

Israel's old enemy, Aram, is now much weaker, and the powerful Assyrians are busy fighting elsewhere. Jeroboam wins back land that has been lost in recent years, and restores Israel's boundaries as they were in the days of David and Solomon. The prophet Jonah (born a few miles north of Nazareth) predicts that God will give Jeroboam success.

Although Israel is strong and prosperous, the historian records that this is an evil reign. For him it is not power or wealth that counts, but faithfulness to God. The rich (especially the royal family) are living in luxury by crushing the poor. Idolatry is rife, with Baal-worship far more popular than the worship of the Lord, the God of Israel.

The prophet Amos is not mentioned here, but he travels north from Judah to preach in Israel at this time. He denounces the shallow faith and cruel injustice of Israelite society. This could have been a reign of peace and spiritual renewal. Instead, the northern kingdom continues on a course which will lead to its destruction.

Azariah, king of Judah (2 Kings 15:1–7)

Azariah (Uzziah) comes to the throne as co-regent with his father, in about 790 BC. This arrangement continues for twenty-four years, until he becomes king in his own right, in about 767 BC.

Azariah is often called Uzziah and is the greatest king of Israel since David. He reigns for a total of fifty-two years, including his years as regent. Although our historian says that Azariah does 'right', he notes that he fails to demolish the 'high places' – the hilltop shrines used for pagan worship.

Azariah (Uzziah) suffers from leprosy – a highly contagious skin disease. He has to live in isolation for the last years of his life. His son Jotham becomes regent and takes over the day-to-day government of the kingdom.

We know more about Azariah from 2 Chronicles. He has a well-trained, well-equipped army, which he uses to defeat both Philistines and Arabs. He strengthens the defences of Jerusalem. He also builds watchtowers to warn of approaching enemies and digs wells in the desert to provide water for people, cattle and crops.

But Azariah grows proud. He tries to act as a priest by burning incense in the temple. It is for this that God punishes him with leprosy (2 Chronicles 26:6–23). Isaiah mentions the year that Azariah dies, using the name Uzziah, as though an era of strength and stability is coming to an end (Isaiah 6:1).

The final kings of Israel (2 Kings 15:8–31)

The kings of Israel now follow one another in quick succession. There are six of them in twenty years, and all but one are assassinated.

The 'sins of Jeroboam I' still shape the nation's religion. Jeroboam had made two gold calf idols for worshipping the Baal-gods. He installed them in shrines in the north and south of Israel, to divert attention from the one true temple in Jerusalem. He also appointed his own order of priests.

Zechariah is assassinated by Shallum, bringing to an end the line of Jehu. Shallum reigns for only one month, before himself being assassinated by Menahem. Menahem is a tyrant who is capable of merciless cruelty.

The king of Assyria is Tiglath-Pileser III, whose personal name is Pul. From 743 BC he leads campaigns on the western borders of his empire. If paid enough, he will leave a people in peace.

Menahem of Israel reigns for a decade – clinging to power by paying tribute to Assyria. He passes on the cost to his people. Menahem manages to save both his life and his throne, and is the only king of this period to die of natural causes.

Menahem is succeeded by his son Pekahiah. He reigns for two years at the time Uzziah's reign is drawing to a close in Judah. Pekahiah is assassinated by Pekah, one of his leading generals, who then becomes king.

Our historian says that Pekah reigns for twenty years, but it is difficult to know how this is calculated. Some scholars think he reigned for only two years. Pekah resists Assyria's demands for tribute, and in the end refuses to pay. In reply, Assyria starts to invade Israel.

The first Assyrian campaign captures northern Galilee and Gilead (Trans-Jordan). The area becomes part of an Assyrian province ruled from Megiddo. Many leading Israelites are taken into exile in Assyria, so weakening the nation's power to recover.

Pekah is attacked and killed by Hoshea, who succeeds him as king. Tiglath-Pileser records how he puts Hoshea on the throne and makes him pay tribute in gold and silver.

The narrative of the fall of Israel continues at 17:1.

Meanwhile, in Judah... (2 Kings 15:32–16:20)

In the southern kingdom of Judah, we read of two more kings – Jotham and his son Ahaz.

King Jotham of Judah

Jotham (15:32–38) is the son of the great Azariah (Uzziah) who has been regent and then king for a total of fifty-two years.

Jotham is twenty-five. He is regent for most of his reign – the twelve years during which his father is still alive, but suffering from leprosy. After Uzziah's death, Jotham is king in his own right for only four years.

The writer of Chronicles tells us that Jotham is a good king (2 Chronicles 27:2). He avoids the pride that made Uzziah try to act as a priest. He defeats the Ammonites and forces them to pay a large amount of tribute money. He defends Judah against an invasion of Syrians and Ephraimites (Aram and Israel) from the north. But he fails to demolish the 'high places' of pagan worship.

King Ahaz of Judah

Ahaz becomes king at the age of twenty (16:1–20). He plunges Judah into further acts of idolatry. He even burns his own sons as sacrifices.

The writer of Chronicles tells how God punishes Ahaz with defeat by both Aram and Israel. There is terrible loss of life, and thousands of his people are taken to be slaves. However, a prophet challenges Israel to be merciful. Many of the hostages are well treated and allowed to return home (2 Chronicles 28:5–15).

Ahaz asks the king of Assyria, Tiglath-Pileser, for help against Aram (Syria) and Israel. He pays him with treasures from the temple and palace. Tiglath-Pileser invades Judah's northern enemies, capturing

Damascus and sending its people into exile. It is this event which is the context of the 'Immanuel' prophecy: that a young woman will give birth to a son as a sign of hope for the future (Isaiah 7:14).

Ahaz visits Damascus – perhaps to pay tribute to his Assyrian master. There he sees an altar which he greatly admires. He has a similar one made for the temple in Jerusalem – moving the old altar to the side of the new.

The new Assyrian altar is larger than the old bronze altar. It is used for offering sacrifices to the gods of Assyria, which seem to be at least as powerful as the God of Israel and Judah.

Ahaz makes many outrageous changes to the temple and its worship. He himself acts as a priest, offering every kind of sacrifice as Solomon once did. He also breaks up much of the bronze furniture to cash its wealth – either for his own treasury or to pay tribute to Assyria.

Judah's worship is now in chaos. Through all the years that the northern kingdom has had pagan shrines at Dan and Bethel, the southern kingdom has kept its temple for the exclusive worship of the living God. Now pagan practices are brought into the very heart of the Jerusalem temple. The God of Israel is worshipped alongside the gods of Assyria.

The fall of Israel, the northern kingdom

Hoshea, the last king of Israel (2 Kings 17:1–6)

Hoshea reigns for nine years. He tries to escape from Assyrian rule by making an alliance with Egypt. This provokes a second Assyrian campaign against Israel.

Assyria, now ruled by Shalmaneser, overruns the northern kingdom and lays siege to its capital, Samaria. After three years, Samaria falls and the Israelites are taken away from their land into captivity.

So ends the history of the northern kingdom of Israel. Her people are in exile in Assyria. In time they will be dispersed among people of other races and religions – and be lost without trace.

The reason why (2 Kings 17:7–23)

The writer explains that the fall of Israel is God's punishment for her sin.

Despite many warnings to turn back to God, the Israelites have been no different from the other nations. They have worshipped the fertility gods of their pagan neighbours. They have indulged in astrology, witchcraft and child sacrifice.

The Israelites have rejected the life of holiness to which God called them through his law and prophets. As the writer says: 'They followed worthless idols and themselves became worthless' (17:15).

With the tribes of the northern kingdom dispersed, there is now only the tribe of Judah left. Judah, the southern kingdom, must bear the name of God alone, and be his people among the nations.

The Samaritans (2 Kings 17:24–41)

People from various races are brought into Samaria to replace the Israelites. At first there is some fear of the God of Israel, because they believe that he still has power in the land – and because they are attacked by lions! Gradually the new 'Samaritans' adopt a mixture of religions, worshipping their various national gods rather than the Lord.

In later centuries the Samaritans will worship the God of the Old Testament. Their sacred books will be the books of Moses – the first five books of our Bible. But their mixed race and incomplete religion will make the Jews regard them as enemies.

Jesus sees Samaritans differently. He travels through Samaria on his way between Galilee and Jerusalem. He has a famous talk with a Samaritan woman whom he meets by a well, and makes a 'good' Samaritan the surprise hero of a well-known parable (Luke 10:25–37).

Judah, the southern kingdom, until the fall of Jerusalem

The historian tells us of the last 100 years of the southern kingdom of Judah. Although his story will end in disaster, he begins with the reign of a great and good king, Hezekiah.

King Hezekiah of Judah (2 Kings 18:1–20:21)

Hezekiah is twenty-five years old when he becomes king. The historian describes him as doing 'right' in the eyes of the Lord, as his ancestor David had done.

Hezekiah's reforms

Hezekiah does what so many of Judah's kings have failed to do. He tackles paganism. He removes the 'high places' of Baal-worship from rural hilltops and the platforms in towns and villages. He smashes the sacred stones which are used for altars. He chops up the poles of the goddess Asherah, which are fertility symbols. He even destroys the bronze snake which Moses once made for healing in the wilderness (Numbers 21:9), because people regard it as magical.

The Assyrian threat

Great events now overtake the reign of good king Hezekiah. Assyria is on the march (18:5–19:8).

The king of Assyria, Sennacherib, invades and conquers Samaria (the northern kingdom of Israel). From there he continues to move south, besieging and capturing the population of Judah. His own account of the campaign survives, with his record of forty-six walled cities captured and 200,150 people taken prisoner.

Sennacherib threatens to besiege Jerusalem. Hezekiah desperately tries to pay him off with large amounts of silver and gold, national treasures from the temple and palace, and the gold linings of the temple doors. But it isn't enough.

The Assyrian king sends a delegation to the outskirts of Jerusalem. His field commander speaks to the people of Jerusalem in their own language, and calls on them to surrender. He promises them safety and a new life. If they refuse, they will be destroyed.

The big question is whether the Lord God of Israel has enough power to defend his people. So far the armies of Assyria have proved stronger than every foreign god. Even the northern kingdom has been defeated...

In grief and near-despair, King Hezekiah seeks advice from the prophet Isaiah. This is the first we hear of Isaiah in the history books of the Bible. We know from his prophecies (in the book of Isaiah) that he is against turning to Egypt for help against Assyria (Isaiah 30:1–7).

Isaiah urges a straightforward trust in God. He sends a message to his king that there is no need to be afraid. The Assyrians will suddenly withdraw!

Isaiah is right. The Assyrians lift their siege of Jerusalem. Our historian explains that they were afraid of being attacked by the king of Egypt. Sennacherib's own record says that he has already defeated the Egyptians at the battle of Eltekah (701 BC). It seems more likely that the Assyrians receive news of trouble at home and go to attend to it. However this deliverance comes about, we see God's action in its perfect timing and completeness.

Hezekiah's prayer

King Hezekiah receives a threatening letter from the Assyrian king, Sennacherib. In it he says that Jerusalem's fate is sealed. Hezekiah needn't think that the God of Israel will be strong enough to save him.

Hezekiah spreads out the letter in the temple, in God's presence. He prays to God, who is the Lord of heaven and earth and king of all kingdoms. He begs him to help and deliver his people (19:9–19).

Isaiah's taunt song

God answers Hezekiah through his prophet Isaiah. Isaiah delivers a poem or chant which taunts Sennacherib for his pride (19:20–37).

Isaiah says that the Assyrian king has only been allowed such conquests as God permits. Now Sennacherib will be forced to withdraw from Judah. The land will recover from his invasion and the survivors will be able to harvest it once again in three years' time. Jerusalem is

---

The prophecies of Isaiah

Isaiah's early prophecies date from Jotham's reign. It is a time of pride and prosperity, but Isaiah sees disaster looming, because of Judah's resistance to God. He predicts a terrible destruction, but beyond it will come God's perfect reign. God will establish a new society, founded on the truth, justice and peace which he alone can give (Isaiah 2–5).

being protected for God's own sake, and for the sake of David, the faithful king who established it.

That night the Assyrian army suffers a disaster. Some kind of plague or dysentery sweeps through the camp. Our historian says that God does this – his angel killing 185,000 men. Sennacherib has no choice but to return to Nineveh. It is in Nineveh, some years later, that he is assassinated by his own sons.

Hezekiah's illness

Hezekiah is gravely ill – perhaps with a blood disease which has caused the eruption of a painful boil (20:1–11). Isaiah's verdict is that the king will die.

Hezekiah 'turns his face to the wall' and prepares to die. He asks God to remember the good deeds of his life, and weeps over his fate.

Suddenly God prompts Isaiah to return to the king. He promises him fifteen more years of life, and deliverance from the threat of Assyria. He also applies a poultice of figs to heal the boil. No doubt Isaiah has faith in the power of prayer – but medicine can do wonders, too!

As a sign that he will recover, the king is allowed to ask that the sun's shadow will move back ten steps on King Ahaz's stairway. Is this a miracle to show that God is giving Hezekiah extra time?

The shadow of Babylon

Hezekiah receives a delegation from Babylon – the power which will dominate the region after Assyria declines (20:12–21). Hezekiah treats his visitors as potential allies and shows them all his treasures. Isaiah

> ### The aqueduct of the Upper Pool
>
> The aqueduct where the Assyrian commander calls on Jerusalem to surrender (2 Kings 18:17) is the same place that Isaiah had once met King Ahaz. He urged him on that occasion to trust God against the threats of Rezin and Pekah, the kings of Aram and Israel (Isaiah 7:3–4). The Upper Pool is probably the Gihon spring on the east side of Jerusalem. It waters the fields as the stream follows the conduit (aqueduct) to a lower pool.

warns that one day all this wealth will be carried off to Babylon, together with members of the royal family.

The historian closes his account of Hezekiah's reign. He mentions the tunnel which Hezekiah has built, to supply Jerusalem with water during a siege. Hezekiah's Tunnel was discovered in 1880, running from the Gihon spring to the Upper Pool near Ophel and the Lower Pool in Jerusalem.

Manasseh, king of Judah (2 Kings 21:1–18)

Hezekiah, one of the best kings, is succeeded by his son Manasseh, who is one of the worst.

Manasseh has the longest reign of any king in Judah. As regent and king he rules for a total of fifty-five years. Assyria is strong and prosperous at this time, and there is peace for Judah because she is subject to Assyria.

Manasseh reverses the good work of Hezekiah. He brings back the worship of the Baal-gods. He rebuilds the 'high places' for pagan worship. He puts altars in the temple in honour of the stars. He encourages all kinds of occult practice, including witchcraft, communication with spirits and child sacrifice.

Manasseh's sins are as dreadful as anything that was done by the Canaanites in the past and for this reason Judah will be punished as they were. It is because of these sins that Judah is to suffer the same fate as Samaria (the northern kingdom of Israel) and the line of Ahab (Israel's most wicked king). She will be measured and judged by the same standard. Jerusalem will be wiped out and left upside down, like an empty dish, when she is sacked of people and property in 587 BC.

This is the only time that a king of Judah is compared to a king of Israel. Like Ahab, Manasseh slaughters innocent people, including God's prophets. There is a story among the Jews that Manasseh had Isaiah sawn in two (Hebrews 11:37).

Amon, king of Judah (2 Kings 21:19–26)

Amon's evil reign lasts for only two years. He sets out to be as wicked as his father, but his rule is cut short when he is assassinated by his own officials.

The reforms of King Josiah (2 Kings 22:1-23:30)

Josiah becomes king of Judah at the age of eight. He is the ideal king – ranking with his great-grandfather Hezekiah as a fitting descendant of King David.

Assyria's power is fading, which leaves Josiah free to make religious reforms. He organizes some repair work on the temple. It is while this work is being carried out that the old Book of the Law is found.

The Book of the Law

We don't know what the Book of the Law contains. It seems likely to be at least a large part of the book of Deuteronomy (22:8-13).

Deuteronomy contains Moses' farewell speech to the Israelites, when they are about to enter the Promised Land of Canaan. It lists the blessings that will come with obeying God's law and the curses that will result when it is broken (Deuteronomy 28:1-68). The final curse is that Israel will be uprooted from her land and her people scattered as slaves in exile (Deuteronomy 28:63-64).

When King Josiah hears this he tears his clothes in dismay. Judah has fallen so far from God's standard and committed so many of the sins that are forbidden. A prophetess called Huldah confirms that God is going to punish Judah – but not in Josiah's time, because of his humility and repentance.

King Josiah renews the covenant

Josiah calls everyone together. They meet in the temple – king, priests, prophets, leaders and ordinary folk.

Josiah reads aloud from the Book of the Covenant – the newly discovered Book of the Law. Then he leads his people in making a new commitment to God (23:1-3). This is a covenant – a marriage between God and his holy people Israel. He will always provide for them and protect them. They will always worship and obey him.

Josiah purges paganism

Now Josiah clears Judah of every trace of pagan worship (23:4-25). He pulls down shrines and altars, dismisses priests and prostitutes, and destroys the paraphernalia of fertility rites and astrology.

The Asherah pole (the symbol of Astarte, Baal's goddess) is removed from the temple, burned to ashes, ground to dust and scattered on graves. The grisly altar of Topheth, where children have been sacrificed to Molech, is desecrated and destroyed. The valley of Topheth, called Ben Hinnom, becomes Jerusalem's ever-burning rubbish tip. It will be known as 'Gehenna', and used by Jesus as an image of hell.

Josiah goes north across the border to Samaria and Bethel. Here Jeroboam built one of two shrines for golden Baal-calves. This is where so much trouble began, with Jeroboam preventing his people from worshipping God in Jerusalem. The Bethel shrine is now demolished, burned and littered with dead men's bones.

When all is ready, Josiah summons his people to celebrate the Passover. This is the meal by which the Jews remember how God rescued them from Egypt in the time of Moses.

Nevertheless...

Josiah's reforms have been thorough and complete. Nevertheless, God will still judge Judah for her sins. Her king, people, city and temple will soon be conquered and crushed (23:26–30).

The political balance of the region is shifting as the power of Assyria fades. Nineveh, the capital of the Assyrian empire, is defeated by the combined armies of the Medes and the Babylonians in 612 BC. This creates a power vacuum which will be quickly filled by Babylon.

Pharaoh Neco II, seeking some advantage for Egypt, marches north. He intends to join forces with Assyria against Babylon. Josiah also campaigns to the north to prevent any help getting through to Assyria. At Megiddo, Egypt and Judah engage in battle, and King Josiah is killed. Mount Megiddo gives its name to 'Armageddon' – a great battle between the powers of good and evil.

The fall of Judah (2 Kings 23:31–25:30)

Now events rush to their terrible conclusion. In a mere twenty-two years Judah will have four kings and Jerusalem will suffer three invasions. God's judgment is breaking over his own people.

Jehoahaz and Jehoiakim

Jehoahaz is a popular choice for king. His personal name is Shallum. His reign is evil and short. Pharaoh Neco takes him captive, demands tribute from Judah and makes Eliakim king instead. Eliakim is Jehoahaz's elder brother – they are both Josiah's sons. He is given a throne-name, Jehoiakim, and rules for eleven years.

Jehoiakim, king of Judah

Nebuchadnezzar invades Judah around the time he becomes king of Babylon in 605 BC. For three years Jehoiakim becomes a vassal of Nebuchadnezzar, but then he rebels. The writer of Chronicles tells us that Nebuchadnezzar takes Jehoiakim captive to Babylon. Our historian merely says that Jehoiakim 'rested with his fathers'. Jeremiah predicts that he will have 'the burial of a donkey' – his body thrown out of Jerusalem and left to rot (Jeremiah 22:19).

Judah suffers invasion by a number of enemy raiders. The writer explains that this is God's punishment for her sins. When the prophets Jeremiah and Uriah predict this situation, Uriah is executed for his message. Jeremiah narrowly escapes the same fate (Jeremiah 26:20–24).

Jehoiachin, king of Judah

Jehoiachin is Jehoiakim's eighteen-year-old son. He reigns for only three months, during which Jerusalem is besieged by Nebuchadnezzar and the Babylonian army (24:8–17).

Our historian now starts to date history by the years of a foreign reign – the reign of Nebuchadnezzar. In the eighth year of his reign, Nebuchadnezzar captures and ransacks Jerusalem and starts to deport her leading citizens. A Babylonian tablet records the date as 15/16 March (2nd Adar) 597 BC. The Jewish exile has begun.

Nebuchadnezzar leaves only the poorest people in Judah, and appoints Jehoiachin's uncle to be their king. His name is Mattaniah, and he is given the throne-name Zedekiah.

Zedekiah and the fall of Jerusalem

Judah is now weakened by the loss of her leaders. She is also divided in her opinions and loyalties. Some people want to rely on Egypt to rescue them. Others (like Jeremiah) preach dependence on God alone. False prophets (like Hananiah) advise that the grip of Babylon will soon be broken (Jeremiah 28:10–11).

The prophet Jeremiah supports King Zedekiah and writes letters to the exiles in Babylon. Our historian sees Zedekiah as king of all the Jews and not just those left in Judah. But Zedekiah fails in several ways. He doesn't listen to Jeremiah. He actively seeks to join Egypt in rebellion against Babylon – so breaking a solemn vow he has made to Nebuchadnezzar. He allows idolatry to seep back into Judah's worship.

The siege of Jerusalem

On 15 January 588 BC, Nebuchadnezzar again lays siege to Jerusalem (25:1–12). He plans to starve the inhabitants into surrender, and does so over a period of nineteen months. At the end of this time Zedekiah and his army try to break out. They are defeated by the Babylonians on the plains of Jericho.

Zedekiah is forced to watch while his sons are killed. He is then blinded and taken to Babylon where he will die. The temple, palace and all Jerusalem's main buildings are destroyed by fire. The Babylonian soldiers break down the city walls. Everyone is deported, except for some very poor people who are left to work the fields and tend the vineyards.

The temple is ransacked

The writer describes how the temple bronze is broken up and carted away to Babylon (25:13–17). It is the dismantling of David and Solomon's dream. It is also the final evidence that God has withdrawn his presence and support from his people. The leading citizens are rounded up, taken to Riblah, and executed. Every source of resistance is snuffed out.

Gedaliah

Nebuchadnezzar appoints Gedaliah as governor of Judah (25:22–26). Gedaliah advises his people to settle down and cooperate with the Babylonians. His approach is gentle and wise, and agrees with the advice of Jeremiah to the exiles. But this is too tame for a small group of resistance fighters. They assassinate Gedaliah and his pro-Babylonian friends, and flee with the remaining survivors to Egypt.

Jehoiachin is released

After thirty-seven years of exile, a new king comes to the throne of Babylon. He releases Jehoiachin from prison and gives him a place at the royal table (25:27–30).

So the history of the Kings ends on a note of hope. The Jews have no homeland, no city, no temple and no royal throne. But there is a descendant of David – alive and well, and living in Babylon.

1 and 2 CHRONICLES

The books of Chronicles are the 'Family Bible' of the Jewish Scriptures. They trace the whole story of Israel from Adam to the present day.

The Chronicles are written some time after the Jews return from exile in Babylon. They look back 500 years to the golden age of Israel's history: the reigns of the great kings, David and Solomon, and the building of the temple.

These are books which record family names, listing people by their tribes and roles. There is particular interest in the history of the royal tribes of Judah and Benjamin, and in the priestly tribe of Levi.

The person or group who wrote the Chronicles (sometimes called 'the Chronicler') wants to show how God has dealt with his people throughout their history. The great kings and the temple may be long gone, but God's promises and purpose for Israel still continue.

OUTLINE

The family lines of Israel (1 Chronicles 1:1–9:44)
The reign of King David (1 Chronicles 10:1–29:30)
The reign of King Solomon (2 Chronicles 1:1–9:31)
The kings of Judah (2 Chronicles 10:1–36:23)

Introduction

The books of Chronicles are really one book. Together they tell the whole story of God's people, Israel, from earliest times to the years following the return from exile in Babylonia. Their story continues in the books of Ezra and Nehemiah.

The Chronicles were originally the last books in the Hebrew Scriptures. They give the overall view of God's dealings with his people and inspire readers to continue the great adventure of faith.

Who wrote the Chronicles?

We don't know who wrote or edited the Chronicles. For convenience, the writer is called 'the Chronicler', and for a long time it was thought the writer might be Ezra.

Ezra would have been an expert in the long list of ancestors. He would also have understood the history of Israel in the light of God's purpose for his people. However, the story continues after the time of Ezra, and is obviously the work of another person or group as well.

The Chronicler shows that God is the true king of his people Israel. He blesses them when they are faithful to him and punishes them when they worship other gods.

When were the Chronicles written?

We don't know exactly when the Chronicles were written. The most likely time is around 430 BC – about 500 years after the reign of King David. The last episode in the history is the decree of Cyrus, king of Persia, by which the Israelites can return from exile in Babylon to rebuild their temple in Jerusalem. This is in 537 BC.

The last people listed as descendants of King David are Elioenai and his sons. They are probably still alive as the Chronicles are written (1 Chronicles 3:24).

The message of the Chronicles

The high point of Israel's history is when they have a king who is faithful to God. This is the reign of David. After David comes Solomon, who is

A range of names

The books we call 'Chronicles' have had various names. The Septuagint version of the Old Testament divided the Chronicles into two parts and called them the 'Annals'. Roman Catholic versions of the Bible have called the Chronicles 'Paralipomena', meaning 'Things which were left out'. This is because the Chronicles provide extra information which is missing from the books of Kings.

granted God's wisdom and builds the temple. Again, God is at the very centre of Israel's life.

The Chronicles begin with long lists of names. These names trace the family lines of the tribes of Israel from earliest times. Some of the tribes, such as Dan and Naphtali, are barely mentioned. However, the royal tribes of Judah and Benjamin and the priestly tribe of Levi are recorded in considerable detail.

The Chronicler then gives special attention to the reigns of David and his son Solomon. This is Israel's golden age when the kingdom is made secure, the capital city of Jerusalem is established and the temple is built and dedicated.

After Solomon's reign, the nation is divided. The Chronicler follows the history of the southern kingdom of Judah. He records the reigns of all the kings who are descended from David, until the fall of Jerusalem in 587 BC. He then deals very briefly with the years of exile in Babylon until the decree of King Cyrus that the people can return to their land.

Chronicles is a book of 'roots'. It is compiled and written for the Israelites who have returned from exile, to remind them who they are. It may seem that Israel is a poor, small, weak nation on the fringes of the Persian empire. However, the reality is that God is still their king and he has a continuing calling and mission for his people.

The message of the Chronicles is that God is with Israel, just as much as he was in the days of David and the ark of the covenant, or Solomon and the temple. The royal and priestly lines continue to the present day, and so does God's promise to bless his people if they are faithful to him.

Saul, David and Solomon

The Chronicles are written to inspire the people of Israel with the story of their past. God has been guiding, blessing and judging them from the very beginning. Their greatest successes and most terrible failures can all be understood in the light of their obedience or disobedience to God's law and God's calling.

The first king, Saul, is a failure, because he is disobedient to God (1 Chronicles 10). David, who succeeds Saul, is Israel's greatest king. He brings the ark of God to Jerusalem, conquers Israel's enemies and prepares for the building of the temple. God is pleased with David and promises him that his royal line will continue for ever (1 Chronicles 17). There is no mention of David's failings, such as his adultery with Bathsheba, the wife of one of his soldiers.

David is succeeded by his son Solomon. The Chronicler presents Solomon as a magnificent king who reigns with all the wisdom and wealth that God gives him. It is he who builds and dedicates the temple as the focus of God's presence among his people. There is no mention of Solomon's failings – his many foreign wives, his experiments with idolatry or the lifestyle which causes many of his people to become slaves.

The kings of Judah

After Solomon's death, the nation of Israel divides, with a northern kingdom of Israel and a southern kingdom of Judah. The Chronicler blames the split on the rebellion of the northern tribes against the southern tribe of Judah, which is the royal house of David (2 Chronicles 13).

The Chronicler follows the history of Judah, measuring each king by the standard of David. He records a small amount of detail about each reign and especially notes whether the king is obedient to God or not. The worst king of all, at least according to the Chronicler, is Ahaz (2 Chronicles 28).

Although the Chronicler is telling the same history as the books of Kings, the writer has his own way of presenting the story. He is portraying people and events from God's point of view. His many extra items of information and insight are used to highlight the shape and meaning of events.

The Chronicler shows how God blesses those who obey him, but disobedience results in judgment and disaster. The Chronicler is using history to highlight spiritual truths. For example, Manasseh is one of the worst rulers in the books of Kings. In the Chronicles, however, he is taken captive to Babylon where he repents and turns to God. He then returns to Jerusalem to strengthen the city and purge it of foreign gods. This is a picture to inspire the exiles. If Manasseh can change, then so can they (2 Chronicles 33)!

The Chronicles end with the fall of Jerusalem, the city of David. The temple is completely destroyed by the armies of Babylon, and the people are carried away into exile. The royal line survives, but with the kings in captivity. The land of Judah is left to rest for seventy years, catching up on the sabbaths it has missed (2 Chronicles 36:17–21). God is merciful. The Chronicles close with the Persian king's decree that the Israelites can return to their land.

DISCOVERING 1 AND 2 CHRONICLES

The family lines of Israel

The Chronicler begins with lists of ancestors. He traces the ancient nation of Israel from Adam, the first man, all the way to the 5th century BC, when he himself is writing.

From Adam to the sons of Israel (Jacob)
(1 Chronicles 1:1–2:2)

Here are some famous names: Enoch who 'walked with God', Methuselah who lived for 969 years, Noah from the time of the flood. The family line continues from Noah through his son Shem, until it arrives eventually at another famous name – Abraham.

With Abraham we step from 'prehistory' into history. God calls Abraham to be the father of a nation through whom the whole world will be blessed.

Abraham's first son, Ishmael, is the ancestor of the Arab nations. His second son, Isaac, is the father of the twins, Esau and Jacob. Esau, the elder twin, is the ancestor of the nation of Edom. The younger twin is Jacob, whom the Chronicler calls Israel. Israel is the father of twelve sons. Their descendants become the twelve tribes which make up the nation of Israel.

The 'twelve' tribes (1 Chronicles 2:3–9:44)

The Chronicler takes each of the tribes in turn. He gives the most attention to the royal tribe of Judah, while Naphtali has only one verse.

Judah

Judah is the most important of the tribes, because it produces the royal line of David. The Chronicler traces the family line from fathers to sons, and the branching off of families and clans (2:3-4:23). Some men have given their names to places (Bethlehem and Tekoa), while some places have become known for their trades or crafts.

The Chronicler occasionally brightens his lists of names with colourful comments. We meet Hezron who got married at sixty (2:21), Sheshan who enlisted his Egyptian servant as a son-in-law (2:34), and we learn how Jebez got his name (4:9). We also discover the names of David's nine lawful sons and his one daughter (3:5-9).

Simeon

Among the descendants of Simeon (4:24-43), Shimei has sixteen sons. He is the exception, however, as the Simeonites are not very successful breeders. Until David's reign they live in towns and villages around the area of Beersheba, where they are outnumbered by the more successful tribe of Judah. More recently, they have won some land from the Amalekites, and are currently living on it.

Reuben, Gad and Manasseh

The Chronicler explains why Reuben is not listed first among the tribes, although he is the eldest son of Jacob. Reuben lost his rights as the first-born son when he slept with his mother's maid, Bilhah (Genesis 35:22). The birthright passed instead to the sons of Joseph, who were called Ephraim and Manasseh. Manasseh exists as two 'half-tribes', on the east and west banks of the Jordan.

Three tribes live to the east of the River Jordan. They are the Reubenites, the Gadites and the eastern branch of Manasseh (5:1-26). It was Moses who decided their allocation of land (Joshua 13:8).

These tribes once enjoyed military strength and success. Centuries ago, they won a famous victory over the Hagrites. They cried to God for help in the battle, and he answered their prayers (5:20). More recently, however, they have worshipped pagan gods and been defeated and carried off by the Assyrians. This was God's punishment for their idolatry (5:25-26).

Levi

The Chronicler has a special interest in the Levites, because they are the priestly tribe (6:1–81).

Levi has three sons. It is from the second son, Kohath, that Aaron, Moses and Miriam are descended (6:2–3). Aaron becomes the first high priest of Israel, and the father of the high-priestly line.

The Chronicler also traces the descendants of Levi's other sons, Gershom and Merari.

The Levites are musicians. King David appoints them to provide music for the worship of the tabernacle. The tabernacle is the tent of meeting which houses the ark of God in the years before the temple is built. Meanwhile, it is the descendants of Aaron who become the priests and offer sacrifices in the Most Holy Place.

When the land of Canaan is divided between the tribes, the Levites are not given any territory of their own. This is to show that God himself is their inheritance. Instead, they are given a number of towns and villages throughout the land. The Levites are to be holy – set apart as a spiritual sign and influence among all the other tribes.

Issachar and Benjamin

The tribe of Issachar was known as a fighting force in the days of King David. Benjamin, too, was a tribe which was proud of its military muscle. Now those days are gone. But God isn't weak or captive, and his purposes have not expired.

The remaining tribes

The Chronicler traces the ancestors of the remaining tribes (7:13–40): Naphtali, the western branch of Manasseh, Ephraim and Asher. Dan and Zebulun are not mentioned, and the total number of 'twelve' tribes is in fact only eleven.

Benjamin

The Chronicler turns his attention again to the tribe of Benjamin (8:1–40). He provides a much longer list of ancestors, a list which has little in common with his previous one! The family lines can omit several generations; or a single name can represent an entire branch of the family tree. The Chronicler now brings us to Saul, who is the first king of Israel.

> **How many tribes are there?**
>
> The calculation and listing of the twelve tribes has many variations in the Old Testament. Most lists of the tribes have eleven or twelve names, but they aren't always the names of the original sons of Jacob.
>
> Jacob's (Israel's) twelve sons give their names to the tribes in theory. There is in fact no tribe named after Joseph. Instead, there are two tribes named after Joseph's sons, Ephraim and Manasseh. This gives the possibility of thirteen tribal names.
>
> When the tribes settle in Canaan, the Levites have no land of their own. This reduces the number of tribal territories to twelve. Of these, Simeon seems to get absorbed into Judah, and Dan and Zebulun have also disappeared by the time of the Chronicler's list. However, Manasseh is divided into two half-tribes, and its territories count for two.
>
> The 'twelve tribes of Israel' is perhaps an ideal picture of completeness rather than a factual description.

The Benjaminites have had their moment as a royal tribe, and their present descendants can take pride in their pedigree. There is some further detail of Saul's descendants at the end of chapter 9.

The families now resettled in Jerusalem

The Chronicler explains that the people of Judah were captured by the Babylonians and taken into exile. This was God's punishment for their unfaithfulness. However, they have now returned (9:1–34).

Among the returnees are descendants of the main tribal groups. There are people from the tribes of Judah and Benjamin, which had formed the southern kingdom of Judah. There are also survivors of the tribes of Ephraim and Manasseh, which had broken off to form the northern kingdom of Israel. Now they are a united nation once again, as they return to inhabit Jerusalem.

The Chronicler lists the names of the priests and Levites, and outlines their duties. He records gatekeepers, keyholders, sanctuary attendants, spice-mixers, bread-bakers and music-makers. Some of the gatekeepers of the past were great people, responsible for the security and dignity of the temple precincts. Now their descendants are once again taking up these historic tasks.

The priests and Levites are a living link with the past. The holy work of the Levites was first planned by King David and the prophet Samuel. Now times have changed and the temple is different, but the worshipping heart of Israel is starting to beat again.

The family line of Saul

The family line of Saul has been listed already (8:29–40), but is now repeated as the Chronicler prepares to narrate Saul's death (9:35–44). It is strange to see 'baal' appearing as part of an Israelite name. Baal means 'lord' and is used by the Canaanites for their pagan gods. The Jewish scribes who dislike writing 'baal' replace it with 'bosheth', which means 'shame'. So Saul's son Esh-baal becomes 'Ishbosheth'. Jonathan's son Merib-baal is 'Mephibosheth', who was disabled as a child and befriended by David in later life (2 Samuel 9).

The reign of King David

The Chronicler begins his presentation of the reign of King David. He uses much of the material we already have in the books of Samuel and Kings. He also has other stories and documents to hand. However, he is not setting out to tell again a story that his readers already know.

The Chronicler's interest is in the lasting importance of kingship and priesthood. Human kings represent God's authority over people. Human priests represent the people's worship of God. One day these imperfect examples of kings and priests will find their perfect expression in Jesus Christ. He is the king of kings and the great high priest.

The death of Saul (1 Chronicles 10:1–14)

The Chronicler tells us that King Saul dies because 'the Lord put him to death' (10:14). Saul has become completely out of touch with God. He is unfaithful to the Lord, he does not obey the Lord's word and he has even called on an occult medium for guidance.

This is how our writer is going to handle this history. He will show us how God rules. It is God who puts Saul to death. It is God who gives the kingdom to David.

David becomes king (1 Chronicles 11:1–12:40)

David becomes king because God has appointed him and because the people want him. David has shown himself to be at one with the people, fighting for them against their enemies.

David wastes no time in capturing Jebus – the last stronghold in Canaan to resist the Israelites. Jebus becomes Jerusalem, the city of David. The 'Mount Zion' on which Jerusalem is built will become an earthly image of the eternal city of God.

David is an outstanding leader. He draws warriors to him, inviting their loyalties, enlisting their skills and releasing their strengths. They will give their lives for him.

Three of David's finest champions break through enemy lines at night to fetch him some water from the well at Bethlehem. But David is too moved to drink it. Instead, he pours it out as an offering to the Lord.

It is a mark of David's leadership style that so many of his warriors are remembered by name. He prizes their commitment and brave deeds. Now their descendants can read their names on the roll of honour, and reflect on their own potential for greatness.

David and the ark (1 Chronicles 13:1–17:27)

David consults his people about bringing the ark of the covenant to Jerusalem. It will be an act of supreme importance, because it will unite the symbol of God's presence with the throne of David and his capital city. David is only willing to do this if the people want it.

The ark of the covenant, or the 'covenant box', has been kept in the southern town of Kiriath Jearim for twenty years – ever since the Philistines captured it but found it too dangerous to keep (1 Samuel 4:17–7:2). From Kiriath Jearim to Jerusalem is a journey of eight or nine miles.

The ark is brought to Jerusalem, but not without a shocking accident. One of the attendants, Uzzah, tries to steady the ark on its ox cart, and is struck dead. The Chronicler is showing us that the holiness of God is not to be treated casually. The ark is left to rest in the house of Obed-Edom for three months, where it brings great blessing to his family. Obed-

> ## The ark
>
> The ark was made in the days of Moses. It was constructed of acacia wood, overlaid with gold, and with two golden cherubim standing at each end. Its solid gold cover is God's throne, the 'mercy seat', where forgiveness or 'atonement' is granted for sins. Inside the ark are the stone tablets on which are engraved the Ten Commandments.
>
> The ark symbolizes God's presence among his people. It was carried ahead of them on their wilderness journey and rested in the tent of meeting when they camped. It stood guard when they crossed the River Jordan, and led them into battle in the days of the judges.

Edom is a Levite. When the ark is finally transported to Jerusalem, only the Levites are allowed to handle the precious cargo.

The ark is brought into Jerusalem with music and dancing. The Chronicler describes David as dressed in a linen ephod like a priest, dancing and celebrating with the rest. He also notes that David's wife despises him. She is Saul's daughter and expects her king to behave with more dignity.

David has the ark installed in the tent that he has prepared. He takes great care to make appropriate sacrifices and offerings, and to appoint suitable attendants and musicians. This is the kind of attention to detail which David will one day give to the planning of the temple and its worship.

David praises the God who keeps his covenant promises. His song is a combination of the Psalms we know as 96, 105 and 106:

Give thanks to the Lord, for he is good;
his love endures for ever. (16:34)

Meanwhile, the original tabernacle, or tent of meeting, is at 'the high place in Gibeon'. There is an altar there, and Zadok the priest is in attendance to offer sacrifices.

The ark and the tabernacle do not need to be in the same place. There is a growing understanding that God can be worshipped anywhere, with or without an ark or tabernacle. This is an important insight for the Israelites who are living after the exile, because they have lost both.

David begins to ponder an irony. He is living in a palace, while the ark of the Lord is housed in a tent. He talks it over with the prophet Nathan.

That night, God speaks to Nathan with a message for David. He says that he has no need for a permanent house. The tent of meeting perfectly expresses his desire to be with his people wherever they are. But God himself will build an enduring house for David – a kingdom and a line of successors that will never end. As for a physical house or temple, the son who succeeds David will build it.

David is deeply moved by Nathan's message. He goes into the tent where the ark is and prays. He wonders at the uniqueness of such a God, who loves and saves a people like Israel. He asks God to fulfil his promise: that the royal house of David will be established and honour the Lord for ever.

David's victories (1 Chronicles 18:1–20:8)

God gives David victories over all his enemies. The Philistines are conquered and Gath is captured. Gath was the home of the giant Goliath. The Moabites are defeated and made to pay tribute. The Aramaean (Syrian) peoples of Zobah, Damascus, Maacah and Mesopotamia are soundly beaten.

The Chronicler repeats that it is God who gives David these victories. In return, David devotes all his captured treasure and tribute to the Lord.

This is very different from Saul's approach to his plunder from the Amalekites (1 Samuel 15:19). The superb haul of bronze that David takes from Tebah and Cun will be used to make the famous bronze 'sea' for ablutions in Solomon's temple.

Preparing to build the temple (1 Chronicles 21:1–22:19)

Satan comes in the wake of David's victories. This is a rather different explanation to the account in the book of Kings. Perhaps the idea is to lessen the blame on David.

Satan tempts David to take a census of his armed forces, to see just how strong he is. Joab, the army commander, knows this is foolish. Israel's triumphs are not because her armies are numerous, but because God is on her side.

God is angry. Through his prophet Gad, he offers David a choice of punishment – famine, defeat in battle or plague. Because plague is 'the sword of the Lord', David chooses to endure God's wrath and hopes also for his mercy.

The plague takes a tremendous toll of life, but the Lord calls the angel of death to halt before it ravages Jerusalem. The point at which the plague stops is the threshing-floor of Araunah. Here, where judgment and mercy meet, David offers a sacrifice.

This story is puzzling. Why should God give David a choice of punishment? Is the Chronicler himself making 'faith' connections between a series of dramatic events?

The threshing-floor of Araunah has been used by the Jebusites for centuries. It is on Mount Moriah, at the northern end of Jerusalem, where Abraham once prepared to sacrifice Isaac. In 1,000 years' time the same place will be Golgotha, where Jesus will offer up his life for the sins of the world. But for now, this is to be the site of the new temple. Although the owner is a Jebusite whom David has defeated, he insists on paying fifteen pounds of gold for the land – the full price.

Soon David is busy with the preparations for a magnificent building. He is not allowed to build the temple himself, because he has been a warrior and has shed blood. This will be a task for his son Solomon, who is a man of peace.

Before he dies, David assembles the materials and workforce that are needed for the huge task. He gives Solomon a careful briefing. The key to success is to obey the law of the Lord, and to proceed boldly in faith. He assures Solomon that God will secure Israel's peace while the work is going on. He also commands all the leaders of Israel to support his son. All is to be done in, and for, the name of the Lord.

The special role of the Levites (1 Chronicles 23:1–26:32)

David introduces Solomon to the work of kingship. For the last period of David's life, their reigns will overlap.

The Chronicler outlines the part the Levites are to play in the building and administration of the temple. David decides that they will have four main functions: supervisors of the building work, gatekeepers, musicians, and 'officials and judges'.

The numbers of Levites are huge, but so is the task. The Levites are to provide all the practical support needed for the smooth running of the temple and the sacred work of the priests. They themselves are to be active worshippers, joining in the morning and evening prayers, as well as the other occasions when sacrifices are offered.

David organizes rotas of duties which will still be used 1,000 years later. Zechariah will be taking his turn in his division's tour of duty when the angel appears to announce the birth of John the Baptist (Luke 1:8).

All the duties of the temple are outlined with great care. The purpose is that the worship will be well-ordered and deeply honouring to God. In case there is too little room for God's Spirit to move, there are singers whose ministry is to prophesy (25:1–3).

The long lists of names, and the fascinating personal details, convey the involvement of real people in this great work. No doubt the apostle Peter had this picture in his mind when he wrote to the early Christians:

You also, like living stones, are being built into a spiritual house to be a holy priesthood, offering spiritual sacrifices acceptable to God through Jesus Christ. (1 Peter 2:5)

The day will come when the temple is no more. But God's people have never relied on a temple or any other building to enable them to worship God (John 4:23).

The leading Israelites (1 Chronicles 27:1–34)

The Chronicler lists the twelve army divisions which each serve for one month of the year. Their commanders are named and come from a number of different tribes. We recognize Behaiah, one of David's Thirty 'mighty warriors', and Asahel, the brother of Joab.

The idea of serving for a month in the year enables the men to continue to live with their families and attend to their farms or businesses. It also reduces the size of any standing army, which can be both expensive and a source of rebellion.

The officers responsible for each tribe are listed. There are thirteen tribes by this count, with Aaron, Ephraim, and both half-tribes of Manasseh included, but Gad and Asher left out. Dan makes a reappearance, having been omitted from a previous list.

There is a move to count the people, but this provokes God's anger. Joab has advised David against this before, and was proved right (21:3). Now it is Joab who starts to number those under twenty years old, but stops in the face of God's wrath. It is the Lord's protection, not the number of warriors, that guards Israel.

The Chronicler lists the individuals who are in charge of David's property. There are twelve of them (of course!) and they have oversight of his farmlands, vineyards, animals, produce and provisions. Here is a well-ordered royal household.

Finally, we have the names of David's close circle of advisers. Including David, they form a group of six. When Ahithophel turns traitor and then hangs himself, he is replaced by Jehoiada (2 Samuel 17:23). Joab is an uncomfortable colleague who must be included because of his power. His influence is balanced by Hushai, who is there simply as David's friend.

David is a leader of genius, a shepherd of people. He is a master of team-building, organizational structure and delegation. He knows his people, trusts them and gets the best from them. Everyone knows where they belong in the life of the nation, what is expected of them and when. They know to whom they are responsible, who they are working with and why they are doing what they do.

The measure of David's success is that he is able to unite the tribes of Israel and enlist a large number of incomers and foreigners in his service. People of differing backgrounds, abilities and temperaments work together for the common good, and many an enemy becomes a friend. We will see these gifts at work again in the approach of Jesus to his disciples, and in the mission of the early church.

Solomon is made king (1 Chronicles 28:1–29:30)

David summons a great assembly. He is old and nearing death. He does everything in his power to ensure a safe transfer of authority to his son Solomon.

David opens his heart to his people. He tells them how God has barred him from building a temple, because he has been a warrior and has shed blood. Nevertheless, God has chosen one of his sons to reign after him and to build the house of the Lord.

David commissions Solomon for the task ahead. He charges him to follow God's commands. This is the first principle of security and success, for himself, for his people and for the future. The Lord has chosen Solomon for a great work. Now the young man must respond with an open heart, strong determination and a humble dependence on God.

David hands the plans for the temple to Solomon. He explains that God's Spirit has inspired him with the vision of it, and guided him in every detail. He assures him that the same God will be with him, together with all the people, to see the work completed.

Now David turns to the people. He invites them to commit themselves to the building of the temple. This is not to be a grandiose project for the glory of an extravagant king. This is to be a fine and fitting place, provided by all the people for the praise of their God. In response to David's invitation, the nation's leaders give willingly, with generosity and joy.

David praises God. He acknowledges that all glory belongs to him and all gifts come from him. These same words are used around the world to this day, especially for the presentation of offerings to God:

All things come from you, and of your own have we given you. (29:14 NRSV)

The following day, in a great festival, Solomon is acknowledged and anointed as king. The Chronicler says this is Solomon's second anointing. There has already been a hasty ceremony, to confirm his right to the throne. This was to counter a claim from Adonijah, another of David's sons (1 Kings 1:39).

As Solomon starts to emerge as the most glorious of Israel's kings, David dies full of years and honour.

The Chronicler has spared us the mistakes, failures and gossip of David's reign. They are there for all to see in the books of Samuel and Kings, and were as well known in the Chronicler's day as they are in our own.

Instead, the Chronicler shows us the ideals and dignities of kingship. He reveals the ultimate reign and purposes of our only true king, which is God. He awakens in us a longing for that just and gentle rule, which will be Christ's at his coming. Jesus is 'Great David's greater Son'.

The reign of King Solomon

Solomon inherits the throne of Israel from his father David.

David's reign has been outstanding. He has won security for his people and given structure to their government. But David's rule involved him in many battles and much bloodshed. Solomon's reign, by contrast, will be a time of peace.

The new king will be free from powerful enemies, so that he can build the temple which his father has planned. He will have room in his life for learning and reflection. He will become a living legend for both his wealth and his wisdom.

Nearly all that the Chronicler tells us about Solomon is already recorded in the books of Kings (1 Kings 1–11). However, as with his account of the reign of David, he does not relate Solomon's failures.

According to the books of Kings, Solomon was wise in his decisions but unwise in his affections. He not only married a huge number of foreign women, but also committed idolatry by worshipping their pagan gods.

The Chronicler knows about this – and he knows that we know. His concern, however, is to highlight the great and remarkable achievements of Solomon's reign. His purpose is to demonstrate the enduring and eternal rule of God, and to reveal his glory and wisdom to Israel.

By the time the Chronicler writes this book, the reigns of David and Solomon are in the distant past. But God's reign is always *now*, and his purpose is for ever waiting to be discovered.

Solomon's early years (2 Chronicles 1:1–17)

Solomon makes a good and wholehearted beginning to his reign. He imposes his authority on his people, but he submits himself to God.

The young king goes to Gibeon, where the wilderness tabernacle, the tent of meeting, is kept. There, at the bronze altar, Solomon commits himself to God with a thousand burnt offerings.

That night God appears to Solomon and makes him an offer in return. He can ask for whatever he wants. It is typical of God to invite a specific request from someone who is wholly committed to his will (Mark 10:51; John 16:24). Solomon asks for wisdom and knowledge, so that he can govern God's people well.

It is a superb prayer – far better than the usual pleas for wealth, honour, long life or revenge. God not only grants Solomon's request for wisdom, but promises him wealth and honour as well.

David's victories now enable Solomon's prosperity. The new king has the respect and resources to trade with all the surrounding nations. Chariots and horses are the status symbols of the day, and Solomon has the very finest from Egypt.

Jerusalem grows wealthy at last, with silver and gold 'as common as stones'. Such an influx of wealth is a sign of God's blessing. The vision of the world's kings bringing tribute to Zion is one of the Bible's pictures of God's universal reign and Israel's superiority (Psalm 72:10; Revelation 21:24)!

The building of the temple (2 Chronicles 2:1–5:1)

Solomon prepares for the building of a temple for God and a palace for himself. He writes to his father's old friend, Hiram king of Tyre.

Solomon asks Hiram to supply cedar wood from Lebanon for the new buildings. Hiram agrees. The trees will be logged and rafted by sea to Joppa, as they were in David's time for his royal palace. Joppa is the nearest port to Jerusalem.

Solomon also asks Hiram to send him a skilled worker. The Israelites have little skill in the arts of metalwork, embroidery and engraving. Hiram responds by sending Huram-Abi, a gifted craftsman whose mother was an Israelite from the northern tribe of Dan.

A place for us

Mount Moriah was where Abraham once prepared to sacrifice Isaac (Genesis 22:9–14). In the future, it will be the hill to the north of the city where Jesus is crucified (John 19:17). Today the site is covered by the Dome of the Rock, one of Islam's holiest shrines.

The temple is built on Mount Moriah. This was Araunah's threshing-floor, where God halted the plague which was about to devastate Jerusalem (1 Chronicles 21:15). David offered a sacrifice here, and bought the site for the temple.

As the building takes shape, Solomon attends to every detail.

The main hall is ninety feet long and thirty feet wide. It is panelled with pine and lined with gold. At one end is the Most Holy Place, thirty feet square, the same width as the rest of the temple.

Two carved cherubim, covered with gold, stand facing the worshippers. Side by side, with wing-tips touching, they span the temple from wall to wall. A curtain, beautifully worked in coloured thread on fine linen, screens off the Most Holy Place. It is in the Most Holy Place that the ark of God will be kept.

Outside, in the courtyard, two great pillars called Jakin and Boaz ('solid' and 'strong') stand north and south at the front of the temple.

Solomon has a huge altar for sacrifice and a vast basin for ablutions cast in bronze. The new altar is four times the size of the old one (which Solomon had used at Gibeon) and twice as high. The basin, called 'the sea', is shaped like a lily and measures fifteen feet across. It stands seven feet high, supported by twelve bronze bulls, and holds 14,500 gallons of water.

The master craftsman, Huram-Abi, works furnishings, decorations and implements in bronze. Solomon commissions some delicate items in gold – the small altar, the tables for the bread of the Presence, the lampstands and lamps, the bowls and dishes.

Finally, the doors of the temple, the hall and the Most Holy Place are all lined with gold. No detail is too small; no effort or expense too great. Nothing but the best is fit for God.

The temple is dedicated (2 Chronicles 5:2–7:22)

When all is ready, Solomon summons the Israelites for a festival in Jerusalem. It is the month of the Day of Atonement and the Feast of Tabernacles.

The ark of the covenant is brought by the Levites from Zion (the part of Jerusalem called the city of David), to the temple. It is reverently installed in the Most Holy Place. This was always David's hope, that the ark which led the Israelites through the wilderness might finally come to rest in a permanent house for God.

As the priests withdraw from the Holy Place, the musicians burst into a mighty psalm of praise. One hundred and twenty priests sound their rams'-horn trumpets, and the temple is filled with the cloud of God's glory.

Solomon blesses the people. He praises God, who has chosen Israel to be his nation, David to be his king, Jerusalem to be his city and this temple to be his house.

This moment, with the cloud of glory filling the temple, sees God's promises fulfilled and David's and Solomon's dream come true. The ark

The rebuilt temple.

> ### Fire from heaven
>
> Moses and Aaron saw fire fall from heaven when they first set up the altar to God in the wilderness (Leviticus 9:24).
>
> David had the same experience when he first offered sacrifices on the temple site, while it was still the threshing-floor of Araunah (1 Chronicles 21:26).
>
> Elijah will have his prayer answered by fire when he challenges the pagan prophets of Baal on Mount Carmel (1 Kings 18:38).
>
> Each occasion is a public event. 'All the people' see what God has done – and worship him.

of the covenant, the royal line of David, the city of Jerusalem and the house of God are all brought together for the first time.

On a bronze platform in the temple forecourt, Solomon kneels to pray. He thanks God for fulfilling his promises to David. He prays that David's line of kings will continue to reign in Israel.

Solomon brings to God the situations that may arise in the future – times of dispute, defeat, drought, disaster, pilgrimage, war or exile. He asks that in every kind of need, the temple will be a source of justice, mercy, healing and help; that God's 'eyes will be open and his ears attentive' to his people's prayers.

Solomon calls on God to answer him – to make his presence known. With that, fire falls from heaven and consumes the burnt offerings and sacrifices. The glory of the Lord – the cloud of his presence – fills the temple.

After two weeks of high festival, the people return to their homes. Soon afterwards, the Lord appears to Solomon again one night. He promises to hear and answer his people's prayers when they approach him in the temple. He also promises to sustain the royal line, the city and the temple, if Solomon will keep his laws. But if the Israelites turn to other gods they will be uprooted from their land and their temple will be destroyed.

Solomon's greatness (2 Chronicles 8:1–9:31)

The Chronicler concludes his account of Solomon's reign. He makes no mention of the king's foreign wives or idolatries. Instead, he describes

> **Tearing up the kingdom**
>
> During the reign of Solomon, the prophet Ahijah had met Jeroboam on his way out of Jerusalem one day. The prophet dramatically tore his new cloak into twelve pieces. He gave Jeroboam ten of the pieces, as a sign that he would become king of the ten northern tribes. Two pieces (Judah and Benjamin) would remain to form the kingdom of Judah under the rule of Solomon's son Rehoboam (1 Kings 11:29–39).
>
> The kingdom is to be torn out of Solomon's hand because of his idolatry with pagan gods. However, this will not happen during his lifetime, because of God's promise to David that his kingdom will continue through the reign of his son.

Solomon's building and restoration projects, his treatment of foreigners, his faithful worship and his successful sea trade.

When the queen of Sheba comes to visit Solomon, she is overwhelmed by his wealth, wisdom and lifestyle. Like Hiram of Tyre, she recognizes that God must love his people very much to give them such a king. Although Solomon's wealth is impressive, it is his wisdom which is truly remarkable. It is his wisdom which gives his people guidance and justice.

Solomon is now fabulously wealthy. The queen of Sheba brings gold, spices and precious stones. Traders bring gold and fine wood from legendary Ophir. The kings of Arabia bring gold and silver.

Solomon lines the hall of his palace with hundreds of solid gold shields. He furnishes his table with solid gold goblets. He has a throne made of ivory with a footstool of gold. His horses (of which he has thousands) are Egypt's finest. In the end, he has nothing made of silver, because silver has become too common.

Solomon dies after forty years on the throne of David. The Chronicler leaves us in no doubt that this was one of Israel's greatest kings.

Solomon's greatness was all from God. It was God's throne that Solomon occupied. It was God's wealth that Solomon accumulated. It was God's wisdom that he acquired.

Jesus in the Gospels describes himself as 'greater than Solomon' (Luke 11:31). He will give his followers a better wealth than Solomon's (Matthew

6:29) and gifts that are greater than gold (1 Corinthians 12:7–11). He is the wisdom of God, who leads his people into all truth (John 16:13).

The kings of Judah

After the reign of Solomon, the kingdom of Israel is torn apart. The nation divides to form the northern kingdom of Israel and the southern kingdom of Judah.

While the books of Kings give us a parallel history of both kingdoms, the Chronicler tells us only about the southern kingdom of Judah. It is Judah that has David's city (Jerusalem) for its capital, Solomon's temple for its holy place and the descendants of David for its kings.

King Rehoboam (2 Chronicles 10:1–12:16)

King Solomon is succeeded by his son Rehoboam. Where Solomon began his reign by asking God for wisdom and understanding, Rehoboam is brash and ignores all good advice.

Solomon's reign has been hard for the common people. He has taken them from their homes to staff his luxurious palace. He has taken them from their farms and vineyards to work like slaves on his building projects. The elders now counsel Rehoboam to lighten his people's burdens.

But Rehoboam doesn't listen to the advice of the elders. Instead he takes the advice of friends his own age. They say he should increase his people's burden and sharpen their suffering; and this is what he decides to do.

But the people have a champion in Jeroboam. Jeroboam is a leader of the tribe of Ephraim. He was seen as a rival by Solomon and has been hiding in Egypt. Now he returns to challenge Rehoboam.

The prophet Ahijah has told Jeroboam that he will become king of ten of the tribes of Israel (1 Kings 11:26–40). Only the tribes of Judah and Benjamin will remain under the rule of Rehoboam and the descendants of David.

The books of Kings tell us that the division of the nation is God's punishment for Solomon's idolatry with his foreign wives. The Chronicler (who is kinder to Solomon's reputation) says that the split is in fulfilment of God's word through the prophet Ahijah (10:15). The

> **Which nation is 'Israel'?**
>
> In the books of Kings, the ten northern tribes are called 'Israel' after the kingdom divides. The two southern tribes are called 'Judah'.
>
> In Chronicles, the name 'Israel' refers to the people of God wherever they are, and is used for both northern and southern kingdoms. Both are part of the true 'Israel', and both have a capacity to either obey or rebel against God.

Chronicler explains the division in terms of Jeroboam's rebellion against Rehoboam's headstrong, bullying policies.

At first, Rehoboam gathers his forces to attempt to conquer the northern tribes and unite the kingdom again. However, one of the prophets, Shemaiah, persuades him against this. He explains that the division of the kingdom has been God's doing and is to be accepted.

Rehoboam then strengthens his little kingdom, by fortifying the towns along its southern border. The main threat is from Egypt, whose pharaoh Shishak is likely to prove a friend and ally to Jeroboam.

Priests and Levites come from the northern kingdom to join Rehoboam in Jerusalem. They are offended by Jeroboam, who is setting up his own religion around goat and calf idols. Jeroboam's plan is to combine the worship of the Lord with the idols of Canaan. In this way he hopes to stop the people of the northern kingdom looking to the Jerusalem temple as the centre of their religion.

Rehoboam is well connected to David's line, both through his father Solomon and by his marriages. His favourite wife is Maacah, who is a granddaughter of David's popular but treacherous son Absalom.

Rehoboam is wiser than David in the way he treats his sons. He provides for them so that they aren't resentful, gives them responsibilities so that they aren't restless, and uses their marriages to forge alliances which strengthen the kingdom.

Despite a good start, the southern kingdom slips into idolatry. The Chronicler says that Rehoboam and 'all Israel' (by which he means Judah, which is supposed to be the true people of God) now abandons the law of the Lord (12:1).

> **The thirty-sixth year of Asa's reign**
>
> The Chronicler says Baasha, king of Israel, invades Judah 'in the thirty-sixth year of Asa's reign'. This clearly is a mistake as Baasha would have been dead some ten years by then. One possible explanation is that the thirty-sixth year is counted from the beginning of the divided kingdom. It is the thirty-sixth year of Judah's history and the sixteenth year of Asa's reign.

God punishes Judah's unfaithfulness with a costly invasion by Shishak of Egypt. Treasures are taken from both the temple and the palace – including the famous gold shields which had lined Solomon's royal hall.

Shishak's own account of his invasion is recorded on the outside wall of the temple of Karnak. The Chronicler tells us that Jerusalem is spared worse punishment, because Rehoboam and the other leaders repent of their idolatry.

The prophet Shemaiah explains that Judah is being abandoned because she has first abandoned God. The Chronicler often shows how God's judgment of a person or people reflects very precisely their own behaviour.

The Chronicler's verdict on Rehoboam is that there is some good in his seventeen-year reign. However, he fails to seek the Lord wholeheartedly. The fatal flaw which is apparent at the very beginning continues to spoil his government.

King Abijah (2 Chronicles 13:1–22)

Rehoboam is succeeded by Abijah, who is his favourite son by his favourite wife.

Abijah makes a determined attempt to conquer the northern tribes and reunite the kingdom. Drawing up in battle array against Jeroboam, Abijah makes an important speech. He sets out the differences between the northern and southern kingdoms, and claims that God is on the side of Judah.

It is Judah whose king is descended from David. The royal line is guaranteed by God 'by a covenant of salt', an unbreakable promise. It is also Judah that has the true priests and the true worship. Her priests are descended from Aaron, and they have the Levites to assist them. In the temple in Jerusalem, the true God is being worshipped in the manner he has ordained. All this is additional to the record of the books of Kings, and shows the Chronicler's bias to the south. By contrast, Jeroboam has been appointing his own false priests for a false religion.

While Abijah declares a holy war against the north, and urges the men of Israel not to fight God, Jeroboam sends forces to ambush him from behind. Despite this, God enables the armies of Judah to defeat the Israelites and capture some of their towns.

King Asa (2 Chronicles 14:1–16:14)

The Chronicler reports that Asa is a good king. He does what is 'good and right in the eyes of the Lord his God' (14:2).

Asa tackles the pagan worship that is taking place in Judah. He removes the altars of foreign gods and breaks up sacred stones. He even deposes his grandmother Maacah from being queen mother, because she has made an Asherah pole (a fertility symbol of the Canaanite mother goddess).

Asa strengthens Judah's defences, builds up his army and enjoys a period of peace. God then gives him victory against the superior forces of Zerah the Cushite, who invades Judah from Ethiopia. Before the battle, Asa prays, 'Help us, O Lord our God, for we rely on you, and in your name we have come against this vast army.' The prophet Azariah commends Asa for his trust in God: 'The Lord is with you when you are with him.'

Asa continues his purge of Judah's paganism, and repairs the bronze altar in front of the temple portico. When he summons an assembly, the numbers are swelled by people from the northern tribes who make their way to Judah because they hear of Asa's reforms. The whole gathering renews its covenant with the Lord in the Feast of Weeks.

Later in Asa's reign, his faith in God starts to falter. The king of Israel, Baasha, starts to blockade Judah. To counter this, Asa uses temple treasure to buy an alliance with Ben-Hadad, king of Aram (Syria).

The alliance is successful, with Ben-Hadad forcing Israel to withdraw from Judah. However, Asa is condemned by the prophet Hanani for turning to Syria for help instead of relying on God. Asa is in no mood to be lectured, and puts Hanani in prison. This is the first occasion that the Bible records a prophet being punished.

In the years that follow, Asa's resistance to God continues. Even when he is stricken by a disease in his feet, he seeks the help of physicians (perhaps occult healers) rather than healing from the Lord.

Despite his faults, both the Chronicler and the people of Judah regard Asa as a great king. When he dies, after forty-one years on the throne, Asa is given a funeral of special honour, with a huge fire of burning spices.

King Jehoshaphat (2 Chronicles 17:1–20:37)

Asa's son, Jehoshaphat, is a fine king. He strengthens his fortifications against the northern kingdom, removes the 'high places' of pagan worship and commissions priests and Levites to teach the law of Moses in the towns of Judah.

From the beginning, Jehoshaphat takes David as his example. The Chronicler records that his heart is 'devoted to the ways of the Lord'. Because Jehoshaphat fears the Lord, the fear of the Lord falls on the surrounding nations. The Philistines bring him tribute; the Arabs bring him flocks. His power and wealth – and the organization of his army – are reminders of the great days of Israel's history.

But Jehoshaphat makes a mistake. He involves himself with Ahab, king of Israel. Perhaps he feels that the time is ripe for the two kingdoms to work together again. At first he makes a marriage alliance with Ahab. Some years later he agrees to join him in a military venture – a campaign to recapture Ramoth Gilead from Aram (Syria).

As they discuss their alliance, Jehoshaphat urges Ahab to seek God's counsel. Ahab summons 400 prophets. All of them tell him what he wants to hear: that God will give him victory. Jehoshaphat still has doubts, and asks if there is a more authentic prophet to consult. Ahab admits that Micaiah speaks from the Lord, although he has never enjoyed a favourable prophecy from him.

When Micaiah arrives, he mimics the mindless advice of the other prophets. One of them, Zedekiah, has been capering around with a pair of iron horns, as a sign that the Syrians will be gored to death. But, when pressed, Micaiah predicts that the armies of Israel will be defeated and scattered. The prophets who predict victory are being deceived by God himself, to lure Ahab to his death.

Ahab decides to ignore Micaiah's prophecy, and has him thrown into prison until they return. However, Ahab is alarmed enough to propose that he should go into battle in disguise, and that only Jehoshaphat should be seen wearing royal robes.

When the battle begins, the Arameans prepare to attack Jehoshaphat, because he is the only visible king. He cries out to God for help, and the Arameans realize he is not Ahab. However, an arrow fired at random finds a chink in Ahab's armour, and gives him a fatal wound. He dies in his chariot at sunset. When Jehoshaphat returns to Judah, he is rebuked by the prophet Jehu for his unholy alliance with the king of Israel.

Back in Jerusalem, Jehoshaphat continues to put in place good structures of government. He appoints judges in each of the fortified cities, giving them a careful and solemn briefing that they are to do the Lord's work. In Jerusalem, he appoints priests and senior people to administer the law of Moses. He warns them that the Lord will punish them if they don't tell people not to sin.

A severe military threat now arises. Moabites, Ammonites and Meunites (from Edom) are advancing on Judah. Jehoshaphat calls all the people to fast, and to come together to seek God's help.

Standing in the great assembly, Jehoshaphat leads his nation in prayer. This is one of the great prayers of the Chronicles, second only to Solomon's prayer when he dedicates the temple.

Jehoshaphat praises God as the only God, the God of their ancestors and the ruler of all nations. He recalls how God conquered their enemies in the past, and promised the land to the descendants of Abraham for ever. God also promised that the temple in which they now stand would be the place where he would hear and help in times of need. Now, in this crisis, Jehoshaphat acknowledges their helplessness and appeals to God to save them.

The Lord's answer comes through Jahaziel, who is one of the Levites. He tells Jehoshaphat and all the people not to be afraid. The battle is the Lord's. Jahaziel describes where the army is to take its stand the following day, but assures them they will not have to fight. In the morning, they march out with the praises of God on their lips.

While the people of Judah praise God, their enemies are overtaken by ambushes and infighting. By the time Jehoshaphat and his army arrive at their vantage point, there is nothing to be seen of their enemies but dead bodies. It takes them three days to collect the plunder.

Jehoshaphat reigns for twenty-five years, and the Chronicler rates him as a fine king. His only fault (apart from getting too close to Ahab) has been that he fails to remove all the sites of pagan worship. They spring up as fast as they are suppressed. The attraction of fertility rites and the influence of superstition go too deep, unless the people themselves resolve to turn to the Lord.

King Jehoram (2 Chronicles 21:1–20)

Jehoshaphat's heir is Jehoram. He begins his reign with an act of sheer brutality, by having his six brothers killed.

While his father had modelled his reign on David, Jehoram takes after his father-in-law, Ahab. Jehoshaphat's involvement with the wicked king of Israel, by making a marriage alliance, is now proving costly for the next generation – and it will prove costlier still.

Jehoram proceeds to lead the people of Judah into idolatry. God only spares him because of his promise to preserve the royal line of David. However, God sets about warning and judging the wayward king, beginning with a letter from the prophet Elijah.

Elijah has been a stern opponent of King Ahab in the northern kingdom, but this is the only occasion when the Chronicler mentions him in connection with the south. It is fitting that it is Elijah who condemns Jehoram for behaving like a king of Ahab's line rather than David's. Jehoram has led his people into religious prostitution – committing idolatry with the Baal-gods of Canaan.

Elijah's message to Jehoram is that God has seen all his wickedness. He is now to lose his family, as he has robbed others of theirs; and he will die a dreadful death.

The Chronicler tells how God stirs up the Philistines and the Arabs to attack Jehoram. They raid Judah, plunder Jehoram's palace, kill his sons and carry off his wives. The king who murdered his brothers is now bereaved of all his sons except one. When the rest of Elijah's prophecy is fulfilled and Jehoram dies of bowel disease, he is buried without any great ceremony or sign of mourning.

King Ahaziah (2 Chronicles 22:1–9)

Jehoram's youngest and only surviving son is Ahaziah. He becomes king at the age of twenty-one and reigns for just one year.

His mother is Athaliah – a granddaughter of wicked king Omri, and daughter of Ahab and Jezebel. She runs true to her evil pedigree in every way, encouraging brutality and idolatry in her son's brief reign. When Ahaziah is put to death by Jehu, Athaliah has her grandsons slaughtered to secure the throne for herself. She may have some idea of uniting the monarchies – in favour of the north.

Athaliah and Joash (2 Chronicles 22:10–23:15)

One of the royal princes escapes Athaliah's massacre. His name is Joash. He is only a baby when his aunt Jehosheba saves him, by hiding him in the temple, where her husband Jehoiada is a priest. Queen Athaliah rules Judah, unaware that a true heir of David is being raised in the temple nearby.

After six years, the priest Jehoiada becomes the king-maker. With careful secrecy, he makes covenant alliances with the army commanders and summons the Levites and heads of families to Jerusalem. Together, they pledge their loyalty to the young king who is hidden in the temple.

Jehoiada plans his coup with military and religious precision. The prince is to be presented to his people in the temple and crowned as their rightful king. The Levites perform their traditional duty as God's warriors, shielding David's heir with their weapons as they bring him for coronation. The priests bring him forth, like a long-kept secret or the anointing of the shepherd-boy David. They place the royal crown on his head, present him with a copy of the covenant and proclaim him king.

The first Athaliah knows of all this is a sound of cheering coming from the temple. Going to investigate, she is dumbfounded to see the seven-year-old King Joash standing in his place at the entrance. In fury, she tears her robes and cries, 'Treason!' but is powerless to alter events. As she leaves the temple precinct and reaches her palace gate, she is overtaken and killed by her own troops.

King Joash (2 Chronicles 23:16–24:27)

At the beginning of Joash's reign, the young king is only seven years old. Jehoiada the priest is his chief adviser in his early years.

Jehoiada oversees the making of a covenant between himself, the people and the king. They commit themselves to be faithful to the Lord. The temple of Baal is destroyed and its priest executed. The temple of the Lord is placed in the care of the priests and Levites. The people's donations are properly administered for repairs to the fabric and for the commissioning of new furnishings and equipment.

Jehoiada lives to a great age. He has been such an influence for good that, when he dies, he is given a state funeral and buried with the kings.

After Jehoiada's death, Joash falls under a very different influence. Officials from Judah persuade him to adopt Baal-worship, with disastrous results. Jehoiada's son, Zechariah, warns the people that the Lord will reject them if they reject him. On Joash's orders, the faithful Zechariah is stoned to death.

The stoning of Zechariah is a tragedy and a scandal. Because Chronicles is placed as the last book in the Jewish Scriptures, Zechariah's martyrdom stands as an appalling rejection of God's messenger. Many Jewish rabbis teach that the destruction of Solomon's temple is God's punishment for the death of this good man. Jesus himself refers to it (Matthew 23:35).

In all, Joash reigns for forty years. Because of his unfaithfulness, God inflicts defeat on him by the armies of Aram (Syria). The king is severely wounded in battle, and murdered in his bed by his own officials. The two men who kill him both have foreign mothers – an Ammonite and a Moabite.

Joash is not a wholly bad king. He begins well but ends tragically. In some ways his reign is like a mini-history of Israel.

King Amaziah (2 Chronicles 25:1–26:2)

The Chronicler says Amaziah does 'what is right in the eyes of the Lord, but not wholeheartedly'.

On becoming king, Amaziah avenges the death of his father, but only executes those who actually committed the murder. He doesn't kill their children, because he discovers that the law of Moses forbids it (Deuteronomy 24:16). This is the first sign that the bloodletting ways of Jehoram and Athaliah are coming to an end.

Amaziah counts his fighting force and finds the numbers much lower than in the days of Asa. He hires mercenaries from Ephraim to increase his military strength, but is warned against using them by 'a man of God', a prophet. Amaziah accepts the prophet's advice, although he regrets the waste of money in paying the Ephraimites and then not using them. The prophet assures the king that God can very easily compensate him for his losses.

God honours Amaziah's trust, and grants him a great victory over the Edomites. Meanwhile, the Ephraimites whom he had sent home prove their unreliability by going on the rampage in the north.

Now Amaziah makes a big mistake. Although he has conquered the Edomites, he brings their gods back to Jerusalem and starts to worship them. He is trying to add the power of the Edomite idols to that of the God of Israel. The king shouts down a prophet who tells him that this is a stupid and dangerous thing to do, and that God will judge him for it.

Amaziah is bold after his success against Edom, and decides to challenge Jehoash of Israel. Jehoash warns him that this will be an unequal fight. Amaziah approaching Jehoash is like a thistle asking to marry a cedar. The cedar will turn into a wild beast and trample him.

Amaziah ignores the warning. The Chronicler explains that this is God bringing about Amaziah's downfall because of his idolatry with the worthless gods of Edom.

Jehoash inflicts a crushing defeat on Amaziah. He breaks down a large section of Jerusalem's wall, ransacks the temple and palace treasures, and keeps Amaziah captive in Samaria for ten years.

During his imprisonment, Amaziah's place on the throne of Judah is taken by Uzziah, his sixteen-year-old son. After his release, Amaziah lives another fifteen years, but his authority is broken. He is a discredited and unpopular king, whose troubles date from the day he turned away from the Lord.

King Uzziah (2 Chronicles 26:3–23)

Uzziah (Azariah) is one of Judah's great kings. He comes to the throne when he is sixteen years old, to act as regent for his father Amaziah. Amaziah is being held captive in Samaria, the capital of the northern kingdom of Israel.

The ten years of Amaziah's imprisonment are followed by a further fifteen years of co-regency. This means that half of Uzziah's reign overlaps with that of his father. In all, Uzziah reigns for fifty-two years and is the finest king since Jehoshaphat, who ruled Judah one hundred years earlier.

Like Amaziah and Joash (his father and grandfather) Uzziah begins his reign well. The Chronicler says that Uzziah does 'right in the eyes of the Lord'. His teacher and counsellor is a man called Zechariah, who is an excellent influence on the king for most of his reign.

The Chronicler says that Uzziah is 'greatly helped'. The name Uzziah means 'The Lord is My Strength'. As king he is also called Azariah, which is possibly a throne-name given him at his coronation. Azariah means 'The Lord Has Helped'.

It is a mark of Uzziah's strength and vision that he recaptures and restores the Red Sea port of Elath. Elath had been developed for industry and trade by Solomon but then lost to the Edomites. Today it is the holiday resort of Eilat.

Uzziah is an all-rounder. As soldier, farmer and administrator, he brings energy and ability to every aspect of his nation's life. He conquers Judah's old enemies – the Philistines to the west and the Arabs to the south. He strengthens Jerusalem's fortifications, provides the army with new equipment and introduces the latest means of defence. He tends his cattle by building watchtowers and digging wells, and takes a lively interest in his vineyards and farms.

Uzziah's reign in Judah runs parallel to Jeroboam II's reign in Israel. Both kingdoms become strong and prosperous at this time, because their enemies are weak. Assyria in particular is experiencing a short-term decline.

Sadly, the last ten years of Uzziah's reign are spoiled by an act of pride and folly. Although Uzziah has a unique role among his people as their king, he tries also to act as their priest. He enters the temple and prepares to burn incense.

The roles of king and priest are strictly separate – the first is secular and the second is sacred. The king represents God to the people, while the priest represents the people to God. The roles are not to be combined in Israel, unlike some other nations, because there is a danger that they will become confused or their significance lost.

As Uzziah approaches the altar of incense, some brave priests challenge him. As the king rages at them in his defiance, he breaks out in leprosy.

Leprosy is a living death – a highly contagious skin disease which eats the flesh and slowly disables the body. In Uzziah's case it is regarded as a dramatic symbol of sin and a sign of God's judgment.

Because of his disease, Uzziah is forced to live in isolation for the last ten years of his life. Nevertheless, his great achievements and length of reign have made him a landmark for his people. When he dies, in 740 BC, the prophet Isaiah is consoled by a vision of the far greater and eternal kingship of God (Isaiah 6:1).

King Jotham (2 Chronicles 27:1–9)

Uzziah is succeeded by his son Jotham, who is a good king. He is one of only two kings of whom the Chronicler has nothing bad to say – the other being Solomon's grandson Abijah.

Jotham reigns for sixteen years. He continues his father's sound policies, conquering the Ammonites and extracting tribute from them, and strengthening Judah's defences. At the same time, he is careful not to make his father's mistakes. The Chronicler notes that although the king is good, the people of Judah are corrupt.

King Ahaz (2 Chronicles 28:1–27)

When Ahaz succeeds his father Jotham, he continues the royal line of David. However, his sixteen-year reign falls far short of the righteousness and justice of his great ancestor.

Under Ahaz, pagan worship becomes rife in Judah. Ahaz himself offers sacrifices to the ancient Baal-gods, even to the extent of burning his own sons. The people of Judah are now behaving in the same way as the Canaanites whom they originally drove from the land.

God's judgment falls on Ahaz in the form of heavy defeats, first by the Arameans (Syrians) and then by the Israelites from the north. The king of Israel, Pekah, takes a terrible toll of human life and seizes a huge number of prisoners.

As the Israelites return to Samaria with their captives, they are met by a prophet named Oded. Oded declares that they have gone far beyond God's will with their atrocities, and commands that the survivors be sent home. These captives are their brothers and sisters, and fellow members of God's people.

The prophet's words are echoed by the leaders of Ephraim. The soldiers give up their prisoners with great grace and generosity. They provide them with food and clothes, put balm on their wounds and transport them back to Jericho on donkeys. Here is the act of kindness to enemies which will one day inspire the parable of the Good Samaritan (Luke 10:33–34).

Ahaz continues to suffer defeats, but they don't make him turn to the Lord. Instead, he appeals to the king of Assyria, Tiglath-Pileser, for help. Tiglath-Pileser merely adds to Ahaz's humiliation by taking his treasures while giving nothing in return.

Ahaz tries worshipping the gods of Damascus, because they have helped Syria defeat him. Finally, he shows all-out defiance of the Lord by closing down the temple and setting up pagan altars on every street corner. When Ahaz dies, he is not buried with the kings of Israel, because he has not been God's king for God's people in any true sense.

Ahaz's reign has been a disaster for Judah. The Chronicler shows how God punishes disobedience with defeat and captivity – and in so doing gives a hint of what is to come. In the past it has been the northern kingdom which has abandoned its loyalty to God; now the southern kingdom is as bad.

King Hezekiah (2 Chronicles 29:1–32:33)

When Hezekiah succeeds his father as king of Judah, his inspiration is the great King Solomon. Hezekiah's vision is to restore the temple and its worship as it was at the beginning. To this end he sets to work on the very first day of his reign.

Hezekiah calls together the priests and Levites. He tells them of his intention to make a covenant with the Lord. After the years of unfaithfulness and idolatry, Judah is now to commit herself again to the one true God. Hezekiah urges the priests and Levites to dedicate themselves to this holy task, and to thoroughly cleanse both themselves and the temple.

The priests and Levites accept the challenge. They set about clearing the rubbish that has accumulated in the temple during the years of neglect. The priests turn out all the trappings of pagan worship from the sanctuary, and the Levites throw them into the Kidron Valley. When all is clean and ready, they report back to the king.

The king and his officials come to the temple with animals for sacrifice: seven bulls, seven rams, seven male lambs and seven male goats.

The bulls, rams and lambs are for burnt offerings on behalf of the different groups – seven being the 'perfect' number that stands for the relationship of God and humanity.

The male goats are for a sin offering. The king and the assembly lay their hands on the goats before they are killed, to show that it is for their sins that the animals are being sacrificed.

While the offerings are being burned, the Levites play psalms from the days of David, on the instruments which David himself appointed. Even after the offerings are completed, they continue to worship God in psalms, with the priests joining in with their trumpets.

All is now ready for the people to bring their sacrifices and thank-offerings. The number of sacrifices is small compared with the day when Solomon dedicated the temple. In any case, there are not enough priests who are ceremonially clean to cope with the skinning of the animals. The Levites, who have taken the time to prepare themselves properly, are able to help.

With the temple cleansed and rededicated, Hezekiah and all the people praise God. They are full of joy that so much has been achieved so quickly.

Hezekiah sends out an invitation for all Israel and Judah to join in a celebration of the Passover. Sadly, the northern kingdom has now been conquered by the Assyrians (in 723 BC), and only the tribes of Ephraim and Manasseh, Issachar and Zebulun have survived in any numbers.

The Passover is held in the second month of the year, which is a month later than usual. The date is delayed to allow extra time for spiritual, ritual and practical preparation. Hezekiah needs time to send out the messengers with invitations. The priests need time for the lengthy process of consecration. The people who are travelling to Jerusalem need time to make their journeys.

Hezekiah sends messengers throughout the land, from Dan in the north to Beersheba in the south. After more than two centuries of painful division and defeat, this Passover is a festival of reunion and reconciliation. Even those who are not ceremonially clean are welcome to take part. Hezekiah prays that God will pardon all those who are genuinely seeking him.

The festival is so successful that the Feast of Unleavened Bread is extended for a further week. Hezekiah contributes most generously, as befits a true descendant of David. He and his officials donate thousands of animals for sacrifice. These are not burnt offerings but peace offerings – to be offered to God and then shared as food among the worshippers. On their way home, the pilgrims joyfully destroy the sites and symbols of pagan worship.

Now Hezekiah organizes the day-to-day running of the temple. He invites the people of Jerusalem to bring their tithes of grain and produce for the support of the priests and Levites. The response is overwhelming – echoing the glad and generous commitments that were made in the days of David. For four months the offerings are simply piled in heaps, until Conaniah can get the storerooms sorted out!

In Hezekiah, the Chronicler has found his hero. Here at last is a king who seeks God, obeys his law, serves the temple and works hard. He does the right thing with all his heart all the time for the glory of God. And God blesses him.

When Hezekiah has been on the throne for fourteen years, everything he has achieved is threatened with destruction. Sennacherib, the king of Assyria, invades Judah and prepares to lay siege to Jerusalem.

The armies of Assyria are a formidable fighting force. In human terms, Judah stands no chance. But Hezekiah makes safe his water supply, doubles his defences and stockpiles his weapons. Most of all, he encourages his people with the assurance that God is with them and will fight their battles for them.

Sennacherib sends his officers to Jerusalem to intimidate the defenders and destroy their morale. He declares that no god has ever been able to resist the might of Assyria – and that the God of Hezekiah will be no exception. In his pride and ignorance, Sennacherib does not realize that Hezekiah's faith will prove more effective than any army.

King Hezekiah and his prophet Isaiah cry out to God for help. And help comes, in the form of an angel who destroys the Assyrian army in a single night. Sennacherib has no choice but to retreat. He returns to his own land, where his sons assassinate him in the temple of his god.

Before the Chronicler leaves his account of Hezekiah, he gives some final glimpses of this great king.

He records how God spared Hezekiah from death when he was dangerously ill. The books of Kings tell how Hezekiah was suffering from a septic boil, and that Isaiah declared he would die. However, God had pity on him and healed him, promising to add another fifteen years to his life. He made the sun's shadow retreat ten steps on Ahaz's stairway as a sign that this healing was a miracle (2 Kings 20:1–11).

The Chronicler mentions Hezekiah's pride, which aroused God's anger. When envoys came from Babylon to enquire about his healing, Hezekiah failed to give the glory to God. He also foolishly showed off his treasures to his visitors, and talked no doubt about a possible alliance against Assyria. All this gave the impression that Hezekiah was secure in his own strength, when in fact he was totally dependent on God for protection.

King Manasseh (2 Chronicles 33:1–20)

Hezekiah's son, Manasseh, is twelve years old when he becomes king of Judah. He reigns for fifty-five years – the longest and most wicked of all the reigns.

The Chronicler, like the writer of 2 Kings (2 Kings 21:1–9), describes Manasseh's wickedness. The new king allows back into Israel all the pagan gods and evil practices which had been driven out by Joshua and David. He even sets up pagan altars in the temple itself, and offers his own sons as human sacrifices in the Valley of Hinnom. This terrible place is sometimes known as Gehenna and will be used by Jesus as an image of hell.

It may be that Manasseh is very religious, and that he is enlisting all the forces of foreign gods, astrology and magic to strengthen his kingdom. But this is exactly what God has always forbidden. It is his name only that is to be worshipped in Israel; and he will prove himself greater than all gods in saving and protecting his people.

Unlike the writer of 2 Kings, the Chronicler tells us that God punishes Manasseh. The evil king is taken captive by the Assyrians and led away by a hook through his nose. In exile, he repents and God restores him to his throne. In the closing years of his reign he is able to strengthen the walls of Jerusalem, protect his people and throw out the pagan idols and other trappings of idolatry.

The book of Kings blames Manasseh for the punishment that falls on Judah and the people of Jerusalem in later years. The Chronicler gives a different account. He describes Manasseh's captivity, repentance and the good achievements of his reign. In this way, Manasseh's life can be seen as a miniature of what is to happen to Judah and Jerusalem. They will be conquered by the Babylonians for their sins, and sent into exile, but later restored.

King Amon (2 Chronicles 33:21–25)

Manasseh is succeeded as king of Judah by his son Amon. Amon is twenty-two years old, and his reign is brief and bitter.

Amon follows the idolatrous ways of his father, but without the repentance which transformed Manasseh's last years. He is assassinated by his own officials. They in turn are slaughtered in a popular movement which brings Josiah to the throne.

King Josiah (2 Chronicles 34:1–35:27)

Josiah, Amon's son, becomes king in 641 BC, when he is eight years old. At this time, Judah is a small and unimportant part of the Assyrian empire, and it is to Assyrian gods that many people look for influence and help. But Josiah's hero is King David. When he is sixteen, he seeks God's help to become a just and godly ruler, like his great ancestor.

By the time Josiah is twenty, the Assyrian power is beginning to wane. The empire has become very large and is proving difficult to control. Josiah takes advantage of this situation to rid Judah of Assyrian gods – breaking down their altars, cutting up the fertility poles of the goddess Asherah and destroying idols.

Josiah's reforms are very thorough, including burning the bones of pagan priests, grinding their ashes to powder and sprinkling them over altars and graves to defile them. However, the worship of Baal-gods has been widespread in Judah for many years; there is no evidence that Josiah's purge is popular.

Josiah's next project is to restore the temple, which has fallen into disrepair. He enlists the money and skills of many of the Israelites from the tribes of Manasseh and Ephraim in the northern kingdom. They have been conquered by the Assyrians in 722 BC, and thousands have become displaced persons. Some have come as refugees to the southern kingdom of Judah, where Josiah puts them to work under the direction of the Levites.

As the work on the temple begins, the high priest discovers the Book of the Law of the Lord. This is probably part of the book of Deuteronomy, which includes the blessings and curses that follow from keeping or breaking the covenant (Deuteronomy 27–28).

When Josiah has the law read aloud to him, he is devastated. God's people have defied and broken it in every aspect, and a terrible judgment must be about to fall. The king consults a prophetess, Huldah, who confirms his worst fears. However, she declares that Josiah himself will be spared the disaster, because he has repented and tried to do what is right.

As events prove, Josiah is the last good king of Judah. He renews the covenant and encourages his people to do the same. He also provides for the greatest Passover celebration since the days of Samuel.

Meanwhile, the international scene is changing. The rising power is Babylon, which is emerging to challenge the dominance of Assyria and Egypt. Pharaoh Neco takes an Egyptian army to support Assyria against the Babylonians at Carchemish. As they pass by Judah, Josiah decides to challenge the pharaoh to battle. It is in this needless skirmish that Josiah is killed at Megiddo. He has been king for thirty-one years.

King Jehoahaz (2 Chronicles 36:1–4)

Josiah is succeeded as king by his son Jehoahaz. The young man's reign lasts only a few months. He is deposed and deported by the king of Egypt, who puts another of Josiah's sons on the throne instead.

King Jehoiakim (2 Chronicles 36:5–8)

The new king, Eliakim, is an elder brother of Jehoahaz. The king of Egypt changes his name to Jehoiakim, and demands tribute of silver and gold from Judah.

With the Assyrian empire overthrown, Judah now finds herself squeezed between Babylon and Egypt. Jehoiakim's reign lasts eleven years under the protection of Egypt. However, the king of Babylon, Nebuchadnezzar, defeats Pharaoh Neco in 605 BC and later lays siege to Jerusalem. He takes Jehoiakim captive and raids the Jerusalem temple for treasures to take back to Babylon.

King Jehoiachin (2 Chronicles 36:9–10)

The next king is Jehoiachin. He reigns for a mere three months, before Nebuchadnezzar exiles him and appoints his uncle, Zedekiah, to be king.

King Zedekiah (2 Chronicles 36:11–14)

Zedekiah becomes king when he is twenty-one years old. His country is tossed on the stormy sea of international conflict, but he survives for eleven years. However, he does so without seeking God's help and in defiance of the messages of the prophet Jeremiah.

The fall of Jerusalem (2 Chronicles 36:15–19)

The Chronicler shows us, in this series of short reigns, the death throes of Judah. She has abandoned God and God is now abandoning her. The armies of Assyria, Egypt and Babylon are all his instruments of judgment. But Judah is corrupt and ready to fall, her people unfaithful and her leaders ungodly.

Zedekiah tries to double-cross Nebuchadnezzar, and so provokes the final assault on Jerusalem by the Babylonians. Jerusalem is destroyed, her population mercilessly slaughtered or captured, and her temple sacked. The Chronicler says that it is God who brings Nebuchadnezzar against his own people, and God who hands them over to their enemy. It is 587 BC.

The exile in Babylon (2 Chronicles 36:20–21)

Even when the worst has happened – Jerusalem in ruins and her people dead or deported – the Chronicler gives glimmers of hope. After all, he is writing of these events from the other side of the years of exile. He and his readers know that God's people will survive.

Some of the survivors become servants to the king of Babylon. In the past, God made Joseph prime minister of Egypt, and Moses one of its princes. In the future there will be fine servants of pagan kings, such as Daniel and Nehemiah. God hasn't ceased to exist because his people are no longer in their own land and temple. His purpose moves on, even in the darkest of times.

The Chronicler says that the land enjoys her sabbath rests. It seems that Judah's kings have never enforced the sabbath year during which the land could recover strength and fertility. Now, with few people to cultivate them, the fields lie fallow. There is peace after tension and bloodshed. The damage and din of pagan worship have finally ceased.

The decree to return (2 Chronicles 36:22–23)

After seventy years, a new world power emerges. This is the Persian empire, and Cyrus is its king.

Cyrus is interested in religion and tolerant of all faiths. Just as Nebuchadnezzar was God's instrument for judging his people, so Cyrus is his means of restoring them. One of the new emperor's first actions is to decree that a temple shall be built in Jerusalem. Anyone who wishes to return home to help with this work may do so!

EZRA and NEHEMIAH

The books of Ezra and Nehemiah tell how the Jews return from exile in Babylonia and rebuild the city of Jerusalem and the temple. This takes place over a long period of time and with great difficulty.

The returning exiles meet strong opposition from their enemies in the region. The Samaritans don't want to see Jerusalem established as a strong, secure city. At the same time, the Jews have to rediscover their nationhood and renew their commitment to God's law.

Nehemiah is appointed governor of Jerusalem by Cyrus, the emperor of Persia. He is granted permission to rebuild the walls of Jerusalem.

Ezra arrives in Jerusalem with a group of returning exiles. It is difficult to tell whether he comes before or after Nehemiah. Ezra is a teacher or scribe who sets God's law at the heart of Jewish life.

OUTLINE

The return from exile and rebuilding of the temple (Ezra 1:1–6:22)
Ezra's return and leadership (Ezra 7:1–10:44)
The rebuilding of the walls of Jerusalem (Nehemiah 1:1–7:73)
Ezra reads the law and the people agree to obey it (Nehemiah 8:1–10:39)
Resettlement and Nehemiah's reforms (Nehemiah 11:1–13:31)

Introduction

The book of Ezra continues the history of the Jewish people from the end of the books of Chronicles. It records how two major groups of people return to Jerusalem from exile in Babylon. The first group is led by Zerubbabel, a governor of Judea. The second is led by Ezra, who is a scribe or teacher. Although the book is named after Ezra, he doesn't enter the story until chapter 7.

Personal memoirs

The books of Ezra and Nehemiah are compiled from personal memoirs, imperial edicts, official letters and lists of people. Between Ezra 7 and Nehemiah 13, the memoirs of the two main characters are merged:

Ezra 7:1–10:44 Ezra's memoirs 1
Nehemiah 1:1–7:73 Nehemiah's memoirs 1
Nehemiah 8:1–12:26 Ezra's memoirs 2
Nehemiah 12:27–13:31 Nehemiah's memoirs 2

The people of Israel are suffering from poverty, bewilderment and low morale. The confidence and wealth of the days of David and Solomon are gone, never to return. The new temple won't be as fine as the old one, and will only be built after much discouragement and long delay. Idolatry and immorality have weakened the people's spiritual health and corrupted their society. They have been conquered and displaced for two generations. They have no king, no army and no empire.

Now, at last, there is the opportunity for rebuilding and a new beginning. The prophets have a great sense that God is with his people. Ezra and Nehemiah both believe it is God who moves the Persian king to provide for the temple and give permission for the walls of Jerusalem to be rebuilt. Despite the trauma of the past centuries, God still has a purpose for Israel. He is their king and his law will be their way to a new life.

Purity... and understanding

The early chapters of Ezra tell how Zerubbabel brings a group of exiles back to Jerusalem. They offer sacrifices and start to rebuild the temple. Once Ezra enters the story (in chapter 7), there is more attention to the rebuilding of the people themselves. Ezra's hard task is to teach God's law and to lead the people by his own example. In particular, there is a rigorous policy that the Jews should not intermarry with pagan nations.

The books of Ezra and Nehemiah are very strict about the religious purity of the community. Both leaders take action to dissolve mixed marriages. Intermarriage with pagan tribes has led to idolatry in the past, even for wise King Solomon himself. The book of Esther takes a more open view, that God can bless and use a marriage which takes place across a racial boundary. Moses himself had foreign wives.

Scholars have wondered whether the final editing of Ezra and Nehemiah was done by the same person who compiled the books of Chronicles. The Chronicler seems more relaxed about including outsiders in the people of God. 2 Chronicles 30 welcomes the northern tribes after the conquest of Israel. In Ezra and Nehemiah we find a more exclusive view – that only those who have taken part in the Babylonian exile are the true Israel. This fact is simply recorded, without any clue as to whether the writer approves of the statement.

Ezra and Nehemiah are men of great vision and determination. However, they are sometimes narrow and insensitive. At the end of the book of Nehemiah, we see a nation under a dictatorship of strict moral and religious rules. Nehemiah is proud that he has excluded foreigners and evicted his enemy Tobiah from the temple. He is pleased to have forced visiting traders to observe the sabbath rest. He has dealt severely with Jews who have foreign wives and children. But the regime does not convey the real nature and love of God; and it doesn't work.

Nehemiah is a faithful and energetic leader, but we long for more understanding and gentleness in his actions.

Ezra also may be missing a great opportunity when he refuses the help of outsiders (Ezra 4:1–4). Isaiah had prophesied that foreigners would come to love God and serve him in Jerusalem, swelling the number of returning exiles (Isaiah 56:6–8). No doubt Ezra feels that these are desperate times and he needs a pure nucleus to start with.

The search for exclusive holiness continues among the Pharisees of Jesus' day. It is one of the hardest barriers that the early church has to overcome, if the gospel is really to reach all the nations of the world (Acts 10 and 15).

Who came first – Ezra or Nehemiah?

The Bible's order of books has Ezra before Nehemiah. However, in some ways the story would make more sense if Nehemiah came first. That way,

Ezra and Nehemiah

Ezra and Nehemiah were originally one book. They are the last part of the history which tells the story of Israel from Adam to Nehemiah.

It is possible that Ezra is the person who wrote or edited Chronicles. His 'memoirs' in Ezra 7–10 are continued in Nehemiah 8:1–12:26. However, the tone of Chronicles is more accepting of foreigners than Ezra is.

The prophets

Two prophets, Haggai and Zechariah, are important figures in the restoration of Jerusalem. Their books give us added insight into the situation at this time. Malachi may also have been written shortly before the return of Ezra and Nehemiah to Jerusalem.

Nehemiah rebuilds the walls of Jerusalem and then Ezra comes to teach the people the law of God.

The dates given in the Bible show the Jews returning to their homeland over a period of ninety years. If Zerubbabel returns in 536 BC and Ezra in 458 BC, then Nehemiah's journey to Jerusalem was probably twelve years later, in 445 BC.

We know that Nehemiah was in Jerusalem for twelve years from 445–433 BC. This is from the 20th year of the reign of Artaxerxes I to the 32nd year (Nehemiah 2:1 and 13:6). Nehemiah returned to the Persian court for a while (probably quite a short time), and then came back to Jerusalem to make further reforms.

The traditional view is that Ezra arrived in Jerusalem some years before Nehemiah, in 458 BC. This means that his king, too, is Artaxerxes I (Ezra 7:7). If this date is right, then Ezra comes before Nehemiah, as we would expect from the order of their books in the Bible.

Another theory is that Ezra returned to Judea much later, in 398 BC. This would mean that his king (Ezra 7:7) is Artaxerxes II, not Artaxerxes I. But is it likely that Ezra and Nehemiah would both be living in Jerusalem at the same time, without mentioning each other?

Discovering Ezra and Nehemiah

The return from exile and rebuilding of the temple

Cyrus allows the Jews to return home (Ezra 1:1–2:70)

Cyrus has become king of Persia and has conquered the evil empire of Babylon. One of his first acts is to allow the Jews to return home from exile (1:1–11). He encourages them to rebuild their temple in Jerusalem.

The Israelites once escaped from Egypt, laden with the wealth of their captors. Now the Jews are sent on their way back to Judah, with money, goods, livestock and offerings from their Babylonian neighbours.

The writer is in no doubt that it is God who is doing all this for the Jews. Everything is happening to fulfil the prophecy of Jeremiah. Jeremiah had foretold that the land of Judah would be laid waste and its people made slaves in Babylon for seventy years; but at the end of that time, Babylon herself would be defeated (Jeremiah 25:11–12).

Cyrus is not a worshipper of the Lord. We know from other records that he worships pagan gods, including Marduk and Sin. But he respects

What's been going on?

The Babylonians have conquered the kingdom of Judah and destroyed its capital city Jerusalem. All the leading citizens of Jerusalem have been deported to Babylonia, where they and their families have lived in exile for seventy years.

Now Babylon has in turn been defeated by the combined force of the Medes and the Persians. The city of Babylon fell in 539 BC.

The new Persian king is Cyrus. He is tolerant towards the peoples of his empire. He gives permission for those who have been displaced by the Babylonians to return home. This enables a group of exiled Jews to return to Judea and Jerusalem in 538 BC.

Cyrus wants his subjects to govern themselves, while still paying tribute to his empire. He is willing to encourage national religions and has a great respect for the God of Israel.

the God of Israel. He is careful to return the temple treasures which King Nebuchadnezzar had carried away to Babylon in 597 BC and 587 BC.

The list of the exiles who return

The journey from Babylon to Jerusalem takes about four months. This list of leaders, tribes and families is repeated in Nehemiah (Nehemiah 7:6–73), although there are some differences of detail. Here eleven main leaders are listed. In other lists there are twelve, which corresponds to the twelve tribes of Israel.

Zerubbabel is to be the governor. Jeshua (or Joshua) is the first high priest after the exile. He is the grandson of Seraiah, who was the last high priest before the exile. The 'Nehemiah' who is mentioned here is not the governor who will rebuild the walls of Jerusalem, but someone else with the same name.

The families who are returning to Judah are named after their ancestors or their home towns. A huge number – 4,289 – of the returnees are priests. They are looking forward to building and serving in a new temple. Surprisingly, there are only 342 Levites. They include the singers and gatekeepers, who will play an important part in the daily life of the temple. When Ezra returns, he has to call in extra Levites because there aren't enough in his group.

Zerubbabel's title of 'governor' is the Persian for 'the one to be feared'. It will also be used of Nehemiah.

Urim and Thummim are the stones which the high priest uses to give God's guidance. They are kept in the high priest's breastplate and drawn out to indicate 'Yes' or 'No'. There is no other mention of them after the exile.

The first thing the people do on arriving in Jerusalem is to visit the site of the temple, the house of the Lord. This is the moment they have been longing for. They give money for the rebuilding and robes for the priests.

Worship begins again on the temple site (Ezra 3:1–6)

Although the temple is in ruins, the Israelites rebuild the altar and offer sacrifices there once again. They follow the instructions in the law of Moses – that is, the books of Leviticus and Numbers.

The first major festival they celebrate is the Feast of Tabernacles. This is one of the three great annual feasts, when as many people as possible come to Jerusalem. The festival is sometimes called the 'Festival of Booths', because the people build shelters or 'booths' to recall the days when their ancestors lived in the wilderness. Now it will also remind them of their journey of return from exile.

At last the old pattern of worship and sacrifice is in place. The New Moon sacrifices are not in honour of the moon, but to mark the first day of a new month and make it a holy day.

The foundations of the new temple are laid (Ezra 3:7-13)

The preparations for building the temple sound similar to the work done by Solomon for the first temple.

Once again the strength and skills of the people of Tyre and Sidon are enlisted to bring cedar wood by sea from Lebanon to Joppa. Joppa is the nearest port to Jerusalem. It is a sign of the times that the permission to do this comes from a foreign overlord, Cyrus of Persia.

It is an emotional moment when the foundations of the new temple are laid. While the young Levites carry out the work of building, the old priests weep or shout for joy. Jeremiah had prophesied that one day sounds of celebrations would be heard again in the streets of Jerusalem (Jeremiah 33:10-11). The refrain of their praise is: 'The Lord is good; his love endures for ever' (3:11).

Perhaps the whole song is the one written by David, which is recorded in 1 Chronicles 16:8-36.

Enemies offer to help – and are refused (Ezra 4:1-3)

The Israelites' enemies offer to help them with the rebuilding. These are people who have been resettled in Samaria by the Assyrians. They come from a variety of races and nations, but claim to worship the God of Israel now that they live in his area.

The Jewish leaders are very firm in their refusal. The new temple and the new Jerusalem are to be purely Jewish. This sounds exclusive and unkind. However, their problem is to keep Israel's vision clear and her

The Persian kings

559–530 Cyrus
530–522 Cambyses
522–486 Darius I (Hystaspes) (the Great)
486–465 Xerxes I (Ahasuerus)
465–424 Artaxerxes I (Longimanus)
424–423 Xerxes II
423–404 Darius II
404–358 Artaxerxes II (Mnemon)

faith focused. Mixing with pagan religions has brought disaster in the past. Allowing people to join the work who don't really want it to succeed might prove bad for progress and morale.

Letters of protest to the kings of Persia (Ezra 4:4–6:12)

The opposition hardens against the rebuilding of Jerusalem and the temple. The Israelites' enemies do all in their power to criticize and undermine the project. Their scorn, political lobbying and physical attacks continue through the reigns of several Persian kings.

A letter sent to Xerxes

The writer now mentions some of the letters of protest which are sent to the Persian kings. The first is at the beginning of the reign of Xerxes, in 486 BC (4:6). Xerxes is called Ahasuerus in the Bible and he reigns from 486–465 BC.

Samaritan leaders write to Artaxerxes

The leaders in Trans-Euphrates send a strong letter of warning to another Persian king, Artaxerxes (4:7–24). 'Trans-Euphrates' or 'beyond the river' is the part of the Persian empire to the west of the River Euphrates. It includes the province of Samaria, which is the centre of opposition to the rebuilding of Jerusalem.

The Samaritan leaders warn the king that Jerusalem has been a well-defended city in the past, and that its people have a reputation for being rebellious. If the Jews succeed in rebuilding Jerusalem, they will stop paying tribute to Persia and pull the whole region away from the empire.

King Artaxerxes checks his records and find that what the Samaritans say is true. He orders the rebuilding work to stop immediately, a message which the Samaritans are pleased and quick to deliver. Later, Artaxerxes changes his mind and commissions Nehemiah to rebuild Jerusalem's walls (Nehemiah 2:7-9).

Prophets encourage the work to restart

It is now the second year of the reign of King Darius of Persia in 520 BC. The work of rebuilding the temple has been halted for about sixteen years. The Israelites have concluded that God doesn't want the work done, and have settled for building their own houses instead (Haggai 1:9).

Into this depressed situation come two great prophets, Haggai and Zechariah. We have books of their prophecies in the Bible, towards the end of the Old Testament.

Haggai challenges the people to return to God again (5:1-2). Every part of their lives is impoverished because they are failing to honour God and complete his house, which is the temple (Haggai 1:5-8).

Zechariah inspires the people with his promises of God's presence in the city and the great days of peace and prosperity that are to come. He, too, urges them to complete the temple (Zechariah 8:9). With their vision renewed, the Israelites set to work and finish the building.

Samaritan leaders write to King Darius

Another governor of Trans-Euphrates now writes to another king of Persia. This time the king is Darius, who reigns from 522 to 486 BC (5:3 - 6:12). The governor is Tattenai. He is not hostile like the previous Samaritan governor, but simply asking for information.

Tattenai asks the Israelites who gave them permission to build the temple. He then writes to King Darius, alerting him to the scale of the project, the size of the stones and timbers and the vigour of the work.

Tattenai tells the king that the Jews are claiming Cyrus issued a decree for their temple to be rebuilt. The governor asks Darius to confirm this and give him any further instructions.

The original decree is not found in the archives at Babylon, but a note of the main points has been kept in the summer palace at Ecbatana. The contents agree entirely with the Jews' account of events.

Darius writes to Tattenai with a strong confirmation that the temple is to be completed. He commands that the cost of the building and supplies for the priests are to be met from the revenues of Trans-Euphrates. So the Samaritans are compelled to pay for the work they have been trying to stop!

The temple is completed and dedicated (Ezra 6:13-18)

The temple is completed on 12 March 515 BC, just seventy years after it was destroyed. Artaxerxes is mentioned among those who have helped the project, although he has not yet been made king. His name may be included because he makes a contribution at a later date.

The celebrations remind us of the festival at the dedication of Solomon's temple, although the number of sacrifices is smaller now because the people are poorer.

The Passover is celebrated (Ezra 6:19-22)

A month after the dedication of the temple, the Jews celebrate the Passover.

Passover is the most important feast in the Jewish year. By it, the Jews celebrate their birth as a nation. It was during the first Passover night, when they were slaves in Egypt, that God slew the first-born sons of their Egyptian persecutors and 'passed over' the homes of the Israelites. It was this terrible act of judgment which finally persuaded the Pharaoh to release them.

The Levites slaughter the Passover lambs – one for each household. Those who are allowed to take part in the meal are the people who have returned from exile and anyone else who has renounced the pagan practices of neighbours such as the Samaritans.

The lamb is roasted and eaten with unleavened bread. The bread at the first Passover was made without leaven (yeast), so that it could be prepared quickly, needing no time for the dough to rise. The Passover meal was then eaten in a hurry, with each family member dressed ready to leave Egypt in the morning. Now the Passover meal marks the beginning of a week-long 'Feast of Unleavened Bread'.

The king of Assyria is suddenly mentioned as having assisted with the work! This should, of course, be the king of Persia, who is now ruling the old Assyrian empire.

Ezra's return and leadership

Ezra comes to Jerusalem (Ezra 7:1–10)

The story moves on sixty years. Zerubbabel and Joshua are now dead, and we have no details of what has happened in the meantime.

Ezra at last enters the book which bears his name. He has an excellent pedigree, being able to trace his family line from Aaron, the first high priest. The 900-mile journey from Babylon takes Ezra and his group four months.

Ezra arrives in Jerusalem in 458 BC. He is a teacher, or 'scribe'. The scribes are secretaries who write letters or make copies of the Scriptures in these days before printing. Now they are to become more important in the life of Israel, because they 'keep' the law in every sense. Ezra studies, practises and teaches the law of God. Now he will bring God's law to the heart of Israel's national life.

Ezra's letter from King Artaxerxes (Ezra 7:11–28)

Ezra is given a powerful mandate by the king of Persia. He is to impose the law of the God of Israel on the whole region of Trans-Euphrates. This is the fifth district of the Persian satrapy, or government, and includes the whole of Palestine and Syria.

Ezra is sent to Jerusalem with money for sacrifices. He also has the king's command that the treasurers of Trans-Euphrates shall provide silver, wheat, wine, oil and salt for the temple. Also, the temple staff are to live tax-free. The king clearly wishes his empire to be protected from the wrath of the God of Israel.

Ezra's main task relates to the law of God. He is to appoint magistrates and judges who are trained in God's law, and to teach those who aren't.

Ezra praises God

Suddenly we hear Ezra's own voice (7:27–28). The language changes to Hebrew (until now it has been Aramaic), and we have Ezra's account of events. He praises God for prompting the king to this action, and rejoices that the temple in Jerusalem is to be honoured. He decides to take some leading Israelites with him on his mission.

A list of the leaders who return with Ezra (Ezra 8:1-14)

While in exile, the Jews have kept their sense of family and nation alive. All the people know to which clan they belong and from whom they are descended. Now Ezra lists the leaders who return with him to Jerusalem, together with their clans. The total number of people is 1,496.

Ezra's leadership (Ezra 8:15-30)

Ezra is a careful organizer. He assembles the people by the Ahava Canal, to prepare for the journey. They fast and pray, asking God for protection. They have enemies in the region and may well be attacked; but Ezra does not ask the king for an armed escort. They rely completely on God to look after them.

No doubt Ezra is thinking of the exodus from Egypt, when a similar journey to Canaan took forty years. This time he wants the people to live in strict obedience to God. Nehemiah, on the other hand, has no hesitation in asking for the emperor's help. He lists his requests – and they are granted.

Ezra finds there is a shortage of Levites to serve in the temple when they get to Jerusalem. As this is one of the main purposes of the journey, he sends for reinforcements.

Ezra entrusts twelve priests and the twelve newly recruited Levites with the temple treasure. It is worth a fortune.

The exiles arrive in Jerusalem (Ezra 8:31-36)

When the returning exiles arrive in Jerusalem they rest after their long journey. Then they hand over the temple treasure, weighing and accounting for every item. When they have completed this duty, they fulfil a long-held dream. They offer sacrifices in the temple – whole offerings on behalf of the whole people to a holy God.

Ezra and his colleagues deliver the king's orders to the satraps – the provincial governors of the Persian empire. The governors ensure that the king's orders are carried out. The Israelites are given every assistance in providing for the temple worship and establishing God's law.

The scandal of marriage to pagans (Ezra 9:1–10:44)

Now there is a problem. It is revealed that many Israelites, including priests and other leaders, have married pagan wives. When Ezra hears of this, he is deeply shocked. He tears his clothes and beard as a sign of grief.

For Ezra, the distinctiveness of the community is an important part of religious purity. It is through intermarriage with pagan peoples that Israel has been corrupted by idolatry. It is probably the men of the first group to return from exile who have married foreigners, because of the shortage of Israelite women. They have broken God's law, which says, 'Do not intermarry with them… for you are a people holy to the Lord your God' (Deuteronomy 7:1–6). However, there is a law allowing Israelites to marry foreign captive women (Deuteronomy 21:10–14).

Ezra's prayer

Ezra prays to God (9:3–15). He confesses the people's sin as if it is his own. He freely admits that they have broken God's law, despite the Lord's goodness to them in giving them a new start. He makes no excuses and suggests no remedy.

The people repent

While Ezra prays, the people gather round him and weep (10:1–17). One of them, Shecaniah, declares that the answer is in their own hands. All the men are summoned to appear in Jerusalem within three days. Meanwhile, Ezra retreats to fast and pray in the room of Jehohanan. Jehohanan will become high priest one day, succeeding his father and great-grandfather.

The men assemble in the temple forecourt in December. It is raining heavily, as though the weather itself is reflecting their grief.

When Ezra speaks to the men, he solemnly commands them to confess their sin and dismiss their foreign wives. They nearly all agree, but suggest that the matter will be best handled by the elders and judges of their home towns. In the event, the whole process takes three months.

A list of leaders who married foreigners

The book of Ezra ends with a list of the men who have married foreign women (10:18–44). They include priests and Levites, as well as Israelites from eleven clans. Some of them have had children.

However carefully and considerately the divorces are accomplished, this is an agonizing episode in Israel's history. We are not told that God required this inquisition or approved it. Not every human response under repentance is necessarily right. As with Achan's sin after the victory at Jericho, so here: there is a painful backlash to the joy of the return from exile.

The rebuilding of the walls of Jerusalem

Nehemiah receives bad news (Nehemiah 1:1–3)

Nehemiah is a trusted official in the Persian royal court. He is cupbearer to the king, Artaxerxes I. As Nehemiah begins his story, he is in Susa, where Artaxerxes has a winter palace. Kislev is the ninth month of the year.

News comes to Nehemiah from Jerusalem. The Jews who have returned to their capital after years of exile are struggling to survive. In particular, they are without walls or gates to defend their city.

Nehemiah prays to God for help (Nehemiah 1:4–11)

Nehemiah is devastated by the news. He is in a difficult position. Some years ago, the king received a report from local officials about Jerusalem, which warned him that the city had a history of rebellion. In their opinion, a restored Jerusalem would make the region ungovernable. Following their advice, the king had issued a command that the rebuilding work should stop. It is very hard to reverse a royal decree!

Nehemiah prays about the problem. He accepts his own part in Israel's disobedience. He draws on the warnings and promises of the books of Moses. The exile has been the fulfilment of a solemn warning, that if Israel was unfaithful to God, he would scatter her people to far countries (Leviticus 26:33). But there is also mercy. If God's people repent, he will gather them back to their homeland (Deuteronomy 30:1–5). Nehemiah asks God to open the way for him to talk to the king – who is, after all, only a fellow human being.

Permission to rebuild Jerusalem (Nehemiah 2:1-10)

As royal cupbearer, Nehemiah has daily access to the king. His task is to taste the king's wine, to prove that it isn't poisoned. As Nehemiah also serves in the presence of the queen, he has almost certainly been made a eunuch.

After some months of mourning, praying and waiting, Nehemiah has his opportunity. It is Nisan, the first month of the year. The king notices that Nehemiah looks sad. It is a punishable offence to appear sad in the presence of the king. Nehemiah explains that his sadness is because of the desperate state of Jerusalem, his ancestral home.

When the king asks Nehemiah what he wants, the cupbearer sends up the briefest of prayers and begs the royal permission to rebuild the city. He sets a timescale, requests letters of safe conduct and negotiates a supply of wooden beams for the various buildings.

Suddenly all is going well. The king is on Nehemiah's side, but some powerful opposition awaits.

The king's letter comes to the regional governors, Sanballat and Tobiah. We know from a document called the Elephantine Papyrus that Sanballat I is governor of Samaria. Tobiah may be the Persian governor of the Ammonites in east Judea. Neither of them wants to see Jerusalem restored, because they would lose their dominance of the region.

Nehemiah surveys the ruins and begins
(Nehemiah 2:11-18)

Once in Jerusalem, Nehemiah inspects the ruined walls. He does so at night, so that no one will guess his plans.

He starts at the Valley Gate, on the south-west corner of the city. From there he visits the Dung Gate to the east, the Fountain Gate on the eastern wall and the King's Pool, which is probably the Pool of Siloam. He also goes some way along the Kidron Valley to review the damage there. He has now seen the worst of the destruction.

After completing his inspection, Nehemiah talks to his officials. He encourages them to work with him to rebuild the city's defences. In this way they will regain their self-respect. He tells them of his experience that God is with them.

Nehemiah defies his enemies (Nehemiah 2:19–20)

As the work begins, Sanballat and Tobiah arrive to pour scorn on the project. They are joined by Geshem, a powerful Arab chieftain who rules the desert country to the south and south-east of Judah. Jerusalem is almost completely surrounded by enemies.

The critics ask if the Jews are rebelling against their Persian overlord. They are not, of course, but the suggestion is meant to stir up trouble. Nehemiah answers that this is God's work and God will grant them success. Jerusalem's enemies must stay away. They have no part or share in what is going on.

The work progresses well (Nehemiah 3:1–32)

Nehemiah allocates sections of the wall to different people and groups. There are forty-two sections in all. They are listed in order, anticlockwise from the Sheep Gate on the north-east corner of the city.

Every kind and class of person takes part in the work – men and women, fathers and daughters, priests and Levites, officials and merchants, goldsmiths and perfume-makers. Most of them are working on the stretch of wall near their homes. In each section, the gatehouse is rebuilt and its doors restored and rehung.

Nehemiah organizes defence (Nehemiah 4:1–23)

Sanballat's scorn turns to fury. To him the task seems impossible, with a puny workforce and damaged materials. Tobiah gives his opinion that even a fox could dislodge the whole structure. But the workers press on, fired up by prayers for help – and revenge. When the enemies threaten to attack, Nehemiah organizes half the people to provide an armed guard while the other half carry on with the work.

Nehemiah is a great motivator. He reminds people that they are fighting for their homes and families – and that God, the greatest fighter of all, is on their side.

Nehemiah secures a fair deal for the poor
(Nehemiah 5:1–13)

As the danger from enemies is confronted, another problem breaks out among the Israelites themselves.

Some of the poor people have had to forfeit their lands and are now having to sell their children into slavery. This is because there is a famine and food is scarce and expensive. In addition, all the Jews are paying taxes to the Persian king, supporting the Persian officials and their Jewish governor *and* providing tithes for the priests and temple.

Nehemiah is angry that wealthy Jews are charging their poorer neighbours 'usury', or interest on loans. This is forbidden in the law of Moses (Exodus 22:25), because all Jews are members of one family. It is wrong to charge interest on a loan within the family.

To tackle the problem of poverty, Nehemiah commands that all land and property shall be returned to its original owners. He also instructs the lenders to return the money and produce that they have taken as interest. This is a mini-Jubilee – good news for the poor and the cancelling of debts.

Nehemiah notes his self-restraint (Nehemiah 5:14–19)

Nehemiah records that he has not behaved like other governors. He has not claimed a food allowance from the people. He has been sensitive to their poverty and unwilling to add to their burdens. He has been a hard-working governor, overseeing the rebuilding of the city wall and feeding a large number of officials at his own table.

Nehemiah's enemies try to intimidate him
(Nehemiah 6:1–19)

Sanballat and Geshem repeatedly invite Nehemiah to meet with them. Knowing that they plan to harm him, Nehemiah tells them he is busy with something far more important. Next, they send him a blackmail letter, left open so that the messenger can read it. In the letter they claim that the wall is being built in preparation for revolt, and Nehemiah is about to use prophets to proclaim himself king.

Nehemiah gives a simple and straightforward answer. None of what they say is true; it is all the product of their imagination. He denies the charges and prays that he will not be distracted from his task.

Now Tobiah and Sanballat send a false prophet to Nehemiah. The prophet's name is Shemaiah. He tries to frighten Nehemiah into hiding from his enemies in the temple, but Nehemiah has plenty of faith that God will protect him.

If Nehemiah is a eunuch, this suggestion is an attempt to compromise him. The law forbids a eunuch to enter the temple (Deuteronomy 23:1).

The wall is completed!

The wall is completed on 25th Elul, in early September (6:15). The work has taken only fifty-two days. This is an amazingly short time, and a tribute to Nehemiah's inspiration, the people's dedication and the urgency of the situation.

The surrounding tribes are shaken by Israel's achievement. They had not thought it possible. Nehemiah regards the success as proof of the Lord's help.

Nehemiah appoints guards for the gates
(Nehemiah 7:1–3)

Nehemiah continues to protect Jerusalem by appointing gatekeepers and guards. He chooses only those who are trustworthy (many of them from the temple staff) and gives them clear instructions.

A list of those who first returned from exile
(Nehemiah 7:4–73)

Although the city is now secure, the population is very small. It seems that Nehemiah takes a census of the people to see how many there are. He uses a checklist of returned exiles, which is the same as the list in Ezra 2.

Ezra reads the law and the people agree to obey it

Ezra reads the Book of the Law (Nehemiah 8:1–12)

The story moves now to Ezra's memoirs.

The people ask Ezra to bring out the Book of the Law and read it to them. Standing high on a platform in the midst of a great gathering, Ezra reads the law aloud. The Levites also help him by explaining it to the people.

The reading of the law makes the Israelites weep, because they have failed to keep it. However, Nehemiah persuades them to see the joy of it – that God has revealed the right way to live. The law is a gift to be celebrated.

The oldest version of this text, in 1 Esdras, does not mention Nehemiah. This is part of the problem of knowing whether Ezra and Nehemiah were in fact in Jerusalem at the same time.

The people celebrate the Feast of Booths
(Nehemiah 8:13–18)

In the reading of the law the people rediscover the Feast of Booths. This is a week-long festival during which the Israelites live in shelters (booths or tabernacles) made from branches and palms.

The festival is a thanksgiving for the wilderness journey which brought the Israelites to the Promised Land. Living in booths is a reminder of the simple life of daily trust in God. Having found the instructions (Leviticus 23:39–43), they celebrate as never before. There are booths everywhere!

The Israelites confess their sins (Nehemiah 9:1–37)

The Feast of Booths is followed by a great national act of repentance. The people gather together. They fast as a sign of sorrow for their sins. They wear sackcloth and sprinkle dust on their heads as a mark of desolation.

For three hours they stand to hear the law of God read aloud to them. Then for three hours they worship God and confess their sins.

We assume it is Ezra who offers a great prayer. He tells of God's goodness in calling Abraham and promising him descendants and a land. He praises God for rescuing their ancestors from Egypt, giving them his law at Sinai and providing for them in the desert. He confesses the many times when, as a nation, they have rebelled and deserved punishment; yet even in judging them, God has been merciful.

Now Ezra comes to the point of his prayer. The Israelites are back in their own land, but they are slaves. They do not own their cattle, or even their own bodies. Their harvest is not their own to enjoy, but the tribute due to a foreign overlord.

They agree to follow God's law (Nehemiah 9:38–10:27)

A binding agreement is made with God and signed by everyone. This is a new start.

Nehemiah's name is the first on the list, but has probably been added later, if his time in Jerusalem was after that of Ezra.

The people's promises (Nehemiah 10:28–39)

The priests, Levites and ordinary people promise to keep God's law.

They promise not to intermarry with pagan nations.

They promise not to trade on the sabbath.

They promise to allow the land to rest, and cancel all debts every seventh (sabbath) year.

They promise to pay their dues to the temple, to provide for the offerings, sacrifices and maintenance of God's house.

They promise to provide wood for burning on the altar.

They promise to bring their harvest offerings each year.

They promise to dedicate their first-born children to the Lord, and the first-born offspring of their animals.

They promise to bring a tenth of their produce to the temple stores, to provide for the Levites, priests and temple staff.

Resettlement and Nehemiah's reforms

The people who are settled in Jerusalem
(Nehemiah 11:1-24)

Here is a list of the people who are living in Jerusalem, or are deputed to move there. It is decided to increase the population of the city by moving 10 per cent of people from the other towns of Judah.

The people who live in the villages
(Nehemiah 11:25-36)

This is a list of the towns occupied by the descendants of Judah and Benjamin. The Valley of Hinnom and Beersheba mark Judah's northern and southern boundaries.

A list of priests and Levites (Nehemiah 12:1-26)

The historian lists the priests and Levites who returned from exile in Babylon with the group led by Zerubbabel. Some other details are also included, tracing the pedigree of famous names such as Eliashib and Jonathan, and noting some of the tasks and responsibilities that people had.

The dedication of the wall of Jerusalem
(Nehemiah 12:27-43)

Now we return to the memoirs of Nehemiah.

The rebuilding of Jerusalem's walls has been completed. They are dedicated by the priests with a festival of music – Levites playing instruments, the singers forming two choirs and priests blowing trumpets. The choirs lead two groups around the wall, processing in opposite directions; then all converge in the temple forecourt. It is an occasion of exceptional joy.

Ezra is credited with leading the procession, but this is impossible as he doesn't come to Jerusalem until much later.

Providing for the temple staff (Nehemiah 12:44–47)

The stores of supplies for the priests, Levites and temple staff are successfully organized. This is how David and Solomon intended it to be.

Zerubbabel and Nehemiah have at last restored the temple, its offerings, music and administration to its original design. They have also organized the arrangements for the Levites to live on the tithes brought in by the other tribes. The Levites in their turn give their tithe to provide for the priests.

Nehemiah's reforms (Nehemiah 13:1–31)

Foreigners are excluded from Israel.

It is discovered in the book of Moses that the Ammonites and Moabites are to be banned from the assembly of God's people. This command is one of the laws in the book of Deuteronomy (Deuteronomy 23:3–4).

The Moabites became enemies centuries ago, when the Israelites were passing through their land on the way to Canaan. The Moabites hired a prophet called Balaam to curse the strange new people who were so quickly becoming a powerful nation (Numbers 22:4–6). In fact Balaam was a true prophet, and found he could only bless the Israelites and predict their ultimate victory. He even foresaw the 'star' of the Messiah (Numbers 24:17–19).

In the book of Ruth, we have a story which begins with two Israelite brothers marrying Moabite women. It is by her 'mixed' marriage that Ruth, a Moabite, becomes a member of the people of God, and an ancestor of Jesus Christ. After the exile, there is a move against such marriages. Nehemiah ensures that foreigners are excluded from Israel.

Tobiah is evicted from the temple

There is also a crisis over Tobiah, who is an Ammonite (13:4–9).

In 433 BC, after twelve years as governor, Nehemiah leaves Jerusalem to visit the Persian court. While he is away, Eliashib the high priest allows

Tobiah, the Samaritan governor, to make his home in one of the temple storerooms!

As well as being a foreigner, Tobiah has also been one of the main opponents of the rebuilding programme. When Nehemiah returns, he takes swift action to evict him. The temple room is thoroughly cleaned and restored to its proper use.

There is a strong sense that God's house can be contaminated if non-Jews come into it. Paul will one day be accused (wrongly) of bringing a Gentile into the Jewish part of the temple (Acts 21:27–29).

The Levites are provided for

Nehemiah finds that the arrangements which provide for the Levites have been allowed to lapse (13:10–14). This means that the temple staff have dispersed, as the Levites have had to go home to their fields to support themselves.

Nehemiah summons the Levites to return to their temple work, and calls on the people to bring in their tithes. He puts responsible people in charge of the stores.

Sabbath trading is forbidden

Nehemiah is angry when he sees Israelites working on the sabbath day (13:15–22). The commandment is that God's people shall do no work on the seventh day of the week, but set it aside as a holy day for worship and rest (Exodus 20:8–11). Foreign traders are also bringing their goods and produce into Jerusalem on the sabbath.

Nehemiah sees sabbath trading as inviting God's punishment. He forbids all commercial activity on the sabbath, by both Jews and non-Jews, both inside and outside the city. He uses the Levites to police the situation.

Foreign marriages are annulled

Finally, Nehemiah is outraged when he sees the evidence of mixed marriages (13:23–31). Some Israelites have married Philistine women from Ashdod, or taken wives from the nations of Ammon and Moab. Many of their children are unable to speak Hebrew, and have a foreign language as their native tongue.

Nehemiah believes that these marriages will destroy the purity of the Israelite people and their faith. He curses and angrily attacks the men who have behaved in this way, and commands them to stop intermarrying.

Nehemiah reminds the offending Jews that King Solomon made the same terrible mistake, and with disastrous consequences. Foreign marriages were the means by which pagan gods came into Israel. The resulting idolatry was one of the sins which led to the exile.

Even one of Eliashib's sons has married a daughter of his old enemy Sanballat. While Nehemiah has been at the Persian court, Tobiah and Sanballat have forged a close alliance with Israel's high priest. They have achieved a degree of influence through friendship which they never managed by being enemies. Now Nehemiah purges the priesthood and sets them afresh to their tasks and responsibilities.

Nehemiah is a great leader with a deep trust in God – although we wince when he starts pulling out other men's hair! Perhaps his greatest example to us is the way he so constantly prays for God's help and so consistently seeks to obey God's word.

Nehemiah's rigorous approach may seem harsh to us, but was greatly needed at that time. In the face of Israel's enemies, Nehemiah built a physical wall around Jerusalem. In the face of compromise with foreign nations and their worthless idols, he raised the protection of God's law.

As a result of the work of both Ezra and Nehemiah, the Jews were able to become established again in their homeland. They were able to recover from the nightmare and disintegration of the exile, to serve God once again as his holy and distinctive people.

ESTHER

Here is an exciting tale, full of colourful characters, strong passions and extraordinary coincidences. It is a typically Jewish story. Its purpose is to remind its hearers that God is able to protect his people against any danger, even in a foreign land.

OUTLINE

Esther becomes queen (1:1–2:18)
Mordecai saves the king's life (2:19–23)
The plot to destroy the Jews (3:1–7:10)
The Jews are allowed to defend themselves (8:1–17)
The origin of the Feast of Purim (9:1–32)
The greatness of Mordecai (10:1–3)

Introduction

The story

Esther is a Jewess, living in Persia with her cousin Mordecai. She is very beautiful. The king of Persia, Xerxes, falls in love with her and makes her his queen, not realizing that she is a Jew.

Meanwhile, Mordecai makes an enemy. This is Haman, who is one of the most powerful people in the land. Haman plans not only to kill Mordecai, but also to exterminate the Jews in every province of the empire. But Mordecai is in close touch with his cousin, the queen...

Encouraged by Mordecai, Esther risks her life. She goes into the king's presence without being summoned. Mercifully, Xerxes spares her and asks her request. As an answer, Esther invites the king to dine with her, with Haman as their honoured guest.

After the meal, Haman returns home elated at his good fortune. He decides to build a monstrous gallows on which to hang Mordecai.

Did the story of Esther really happen?

The story of Esther is quite extraordinary, with its pantomime characters and fantastic timing. Esther is a beautiful princess in danger of her life. The Jewish people are threatened with extinction by the wicked vizier, Haman. King Xerxes is as unpredictable as he is powerful, and can command anyone's death at any moment.

But although the story sounds as though it has leapt from the Tales of the Arabian Nights, or the Histories of Herodotus, it is carefully written. The author quotes the place in which the story is set (a provincial capital, Susa) and the date (the third year of the king's reign). If this is a novel, it is based on many accurate facts. The person writing has inside knowledge of the Persian court and government, as well as strong sympathies with the Jewish people caught up in its power play.

The truth of the book of Esther may be even more exciting – that this is an account of God's amazing and timely deliverance of his people. This is, after all, the way the author tells it – and the reason why Esther is a popular and frequently read book among the Jews even today.

Meanwhile the king passes a sleepless night reading the records of his reign – and is reminded that he owes Mordecai a favour.

When the king and Haman meet the next day, they are delightfully at cross purposes. The king asks Haman's advice on how best to honour a man. Haman (thinking he is the one to be honoured) prescribes a procession fit for a prince – only to find himself having to arrange it all for Mordecai!

At a second banquet, Esther asks the king to spare her life and avert the slaughter that has been decreed for the Jews. The king is furious that such an outrage has been planned, and demands to know the culprit. Esther reveals that Haman, who is dining with them, is the villain. Now Haman is exposed as a coward and a bully. As he pleads for his life, he seals his fate by appearing to assault the queen. Xerxes has Haman hanged on the very gallows he had built for Mordecai.

At last Esther is able to tell the king how she and Mordecai are related. The king gives Haman's estate to Esther and his ring to Mordecai. But how is the extermination of the Jews to be averted? The royal command has gone out to every province of the empire that all Jews are to be killed on a certain day – the 13th day of the month of Adar. The day was chosen by Haman through the casting of *pur* or lots.

The king's order must stand, but Esther and Mordecai persuade him to send out a further decree. At Mordecai's dictation, the scribes and translators dispatch orders that the Jews are allowed to defend themselves. They have the right to kill anyone who attacks them. His task completed, Mordecai leaves the king's presence dressed splendidly in crown and royal robes.

When the 13th day of Adar arrives, the Jews defend themselves with great success, and avenge many scores with old enemies. The date becomes the Feast of Purim for future generations – the last feast in the Jewish year.

In English Bibles, the book of Esther is placed with those of Ezra and Nehemiah. They all record events that take place in the days of the Persian empire.

The book of Esther never mentions God directly. For this reason many scholars (including Martin Luther) have challenged its right to a place in the Bible. All the same, it is very much a Bible story, showing how God uses those who are faithful and brave to do his will. Esther and Mordecai in Persia are like Joseph in Egypt or Daniel in Babylon – all of them raised to high office under a pagan ruler, for the glory of God and the safe keeping of his people.

Living in a pagan world

On a serious note, the story of Esther raises the question of how Jews should maintain their distinctive standards and way of life in a pagan world. The answer seems to be that they must seek the good of their ruler and their neighbours, and put their trust in God in times of persecution. Although the Jews kill many of their enemies at the end of the story of Esther, and see the sons of Haman hanged, there is a strong message in their refusal to take any plunder from their victims. They will defend themselves against injustice, but their welfare and hope is in God alone.

DISCOVERING ESTHER

Esther becomes queen (1:1–2:18)

King Xerxes is the Persian emperor. Xerxes is his Greek name, but he is also known as Ahasuerus or Khshayarshan. His empire is vast, stretching from India to Cush – the Upper Nile in Egypt.

Our story is set in Susa. This is the ancient city of Elam which Darius had rebuilt, and which is now the place where Xerxes has his winter palace.

King Xerxes invites the leading figures of his government and armies to a magnificent banquet. During it he summons Queen Vashti to show off her beauty, but she refuses to appear. This act of female defiance is considered a dangerous example to other wives. The queen is banished by royal decree. Here we see something of the style of the Persian empire as well as the character of its king.

The Persian empire... and Xerxes

The Persian empire is founded by Cyrus, who conquers the Babylonians in 539 BC. Cyrus is generous to the religious and national groups in his realm, and gives permission for Jews to return to Jerusalem after their years of exile in Babylonia. However, some Jews remain scattered throughout the Persian empire, and it is part of their story that the book of Esther has to tell.

Cyrus is succeeded as king by Darius, who establishes the administration of the mighty empire. He in turn is succeeded by his son Xerxes, who reigns from 486 to 465 BC.

The Greek historian Herodotus wrote his books in the 5th century BC, not long after the reign of Xerxes. He describes the great king as cruel and unpredictable.

The Persian emperor's own words are recorded on a monument found at Persepolis:

I am Xerxes, the great king, the only king, the king of all countries which speak all kinds of languages, the king of the big and far-reaching earth.

Mordecai

Mordecai, with Esther, is the hero of this story. A baked clay tablet has been found at Borsippa, near Babylon, which names a man called Marduka as a leading official in the court of Susa in the early years of King Xerxes. If Marduka is Mordecai, then perhaps he is already an important person at court, even before Esther becomes queen. This explains the jealousy and racial hatred of other ambitious courtiers, such as Haman. The book of Esther is an early story of anti-Semitism – persecution of the Jews.

In future reigns, under Artaxerxes I and Darius II, there will be many Jews in prominent positions in the Persian government. Perhaps it is Mordecai who paves the way for other members of his gifted race to be entrusted with high office.

The king is easily led by his advisers when they suggest that he should choose a new queen from among the most beautiful virgins in the empire. Among them – and already living in Susa – is Hadassah, or Esther. Hadassah is the Hebrew word for 'Myrtle', while Esther may be the Persian word for 'Star'. The young woman lives under the guardianship of her older cousin, Mordecai.

While Esther awaits her call to the king, she becomes a favourite with Hegai, the eunuch in charge of the royal harem. Like Daniel in the court of Babylon, she acts wisely as befits one of God's people.

Daniel and his friends refused the royal food and wine, in order to keep their self-discipline and devotion to God. Esther adopts a different policy, forging a friendship with Hegai and enjoying his protection and good advice. She also obeys Mordecai in keeping her Jewish identity a secret.

When the time comes for Esther to go to the king, she wins his heart with her pure beauty and unaffected manner. Xerxes makes her his queen, with great celebration.

Mordecai saves the king's life (2:19–23)

Meanwhile, Mordecai sits at the king's gate. This may be so that he can keep in touch with Esther, or because he is in fact a royal official overseeing the business of the palace. From this vantage point, Mordecai overhears a plot being made to kill the king (2:19-23). He is able to warn Esther of the danger, with the result that the king's life is spared. Mordecai's good service is recorded in the official history of the reign – to be remembered later in the story!

The plot to destroy the Jews (3:1-7:10)

Haman plots to destroy the Jews

Esther has complied with all that has been asked of her – and has become queen. Mordecai, on the other hand, now runs into trouble. He is required to bow down before the newly promoted Haman – something he refuses to do. Haman is described as an Agagite. This may mean that he is descended from Agag the Amalekite, and is therefore one of Israel's traditional enemies (1 Samuel 15:32-33). In any case Mordecai is a devout Jew and will bow only to God. This, again, was the same dilemma Daniel and his companions had faced in a pagan culture (Daniel 3).

Haman is furious. However, it seems too small a thing merely to kill Mordecai. He seeks to exterminate the entire Jewish population of the Persian empire (3:1-15). To discover a lucky date for the massacre, Haman has a lot (*pur*) cast to reveal the ideal month and day. The lot falls on the month of Adar, at the end of the year. It is the *pur* which will give its name to the Jewish Feast of Purim – but Haman will not live to see it.

King Xerxes agrees that Haman may issue a royal decree for the destruction of the Jews. Haman offers a huge amount of silver to pay those who will carry out the massacre. The king declines the money, but gives Haman his personal ring to sign the orders. Haman is now the king's grand vizier, with unlimited powers.

The royal command is sent out to every province in every language of the empire, using the fine postal network created by Cyrus. Once sent,

---

The survival of the Jews

The story of Esther reminds us that the Jews have suffered hatred and persecution throughout their history, not least in the pogroms and death camps of the 20th century. The Feast of Purim is a celebration of their deliverance, and of the God who keeps his promise to protect them.

such a decree can never be changed or cancelled. The 'Law of the Medes and Persians' is still a byword for something immutable; but it is more to do with pride than perfection, both then and now.

Esther risks her life

As the king's decree becomes known, Mordecai and his fellow Jews cover themselves in sackcloth and dust themselves with ashes. This is a sign of grief and desolation in the face of death.

When Esther hears of Mordecai's state, she sends a eunuch to discover what has happened. Mordecai tells him of the dreadful situation, supplies him with a copy of the decree, and sends a message asking Esther to plead with the king for mercy (4:1–5:3).

This is not as easy as it sounds. Esther sends a message back to Mordecai that even the queen cannot go into the royal presence without being summoned. To do so is to risk an immediate sentence of death. Furthermore, she is not sure that she is in favour with the king at this time.

Mordecai's answer is a high point of the story, and the clearest statement of his faith in God's power to deliver them. He warns Esther that she will not escape the massacre herself. God will of course make sure his people survive, but Esther's own branch of the Jewish nation will certainly be destroyed. What has she to lose by going into the king's presence? Might it not be for this very purpose that she has become queen?

Esther, after much fasting and prayer, takes her life in her hands and goes into the king's presence unbidden. To her great relief Xerxes extends his sceptre towards her – the sign of mercy and permission to approach his majesty. He invites his queen to make her request, but Esther merely opens the way for a special meal together – with Haman.

Haman's hatred of mordecai

Haman is delighted at the honour of dining with the king and queen. Only one thing spoils his glee, and that is the sight of Mordecai, who stubbornly refuses to bow to him as he passes through the king's gate (5:9:14).

On the advice of his wife and friends, Haman resolves to build the tallest of gallows, and get the king's permission to hang Mordecai on it the very next day.

We cannot help but compare the wisdom and humility of Mordecai and Esther, who seek God's guidance in fasting and prayer, with Haman who is ruled by ambition, jealousy, rage, superstition and peer pressure.

Mordecai is honoured, and Haman hanged

By one of those extraordinary coincidences which bring excitement to the story, the king has a sleepless night. To pass the time he sends for the record of his reign and has it read aloud until morning.

The passages of the chronicles which are read include the account of Mordecai saving the king's life. Xerxes has forgotten all about this until now, and is dismayed to find that Mordecai has never been rewarded. He resolves to honour the Jew as soon as possible. At that very moment Haman arrives, and is asked his advice on how this might be done!

Assuming the honour is for him, Haman suggests a procession through the streets, dressed in royal robes and riding a royal horse. The horse is to wear a royal headdress, and is to be led by a noble prince. The king is pleased with the idea, and commands Haman to carry it out in every detail for Mordecai. Haman himself is to lead the horse and shout out Mordecai's fame. Afterwards, it is Haman's turn to cover his head in grief!

That evening the king and queen dine with Haman again, and Xerxes again invites Esther to make her request. At last she feels the time is right. She tells the king about the decree to destroy her people, and pleads that both she and they may be spared.

The king is furious at the situation and demands to know who has engineered it. The culprit is with them at the table, and Xerxes strides out into the garden in a rage to decide what action to take. Left alone with the queen, Haman throws himself on her in desperation and terror. When the king catches him like this, his fate is sealed. Haman is led away with his face covered. He is as good as dead.

When Xerxes hears that Haman has prepared a gallows for Mordecai, he orders that the grand vizier be hanged on it himself. This is typical of the vindication the Jews expect when God saves them from their enemies:

> They make a pit, digging it out,
> > and fall into the hole that they have made.
> Their mischief returns upon their own heads,
> > and on their own heads their violence descends. (Psalm 7:15–16 NRSV)

The Jews are allowed to defend themselves (8:1–17)

With Haman disgraced and executed, the king gives his estate to Esther. She is finally able to tell Xerxes (who is always the last to know anything) that Mordecai is her cousin. The ring the king had given to Haman is now presented to the Jew. Mordecai is the new grand vizier.

There is one more favour for Esther to ask, and it is that Haman's plan to annihilate the Jews should be averted. Xerxes puts the matter in Mordecai's hands, to publish a further decree granting the Jews the right to assemble together and defend themselves (8:1–17). The first decree may never be revoked, but at least a further decree can give the Jews a fighting chance.

Mordecai leaves the king's presence dressed in royal robes – not this time as a short-lived honour, but as the rightful regalia of his office. As the decree reaches the provinces of the Persian empire, there is joy and celebration in every Jewish community. In Susa itself, perplexity changes to gladness. People of other nations see what has happened, and put their faith in the God of the Jews.

The origin of the Feast of Purim (9:1–32)

When the 13th day of Adar arrives, the Jews are well prepared. Many of their enemies dare not stand against them, but others do so and are destroyed.

In Susa there is widespread bloodshed, and the ten sons of Haman are among those who are killed. Esther asks the king's permission for the time of revenge to be extended, so that Haman's sons may be hanged the following day. Their humiliation has continued down the ages, with a Jewish tradition that their names are printed vertically. They are still left hanging!

Even though the Jews are carrying all before them, they steadfastly refuse to take any plunder. It is the principle that counts, not the profit.

The author describes how the Feast of Purim comes about (9:1-32). It is a two-day festival on the 14th and 15th days of the month of Adar, the anniversary of the Jews' deliverance from certain death and their revenge on their enemies. The fast and feast, with presents and partying, fall exactly a month before Passover.

Mordecai and Esther write to their fellow Jews in all the provinces of the Persian empire, instructing them when and how to keep the festival. This is not a feast which is centred on Jerusalem or the temple, but on the celebration of the God who protects his people even in exile.

The greatness of Mordecai (10:1-3)

The author closes the book of Esther by referring the reader to the official records of the Mede and Persian kings. In them is recorded the extent of Xerxes' empire and the distinguished role of Mordecai the Jew (10:1-3).

Like Joseph in Egypt and Daniel in Babylon, Mordecai is a man who, in the providence of God, has been found worthy of the highest responsibility in a pagan administration.

JOB

Job is a good man – an exceptionally good man! He has been blessed with children and great wealth. Indeed he is described as 'the greatest of all the people of the east' (1:3 NRSV).

One day, and for no apparent reason, Job is plunged into terrible suffering. In a series of disasters, his children are taken from him, his cattle are seized and his property is destroyed. As if this isn't enough, he also loses his health. He is afflicted with painful sores from head to foot. Even his wife urges him to abandon his faith in God. She says to him, 'Are you still maintaining your integrity? Curse God and die!' (2:9).

But Job refuses to curse God. When his friends (Eliphaz, Bildad and Zophar) come to visit him, they at first sit in silence for a whole week. Then, in a complex and beautifully expressed debate, they consider the problem of human suffering. Is our suffering a punishment for our sins? Does God know about our suffering? Does he care about it, or is he the one who inflicts it?

The discussion is lengthy but orderly, with each of Job's friends exploring a point of view and Job answering. Despite his anguish, he maintains both his innocence and his faith. The debate goes round three times, with each friend contributing and Job answering. A young man, Elihu, expresses his exasperation that they have found no answer. Elihu says that God is able to rescue from suffering, but can also use it to punish or teach us. Above all, God is immeasurably great and unknowable.

When all has been said, God himself speaks to Job. He challenges Job to contemplate the vastness and wonder of creation and invites him to consider his own littleness and lack of understanding. Job humbles himself before the majesty and wisdom of God; and the story ends with God upholding Job's righteousness and restoring to him family and fortune.

Outline

Job's troubles (1:1–3:26)
The three rounds of discussion (4:1–31:40)
 The first round of discussion (4:1–14:22)
 The second round of discussion (15:1–21:34)
 The third round of discussion (22:1–31:40)
Four speeches by Elihu (32:1–37:24)
The Lord speaks (38:1–41:34)
Job acknowledges God and is restored to life (42:1–17)

Introduction

The problem of suffering

The book of Job is one of the world's greatest poems. It probes deeply into human suffering, exploring it from every angle.

Does suffering come because we have done something to deserve it? Is it God's punishment for our sins?

There are many occasions in the Bible when people get what they deserve; but the story of Job is different. While most people can think of a reason for their suffering, Job is convinced that he is innocent.

Three of Job's friends – Eliphaz, Bildad and Zophar – come to be with him. They discuss his situation, each giving their opinion on why this disaster has befallen him.

Job and his friends believe that God rules the world. Both blessing and suffering come from his hand. He rules the world by blessing good behaviour and punishing wickedness. But here is the exception to the rule. Job is a good person – as near perfect as is humanly possible – and yet he is inflicted with every kind of pain.

Even in the depth of his suffering, Job continues to have faith in God. He has enjoyed God's blessing and now he will endure God's trouble. Meanwhile, his friends suspect that he is being punished for some secret sin, and they urge him to confess it and get rid of the guilt. For his part, Job longs to be rescued and restored. He wants everyone to know that this terrible experience is not his fault.

Was Job sinless?

The book of Job never claims that Job is sinless. It simply says that he has done nothing to deserve his suffering. He himself admits that he isn't perfect. God knows, for example, the sins he committed when he was young (13:26). Of course Job is not entirely innocent – no one is. But his suffering is way beyond anything that he can possibly have deserved. If this is punishment for things he did when he was young, then it is out of all proportion to his faults. Here is an almost perfect human being who is undergoing every suffering short of death. Why is God allowing this to happen?

Perspective

The book of Job is not only a beautiful poem, it is also an absorbing discussion. It breaks new ground in the Old Testament's understanding of God's dealings with human beings. It is both a great masterpiece of literature and a superb exploration of our experience of life. It challenges all the popular ideas of why we suffer and how God governs the world. 'What have I done to deserve this?' 'There's no justice.' It also challenges the popular idea that we are being punished for the sins we have committed in a previous life.

Meanwhile, the story takes us behind the scenes to see what is happening in heaven. We find that Job is indeed blameless in the way he lives, and that God is pleased with him. But Satan argues that Job finds it easy to live a godly life because he is blessed with health and wealth. If all that were snatched away, he would soon turn against God. But God has complete faith in Job. He gives Satan permission to test him, but without taking his life.

Satan – evil with attitude

The book of Job tells us more about Satan.

Satan first appears in the Bible as the serpent who tempts Eve in the Garden of Eden (Genesis 3:1–5). The story of Job is older than any of the Bible books – so this is the earliest portrayal of Satan that we have.

The meaning of 'Satan' seems to be 'To Obstruct'. Satan is the one who hinders God's purposes, criticizes human motives and is sceptical that goodness can ever be genuine.

In the Hebrew Bible, 'Satan' can be anyone who adopts the stance of an accuser or adversary – so 'Satan' is not as much a particular person as an attitude (2 Samuel 19:22; 1 Kings 11:14).

In the book of Job, Satan is a member of God's council. When God expresses pride in Job's blameless and upright life, Satan sets out to prove that Job's goodness is shallow. According to Satan, Job is only good because it suits him. Job's righteousness will soon disappear if he is plunged into poverty, bereavement, physical pain and mental anguish.

So Satan is at the heart of the debate about where evil comes from, and whether evil is under God's control. Other religions have tackled the same problem – sometimes deciding that there must be two equal and opposite powers striving for control of the world – good and bad. This is called 'dualism'.

The Bible does not offer us dualism, but nor does it tell us where evil comes from. When Satan appears, he is clearly a part of God's creation who is critical and rebellious, but ultimately under God's authority.

In the books of Genesis and Job, Satan tries to prove to God that human beings are worthless. Satan stirs up criticism and doubt, to spoil the relationship between humankind and God. He wants God and humans to mistrust each other and so fall out.

At the same time, the writer of Job avoids saying that Satan is the cause of Job's suffering. Job is suffering because God allows it. At the end of the book, the writer says, 'They comforted and consoled him over all the trouble the Lord had brought upon him' (42:11). We never really know why God responds to Satan's challenge by allowing Job to suffer.

Who wrote the book of Job?

We don't know who wrote the book of Job, nor when it was written. It has been placed in the Bible after the history books and alongside the Psalms and the writings of Solomon. These books contain deep reflections on the relationship between God and human beings. There are angry outbursts at the silence of God and the pain of the human condition. Some people think that the book of Job is an attempt to understand why God's people suffered so terribly when they were overrun by their enemies and carried off into exile. But, as the history books show us, such suffering was hardly undeserved!

Why do bad things happen to good people?

When tragedy strikes innocent people, it challenges our belief that God is good, wise and powerful.

The book of Job explores these great questions, and gives us some bearings.

First of all, God entirely desires the well-being of his creation. He has pleasure in Job's upright life, and trusts that he will keep his faith even through intense and prolonged trial.

Satan works hard to destroy the trust between human beings and God, but his power is limited.

All the speakers in the poem believe that God is both the creator of the universe and the perfect judge of right and wrong. He is holy and majestic, yet concerned with the smallest detail in the lives of his creatures.

Clearly, God is stronger than evil, but allows evil to have its effect for the time being. This world is a place in which we can make moral decisions and develop godly character. Hardship and temptation play their parts in getting us spiritually fit.

It is true that in this world we often suffer for our mistakes and reap the consequences of our actions. But it isn't always so. There are exceptions. The Bible shows us people who get what they deserve *and* people who don't deserve what they get.

The book of Job shows us undeserved suffering. We cannot simply say that God always blesses the good and always punishes the wicked. Every day we see good people suffering while wicked people prosper.

The New Testament takes the whole matter much further. We see God *involved* in human suffering. God comes to us, not with smooth excuses or brisk retorts, but in the shape of his dreadfully rejected and brutally murdered Son. All our indignant questions and challenges fall silent in the presence of Christ on his cross, the crucified God.

We may not find all the answers to our questions in Job. But, like Job, we have a question put back to us: 'Will we let God be God?'

Discovering Job

Job's troubles

Job is introduced (1:1–5)

Job is a man of all-round goodness. He is at peace with God, prosperous in his possessions and blessed with a large family. He lives an upright life and is careful to offer sacrifices for any possible sins of his children.

God gives permission for Satan to test Job (1:6–2:10)

The scene changes. The story moves to God's council in heaven and a conversation between the Lord and Satan. God asks Satan if he has noticed Job's wholesome attitude and lifestyle; but Satan accuses God of giving Job special protection. If God changed Job's circumstances, he would soon start to curse him!

And so God gives Satan permission to test Job in every way, short of taking his life. There follows a series of disasters in which Job's sons and daughters are seized and his servants killed, his sheep consumed by a fire from heaven and his camels carried off by raiders. Finally, a hurricane destroys the house of his eldest son and takes the lives of his remaining children.

Job is devastated by this turn of events. In grief he tears his robe, shaves his head and lies face forward on the ground before God. But, in all his anguish, he refuses to blame or curse God. All that he had was given him by God, and if God chooses to take it away again, so be it.

When Satan finds that Job's faith is still firm, he covers him in sores from head to foot. As Job sits desolate among the ashes of grief and loss, even his wife urges him to curse God and die.

Job's friends (2:11-13)

As he sits on an ash heap – bereft of his family and covered in sores – Job is visited by three friends. Each of them tries to help him understand why he is suffering so terribly. They all say things that are true and right – but they don't apply to Job! Even today we speak of 'Job's comforters' – people who come alongside us, and think they are being helpful, but leave us feeling rather worse.

Job is already thinking deeply about his situation. He is experiencing acute pain in his mind, body and spirit. However his friends explain the suffering, it is he who is having to endure it. To their credit, the three friends begin by sitting with Job in silence, day and night, for a week. Their silent company and sympathy is probably the best thing they can offer him – certainly better than the words that are to come.

Job's cry of anguish (3:1-26)

Such is his pain that Job wishes he had never been born. It would have been better to be stillborn or to have died at birth. He desires death like a treasure – to allow him to escape his suffering and be at peace. It is a dreadful torture to have light without sight and life without happiness and freedom.

The speeches of Job's friends

The first round of discussion (4:1-14:22)

- Eliphaz's first speech and Job's reply (4:1-7:21)
- Bildad's first speech and Job's reply (8:1-10:22)
- Zophar's first speech and Job's reply (11:1-14:22)

The second round of discussion (15:1-21:34)

- Eliphaz's second speech and Job's reply (15:1-17:16)
- Bildad's second speech and Job's reply (18:1-19:29)
- Zophar's second speech and Job's reply (20:1-21:34)

The third round of discussion (22:1-31:40)

- Eliphaz's third speech and Job's reply (22:1-24:25)
- Bildad's third speech and Job's reply (25:1-26:14)

The three rounds of discussion

Each of Job's friends speaks in turn and Job replies.

Eliphaz

The first of the friends to speak is Eliphaz. He is probably the oldest and certainly the kindliest of the three. He believes firmly in the holiness of God – and has some experiences of his own that he is eager to share. Of course, he has no idea (as we do) that the cause of Job's suffering is that God has allowed Satan to test him. Instead he rather suspects that Job has done something to deserve this punishment. Surely no one has ever suffered without deserving it?

Consider now: Who, being innocent, has ever perished?
  Where were the upright ever destroyed?
As I have observed, those who plough evil,
  and those who sow trouble, reap it. (4:7–8)

Throughout this debate, Eliphaz and his friends assume that God rules the world in such a way that good is always rewarded and evil is always punished. But Job is a test case which proves otherwise. Sometimes God allows people to suffer who *don't* deserve it.

Meanwhile, Eliphaz prescribes his remedy:

If it were I, I would appeal to God;
  I would lay my cause before him. (5:8)

Job should take his punishment courageously. It will do him good:

How happy is the one whom God reproves;
  therefore do not despise the discipline of the Almighty.
For he wounds, but he binds up;
  he strikes, but his hands heal. (5:17–18 NRSV)

Job's reply is that he is indeed bearing the discipline of the Almighty – and nobody knows that better than he does. He needs the support of his friends, not their accusation.

When Eliphaz speaks again (in chapter 15) he increases the pressure on Job to admit his guilt. Job has far too high an opinion of himself:

Are you the firstborn of the human race...
What do you know that we do not know? (15:7, 9 NRSV)

Eliphaz feels that Job has gone quite far enough in criticizing God and dismissing the advice of his friends. He describes the defiance of wicked people, followed by their ruin. He implies that Job fits the description rather well.

Job longs that Eliphaz would stop crafting fine speeches and instead give him the comfort of genuine understanding. It's bad enough being used as target practice by God without also being subjected to the harsh opinions of friends.

When Eliphaz speaks again (in chapter 22) he tries to convince Job that he is guilty of self-righteousness. Probably God isn't that bothered anyway:

What pleasure would it give the Almighty if you were righteous?
What would he gain if your ways were blameless? (22:3)

Surely Job isn't being punished for being good. There must be some underlying sin. Perhaps he didn't lend freely to his family, or respond to the needs of the thirsty and hungry, or made the plight of widows and orphans worse.

Eliphaz advises him to repent:

Submit to God and be at peace with him;
in this way prosperity will come to you. (22:21)

But Job knows that he *is* submitting to God. There is nothing more he can do to get right with God. Eliphaz is failing to see that Job really *is* innocent, and to hear the cry of desolation and anger coming from Job's heart.

Bildad

The second of Job's friends is Bildad. From the start, he takes a rigorous approach to the problem. As far as he is concerned, God always acts justly. If Job's children have died, it can only be because they have deserved it. If Job is innocent – as he claims he is – then he can confidently appeal to God and get some action.

If you will seek God earnestly
and plead with the Almighty,
if you are pure and upright,
even now he will rouse himself on your behalf
and restore you to your prosperous state. (8:5–6)

Bildad believes that the world runs in a predictable way. Just as certain laws of nature are always true (for example, that papyrus reeds grow best in marshland) so there is a moral law at work. God can never reject a blameless person – it would be against his nature to do so.

When Bildad speaks again (in chapter 18), he is offended that Job is rejecting all this good advice. Job is being far too arrogant in claiming to be a special case. He warns Job of the terrible fate that awaits the wicked:

They are thrust from light into darkness,
and driven out of the world.
They have no offspring or descendant among their people,
and no survivor where they used to live. (18:18–19 NRSV)

Job's redeemer

Even in his torment, Job believes that someone will come and prove him right. This person is his 'redeemer':

I know that my Redeemer lives,
and that in the end he will stand upon the earth. (19:25)

Mention of a redeemer makes Christians think of the Lord Jesus Christ, who rescues us from sin, delivers us from death and restores our status as children of God. This, of course, is far more than Job can hope for – living as he does many hundreds of years before the time of Christ. But his experience of undeserved suffering helps us to understand what will happen to Jesus. Jesus didn't deserve to suffer either – but he took the punishment that should have been ours.

But Job begs his friends to change their minds:

Have pity on me, my friends, have pity,
for the hand of God has struck me.
Why do you pursue me as God does?
Will you never get enough of my flesh? (19:21–22)

In his third speech (in chapter 25), Bildad tries to give a different perspective. He reminds Job that God is perfect. However innocent Job feels himself to be, he can hardly be pure enough for God:

How then can a mortal be righteous before God?...
If even the moon is not bright
   and the stars are not pure in his sight,
how much less a mortal, who is a maggot,
   and a human being, who is a worm! (25:4–6)

Job responds with heavy sarcasm. Bildad's track record of good deeds and insight leaves him little reason to boast – and still less to advise others! Job continues to insist that he hasn't deserved his fate:

I will never admit you are in the right;
   till I die, I will not deny my integrity.
I will maintain my righteousness and never let go of it;
   my conscience will not reproach me as long as I live. (27:5–6)

Zophar

Job's third friend is Zophar. He is indignant that Job still maintains his innocence. He wishes that God himself would intervene to declare the true state of affairs. It is not for human beings to pass judgment on God's ways. His mysteries are too deep for us to probe. Whatever he decides must be right and there can be no appeal.

Like the others, Zophar's advice is that Job should repent:

If you devote your heart to him
   and stretch out your hands to him,

if you put away the sin that is in your hand
  and allow no evil to dwell in your tent,
then you will lift up your face without shame;
  you will stand firm and without fear. (11:13–15)

But Job dismisses this advice. The answer to his suffering does not lie in repentance – because he has nothing of which to repent. It is simply not true that he has only to repent and his happiness will be restored:

I desire to speak to the Almighty
  and to argue my case with God. (13:3)

In his second speech (in chapter 20), Zophar describes the fate of the wicked. They are punished for their sins:

For they have crushed and abandoned the poor,
  they have seized a house that they did not build...
The heavens will reveal their iniquity,
  and the earth will rise up against them.
The possessions of their house will be carried away,
  dragged off on the day of God's wrath.
This is the portion of the wicked from God,
  the heritage decreed for them by God. (20:19, 27–29 NRSV)

Job answers that this simply isn't true. God may be a moral God, and the universe may hold consequences for those who are wicked. But Job's point is that people like him are suffering innocently – and the wicked are having a very good time!

Why do the wicked live on,
  growing old and increasing in power?
They see their children established around them,
  their offspring before their eyes.
Their homes are safe and free from fear;
  the rod of God is not upon them. (21:7–9)

Job's cry of despair – and hope

Job's friends are eloquent and well meaning. They are rich in their knowledge of God. But in the end they can't relate to Job's trouble. He describes them as 'miserable comforters' (16:2)!

But then, from the depths of his agony, Job makes a ringing declaration of faith:

I know that my Redeemer lives,
  and that in the end he will stand upon the earth.
And after my skin has been destroyed,
  yet in my flesh I will see God;
I myself will see him with my own eyes – I, and not another.
  How my heart yearns within me! (19:25–29)

A 'redeemer' is a kinsman you can rely on for help. He is the next of kin who pays a debt or avenges a wrong. In the story of Ruth, Boaz is the kinsman-redeemer who cares for Naomi and marries her widowed daughter-in-law.

The God of Israel is a redeemer to his people. He rescues them in time of need. Now Job expresses his faith that this saving God will appear as his redeemer. His vindicator will stand up and tell everyone that Job is right – despite all the mystery of his present suffering.

As Christians, we have problems with suffering. Is it that God doesn't care? Or is the evil in this world too strong for him? But we see, in Jesus on the cross, that God enters into our suffering and bears it and redeems it. Jesus Christ is our kinsman-redeemer – the next of kin we can rely on.

Where can wisdom be found?

Humans can tunnel underground for precious metals and jewels, but they won't find wisdom there. It isn't under the ocean either; and it can't be bought for money.

Wisdom belongs to God – then and now (28:1–28). It isn't to be found through any human endeavour of science or engineering. It can't be acquired like knowledge or deduced by reason. There is only one source of wisdom, and that is God. True wisdom is a life lived in the fear of the Lord.

If only...

Job wishes he could call on God somewhere – go and knock on his door and argue his case:

If only I knew where to find him;
  if only I could go to his dwelling!
I would state my case before him
  and fill my mouth with arguments. (23:3–4)

Job isn't looking to win an argument with God. He simply longs to be in fellowship with him. But God is unobtainable. Remote. High-handed. Job doesn't know where the next blow is going to fall:

He stands alone, and who can oppose him?
  He does whatever he pleases.
He carries out his decree against me,
  and many such plans he still has in store.
That is why I am terrified before him. (23:13–14)

And why doesn't God step in and sort out some of the wrongdoers? What about bullies, kidnappers, murderers and adulterers?

Why does the Almighty not set times for judgment?
  Why must those who know him look in vain for such days? (24:1)

But, despite his indignation and bewilderment, Job clings to his faith in God – and defies the opinions of his friends:

As surely as God lives, who has denied me justice...
I will never admit you are in the right. (27:1–5)

Letting it all out!

Job is going through the worst experiences that anyone can endure. He is poverty-stricken, bereaved, in acute pain, misunderstood by friends and abandoned by God.

And because he is thoughtful and eloquent, we have been able to follow his response. At first he was in a state of shock. Then he was by stages grieving, angry and despairing. But now he has begun to hope again, even in the face of God's silence.

Job clings to his integrity as the only thing left to him – and dares to believe that God has integrity too:

> *I will not deny my innocence.*
> *I will maintain my righteousness and never let go of it;*
> *my conscience will not reproach me as long as I live.* (27:5-7)

Job's final plea

In a powerful speech Job reviews his life: the days of his prime, his good reputation and the kindnesses he showed to others (31:1-40). Now he is a despised and tragic figure, who has done nothing to deserve his misfortune. Will *nobody* take his side?

Job offers an eloquent and compelling account of his innocence. In every aspect of his life he has been open, honest and generous. God has seen and can judge his every move and motive.

In his sexual behaviour, he hasn't lusted after girls or had affairs with other men's wives.

He has always been fair to his servants, treating them as fellow human beings.

He has not held back from helping the bereaved and the poor; nor has he used bullying or influence to get his way.

He hasn't relied on his wealth instead of trusting God; nor has he paid any attention to astrology.

He hasn't gloated over an enemy's misfortune, or cursed anyone, or refused hospitality to a stranger.

He hasn't concealed secret sins, or harboured guilt, or done anything to make him fear public opinion.

All this is a wonderful statement of Job's moral values in private, public, social and sexual matters. With such a blameless record, small wonder he cries out:

> *Oh, that I had someone to hear me!*
> *I sign now my defence – let the Almighty answer me.* (31:35)

Four speeches by Elihu

Now a young man steps forward who has been waiting for his chance to speak. And he is angry! Angry with Job for being so self-righteous, and angry with the friends for being so dim:

Not one of you has proved Job wrong;
  none of you has answered his arguments. (32:12)

Elihu believes that God is not as remote as Job claims. God speaks in a variety of ways – through dreams and visions, for example, or through healing. And Job should beware of being so scornful of God's justice:

It is unthinkable that God would do wrong. (34:12)

Job and his friends are in danger of reducing God – calling him to account for his actions as though he is just another human being. But God is different:

How great is God – beyond our understanding! (36:26)

The question Elihu raises is not, 'Why has God done this *to* us?' but, 'What is God doing *in* us?'

The Lord speaks

And now, at last, God speaks (38:1–41:34). He speaks to Job out of the storm. A storm, like an earthquake, is nature's echo of the tumult in our human hearts. God is speaking amid the storm of Job's suffering and protest.

God shows Job the vastness of his creation – the foundations of the earth, the springs of the sea, the abode of light and the gates of death. He reviews its splendour: the storehouses of the snow, the networks of stars, the complexities of nature and of the human heart. Look at any of God's creatures – and wonder at the mind and majesty of the creator!

Does Job have any questions about all this? Does he have any advice to offer? Perhaps he would like to take over and run the world better?

Have you an arm like God...
Deck yourself with majesty...
Pour out the overflowings of your anger...
Look on all who are proud, and bring them low;
  tread down the wicked where they stand...
Then I will also acknowledge to you
  that your own right hand can give you victory. (40:9–12, 14 NRSV)

God doesn't apologize to Job. He doesn't explain that Satan wanted to test him. He doesn't promise to put everything right in the end. He simply presents Job with the fact that God alone is the creator and he alone has the right and power to judge.

'Look at the behemoth...' (40:15)

Look anywhere in creation. Look at behemoth, the hippopotamus. Look at Leviathan, the crocodile. Both of them are majestic monsters – beyond human power to create or control! Doesn't the God who made these awesome creatures also have power over the uncontrollable forces of chaos, evil and suffering? And doesn't he have every right, as God, to do things his way?

Job acknowledges God and is restored to life

And so Job submits to God (42:1–17). He is silent in the face of God's awesome majesty and unsearchable wisdom:

I am unworthy – how can I reply to you?
  I put my hand over my mouth. (40:4)

At the end of the day, Job must let God be God:

I know that you can do all things;
  no plan of yours can be thwarted...
  Surely I spoke of things I did not understand,
  things too wonderful for me to know. (42:2–3)

Epilogue (42:7–17)

At last Job's ordeal is over. The poetry of the great debating speeches gives way to the prose of the story. God says that the opinions of Job's three friends have made him angry. They have not been speaking the truth about God. However, the fourth speaker, Elihu, is not condemned. He alone has pointed out that suffering is not necessarily a punishment for sin, nor does it always fit the crime.

God tells Job to pray for his friends as they offer sacrifices and seek forgiveness. Job's prayer counts with God, because it springs from a faithful and integrated life. 'The prayer of the righteous is powerful and effective,' writes James in his New Testament letter (James 5:16).

God restores to Job all that he has lost in family, friends and fortune. Indeed, God grants Job even greater prosperity than he had enjoyed before – and makes him the father of the three most beautiful women in the land. Job, in turn, gives his daughters an equal inheritance along with his sons. He has been a champion of a clear conscience and fair dealing; and he dies at a great age, at peace with his God, his neighbours and himself.

PSALMS

The book of Psalms is a collection of hymns and prayers. They are written by various people over a long period of time. King David wrote some of them, and priests and directors of the temple music wrote others.

The Psalms cover the whole range of our experiences of God, from praising him for our creation and salvation, to complaining about our situation or circumstances. Above all, they are honest with God, and help us to talk to him straight from the heart. Even a lament, when addressed to God, is regarded in the Psalms as 'praise'. The title 'Psalms' means 'praises'.

OUTLINE

Book 1: Psalms 1–41
Book 2: Psalms 42–72
Book 3: Psalms 73–89
Book 4: Psalms 90–106
Book 5: Psalms 107–150

Introduction

The Psalms were probably collected together after the Jews' return from their exile in Babylon. Psalm 137 recalls those sad and desperate days:

By the rivers of Babylon we sat and wept
  when we remembered Zion.
There on the poplars
  we hung our harps,
for there our captors asked us for songs,
  our tormentors demanded songs of joy;
  they said, 'Sing us one of the songs of Zion!'
How can we sing the songs of the Lord
  while in a foreign land? (137:1–4)

The Psalms are arranged in five sections, or books. The sections don't always follow a theme and are not in order of date. Their arrangement is often informal; but some of David's Psalms are grouped together, and there is an extended collection of praise Psalms at the end.

Each group of Psalms closes with words of praise (a doxology) such as:

Praise be to the Lord, the God of Israel,
from everlasting to everlasting.
Amen and Amen.

Some of the Psalms are very personal, while others are suitable for a congregation, or for singing at a festival. Jesus knew the Psalms well, and made their words his own. Both Jews and Christians have used them constantly, both for private prayer and public praise.

Who wrote the Psalms?

Many of the Psalms are written by David or associated with him. Book 2 ends with the words, 'This concludes the prayers of David son of Jesse' – but there are other Psalms by David later on in the collection. When a psalm is described as 'of David', it can mean that it is either by him or for

The editors

In the early Middle Ages, scholars called the Massoretes edited the Psalms. They put in vowel sounds (there are no vowels in written Hebrew) and accents, and marked the Psalms for public reading and singing. Their work was carried out between about AD 600 and 1000. They did the same for the poetic books of Job and Proverbs.

Simple and subtle

The Hebrew language is full of fun. It enjoys wordplay and double meaning. It can express the heights of praise as well as the depths of despair. Many of the Psalms have a rhythm, and the lines often run in couplets – the thoughts echoing and complementing each other. When this happens it is called 'parallelism'.

him. Half the Psalms (seventy-three of them) are headed 'of David'. Some of these are linked with particular episodes of his life – his exile in a cave, his victories in battle or his repentance after his adultery with Bathsheba.

These are personal poems and prayers which are soaked in the blood, sweat and tears of a great believer, and forged in the heat of his experiences, both good and bad.

Some Psalms (at the beginning of Book 2) are the work of the Sons of Korah – a family which served as temple officials. Psalms 73–83 in Book 3 are by a musician called Asaph, who was a founder of one of the temple guilds.

Over a third of the Psalms are headed 'for the director of music' – perhaps written for use in the daily temple worship, or arranged for a special occasion.

Soul music

In the Psalms we hear a voice which is new to scripture. It is the voice of personal prayer, soul-searching, praise and hope.

During the years of exile, the prophets challenged the Jews to be responsible for their own heart attitude to God. Without a temple or king, it was up to individuals and local communities to establish their own pattern of worship. The result was a deeper personal faith for some and the development of the synagogue as a place for local prayer and teaching.

A variety of psalms

The Psalms may have been written and collected over a period of 600 years. They include hymns of praise to God for his greatness. They provide songs and chants for pilgrim festivals and royal events. They recall and teach the mighty acts of God in rescuing and helping his people. They express personal prayers of joy and sadness, exaltation and grief.

Book 1 (Psalms 1–41)

Most of the psalms in the first book (or collection) proclaim a truth about God or the godly life. They speak of God as 'Yahweh' (Lord).

In the whole of his creation, the Lord has given a unique place of honour to humankind (Psalm 8). The Lord lives with people who are innocent, honest, trustworthy and generous (Psalms 15, 24). Those who delight in the law of the Lord will be spiritually strong, fresh and fruitful (Psalm 1). All peoples should find their security in the Lord's power and wisdom (Psalm 33).

Many psalms are intensely personal: asking for help against enemies (Psalms 3, 12, 25, 35), or for revival (Psalms 6, 38, 39), or for protection (Psalms 7, 15, 36).

Sometimes the psalmist cries out to the Lord to rescue the good and punish the wicked (Psalms 10, 17), or to look on his longing and count him among the righteous (Psalms 26, 27).

Often, the psalmist sings of love for the Lord and reliance upon him, using images from everyday life: the Lord is a rock, fortress, shield, stronghold, shepherd and light (Psalms 18, 23, 27). Similarly, the psalmist might describe his own plight as caught in a net, fallen into a pit or like a city under siege (Psalms 31, 40).

A psalm may narrate a personal experience of the Lord, which has changed a perspective and brought release (Psalms 32, 34, 37, 40, 41). Some psalms ask that the blessings on an individual may become blessings for the whole people of God, Israel (Psalm 28).

Book 2 (Psalms 42–72)

In this group, the psalms tend to use the word 'Elohim' for God. As one or two of the psalms are repeats from Book 1 (Psalms 53, 70), it may be that this is a collection for people who have a different tradition. We certainly have such preferences and choices in our hymns today.

Here are wonderful psalms of personal devotion, typical of David (Psalms 62, 63). There are prayers for revival (Psalm 42) and rescue (Psalms 43, 54, 55, 58, 59, 69, 70, 71) and forgiveness (Psalm 51). Some psalms remind God of his great deliverance in the past, and ask that he will do the same again (Psalms 44, 60). Others put worries, fears and jealousies in their proper perspective (Psalms 49, 52, 56, 57).

The psalms of the Korahites start to expand from the private and personal to the public and congregational (Psalms 46, 47, 48): 'Clap your hands, all you nations!' There is a great sense of God making himself known and calling people to worship him (Psalm 50). There are mighty praises to God for his acts of creation and deliverance (Psalms 65, 66, 68) and requests for his ongoing mercies (Psalm 67).

Book 3 (Psalms 73–89)

Book 3 has many psalms of Asaph, as though these may have been by him or were in his collection as a choirmaster.

Again, there are psalms for personal use: a reflection on jealousy (Psalm 73) and pleas for guidance (Psalm 86) and deliverance (Psalm 88). But several of the psalms are for public and national repentance and praise. There is a corporate memory of defeat and desecration (Psalms 74, 79), the cry for rescue and restoration (Psalm 80), and celebration that God alone is sovereign and judge (Psalms 75, 76).

Here is the sweep of narrative, recounting God's actions in nature and history (Psalm 78) and his covenant with David (Psalm 89). There is the call for people to turn to God (Psalms 81, 82), the longing for God to overthrow enemies (Psalm 83) and the aching desire for peace (Psalm 85).

In this book, too, there emerges the sense of Zion as God's holy mountain and city – the centre and joy of the whole earth (Psalm 87).

Book 4 (Psalms 90–106)

The fourth book begins with reflection on human life and history in the light of eternity (Psalm 90) and the absolute reliability of God (Psalm 91). There is thankfulness for the blessings of a God-centred life (Psalm 92).

Then follows a group of psalms which praise God for his kingship of the world (Psalms 93–100), and some beautiful psalms of David, brimming with righteousness (Psalm 101), longing (Psalm 102) and praise (Psalm 103). Again, there are psalms which draw on God's provision in nature (Psalm 104) and dealings with Israel (Psalms 105, 106). They evoke wonder and joy.

Book 5 (Psalms 107–150)

Book 5 begins with a review of God's rescue from desperate situations (Psalm 107), and David's determination to honour him (Psalm 108). David also calls down curses on the head of an enemy (Psalm 109)!

There is a psalm in honour of the Lord's chosen king, who will be both priest and judge (Psalm 110), which is followed by praise of God (Psalm 111) and his faithful people (Psalm 112).

There is a selection of songs for Passover, known as the 'Egyptian Hallel' (Psalms 113-118). 'Hallel' lives on in our word 'Hallelujah!', which means 'Praise God!'

The longest psalm is personal – praising God for his law and asking for help in keeping it (Psalm 119). There follows a collection of 'Songs of Ascent', to be sung by Jewish pilgrims as they journey up to the temple in Jerusalem (Psalms 120-134). There are also psalms praising God for his Passover rescue and victory over pagan tyrants and idols (Psalms 135, 136).

Suddenly we are plunged into the painful memory of exile (Psalm 137), but surface to recall the kingship of God (Psalm 138) and his complete knowledge of us (Psalm 139). Next come some psalms of David asking for protection and vindication in the face of his enemies (Psalms 140-143), and praises which testify to God's power and grace (Psalms 144, 145).

The book of Psalms ends with a final Hallel, calling all of creation to praise God (Psalms 146-150).

Hymns of praise

The basis of all praise is that God has created the world. He has conquered the forces of chaos, and defeated all other gods:

He set the earth on its foundations;
　　it can never be moved.
You covered it with the deep as with a garment;
　　the waters stood above the mountains.
But at your rebuke the waters fled,
　　at the sound of your thunder they took to flight.... (104:5-7)

However, God has done more than create the world. He has chosen and saved a nation for himself – the people of Israel. A popular theme in the Psalms is the great deliverance of Israel at the exodus, when God brought his people out of Egypt through the Red Sea:

With your mighty arm you redeemed your people,
  the descendants of Jacob and Joseph.
The waters saw you, O God,
  The waters saw you and writhed;
  the very depths were convulsed. (77:15–16)

After the exodus, there were hard lessons to be learned in the years of wandering in the desert. Some psalms recall what happened in those days of friction and discontent:

How often they rebelled against him [God] in the desert
  and grieved him in the wasteland!
Again and again they put God to the test;
  they vexed the Holy One of Israel. (78:40–41)

The Psalms remind Israel of God's ways and his standards, so that they can avoid making the same mistakes in the future. They make

What the scholars say about the Psalms

Hermann Gunkel, in 1904, identifies different types of Psalms. He finds hymns, thanksgivings, laments and epic dramas for royal occasions. He notes how the Psalms belong to the great occasions of national life – the miracle of the exodus, the wonder of the Torah (law) and the majesty of God and of his anointed king.

Sigmund Mowinckel, in the early 1920s, traces the Psalms to the golden age of the monarchy with its festivals and celebrations. He thinks that the Feast of Ingathering and Tabernacles was a time for enacting the glorious victory and kingship of God.

In the Psalms, Mowinckel finds the scripts for great battles with the forces of chaos, the victory procession of God to his holy place (Mount Zion) and the renewing of his covenant commitment with his people.

Suddenly the Psalms come alive – springing from their dusty pages to share the shouts and sobs, laughter and music, dancing feet, clapping hands and swirling robes of God's praising people. God's salvation is to be remembered from the past and celebrated in the present. It is to be enjoyed by everyone now!

> **Music to our ears**
>
> The book we know as 'Psalms' is called 'Praises' in the Hebrew Scriptures. Our word 'Psalms' comes from the Greek word 'psalmoi', which means 'music played on instruments'.

history come alive, to encourage repentance and praise in the present, and to give hope for the future.

The Psalms provide songs and prayers for every human situation. Hymns of praise spring from the great things God has done, both for Israel as a nation and for individuals in their own lives:

Praise the Lord, O my soul;
  all my inmost being, praise his holy name.
Praise the Lord, O my soul,
  and forget not all his benefits –
who forgives all your sins
  and heals all your diseases,
who redeems your life from the pit,
  and crowns you with love and compassion,
who satisfies your desires with good things
  so that your youth is renewed like the eagle's. (103:1–5)

Some psalms are in praise of Zion – the name for Jerusalem as God's holy city. Pilgrims approaching the capital might sing these hymns as they approach their destination – the city of their king and the temple of their God:

Great is the Lord, and most worthy of praise,
  in the city of our God, his holy mountain.
It is beautiful in its loftiness,
  the joy of the whole earth.
Like the utmost heights of Zaphon is Mount Zion,
  the city of the Great King.
God is in her citadels;
  he has shown himself to be her fortress. (48:1–3)

God is the true king, not only of Israel, but of the whole earth. It is he who gave his people victory over the pagan nations around:

Clap your hands, all you nations;
　shout to God with cries of joy.
For the Lord Most High is awesome,
　the great King over all the earth!
He subdued nations under us,
　peoples under our feet. (47:1–3)

The Lord, the God of Israel, is God of the whole world. The nations are summoned to celebrate the history of Israel – because this is to be their story too. The kings of the nations will assemble as the people of the God of Abraham (47:9).

For most people today, both Jews and Christians, the Psalms provide beautiful expression for personal worship:

I love you, O Lord, my strength.
The Lord is my rock, my fortress and my deliverer;
　my God is my rock, in whom I take refuge.
　He is my shield and the horn [strength] of my salvation, my stronghold.
I call to the Lord, who is worthy of praise,
　and I am saved from my enemies. (18:1–3 NIV)

A large number of psalms are devoted to the cries of pain or longing:

As the deer pants for streams of water,
　so my soul pants for you, O God.
My soul thirsts for God, for the living God.
　When can I go and meet with God? (42:1–2)

Most of these psalms emerge into confidence and praise. They sing with the wisdom that comes from knowing God's rescue at first hand:

Once God has spoken;
　twice have I heard this:

> *that power belongs to God,*
> > *and steadfast love belongs to you, O Lord.*
> *For you repay to all*
> > *according to their work.* (62:11–12 NRSV)

Some psalms are concerned with royal occasions and the special status of the king. They are written for coronations, weddings and anniversaries, but they can also look forward to the Messiah. This one, for example, is quoted by the Gospel writers when Jesus is baptized:

> *He [God] said to me, 'You are my son;*
> > *today I have become your Father.*
> *Ask of me,*
> *and I will make the nations your inheritance,*
> > *the ends of the earth your possession.*
> *You will rule them with an iron sceptre;*
> > *you will dash them to pieces like pottery'.* (2:7–9)

Jesus and the first Christians knew the Psalms and drew inspiration from them. Quotations from them are an integral part of the Gospels and letters of the New Testament. But this is also a book of prayers for us to use today. Here are beauty and honesty, praise and petition, laughter and tears. Here is soul music to which we can tune the song of our own spirit.

The Psalms help us to enter into the supreme privilege of being human, which is to praise God from our own hearts and with our own lips: 'Praise the Lord, O my soul!'

The king

The king has an important part to play in the Psalms. He is God's Son – holy and set apart as the Lord's anointed servant. On rare and special occasions he may even act as a priest, offering prayers and sacrifices to God on behalf of his people. Of course, all Israel's kings are merely human – but their special status points forward to the Messiah. He will be the perfect king and great high priest.

DISCOVERING PSALMS

A selection of Psalms:

Psalm 1 The good life
Psalm 2 God's supreme rule
Psalm 8 Glory in the heavens and humankind
Psalm 19 The cosmos and the commandments
Psalm 22 Pain and praise
Psalm 23 The Lord, my shepherd
Psalm 51 A plea for forgiveness
Psalm 73 True wealth
Psalm 95 A call to worship
Psalm 100 The gladness of access
Psalm 103 Amazing grace
Psalm 107 Thanks for the memories
Psalm 119 The way of life
Psalm 121 All-round protection
Psalm 139 'All yours!'
Psalm 150 Hallelujah chorus

The good life (Psalm 1)

The first psalm provides an introduction to the whole collection. It describes the happiness of people who delight in God's law – chewing it over like a dog with a bone. The law feeds and refreshes them, enabling them to live good, happy and fruitful lives. The truth that they hold in their hearts shapes their everyday behaviour, so that they avoid those who plot wickedness, do wrong or scorn godliness.

By contrast, those who reject God's law are like chaff. They have no substance or stability. Like the husks which the wind blows away when grain is winnowed, they will never survive in the furnace of God's judgment. They will have no place among God's people.

Here is a choice which everyone must make and there is no escaping. Either we go the way of God's law or the way of the wicked. The first leads to life, but the second leads to destruction.

God's supreme rule (Psalm 2)

The nations of the world think they can overthrow God's purpose and his anointed king – but their plans are paltry and pitiful. They stand no chance, as God well knows. Once he has stopped laughing at their feeble efforts, he gives a ringing declaration of his authority: 'I have installed my king on Zion, my holy hill.'

This is a psalm about the certain triumph of God's kingdom, through his partnership with the king, his obedient servant and Son. It may look back to the day of coronation, when God endorsed and enthroned his chosen king David. It certainly looks forward to the coming of Christ (which is the Greek word for 'anointed one').

These verses are quoted many times in the New Testament, and especially at the baptism and transfiguration of Jesus (Mark 1:11 and Matthew 17:5). Paul quotes them in a sermon about the resurrection of Jesus (Acts 13:33). The disciples see the hostility of kings and rulers when Herod and Pilate conspire to crucify Jesus, the Lord's anointed (Acts 4:25–28).

For Christians, this psalm has many glimpses of Jesus. For Jews, it is about the crucial kingship of David and his descendants. Here is the promise that David's line will rule the whole earth, and that all nations must reckon with his God-given authority in the end (Revelation 2:27). They will be wise to bow to him while they still have the chance. They will find both peace and safety in his just and gentle rule.

Glory in the heavens and humankind (Psalm 8)

Here is a majestic, thoughtful hymn of praise.

The psalmist reflects that God has shown his glory in the vastness and beauty of the heavens. But, just as wonderfully, he allows his name to be praised by the lips of human babies.

God's enemies and critics (of whom the chief is Satan) are dumbfounded that God should share his honour (and risk his reputation) by making humankind in his own image (Genesis 1:26).

Human beings are tiny specks in the scales of creation, yet we are the supreme object of God's compassion. We are also the ones who will share God's eternal glory. Meanwhile, it is to us that God has entrusted the charge and care of his creation in all its variety.

The psalmist closes as he began, with words of wonder, submission and praise. The Lord of creation is *our* Lord!

The cosmos and the commandments (Psalm 19)

There are two great witnesses to the power and perfection of God – they are his creation and his law.

The psalmist describes the heavens as a silent, eloquent declaration of God's greatness. If the heavens are full of wonder, how much more wonderful must their creator be! Not a word is said, but the glorious evidence of his majesty is transmitted continually everywhere and to everyone.

The sun is a supreme example of God's creation. Every day it rises in a blaze of light and heat – like a bridegroom setting out for his wedding. Yet the heavens are a mere tent that God has pitched; and the sun runs the course that God has set.

Now the psalmist turns to the other great witness, which is the law. In its way the law is just as glorious, bright and life-giving as the sun. The two belong together – the sun ruling the cosmos and the law ruling the conscience. Without them, there would be darkness in both the outer world and the inner heart.

The psalmist praises God's law for its perfect revelation of his will. He uses the term 'the Lord', which has a greater sense of relationship than the more general title 'God'. This is God's personal law, with its reliable statutes, true precepts and enlightening commands.

The psalmist finds that God's law helps him to stay pure, gives him a clear conscience and alerts him to moral danger. It is more valuable than gold, more delicious than honey and endlessly rewarding. It keeps him in step with God's will.

Just as there is nothing hidden from the sun, so there is nothing hidden from the law. The psalmist asks God to forgive the faults he is unable to see in himself, because they are so much a part of his human nature and the society in which he is set. Moses taught that some sins

are unconscious or accidental – but they are sins all the same.
The psalmist begs God's help, too, when he has a strong desire to do wrong.

The psalmist ends with a prayer that his words and thoughts may please God, who sees everything. God is like a rock that shelters from the sun. He is like a redeemer or next of kin, who rescues from the penalty of breaking the law.

Pain and praise (Psalm 22)

This is the psalm that Jesus cries out as he hangs on the cross. We cannot read it without thinking how completely its words are fulfilled in the suffering and salvation of Christ.

The psalmist feels abandoned by God, as he calls out ceaselessly for help. There is no occasion in David's life that we can link very closely with this description, although he was often in danger and persecuted for long periods of time.

Despite his pain and dereliction, the psalmist still trusts in God. He doesn't curse God or deny him. He knows that the Lord is holy, righteous and enthroned as king. He recalls that God has rescued and delivered others in the past.

The sufferer describes himself as 'a worm' – reduced and diminished, devoid of any sense of worth or significance. He is despised, mocked, insulted, taunted... Yet he never sinks into self-pity, never blames himself for his fate and never seeks revenge.

So many of these details only make sense when they are fulfilled in the crucifixion of Jesus: the animal behaviour of the crowd, the blasphemous taunts about God's rescue, the dislocation of the body stretched in torture, the desperate thirst, pierced hands and feet, the disposal of the clothes... (Matthew 27:33–46).

In all that is happening to him, the sufferer continues to confide in God. He calls out for deliverance from the enemies which surround him. He remembers God's lifelong care of him, right from the moment he was born. He lifts up his heart in hope... then suddenly makes a bold declaration: 'He has listened!'

Now the psalmist's words turn from pain and abandonment to praise and hope. He knows that he will live to celebrate God's deliverance – sharing a sacrificial meal of thanksgiving with the poor and needy.

His good news will travel, so that all the families and nations of the world will hear it. Even the wealthy and self-sufficient, even the dying, even the countless generations yet to come, will hear about this saving God and put their trust in him.

The Lord, my shepherd (Psalm 23)

This is the best known and most popular of all the Psalms. It speaks of God's love and faithfulness in every circumstance of life, both now and in the future.

We are invited to imagine the eastern shepherd at work. He is the leader, provider and protector of his flock. He knows every animal by name, and values each one more than his own life. As David was a shepherd-boy, and Jesus describes himself as the 'good shepherd', these verses take us to the heart of pastoral care.

Walking ahead of his sheep and calling them to follow, the shepherd finds fresh pasture to graze and safe places to drink. Even when the flock has to squeeze through a narrow defile, the sheep have nothing to fear. The shepherd can haul them to safety with his staff, or beat on the rock wall with his rod to let them know he is near.

The shepherd tends his sheep in every way. He clears the pasture of stones and levels the potholes – then stands guard while they eat. He checks their heads for sunburn and treats their wounds with soothing oil. When they are thirsty, he fills the drinking trough to the brim. At night he takes them into his own home.

This is how God is with his people, says the psalmist. He is like a shepherd, and I am in his constant care. His goodness and love will never fail me. In old age and in the face of death, I will continue to live with him.

A plea for forgiveness (Psalm 51)

David is in extreme mental anguish and heart-guilt. He has committed adultery with Bathsheba and then arranged for her soldier–husband,

Uriah, to be killed in battle. Now the prophet Nathan has confronted David with his crimes – and he is devastated (2 Samuel 11–12).

This is the greatest of the psalms which deal with sorrow and repentance. David cries out to God for mercy, cleansing and a new start. Although he has ruined the life of a beautiful woman and destroyed a brave and faithful man, his main crime has been against God.

David is aghast that he could have done such a thing. He accepts that it is all entirely his fault. He doesn't blame ignorance, depression or unruly passion. He doesn't plead that Bathsheba was half-responsible, or accuse Uriah of neglect. It is from his own sinful nature that these acts have sprung – from the sin ingrained in him and in all humanity from birth.

There is no sacrifice that David can offer for the sins of adultery and murder. Unless God forgives him and recreates him, he is lost. But he is not despairing. He holds on to what he knows of God – that he is compassionate and yearns for his people with the utmost love. David prays that his gracious God will wipe away this appalling sin and thoroughly cleanse his heart and soul.

David is asking God for a miracle. He begs to be 'cleansed with hyssop' – as a leper is sprinkled with the blood of a sacrifice, using a bunch of hyssop (a common herb). This is a sign to the leper that he is now fully restored to health and can rejoin the community (Leviticus 14:1–9). David pleads that the bones of his soul, so shattered in shame, may be mended by forgiveness and dance for joy.

David asks for nothing less than a pure heart, which God alone can create in him. He asks that God will restore him to fellowship, giving him a fresh delight in his saving love. He prays for a new spirit within, so that he may be gladly obedient in the future.

David realizes – and tells God – that he will have so much to offer others if he comes through this nightmare of guilt and grief. The fact that we have this psalm is proof that his prayer is answered. It has helped countless numbers of Jews and Christians to confess their sins and find forgiveness, new life and peace with God.

David realizes that, in worship, it is the heart attitude that counts. Sacrifices are meaningful and helpful only if they are offered with genuine repentance, commitment and love. It is this complete openness that God delights to see, and which he will never reject.

The psalm closes with a prayer which is probably added later. It asks that God will restore Jerusalem, his holy city of Zion. The people who endure the years of exile in Babylon, or who long to see Jerusalem and the temple rebuilt, may be making David's confession and prayer their own. The book of Nehemiah tells us how this prayer, too, is answered (Nehemiah 12:43).

True wealth (Psalm 73)

This great psalm is written by Asaph, who is the founder of one of the temple choirs.

Asaph has been eaten up by a jealousy that has almost robbed him of his faith. He has seen that proud and wicked people lead comfortable and successful lives, without shame or punishment for their sins. He has agonized whether he has made the wrong choice in devoting himself to God.

Asaph has watched unbelievers. They are healthy, wealthy and self-confident. They buy their way out of problems or employ others to shoulder their burdens. They get away with murder, cruelty and unbridled greed. They mouth arrogant opinions, despise goodness and plot evil. They talk of the universe as though they made it themselves and own it. People flock to them, because they admire their attitude and aspire to their achievements.

Meanwhile, Asaph has devoted himself to a godly life. He has spent much time and effort keeping his conscience clear and his actions pure. But he feels it has got him nowhere. It seems that trusting God is for no-hopers who can't face up to life in the real world. But, of course, to express such doubts would be to betray his faith and mislead his fellow believers…

After long days of heart-searching, Asaph brings his problem to God in prayer. At last, in the sanctuary of the temple, he sees an entirely different perspective.

The truth about the proud and wicked is that they are far from God. Their deaths may be peaceful, without fear, pain or regret; but they will awake to the reality of eternal judgment.

Soon it will be God's turn to express his opinion of them – which is that he doesn't know them. Their much-vaunted standard of living is a fleeting and futile dream. Their primrose path is really a road to ruin.

Asaph reflects on his new-found understanding. He has been blinded by envy and ignorance, knowing no more of God than a stubborn and stupid animal. Now he sees that he is truly rich.

Asaph has a friendship with the living God which will never fail or end. God is all he needs or can ever need. He may not have houses or lands or the admiration of others – but he has God, whose presence and protection is priceless, and whose purpose is to share his glory with all who love him.

And yes, holiness is exciting, and God is good to those who keep their hearts pure.

A call to worship (Psalm 95)

This psalm begins with an invitation to worship God together. For centuries it has been called the 'Venite', from the Latin word meaning 'come'. It is a summons to all-out praise, with joyful singing, loud shouts and every kind of music.

God is 'the Rock of our salvation' – the one on whom all our security and peace is built. He is supreme over all the other false and mistaken gods that humans may worship – gods of the depths, the heights or the turbulent seas. The God of Israel is the One who created these things, and who holds them even now in the palm of his hand.

God's majesty and power prompt us to honour him – bowing, kneeling or lying face down in his presence. We belong to him and he cares for us like a shepherd with his sheep.

Suddenly there is a solemn warning. God's word is not only for certain people in the past. It is also for us – now. Today may be the day when *we* hear his voice and receive his command. If so, we must not be resistant like the Israelites on their desert journey to Canaan.

At Meribah, the Israelites argued with God. At Massah they tested him. Despite their great deliverance from Egypt and the miracles of manna, quail, water and protection, they refused to believe that God could bring them safely to their Promised Land (Exodus 17:1–7).

God turned those rebellious people back to the desert, to wander for forty years until the older generation died out. Because of their unbelief they never entered their 'rest' – the freedom, peace and plenty of Canaan. Even Moses, their great and godly leader, was ruled out.

It is an awesome privilege to receive God's word. We ignore or resist it at our peril (Matthew 7:26–27). Today there is still a 'rest' for us to enter into and enjoy. It is nothing less than the salvation Jesus has won for us on the cross. The writer of the letter to the Hebrews takes these verses and urges us to enter God's rest – by hearing and believing the gospel (Hebrews 4:1–2).

The gladness of access (Psalm 100)

This psalm is often known as the 'Jubilate', which is Latin for 'O be joyful'. It is one of the most popular and often-used psalms for public worship. Many other anthems, hymns and worship songs are based on it, the most famous being William Kethe's 'All People That on Earth Do Dwell'.

Here is an invitation to the whole earth (not just separate 'lands') to offer a great shout of joy to the Lord, and to enter his presence, singing with uninhibited joy! It may originally have been a psalm for bringing a thank-offering.

The joyful shout is that of a crowd offering loyalty and welcome to a king. It is not to be given lightly, as it implies a total commitment. The people of Israel shouted in such a way when Saul became their king (1 Samuel 10:24). It is a fanfare of human hearts and voices.

This is a psalm of vast and eternal perspective. God has made us and we belong to him. We are his people, his sheep. His love and purpose cover the whole context of our lives, both now and for ever. To worship this God is also to serve him with our whole self (Romans 12:1).

Knowing that the Lord is God is a sure foundation for our praise. We are secure in his creation and saving love. We are sure of his welcome. We belong to him.

It is because God has made us and he welcomes us that we can come into his presence with such confidence and praise. The courts are the courts of the temple, where nothing unholy is allowed – and yet we may enter. This is God's house, his place – and we can come in!

Finally, the psalmist realizes that this privilege is ongoing. God's nature doesn't change, so his goodness will continue. His love will last for ever. This invitation to acknowledge him is to all people, in every place and age.

Amazing grace (Psalm 103)

Here is one of the greatest psalms. Beginning with his own heart and experience, David reviews the quality of God's love for all people. He calls on the whole of creation to praise this endlessly merciful and gracious God.

'Count your blessings'

David begins by talking to himself (103:1-5). He urges his soul to praise the Lord. It is easy, but very wrong, to ignore or forget the infinite goodness of God.

The Lord blesses David in so many ways, forgiving his sins and healing his diseases. The Lord redeems him, like a close, reliable and generous relative coming to his aid. Even 'the pit' of despair, disaster and death is not beyond God's saving reach. The Lord gives every appetite its proper satisfaction, and restores the spring of youth, like the strong and soaring eagle.

David is in good heart. He is not burdened with problems, besieged by enemies or racked with guilt. He is free to stand and survey the great vistas of God's mercy and love. This psalm inspired H.F. Lyte to write the wonderful hymn, 'Praise, My Soul, the King of Heaven'.

The quality of Mercy

God's character is clear from the way he has dealt with his people (103:6-18). His heart goes out to the needy. He secures justice for the oppressed. He rescued Israel from captivity and gave them his law. He was patient and considerate with their complaining; and even his anger was strictly limited.

This is what God is like. Even when he disciplines, his motive and goal are love. He doesn't prosecute without mercy, or hold long-running grudges, or insist on the fullest punishment. His love is as high as the heavens; his forgiveness as wide as space. The New Testament reveals that God's forgiveness is not because our sins don't matter to him, but because he himself bears the cost of them.

God's love is gut-felt like a father's love, and is as close as a mother's womb. We are human, fallible and finite – formed from dust and as short-lived as a flower. But God's love gives us a lasting value and meaning; his goodness will continue to future generations. The last word is not our futility, but God's faithfulness.

Creation praise!

David calls on the whole of creation, in heaven and on earth, to praise the Lord (103:19–22). Angels and humans alike owe their existence and service to God. Finally, David returns to his own first thought: that he, from his own soul, can add his voice. No one else can offer my praise.

Thanks for the memories (Psalm 107)

God's people should thank him. He has been good to them. He has rescued and gathered them from all parts of the world and from every trying circumstance. He has been a 'redeemer' – a strong, reliable next of kin. And he loves them.

This psalm could be based on the exodus or the return from exile. It describes how God saved his people from four contrasting situations: desert, darkness, disobedience and disaster.

A God who saves and satisfies

Here is a God of action. He can be seen in what he does. He turns situations around: rivers become deserts and vagabonds become prosperous farmers. Nobles are reduced to poverty, while the needy are made rich. This is the God of reversals, of whom Hannah sang when her barrenness ended (1 Samuel 2:6–8); and Mary, too, when she was pregnant with Jesus (Luke 1:52–53). He is a God who is worth praising.

The disciples of Jesus saw him do these works of God. He fed a multitude in the desert and called himself 'the bread of life' (John 6:35). He rescued his disciples in a storm – and brought their boat swiftly to land (John 6:18–21). He offered himself as 'living water', the only remedy for spiritual thirst (John 7:37–38).

The Christian church looks forward to a 'city', which will be a perfect community centred on God. Abraham journeyed and died in the hope of it. Jesus died and rose to establish it. It is the new Jerusalem, which God himself will give (Hebrews 11:10; Revelation 21:1–5).

Desert

The desert is a place of wandering and rootlessness (107:4-9). It is a place where survival is a struggle and death is always near.

The Israelites experienced the desert in body and spirit during their wilderness wanderings – on the way to Canaan and in the return from Babylon. But they found that God answered their cry for help. He rescued them from distress. He brought them out of trouble by the most direct route. Instead of the trackless wilderness, he gave them a secure and settled city.

Darkness

The darkness the psalmist describes is that of prison and slavery (107:10-16). It is also the spiritual darkness of rebellion against God. It is the gloom of living with guilt and its consequences, without choice or hope.

Israel knew this darkness during the long years of slavery in Egypt and the generation of exile in Babylon. Many individuals knew it through their own fault: their darkness fell when they rejected the light of God's law.

But God heard the cry of those in prison. He released the chains of captivity and broke open the confines of despair.

Disobedience

God's people became fools. This does not mean that they were ignorant or unintelligent. It means that they wilfully rejected God's way (107:17-22). Their foolhardy attitude almost cost them their lives. But God heard their cry for help. By his powerful word he rescued and healed them.

Disaster

Finally, the psalmist describes God's people who were almost lost at sea (107:23-32). They were at the mercy of the awesome forces of wind and water. But they cried out to God – and he rescued them. He hushed the storm to a whisper. He brought them safely to land.

Here is an image of circumstances beyond human control, when chaos reigns and all is lost. But the Lord, with sovereign power and love, is strong to save.

Dire straits and divine reversals

The psalmist has described four kinds of extreme need. In each of them, God has answered the call of his people. He has not only rescued them from their trouble, but positively transformed their situation for good.

The psalmist summarizes God's activity in the world (107:33–42). The water of life is his blessing and gift; so is security, plenty and fertility. But hardship, dearth and suffering can be a sign of his displeasure.

'Whoever...'

The psalmist closes by pointing out that these memories are not just history (107:43). They are lessons for today – for whoever will listen and learn.

The way of life (Psalm 119)

This is the longest psalm. It is a prayer to God which sings the praises of his law, and reflects on the security and happiness of those who live by it. To keep God's law is to walk in the light, to run on the freeway:

I run in the path of your commands, for you have set my heart free. (119:32 NHEB)

The psalm uses several different terms for God's word: law, statutes, precepts, decrees and commands. By one term or another, God's word and way are mentioned in every verse.

The whole psalm is carefully constructed around the twenty-four letters of the Hebrew alphabet. Each letter introduces an eight-verse section or stanza. Each stanza extols a fresh aspect of God's wonderful law, its beauty and benefits. It is like a great love poem.

God's law is his truth, his teaching. It has been revealed so that we may live fully, safely, wisely and well. It is found in all the Scriptures, but in the Pentateuch (the books of Moses) in particular.

When Moses presented the people with God's law, he urged them to 'choose life'! He wrote all the laws in a Book of the Law and gave directions that it should be kept beside the ark of the covenant (Deuteronomy 31:26).

The psalmist refers to God's guidance as *law, precept, statute* and *commandment*.

The psalmist has great delight in God's *law*. It thrills him to have God's truth in his mind and God's wise counsel in his heart:

Your statutes are my delight;
  they are my counsellors. (119:24)

God's *precepts* are important points of detail. They are to be applied, checked and attended to. They enable the fine-tuning of a well-ordered life:

You have laid down precepts
  that are to be fully obeyed. (119:4)

God's *statutes* are binding and permanent landmarks for living. Their permanence is expressed by writing them down and preserving them for future generations. Their truth will never lessen and their relevance never wane:

Your statutes are always righteous;
  give me understanding that I may live. (119:144)

The *commandments* emphasize God's authority. He is the creator, the Lord. These are his 'maker's instructions' – not a matter of opinion, but a necessity. The psalmist humbles himself to receive them:

I wait for your salvation, O Lord,
  and I follow your commands. (119:166)

Freedom and protection

Loving God's law is not to be confused with legalism. Legalism binds us in fearful and obsessive effort, lest we fail to do everything correctly. But love for God's law sets us *free*.

God's law protects us from the opinions of others, and from self-deceit. It steers us away from wrongdoing, hurtful consequences and guilt. It releases us to do right:

How can young people keep their way pure?
By guarding it according to your word. (119:9 NRSV)

Discovery and delight

The psalmist loves God's law because he loves God. He can't get enough of God's guidance, because it is so good! For him, it is a constant voyage of discovery; a feast of delectable insights:

Open my eyes that I may see
  wonderful things in your law. (119:18 NIV)
How sweet are your words to my taste,
  sweeter than honey in my mouth! (119:103)

Light and life

To know God's law is to have a light for the path of life:

Your word is a lamp to my feet
  and a light for my path. (119:105 NRSV)

It gives access to wisdom – like a door opening. This is wisdom which we could never discover by our own efforts; and yet the simplest person can understand it:

The unfolding of your words gives light;
  it gives understanding to the simple. (119:130)

A cry for help

As the psalmist ends his prayer, he cries out for help. He knows God's law is good and right, but he hasn't been able to keep it. He has strayed away and become lost, like a sheep. He asks that God will be his shepherd and come to find him:

Seek your servant,
For I have not forgotten your commands. (119:176)

God's law is wonderful, permanent and true, but it is only with his constant help that we may live by it.

All-round protection (Psalm 121)

This is a psalm for pilgrims as they make their way up to Jerusalem. It's a journey where one is aware of the hills, as a place of refuge or a source of danger.

The psalmist looks at these hills. They are the last resort in times of trouble: 'Flee to the mountains!' says Jesus (Mark 13:14). They are the natural defences of Jerusalem, which (as the city of Jebus) was the last stronghold in Canaan to fall to the Israelites.

The hills stand for stability, permanence and protection; but the psalmist doesn't rely on them. His protector is the One who *made* the hills!

The care which God gives to his people is for every individual at all times. God never sleeps; his attention never wavers. There is no circumstance which is beyond his control. The Lord himself guarantees safety in every enterprise, for the whole of life. And the cover starts now.

'All yours!' (Psalm 139)

This is a psalm about the completeness of God's knowledge and care for every individual.

'O lord, you know!'

David is amazed at how completely God knows him (139:1-16). It is as though God has sifted through him in painstaking detail, to know him in every part.

God has always been at work in David's life. He formed him in his mother's womb. He sees his every action and knows his every thought. There is nowhere David can go which is beyond God's saving presence and love. The vastest distance, the deepest darkness – even death itself – are no barriers to God.

'Still with you'

David turns his wonder to praise (139:17:18). God thinks about him constantly! This gives him total security. When he wakes, whether in the morning after sleep or at resurrection after death, he is still with God.

An outburst

Suddenly David flashes with anger at the violence and blasphemy of the wicked (139:19–22). If God is so powerful, why doesn't he rid him of them? After all, they are God's enemies too.

There is no answer. But the psalm prompts us to realize that God has also made these enemies. Like David, they are never beyond God's reach. He doesn't destroy them, because his patient love waits for them to become friends.

'Lead me'

The outburst over, David invites God to test his inner thoughts and worries (139:23–24). He wants more of God's perfect knowledge of him. He wants all of God's way to life.

Hallelujah chorus (Psalm 150)

The Psalms end with a glorious summons to 'Praise the Lord!' – which is the meaning of 'Hallelujah!'

All of God's creatures, on earth and in heaven, are called to praise him. He is to be praised by humans in his sanctuary, the temple. He is to be praised by angels in the mighty heavens, which are the vastness of his making.

God is to be praised both for his own greatness and for the great things he has done. He has created the universe. He has rescued his people and made them his own.

God is to be praised with the full orchestra: the blowing of ram's-horn trumpets, plucking of strings and shaking of tambourines. This is a triumph of heart over art. Hands and feet, hearts and voices are to join with every kind of instrument – played with gusto.

Isaiah speaks of a day when every knee will bow before God and every tongue will pay homage to his name (Isaiah 45:23). The writer of the book of Revelation hears 'every creature in heaven and on earth and under the earth and on the sea, and all that is in them', singing God's praise (Revelation 5:13–14).

This is the ultimate purpose and fulfilment of all God's creatures, angels and humans: to unite in praising him.

PROVERBS

Proverbs are sayings which distil God's truth for everyday life. They are usually brief, always perceptive and often amusing. They are essential advice for good living. Above all, they introduce wisdom as the perfect companion – attractive, liberating, constant and delightful.

God's truth is true for the whole of life, whoever we are and wherever we live. The Proverbs show how God's truth applies to our everyday situations – at home and at work; in marriage and family; in government and commerce; and in the heart attitudes which shape our reactions, lifestyles and habits. In all these areas, the Proverbs light the way to life and post hazard signs on every road to ruin.

OUTLINE

The first collection of proverbs (1:1–9:18)
The second collection: proverbs of Solomon (10:1–22:16)
The third collection: sayings of the wise (22:17–24:22)
Further sayings of the wise (24:23–34)
The fourth collection: more proverbs of Solomon (25:1–29:27)
Other collections of proverbs (30:1–31:9)
Epilogue: the treasure of a wise wife (31:10–31)

Introduction

The book of Proverbs is a collection of wise sayings. It ranges over every aspect of life, showing that there is always a choice between acting wisely and acting foolishly. The two ways of life are presented like people – Wisdom and Folly – who each call us to follow their path.

At the heart of all wisdom is 'the fear of the Lord' (1:7). To fear God is to be in awe of his majesty and reliant on his truth. He is our creator, and he knows what is best for us. The Proverbs are everyday examples of God's truth in real life.

The Proverbs point to Jesus

Proverbs are the light of God's wisdom, broken into a myriad beautiful colours. This is the light which will be seen in its purity and completeness when Jesus comes. He is the light of the world. He is wisdom in person (John 1:9; 1 Corinthians 1:24).

Famous proverbs

Some proverbs are best known from the King James Bible, which was published in England in 1611 and became known as the 'Authorized Version'. Here are some of them as they appear in the King James Version of the Bible:

Whom the Lord loveth he correcteth. (3:12 KJV)

Go to the ant, thou sluggard; consider her ways, and be wise. (6:6 KJV)

Wisdom is better than rubies. (8:11 KJV)

A virtuous woman is a crown to her husband. (12:4 KJV)

He that spareth his rod hateth his son. (13:24 KJV)

Righteousness exalteth a nation. (14:34 KJV)

A soft answer turneth away wrath. (15:1 KJV)

Better is a dinner of herbs where love is, than a stalled ox and hatred therewith. (15:17 KJV)

A word spoken in due season, how good is it! (15:23 KJV)

Pride goeth before destruction, and an haughty spirit before a fall. (16:18 KJV)

A friend loveth at all times, and a brother is born for adversity. (17:17 KJV)

A good name is rather to be chosen than great riches. (22:1 KJV)

Train up a child in the way he should go: and when he is old, he will not depart from it. (22:6 KJV)

The 'Wisdom' books

The writings of wise people are included in the Bible alongside the works of prophets and priests. They are known as the 'Wisdom' books – Job, Ecclesiastes and Proverbs.

Job explores the mystery of suffering, especially when it is undeserved. He cries out, 'Why?'

The book of **Ecclesiastes** reflects on the meaninglessness of life, because nothing seems to last. The preacher asks, 'What does it all mean?'

The **Proverbs** draw our attention to God's wisdom, which reaches into every part of life. They teach us 'how to live wisely and well'.

Boast not thyself of tomorrow, for thou knowest not what a day may bring forth. (27:1 KJV)

Faithful are the wounds of a friend. (27:6 KJV)

A continual dropping in a very rainy day and a contentious woman are alike. (27:15 KJV)

He that maketh haste to be rich shall not be innocent. (28:20 KJV)

Where there is no vision, the people perish. (29:18 KJV)

Who can find a virtuous woman? For her price is far above rubies. (31:10 KJV)

Wisdom

Wisdom gives life! Wise people are life-givers, because their searching sayings, shrewd comparisons and teasing riddles make us *think*. They make truth intriguing and attractive.

The most famous wise person in Israel's history is King Solomon. But there were wise men and women in Israel and other nations for centuries before his time. Egypt and Arabia, Babylon and Phoenicia all honoured the wise and treasured their wise sayings.

There is something special about the wisdom of Israel. In Israel, wisdom springs from the mind and will of the living God. This makes

Israel's wisdom very different from the fear for safety and the hope of good luck which shapes the behaviour of pagans. In Israel, all forms of magic and fortune-telling are rejected as guides to behaviour. In Israel, all forms of immorality – unfaithfulness, indecency and permissive sex – are always wrong. God himself may be hidden, but the way to live a godly life is absolutely clear. Wise behaviour and good behaviour will always be the same thing.

Who wrote Proverbs?

The book of Proverbs is made up of at least five separate collections of wise sayings. Three authors (or collectors) are named – Solomon, Agur and Lemuel. Some proverbs are simply described as 'the sayings of the wise'. The last section makes no mention of an author at all.

Of all the authors, Solomon is by far the best known. He is the son of David and has inherited his father's gift for words. While David is associated with the Psalms, Solomon is associated with the Proverbs. Many of the Proverbs in the third collection (22:17–24:22) have also been found in Egyptian writings from as far back as 1300 BC. Agur (whose collection we have in 30:1–33) may be an Arab writer. His style is similar to the book of Job, which comes from the same area. We know nothing more about Agur or about King Lemuel; nor do we know when all the collections were compiled together into one book. A reasonable guess is that the final collection was made after Israel's years in exile, and probably in the 5th century BC.

Solomon

The book of Kings tells how King Solomon was the wisest of the wise people.

God gave Solomon very great wisdom, discernment, and breadth of understanding as vast as the sand on the seashore, so that Solomon's wisdom surpassed the wisdom of all the people of the east, and all the wisdom of Egypt... his fame spread throughout all the surrounding nations. He composed three thousand proverbs, and his songs numbered a thousand and five. He would speak of trees, from the cedar that is in the Lebanon to the hyssop that grows in the wall; he would speak of animals, and birds, and reptiles, and fish. People came from all the nations to hear the wisdom of Solomon; they came from all the kings of the earth who had heard of his wisdom. (1 Kings 4:29–34 NRSV)

Discovering Proverbs

The first collection of proverbs

Solomon, the son of David and king of Israel, gives us his fatherly advice. At the heart of it all is 'the fear of the Lord', which he describes as 'the beginning of knowledge' (1:7).

Solomon shows us that life is all of a piece, that belief and behaviour belong together. There are many choices to be made between wisdom and folly and between life and death. Solomon describes wisdom as like a woman calling out in public for people to listen to her advice (1:20–23). To those who listen and take her words to heart, she promises a safe, confident and contented life (1:33).

Solomon urges his son to trust in God completely:

Trust in the Lord with all your heart
 and lean not on your own understanding;
in all your ways acknowledge him,
 and he will make your paths straight. (3:5–6)

The whole of life belongs together, and all our relationships overlap.

Between God and human beings: God is to be honoured with the first and best of our produce:

Honour the Lord with your wealth,
 with the firstfruits of all your crops;
then your barns will be filled to overflowing,
 and your vats will brim over with new wine. (3:9–10)

Among human beings and between human beings and nature: We are to be open, prompt and compassionate in our dealings with one another:

Do not withhold good from those to whom it is due,
 when it is in your power to act.

Do not say to your neighbour,
   'Come back tomorrow and I'll give it to you' –
   when you already have it with you. (3:27–28)

A warning against adultery (5:1–23)

Solomon warns his son not to fall into adultery. Another man's wife may look and sound perfect, but an affair with her will end in bitterness, injury and death. It is best to keep a long way from her door! The consequences of adultery are terrible. It will ruin your whole life.

But what is the alternative?

The greatest defence against adultery is a truly devoted marriage. 'Drink water from your own cistern', says Solomon (5:15). At its heart, a good marriage is exclusive of others, although many will benefit from its warmth and example. As in the Song of Songs, the author encourages good sex with the right person. 'May her breasts satisfy you always, may you ever be intoxicated with her love' (5:19). Compared with married sex in the security of committed love, an affair with a fellow cheat is cheap, furtive and futile. Even if it stays a secret from other people, it is all known to God. 'For human ways are under the eyes of the Lord' (5:21 NRSV).

How to handle a crisis (6:1–5)

Solomon tells his son what to do when a business deal goes wrong. He is to make every effort to get out of debt and not to give up until he is forgiven or free.

Advice for a sluggard (6:6–11)

We meet the sluggard – the lazy person who never really gets organized. Such a person puts off decisions and evades responsibilities. The sluggard wastes the life, gifts and opportunities that God has given.

Solomon chooses a favourite picture from the world of nature. 'Go to the ant, you sluggard; consider its ways and be wise!' (6:6).

The ant is the harvester ant, which is found in Palestine – always busy, hard-working and effective. The harvester ants store food in the summer to last them through the winter – as Agur will again point out later in the book (30:25). By contrast, the sluggard, with heavy sleeping and many little naps, is storing up poverty for the future. When the sun shines, the sluggard likes to stretch out and relax, while the ant uses the fine weather to do its work.

The scoundrel (6:12–15)

Solomon tells his son how to recognize crooks – by their cunning speech and crafty signals. They are always planning mischief for others, but one day they will get what they deserve.

Solomon isn't afraid to predict consequences. He has noticed how things turn out. Lazy people fall on hard times. Honesty and faithfulness bring great rewards. Villains will face a day of reckoning.

Another warning against adultery (6:20–7:27)

Solomon teaches that adultery begins not in a bed, but in the mind. 'Do not lust in your heart after her beauty', he warns (6:25). A thousand years later, Jesus will say the same: 'Anyone who looks at a woman lustfully has already committed adultery with her in his heart' (Matthew 5:28). It's the thought that counts. Eyes and ears must be defended. They are the doors through which temptation comes.

The consequences of adultery are terrible. 'Can fire be carried in the bosom without burning one's clothes?' (6:27 NRSV). 'A man who commits adultery has no sense; whoever does so destroys himself' (6:32).

As an example, Solomon describes a foolish young man getting involved with a brazen prostitute. The young man thinks he is free to take advantage of the woman's invitation and the husband's absence; but he is 'like a deer stepping into a noose' or 'like an ox going to the slaughter' (7:22).

Solomon tells how to avoid adultery. Firstly, we are to control our hearts – not letting ourselves drift in a wrong direction. Secondly, we must stay away from obvious temptation (the young man just happened to be going past the prostitute's door at twilight!). Finally, we should look at what has happened to others – the multitude whose lives have been wrecked.

Special proverbs

Every proverb is a gem, but here are some special treasures:

Ill-gotten treasures have no lasting value,
    but righteousness delivers from death. (10:2)

Hatred stirs up conflict
    but love covers over all wrongs. (10:12)

The Lord detests dishonest scales,
    but accurate weights find favour with him. (11:1)

A gossip goes about telling secrets,
    but one who is trustworthy in spirit keeps a confidence.
    (11:13 NRSV)

For lack of guidance a nation falls,
    but victory is won through many advisers. (11:14)

Like a gold ring in a pig's snout
    is a beautiful woman who shows no discretion. (11:22)

A generous person will be enriched,
    and one who gives water will get water. (11:25 NRSV)

A wife of noble character is her husband's crown,
    but a disgraceful wife is like decay in his bones. (12:4)

A heart at peace gives life to the body,
    but envy rots the bones. (14:30)

Those who oppress the poor insult their Maker,
    but those who are kind to the needy honour him. (14:31 NRSV)

A gentle answer turns away wrath,
    but a harsh word stirs up anger. (15:1)

The eyes of the Lord are everywhere,
    keeping watch on the wicked and the good. (15:3)

> Better a dish of vegetables with love,
> than a fattened calf with hatred. (15:17 NIV)
>
> Commit to the Lord whatever you do,
> and he will establish your plans. (16:3 NIV)
>
> Starting a quarrel is like breaching a dam;
> so drop the matter before a dispute breaks out. (17:14 NIV)
>
> He who finds a wife finds what is good
> and receives favour from the Lord. (18:22 NIV)
>
> A stupid child is ruin to a father,
> and a wife's quarrelling is a continual dripping of rain. (19:13 NRSV)
>
> The human mind may devise many plans,
> but it is the purpose of the Lord that will be established. (19:21 NRSV)
>
> Wine is a mocker and beer a brawler;
> and whoever is led astray by them is not wise. (20:1 NRSV)
>
> The human spirit is the lamp of the Lord,
> searching every inmost part. (20:27 NRSV)
>
> The horse is made ready for the day of battle,
> but victory belongs to the Lord. (21:31 NRSV)
>
> A good name is more desirable than great riches;
> to be esteemed is better than silver or gold. (22:1)
>
> Train children in the right way,
> and when old, they will not stray. (22:6 NRSV)

Wisdom's call (8:1–36)

Solomon has already described wisdom as like a woman calling out to people in the street. Unlike the prostitute, Wisdom speaks the truth. The prostitute leads to destruction and death, but Wisdom guides to truth and life. Her instruction makes us truly wealthy – more than any amount of silver, gold and precious stones.

There is nothing secret about Wisdom. She is to be found on the highways and at the city gates – freely available to all. There is no talk of only finding her in church, or through reading books, or by making a pilgrimage to a guru. Wisdom is found in everyday situations, wherever there is the choice between right and wrong.

The wisdom we first met at the street corner is infinitely greater than we first imagined. The Lord God prized Wisdom and made her supreme before ever he created the universe. When God made the world, Wisdom was with him – attending to every detail. 'I was the master worker at his side' (8:30 NRSV), delighting in God's presence and rejoicing in his creativity. The greatest joy of all was the creation of the human race.

Wisdom is an indispensable part of the way the world works. If we want to enjoy this world as our maker intends, we must live by the same wisdom with which he made it. When Jesus comes, he will be seen as this wisdom in person:

He is the image of the invisible God, the firstborn of all creation; for in him all things in heaven and on earth were created, things visible and invisible, whether thrones or dominions or rulers or powers; all things have been created through him and for him. He himself is before all things, and in him all things hold together. (Colossians 1:15–17 NRSV)

Jesus Christ is none other than the wisdom of God (1 Corinthians 1:24).

Solomon sums up Wisdom's invitation by stating a simple and wonderful fact:

Whoever finds me finds life. (8:35 NRSV)

The invitations of wisdom and folly (9:1–18)

Solomon describes Wisdom and Folly as like hosts inviting people to dine. The food and drink which Wisdom offers are understanding and the fear of the Lord. Even the simplest people are invited most warmly to share them. Folly, by contrast, is slovenly and ignorant. Her food and drink are exciting only because they are stolen. Hers is an invitation as old as the serpent's to Eve (Genesis 3:6); and the consequences are the same.

The second collection: proverbs of Solomon

Here is a second collection of Solomon's proverbs. In this collection there are no hymns in praise of wisdom or warnings against folly. Instead, there is a wonderful variety of one-off sayings. They contain all kinds of advice and insight on how to understand the ways of the world and live a good life.

Solomon teaches that self-control is very important, especially in the things we say. There are many things which are beyond our knowledge, and which are known only to God. We must be humble in the face of these deep mysteries of life. Now and again a proverb reminds us that God is working out his purposes – in us, around us and sometimes despite us.

Some underlying principles

Making peace

We belong to one another and are responsible for the poor. Regardless of worldly wealth, it is the righteous who are truly rich. Conflict is harmful when it is unresolved. Hatred makes for discord, but love makes for peace (10:12).

Real wealth

Our quality of life does not depend on whether we are rich or poor. However, the truth is that poor people have a harder life and fewer friends than rich people (10:15). What we do with our money says a lot about us (10:16).

Straight talk

The words we say with our tongues indicate our inner thoughts; the thoughts of our hearts. God cares about our business dealings; he loves to see honesty and fairness (11:1).

Gaining by giving

We gain by giving – both of our goods and of ourselves (11:25). The things we say can cause terrible hurt, or lasting healing (12:18).

A whole world

Good people honour and care for the whole of God's creation. They treat their animals as their neighbours (12:10).

The advice of the Proverbs is summed up in a single saying:

Commit to the Lord whatever you do,
  and he will establish your plans. (16:3)

The third collection: sayings of the wise

Here are thirty sayings which are perhaps to be learned by heart. They are written like a father speaking to his son. They show how to live wisely, with dignity, respect and self-control.

Scholars think that these sayings come from an Egyptian collection. They are very like the 'Instruction of Amenemope', an Egyptian wise man, and there are many parallels between the two. The Egyptian text seems to be much older. Amenemope lived long before the time of Solomon.

Some gems

Do not wear yourself out to get rich;
  be wise enough to desist. (23:4 NRSV)

Do not speak in the hearing of a fool,
  who will only despise the wisdom of your words. (23:9 NRSV)

Like many other proverbs, this teaching is echoed in the teaching of Jesus and especially in the Sermon on the Mount. 'Do not give dogs what is sacred; do not throw your pearls to pigs. If you do, they may

> ### A sharper focus
>
> Most proverbs are written as couplets, or set in pairs. Just as seeing with two eyes gives a better perspective, so the pairing of Proverbs gives a sharper understanding. The second statement often puts the same point but in an opposite way – enabling us to compare wise and foolish, rich and poor, righteous and wicked, proud and humble.

trample them under their feet, and then turn and tear you to pieces' (Matthew 7:6).

It is important to discipline children; but the real joy comes when children share their father's values of their own free will:

The father of the righteous will greatly rejoice;
he who begets a wise son will be glad in him. (23:24 NRSV)

And there is warning. Prostitutes and unfaithful wives are dangerous predators. They riddle society with lies, guilt and broken relationships.

A warning against getting drunk (23:29–35)

The father warns his son against becoming a drunkard. Red wine, like a wicked woman, can be seductive and damaging. He describes the living nightmare of a drink problem.

No need to be jealous (24:1–2, 19–20)

The father advises his son not to be envious of the friendships or successes of wicked people. They are troublemakers whose lives won't last long.

Further sayings of the wise

This little collection contains excellent advice about fairness, honesty, priorities and hard work.

It is best to sort out your land (which is going to support you) before you start your family (24:27)!

The fourth collection: more proverbs of Solomon

These are Solomon's proverbs, which have been arranged and copied by the scribes of King Hezekiah. It seems that they have grouped them by topic, to avoid repetition.

Hezekiah was the godly king of Judah whose twenty-nine year reign coincided with the ministry of Isaiah.

The collection opens with advice to kings to be thorough in their government (25:2) and for their courtiers not to be proud (25:6–7). There is a feast of observations which give guidance on relationships:

A word fitly spoken
is like apples of gold in a setting of silver. (25:11 NRSV)

Like a broken tooth or a lame foot
is trust in a faithless person in time of trouble. (25:19 NRSV)

There is also some very practical, hard-won wisdom, such as 'too much honey makes you sick' (25:16)!

Caring for enemies (25:21–22)

Here is advice we have met before, and which Paul will repeat in his letter to the Romans (Romans 12:20). By treating your enemies with kindness and generosity, you 'heap coals of fire on their heads'. They burn with shame when they think of the way they have treated you.

Fools, sluggards and mischief-makers (26:1–28)

Solomon draws on a host of pictures from everyday life to warn against getting involved with unreliable people.

Fools are weak and will let you down like 'the legs of a disabled person' (26:7). The sluggard is attached to the bed 'as a door turns on its hinges' (26:14). Mischief-makers, with quarrels, gossip and deceit, are downright dangerous, 'though their speech is charming, do not believe them' (26:25).

Right attitudes (27:1–27)

Now the collection turns to personal attitudes. We mustn't assume what the future holds (27:1). It is better to be praised by someone else than to praise ourselves (27:2). Faithfulness in friendship, wisdom and prudence are fine qualities. But beware of being jolly too early in the day, or of a wife who picks fights (27:14–16).

Solomon takes us to the shepherd to see the benefit of good work. Doing today's work well gives satisfaction in the present and provides for the future (27:23–27).

Deep thoughts (28:1-29:27)

The Proverbs now probe the realities of government and justice:

When a land rebels it has many rulers;
   but with an intelligent ruler there is lasting order. (28:2 NRSV)

The northern kingdom of Israel has discovered this truth the hard way. She has been ruled by a series of nine kings, of whom eight have been assassinated. Meanwhile, the southern kingdom of Judah has enjoyed the stable rule of David and his descendants.

Smile!

The Proverbs take a long-range view of life – smiling at its ironies and reverses (28:8). The wealth amassed so ruthlessly by one person is generously given away by another!

Goodness works

God sees, values and blesses the person who leads a good life (28:18-28). Faithfulness, fairness and hard work are richly rewarded. The person who relies on God's wisdom will always be safe. The people who are generous will find themselves provided for.

Chaos and order

A society may fall into wickedness, but goodness will prove stronger in the end (29:16-18). Every parent can contribute to the health of society by raising children well. The antidote to anarchy is to live humbly in the light of God's law.

Other collections of proverbs

Sayings of Agur (30:1-33)

Agur is another of the wise men of Judah. He speaks towering wisdom from a humble heart. He has a simple faith, plainly expressed:

Two things I ask of you, O Lord;
   do not refuse me before I die:
Keep falsehood and lies far from me;
   give me neither poverty nor riches,

but give me only my daily bread.
Otherwise, I may have too much and disown you
  and say, 'Who is the Lord?'. (30:7-9)

He is a fascinated observer of the world around him. He wonders at its mysteries:

There are three things that are too amazing for me,
  four that I do not understand:
the way of an eagle in the sky,
  the way of a snake on a rock,
the way of a ship on the high seas,
  and the way of a man with a young woman. (30:18-19)

Outcomes

Agur warns against behaviour which leads to trouble (30:20). He is amazed that a woman can commit adultery as though it's as harmless as eating a snack. He warns about the consequences of foolish, proud or wicked behaviour:

As churning cream produces butter,
  and as twisting the nose produces blood,
  so stirring up anger produces strife. (30:33)

Sayings of King Lemuel (31:1-9)

This little collection of sayings was passed on to King Lemuel by his mother! Lemuel is not mentioned anywhere else in the Bible and is not a king of Israel.

Lemuel's mother warns him against wasting his energy on women, or befuddling his wits with wine. Instead, he should speak up for the powerless and protect the poor. This is a brilliant insight into Israel's standards for political authority – and finds many of her kings falling short!

Epilogue: the treasure of a wise wife

The book of Proverbs ends with a poem in praise of the perfect woman. It is as though the lady Wisdom of the early chapters has got married and is now running a home. She is trustworthy, hard-working and far-sighted. She is good at business, clever with her hands and generous to the needy. She looks good, speaks wisely and teaches well. Her secret is that she fears the Lord and the outcome is that her family is proud of her.

Many modern women have no desire at all to be super-competent in all these ways. But at least they may accept the compliment to their sex. The book of Proverbs ends with an example of all the good qualities praised in the book, and describes them in the form of a woman.

ECCLESIASTES

Ecclesiastes is a book of wise sayings. They come from a man called Qoheleth (pronounced Ko*hell*et), which means 'teacher'. He is outstanding among wise people, and is strongly linked with Solomon. Although the book may sound like Solomon, most scholars believe it was written much later.

The Teacher has looked long and hard at life on earth – and found nothing of lasting value. His opening cry is 'Meaningless! Meaningless! Utterly meaningless! Everything is utterly meaningless' (1:2). By 'meaningless', he means that life is as fleeting and ephemeral as a breath.

But there is more to his message than despair. The Teacher wants us to stand back from short-term goals and pleasures and find our long-term trust in God.

Ecclesiastes takes its place alongside the other 'wisdom' books of the Bible – Job and Proverbs. Together they show us that 'the fear of the Lord is the beginning of knowledge' (Proverbs 1:7). The Teacher wants to bring us to hope in God by showing us how empty and pointless life is without him.

The Teacher clearly believes in God, but probes human experience to see if faith in God makes any difference. He sounds listless, disillusioned and cynical. We have to realize when he is merely putting a point of view to test us – to make us think. He exposes the selfishness and blind ambition which blights our lives – and reminds us that our time is short.

OUTLINE

Meet 'The Teacher' (1:1)
'Vanity of vanities' (1:2)
The world is boring (1:3–11)
There is no meaning in anything (1:12–2:25)
A glimmer of light (2:26)
A time to enjoy (3:1–15)
A big question (3:16–4:3)

Alienation (4:4-12)
Be wise (4:13-16)
Mind how you come (5:1-2)
And mind how you go (5:3-7)
The balance of power (5:8-9)
The poverty of riches (5:10-17)
Simple pleasure (5:18-20)
They were robbed (6:1-6)
Life sentences (6:7-12)
Get real - get wisdom (7:1-13)
Stay cool? (7:14-22)
Wisdom is deep (7:23-8:1)
Living in the circumstances (8:2-15)
A glimpse of God (8:16-17)
All the same (9:1-6)
Good cheer (9:7-10)
Just our luck (9:11-12)
A sad case (9:13-18)
Seeds of sense (10:1-20)
Just do it! (11:1-10)
The heart of the matter (12:1-8)
In conclusion (12:9-14)

Introduction

A humdrum world

The Teacher says that, in spite of the wonders of creation, life in this world is tedious. There is so much drudgery and dreary routine:

It is an unhappy business that God has given to human beings to be busy with. I saw all the deeds that are done under the sun; and see, all is vanity and a chasing after wind. (1:13-14 NRSV)

Life isn't fair

The Teacher says that life is unpredictable. Even what we have can be snatched away at any time. Whether our lives are a success or failure in human terms, we all end up in the grave:

Those to whom God gives wealth, possessions, and honour, so that they lack nothing of all that they desire, yet God does not enable them to enjoy these things, but a stranger enjoys them. (6:2 NRSV)

A longing for more

The frustrations of life make us cry out for meaning. Sometimes we think we see a purpose or glimpse a pattern. But God is too great for us. We cannot read his mind. His thoughts are too deep:

God has made everything beautiful in its time. He has also set eternity in the human heart, yet no one can fathom what God has done from beginning to end. (3:11)

The Teacher says that even wisdom and knowledge have their limits. In the end, wisdom just shows our stupidity and knowledge reveals our ignorance. In the end, neither wisdom nor knowledge can show us God. We are still left guessing. We are still in the dark.

God

For all that he sounds world-weary, the Teacher is utterly serious about God. God is completely different from us, and his ways are beyond our understanding. We must not be frivolous and shallow when we talk of him:

God is in heaven
    and you are on earth,
    so let your words be few. (5:2)

The Teacher urges us to take our worship and our vows seriously. God is the creator. We are merely a tiny part of his creation. We must realize our littleness and ignorance:

As you do not know the path of the wind,
    or how the body is formed in a mother's womb,
so you cannot understand the work of God,
    the Maker of all things. (11:5)

God has not made us to be robots, mindlessly reacting to his signals. We can think, reflect and judge. We are responsible for our behaviour. Most of the troubles we experience are our own fault:

God made human beings straightforward, but they have devised many schemes. (7:29 NRSV)

The Teacher's conclusion

We should enjoy life while we are young – knowing that our youth won't last for ever. We should learn to fear God and keep his commandments while we have our health and strength. This will stand us in good stead when we grow old, and our sight, hearing, strength and courage fail:

Fear God and keep his commandments; for that is the whole duty of everyone. (12:13 NRSV)

Some thoughts on time

The Teacher sees 'time' as a period of opportunity. There are different stages and chapters of our lives, and we must accept the freedoms and limitations that come with each of them. Above all, there is time for everything God wants us to do!

*There is a time for everything,
and a season for every activity under the heavens:
a time to be born and a time to die,
a time to plant and a time to uproot,
a time to kill and a time to heal,
a time to tear down and a time to build,
a time to weep and a time to laugh,
a time to mourn and a time to dance,
a time to scatter stones and a time to gather them,
a time to embrace and a time to refrain from embracing,
a time to search and a time to give up,
a time to keep and a time to throw away,
a time to tear and a time to mend,
a time to be silent and a time to speak,
a time to love and a time to hate,
a time for war and a time for peace.* (3:1–8)

Some of the Teacher's sayings

A cord of three strands is not quickly broken. (4:12)

When you make a vow to God, do not delay fulfilling it. (5:4 NRSV)

Whoever loves money never has enough. (5:10 NIV)

As they came from their mother's womb, so they shall go again, naked as they came. (5:15 NRSV)

A good name is better than fine perfume. (7:1)

Wisdom preserves the life of those who have it. (7:12)

Cast your bread upon the waters, for after many days you will find it again. (11:1 Berean Study Bible)

Remember your Creator in the days of your youth. (12:1)

Discovering Ecclesiastes

Meet 'The Teacher' (1:1)

The writer introduces himself in a mysterious way. He calls himself 'The Teacher'. The Hebrew word is Qoheleth, which has often been translated 'The Preacher'.

The writer says he is 'the son of David, king in Jerusalem'. This sounds like Solomon, the son who succeeded David as king, and to whom God gave the gift of wisdom.

Solomon's name is given to other books in the Bible (the books of Proverbs and the Song of Songs) – but not to Ecclesiastes. If the writer is Solomon, why doesn't he say so? Is he writing in a private way, presenting his 'other side' – like a president giving a history lecture, or a prime minister writing a novel? Or is this someone else, who wants to put his wisdom in the super-league alongside Solomon's? We don't know.

Later in this chapter, the writer says, 'I have acquired great wisdom, surpassing all who were over Jerusalem before me' (1:16 NRSV). This echoes what the Bible tells us about Solomon: 'God gave Solomon very great wisdom, discernment, and breadth of understanding as vast as the sand on the seashore, so that Solomon's wisdom surpassed the wisdom of all the people of the east, and all the wisdom of Egypt. He was wiser than anyone else... He composed three thousand proverbs, and his songs numbered a thousand and five' (1 Kings 4:29–32 NRSV).

There is further information about the Teacher towards the end of Ecclesiastes. He 'taught the people knowledge, weighing and studying and arranging many proverbs. [He] sought to find pleasing words, and he wrote words of truth plainly' (12:9–10 NRSV). This makes him sound like a scholar and teacher rather than a man of action and affairs of state, such as a king. But it is possible to be both.

'Vanity of vanities' (1:2)

The Teacher says that everything there is – creation, history, human life – amounts to 'vanity'. By vanity he means something that is 'in vain' – pointless, fruitless and empty. Life amounts to nothing. It is all meaningless. This isn't merely a sound bite to attract our attention. It's his conclusion. He's serious.

But what about the reality of God and the joy of leading a godly life? Is the Teacher saying that's vanity as well? No he isn't. He is talking about everything in this world *apart from* God – everything 'under the sun' (1:9). He is talking about life as most people live it, with our perpetual striving for possessions, pleasure, security and success.

The Teacher will reveal himself, in the end, as a person of deeply worked faith. But first he is going to make us take a long, hard (and scary) look at our situation.

The world is boring (1:3–11)

The Teacher surveys the scene. Life on earth is tiring, tedious and predictable. People live and die, the sun rises and sets; air circulates and water runs downhill. So where's the benefit? What's the point? It's so boring!

The Teacher says there's nothing new to discover or do. That's not true, of course – human history has been a continuing adventure of enterprise and discovery. But the Teacher is challenging us to look at our endless stress and busyness. What's it all about? It's all been done before.

We don't know or care about the people in the past, and in the future no one will know or care about us.

There is no meaning in anything (1:12–2:25)

The Teacher describes how he set out to discover the meaning of life. Is it to be found in wisdom? Is wisdom any better than foolishness? After all, wisdom can be worrying and knowledge can be disturbing; but fools seem happy and carefree.

The Teacher reckons that everything is futile. At base, nothing changes – and what will be will be. He sums up the situation in a proverb: 'What is crooked cannot be made straight, and what is lacking cannot be counted' (1:15 NRSV).

The Teacher tells how he tried to laugh away the problems and experimented with drink. Then he tried being constructive: building houses, planting vineyards and planning gardens and parks. He made a fine collection of fruit trees, all carefully irrigated. He gathered people and animals: slaves and flocks and herds. He acquired enormous wealth in gold and silver and treasure. He was surrounded by music and sated with sex.

It was fun! But it had no meaning. The pleasure was in the effort, not in the result. Wisdom is better than madness only because it is aware of itself. Wisdom knows what it is doing: 'The wise have eyes in their head, but fools walk in darkness' (2:14 NRSV).

In so many ways, the wise person and the fool are both the same. The wise person dies just as certainly as the fool. The Teacher has come to regret his wealth and achievements. They give him no advantage in this life and might be inherited by a fool when he dies. The pain and strain and sleepless nights are a waste of time. Like chasing the wind.

A glimmer of light (2:26)

Suddenly the Teacher gives a glimpse of what he really believes. He has been describing life without God as a ceaseless quest for fulfilment which is doomed to failure. But *with* God there is the joy of wisdom and knowledge.

There is a world of difference between life as a mindless drudgery and life as a God-given gift. Without God we invest our life in 'gathering and heaping', like an occupational therapy to fill the time. Working so hard without purpose or hope is empty and meaningless. But *with* God there is an exciting dimension to life which is endlessly intriguing and fulfilling.

A time to enjoy (3:1–15)

The Teacher considers the way the world is. Life is made up of seasons and opportunities. The seasons come round again, but opportunities may not. Being born and dying are things we do only once, and about which we have no choice. For other things – planting and building – we must choose the right moment for success. Other actions and reactions must be appropriate to a relationship or circumstance: to kill or to cure, to break or to mend, to make love or to wage war.

The Teacher says that God has given us this context of rhythm and reliability, crisis and change. We take our place in an unfolding drama and purpose, having missed the beginning and being unable to guess the end. We have our defining moments of usefulness or success, but our contribution is tiny and brief. It is God who knows the purpose and sees the whole. It is his work alone that endures.

Having confined us to a prison of time and circumstance, the Teacher opens a door to freedom in the present. Enjoy! Food and drink and all the varied activities of daily life are God's good gifts. When our life engages with God's love, we experience something of eternal value.

A big question (3:16–4:3)

The Teacher advises that life is to be enjoyed, but for many people that is impossible. What about those for whom life is a misery, because of exploitation, persecution or disaster? Life isn't fair.

The Teacher wants to believe that God will sort everything out, punishing the wicked and rewarding the good. But that hasn't happened. Maybe God is allowing humans to behave like animals until they come to their senses and realize their dignity. But *are* humans a higher form of life than animals? Don't both die and disappear, without significance or hope?

Sometimes life is so bad that death seems better. And many must wish they had never been born.

Alienation (4:4–12)

As well as injustice and suffering, there is the problem of alienation. People can't relate to each other and society becomes fractured by isolation and loneliness. For some, their driving envy or ambition make more enemies than friends. Others are marginalized because they can't or won't compete. Both the tycoon and the drop-out are too self-absorbed to build a united and caring society.

The Teacher pleads for a balance which he describes as 'a handful with quiet' (4:6 NRSV). Everyone should have enough to be content, without the extremes of overwork or underachievement.

The Teacher sees single people without any dependent relatives, who work all hours and still don't feel they have enough. He advises that it's better to work with a partner, to share in times of success and help in times of hardship. Partners can also encourage each other – and stand together against a foe.

Be wise (4:13–16)

The Teacher offers some more advice. It is better to be poor and wise than old but foolish. He has seen a young man come from prison to replace a king, because the young man was wise while the old king was foolish. The new young king will be popular for a while; but experience shows that his novelty will fade. As with everything else, there's nothing new.

Mind how you come (5:1–2)

The Teacher advises on how to approach God. It is better, when coming to worship, to remember the greatness of God. Don't rush in with your contribution and your noise, as though you are the centre of attention. Instead, wait quietly so that God can speak to you.

And mind how you go (5:3-7)

Just as worries come out in our dreams, so do fools come out with chatter (5:3).

The Teacher warns us not to let our words run away with us when we make our vows to God. We should keep the promises we make to God – and do so as soon as possible. God is angry when we make a vow and then don't fulfil it – or pretend it was a mistake. We should say what we mean and mean what we say (5:4-7).

The balance of power (5:8-9)

The Teacher has a word about social order. A hierarchy of authorities can lead to corruption and abuse – the poor being oppressed by those with power or privilege. It's not surprising, because power corrupts (5:8).

But, overall, an authority structure is a good thing, because it imposes duties on people. The Teacher summarizes the benefit in a proverb: 'A king for a ploughed field' (5:9 NRSV). A king is the price you pay for a settled and ordered society. If there is a clear leader, the needed work is done.

The poverty of riches (5:10-17)

The Teacher talks about wealth. The person who loves money will never be satisfied, but always crave more (5:10). And when wealth increases, so does expenditure – so the rich have to watch their assets being consumed (5:11). By contrast, poor labourers are well off, because their work results in a good night's sleep – unlike the wealthy who are kept awake by worry and indigestion (5:12).

There is another problem with wealth. It can be lost very suddenly (5:13). A ruined person's children inherit nothing (5:14). In any case, death takes us from our riches. We leave this world as naked as we arrived and can take none of our profits with us (5:15).

A preoccupation with wealth makes rich people poor. It robs them of the simple joys of life, shutting them in a gloomy world of stress, illness and dissatisfaction (5:16-17).

Simple pleasure (5:18–20)

The Teacher offers a better attitude to life than being eaten up by envy. Why not enjoy each day as it comes, with its food and drink and work? After all, God gives us life a day at a time. See all that you have as God's gift and savour every moment. You will find you have no time to be jealous of others or to worry about growing old.

They were robbed (6:1–6)

The Teacher returns to a situation that puzzles him. He has seen people acquire wealth and then not have the chance to enjoy it. Why should someone they don't even know reap the benefit (6:1–2)? It seems to the Teacher that it would have been better to be stillborn, because in that state is peace. Ignorance is bliss. You may have 100 children and live 2,000 years, yet still end up in the same place as the baby that had no life at all (6:3–6).

Life sentences (6:7–12)

The Teacher sums up the basic dilemmas of human life. We work to eat, but for ever get hungry (6:7). In this, the wise and the foolish are both the same. Poor people may lead better lives than the rich, but never receive any advantage or reward (6:8). It is better to delight in seeing something than to become obsessed with the desire to possess it (6:9).

The Teacher says there is nothing new left to discover, either outside us in the world or within our human nature. We can't argue with someone stronger than us and that's a fact (6:10). The more we talk, the more meaningless everything becomes; for who really knows what is best for us in this fleeting life? And no one knows what is to come (6:11–12).

Get real – get wisdom (7:1–13)

The Teacher has presented us with bleak realities. Life is constraining, perplexing and short. But now he changes the pace and starts to gather some fragments of truth.

Little by little, the Teacher puts in place a foundation for living, although not everything he writes is reassuring. He doesn't say, 'This is what God wants,' but rather, 'This is hard-won common sense.'

Firstly, a good name is more precious than any material luxury (7:1). Secondly, it is wise to accept the certainty and finality of death. This may mean that we are sad at heart, but that in itself can be liberating – it frees us from pretending to be happy (7:2-4). Foolish people may try to lighten the situation with laughter, but their cackling is like the fierce and futile crackle of a flash-fire (7:5-6).

The Teacher advises us to notice the influences that change us. Hardship can make us wise, because it forces us to wrestle with resentment and longing. A bribe, on the other hand, can make us foolish – undermining our integrity at a stroke (7:7).

It is better to judge something by its end result than to be misled by the promise of its beginning. Patience is a better attitude than pride, because patience is open and looks forward, while pride is closed and looks back (7:8).

The Teacher warns against anger. Only fools let anger take root in their hearts (7:9).

It is vain to hark back to 'the good old days'. They weren't that good, and you fail to live fully in the present (7:10).

Wisdom has great value. It is just as much an advantage in life as owning money or land. Wisdom is an asset which gives protection and independence (7:11-12).

The Teacher advises a realistic, almost fatalistic, approach to life's problems. If God has made a thing in a particular way, it is futile to try to change it (7:13).

Stay cool? (7:14-22)

The Teacher's tone turns sarcastic. Why not simply stay cool? Life may be easy or life may be tough; but either way, stand well back. Don't get too involved. This is just the way things are (7:14).

Don't be surprised when good people suffer and wicked people prosper. Life doesn't fit into neat patterns of punishment and reward (7:15).

Be good but not too good. No one's perfect, so why strain yourself (7:16, 20)? But don't just throw your life away by deliberately being evil or playing the fool (7:17). Try to find a balance. That way you've covered both bases. Fear God and do what you like (7:18).

But seriously, when you overhear someone say something bad about you, remember you have said the same of others. And when you see a fault in someone else, notice it in yourself as well (7:21-22).

Wisdom is deep (7:23–8:1)

The Teacher has found it hard to discover wisdom and define it. He feels as though he has dug deep, but mined only a few nuggets. He is sure that wisdom is the key to life and that wickedness and folly lead to disaster (7:23-25). A deceitful and manipulative woman, for example, is definitely to be avoided (7:26)!

The Teacher believes that God has made humans 'straightforward' (7:29 NRSV). Men and women can stand upright physically and live upright morally. They *can* but the Teacher finds they *don't* (7:28).

Only the wise person has really got it all together. Wisdom shines out in a joyful face and a relaxed manner (8:1).

Living in the circumstances (8:2-15)

The Teacher points out that everyone has to live within the limits of status and circumstance. There is no avoiding the commands of those in authority, so it's wise to obey them promptly and without fear (8:2-5).

But rulers don't have it easy either. The future is uncertain for them as well. They can't control the elements, or avoid death, or evade a battle. If they act wickedly, wickedness won't defend them (8:8).

But what about the wicked? How do they get away with it – even to the extent of being admired and praised by the community they exploited (8:10)? The Teacher is sure they will be judged by God. It may not happen quickly, but it will happen certainly (8:11-13).

The Teacher notes again that good people don't get the rewards they deserve in this life, while some wicked people win all life's prizes. It doesn't make sense (8:14). Again, he recommends enjoyment as the rule of this God-given road (5:18; 8:15).

A glimpse of God (8:16–17)

The Teacher pauses to state a conclusion – which is that he can't find one! Except that he believes it is God's work he is surveying and God's meaning he is pondering. No one knows the purpose and end of it all – and if they claim to, don't believe them.

All the same (9:1–6)

The Teacher sees that life is the same for everyone. It isn't clear whom God loves and whom God hates, because all are treated the same (9:1–2). There is no distinction between the good and the wicked, or those who keep the law and those who don't, or those who practise religion and those who don't (9:2).

The only thing that is certain is that everyone dies in the end. Everyone shares the same fate – and the same wicked, crazy human nature (9:3). But if one has to choose between life and death, it is better to be alive. While we are alive we have awareness, hope and a share in what's going on (9:4–5). The dead have nothing – no passion and no power (9:6).

Good cheer (9:7–10)

The Teacher urges us to live life joyfully. It pleases God if we enjoy our food and drink, wear fine clothes and indulge in life's luxuries (9:7–8). Marriage, work – everything is to be enjoyed! Life is for living, so we must live it while we can. When we come in the end to Sheol (the world of the dead) there will be no such dimensions to existence (9:9–10).

Just our luck (9:11–12)

The Teacher has found no rhyme or reason to human success. Races aren't always won by the fastest, nor are battles always won by the strongest. Wise, intelligent and skilful people can all suffer setbacks (9:11). Disaster can overtake anyone at any time, and without warning (9:12).

A sad case (9:13-18)

The Teacher tells a story. There was a wise man who was very poor, but his wisdom saved his little city from being conquered. Sadly, everyone forgot him afterwards (9:13-16). Quiet wisdom is superior to bombastic speeches and heavy armaments. But a fool can do a lot of damage (9:17-18).

Seeds of sense (10:1-20)

The Teacher offers some proverbs which make sense of life as we find it.

A moment of foolishness can ruin a lifetime of achievement – like a fly spoiling an ointment (10:1).

Wise people and fools lead very different lives. The wise seek the right, while the fool does wrong; yet the wise may sink and the fool may rise (10:2-3, 5-7).

If your boss is angry with you, stay calm. Don't flare up or walk out. Your steadiness and maturity will do a lot to put the matter right (10:4).

Life has consequences. If we live dangerously, we are likely to get hurt (10:8-9). However, wisdom can help us stay safe, by learning from the past and anticipating the future (10:10-11).

Our words matter. They reveal us as wise or foolish, and shape our relationships. All the more reason to speak from wisdom – and to know what we don't know, whether it's the future or the way to town (10:12-15).

A mature ruler is the key to a people's well-being. If a ruler is disciplined in his own life, he can give a good structure to the lives of others (10:16-18).

Laziness will show through the holes in your roof (10:18)!

Everything has a purpose: feasting covers sadness and money covers need (10:19). Be careful what you think. It's amazing how other people will get to hear of it (10:20).

Just do it! (11:1-10)

The Teacher has been advising caution, but now he commends some positive actions.

Be generous and share what you have. You will receive back the benefits many years later (11:1). Spread your assets to benefit several causes, for you don't know what's going to happen to them or you (11:2).

You can't help the onset of rain or the fall of a tree, but if you're too cautious you'll never do anything (11:3-4). There is so much of God's work that we don't understand – even the basic things about creation (11:5).

Rather than avoiding risk, make time and chance work for you. If you've done your main work in the morning, then use your spare time for another project which may do just as well (11:6).

Life is too good to waste a single day. Be glad of it, right into old age. After all, you'll be dead a long time (11:7-8)!

Are you young? Then delight in the health and strength of your body. There's a whole world to be explored, and you have the energy and enterprise to do it. Your senses and emotions will lead you – but remember there's a reckoning with God (11:9). Don't lose your early years to worry or pain, because this is a time to be free (11:10).

The heart of the matter (12:1-8)

Finally, the Teacher tells us what he really thinks and believes.

The best advice for living is to begin with God. Commit yourself to God and build your relationship with him while you are young (12:1). Then, when troubles come or old age creeps on, you'll have a firm grasp of your creator's presence and purpose (12:13-14).

The Teacher describes the ageing process in exquisite images. Our appetite and desire begin to fade (12:2). Heaven and earth seem to close down, as we sink into a twilight world, where we can no longer stand, or work, or see, or hear as we used to do (12:3-4). We become frail, anxious and vulnerable as our defences and resources crumble (12:6). We glimpse a funeral; and one day those mourners will be ours (12:5). At the end, our bodies return to dust and our breath or spirit returns to God (12:7).

Is all empty and meaningless? Not at all. All is created, God-given and God-intended. And you aren't dead yet. You're young! Your time to know God is now.

In conclusion (12:9–14)

The book of Ecclesiastes closes with a description of the Teacher himself. He not only taught and collected proverbs, but put plain truth in beautiful words (12:9–10).

Wise sayings are short and sharp – much better for guidance than many long books (12:11). The point of all things is to know God – to live our lives in the light of his holiness and will (12:13). One day we, with everyone who has ever lived, will find the meaning of our lives at his judgment seat (12:14).

SONG OF SONGS

The Song of Songs is about the longing of love and the joy of sex. The Song is a collection of love songs. No one is quite sure how many songs there are, or whether they form a continuous story. A woman (the beloved) and a man (the lover) adore one another and tell each other of their love. There are also some friends or attendants who join in with their questions and praises.

These songs may have been sung for many years before they were written down. They may have been used as part of a marriage ceremony or the lengthy celebrations afterwards. They are a lovely, pure antidote to the lewdness and immorality of pagan sex, and especially of the Canaanite fertility rites.

Both Jews and Christians have found in the Song a picture of God's love for his people. This is why it was included in the Bible. But in fact the Song never mentions God. It is good to have the Song in the Bible for its own sake, as a book which describes the tender, mutual and wholesome enjoyment of sex between a man and a woman.

OUTLINE

Two lovers (1:1–2:7)
Spring in the air (2:8–17)
A restless night (3:1–5)
A royal procession (3:6–11)
A natural beauty (4:1–7)
The secret garden (4:8–5:1)
Longing and loss (5:2–8)
Simply the best (5:9–16)
Inside knowledge (6:1–3)
An awesome beauty (6:4–10)
Awakening desire (6:11–8:4)
Love is... (8:5–7)
Chastity and fulfilment (8:8–14)

Introduction

A continuous story?

Some scholars think that the poems of the Song make up a story. King Solomon tries to get a beautiful country girl, a Shulammite, to join his harem in the royal palace. But her true love is a shepherd, and she is eventually reunited with him.

Love is good

The Song of Songs speaks to a society where sex has been abused and degraded. The Israelites are constantly tempted by the permissive and promiscuous sex which other nations so clearly seem to enjoy.

The Song shows that love is good – God's own holy flame within humankind (8:6). The desire and pleasure of sex are his gift. The human body is a treasure trove of sensual delights, to be rightly reserved for, and gladly given to, the right partner when the time is ripe.

The Song's repeated advice is: 'Do not arouse or awaken love until it so desires.' It goes as deep as any proverb (2:7; 3:5; 8:4). A sexual relationship is not to be contrived, manipulated or forced. The Song portrays a love which flourishes on assured commitment, a sharing of souls and mutual delight.

The 'Song of Solomon'?

The Song of Songs is sometimes called the 'Song of Solomon', because it was thought to be by him or to belong to his collection. Solomon was certainly a writer of poems and proverbs, and had a vast knowledge of plants and animals. However, his love life had nothing of the excited adoration and delighted faithfulness which is portrayed here.

Solomon was married many times, with 700 wives and 300 concubines. His sex life was busy but disastrous. By marrying foreign princesses he forged alliances with other nations, which secured peace and good trade for his country. Unfortunately, his wives brought pagan idols into the royal household and Israel's public life. This damaged Solomon's own devotion to God and weakened the faith of his people (1 Kings 11). It also damages his reputation as the wisest person who ever lived.

The meaning of the Song

The 'Song of Songs' means 'the most excellent song'. The Jews did not include it in their Scriptures (our Old Testament) until AD 70. Even then, some rabbis felt it was unsuitable because it doesn't mention God and its images are very sexy.

The main argument for including the Song in the Bible has been that it portrays God's love for his people. The love between the man and the woman is seen as a picture of the covenant marriage between God and Israel.

Christians, too, have seen the Song as a beautiful image of the love between Christ and his church. The scholars of the Middle Ages (many of them monks) went to great trouble to find parallels between the lover, Christ, and his beloved, the church. Bernard of Clairvaux did particularly well, finding eighty-six such meanings in the first two chapters alone!

It is true that the prophets picture the covenant as a marriage between God and his people. Hosea, Jeremiah and Ezekiel all accuse Israel of being an unfaithful bride. Even so, they never portray the covenant as an overtly physical and sexual relationship. That would be much too close to the rites of the pagan fertility cults.

It is best to see the Song as a collection of poems in praise of sexual love. By including them in the Bible, the Scriptures refuse to let the devil have all the good sex. They remind us that sex is God's gift for creation and recreation, the marriage covenant and mutual joy.

Like all God's gifts, sex is to be used according to his laws and the wider teaching of scripture. Both Christians and Jews believe that the right place for sex is the safe and loving context of lifelong marriage.

DISCOVERING THE SONG OF SONGS

Two lovers (1:1–2:7)

The woman longs for her lover, her king. She is dark and beautiful, suntanned by her open-air life. Her brothers have made her look after the vineyards, which means she has had no time to groom herself. Now she looks for an opportunity to be near her lover by finding where he rests his sheep.

The man and woman are utterly absorbed in each other's beauty, fragrance and touch. Their descriptions of one another draw on lovely images from the world of nature. She reminds him of one of Pharaoh's finest mares, or a lily among thorns. For her, he is like a scented sachet of spices, or a beautiful and sweet apple tree, where she is shaded and refreshed.

Spring in the air (2:8–17)

The signs of spring are all around and love too is awakening. The lover is like a strong and graceful young stag, bounding over the hills. The beloved is like the peaks in which he delights and the lilies where he grazes.

A restless night (3:1–5)

The woman dreams that she has lost her lover. She is looking for him and can't find him. There are ancient myths which tell stories like this, which deal with anxiety, loss and grief. At heart they express a fear of death. But this story has a happy ending. Suddenly she finds him and all is well.

A royal procession (3:6–11)

A grand procession is coming up from the desert. Is this King Solomon arriving for his coronation, or one of his many foreign brides arriving for her wedding?

This may be a song which was first used for royal occasions and has now become a part of other wedding celebrations. Every bride and groom are a royal couple on their wedding day.

A natural beauty (4:1–7)

The lover praises his partner's beauty. She is altogether lovely and every part of her is perfect. Her eyes are like gentle doves, her hair flows like goats down a hillside, her teeth are like newly washed sheep and her lips like scarlet ribbon. He looks forward to spending the night exploring her fragrant mountains!

The secret garden (4:8–5:1)

The lover calls his bride to come from the remoteness and dangers of mountain ranges to the intimacy and safety of his love. He calls her his 'sister', which is a common term in Egypt for one so dearly treasured.

The man is absorbed in the wonder, taste and smell of his beloved. She has captured his heart.

The bride is a virgin who, like a locked garden, is to be discovered and delighted in. She is an orchard of pleasures, a Persian paradise. The bride calls the winds from north and south to carry the fragrance of her garden to her husband and draw him to her choicest fruits.

When they finally come together, their lovemaking is like breathing in myrrh, feasting on honey and drinking both wine and milk. Every sense is sated and every longing satisfied.

Longing and loss (5:2–8)

As the girl sleeps, she hears her lover at the door. He is eager for her, calling to be let in. Ready for love, she opens the door, only to find that he is not there. The song takes on a nightmare quality as the young woman searches the streets for her lover and is abused by the night watchmen.

Simply the best (5:9–16)

Now it is the woman's turn to describe her man. He is far more handsome than other men and glowing with health. His head is noble,

Jesus as lover?

The Song of Songs has often been used by Christians to illustrate Jesus' love for his church. He stands at the door asking to be let in (Revelation 3:20).

The New Testament pictures Christ as the church's bridegroom, but it is misleading to think of Jesus and Christians having a sexual desire for each other. Jesus describes his love in terms of service and sacrifice. He asks his friends to respond not with love songs but with obedience and faith (John 15:12–14).

his hair luxuriant, his eyes limpid but striking, his cheeks fragrant and his lips sweet. His body is strong, well proportioned and finely formed. She adores him and is proud of him, both as a lover and as a friend.

Inside knowledge (6:1–3)

The woman's friends offer to help her find her lover, but she knows very well where he is. He is already browsing among her lilies!

An awesome beauty (6:4–10)

The lover describes his woman in terms of awe bordering on fear. She has the beauty of Tirzah, the old capital of the northern kingdom. She is formidable, like an army in full array.

Parts of this description echo the worship of Ishtar, the Canaanite goddess of love and war. She was as 'fair as the moon, bright as the sun' and as terrifying as an army. Now the same phrases are used to praise this strong, independent and beautiful woman – a woman who commands the admiration and respect of her lover.

Awakening desire (6:11–8:4)

The bride is a Shulammite woman. Her name comes from 'Salem' – the old name for Jerusalem. She dances, stately and regal, for the delight of her lover. He desires her so much that he wishes he could scale her like a palm tree and take her breasts like bunches of grapes. For her part, she would gladly be consumed by him.

The woman calls her lover to go with her to the countryside and make love amid the signs of spring. Mandrakes are 'love plants' which open in May, and are used as an aphrodisiac to heighten sexual hunger. She wishes she could kiss her lover openly, as she would be able to if he were her brother. She longs to take him home and give herself to him in love.

Love is... (8:5–7)

The friends see the woman approaching, leaning on her lover. She recalls how they first made love in his family home, where he himself was conceived and born. She asks him to wear her love like an ornament over his heart and on his arm. She reflects that true love endures for ever, as strong as death. It blazes like the fire of God. Rivers cannot quench true love, and a fortune can never buy it.

Chastity and fulfilment (8:8–14)

The friends ask advice concerning their young sister. How may they best protect her virginity until she is married? If she protects herself, like a wall, they will adorn her with silver. If she is vulnerable, like a door, they will take care to cover her.

The bride likens herself to a wall. She has kept herself a virgin for her true love. Now she is mature, and ready to give herself fully to him. She thinks of Solomon, hiring out his vineyard for money. She too has a vineyard – herself – which is hers alone to give. She will never yield herself for money.

The Song ends with her joyous call for her lover to come away with her, and play the gazelle on her fragrant mountains.

ISAIAH

Isaiah is a prophet who lives in Jerusalem in the 8th century BC. He is called to be a prophet in 740 BC and his ministry lasts for some forty years. He is a valued counsellor to two of Judah's kings – Ahaz (736–716 BC) and Hezekiah (716–687 BC).

At this time Judah is threatened by the military might of Assyria. Isaiah is sure that God will protect his people and that Jerusalem will be kept safe. He advises quietness and confidence in the face of the crisis.

At the same time, Isaiah delivers probing messages on the state of society and religion in Judah. He looks forward to a perfect Judah, ruled by a perfect king.

OUTLINE

Prophecies to Judah before the exile (1:1–39:8)
 Prophecies to Judah and Jerusalem (1:1–12:6)
 Prophecies against foreign nations (13:1–23:18)
 Future judgment and hope (24:1–27:13)
 Promises and judgments for Judah (28:1–33:24)
 God will judge the nations (34:1–17)
 A blossoming desert and a highway home (35:1–10)
 Assyria threatens Judah (36:1–39:8)
Prophecies to God's people during their exile in Babylon (40:1–55:13)
 God still cares for Israel and will forgive (40:1–48:22)
 God will rebuild Jerusalem (49:1–55:13)
Prophecies to Israel after the exile (56:1–66:24)

Introduction

The prophecies in the book of Isaiah cover three periods of Judah's history:

 Chapters 1–39: Isaiah's ministry in Jerusalem
 Chapters 40–55: prophecies for the exiles in Babylon
 Chapters 56–66: prophecies for the return from exile.

Israel and Judah

After the reign of King Solomon the nation of Israel divides into two kingdoms. Ten tribes in the north become the kingdom of Israel with Samaria as the capital city. The tribes of Judah and Benjamin form a smaller kingdom of Judah in the south, with Jerusalem as the capital. It is in Jerusalem that Isaiah lives.

Both Israel and Judah are little 'buffer' states between the greater powers of Assyria to the north and Egypt to the south. If Assyria pursues her ambition to conquer Egypt, her advance will crush the Hebrew states.

In this situation Isaiah advises the king to stay neutral. Judah should rely on God to defend her – and avoid all foreign alliances. A foreign alliance means compromising with pagan gods – an unthinkable act of unfaithfulness to the Holy One of Israel.

Isaiah's ministry in Jerusalem (1:1–39:8)

The prophecies of Isaiah are not necessarily in the order in which they were first delivered.

Isaiah warns the people of Judah that they are guilty of sin. Their worship is shallow, their greed is breaking up society and they are failing to protect the poor and the weak.

They will suffer severe punishment when God will use Judah's enemies to discipline her. But beyond these dark days is a perfect future when God's reign will bring justice and peace to the whole world.

Politics and religion

Isaiah refuses to separate politics and religion. Each time there is a military threat to Jerusalem, Isaiah urges the king to trust in God for defence.

King Ahaz decides to compromise with the Assyrians. He asks for, and receives, help against Syria and Israel. The Assyrians protect him by capturing the Syrian capital, Damascus. To show his gratitude, King Ahaz has an Assyrian altar designed and installed beside the altar of the Lord in Jerusalem. So he hopes to get the best from both religions (2 Kings 16:11–14).

King Hezekiah, on the other hand, destroys the pagan shrines. With Isaiah's encouragement, he learns to bring his fears to God and rely on him for help.

God's voice in the situation

Isaiah's prophecies span a period from 740–701 BC. We can trace his ministry through the dates and episodes that are mentioned in his book.

He is called to be a prophet when King Uzziah dies and his son Ahaz becomes king of Judah (6:1).

When Syria (Aram) and Israel (Ephraim) join forces to march on Jerusalem, Isaiah and his son meet King Ahaz. Isaiah says of the danger:

It will not take place,
   it will not happen...
If you do not stand firm in your faith,
   you will not stand at all. (7:7, 9)

Isaiah invites the king to ask God for a sign – but the king refuses. He doesn't want to acknowledge that Isaiah's advice may be right. But Isaiah declares a sign anyway:

'The young woman is with child and shall bear a son, and shall name him Immanuel' (7:14 NRSV). 'Immanuel' means 'God With Us'. By the time this child knows wrong from right, the nations they fear will have vanished.

When the Assyrians capture the Philistine stronghold of Ashdod, they are clearly too close for comfort. There is an overwhelming temptation to make an alliance with Egypt in the face of this threat.

But God tells Isaiah to go stripped and barefoot in the streets of Jerusalem for three years! This is how the Egyptians will look when they themselves are led away captive. There is no future in relying on them (20:1–6).

When the Assyrians threaten to attack Jerusalem in Hezekiah's reign, the question is: 'Whose god is the stronger?' The Assyrian field commander taunts:

If you say... 'We are depending on the Lord our God' – isn't he the one whose high places and altars Hezekiah removed? (36:7)

He goes on to make a counter-claim:

The Lord himself told me to march against this country and destroy it. (36:10)

In desperation King Hezekiah turns to Isaiah for a word from the Lord. Isaiah promises the king that the Assyrians will hear a report of action elsewhere and be distracted away from Jerusalem.

When the Assyrian emperor sends a threatening letter to Hezekiah, the king spreads it before the Lord in prayer (37:14). Isaiah assures the king that his prayer has been heard, and that God will protect Jerusalem:

I will defend this city and save it,
for my sake and for the sake of David my servant! (37:35)

With that, the Assyrian camp is swept by plague. The Assyrian king, Sennacherib, returns home – to be murdered by his sons (36:1–37:38).

Prophecies for the exiles in Babylon (40:1–55:13)

We come to the second main section of the book of Isaiah.

Jerusalem has now fallen to the Babylonians. Most of her population has been carried off into exile in Babylonia.

The prophecies in this section are full of comfort and hope. The destruction of Jerusalem and the exile of her people are God's punishment for sin. But God hasn't forgotten or abandoned his people. His plan is to teach them his ways, renew their commitment and bring them joyfully home to Zion (Jerusalem).

God will summon Cyrus of Persia to conquer Babylon and rescue his people. Meanwhile, there is an opportunity for Israel to reflect on her suffering – and her calling.

Although it is possible that Isaiah of Jerusalem could have uttered these prophecies, most scholars think they are by someone else. The scholars' name for this unknown prophet is 'Deutero-Isaiah' (or 'Second Isaiah').

Prophecies for the return from exile (56:1–66:24)

This is the final part of the book of Isaiah. The prophecies here are addressed to the people who have returned from exile.

Back in Jerusalem, God's people must still live by faith. All the old lessons of obedience to God and hope in his future are to be learned and applied by the next generation.

Jerusalem is at the centre of God's plan for the whole world. All the nations will be able to see God at work in the rebuilding of the city and her righteous community. God is bringing about a new creation – a glorious kingdom of peace and everlasting joy.

The Holy One of Israel

Although the book of Isaiah falls into three sections, it explores the same great themes throughout. Isaiah teaches that God is holy. He is the Lord and judge of all the nations. And Israel – even an Israel that has dwindled to a few scattered survivors – is the focus of God's love and the means by which the world will see God's glory.

DISCOVERING ISAIAH

Isaiah's prophecies are delivered to Israel at three distinct stages of her history: before, during and after the exile in Babylon.

Prophecies to Judah before the exile

Prophecies to Judah and Jerusalem (1:1–12:6)

Judah's worship is false

Isaiah challenges the credibility gap between the worship people offer and the lives they actually live. God is sick of burnt offerings. They are just a front behind which people commit crime and oppress the poor. And yet God longs that his people should relate to him again:

'Come now, let us settle the matter,' says the Lord.
'Though your sins are like scarlet,
they shall be white as snow...
If you are willing and obedient.' (1:18–19)

The magnet of Zion

One day God will establish Jerusalem as the centre of his universal reign of peace.

Isaiah describes Jerusalem as 'Mount Zion' rising higher than any other mountain. She will be the place where God lives and from which he reigns. All the nations will make pilgrimage to her, and God's wise judgments will be issued from her.

God's wise ruling will bring peace to the nations, so that the weapons of war can be turned into implements for farming and fruit-growing (2:4).

Micah has the same prophecy as Isaiah (Micah 4:1-3). Either one has copied from the other, or both have used a popular poem or song.

Warnings of judgment...

Although Isaiah foresees a perfect future for Jerusalem, her present state is compromised and corrupt. She harbours superstition and deals with pagan powers (2:6). She relies on wealth and military might (2:7). She worships gods of human origin (2:8).

Isaiah declares that God will humble these proud and self-important people. Soon they will hide in caves and grovel in the dust, to escape the awesome judgment of God (2:9-11, 19).

Isaiah lists the heights and strengths of the natural world – the cedars of Lebanon, the oaks of Bashan and all the mountains and hills. He mentions the towers and fortifications built by people, and their powerful ocean-going ships. All will be humbled on God's Day of Judgment (2:12-17).

God is going to bring famine and drought on Jerusalem (3:1), and deprive her of every kind of leader (3:2-3). Instead, her rulers will be

Today Jerusalem – tomorrow the world

Isaiah exhorts his people, the 'house of Jacob', to live in the light of God's truth. This is the light which will shine out to the whole world (2:5).

God once called Abraham, to make him a great nation and to bless all the nations of the world through him (Genesis 12:1-3). Now he promises to establish Jerusalem as a geographical centre where all may find God's truth.

immature and ineffective. Her social order will collapse in violence and abuse (3:4-5).

God stands up in court to accuse his people (3:13). He blames the rulers of Judah for the coming disaster. They have ruined 'the vineyard' (the land God gave to his people) and exploited the poor (3:13-15). The women, too, are proud, permissive and self-indulgent. Just as they have spoilt themselves, now he will spoil them (3:16-4:1).

... and a message of hope

Suddenly, Isaiah reveals that God's Day of Judgment will also be a day of glory. The 'branch of the Lord' will appear – that is, a king from the family tree of David (4:2). There will be survivors in Jerusalem whom God will himself cleanse from immorality and bloodshed (4:3-4).

God will make Mount Zion a great landmark, with a pillar of cloud by day and of fire by night – the signs of God's presence on Israel's journey through the wilderness (4:5). Over everything will be a canopy, so that Zion becomes a great tent or tabernacle – a place of shelter where God is present: an image of the perfect temple (4:6).

Judah is like a vineyard producing bitter grapes

Israel and Judah are like a vineyard God has planted (5:1-7). They are a chosen people in a promised land. God has done everything to ensure their safety and success. But when he comes looking for a vintage crop, his hopes are dashed. Instead of righteousness and justice he finds bloodshed and distress.

Surely God is within his rights to abandon such an unrewarding project.

God is going to show his holiness by judging his people

God is going to judge those who have grown rich at the expense of others, by squeezing them off their land (5:8). He is going to lay waste their houses and bring dearth on their vineyards and fields (5:9-10).

God condemns those who live only to get drunk. Their festivals are music and wine, without any celebration of God's goodness and purpose in their lives (5:11-12). Because of such people, both rich and poor are starved of the knowledge of God – and Israel will be led away to exile (5:13).

Sheol (the place of departed spirits) is a cavernous mouth, swallowing the leaders of Judah and her people down into death (5:14).

God takes issue with those who have turned his values upside down. They pretend they want the day of God's judgment to come – as though they welcome his action in the world (5:19). They are liars and posers – brave with the booze and busy with injustice (5:22–23). God will destroy them like a field fire after the good crop has been harvested (5:24).

God is summoning Assyria to Judge Israel

God is Lord of all the nations. He will summon a nation from far away to execute his judgment on Judah and Jerusalem (5:26–28). This is Assyria – powerful, swift and well equipped – bounding towards Israel like a lion to its prey (5:29). A storm is about to break over God's people – a destruction which none can escape (5:30).

Isaiah's vision of God and his call to be a prophet

Isaiah is called to be a prophet in 742 BC – the year of King Uzziah's death. Uzziah has enjoyed a long reign, but lived in isolation as a leper during his last years.

Isaiah has an awe-inspiring vision of God (6:1–13). The Lord is enthroned in his temple, surrounded by seraphs – the winged beings that worship and serve him continually.

God is utterly holy. He is infinitely higher than his creatures. He is completely pure in his character.

Isaiah, in stark contrast, sees himself as a moral leper. He is riddled with sin, and can have nothing to do with this holy God.

But, as Isaiah cries out in despair, a seraph touches his mouth with a live coal from the altar. God in his mercy reaches out to purge Isaiah's sin and remove his shame. His lips are consecrated to speak God's word.

When he hears God asking, 'Whom shall I send?' Isaiah gives the heartfelt response, 'Send me!'

God commissions Isaiah to a difficult and unrewarding task. He has to take God's message to people who will listen but never understand. Their senses will be dulled by self-interest. They won't allow God's word to reach their hearts because they don't want to change their lives. This is the experience of many prophets, from Jeremiah to Jesus (Jeremiah 5:21; Ezekiel 12:2; Mark 11:17–18).

A sign of hope: A baby called Immanuel

A sign of hope for King Ahaz

Isaiah is evidently well respected in Jerusalem, and no doubt a familiar figure at court. Two kings – Ahaz and his son Hezekiah – consult him on important matters of state.

In 735 BC Judah's northern neighbours, Aram (Syria) and Israel (Ephraim), move to attack Judah. They are putting pressure on Judah to form an alliance with them against Assyria.

Isaiah advises King Ahaz against such an agreement. If Judah is to keep her political independence and her own religion, she must resist all temptations to compromise. She must simply trust God.

A baby called Immanuel

Isaiah invites Ahaz to ask for a sign of God's protection. The king declines, because he doesn't want to get involved with God. But Isaiah gives him a sign anyway:

The virgin will conceive and bear a son, and will call him Immanuel. (7:14)

The name means 'God With Us' – the assurance of victory.

By the time the child is old enough to make choices, Israel and Syria will be deserted. But Judah will have another enemy to contend with – Assyria.

God will use Assyria as his weapon

Disaster looms

Isaiah predicts that Assyria and Egypt will mass against Judah like swarms of bees and flies. This happens in 735 BC. Ahaz will be humiliated – like having a body shave (7:17–8:4).

'They will call him Immanuel'

The naming of the baby in Isaiah's prophecy becomes a pointer to the birth of Jesus (Matthew 1:23). There has been much discussion as to whether Isaiah's baby had a virgin mother. The Greek version of the Hebrew Bible uses a word which means 'virgin'; but the original Hebrew word means 'young woman'.

Isaiah's wife gives birth to a son. The prophet gives him the name 'Quick to the Plunder, Swift to the Spoil'. This will be the Assyrians' approach when they sack Damascus (capital of Syria) and Samaria (capital of Israel). The name matches that of the baby 'Immanuel'. One name assures Ahaz of God's presence and the other of the defeat of his enemies.

Troubled waters ahead

One of the places Isaiah meets King Ahaz is 'at the end of the aqueduct' (7:3). Jerusalem relies on its gently flowing water supply – a symbol of God's grace. But Isaiah sees that people are rejecting their God – and will soon be overwhelmed by a tidal wave from Assyria (8:5–10).

Fear only God

God tells Isaiah not to be infected with the plans and fears of the people among whom he lives (8:11–12). The only thing that matters is God's holiness, and to fear him alone (8:13).

God will be a rock of sanctuary for his faithful people, but a stumbling block to the spiritually blind. They will trip over God's will and fall headlong to their doom (8:14–15).

Isaiah wants his words sealed up and kept by his disciples, so that what he has said will be seen to come true (8:16–17).

Light or darkness

Isaiah has around him a small community – his 'children'. Their faith is a sign to the wider community of Israel, because they live with reference to the Lord God of Mount Zion, the true Jerusalem (8:18).

Many people are looking to spiritualism and the occult for guidance – as Isaiah says, consulting 'the dead on behalf of the living' (8:19)! But there is no light in those dark rooms – only spiritual famine, physical exile, exasperated rage and outer darkness (8:21–22).

God will raise up a king like David

David was Israel's greatest king, and there was always hope for another one like him. He combined wisdom and strength with a compassion for people and the ability to establish peace.

Here Isaiah celebrates the birth of a royal heir, or perhaps a coronation (9:1-7). The king's reign will be an extension of God's rule. These words enjoy lasting fame as a prophecy of the birth of Jesus. They are a superb description of the Christ.

God's hand raised in judgment

Isaiah sees that God is stretching out his hand to judge his people and punish them for their sins.

God spoke to the northern kingdom of Israel through his prophets, Amos and Hosea (9:8). They warned Ephraim (Israel) of judgment and everyone heard; but they were proud and determined to survive (9:9). When the destruction was past, they planned to build bigger and better than before (9:10).

God punished the northern kingdom through her old enemies, the Arameans and the Philistines (9:11-12). Israel was destroyed 'head and tail' - leaders and prophets, the virile and the defenceless (9:13-17).

Israel was torched for her wickedness (9:18-19). The different tribes consumed each other - even the brother tribes of Ephraim and Manasseh, which were both descended from Joseph (9:18-21).

Isaiah speaks against the cruel and cunning judges of his day. They twist the law to rob the poor and cheat the helpless (10:1-2). Where will they hide when the judgment comes (10:3-4)?

In all these events God is reaching out his hand in judgment - and he hasn't withdrawn it yet. There is more punishment to come (10:4).

But God will also humble Assyria

God is using Assyria as his instrument to punish Israel. Assyria is the club in God's hands (10:5). But Assyria is arrogant and takes the glory of God's victory for himself (10:13). Now God is going to rein in proud Assyria, weakening him with sickness and destroying his splendour in the fire of his holiness (10:16-17).

A small part of Israel will survive

Isaiah has a son called 'Shear-Jashub', which means 'A Remnant Will Return' (7:3 NIV footnote). By his naming of his son, the prophet expresses his hope that God's people will survive. Although the coming punishment will be terrible, a small group will return from exile and (more importantly) return to the Lord.

Countdown to conquest?

The Assyrians are advancing on Judah and Jerusalem from the north – and moving swiftly. Aiath is probably Ai, fifteen miles from Jerusalem (10:28). Supplies are checked and stored at Michmash and the advance continues across a steep valley – over the border of Judah and up to encamp at Geba.

Gibeah is a fortified town which guards the approach to Jerusalem – but its inhabitants have already fled (10:29). Anathoth, five miles northwest of Jerusalem, is captured (10:30), and the Assyrian horde sweeps on to Nob, within a mile of Jerusalem (10:32)!

In the face of the emergency, Isaiah speaks of the sovereignty of God. The Lord will lop off these powerful branches of Assyria and cut down even the tallest trees (10:33). God has set his heart to bless a different stump altogether – the root of Jesse, which is the royal line of David (11:1).

A descendant of David

Judah is like a tree about to be felled: cut down by God's judgment because of its disease. There will be nothing left of David's dynasty but a stump – 'the stump of Jesse' (the name of David's father).

Isaiah prophesies that, against all the odds, a new shoot will grow from the old stump. It will become strong and significant: a fruitful branch. So he describes the Messiah who is to come (11:1–9).

The Messiah will be endowed with the fullness of God's Spirit – wisdom and understanding, counsel and power, the knowledge and fear of the Lord – and delight in doing God's will.

David's great descendant won't judge by appearances, for he will understand people's hearts. He won't rely on hearsay, because he will know the truth at first-hand. He will find in favour of the poor and needy. He will rule with the authority of his word. Even the divided realm of animals and humans will find peace and harmony under his government.

These words of Isaiah are the Bible's finest description of the leadership style of Christ and the well-being of his perfect kingdom.

A song of praise for God's salvation

God's people will experience a new exodus. God will rescue them and bring them home from all directions (11:11).

Isaiah allows his future hope to shine into the present crisis (12:1). He will trust in God and take complete comfort in God's protection and salvation (12:2). He calls the inhabitants of Jerusalem to praise God already for what he is certain to do (12:3-6).

Prophecies against foreign nations (13:1-23:18)

All nations are under God's rule, and subject to his judgment. He knows their ways, humbles their pride, sets limits on their power and uses them for his own great purpose.

Isaiah shows God's command of all the nations – the whole earth is God's kingdom. He delivers God's judgments of punishment and hope in the form of 'oracles' or public announcements. An oracle is a 'lifting up' of the voice.

Prophecies against Babylon and Assyria

Isaiah declares that God will send his armies on the day of his wrath (13:3, 9) to execute his judgment on the nations of the earth (13:5). He will use the Medes to overthrow the terrible power of Babylon (13:19).

Babylon (herself the conqueror of Assyria) will be defeated in 539 BC. In the Bible she is a symbol of all worldly power which is opposed to God, and the spiritual descendant of the tower of Babel (Genesis 11:1-9).

When God has restored his people to their land, they will be able to sing of Babylon's fall (14:1-23). This is the Lord's triumph (14:24-27).

God's judgment on the nations

Isaiah declares God's judgment on the Philistines (14:29-32), Moab (15:1-16:14), Damascus (17:1-14), Ethiopia (18:1-7) and Egypt (19:1-15). However, there is a prediction of hope for Egypt (19:16-25). She will have an altar to the Lord God at her centre and a pillar of the Lord's protection at her border (19:19-20).

Naked and barefoot

In 711 BC, an Assyrian force is sent by King Sargon to capture Ashdod. Ashdod is a Philistine city which had revolted against the Assyrian empire and thrown out an imposed king (20:1). Ashdod has hoped for support from Egypt and Ethiopia – and indeed from Judah – but the proposed rebellion never materializes.

At this time, God tells Isaiah to go about Jerusalem naked and barefoot. Isaiah does this for three years – acting the part of a captive (20:3). This will be the fate of anyone who rebels against Assyria or trusts the support of Egypt! Egypt herself will be defeated and her people deported (20:4–5).

Desert storm for Babylon

Isaiah delivers further oracles about the surrounding nations.

The first oracle begins with a vision of 'the wilderness of the sea' (21:1). The forces of Elam (Persia) and Media are sweeping up like a desert storm, dark and destructive (21:1–2). Isaiah realizes that this is the force that will overwhelm Babylon – and he is appalled (21:3–4). Babylon's commanders are taken by surprise as they feast (21:5).

Isaiah sees himself as a watchman, on the lookout for invaders (21:8). God tells him that Babylon has fallen and her idols lie shattered (21:9). Isaiah reports Babylon's fate to Israel, his 'threshed and winnowed one'. God's people have suffered so much upheaval and distress at Babylon's hands (21:10).

The silence of night

Isaiah speaks an oracle concerning Dumah – a place in Edom whose name means 'Silence'. Someone is asking the watchman what time it is – how long will the night of judgment last? The answer is: 'Inquire and come back' – which is an invitation to return to the way of God (21:12).

Brief respite

Isaiah speaks to the peoples of the Arabian desert. The oasis at Tema must give water to the Dedanites. They are fleeing from the destruction of the Assyrians (21:14–15). But any relief will be short-lived. In 703 BC the whole area of Kedar is conquered by Sennacherib (21:16–17).

Crisis for Jerusalem

Isaiah has an oracle for 'the valley of vision' – that is, Jerusalem, where he himself lives (22:1). Jerusalem is surrounded by mountains.

Isaiah weeps for his city (22:4). He foresees an attack and destruction which features Elam, an ally of Babylon (22:6). People are both taking up weapons and partying. The weapons are kept in the House of the Forest – a hall in the royal palace (22:8; 1 Kings 10:17). The partying is a last celebration before people die – or perhaps because there is a lifting of a siege (22:13). Isaiah knows that the fun is out of place because worse is to follow.

Isaiah has messages for two individuals – Shebna and Eliakim (22:15–25). Shebna is the royal steward who has been busy with his status symbols: his chariots and his tomb. Isaiah says that God will demote him and throw him out – far into the desert (22:18).

Eliakim will be promoted in Shebna's place and people will rely heavily on him (22:24). He will have the authority of the royal key and make high-level decisions (22:22). Even so, he is merely human and will ultimately fail (22:25).

Tyre

Isaiah predicts that the Chaldeans (Babylonians) will destroy Tyre – the wealthy seaport whose trading reaches around the known world. This will be God's judgment on her pride (23:9) and will last for a lifetime (23:15). Afterwards her prosperity will be restored, but she will consecrate her wealth to the Lord (23:17–18).

Future judgment and hope (24:1–27:13)

God's worldwide judgment...

Having spoken to individual nations, Isaiah now addresses the whole world. God is going to judge all alike – priest and people, owner and slave, buyer and seller (24:2). The earth is to fall under God's curse (24:3–13).

Far away to east and west the praises of the survivors, the 'remnant', can be heard. They are praising God, the Righteous One, for his splendour (24:14–16). But Isaiah still grieves under the weight of his people's sins (24:16).

A cosmic judgment is about to fall. God will call all powers in heaven and on earth to account (24:21–22). The light of sun and moon will be dimmed by the glory of God shining out from Mount Zion (24:23).

... and victory

Isaiah praises God for his power and justice (25:1-5). He will establish a community of joy and plenty, life and peace on Mount Zion, the new Jerusalem (25:6-8). All sadness and tears – and death itself – will be things of the past (25:8). This is the God and this is the salvation for which his people have waited so long (25:9).

A longing for God

Isaiah looks forward to the secure strength and welcome of God's city (26:1-2). This is his steadfast hope (26:3-4). He longs for God to bring down the proud, give justice to the poor and set the feet of the righteous on a level path (26:5-8).

Isaiah acknowledges that his people have achieved nothing without God (26:16-18). And yet God will call the dead to life (26:19). In the midst of failure, Isaiah glimpses God's resurrection power – the shining dew of a bright new dawn.

As God raises his people to life, he will also punish the wicked and destroy Leviathan, the chaos monster (26:20-27:1).

Peace with God

At last God rejoices over a fruitful vineyard. This is his people as he has longed them to be – a blessing to the whole world (27:6). What a change from the days of frustration, bitterness and destruction in the past (5:1-7)! The only thorns now are the enemies which the Lord will destroy (27:4).

Israel has come a long way, through much suffering and destruction (27:7-11). But now God is harvesting his people from their far-flung places of exile, and bringing them home to Jerusalem (27:12-13).

Promises and judgments for Judah (28:1-33:24)

Isaiah condemns drunken leaders, hard-hearted worshippers and the futility of seeking protection from Egypt. God is about to shatter the security of complacent women and strong men. But beyond God's judgment lies his promise of mercy, healing and peace.

Jerusalem – God's own city

Jerusalem always had an eternal quality. The mysterious priest–king Melchizedek had come from there. It was called Salem in those days. Melchizedek met Abraham with bread and wine, gave him a blessing and accepted 10 per cent (a tithe) of the plunder from a recent victory (Genesis 14:18–20).

During the conquest of the land of Canaan by Joshua, Jerusalem was never captured. It remained securely in the hands of the Jebusites. It was David who finally captured it and made it his capital city.

David also made Jerusalem God's capital – bringing the ark of the covenant there and making plans for a temple (33:20–22). It was the city 'where God's name dwelt', and where God promised that the line of David would reign for ever. One day Jerusalem would become fully and gloriously 'Zion' – the centre of God's kingdom on earth.

Small wonder that the inhabitants of Jerusalem think God will never let his city fall – and certainly not to a pagan army.

Now Isaiah brings the unthinkable message that God himself will lay siege to Jerusalem – and use foreign armies to do so. Calling Jerusalem 'Ariel', Isaiah speaks for God:

Woe to you, Ariel, Ariel,
  the city where David settled!...
I will besiege Ariel...
  I will encircle you with towers
  and set up my siege works against you. (29:1–3)

The inhabitants of Jerusalem have forgotten that God's protection is conditional on obedience to his commandments. God and his people are married by their covenant. He expects them to be holy as he is. But Isaiah preaches that this once-faithful city has become a prostitute. Her leaders are drunken, idolatrous and corrupt. Her orphans and widows are neglected.

Jerusalem has been unfaithful to God:

See how the faithful city
  has become a prostitute!

> *She once was full of justice;*
> *righteousness used to dwell in her –*
> *but now murderers!* (1:21)

Meanwhile, the temple worship continues. Sacrifices are offered morning and evening, and festivals are very well attended. But they are a sham. They make God angry!

> *When you come to appear before me,*
> *who has asked this of you,*
> *this trampling of my courts?*
> *Stop bringing meaningless offerings!*
> *Your incense is detestable to me.*
> *New Moons, Sabbaths and convocations –*
> *I cannot bear your worthless assemblies.* (1:12–13)

God will judge the nations (34:1–17)

God is going to massacre all the nations and unravel his work of creation (34:1–4). The storm will break on Edom, the long-time adversary of God's people (34:5–10). She will become a wasteland, her strongholds overgrown and inhabited only by wild animals (34:11–17).

A blossoming desert and a highway home (35:1–10)

Meanwhile, another desert will spring into bloom (35:1–2). This is the desert across which God's people will travel when they return from exile to their homeland (35:10).

Isaiah encourages the weak and faint-hearted. God is acting to save them (35:3–4)! The personal handicaps of body and spirit are being healed; the hazards of nature reversed (35:5–7). God is making all things new – a new creation.

Across the desert stretches a highway – a broad route home for God's holy people. No one will be able to lose their way (35:8). The road will be safe from all danger (35:9), and resound with the joyful praises of the free (35:10).

Assyria and Babylon

When Isaiah's ministry begins, the Babylonians are known as Chaldeans. They are ruled by Assyria – having been conquered by Tiglath-Pileser III in 745 BC. Assyrian rulers call themselves kings of Babylon. But Assyria will overreach herself and her power will wane. Babylon will take over as the new superpower in the region.

When Jerusalem is destroyed it will be at the hands of Babylon in 587 BC.

The names of Israel and Judah

The name 'Israel' is used for the northern kingdom after the death of Solomon in about 922 BC. This land and its people are also called 'Jacob' and 'Ephraim' after famous ancestors. The capital of Israel is Samaria and the main centres of worship (for festivals, pilgrimages and sacrifice) are Bethel and Dan.

The southern kingdom at this time is called Judah, and its capital and worship centre (the temple) is Jerusalem.

But 'Israel' can also mean 'God's people'. After the northern kingdom is conquered by the Assyrians in 721 BC, the name of Israel is used for the people of Judah.

Assyria threatens Judah (36:1–39:8)

This is an account of the siege of Jerusalem in King Hezekiah's reign. It is also found in 2 Kings 18–20.

The Assyrian commander is confident of an easy victory over Jerusalem – and King Hezekiah is terrified. Nevertheless the king accepts Isaiah's assurance of God's protection – and the Assyrian army disappears without a blow being struck.

God uses Isaiah to cure Hezekiah of a life-threatening boil. In celebration of his recovery, Hezekiah gives a deputation from Babylon a guided tour round his royal treasures. Isaiah warns that one day they will return to carry them off. The foreign threat is no longer Assyria, but Babylon.

Prophecies to God's people during their exile in Babylon

God still cares for Israel and will forgive (40:1-48:22)

Words of comfort - the exile is nearly over

The scene changes. The Babylonians have captured Jerusalem in 587 BC. Many of God's people have been deported to Babylonia, where they are in exile from their beloved homeland.

The messages in these chapters are the prophet's words of comfort and hope for God's stricken people. The God of Israel hasn't been defeated by Marduk or any of the other gods of Babylon. He himself has been punishing his people for their sin. Now the punishment is coming to an end, and God is going to bring his people back home.

God is here!

Zion is to proclaim good news to the cities of Judah: 'God is here!' God will come to his people with majestic strength and goodness. He will care for his people like a shepherd, paying special attention to the weak (40:11).

Suddenly Israel's problems shrink in the perspective of God's mighty power. Job had a similar experience of seeing his suffering in the light of God's majesty and eternity (Job 38:1-7). The waters of creation (and even of chaos) are a mere pool in the palm of God's hand (40:12). The heavens are a hand's breadth; the earth and mountains little more than dust in his scales (40:12).

This mighty creator God has no need of advice from his creatures on matters of guidance, justice, knowledge or understanding (40:13-14). The forests of Lebanon and all its animals would not amount to a sufficient sacrifice for him (40:16).

The creator who cares

It seems ridiculous to compare the living God to an idol, which is made by people and has to be propped upright (40:18-20). God is the Lord of earth and heaven, time and space: he appoints and removes princes (40:23), sets all the stars in place (40:26) and knows every detail of the lives of his people (40:27). He himself is tireless, and is able to revive and sustain all who look to him for strength (40:28-31).

God stands by his servant

God calls the nations together to take counsel (41:1). He has a question for them: who has stirred up 'a victor from the east' (Cyrus of Persia, 44:28) and allowed him to conquer so many nations? The answer: it is the Lord (41:4).

While other nations rely on the skill of their artisans and the fastenings on their idols, it is God who guards Israel (41:5-10). Israel is his servant, descended from Abraham and Jacob (41:8). God promises to protect his people in the face of their enemies. He is the redeemer – the next of kin on whom they can rely for help (41:11-14).

Is there more than one 'Isaiah'?

The prophet Isaiah had a long life and ministry in Jerusalem, 150 years before the exile in Babylon. It is possible that he could have foretold events so many years ahead, but most scholars think that these messages to the exiles in Babylon are by someone else. If they are, their author is clearly a close disciple of Isaiah, and uses similar teaching and language.

Isaiah in Jerusalem has been speaking of Assyria as the enemy – and the place from which exiles will return. Now these prophecies in Babylon talk of the Chaldeans (Babylonians) as Israel's oppressors, with their gods Bel and Nebo.

Another difference between the prophecies in Jerusalem and the prophecies in Babylon is that Jerusalem has now fallen. Instead of threats of judgment there are words of comfort and hope. The prophet looks forward to Israel's return from Babylon – a deliverance like a great second 'exodus'. The new emperor, Cyrus of Persia, is a welcome conqueror. He will do God's work of rescuing his people.

Because we don't know his name, the prophet in Babylon is called 'Second Isaiah', 'Deutero-Isaiah' or 'Isaiah of Babylon'. He writes beautiful, stylish Hebrew, as he sings the praise of the God of Israel in creation and history.

'Isaiah of Babylon' lives with the people in exile. He may be suffering for the messages of hope he brings. There are chapters here which describe just such a 'suffering servant'.

Israel will be used to judge the nations

God is going to turn his servant, the lowly 'worm' Jacob, into a threshing sledge (41:14-16). A threshing sledge is a heavy piece of machinery which is rolled over the harvested grain to crush it. The grain is then tossed up in the wind, so that the husks can be blown away while the grain itself falls to the ground. The sledge is a symbol of judgment. God is going to use Israel to judge the nations (41:15-16).

God is active, while idols are 'nothing'

God has compassion on the poor and needy. He will ease their journey across the desert by providing water sources and planting shady trees (41:17-20).

God challenges the gods of the other nations to explain what has happened in the past, or predict what will take place in the future. Of course, they are unable to do so, because they are nothing (41:21-24).

It is God who is stirring up the emperor Cyrus to come from the north (41:25). He declares it now, so that he will be seen to be right (41:26). He can communicate this to his faithful people, but not to deluded idol-worshippers (41:27-29).

The first 'servant song'

God introduces his servant to the watching world. In the previous chapter, this servant is Israel, whom God has chosen and will support (41:8). Now, however, an individual person begins to emerge...

God's servant will be inspired and empowered by God's Spirit (42:1). He will deliver justice to the nations, as David did for Israel (42:1). His style will be gentle and affirming, not loud or bullying (42:2-4). He will not grow tired or discouraged, but will continue his task until he has established God's justice and truth (42:4).

God commissions his servant to do his work. He is to be a light to the nations (42:4-5) and an expression of the covenant relationship between God and his people (42:6). The servant is to release people from physical and spiritual darkness, such as blindness and imprisonment (42:7). The God of the exodus is revealing the vision of a new deliverance (42:8-9).

Creation praise!

The whole of creation sings a new song to God, in praise of his supreme initiative (42:10). Sea and coastlands, desert and towns rejoice together (42:11–12). Even old enemies like Kedar and Sela give vent to joyful shouts (42:11).

Although the Lord's servant is gentle and quiet, God himself rides out bellowing fury against his enemies (42:13). Like his people, God has been waiting patiently for this moment (42:14). Now he breaks out in passionate activity – transforming nature, rescuing the blind and wreaking havoc among idol-worshippers (42:14–17).

God promises deliverance

The prophet sees the return of Israel from Babylon as a great 'second exodus'. The mountains and valleys will be levelled to make a royal

The 'suffering servant'

Four poems movingly describe a person enduring pain, rejection and death. His agony is undeserved. He is going through this suffering on behalf of others, so that they can be spared.

The poems are to be found in 42:1–4, 49:1–7, 50:4–9 and 52:13–53:12.

Sometimes the 'servant' seems to be Israel (by which the prophet means Judah in exile). But it is hard to see how Israel's suffering is undeserved.

Sometimes the servant is clearly an individual – perhaps the prophet himself or someone the people know. Is this 'Isaiah of Babylon' being rejected by his people, or punished by the Babylonians?

One day Jesus will find inspiration in these poems. He is the perfect servant of God who brings justice and healing to the nations (42:1–9). He is also the innocent person who will be 'led like a lamb to the slaughter' (53:7) as he undergoes rejection, torture and death for the sins of the world.

The identity of the servant is a puzzle. The Ethiopian who meets Philip was still working on it centuries later, and is pointed to Jesus (Acts 8:32–34). It is best to turn it as a jewel in our hand, and see sometimes Israel, sometimes the prophet, sometimes Jesus.

Later still, Paul sees himself and his missionary colleagues as obeying the mission of the servant in taking the light of the gospel to the Gentiles. He actually quotes Isaiah 49:6 (Acts 13:47).

highway across the desert. The exiles will come home (40:3-5)! One day John the Baptist will echo these words. He will call for people to make a highway in their hearts for the Messiah to arrive and rule (Luke 3:4-6).

In the event, some Jews remain in Babylon where they are settled, rather than sharing the hardship of rebuilding Jerusalem. The returning exiles are still not their own masters, for Judah becomes a province of the Persian empire.

In all this great upheaval, the prophet encourages Israel to know that God is with them. Their punishment is over, and God's future is opening up for them. One day all the nations will look to Israel's God for justice and salvation.

A new exodus

God declares that he will send for his people in Babylon and compel the Chaldeans to release them (43:14). He is the God of the exodus from Egypt, who parts the sea and drowns enemy armies (42:16-17). But there is no need to look back to the past, because the same God is even now at work in the present (43:18-19).

God is about to do a new thing. He is going to bring back his people from their exile in Babylon. He will make a way across the wilderness, protect them from attack by wild animals and provide rivers for their refreshment (43:19-21).

God's offering to his people

God takes Judah to task for not offering him the worship of sacrifices and other gifts. Instead, they have brought him the burden of their sins (43:22-24). But God is determined to forgive Israel, to break the weary cycle of sin and punishment (43:27).

Now God is going to end Israel's spiritual drought, just as he sends rain on thirsty land. He is going to pour his Spirit upon their descendants, so that they will delight to be called 'the Lord's' (44:3-5).

God declares himself to Israel

God is Israel's true king and only redeemer – both her ruler and her Saviour. He was there at the beginning and will be there at the end (44:6). He is unique as God, for all other gods are powerless frauds and delusions. God also predicts the future, which no other god, pagan prophet or medium is able to do (44:7).

God speaks to Israel's anxieties – her insecurity, lack of faith and fear of the future. He tells her there is no need to be afraid; he has always confided in her what is to happen. There is no other god who is working to save her; no other rock on which she can seek security (44:8).

Idol-worship is nonsense

God exposes idol-making as a shameful deceit (44:9–11). The blacksmith gets thirsty and tired as he forges an idol. How can he be making something stronger than himself (44:12)? The carpenter who so carefully draws a human shape and selects a suitable tree, then uses half the wood for an idol and the other half for his fire (44:13–17) – how can his handiwork save him?

The problem with idol-worship is that it is so unthinking. The people who make idols and bow down to them won't face the fact that what they are doing is nonsense (44:18–20).

God's joy in delivering his people

God calls his people to return to him. He has forgiven their sins and recovered them from disaster (44:21–22). Heaven and earth rejoice that God has acted to save Israel and to reveal his glory in her story (44:23).

God declares his power. It is he who has created the cosmos and established truth (44:24–25). He endorses the predictions of his prophets that Jerusalem will be restored and the population of Judah return.

God is the Lord of nature (44:27) and the Lord of history (44:28). Even the emperor Cyrus, the world's most powerful ruler, is like a shepherd caring for people on God's instructions (44:28). With all these assurances, God promises that Jerusalem and her temple will be restored (44:28).

God commissions Cyrus

Cyrus, the Persian emperor, is anointed by God for a divine purpose – just as Israel's kings were anointed for a holy task (45:1).

God will give Cyrus victories over wealthy King Croesus and the mighty Babylon (45:1–2); but Cyrus's most important work will be to restore the exiled Israelites to their land, capital and worship (45:4–6).

Cyrus of Persia

In a series of brilliant military campaigns, Cyrus wins an empire stretching from Asia Minor in the west to India in the east. He conquers Mesopotamia, and takes Babylon without a struggle in 539 BC. The prophecies in this section of Isaiah date from the years of these campaigns: 550–539 BC.

Cyrus is to be God's agent, even though he is unaware of it (45:5). God moves in the great events of nature and history: light and darkness, well-being and disaster, are all his work (45:7–8).

It seems strange and shocking that God will use a pagan emperor to restore his holy people; but God is the Lord of all nations and rulers. Those who criticize what God is doing are like clay questioning the potter that shapes it (45:9). God has raised up Cyrus for this great purpose and he will help him succeed (45:13).

God – the only lord and saviour

The peoples of other nations will bring their wealth and pay homage to Israel – just as if they have been conquered (45:14). They will acknowledge that Israel's God is the only God, although he is invisible (45:15). Idol-makers will be exposed as deluded frauds, while Israel's God will keep her eternally safe (45:16–17).

God declares that he is the creator of order and truth (45:18–19). While idols are dumb and ignorant, God makes his purposes known (45:20–21). He calls all nations to turn to him, acknowledge him as Lord, and receive his salvation (45:22–25).

No contest

The famous idols of Babylon are loaded onto animals. 'Bel' (like 'Baal', and also known as Marduk) and 'Nebo' (Marduk's son) are being carted off into captivity (46:1–2). Their powerlessness is exposed for all to see.

By contrast, the living God has always carried his people – and always will (46:3–4). How can anyone persist in comparing the God of Israel to pagan idols? Idols are merely metal objects that have to be carried around or propped in a corner – incapable of helping themselves or anyone else (46:5-7).

The true and only God is fulfilling his age-old purpose (46:8-10). He is summoning the Persian emperor Cyrus, like a bird of prey, to rescue and restore Israel (46:11-13).

God will judge Babylon

Isaiah sings a lament for Babylon. She sees herself as a beautiful young woman – the loveliest of kingdoms, for ever secure (47:5, 8). But God is going to humiliate her, reveal her true nature and put her to hard labour (47:2-3).

Babylon is proud and cruel. She talks as though she is God (47:8), relies on the occult for guidance (47:12) and has been merciless to captive Israel (47:6). Now God is going to reduce her to ruin (47:1). Her stargazing astrologers and fortune tellers will vanish in the fire of judgment like burning stubble (47:12-14).

'New things'

Isaiah speaks God's word to Israel. Israel claims to rely on God and honour his name, but still continues to sin in thought and deed (48:1-2).

God had long warned Israel that he would punish her, and now he has done it. She can't blame her idols (48:3-5). Now God wants to tell Israel new things – things which have not been so long predicted that they have become dull (48:6-8).

God is going to spare Israel further punishment, because he wants her to live for his glory (48:9-11). He is the living God, the eternal creator and Lord of all (48:12-13). Now he is bringing Cyrus to conquer Babylon (48:14).

The Lord's servant speaks. He has always made himself known – through creation and in wisdom. Now God is sending him to work, in the power of his Spirit (48:16).

If only Israel had obeyed God instead of rebelling! She would have enjoyed prosperity, success and growth (48:17-19). But it is not too late. God commands Israel to leave Babylon – and to do so with joyful praise.

God is releasing his people from captivity. He will provide for them on their desert journey home (48:20-21).

God will rebuild Jerusalem (49:1-55:13)

The second 'servant song'

God's servant announces himself to the world (49:1). The Lord God has called him before he was born, to be his spokesperson – his mouth 'like a sharp sword' – to deliver his message of judgment and love (49:2).

The servant's name is Israel; but this is not the Israel that has failed and is in exile. This is Israel as she should be: the suffering servant of God who restores his people (49:3-6).

But the servant's task is to be greater still. He is to reveal God's glory to the nations and give light to the whole world (49:5-6). The rulers of the nations will bow down before this mysterious, rejected, glorious servant who so perfectly expresses the purpose of God (49:7).

Making up

God is restoring his relationship with his people. He calls them from the prison darkness of exile (49:8) and transforms the landscape to ease their journey home (49:9-11). They come from three directions – north, west and south (Syene is Aswan in Egypt). The whole of creation rejoices in God's love for his people (49:12-13).

Does Zion (Jerusalem) still feel that God has forgotten her? God assures her of his enduring love – greater than the love of any nursing mother (49:14-15). Look at the progress of the building work and the steady influx of people (49:17-18)! God is filling sad Jerusalem with children – and foreign kings and queens to look after them (49:19-23).

Will God be able to free all his people? Isaiah says that God is fighting all Jerusalem's enemies – and will defeat even the strongest (49:24-26).

God regrets the years of Israel's exile. It wasn't because of divorce or debt that she was deported, but for rebellion against God (50:1). He called and no one answered (50:2). However, all that is in the past. Now the God of creation and judgment is rescuing his people (50:2-3).

The third 'servant song'

The Lord's servant is a teacher with the ability to encourage. He listens to God and passes on to others what he hears (50:4-5). His work results in him being punished and tortured (50:6). We see why Jesus draws on these songs to understand his own suffering (Mark 10:33-34).

'Your God reigns!'

Isaiah reminds Israel of her experiences of God in history.

God raised the nation of Israel from the unlikely beginnings of elderly Abraham and barren Sarah (51:1-2). Now he will turn Israel's barren wilderness into the Garden of Eden (51:3). The light of his justice shines out; his salvation reaches all peoples. Heaven and earth are short-lived, but his deliverance is for ever (51:4-8).

God is going to act with sovereign power. He once subdued the mythic forces of evil – Rahab (Egypt), the dragon (Satan) and the sea (Chaos). Now the God of the exodus from Egypt is rescuing his people again – from exile in Babylon – and bringing them home with joy (51:9-11). Israel need not fear any foe, nor famine or death, because she is God's own people (51:12-14).

Jerusalem has drunk deeply of God's wrath. She has been made dizzy by devastation and sent sprawling by destruction. She and her children lie unconscious with no one to pity or help (51:17-20). But God will intervene. He will take his cup of wrath from her and give it to her enemies instead – those who have trampled her (51:21-23).

Isaiah gives Zion (Jerusalem) her wake-up call (52:1). This is more than another day – it is a new life, a resurrection. Jerusalem is to receive again her beauty, holiness, dignity and freedom (52:1-2). This is God's doing, who called his people from captivity in Egypt and Assyria (52:3-6) without question or payment. He is the Lord (52:3-5).

What a wonderful sight – the running feet of the messenger, springing through the mountains. He brings God's declaration of peace, salvation and victory (52:7). The watchmen burst into a song of joy which is echoed by the ruins. God has acted! The Lord himself has comforted his people (52:8-10).

The newly holy nation prepares to leave Babylon. She returns from exile like a procession of priests (52:11). All is done with dignity, without haste or fear (52:12).

The fourth 'servant song'

God's servant is to be raised up (52:13). He has been rendered almost unrecognizable by what he has suffered. The nations and their rulers fall silent at the sight of him (52:14-15).

There seemed nothing special about the servant when he first appeared – like a root out of dry ground. No majesty. No beauty (53:1-2). He suffered in so many ways – sorrow, rejection, illness – that people dismissed him as hopeless and worthless (53:3).

But now we see the servant's suffering in a new light. It was our suffering he was carrying – and we thought God was giving him what he deserved (53:4). The servant was wounded and crushed for our sins – so that we can be healed (53:5). He has been our scapegoat, our sacrifice, our sin-bearer (53:6).

The description of what happened to the servant is, for Christians, a description of what happened to Jesus – and for the same reasons. In his suffering he was meek and unprotesting, like a lamb being shorn or sacrificed (53:7). It was John the Baptist who recognized Jesus as 'the Lamb of God, who takes away the sin of the world' (John 1:29).

Like the servant's trial, Jesus' trial was unfair and his fate undeserved. Crucifixion was the ultimate cut-off from dignity, life and hope (53:8). Most strangely, the servant's grave was 'with a rich man' – and Jesus on his death will be given the tomb of Joseph of Arimathea (Matthew 27:57-59).

Isaiah sees that all this is God's will. Through this innocent suffering and death will come a great forgiveness and mighty resurrection (53:10-11). This terrible death endured means life and victory for all (53:12).

Transformation!

Jerusalem is to rejoice. She was barren, but is now teeming with children. She needs more space to live, and can spread throughout the world (54:1-3). God the creator of all is her husband, restoring their relationship after the miseries of suffering and separation (54:4-8).

The punishment is over and God renews his promises to Israel – as he did to Noah after the flood (54:9-10).

God is going to transform ruined Jerusalem. Her foundations, walls, gates and towers will be of precious stones (54:11-12). Her children will receive God's own teaching and enjoy prosperity (54:13). This is a heavenly city – a place of righteousness, truth and peace (54:14-17; Revelation 21:10-11).

An open invitation

Isaiah calls everyone who is hungry to God's feast. The siege of sin and suffering is lifted. The gates of plenty are thrown open (55:1).

'Why spend your money on junk food?' he asks (55:2 The Message), 'Why waste your life on vain ambitions? Instead, come into the life and love of God – the fulfilment of the kingdom of David' (55:2-3). You will become part of God's mission to the world. God will make you radiant so that others may be drawn to his light (55:4-5).

This is a moment of opportunity. It is time to turn to God while he is so approachable, so near (55:6). It is time to receive God's mercy, share his thoughts and catch the wave of his purposes (55:7-11). The freedom, joy and peace of God's people will cause the whole of creation to rejoice (55:12). Peace will break out – a peace which will be for ever the hallmark of God's reign (55:13).

Prophecies to Israel after the exile

Here are encouraging words for the people rebuilding Jerusalem. God's glory is shining around Israel, and the whole world will be drawn to her light. Jerusalem will be at the centre of God's new creation, where injustice and discord will be replaced by joy and peace (65:17-25).

Again we hear the servant speaking (61:1-11). He proclaims God's grace and favour to everyone in need. Jesus will turn to these words when he teaches at the synagogue in Nazareth. God's jubilee of forgiveness and freedom has arrived – in person (Luke 4:18-21).

All are welcome (56:1–8)

God's salvation is not exclusively for Israel. All who are serious about God's justice and keep the sabbath are welcome to his new community (56:1-2).

Isaiah particularly mentions foreigners and eunuchs. They have been excluded from Jewish worship because of physical or moral defects. But now God wants to include them.

The foreigner or pagan 'outsider' must not assume that God will reject him from his people; nor must the eunuch dismiss himself as a dead and fruitless tree (56:3). The eunuch who lives in God's way will be remembered, even though he has no children (56:4-5). Foreigners, too, who love God and keep his law, may come and worship in his temple (56:6-7).

God's mission, through the Jews, was always to bless the world and draw all nations to him. This was the purpose of God's call to Abraham (Genesis 12:1-2); it will be understood by Jesus (John 10:16); and it is here in the prophecies of Isaiah: 'My house [temple] shall be house of prayer for all peoples' (56:7).

When the watchmen sleep... (56:9-57:13)

The prophets who should be guarding Israel are silent – asleep like dreaming dogs (56:10). Israel's leaders are like drunken shepherds – indulging themselves rather than caring for their people (56:11-12).

As a result, the wild beasts of idolatry invade Israel unchecked (56:9). Trees become the sites of cultic prostitution and rocks are used for child sacrifice (57:5-6). God has tried to ignore Israel's wrongdoing, but he can do so no longer (57:11). The idols will not protect them from God's judgment. Only those who hide in God will be allowed to live in his holy community (57:13).

God is determined to forgive (57:14-21)

The cry goes up to build the road home from exile (57:14); but God needs also to prepare people's hearts for his holy presence (57:15). God wants to put aside his anger and forgive even those who don't deserve forgiveness (57:16-19).

True fasting is love in action (58:1-14)

God tells Isaiah to shout out like a trumpet (58:1). He is to declare that the Israelites are fasting in the wrong spirit. They look sincere and eager, but really they are trying to manipulate God (58:2-3).

While they take time off to fast and pray (perhaps on the Day of Atonement), they are still making their employees work (58:3). Going without food is supposed to make them humble before God; but it makes them bad-tempered and violent towards each other (58:4-5).

God's idea of a fast is very different. True fasting means putting ourselves out to serve others: releasing people from injustice and oppression; sharing our food and home and clothes; and helping our relatives (58:6-7). When we do these things, God's blessing is upon us and he answers our prayers (58:8-9).

It is important to keep the sabbath for God's sake, and not just use it as an extra day off. It is a day to delight in the Lord (58:13-14).

Sin separates but God saves (59:1-21)

Israel's sins are blocking her off from God and preventing God from saving her (59:1-1). All is bloodshed and lies (59:3), dishonesty and the creeping poison of corruption (59:4-5). Society cannot hold together when there is such a complete breakdown of moral standards (59:6). Everyone is bent on doing evil (59:7-8).

Israel is in deep moral darkness (59:9-12), blocked off from the light of God's truth, righteousness and justice (59:13-15).

God sees this desperate situation, and that there is no one to take action (59:15-16). He decides to intervene – coming to the rescue himself armed with radical goodness, intent on salvation and swathed in righteous anger (59:17). He will sweep in like a cleansing flood, giving justice, righting wrongs and punishing the guilty (59:18-19).

And what will be the fate of Israel? He will act as her redeemer: her next of kin who saves her and pays her debts (59:20). He forges an everlasting bond with his people, to put his Spirit of truth within them (59:21).

The panoramic glory of Zion (60:1-22)

The glory of God dawns over Jerusalem like the sunrise (60:1). She becomes a beacon to a world in deep darkness (60:2) and nations are drawn to her light (60:3).

The procession of returning Israelites becomes an influx of people and wealth from all the nations (60:4-7). They bring animals for sacrifice and gifts to beautify the temple (60:7).

Jerusalem's glory and the news of what God has done for her make her the wonder of the world (60:8-16). Her gates are open day and night, so that the royal delegations may flow in (60:11). All nations are judged by their response to Jerusalem (60:12) and old enemies come to pay homage (60:14).

Everything is richer, stronger, better (60:17). The aim of government is righteousness and its driving force is peace (60:17). Jerusalem is surrounded by salvation and accessed with praise (60:18). The glory of God is her perpetual light, and darkness and grief are no more (60:19-20).

Finally, Jerusalem's people will be righteous – planted as God's own, to grow and flourish (60:21-22). Is it all a dream? No – God himself is going to make it a reality (60:22).

The Lord's anointed (61:1-62:12)

God's servant speaks again – this time with the words which Jesus will take to refer to himself (Luke 4:17-21).

God is sending his servant to his people in exile. He has anointed him to deliver good news of rescue, comfort and freedom (61:1). The year of God's salvation has arrived at last – the joyous Jubilee which dispels injustice, mourning and despair (61:2-3). God's people will become splendid examples of righteousness (61:3). They will rebuild and restore the ruins of long ago (61:4).

God's people will be given their true status as his priests and ministers (61:6). Foreigners will be their slaves and the wealth of nations will support them (61:5-6). God is going to give his people double honour, to make up for their double shame (61:7).

God will bring about all that he holds dear. He will establish justice in the world and set his restored people as the centrepiece of his blessing (61:8-9).

Israel rejoices in all that God is doing for her. She is robed in his saving goodness (61:10). She will grow in his purity and praise (61:11).

Seeing red (63:1–6)

Isaiah has an awesome vision of God returning from his work of judgment. He is majestic and dreadful – stained with the blood of his enemies (63:1).

God has been to punish Edom (which means 'red') and her capital Bozrah (which sounds like 'grape-harvester') (63:1–2). He has acted alone in this, because there was no one fit to help (63:3–5). It was a lone feat of ruthless, righteous wrath (63:6).

A cry from the heart (63:7–64:12)

Isaiah cries out to God to have mercy on his people. He has been so good to Israel in the past, caring for them in person (63:7–9).

Israel has rebelled against God and become his enemy (63:10); but now she remembers the mighty deliverance of the exodus. She longs for those great days to return (63:11–15). Even if her ancestors, Abraham and Israel, disown her, will not God have mercy (63:16)?

Israel attributes everything to God – even her own hard heart, her disobedience and lack of faith (63:17). Now she begs God to rescue, restore and rule her (63:17–19).

Israel asks God to intervene by his mountain-moving power (64:1) and like fire in his awesome holiness (64:2). He is the only One who can act in this way, revealing himself in justice to those who wait for him (64:3–5).

Israel admits her sin and guilt – even her best actions are filthy (64:5–6). She feels that she is dying in sin, and that God has turned away and left her to her fate (64:7). And yet she pleads that she is still in God's hands. He can still reform her, like a potter with clay (64:8).

Israel asks God to have pity on her desolate cities – and especially on the ruins of her temple. Is God's silence really final (64:10–11)?

Choices and consequences (65:1–16)

God says that he has been open to those who haven't looked for him (65:1). The apostle Paul understands this to refer to non-Jews (Romans

10:20). Equally, God has held out his hands to people who did know him, but were rebellious (65:2) – which Paul takes to mean Israel (Romans 10:21).

The sins which have offended God and provoked his punishment are pagan offerings and attempts to commune with the dead (65:3-4). The stench of incense and disgusting foods offends him (65:4-5). God has promised that he will pay back these outrages – and he will do so (65:6-7).

And yet, even in his judgment, God will spare a remnant – like a few good grapes that deserve to survive (65:8). He will retrieve some descendants of Israel to reoccupy his promised land (65:9). The pastureland of Sharon will once again have flocks. The Valley of Achor ('bitterness') will be a place of peace (65:10).

However, God will sentence to death all who worship the Syrian gods of fortune and destiny (65:11). There will be a world of difference between the fate of those who turn to God and those who rely on idols (65:13-16).

God's new creation (65:17-25)

God describes the new world that he is creating – so wonderful and different that the present pain will be completely forgotten (65:17).

Jerusalem, which has seen so much suffering and destruction, will become a community of joy and delight (65:18-19). Bereavement and early deaths will be things of the past: to live to 100 will be quite normal (65:20)!

There will be peace and stability. Families will be able to build and plant – enjoying the fruits of their labour through many generations (65:21-23). There will be a new closeness to God and a readiness to speak with him (65:24). The animal world will be at rest, with natural enemies feeding side by side – rather than one eating another (65:25). Only the serpent, the ancient symbol of evil, will continue to be cursed (65:23).

God's judgment and salvation (66:1-24)

God announces himself. He is the One who has heaven as his throne and the earth as his footstool (66:1). What significance, then, does this 'house', the temple, have? Everything comes from God anyway (66:2).

What God looks for in worship is the obedient response of a humble heart (66:2, 4). Without the offering of the heart, a sacrifice is just mindless pagan butchery (66:3). God has no pleasure in receiving worship which is a pretence. He feels mocked – and will mock in return (66:4–5).

Isaiah describes a miracle: a woman gives birth to a son without going into labour. It is unheard of, and yet God is going to bring his new nation to birth in an instant (66:7–9).

Isaiah calls all those who love Jerusalem (and have grieved over her) to rejoice (66:10). She will suckle and nurture her children (66:11). She is the mother of all, giving wealth and well-being, support and comfort to her people (66:12–13).

The other side of God's blessing is that he will punish and destroy his enemies (66:14). He loathes the eating of unclean foods (66:17).

God is drawing people from the far reaches of the earth: Tarshish in Spain, Put and Lud in Ethiopia, Tubal in the north and Javan, which is Greece (66:18–19). They are bringing the Israelites with them – like an offering – on every kind of transport (66:20–21). They will form an enduring community – the worshipping nucleus of the entire world (66:22–23).

At the last, God's restored people will look at the corpses of their enemies – and see the sad and sickening fate of those who resisted God to the end (66:24).

JEREMIAH

Jeremiah is a prophet of disaster and hope. He lives in the southern kingdom of Judah during the years leading up to the fall of its capital city, Jerusalem. For forty years he preaches that this catastrophe is going to happen if the people don't repent and turn to God.

Jeremiah's warnings come true when the armies of Babylon, directed by King Nebuchadnezzar, invade Judah. In 587 BC they destroy Jerusalem and her temple. The king and many of the people are taken away to exile in Babylonia.

But Jeremiah also has a message of hope. He predicts that one day the people will return and that the nation will be restored. He also promises that God will make a new deal with his people. His law will no longer be 'outside' them, written on tablets of stone. Instead, it will be 'within' them – written on their hearts (Isaiah 31:33 NRSV).

In Jeremiah we see the pain and passion of a prophet at work. God's word burns within him, so that he *must* preach. But his message makes him unpopular. At times he is cruelly persecuted. He has a hard life – crushed between the pressing truth of God and the resistance of his people.

OUTLINE

God calls the young Jeremiah to be a prophet (1:1–19)
God's messages to Judah and Jerusalem (2:1–25:38)
Episodes in Jeremiah's life (26:1–45:25)
Prophecies against the nations (46:1–51:64)
The fall of Jerusalem (52:1–34)

Introduction

When did Jeremiah prophesy?

Jeremiah prophesies during the reigns of the last five kings of Judah: Josiah, Jehoahaz, Jehoiakim, Jehoiachin and Zedekiah.

Jeremiah is born towards the end of the reign of Manasseh. Manasseh has led the people of Judah in Baal-worship and occult practices. He has introduced idols into the temple and even sacrificed his own sons on pagan altars. Although Manasseh eventually repents of these acts, his son Amon is an idol-worshipper as well (2 Chronicles 33).

When the young king Josiah comes of age, he sets out to restore the worship of the Lord. He wants to be a king like his ancestor David. He demolishes the pagan altars and destroys their images (2 Chronicles 34:1–7).

Jeremiah is a similar age to his king. When he is called to be a prophet in 627 BC, he pleads that he is 'only a boy' (1:7 NRSV).

Assyria and Babylon

Judah is a small kingdom, tossed between the superpowers of Assyria to the north-east and Egypt to the south-west. Judah's twin kingdom, Israel, has rebelled against Assyria and been overrun; her capital city, Samaria, captured in 722 BC and her people dispersed.

In the early years of Jeremiah's ministry, Assyria dominates the region. But Jeremiah's message is that Babylon will arise and conquer all.

Judah, too, has defied Assyria during the reign of Hezekiah. Hezekiah formed an alliance with Egypt and rebelled against Assyria, but the punishment was swift and terrible. The Assyrians devastated Judah in 701, although Jerusalem itself was protected by God, thanks to the faith of Hezekiah and his prophet Isaiah.

While Josiah is pursuing his reforms, Assyria's power begins to fade. Her strong ruler, Ashurbanipal, has died in 627, and the province of Babylon has broken away as an independent power. Her founder, Nabopolassar, defeats his Assyrian masters in 626 and establishes the beginnings of the Babylonian (Chaldean) empire. His famous son is Nebuchadnezzar.

Josiah's reforms

When Josiah has completed the destruction of pagan altars and idols, he commissions a team to restore Solomon's temple. This results in the discovery of the Book of the Law – the long-lost law of Moses. The effect

Countdown: the decline and fall of Judah

640/39 Josiah becomes king of Judah at the age of eight.
628 He begins his reforms at the age of nineteen.
627 Jeremiah starts to preach.
622 The Book of the Law is found in the temple.
612 The Assyrian empire falls to the forces of Babylon.
609 Josiah is killed in battle at the age of thirty-nine. Jehoahaz becomes king of Judah for three months. Jehoiakim is made king of Judah by Pharaoh Neco of Egypt.
605 The Babylonians defeat the Egyptians at Carchemish. Daniel and other young leaders are deported to Babylon.
604 Jeremiah's scroll is read to King Jehoiakim – and burned.
601 Jehoiakim rebels against Babylon.
598 Jehoiakim is deposed and dies.
597 Jehoiachin is taken off to exile in Babylon, along with 3,000 skilled workers and the temple treasures. This is the first phase of captivity. Zedekiah becomes king at the age of twenty-one.
588 Zedekiah rebels against Babylon. Nebuchadnezzar besieges Jerusalem.
587 Jerusalem falls to the Babylonian army. Eight hundred and thirty-two of her people are taken into exile. This is the second phase of captivity, but Jeremiah is spared and released. Gedaliah is made governor of Judah, and Jeremiah stays with him at Mizpah; but Gedaliah is assassinated by Ishmael. The survivors from Judah go to Egypt, against Jeremiah's advice; they take Jeremiah with them.
582/1 There is a third phase of deportation, with 745 people taken away to exile in Babylon.
561 A new king of Babylon releases King Jehoiachin from prison, but keeps him in the royal court. He has been in exile for thirty-seven years.
539 Babylon falls to Cyrus, king of Persia.
539/8 Cyrus frees the Jewish exiles and allows them to return home.

of hearing the law is dramatic. Josiah leads the nation in repentance. The covenant with God is renewed and the Passover celebrated in a week-long festival (2 Chronicles 34:8–35:19).

Jeremiah plays a key role in Josiah's reforms. He travels the land, proclaiming the covenant and presenting people with its commands and blessings (Jeremiah 11:1-8). Paganism is deep-seated and Jeremiah has his first taste of opposition and rejection. At Anathoth, where he was raised as the son of a priest, there is a plot to kill him. We begin to see his loneliness, as people reject him as a killjoy:

I never sat in the company of revellers,
    never made merry with them;
I sat alone because your hand was on me
    and you had filled me with indignation. (15:17)

The heart of a true prophet

Jeremiah is often angry with both the people and God – but his message consumes him:

You deceived me, Lord, and I was deceived;
    you overpowered me and prevailed.
I am ridiculed all day long;
    everyone mocks me.
Whenever I speak, I cry out
    proclaiming violence and destruction.
So the word of the Lord has brought me
    insult and reproach all day long.
But if I say, 'I will not mention his word
    or speak any more in his name,'
his word is in my heart like a fire,
    a fire shut up in my bones. (20:7-9)

Jeremiah has the heart of a true prophet. His calling makes him lonely in a crowd; yet he loves his people and longs that they will turn to God. He begs God to spare them:

You are among us, O Lord,
    and we bear your name;
    do not forsake us! (14:9 NIV)

Jeremiah's work continues in this way for twenty-three years. He is protected from harm by Josiah – now in his prime and a true king and father to his people.

Changes in Judah's history

But now international affairs change the course of Judah's history. Assyria is hard-pressed by the rising power of Babylon, and the king of Egypt decides to intervene. He marches to support Assyria in the hope of increasing his influence in Palestine. But Josiah wants Assyria to remain weak, and he rides to intercept the Egyptians – only to be killed in battle at Megiddo.

The Egyptian king uses his new-found power to remove Josiah's successor (Jehoahaz) and install another son, Jehoiakim. But in 605 the Egyptians themselves are swept away by the Babylonian armies of Nebuchadnezzar, at the battle of Carchemish.

It is in 605 BC that God tells Jeremiah to have all his prophecies written on a single scroll. Jeremiah's secretary Baruch writes them down, and they are read in public in the temple.

The new king's staff bring the scroll to his attention and he demands that the prophecies be read to him. Jehoiakim is completely unmoved by the warnings they contain. As each section is read, he cuts it away and throws it on the fire (36:23). But Jeremiah and Baruch sit down and write the whole document again – with some further material for good measure!

Jeremiah's messages are regarded as treason. He is preaching against the temple and the city. He is challenging the new wave of paganism and undermining public confidence. Without a king to protect him, Jeremiah is much more severely persecuted. He is beaten, put in the stocks (20:1-2) and threatened with death (26:16).

Now Nebuchadnezzar takes control of the whole region and demands tribute from Judah. When Jehoiakim rebels, he is deposed and dies. His successor Jehoiachin (Jeconiah) also resists the Babylonians, but is soon defeated. He is taken into exile along with thousands of his leading citizens and all the treasures from Solomon's temple.

Judah under King Zedekiah

The next king is Zedekiah. He immediately lays plans to break Babylon's grip. But Jeremiah knows that Babylon's triumph is God's judgment on Judah. They will be wise to submit to it. He enacts Babylon's control by wearing a yoke on his neck – and warns of dire punishments if Judah tries to throw it off (27:8). When envoys from the surrounding kingdoms come to pay their respects to Zedekiah, Jeremiah sends them away with an extraordinary message: the Lord, the God of Israel, is the supreme God, and Nebuchadnezzar is his servant (27:6)!

Jeremiah also writes a letter to the Jewish exiles in Babylon. He advises them to settle down and 'seek the peace and prosperity of the city to which I have carried you' (29:7). This is a stark contrast to the feelings of Psalm 137. Jeremiah declares that it is *God* who has carried them off to Babylonia, when actually it was Nebuchadnezzar! Their exile is to last for seventy years, after which God will answer their prayers and bring them home.

Even with the Babylonian army threatening Jerusalem, Zedekiah is determined to resist. He consults Jeremiah privately from time to time, asking him for a word from the Lord. No doubt he and his advisers hope for a last-minute rescue, as happened with the Assyrian threat in Hezekiah's reign.

Jeremiah is arrested for trying to leave the city. Although he is on personal business, it looks as though he is deserting to the Babylonians. The king has him placed under guard in the courtyard of the palace (37:21). However, his enemies still object to his messages, which they see as disloyal. They seize him and lower him into a cistern, where he might be lost for ever (38:9). Fortunately he is rescued by one of the king's servants, who is an Ethiopian.

When Jerusalem finally falls, the Babylonian commander seeks out Jeremiah. He gives him his freedom and offers to take him to Babylon. The Babylonians treat Jeremiah as an ally, as he has so long preached submission to Nebuchadnezzar. But Jeremiah chooses to stay in Judah, with the poorest survivors of the catastrophe (40:7).

Meanwhile, King Zedekiah has tried to escape. He is captured, blinded and carried off to prison in Babylon. The last thing he sees is his sons being killed in front of him (52:10–11).

No happy ending

Jeremiah hopes to settle with the new governor Gedaliah at Mizpah. Together they will care for the shattered people of Judah and rebuild their community. But Gedaliah is assassinated by Ishmael, who wants the royal throne.

After much bloodshed, Ishmael is driven off. The survivors ask Jeremiah for a word from the Lord. They promise to do whatever he says. When God speaks, it is to assure them of his protection. There is nothing to fear from Babylon. He will bless and restore them if they stay in their land; but if they take refuge in Egypt, they will die (42:17).

The survivors have learned nothing from their terrifying ordeal. They accuse Jeremiah of lying. He and Baruch are trying to get them all killed or exiled. Far from agreeing that Jeremiah has been right all along, they reject him all over again. They defy God's message and leave for Egypt, taking Jeremiah with them.

There is no happy ending to the book of Jeremiah. We leave him in Egypt, still speaking God's word to a resistant and disobedient people. They revive their pagan practices, burning incense to the Queen of Heaven. The God of Israel has failed them, but they always had plenty when they worshipped her. When the time of captivity is over, thousands of Jews return from exile in Babylon. But nothing more is heard of those who went to Egypt.

DISCOVERING JEREMIAH

God calls the young Jeremiah to be a prophet

Jeremiah is a priest's son. He comes from Anathoth – a settlement of priests on the eastern border of Judah by the open wilderness.

Josiah has been on the throne twelve years and is now about twenty. Jeremiah and his king are a similar age. When God calls him, Jeremiah pleads that he is only a child and unable to speak. But God has known and chosen him from before his birth (1:6–7).

Jeremiah is to serve God as his prophet through forty stormy years. In the north, the Assyrian empire will fall and the Babylonian empire will rise. To the south, the power of Egypt will be both a threat and a refuge. And Judah herself, like her kings, will swing between godliness and paganism.

In all this, Jeremiah is to devote himself to speaking God's messages. He must warn the people of judgment, defeat and exile. Jerusalem and her temple will be destroyed. The king descended from David will become a prisoner. The whole nation will be gutted and displaced. Jeremiah's message is not only unbelievable – it is unacceptable. No one will want to listen.

But Jeremiah is God's choice. God touches his mouth and gives him the words to say. He promises to strengthen and protect this hesitant young man against all that his enemies will try to do to him. And he does. He appoints him to an earth-moving, kingdom-toppling, life-giving ministry (1:10).

To a prophet's eyes, ordinary things take on special meaning. Jeremiah sees an almond tree about to blossom – the first sign of spring (1:11). The Hebrew word for 'almond' sounds like 'watchful'. God is awake and alert to fulfil his plans. Jeremiah sees a boiling pot, tilting its contents from the north. In the same way God is about to pour out his punishment on Judah through fierce invaders (1:13–14).

God's messages to Judah and Jerusalem

Jeremiah starts preaching in 627 BC, which is the thirteenth year of Josiah's reign. The king is twenty-one years old. The messages in these chapters (2:1–25:38) come from the remaining years of Josiah's reign, and the following reigns until 605.

Josiah dies in battle at the age of twenty-nine. His son Jehoahaz becomes king for a few months, but is soon deposed by the king of Egypt. The king of Egypt (Pharaoh Neco) puts another son on the throne instead. This is King Jehoiakim, who reigns for eleven years.

Jehoiakim is deposed and taken captive by King Nebuchadnezzar of Babylon. His son Jehoiachin succeeds him on the throne of Judah. He is eighteen years old. Almost immediately, he too is deported to Babylon. His uncle, Zedekiah, becomes king in his place.

Jeremiah prophesies throughout these reigns. Chapters 2–20 contain messages delivered between 627 and 605 BC. In 605, Jehoiakim is king of Judah and Nebuchadnezzar is the new king of Babylon.

God tells Jeremiah to collect his prophecies into a single scroll, which his secretary Baruch writes out for him (36:1-2). This is probably the scroll which is read to King Jehoiakim the following year - and which the arrogant king cuts up and burns.

Israel forsakes the God who loves her (2:1-3:5)

God is like a husband to his people. He remembers the delight of his young love when he rescued her from Egypt, married her in the wilderness and brought her home to a fertile land. But now Israel and Judah have behaved like prostitutes. They commit spiritual adultery by worshipping other gods.

Jeremiah can't believe what he sees. God's people reject him - for what? They lust after fertility gods and goddesses - erecting phallic poles on hilltops and holding orgies under trees. This is like exchanging spring water for the foul contents of a leaking cistern. Idols are made by human beings and they don't work.

God's people are unholy in their behaviour. They are also unfaithful in their politics. They no longer trust God to protect them. Instead they rely on alliances with other nations, such as Egypt and Assyria. But they don't need to be slaves to anyone. They are God's children! And these so-called allies are treacherous. They will just as soon tear them apart.

In all this, the people still call on God as their Father and friend. But their hearts are hard and their eyes are cold. Their actions deny their words.

Jeremiah calls to God's people to return (3:6-4:2)

God shows Jeremiah that the northern state of Israel has behaved like an unfaithful wife. She has played the whore as her people have worshipped Baal ('master') in fertility rites on hills and under trees. Now God has divorced her. The ten tribes of Israel have been captured by Sargon II of Assyria and taken from their land.

God tells Jeremiah to call Israel to return to her true master, who is God (3:14). God promises to give Israel good shepherds - that is, leaders who will nurture and protect her people. God's presence will become far more meaningful to them than in the old days of the ark of the covenant

(3:16). Jerusalem herself will become God's throne where the nations of the world will acknowledge him; and Israel and Judah will be reunited and come into God's blessing (3:18).

Visions of invasion from the north (4:3–6:30)

God urges his people to make a true, deep repentance, like a circumcision of the heart (4:4). Only this will avert the disaster that is about to fall on Judah.

The crisis is breaking. The trumpet must sound the alarm, so that people can take refuge (4:5–6). God is bringing a fearsome army from the north, which is springing forth like a hungry lion from its thicket (4:7). Judah's leaders will be stunned and helpless in the face of the threat (4:9), and fatally deceived by those who have been prophesying that all would be well (4:10).

The enemy will sweep in like a roasting wind: not useful or refreshing, but inescapable and withering all in its path (4:11).

Jeremiah calls on Jerusalem to repent. The terror is approaching. The alarm is sounded from Dan, the northernmost tribe. The names of Judah's cities are on the lips of the invaders (4:14–16). Jeremiah is doubled up with the pain and overwhelmed by the tumult of invasion (4:19–21). God's people have brought this on themselves by their wanton rebellion (4:22). The prophet sees a desolate and deserted landscape (4:23–26); and yet God will still leave room to be merciful (4:28).

To Jeremiah, Judah is like a woman dressing herself for seduction; but she will soon be writhing in anguish as her enemies have their way (4:29–31).

Is there any hope for Jerusalem? Is there a single person, poor or rich, who could be the reason for sparing the city from destruction (5:1–5)? There is no one. And so Jerusalem will be besieged, as though wild animals are lying in wait outside her walls (5:6). This is God's punishment for her wilful idolatry and rampant immorality (5:7–9).

The people of Jerusalem have been deceived by false prophets. They have believed messages that all will be well and Jerusalem can never fall (4:12–14). But now Jeremiah's words are to be like a fire, igniting God's judgment on his people (5:14). This judgment will be executed by the forces of a mighty, foreign nation, which will consume and destroy all that Judah holds dear (5:15–19).

Topheth

The altars of Topheth in the Valley of Ben Hinnom are the scene of the grossest act of all – child sacrifice. People think they are making the supreme offering – but God has never asked them to do such a thing. Now judgment is on its way and must run its course. Only on the other side of judgment will there be mercy and renewal.

'Topheth' rhymes with the Hebrew for 'shame' and is used to mean 'spit'. The Valley of Ben Hinnom becomes 'Gehenna', the rubbish dump outside Jerusalem. Jesus uses its ever-burning fire as a picture of judgment.

Jeremiah preaches in the temple (7:1–8:3)

Eighteen years have passed since Josiah began his reforms and Jeremiah began to prophesy. Now, in his late thirties, Jeremiah stands at the gate of the temple and preaches to the people as they arrive for worship.

The same sermon (or a similar one) is mentioned in chapter 26, where we are told it is preached at the beginning of Jehoiakim's reign (about 608 BC). In that account, Jeremiah is nearly executed for his radical and hard-hitting words.

Jeremiah accuses the pilgrims of treating God's temple in a mindless, shallow way. They assume they can get forgiveness just by walking through the door. They believe God will never desert them, because he will always protect his temple.

But Jeremiah challenges the behaviour and beliefs of his hearers. Are they true believers? If so, why do they abuse foreigners and the weakest members of society? Are they God's people? Then why do they break his commandments and honour pagan idols?

People are coming to the temple for automatic forgiveness and a sense of safety. But God says they are treating his house as a criminals' hideout. One day Jesus will say the same, when he clears the temple of traders and money-changers (Matthew 21:13).

Will God always protect his temple? No! Look how the shrine at Shiloh was destroyed by the Philistines. And remember what happened to Ephraim (the northern tribes of Israel) when they were defeated by Assyria and dispersed. God didn't step in to save either the place or the people. Nor will he save Jerusalem when the time comes for judgment to fall.

God looks for obedience. Pilgrimage and sacrifice are nothing without the offering of hearts and lives.

Jeremiah is forbidden to pray for the people. They have gone too far. Whole families worship the Queen of Heaven – the moon, or the Canaanite goddess Astarte – each doing their bit to light the fire and bake the cakes.

Judah's resistance and Jeremiah's anguish (8:4–22)

God's people are in full rebellion against him. It is as though they have fallen and not got up, or gone astray and not turned back (8:4). They have become perpetual backsliders – being dragged along on their backsides, wilfully resisting the right way with all their strength. They no longer have any instinct for God's will (8:7).

The so-called wise people and the priests are singled out for blame. They have busied themselves with getting rich, giving their people casual assurances that all will be well (8:8–11). The leaders will be punished for their shameless behaviour (8:12). God has looked for a harvest from them, but they are like empty and blighted fruit trees (8:13).

Meanwhile, the sounds of approaching invasion are heard from the north (8:16). God is releasing a swift and lethal enemy upon his people, like a brood of adders, to punish them (8:17).

In the face of all this, Jeremiah is grief-stricken. He has no pleasure at all in being right. He is in anguish for the plight of his people, and longs that a remedy might be found for their condition (8:18–22).

Jeremiah preaches about sin and punishment (9:1–26)

Jeremiah has run out of tears for his people and has nowhere to escape from their wickedness (9:1–2). There is no truth or trust to be found, either in neighbourhoods or families (9:3–4). God is going to punish, but only because he wants to refine and reform them (9:7–9).

Jeremiah sees again the desolation that lies ahead. The landscape will become deserted and Jerusalem destroyed in the judgment that is about to fall (9:10-11). All this will be God's doing, because of the idolatry his people have committed with the pagan gods of Baal (9:12-16).

The only thing that matters is to know God. This is more important than any human wisdom, strength or wealth (9:23). To know God is to realize and embrace his standards and his ways. He is endlessly patient and merciful, just and good. Now he is moving to put his values in the hearts of all peoples (9:24-26).

Jeremiah preaches against idolatry (10:1-16)

People like a god they can see and touch. But the commandments have always stood against this for the Jews (Exodus 20:1-4). They are not to reduce God to the shape of a creature or the size of a doll. He is eternal Spirit and not to be imaged – the great, invisible, holy Lord. The only image of God is the One he himself has given – a living and self-giving human being: Jesus Christ.

Jeremiah ridicules the whole process of manufacturing an idol. Cut, chiselled and bejewelled, it is no more effective than a scarecrow. It can't speak or walk by itself. It has no power to punish or save.

Why trade idol-worship for a relationship with the living God? He isn't a part of the creation – he is the Creator. He isn't a bolt of lightning or a shower of rain – he is the founder of the universe.

Get real! Idols are a con, as everyone who makes them knows. Worship the only maker that matters – the One who made *you.*

Jeremiah's pain and prayer (10:17-25)

Jeremiah tells the people under siege that it is nearly time to leave for exile (10:17-18). He himself is in great distress. His life is like a collapsed tent and there are no leaders to put things right (10:19-21). Away to the north he hears the advancing foe – the Babylonian armies which will wreak such terrible destruction (10:22).

Jeremiah pleads with God. Humans are unable to live as they should and deserve to be corrected. But Jeremiah prays that God's punishment won't completely destroy him. He prays that God's anger would be poured out on the nations that have oppressed Israel (10:23-25).

The reason why (11:1-17)

God speaks to Jeremiah of all that has happened in Israel's history. God rescued his people from the furnace of Egyptian oppression (11:4) and made a covenant agreement with them. They were to obey him and he would bless them (11:7); but they have utterly betrayed his trust (11:9-10). Now God is about to punish his people, and they must turn to their Baal-idols for help (11:11-13).

Jeremiah is forbidden to pray for his people. They are like a much-loved wife who has now gone too far in her adulterous affairs. They are like a once-beautiful fruit tree, which is now fit only for destruction (11:14-17).

Jeremiah's own people plot to kill him (11:18-23)

Jeremiah has been given an insight and a message which have plunged him into trouble. He feels that he got involved quite innocently, like a lamb being led to be slaughtered (11:18-19). Now his own neighbours, the people of Anathoth, are plotting to destroy him (11:19). Jeremiah asks God to avenge him (11:20) and is promised that he will (11:21-23).

Anathoth is Jeremiah's birthplace and the home of a frustrated priestly line. Abiathar was a high priest in the time of David, who was banished to Anathoth by Solomon for trying to make someone else king. This was also God's judgment on the corrupt family of Eli, the priest at Shiloh, from whom Abiathar was descended (1 Kings 2:26-27).

The descendants of Abiathar are no doubt angry that they are barred from the temple in Jerusalem. This anger is now focused on Jeremiah, a priest's son, who is predicting the destruction of all that they hold dear (11:19).

Jeremiah complains and God answers (12:1-17)

Jeremiah knows that God is right, but he still wants to complain about his situation (12:1)! Like Job and David before him, Jeremiah sees wicked people prospering. They are even people who claim to be religious, but the things they say are very different from the things they do (12:2).

For his part, Jeremiah has tried to be genuinely faithful – as God knows (12:3). He begs that God will intervene to judge the wicked, because the whole land is suffering from their evil influence (12:4). In addition, Jeremiah feels discouraged already, because his own family and home town have rejected him, so what chance does he stand in Jerusalem (12:5-6)?

God reveals that he, too, is estranged from his loved ones. He has come to hate his own people and is giving them up to defeat by their enemies (12:7). His own land has been trampled by those who should have treasured it, abused by idolaters and laid waste by violence (12:10-12).

God swears that he will judge the neighbouring nations that oppress Israel. He will pull them up like weeds (12:14). But then he offers mercy. If pagan nations will learn God's ways from Israel, instead of corrupting her, they will be saved (12:15-16).

Warning signs (13:1-27)

God gives Jeremiah some striking images of the judgment which is to come.

God tells Jeremiah to buy a linen loincloth (13:1). The prophet is to wear the loincloth without moistening it with water – so it is stiff and uncomfortable. Afterwards, he hides it in the cleft of a rock near the Euphrates (or, more likely, Perath, which is three miles from Jeremiah's home town of Anathoth). When he next goes to find it, the loincloth is ruined (13:7). God says that his people will be similarly ruined, for their stiffness and pride in failing to cling to him (13:9-11).

God gives Jeremiah a saying: 'Every winejar should be filled with wine.' God is going to treat the people of Jerusalem like large winejars and fill them to the brim. They will be thrown into chaos like a group of helpless drunkards (13:12-14).

Jeremiah again takes issue with Israel's pride. He urges them to humble themselves and turn to God's light before the darkness of doom overtakes them (13:17).

Jeremiah is given a message for the young King Jehoiachin and his mother Nehushta. They are to step down from their thrones, because

God is taking their crowns from them (13:18). They may think of fleeing to the south when the enemy invasion comes, but the towns of the Negeb ('the Dry') will be shut against them. No one will escape captivity and exile (13:19).

Jerusalem is to be overrun by the forces of Babylon, whom she had once considered as an ally (13:20-21). Now she is to be humiliated and violated – the fate of a prostitute – because of her shameless acts of Baal-worship (13:22-27).

Dry land and lying prophets (14:1-16)

Judah languishes in drought, which is a sign of God's punishment for sin (14:1; Deuteronomy 28:23-24). There is great suffering in town and country (14:3-4) and among the creatures of the wild (14:5-6).

Jeremiah grieves that God has become a stranger to his people; and yet he should be at the very centre of Judah's community (14:8-9). The people have wandered away from God and are now realizing what life is like without his blessing (14:10).

Jeremiah is forbidden to pray for the people (14:11-12). They are being deceived by the calming words of lying prophets (14:13-14). These prophets promise that there will be no judgment by sword or famine; but God assures Jeremiah that he is going to afflict them with both (14:15-16).

Jeremiah pleads with God (14:17-15:9)

Jeremiah feels God's grief for the people of Judah. He sees her like a young daughter, violently done to death (14:17). He has visions of slaughter in the countryside and famine in the city (14:18). But the cause of this physical disaster is spiritual. It is the treachery of the prophets and priests, who have failed to guide and lead the people in God's way (14:18).

Jeremiah begs God to remember his kingship and covenant with his people – and to have mercy and send rain (14:19-22). He stands before God to plead for the people, just as Moses once did (Exodus 32:11-14) and Samuel (1 Samuel 7:5). But God is adamant that his punishment is to fall in the form of plague, violent death and captivity (15:1-2).

Judah is to be destroyed by enemy swords, the bodies dragged away by dogs instead of having proper burial, the corpses picked clean by birds or torn by wild animals (15:3). This horrible fate will come because of the cruel and idolatrous deeds done in the reign of King Manasseh (2 Kings 21:10-16). Judah's fate is to be a warning to all the other nations of the world (15:4).

Jeremiah's pain and God's assurance (15:10-21)

Jeremiah wishes he had never been born. He is an innocent bystander who has been caught in the fierce clash between God and his people (15:10). He has committed himself to feed on and deliver God's word (15:16), but it gives him terrible pain. He feels betrayed – like someone who comes to a water source and finds it dry (15:18).

God promises to strengthen Jeremiah for the task of being his mouth and speaking his messages (15:19). His prophet may suffer verbal and physical attack, but God will defend and deliver him. God will make Jeremiah immensely strong – like a bronze wall (15:20-21).

A great grief (16:1-21)

God tells Jeremiah not to marry or have children. A wife and family will only swell the number of victims in the plague and carnage to come (16:1-4). Jeremiah is not to take any part in mourning the deaths of others, or in celebrating marriages (16:5-9). These expressions of community life no longer apply, because the relationship between God and his people has been severed (16:10-12). God is evicting his people from their homeland and sending them far away to exile in a foreign country (16:13).

And yet God gives a strong promise for the future. A day will come when he will bring his people back again, in an act just as great as the rescue from Egypt in the days of the exodus (16:14-15).

The bare facts (17:1-18)

Judah's sin is deeply engraved on the hearts of her people (17:1). Even the children have memories of the pagan fertility rites enacted at landmarks around the country (17:2-3). Now God's judgment is that they are to pay for these sins with their possessions and their freedom (17:3-4).

People who trust in themselves instead of God will endure a living death – like a lonely shrub in the desert (17:5-6). But those who trust in God will be like trees with their roots in streams – fresh and secure in times of drought and constantly fruitful (17:7-8).

The human heart is supremely secretive and cunning. No one can understand it, except God. He sees, he knows and he judges (17:9-10).

Wealth made unfairly is like a chick that a partridge hatches. It flies away (17:11)!

God's throne is Israel's glory and hope and spring of life. Those who reject God's reign will be listed among the dead (17:12-13).

Jeremiah asks God to heal and rescue him. He has been hurt by the scorn of those who reject his message of judgment. He longs for God's word to come true, to vindicate his prophet and punish his enemies (17:14-18).

Keep the sabbath! (17:19-27)

God tells Jeremiah to stand at the various gates of Jerusalem – the People's Gate used by the royal princes and the other gates used by travellers and traders (19:1). He is to warn everyone, as they come and go with their burdens of produce or responsibility, that they should keep the sabbath day as a day of holy rest (17:20-22).

The city gates are a focus of status, access and business. If God is honoured, then these gates will see royal processions and pilgrimages (17:24-26). If God is not honoured, and business continues on the sabbath day, then these gates will be torched and the royal palaces razed to the ground (17:27).

Potter and clay (18:1-23)

Jeremiah is told to go and see the potter at work. He watches the craftsman at his wheel, moulding a lump of clay into a pot.

As he watches, the potter changes his mind. This particular pot isn't working out and he decides to change the shape. He has every right to do so, of course. He's the potter!

The potter is a picture of God. He is skilful and caring in all his making. But, as Jeremiah realizes, God is free to change his mind.

At present a judgment hangs over Jerusalem, ready to fall. But there is time to repent. God is free to change his mind – both about his blessings and his punishments. There is nothing fatal and final about God's promises. They are opportunities to change. Remember, Jonah preached certain judgment on Nineveh – but the people listened, repented and were spared!

The image of God as a potter is often used for individual piety – to reflect on the way God can mould our lives. But for Jeremiah it is an image of God's international sovereignty in history.

Judah is to be broken like a clay jar (19:1–15)

God tells Jeremiah to buy an earthenware jug from a potter (19:1). He is to take it, with some of Judah's leaders, to the Valley of Ben Hinnom. This is a place just outside Jerusalem, which has been used for pagan worship. Its 'high place' is called Topheth, where children have been sacrificed (19:2–5). In the future it will be the city's rubbish dump, with an ever-burning fire which Jesus will use as an image of hell. The Potsherd Gate may be the place where broken pots are dumped (19:2).

Jeremiah is to pronounce God's judgment and disaster on Judah – and smash the pot to smithereens (19:3–10). Clay on the potter's wheel can be remoulded, but once it has been baked and broken it can never be mended. So God passes full and final judgment on his people for their idolatry and bloodshed (19:11).

After his dramatic action, Jeremiah makes the same announcement in the temple court (19:14–15).

Jeremiah is punished in the stocks (20:1–18)

The temple's security officer is a man named Pashhur. He punishes Jeremiah for his outburst by striking him and putting him in the stocks overnight. Stocks are a wooden trap. To be locked in them is a sign of public disgrace – and a warning to others (20:1–2).

When Jeremiah is released, he condemns Pashhur and gives him a new name: 'Terror-All-Around' (20:3 NRSV). Soon it will be Pashhur's turn to be exposed as a fraud. He will be forced to watch while his fellow citizens are killed and their possessions plundered. His predictions of peace have been utterly wrong; now he and the friends he has deceived will be dragged away into exile (20:4-6).

God will fight for Babylon against his own (21:1-14)

Chapters 21-45 contain Jeremiah's prophecies and prayers during the twenty years between King Josiah's death and the destruction of Jerusalem (609-587 BC).

Jeremiah's prophecies are fulfilled. Judah is invaded by the armies of Babylon, and the leading citizens of Jerusalem are deported. Zedekiah becomes king of the poor and pathetic people who are left. He himself is a puppet ruler, put in place by the Babylonian emperor.

Zedekiah is the last in the line of twenty-one kings who have ruled Judah since the reign of Solomon. He becomes king at the age of 21, when Nebuchadnezzar of Babylon promotes him in place of his nephew Jehoiachin. Zedekiah's name was Mattaniah at first. He is given a new name to show that he has a new master. He reigns for eleven years (597-587 BC).

Zedekiah looks for an opportunity to rebel against Babylon, but Jeremiah advises against it. Jeremiah sees the situation as God's punishment, to be patiently borne (27:5-7).

Although Zedekiah makes an agreement with Babylon, he is encouraged to revolt by the possibility of support from Egypt. His rebellion provokes a massive offensive from Babylon, whose armies lay siege to Jerusalem in 587 BC and capture it in July the following year.

God judges the kings of Judah (22:1-30)

God tells Jeremiah to go to the royal palace. He is to preach to the king, Zedekiah, who sits on the throne as a successor of King David (22:1-2).

Jeremiah must challenge the king to rule by God's standards of justice and compassion (22:3). If he does so, his royal line will continue in peace and prosperity. If not, then the palace will be destroyed and become deserted (22:4-9).

God says of another king, Shallum, that he has been exiled and will never return (22:10-12). Shallum is Jehoahaz, who became king after his father Josiah was killed in battle at Megiddo. Jehoahaz had mourned for his father, but really he should be mourning for himself (22:10); he will never see his homeland again (22:12).

God condemns someone who has built a large and luxurious palace, but only by oppressing and exploiting the poor (22:13-17). This is king Jehoiakim, the brother who succeeded Shallum. A godly king is not to be known by the fine cedar panelling of his house, but by his concern for the poor (22:15-16). Jehoiakim will die and his corpse be thrown out like a dead donkey (22:18-19).

God's judgment is to be announced all over the country – in Lebanon to the west, in Bashan to the north-east and Abarim to the east (22:20). The people have had their chance to repent (22:21). Now the wind of judgment will round up and sweep away the shepherds (leaders) and those who have been immoral will be taken captive and exiled (22:22).

God says of King Coniah that he would discard him, even if he were 'the signet ring on his right hand'. A royal signet ring is a symbol of authority, as well as being a treasured and intimate possession (22:24-27). Coniah is King Jehoiachin, who succeeded his father Jehoiakim. He reigned for just three months before being taken away to Babylon. God declares that Jehoiachin will become a dead end, exiled and childless (22:30).

The shepherd king (23:1-8)

The leaders of God's people are often called 'shepherds'. They have the responsibility to guide, feed and protect the nation in their care.

But King Zedekiah and his officers are failing in their trust. They are destroying and scattering God's flock. Now God himself will take action to gather his people, provide for them and increase their number. He will appoint shepherds who will give them peace and security.

God promises that one day he will give his people a king like David. This will be the Messiah, who will be a branch of David's royal line. Unlike most of Judah's kings, he will be wise and righteous. Through him, God's people will share his righteousness – and be saved.

The lying prophets of Judah (23:9–40)

There are other prophets at work besides Jeremiah, but not all of them have a genuine word from the Lord. Many of the prophets and priests are corrupt and compromised. They defile the temple with their vice. They pretend to be holy, but in fact they commit adultery and condone evil.

The false prophets make up messages from their own imagination. They promise the people God's peace and safety – but their message is not from God. They claim to have meaningful dreams, steal each other's insights and even begin their sayings with 'the Lord declares'. But their words are empty, misguided and useless.

The tragedy is that if they had only listened to God ('stood in my council') they would have had life-giving, life-saving words for his people. The nation is sick and heading for destruction because the prophets have failed in their task.

Good and bad figs – exiles and survivors (24:1–10)

God shows Jeremiah two baskets of figs. The figs in one basket are good, but in the other they are bad (24:1–3). God declares that the people who have gone into exile are like good figs. These are King Jehoiachin (Jeconiah) and Judah's leaders (24:1). God will bless them and bring them home (24:4–7). The bad figs are King Zedekiah and the people left in Jerusalem (24:8). God is going to inflict on them further punishment (24:9–10).

Jeremiah might assume that the 'bad figs' are those who have been exiled and the 'good figs' are those who have survived in Jerusalem. In fact it is the other way round.

Jeremiah predicts seventy years of captivity (25:1–14)

Jeremiah has preached to the people of Judah and Jerusalem for twenty-three years, and they haven't listened (25:1–7). Now Nebuchadnezzar has become king of Babylon (25:1), and he will be God's servant in judging and destroying them (25:8–10). The land will lie waste and its people languish in exile for seventy years (25:11–14).

God's judgment on all nations (25:15-38)

Jeremiah is to deliver God's judgment to all peoples – like a cup of wine seething with God's anger (25:15-17). Jerusalem is to drink first, then the rest of Judah (25:18). After them, God's judgment will fall on all the nations of the region and beyond – the Egyptians, the Philistines, the Arabians... Last of all 'Sheshach' is to be judged. Sheshach is a coded word for 'Babel' – that is, Babylon (25:26).

God is like a lion attacking a fold of sheep (25:30, 38); but the sheep are his own people – all the nations of the earth (25:31). There is to be a great judgment and destruction (25:31-33). The shepherds (leaders) will be thrown into confusion (25:34-36) and the fields and folds destroyed (25:36-37).

Episodes in Jeremiah's life

These events are not in the order in which they happen!

Jeremiah's life is threatened (26:1-24)

It is 609 BC – the beginning of King Jehoiakim's reign (26:1). God tells Jeremiah to preach in the temple court. By preaching to the people who have come there to worship, he is in a way addressing the whole of Judah (26:2).

Jeremiah tells the people that there is still time to turn to God and be spared the coming disaster. If they don't repent, the temple itself will be destroyed and become like the ruined shrine at Shiloh (26:3-6).

When Jeremiah has finished speaking, a crowd gathers round him. They are led by the priests and rival prophets – and they demand Jeremiah's death (26:7-9). Some royal officials arrive to hear what has happened (26:10-11) and Jeremiah repeats his message to them (26:12-15). The officials believe that Jeremiah is a true prophet (26:16). Some elders recall that Micah delivered a similar message in his day (26:17-18).

Micah had prophesied that Jerusalem would be destroyed, but his king, Hezekiah, had repented and the city had been spared. Another prophet, Uriah, had preached a message of God's judgment in the days of

King Jehoiakim. Uriah fled to Egypt, but was brought back and executed (26:22-23).

Jeremiah's trial ends, and he leaves under the protection of Ahikam. Ahikam's father, Shaphan, may be the court secretary we encounter later (36:10); his son is Gedaliah – the person Nebuchadnezzar will appoint as governor of Judah after the destruction of Jerusalem (39:14).

Jeremiah wears a yoke (27:1-22)

The year is 594 BC – the beginning of King Zedekiah's reign (27:1). Judah has been defeated by the Babylonians. Her king and national leaders have been deported. However, there are strong hopes that Judah will be able to rebel – perhaps in alliance with Egypt – and throw off the Babylonian oppressors.

God tells Jeremiah to make a yoke – a heavy wooden collar used for controlling oxen. The prophet is to wear the yoke across his own shoulders (27:2). Then he is to send a message back with the foreign envoys who have been to Jerusalem to plot a rebellion against Babylon (27:3).

Jeremiah's message is that the Babylonian rule has been brought about by God. It will continue for three generations (27:4-7). Those who submit to this yoke will be spared; those who throw it off will be punished by God with death, hunger and disease (27:8-11).

Jeremiah gives the same message to King Zedekiah, and to the priests (27:12-16). But the king and priests listen to false prophets and clairvoyants, who say that all will be well (27:9, 14). They say that the great bronze pieces in the temple – the pillars and the 'sea' (the great basin for washing) – will remain in Jerusalem (27:16-22). But it is all wishful thinking. They will be carried off as plunder to Babylon (27:22).

Jeremiah confronts a false prophet (28:1-17)

A rival prophet called Hananiah confronts Jeremiah in public debate (28:1). He tells Jeremiah that God is going to break the yoke of Babylon, and return King Jehoiachin (Jeconiah) and the other exiles to Jerusalem (28:2-4).

Jeremiah welcomes Hananiah's prophecy – if it is true. But the only way to know if a prophecy is true is to wait and see if it is fulfilled (28:5-9)! Hananiah is so angry at this sarcasm that he seizes the yoke from Jeremiah's neck and breaks it (28:10). This, he says, is God's sign that the yoke of Babylon will be broken within two years (28:11).

Later, Jeremiah visits Hananiah (28:12). He tells him that his prediction of a successful rebellion is not from God. Hananiah is guilty of preaching a lie (28:13-15). Jeremiah declares God's judgment on Hananiah; within two months, the false prophet is dead (28:16-17).

Jeremiah writes to the exiles (29:1-14)

Jeremiah sends a letter to the exiles in Babylonia (29:1-3). Instead of assuring them that their captivity will be short, he advises them to settle down. They are to build houses and plant gardens and make a life for themselves (29:4-6). They are also to work hard and pray for the city where they are exiled (29:7). They are not to believe the vain hopes of false prophets and clairvoyants (29:8-9).

Jeremiah is blunt. God is telling him that the period of exile in Babylon will be seventy years (29:10). But God will not forget them and has wonderful plans for their future (29:11). This future will begin when they turn to God with their whole heart (29:12-13). When they finally do this, God will not hide from them (29:13-14). He will gather them from all the places where they are scattered – and bring them home (29:14).

Facing off false prophets (29:15-32)

In Babylon there are false prophets who are preaching that Babylon will be destroyed (29:16-19). Jeremiah condemns them. Their message is not from God (29:19) and their behaviour is disgraceful (29:21-23). God will cause two of these false prophets – Ahab and Zedekiah – to be executed by Nebuchadnezzar (29:21).

Jeremiah also has to deal with a troublemaker called Shemaiah (29:24). Shemaiah has written to the priests in Jerusalem, telling them to suppress the prophets (29:24-26). Shemaiah names Jeremiah in particular, because he has advised the exiles to accept their punishment and make their lives in Babylon (29:27-28).

Jeremiah pronounces God's judgment on Shemaiah. None of his descendants will live to see the exiles return home (29:29-32).

God promises a new covenant (30:1-31:40)

Jeremiah has a dream. God will bring both Israel and Judah back from captivity and restore them to their land! God promises his people will return home, and he will make a new covenant with them. This covenant will be written on their hearts.

There is a tough time ahead, as this deliverance is brought to birth. Babylon's yoke will be broken. God's people will be released. They will once again be ruled by a king like David.

Meanwhile, there is punishment to be endured. Sin can't simply be brushed aside. God's people are guilty, hurting and apparently abandoned by God. But here and now he promises to heal and restore them. He makes a simple, total commitment:

So you will be my people,
and I will be your God. (30:22)

The return from Babylon is going to be like a new exodus. The survivors will, like the Hebrew slaves, 'find favour in the desert' (31:2). Israel will be newly married to God, with great rejoicing. Vineyards will be planted in Samaria – the country that was laid waste over a century earlier. And those who guard Ephraim (Israel) will call people to make pilgrimage to Zion (the heavenly Jerusalem).

All the lost people of Israel will converge on Jerusalem as God brings them home. No one will be left behind because they are useless or weak. Just as they went into exile weeping with despair, now they will return with tears of joy (31:9).

God will take the utmost care of them on the way – treating long-lost Ephraim as his first-born son. Young and old, men and women, priests and people – all will enjoy the freshness, gladness and plenty of Zion (31:12-14).

There has been great grief at the loss of the northern tribes. Ephraim and Manasseh (the two half-tribes descended from Joseph) were lost in defeat and exile. Jeremiah thinks of Rachel, the mother of Joseph and Benjamin, weeping for her children. But now she can dry her tears. They will return. Ephraim, 'the unruly calf', is turning back to God.

Jeremiah wakes from his sleep refreshed. Here at last is a time to build and plant. There will be no more laying the blame for suffering on the sins of a previous generation. Everyone will be equally blessed by God's grace, and equally responsible for their behaviour (31:29–30).

God will make a new covenant with his people. It won't be a covenant like the one on Mount Sinai – defined by laws written on stone. It will be a covenant given and sustained by God's grace and written on human hearts.

In this new covenant, everyone will know the Lord for themselves and *want* to keep his law. The past is forgiven. This is a new start. A fine, enlarged Jerusalem will be built – a glimpse of the glorious Jerusalem that is to come. This is a God-centred community that will never fall again.

Jeremiah buys a field (32:1–44)

The year is 587 BC. Jerusalem is besieged by the armies of Nebuchadnezzar and Jeremiah himself is in prison. But he is dreaming that the Jews will return from exile and that their land will be restored.

God tells Jeremiah to expect a visit from his cousin Hanamel. Hanamel wants to sell a field, which by law must be bought by his next of kin (Leviticus 25:25). Jeremiah is that person.

It's an extraordinary situation. Jeremiah is being asked to buy a field which will be immediately seized by Babylonian invaders. Any day now, the Jews will cease to own any property. Their legal deeds and agreements will be worthless…

But Jeremiah agrees! He counts out the money, puts the documents in a clay jar (for long-term storage) and explains his crazy action. He has bought the field because God has told him to do so. It's a sign of his promise that the Jews will return from exile at some time in the future – and resume their everyday life with houses, fields and vineyards (33:15). His purchase is a sign of hope for when the exile is over.

'Now' and 'then'

Is Jeremiah speaking of the return from exile in Babylon, or the gathering of all peoples into Christ's kingly rule? We have to say 'both'.

There was a return to Judah by exiles from Babylon in 538 BC. But it didn't include the exiles of the northern kingdom of Israel ('Ephraim') and it wasn't crowned with the rule of a king like David.

But the return of the exiles was a miracle of God's power to rescue and forgive. It is a glimpse of the great gathering of both Jews and Gentiles on the Last Day. The new covenant is for the whole world. It is sealed in the blood of Christ, who will return in glory to be God's Messiah – the king who is greater than David.

Jeremiah prays. Is Jerusalem going to be spared after all? Is this land deal a sign that normal life will be restored quite soon? Nothing is too hard for God (32:17). But it isn't to be. Judah is being punished for her immorality and idolatry – and God is on the side of the Babylonians.

But then comes the good news. After the calamity, God will give prosperity. There will once again be buying of fields and signing of deeds all over the country. And Jeremiah has acted on God's word as though it's already done.

God promises that Israel and Judah will be restored (33:1–26)

While Jeremiah is still in detention, he receives a wonderful promise for the future (33:1–3). The houses of Jerusalem and the palaces of her king, so brutally destroyed by the Chaldeans (Babylonians), are to be restored (33:4–6). God will give healing and forgiveness, prosperity and joy to Jerusalem – for all the nations of the world to see (33:7–9).

Normal life will be resumed in the towns of Judah: weddings and harvests will be celebrated (33:10–11) and shepherds will tend their flocks (33:12–13).

God promises that one day he will unite the kingdoms of Israel and Judah under one king. This king will be a strong and healthy branch from David's family tree. Like David, his reign will be just and righteous; and his people will be secure (33:14-16).

There will always be a king descended from David and there will always be a high priest from the Levites to offer sacrifices (33:17-18). God is doing this to honour his covenant promises to David and the Levites – a bond he can never break (33:19-26).

Jeremiah tells King Zedekiah his fate (34:1-7)

The Babylonian armies are laying waste the towns of Judah and Jerusalem's destruction seems certain (34:1, 6-7). Jeremiah goes to King Zedekiah to tell him what will happen. Jerusalem will be burned to the ground, but Zedekiah himself will be spared and taken to Babylon (34:2-3).

Jewish slaves should be set free (34:8-22)

Some of the people of Judah have become slaves – through misfortune or debt. But if the nation is conquered by the Babylonians, the entire population will become slaves. King Zedekiah thinks to win God's favour by declaring that Hebrew slaves (those of Judean race) shall be set free (34:8-10). However, the crisis passes and the reform doesn't last (34:11).

God reminds Jeremiah of the old law of Moses: that every seventh year all slaves shall be freed (Deuteronomy 15:12-18). This is because the Israelites had themselves been rescued from slavery in Egypt (34:12-14). Now, if they do not release their brothers and sisters from slavery, God will release punishment on them (34:15-17).

Those who split from their covenant with God will be split themselves – cut in half like a sacrifice (34:18-20). When the Babylonians execute God's judgment (34:21-22), the king and his officials will be severed from their city (34:21-22) and the land will be parted from its inhabitants (34:22).

The Recabites – an example of obedience (35:1-19)

It is, perhaps, 598 BC – towards the end of King Jehoiakim's reign. Babylonian raiding parties are active in Judah. Among those taking refuge in Jerusalem is a group of nomads called Recabites.

God sends Jeremiah to meet the Recabites and invite them to the temple to drink wine (35:1-5). The Recabites tell Jeremiah that their ancestor forbade them to drink wine, or build houses, or plant crops. Instead, they live very simply in tents (35:6-10). They have only come to live in Jerusalem because of their fear of the Babylonian armies (35:11).

Jeremiah is greatly impressed by the obedience of the Recabites. God tells him to use them as an example of faithful, upright living. Why can't the people of Judah obey the commands of God in such a straightforward way (35:12-19)?

King Jehoiakim burns Jeremiah's scroll (36:1-32)

It is 605 BC. God tells Jeremiah to write down all his messages on a scroll (36:1-2). For this great work, Jeremiah enlists the help of a scribe called Baruch (36:4).

Jeremiah is banned from the temple at this time, so he asks Baruch to go there and read out his prophecies (36:5-6). Jeremiah never ceases to hope that people may hear God's word and repent (36:7-8).

In December 604 BC, the Babylonians are advancing through the towns of Philistia. They capture and destroy Ashkelon. Perhaps because of this, the inhabitants of Judah and Jerusalem hold a fast – a day without food, for mourning and prayer (36:9). It is on this occasion that Baruch gives a public reading of Jeremiah's prophecies in one of the rooms of the temple (36:10).

Soon Baruch is asked to read the prophecies to the royal officials (36:11-16). They are shaken by what they hear and advise Baruch to take Jeremiah into hiding (36:16-19). Then one of the royal officials, Jehudi, reads the prophecies to King Jehoiakim (36:20-21).

It is winter, and the king is sitting beside a fire burning in an iron brazier. As Jehudi reads out God's word from Jeremiah, the king slices the scroll with his penknife and throws the paragraphs into the flames (36:22-23). The warnings of judgment don't alarm the king at all – except that he orders Jeremiah and Baruch to be arrested (36:24-26).

God tells Jeremiah to write out all the prophecies again on a new scroll (36:27-28, 32). God gives him further messages, including predictions about King Jehoiakim. Jehoiakim's sons will not succeed him on David's throne; and when he dies his corpse will lie unburied (36:30).

Baruch – faithful secretary

Baruch is the brother of Seraiah, the quartermaster to King Zedekiah. He becomes a faithful secretary to Jeremiah, writing down the prophet's messages at his dictation (36:4) and courageously reading them in public (36:8).

Baruch stays with Jeremiah and shares his fate when Jerusalem is destroyed. He is accused of influencing Jeremiah in favour of the Babylonians, and taken with Jeremiah and other survivors down to Egypt (43:3, 6).

Baruch is only the scribe who writes down Jeremiah's messages. But there are short links of narrative in the book of Jeremiah which may well be his work.

Jeremiah is put in prison (37:1–21)

The scene changes and the story moves to a later time. The Babylonians have been laying siege to Jerusalem, but have left to deal with a challenge from the Egyptian army. The people of Jerusalem had been hoping that the Egyptians would come to their rescue (37:5).

There has been a change of king. Jehoiakim is in exile, and in 597 BC Zedekiah is appointed as puppet king by Nebuchadnezzar of Babylon.

King Zedekiah asks Jeremiah to pray to God and find out what is going to happen (37:3). Jeremiah predicts that the Egyptians will return home and the Chaldeans (Babylonians) will complete the siege and destruction of Jerusalem (37:6–10).

During the lull in the siege, Jeremiah tries to leave Jerusalem on business. He is accused of trying to go over to the Babylonians. For punishment, he is imprisoned in the cistern of the house of the secretary of state (37:11–16). It is dark and airless.

King Zedekiah sends for Jeremiah and asks him privately about his messages. Jeremiah has no good news for him – only that God will give him over to the king of Babylon (37:17). But Jeremiah asks for better prison conditions and is transferred to the court of the guard. There he is given a regular allowance of bread, right through the siege of Jerusalem (37:20–21).

Jeremiah is lowered into a muddy cistern (38:1-13)

Jeremiah continues to make predictions which sound disloyal and defeatist. He advises people to surrender to the Babylonians, and says that the fall of Jerusalem is certain (38:1-3). Jeremiah's enemies complain to the king, who gives them permission to ill-treat him (38:4-5).

Jeremiah is lowered into a cistern, where he sinks in the mud and is left to starve (38:6). Fortunately he has a friend – an Ethiopian eunuch – who tells the king what has happened and is allowed to haul him out (38:7-13).

Jeremiah advises the king to surrender (38:14-28)

King Zedekiah again seeks Jeremiah's advice. This time he promises to take notice of his words and protect him (38:14-16). Jeremiah tells the king that the only way out is to surrender to Babylon (38:17-20). If he doesn't, he will find himself well and truly stuck – and Jeremiah knows how that feels (38:21-22)!

The king insists that their conversation must remain a secret (38:23-28).

Nebuchadnezzar captures Jerusalem (39:1-18)

In July 587 BC, after a siege lasting a year and a half, the Babylonians breach the walls of Jerusalem (39:1-2). They capture the city and set up a ruling council in a gatehouse (38:3). Meanwhile, King Zedekiah and his officials escape by night through the Fountain Gate. They flee towards the Arabah – the Jordan Valley to the north of the Dead Sea (39:4).

The king and his staff are pursued and caught. They are brought before Nebuchadnezzar in his camp at Riblah (39:5). Nebuchadnezzar forces Zedekiah to watch his sons being slaughtered, and then has him blinded and deported to Babylon (39:6-7). The other nobles are also killed and Jerusalem is sacked and burned (39:8).

When all is done, only the poorest people are left living in the ruins. The Babylonian captain allows them some fields and vineyards (39:9-10). Nebuchadnezzar gives special instructions that Jeremiah is to be well treated (39:11-12). He is placed in the care of Gedaliah, who will become the governor of the survivors (39:14).

Jeremiah's message of reassurance to Ebed-Melech is recorded. Ebed-Melech is the Ethiopian friend who rescued Jeremiah from the boggy cistern (39:15-18).

Jeremiah is rescued and given his freedom (40:1-6)

By some mistake, Jeremiah is shackled and is being led away with the other prisoners (40:1). The Babylonian captain releases him and gives him complete freedom to go or stay. He also gives him food and a present (40:2-5). This treatment by an enemy is an extraordinary contrast to Jeremiah's treatment by his own people.

Jeremiah settles with governor Gedaliah (40:7-16)

Jeremiah goes to join Gedaliah at Mizpah, a few miles from Jerusalem (40:6). Gedaliah has been made governor of the 'remnant' – those who remain in the land after most of the population has been deported.

Gedaliah's policy is to accept the defeat and cooperate with the Babylonians (40:7-9). A number of survivors gather to him and they start to cultivate and harvest the land (40:11-12).

Gedaliah is warned that there is an Ammonite plan to assassinate him, but he doesn't believe it (40:13-16). The Ammonites may be wanting to move into the land left vacant by the departed exiles.

Gedaliah is assassinated by Ishmael (41:1-18)

In October (perhaps of 586 BC) a group of men arrives at Mizpah (41:1). They are led by Ishmael – the assassin about whom Gedaliah has been warned (40:14). As Gedaliah shares a welcoming meal with them, he and his companions are slaughtered (41:2-3).

The following day, some pilgrims arrive from the north. From their shaved heads and self-inflicted wounds, they are in mourning for the temple that has been destroyed (41:4-5). Ishmael massacres them too (41:6-7).

Ishmael rounds up the survivors and prepares to return to the Ammonites (41:10). He is intercepted and defeated by Johanan (41:11-15), who decides to take the group to seek safety in Egypt (41:16-18).

Jeremiah warns the survivors about Egypt (42:1-22)

The group of survivors from the destruction of Jerusalem has gathered near Bethlehem (41:17). Their leader, Johanan, intends to take refuge from the Babylonians in Egypt. But first they ask Jeremiah for a word from God (42:1-3). They promise to do whatever God says (42:4-6).

After ten days, Jeremiah answers their enquiry. God says that they should stay in their own land, where he will keep them safe and restore them. There is nothing to be afraid of from the Babylonians (42:7-12). But if the survivors are determined to go to Egypt, then the very things they dread – starvation, disease and violent death – will follow them there (42:13-22). As always, God wants his people to trust him, rather than using force, deceit or political alliances.

The survivors ignore Jeremiah's advice (43:1-7)

Despite their promise to do whatever God tells them, the survivors reject Jeremiah's advice (43:1-2). They accuse Jeremiah's secretary, Baruch, of trying to hand them over to the Babylonians (43:3). Insolent and obstinate, they make their way south to Egypt (43:2, 4, 7). Jeremiah and Baruch go with them. Either they want to share the people's troubles, or they are forced to go.

Jeremiah prophesies that Nebuchadnezzar will conquer Egypt (43:8-13)

The group of survivors arrives at Tahpanhes in Egypt, on the eastern boundary of the Nile Delta.

God tells Jeremiah to bury some large stones at the entrance to the Pharaoh's palace. Jeremiah predicts that Nebuchadnezzar will conquer Egypt and build his palace on this very spot (43:8-10). The king of Babylon will also destroy the temples of the Egyptian gods (43:12-13).

The Jewish refugees commit idolatry (44:1-30)

The survivors from the fall of Jerusalem continue their idol-worship in Egypt (44:8). They worship the Queen of Heaven, baking cakes for her and pouring out drink offerings (44:19).

Jeremiah warns this last remaining group from Judah that God will wipe them out entirely (44:11–14). The people refuse to listen to Jeremiah (44:15–16) and continue to revive their old acts of idolatry (44:17).

God's promise of safety to Baruch (45:1–25)

As Baruch writes down Jeremiah's prophecies (45:1), the prophet adds one which is just for him (45:2). God knows that Baruch has suffered sorrow and pain through being caught up in the persecution of his master (45:3). Perhaps he hoped at one time to find himself on the winning side and to become famous; but now all seems lost (45:5).

God confides to Baruch that there will be further destruction yet, because the work of judgment is still going on. But he promises that, whatever happens, he will always keep Baruch safe (45:5).

Prophecies against the nations

These messages have no particular date. They have been collected together for the finished book of Jeremiah. In the Septuagint (the Greek version of the Hebrew Bible), they are placed in chapter 25.

Jeremiah prophesies to the nations which surround Judah. His messages address Egypt (46:1–28), Philistia (47:1–7), Moab (48:1–47), Ammon (49:1–6), Edom (49:7–22), Damascus (49:23–27), Kedar and Hazor (49:28–33), Elam (49:34–39) and Babylon (50:1–51:64).

The God of Israel and Judah is the true God of all the nations. He is at work in their circumstances and histories, and he will punish them for their sins.

The longest prophecy concerns Babylon. God has used Babylon to bring his judgment on Judah, but now Babylon herself will be judged. God is going to bring nations from the north – the Medes and the Persians – to attack her (50:9; 51:11). Everyone who sees her destruction will be appalled (50:13).

Jeremiah tells Seraiah, the chief priest (and Baruch's brother), to read out the prophecies against Babylon when he arrives there with the exiles (51:59–60). After he has read them, Seraiah is to tie the scroll to a stone and fling it into the middle of the River Euphrates – the lifeline of Babylonia (51:63). The sinking stone will be a sign that Babylon will sink into oblivion, when God judges her for her wickedness (51:64).

The fall of Jerusalem

The book of Jeremiah ends with a detailed account of Jerusalem's fall (52:1–27). The story has already been told in chapter 39, but it all goes to prove that Jeremiah has been a true prophet.

The numbers of people taken into exile are recorded (52:28–30), with the years counted in Babylonian time. The seventh year is 598–597 BC, the eighteenth year may be 587–586 BC and the twenty-third year 582–581 BC. Where the numbers don't agree with those elsewhere (2 Kings 24:14), it is possible that this record only counts the men, and not their wives and children.

A king, Jehoiachin, survives in Babylon (52:31–34)

Nebuchadnezzar is succeeded as king of Babylon by King Evil-Merodach. The new king treats Jehoiachin kindly, releases him from prison and invites him to dine at his table (52:31–32).

After the terrors and traumas of conquest and deportation, there is a glimpse of a new start, a new relationship and a definite future for the royal line of King David (53:34).

LAMENTATIONS

Lamentations are grief-stricken poems. They are the laments or dirges with which the Jews mourn the terrible destruction of Jerusalem by the Babylonian armies in 587 BC.

God has used his people's enemies to punish them for their sins. Even so, the poems cry out to God for mercy and dare to believe that he will restore them to their land again one day.

Outline

The first poem (1:1-22)
The second poem (2:1-22)
The third poem (3:1-66)
The fourth poem (4:1-22)
The fifth poem (5:1-22)

Introduction

The worst has happened. Jerusalem is in ruins. God's chosen people, the Jews, have lost their city and their land. Now they may also lose their nation and their faith.

The Lamentations are funeral songs for the way of life and the people that have been lost. The songs accept that this disaster is God's punishment, and they look to him as their only help and hope.

The Lamentations give a vivid picture of a desperate situation. All the people of Jerusalem and surrounding Judea have been killed, captured or ruined. Solomon's temple has been torn down. The city's great buildings and fine houses have been reduced to rubble.

The poems admit that this destruction is well-deserved and long overdue. God has punished his people for their sins, by letting their enemies conquer them. But God is also merciful. His people dare to hope and pray that he will accept their repentance and restore them.

A day of grief

The Jews remember the destruction of the temple on 9th Ab – that is, in mid-July. On this day, the 'Lamentations' are read aloud to the east of the temple site.

The temple was destroyed twice in its history. The temple built by Solomon was destroyed by the Babylonians in 587 BC. The temple built by Herod the Great was destroyed by the Romans in AD 70.

Patterns with letters

There are five poems in Lamentations. The first four are cleverly shaped. Each sentence of the first four poems begins with one of the twenty-two letters of the Hebrew alphabet.

The other poem also makes patterns with the letters, and there is much play on the sounds of words.

Who wrote Lamentations?

We don't know for sure who wrote these poems. The Jewish teachers simply call them 'Wailings'. The Vulgate (Latin) version of the Bible calls them 'Lamentations' and says that they are written by the prophet Jeremiah.

Jeremiah had a long and painful career predicting that Jerusalem would suffer God's judgment. He was ridiculed and ill-treated for his prophecies – the king himself shredded and burned his writings. When Jerusalem fell, Jeremiah was caught up in the disaster and migrated to Egypt with a group of survivors.

It is very likely that Jeremiah wrote the Lamentations. If not, then they are the work of someone who sees the destruction of Jerusalem in the same way as he did.

The fall of Jerusalem

The story of the fall of Jerusalem is told in 2 Kings 25.

The king of Babylon, Nebuchadnezzar, lays siege to Jerusalem for two years. At the end of that time, with no food left in the city, the Jewish king Zedekiah and his army try to break out.

The effort is useless. The armies of Judah are overtaken and destroyed by the fast and furious forces of Babylon. Zedekiah is captured, forced to watch his sons killed and then blinded. He is taken to Babylon as a prisoner in chains.

Is this the end of 'the house of David' – the line of kings, descended from David, which God said would last for ever? The author believes that God has not forgotten his covenant promise.

All the leading citizens of Jerusalem are deported. Only the very poor people are left to live in the ruins and look after the land. The Babylonians put a governor in charge, but he is killed by rebels. A group of survivors, including the prophet Jeremiah, goes south to Egypt to find protection and a better life. Jeremiah doesn't approve of this move, but goes with the people to care for them.

Is this the end of the Jews – God's own people? Are God's promises withdrawn and the covenant cancelled? The author believes God still loves them and is with them, even though he is angry. It is his nature to forgive.

Because of the Lord's great love we are not consumed,
  for his compassions never fail.
They are new every morning;
  great is your faithfulness. (3:22–23)

The last poem ends with a prayer:

Restore us to yourself, Lord, that we may return;
  renew our days as of old
unless you have utterly rejected us
  and are angry with us beyond measure. (5:21–22)

The third poem expresses firm faith and a sure hope. The best approach is to wait patiently for God to rescue them:

The Lord is good to those whose hope is in him,
  to the one who seeks him;
it is good to wait quietly
  for the salvation of the Lord. (3:25–26)

Discovering Lamentations

The first poem

Jerusalem is like a desolate widow (1:1–7)

The first poem (1:1–22) begins with an agonizing howl of grief: '*How!?*' How terrible is this tragedy of God's city and temple in ruins! And how has such a dreadful thing happened?

Jerusalem was loved by God and had many children; but now she is a widow (1:1). She was a princess; but now she is a slave (1:1). She had many lovers – nations with whom she could form alliances; now she is alone and her friends have betrayed her (1:2). Her roads used to be thronged with pilgrims, her priests singing and the young girls dancing; now the roads are deserted, the priests groan and the young girls weep (1:4). The princes, which were her pride, are now like starving stags being hunted down (1:6). All she has are her memories – which are of shame and helplessness and loss (1:7).

Jerusalem is being punished for her sin (1:8–11)

Jerusalem's idolatry has been exposed like sexual sin (1:8–9). She feels violated by the pagan soldiers who have trampled her sanctuary (the temple), and touched the sacred vessels with their unholy hands (1:10). She feels degraded and worthless – her once-proud people scratching around for food like beggars (1:11).

Jerusalem cries out for sympathy (1:12–22)

Jerusalem acknowledges that she deserves God's punishment (1:18); but will no one have pity on her (1:12)? God has seared her with the fire of his judgment, tangled and turned her in her efforts to escape, and left her prostrate and stunned (1:13). She feels guilty, rejected and totally alone (1:16–17). She also wants her enemies to become as desolate as she is (1:20–22).

The second poem

The Lord is against his people (2:1–9)

God has vented his anger on Jerusalem. Never mind that she was his daughter, his footstool (2:1); God's rage has obliterated all such niceties. He has ruthlessly demolished the kingdom, its strongholds and rulers (2:2). He has withdrawn his protection when her enemies attacked (2:3) and has himself taken part in the assault (2:4–5). The temple and the royal palaces lie in ruins (2:7); the ramparts and gates are destroyed (2:7); the royal princes are in exile and the prophets are silenced (2:8–9).

The agonies of famine (2:10–13)

The writer looks around. What he sees makes him weep until he has no more tears. His stomach writhes and he can't control his bowels (2:11). The scene is one of abject poverty, famine and despair. The plight of the mothers with their little children is pitiful (2:12).

True and false prophets (2:14–17)

The writer notes how dreadfully the false prophets have failed the people. By preaching that all was well, they have prevented any chance of repentance (2:14).

Prayer and tears (2:18–22)

The writer urges Jerusalem (the wall that surrounds her) to weep out all her grief (2:18) and to pray for the starving children (2:19).

The poem becomes a prayer, arguing with God. It's not right that mothers should be driven to eat their children; that priests and prophets should be slaughtered in the temple (2:20); that every kind of person lies dead in the streets – old and young, men and women (2:21). It seems that God has invited all Jerusalem's enemies round for a party – to destroy all that she holds dear (2:22).

The third poem

A lament of desolation... (3:1-21)

The writer records his own suffering. He feels as if God has beaten him day and night, plunged him into darkness and chained him in prison (3:1-9). He has been subjected to every kind of attack – ambush, abduction, isolation and target-practice (3:10-12). He has been pierced, scorned, and saturated with envy and self-pity (3:13-15). He is crushed and humiliated; all vestiges of peace, happiness, dignity and hope have vanished (3:16-18). He can think of nothing but his own loneliness and anguish (3:19-20). And yet there is one thing of which he is certain...

... and a song of assurance (3:22–42)

The writer is certain of God. God's mercies are as sure as the sunrise (3:22-23). The Lord is all he has – and all he will ever need (3:24). He finds it good to wait for God – to accept his punishment and expect his forgiveness (3:22-30). God's punishment is a sign of his care (3:33): what else can he do when tyranny and injustice are rife (3:34-36)? Are we to protest because God punishes our wickedness (3:39)? It is time to turn to God – to beg his forgiveness (3:40-42).

Rejected by God and people (3:43–54)

The writer addresses God. God has been merciless (3:43) and remote (3:44). He has made his people the scum of the earth (3:45). They have fallen foul of insults, anxiety and traps (3:46-47). The writer's eyes gush tears when he thinks of what has befallen the young women (3:48-51). He himself has been subject to such ill-treatment that he thought he must be dying (3:52-54).

A prayer for revenge (3:55–66)

Very wonderfully, when the writer cried to God from the deepest place of despair, the Lord answered (3:55-57). Now he asks God to take revenge on the enemies who have plotted against him and taunted him (3:58-66).

The fourth poem

From riches to rags (4:1-10)

A great change has taken place in Jerusalem. The gold of the temple is tarnished and her sacred stones – once so reverently cut and built together – are littered around the streets (4:1). The unique and priceless inhabitants of Jerusalem (Zion's children) are as worthless as clay pots (4:2). An unnatural cruelty has seized people, so that they no longer care for their children (4:3-4). People who were once prosperous, stylish, healthy and handsome are now destitute and shrivelled (4:5-8).

It would have been better to have been killed outright than to endure this lingering death by starvation (4:9). Once-loving mothers have cooked and eaten their own children (4:10).

An unbelievable defeat (4:11-20)

The rulers of the nations look in disbelief at the destruction of Jerusalem. They can't believe that God has allowed it to happen (4:11-12). The writer lays the blame on Jerusalem's false prophets and corrupt priests (4:13). They walked through the streets in clothes soaked with the blood of innocent people (4:14). Now they have been expelled and are treated like lepers (4:15-17).

Judah waited in vain for Egypt to come to her rescue (4:17). Now everyone is watched and controlled by the Babylonians (4:18). When the time came for flight, the Judeans were easily overtaken and captured (4:19). The king himself was surrounded and seized – the one who personified God's presence and rule (4:20).

God will punish Edom too (4:21-22)

The neighbouring nation of Edom may rejoice for a while – having withheld support from Judah and been awarded land by Babylon; but her turn for judgment will come (4:21). Her shame will be exposed for all to see (4:22).

The fifth poem

A pitiful state (5:1-18)

God's people are reduced to a pitiful state. They have lost their homes, lands and loved ones (5:2-3). They must buy or bargain for the bare necessities of life: bread, water and firewood (5:4, 6). Danger, discomfort, abuse and torture are their daily experience (5:9-13). There is no pleasure of conversation or music or dancing (5:14-15). They have lost their authority and security because of sin; their hearts, like Mount Zion, are deserted and full of fear (5:16-18).

'Restore us to yourself, O Lord' (5:19-22)

The laments end with a heartfelt cry to God: 'Restore us to yourself, O Lord, that we may be restored' (5:21). Even if God has finally abandoned his people and his covenant, the writer has no doubt that he is still the only God – and therefore the only hope of forgiveness and new life (5:19).

EZEKIEL

Ezekiel is a prophet who shares the early years of exile with God's people in Babylon.

Ezekiel has amazing visions. One is of God moving around in a chariot-throne – with wheels that go in all directions and are full of eyes. Another is of a valley full of dry bones – which collect into skeletons, develop bodies and become a mighty army!

Ezekiel's message is that God is with his people even in exile. God has not abandoned them. He has both the purpose and the power to restore them to their homeland, nationhood and covenant faith.

OUTLINE

Israel's sin and God's judgment (1:1–24:27)
Prophecies against surrounding nations (25:1–32:32)
A perfect future for Israel (33:1–48:35)

Introduction

Ezekiel writes his own story. His visions and messages are all in the order in which they happen. He gives us a well-organized record of all his experiences, paying great attention to detail.

As a young man, Ezekiel is a priest, married and living in Jerusalem. In 597 BC, the Babylonian armies of Nebuchadnezzar besiege the city. Jerusalem is captured, and the temple of Solomon is ransacked of its treasures.

Ezekiel is taken captive, along with many of Jerusalem's citizens. King Jehoiachin and 10,000 of his soldiers, skilled workers and business people, are all deported to Babylonia, 700 miles away.

Ezekiel finds himself living on a barren plain, near the Kebar River. The Kebar may be an artificial canal taking water from the River Euphrates to the land south-east of Babylon.

After four or five years, when Ezekiel is about thirty, God calls him to be a prophet. His messages are to correct and encourage God's people in exile.

Ezekiel's attention is always on what God is doing – in the punishment of Judah, the fall of Jerusalem and the destruction of the temple. In the days before fast news networks, Ezekiel receives visions of what is happening back home.

Of all the prophets of the Old Testament, Ezekiel is the strangest. Like Isaiah, he has a tremendous sense of God's holiness. Like Jeremiah, he acts out some of his prophecies. Like Daniel, he sees visions which leave him speechless. Like Hosea, he experiences heartbreak. But in addition to all these, he seems in some way psychic. He goes into trances, is struck dumb for months and feels himself transported great distances. At one point he visits Jerusalem in a vision and interacts with the people there.

Ezekiel is also a deeply sensitive and passionate man. He is often sad – mourning the fate of the kings of Israel (19:1–14), the death of his wife and the tragic fall of Jerusalem (24:15–27). His last message is dated in the twenty-seventh year of exile, when he is in his early fifties. We don't know what happens to him after this.

Life in exile is not a prison-camp existence. The people are allowed to settle down and form communities. They have their own elders, who organize worship and teaching. Jeremiah advises the exiles to establish a normal life, build houses, plant fields and raise families.

Babylon is an impressive place. The famous 'Hanging Gardens' are one of the seven wonders of the ancient world. The stepped towers, known as 'ziggurats', are formidable temples to seemingly powerful gods. These structures are descendants of the original tower of Babel which tried to reach to God (Genesis 11:1–9). And everywhere are carvings of strange, winged, lion-like creatures – symbols of the might and mobility of Babylon.

The exiles, who have been so proud of Jerusalem, now find themselves dwarfed by the size and scope of Babylon's buildings and businesses. And where is the God of Israel in all this? Is he still alive, or has he been defeated too?

Discovering Ezekiel

Israel's sin and God's judgment

Ezekiel's vision of God's chariot (1:1–28)

Ezekiel can name the very day and place when his visions of God begin.

The year is 593 BC. He is thirty years old. If he were in Jerusalem he would be taking up his priestly duties in the temple. As it is, he is in exile in Babylon, where he has been for five years. And the place? He is on the plain of the Kebar River – the Babylonian 'grand canal'.

Something like a windstorm comes sweeping in from the north. The sky grows dark, the wind builds up to a hurricane and lightning starts to flicker around the landscape.

At the heart of the darkness, Ezekiel sees something dazzling, like white-hot metal. There are four living creatures – of human form, but with wings and hands and burnished legs. Each has four faces – a human being, a lion, an ox and an eagle. They move, wing-tip to wing-tip, in a hollow square and with lightning speed. They are like fiery torches, with fire passing constantly between them. And they travel everywhere in an instant – wherever the Spirit of God takes them – without deviation and in perfect unison.

And then Ezekiel sees the wheels: one for each creature – vast, moving in all directions and full of eyes! Here again is perpetual harmony in motion, for the spirit of the living creatures is in the wheels. The sound of beating wings is overwhelming – like rushing waters and the roar of an army.

Above the creatures is an expanse – a platform, a firmament. This is the throne of God. The unity, harmony, mobility and glory are his. He appears like a human being, but dazzling, full of fire and surrounded by the brilliance of storm and rainbow.

Ezekiel is unable to stand. He falls face down in the presence of the Lord.

What does this awesome vision signify? God is transcendent above his creation. He is indescribably glorious. He is everywhere present and active – all-seeing, all-knowing. Suddenly Ezekiel begins to understand the exile of God's people in a new, altogether different, perspective. God is not absent. God is not powerless. God is overwhelmingly here and now.

The call of Ezekiel (2:1–3:15)

The Spirit of God lifts Ezekiel to his feet. God speaks to him as Son of Man – one small human standing in the presence of the Lord.

God tells Ezekiel that he is sending him as a messenger to his own people, his fellow exiles. There will be no barriers of race or language, but they will still refuse to listen to him. They are a rebellious people – worse than the heathen.

Ezekiel will need to be tough and resolute. God will make Ezekiel's forehead 'harder than flint' (3:9). Isaiah and Jeremiah (his older contemporaries) are similarly fortified (Isaiah 50:7; Jeremiah 1:18).

God gives Ezekiel a scroll, covered on the front and back with messages of woe (2:10). For several years his only words will be warnings of the destruction of Jerusalem. The young prophet is to eat the scroll, taking in these messages and making them his own. He finds it 'as sweet as honey'. John has a similar experience in his vision (Revelation 10:10). The messages may be bitter, but obedience is sweet.

Now Ezekiel is caught up in his new work, and he confesses to feeling angry and bitter. He may feel trapped in a hard and lonely ministry; but it is more likely that he already shares God's own indignation at Israel's rebellion. He moves to the exiles' settlement at Tel Abib ('mound of green barley ears'), where it takes him a week to recover from his ordeal.

To be a watchman (3:16–27)

God commissions Ezekiel to be a watchman – that is, one who is alert to approaching danger. He is to warn the people of Israel that they are responsible for their sins. Even righteous people are to be warned – and God will hold Ezekiel responsible for telling them.

This idea is new: that people are accountable to God as individuals. In the past, people have been treated as a nation or group.

Ezekiel is to lose his freedom for a while. He is to stay at home and be silent, unless God gives him a message to speak. His mouth is dedicated to the delivery of God's word. Apart from the word of the Lord, he has nothing to say. The enforced silence lasts for six or seven years, until the news of the fall of Jerusalem reaches the exiles (33:22).

Actions speak louder than words (4:1–5:17)

Ezekiel doesn't always speak his messages. Sometimes he acts them. He lies on his side, cuts his hair and remains silent, to convey aspects of suffering and grief.

He draws an outline of Jerusalem on a clay tile, and builds a model siege around it. He pretends he is God laying siege to Jerusalem – 390 days for the sins of Israel and forty days for the sins of Judah. It's a terrible shock to realize that God is set against his own people in this way.

Ezekiel allows himself only a small amount of food and water each day. He cooks in disgusting conditions. Neither the exiles in Babylon nor the people under siege in Jerusalem can enjoy a life of plenty or purity. It is dreadful for Ezekiel, a priest, to have to portray such a state of affairs!

One day Ezekiel packs his bags and then, at night, digs his way out of his house. This is how King Zedekiah will try to escape from Jerusalem (12:3–14).

Prophecy against the mountains of Israel (6:1–14)

Ezekiel is to pronounce doom on the land of Israel – the mountains and hills, valleys and ravines (6:2–3). The whole landscape has been defiled by idol-worship. There are pagan altars on the 'high places' (hilltops or platforms) and incense-burning and immoral rites under green trees (pagan symbols of fertility). God is going to bring judgment in the form of war, famine and plague (6:11). The sites where the Baal-gods have been worshipped will be littered with corpses (6:5), and the survivors will be scattered to other countries (6:8).

Israel's day of doom (7:1–27)

The time has come for God's judgment on Israel (7:2–3). She is to be punished for her idolatries and disgusting practices (7:4). The day of doom approaches, when revellers will be plunged into chaos (7:6–7).

Just as a rod grows buds, so Israel's pride has developed; her violence has become full-fledged wickedness (7:10-11). Now God is going to judge every single person (7:12) – those who buy and those who sell, the city dwellers and the country folk (7:12-15).

God's weapons of judgment will be war, famine and plague (7:15). Those who escape will go into mourning (7:18); their money will be useless (7:19) and the women's ornaments will be snatched by strangers (7:20). God will even allow pagan invaders to trample his holy temple (7:22). Prophet, priest and king will all fall silent in the face of the disaster that God will bring upon them (7:25-27).

A visit to Jerusalem (8:1–11:25)

On one occasion Ezekiel feels himself being carried off by his hair, to visit Jerusalem in a vision.

He sees an idol in the temple; the leaders of Israel performing secret rites; women mourning for Tammuz (a pagan god who dies and rises); and men worshipping the sun. In a Passover-type operation, God has all such people killed – but spares those who are innocent.

The awesome chariot-throne that Ezekiel saw by the Kebar River is in Jerusalem as well. As Ezekiel watches, the chariot bears God's glory away from the temple. His presence will no longer be there.

Ezekiel watches the leaders of Jerusalem plotting their wicked schemes. He recognizes some of them and prophesies against them. He watches as one of them, Pelatiah, drops dead (11:1-13)!

When Jerusalem is besieged again, Ezekiel is the first to know. God tells him:

Son of man, record this date, this very date, because the king of Babylon has laid siege to Jerusalem this very day. (24:2)

Later, the terrible news is confirmed:

In the twelfth year of our exile, in the tenth month, on the fifth day, a man who had escaped from Jerusalem came to me and said, 'The city has fallen'. (33:21)

Prophecies against Jerusalem (12:1–24:27)

Ezekiel has announced God's judgment on Jerusalem. Now he tries to persuade the people that this is indeed going to happen. They are a 'rebellious house' – refusing to listen to God's warning or change their ways (12:2–3).

Leaving at night

Ezekiel is to pack his bags and dig his way out of his house at night (12:7). This is to act out the king's attempt to escape when the disaster strikes (12:12). The king will be caught and carried off to exile in Babylon (12:13).

Trembling with fear

Ezekiel is to shake with fear as he eats and drinks (12:17–20). This is how it will be for everyone when the Babylonian invasion sweeps through the land.

You'd better believe it!

People like to say of Ezekiel's prophecies, 'It'll never happen.' Now God assures them that all the predictions will be fulfilled in their lifetime (12:21–28).

Peace smashed to pieces

Ezekiel condemns the false prophets who have assured people there will be peace. Their visions have been like whitewash on the great wall of Israel's sins (13:10). Now God is going to bring judgment on that wall – a deluge of rain, huge hailstones and a stormy gale (13:11). The wall of sins will be broken down and destroyed – and the uselessness and deceit of the whitewash exposed (13:12–16).

Designing women

Ezekiel preaches against women who bind people with superstition (13:17–23). They sew wristbands and make veils, which people wear in the hope of being safe from evil powers. By doing this, the women are introducing a layer of false judgment, fear and hope into people's lives. Their activities are nothing to do with God's standards or purpose (13:22). He will destroy their charms and release their captives (13:20).

Blocked hearts

Some elders come to consult Ezekiel. He realizes that they can't receive God's word because they have allowed idol-worship and sin to occupy their hearts (14:3–5). Such people must repent and dispose of their idols, or God will turn away from them (14:6–8). If a prophet is taken in by one of these enquirers, both of them will be judged for abuse of God's word (14:9–11).

God has the right to judge

In the past, God might spare a people or land for the sake of a righteous person who lived there: a Noah, a Daniel or a Job (14:14). Now God announces that he will still spare righteous people, but their presence will not prevent him destroying the rest (14:15–20). There will be some who escape the destruction of Jerusalem, but it will not be because they are righteous. When people see the evil ways of the survivors, they will understand why God acted as he did (14:21–23).

Fit for nothing

The wood of the vine is useless. It won't even make a coat-peg. It is even more useless when it has been charred by fire. This is how God sees the inhabitants of Jerusalem – the vine he planted in the Promised Land. The people of Jerusalem are to be charred in the fire of God's judgment and discarded in exile (15:1–8).

Jerusalem – God's wanton wife

Ezekiel tells Israel's life story from God's point of view. God first came across Israel as an abandoned baby, unwashed and unloved (16:4–6). He blessed her with life and, when she came of age and beauty, made a marriage covenant with her (16:7–8). This was the covenant at Mount Sinai when God gave Israel his law. He was an adoring, considerate and generous husband who shared his splendour with her (16:9–14).

But Israel devoted her beauty and blessings to other lovers – the neighbouring nations and their pagan idols (16:15–19). She sacrificed her own children to these gods, and forgot all that the true God had done for her (16:20–22). She gave herself over to a series of liaisons – political alliances and mingling of faiths – with Egypt, Philistia, Assyria and Babylon (the Chaldeans). There were platforms for idol-worship, like beds, in every square and at the end of every road (16:23–29). And yet Israel wasn't a whore, because she paid her lovers for the privilege of their alliances (16:30-34).

Now God is going to expose Israel's shame and turn her lovers into enemies (16:35-39). She will be destroyed by them as God's judgment on her unfaithfulness (16:40-43). There is a strand of paganism and immorality in Israel which comes from her Hittite origins (16:44-46). Her sisters are Samaria and Sodom, who are proud and pagan enough – but Israel is worse than either of them (16:44-52).

God promises to restore Sodom and Samaria – and Israel along with them (16:53-58). God will punish Israel by breaking his covenant with her and allowing her to be defeated and exiled; but afterwards he will renew his commitment to her and forgive all she has done (16:59-63).

A riddle of two eagles

Ezekiel tells a story of two great eagles, which represent Babylon and Egypt (17:11-15). Babylon has carried off the leading shoot of Judah, but left an offshoot in Jerusalem (17:3-6). The offshoot grows well, but leans towards Egypt for sustenance (17:7-8). God sees this as rebellious and doomed to failure (17:11-21). It depicts the time in 588 BC, when King Zedekiah of Judah looked to Egypt for help in lifting the Babylonian siege of Jerusalem.

God promises to select and tend a new sprig from the tree of Israel. This shoot will grow on a prominent height and become a landmark and shelter for all the nations of the world (17:22-24). It is a picture of Mount Zion and the kingdom of God.

The soul that sins will die

People are saying that they don't deserve their punishment. It's all the fault of their parents. As the saying goes:

The parents eat sour grapes, and the children's teeth are set on edge. (18:2)

There is a lot of truth in this idea. Israel has always had a strong sense of belonging together, and of being blessed or punished together.

But now Ezekiel declares that each generation is responsible for its own actions. People cannot claim innocence just because their parents were wicked. From now on, each person will stand alone before the judgment of God – not hiding behind someone else's goodness, or blaming someone else for their faults. If anyone dies, it will be for their own sin and no one else's. God's new community will be made up of individuals – each of whom has chosen to do right.

A lament over the kings of Israel

God tells Ezekiel to raise a lament for the princes of Israel (19:1). They have been like young lions – one getting caught in Egypt and another captured and taken to Babylon (19:2–9). These images describe the fates of kings Jehoahaz and Jehoiachin.

Ezekiel pictures a strong and healthy vine. This vine has been pulled up and transplanted to a desert situation. Its strength to rule is gone (19:10–14). This is a reference to King Zedekiah, whose rebellion provoked the Babylonian assault on Jerusalem.

Israel's past...

Some elders come to consult Ezekiel. God asks Ezekiel to challenge their motives (20:1–3).

In the beginning, when God chose the Israelites to be his own people, he commanded them to reject the idols of Egypt; but not one of them did so (20:5–8). God considered punishing Israel there and then, but brought her out of Egypt to prove his power to the other nations (20:9–10).

God led the Israelites through the wilderness and gave them his holy laws, but they did not keep them. Again, God considered abandoning them to death in the desert, but he spared them (20:11–22). He warned them that the consequence of breaking his law would be exile among the nations (20:23–24). There was confusion over the offering for first-born children, which was sometimes interpreted as child sacrifice (20:25–26).

Finally, since the Israelites came into their own land, they have defiled it with idolatry (20:27–29). So why should the elders be allowed to consult God? Their ancestors have never taken any notice of what God has said (20:30–31).

... and God's future

God will never allow his people to settle for idolatry. He is determined to be their king. He will rescue them from captivity and bring them into the wilderness once again. There he will judge them like a shepherd checking his sheep; and he will renew his covenant with them (20:32–38).

The Israelites can choose to worship idols if they wish. What God will not tolerate is the mixing of idol-worship with the worship of the one true God (20:39). God will establish his holy mountain as the centre for Israel's worship, where all can bring their offerings. It will be a place of repentance and forgiveness – a place to realize the grace of God (20:40–44).

Judgment by fire and sword

Ezekiel is given four prophecies of judgment: one by fire and three by sword (20:45–21:32).

Fire in the Negeb

Ezekiel is to preach to the south of Jerusalem, to the forest of the Negeb – the 'dry land'. God promises to kindle there a terrible fire for all to see (20:45–49). Ezekiel himself feels the pain and frustration of such an image. His words are frightening and puzzling, but not understandable.

God's sword against Jerusalem

Ezekiel is to prophesy towards Jerusalem that God is coming to wreak judgment with his sword (21:1–17). The sword is polished and sharp, and is being wielded against God's own people. It will not be sheathed until its task is completed.

Nebuchadnezzar's sword at the crossroads

Ezekiel is to mark a junction in the road. It is the junction where Nebuchadnezzar will pause, to decide whether to march on Jerusalem or Rabbah (the city of the Ammonites – modern Amman). Nebuchadnezzar will choose from arrows with the names of cities written on them; he will consult the teraphim (little idol figures) and inspect the liver of a sacrifice. He will choose Jerusalem and call up the equipment for laying siege to her (21:18–23).

The choice of Jerusalem is no mistake. The time has come for God's judgment on Israel's guilt, which is freshly exposed. Jerusalem's king must prepare to be deposed, and her people must contemplate the unthinkable: that the city will become a ruin (21:24–27).

Ammon's sword turned back

Ezekiel is to prophesy against the Ammonites (21:28–32). They plan to join the attack on Jerusalem, but God tells them to return the sword to its sheath. They themselves are to be judged and destroyed in their own land – and will disappear for ever.

Three prophecies condemning Jerusalem

She is guilty

The time has come for judgment to fall on Jerusalem. The city has brought it on herself with violent bloodshed and vile idolatry (22:1–5).

Jerusalem's crimes affect many sections of the population: murderous princes, despised parents, exploited foreigners, neglected widows, abused religion and broken sabbaths. There is every kind of sexual deviation: orgy, incest, abuse and adultery. There is malpractice in business: bribery, double accounting and extortion. But the heart of all the trouble is that the people have forgotten God and his law (22:6–12).

God announces his verdict. The people of Jerusalem are sentenced to exile – even though their defeat will reflect badly on God's reputation among the other nations (22:13–16).

She is worthless

Jerusalem has become worthless in God's sight (22:17–22). However valuable she once appeared, all her precious qualities will vanish in the furnace of God's judgment.

She is unholy

Jerusalem is spiritually filthy – like an unwashed land in drought. Her leaders are murderous as they intimidate and steal. The priests have failed to teach God's law or observe God's holiness. The officials are corrupt. The prophets are shallow and dishonest. The common people are bullies and thieves. There is not a single righteous person with whom God can start again. He sentences them to the consequences of their behaviour (22:23–31).

The shameless sisters

God describes two sex-obsessed sisters. Their names are Oholah and Oholibah. In telling of their sexual awakening in Egypt and their insatiable lusts ever since, Ezekiel is describing the idolatry of the fertility religions. He is describing Samaria and Jerusalem (23:1–4).

Samaria was the capital of the northern kingdom of Israel. Jerusalem is the capital of the southern kingdom of Judah. Oholah (Samaria) lusted after the Assyrians and their gods. The Assyrians violated her, seized her children, and killed her. Oholibah (Jerusalem) not only lusted after the Assyrians, but also the Chaldeans (Babylonians). She played the whore with the Babylonians, but was disgusted by them. God was, in turn, disgusted by her (23:5-21).

Now God is gathering all Jerusalem's hoped-for lovers into an invading army. They will attack from the north in huge numbers, well-organized and well-armed. They will execute God's judgment on Oholibah for her abandonment of God's law. She will drink the same cup of horror and desolation as her sister (23:22-35).

Ezekiel weighs the crimes of Oholah and Oholibah. They have committed adultery with other nations and idolatry with other gods. They have offered their children as sacrifices and then entered God's holy temple with blood on their hands. They have entertained foreign suitors by playing the whore and used holy incense and oil for their seductions. Any righteous judge would find them guilty.

God declares that Oholah and Oholibah are to be destroyed, together with their children and their houses. God is holy, and lewdness and idolatry are to be eradicated from his holy people (23:36-49).

The cooking of Jerusalem

It is January 588 BC, God tells Ezekiel that Nebuchadnezzar, the king of Babylon, has laid siege to Jerusalem. Jerusalem is like a large copper cauldron, placed on the fire of God's judgment to cook. The pieces of meat in the cauldron are her citizens (24:1-5).

The cauldron is rusty. The rust colours the meat, making it look bloody. The contents are poured out on bare rock, so that the earth doesn't soak up the blood. The citizens of Jerusalem, too, will be slaughtered and thrown out at random – to lie without burial (24:6-8).

Finally, the cauldron itself is left on the fire to melt down completely, destroying the rust within it. So God destroys the filth of Jerusalem, her blood-guilt and immorality. He will not turn back now or change his mind (24:9-14).

The death of a wife

God tells Ezekiel that he is about to take away the delight of his eyes; but he forbids him to mourn or weep. The prophet must put on his turban and sandals as usual, and not give any outward sign of grief. That evening, Ezekiel's wife dies (24:15-18).

Ezekiel's bereavement parallels the tragedy of Jerusalem, who is God's wife. Jerusalem is also the great love of the people in exile. Ezekiel explains to the people that, when the news comes of Jerusalem's death, they are not to give any signs of mourning. But within and between themselves they must pine and groan, because of the sins which have caused this great tragedy (24:19-24).

When the news arrives that Jerusalem has been destroyed, Ezekiel will be able to speak freely again. The worst has happened and his prophecies have come true. Now he will be able to teach and prepare the people for God's new future (24:25-27).

Prophecies against surrounding nations

God gives Ezekiel prophecies to utter against seven nations: Ammon, Moab, Edom, Philistia, Tyre, Sidon and Egypt. The God of Israel is the Lord of all the earth, and his standards apply to all nations. It is not just Israel who comes under his judgment.

Ammon, Moab, Edom and Philistia (25:1-17)

Ammon has rejoiced at Israel's fate. Now God will cause her to be overrun by tribesmen from the east – the Nabateans. Her capital, Rabbah, will become grazing for their camels (25:2-7).

Moab has concluded that the invasion of Judah means that Israel is no different from the other nations. She is wrong and will be invaded herself by the Nabateans (25:8-11).

Edom has taken advantage of the Babylonian invasion of Israel – perhaps by gaining part of southern Judah. Now God will take revenge on her (25:12-14).

The Lord of all

The surrounding nations may gloat over the fate of Israel at the hands of her own God. But ultimately it is the God of Israel who will judge them too.

The Philistines were always hostile to Israel, and joined in her destruction. Now God will avenge himself on them and destroy their coastlands (25:15-17).

Tyre (26:1-28:19)

The proud and magnificent port of Tyre has rejoiced at Jerusalem's fall. She expects to gain from it in plunder and trade (26:2). But, after his destruction of Jerusalem, Nebuchadnezzar will turn his attention to Tyre. He will lay siege to her for thirteen years.

God is against Tyre and will subject her to overwhelming waves of attack. The armies of Babylon will crash over her. She will be broken down and eroded until she becomes merely a bare rock on which to dry fishing nets (26:3-21).

God tells Ezekiel to lament the destruction of such a thriving community. She is like a great trading ship, laden with merchandise, which sinks within sight of the shore (27:1-36). Tyre's pride has been her downfall. Her king has thought himself a god (28:1-10). He was indeed exquisitely wealthy and wise, but his power and pride corrupted him (28:11-19).

Sidon (28:20-26)

Sidon is to fall under the judgment of God, by plague and sword (28:20-23).

God's purpose in judging the nations

God's judgment and destruction of the surrounding nations show his sovereign holiness. He is cutting back the 'briers and thorns' of Israel's enemies, to make a safe place for her to live (28:24-26).

Egypt (29:1-32:32)

In January 587 BC, God declares to Ezekiel his judgment on Egypt. Pharaoh, king of Egypt, is like a great dragon or crocodile ruling the River Nile, his lair. God will hook him up and fling him out (29:1–5).

Egypt is condemned because she was an unreliable support in Israel's need – like a reed staff which breaks when leaned on, tearing the shoulders and buckling the knees (29:6–7). God will punish Egypt by laying waste her land and scattering her people for forty years. Afterwards he will restore her, but only as a shadow of her former power. Israel will never again look to depend on her (29:8–16).

On New Year's Day 571 BC, Ezekiel receives his last recorded prophecy. It is placed here, because it concerns Egypt and Tyre. Nebuchadnezzar has lifted his siege of Tyre around 574 BC. It has been a long and unrewarding venture, lasting thirteen years. Now Nebuchadnezzar will hope to make good his losses (and pay his soldiers) by invading Egypt (29:17–20).

Ezekiel prophesies a day of God's judgment on Egypt – a 'day of the Lord' (30:3). The Babylonian armies of Nebuchadnezzar will sweep through every part of the land (30:4–19).

God will ensure victory for the Babylonians. Pharaoh Hophra's 'arm' was 'broken' in 586 BC, when he tried to relieve the Babylonian siege of Jerusalem. Now God will break both Pharaoh's arms, but strengthen Nebuchadnezzar's (30:20–26).

In June 587 BC, God gives Ezekiel an oracle for Pharaoh and his armies. Egypt is like a mighty cedar of Lebanon, taller and more beautiful than the cedars in the garden of Eden (31:1–9). But Egypt is proud, and her cedar is to be cut down by foreigners – the Babylonians (31:10–14). Pharaoh and his armies will go down to Sheol, the world of the departed (31:15–18).

Pharaoh's fate

In March 585 BC, God tells Ezekiel to raise a lament for Pharaoh, king of Egypt.

Does Pharaoh think himself like the winged lion of Babylon? He is more like a cumbersome crocodile thrashing around in muddy waters (32:2). God is going to bring the armies of Babylon to capture and overthrow him (32:3–16). Other nations and their rulers will be appalled at Egypt's destruction (32:9–10).

In the same month, Ezekiel is given a further lament. Pharaoh and his hordes have been put to the sword and now lie buried in Sheol. There they keep company with the dead of many other pagan nations: Assyria, Elam, Meshech and Tubal, Edom and Sidon (32:17–32).

A perfect future for Israel

Responsible to God and the people (33:1–20)

God tells Ezekiel that he is to be a watchman for Israel – the only one keeping a lookout against attack. He feels an enormous sense of responsibility to tell the people what God is doing, and to warn them of God's judgment. If he fails in his duty, the people will be lost.

Ezekiel is to act as a watchman by warning people. They must stop their wickedness or they will die. They must respond to God *now*. It doesn't matter whether they have acted well or badly in the past. The important thing is to turn to God in the present – and live.

The turning point: 'The city has fallen!' (33:21–33)

And now comes a turning point in Ezekiel's ministry.

For six or seven years Ezekiel has been silent, except when speaking the Lord's messages. Now, at last, the news arrives which Ezekiel has long predicted, 'Jerusalem has fallen!'

Ezekiel already suspected as much, because the previous evening God had enabled him to speak freely again. This was the sign that Jerusalem ('their stronghold, their joy and glory') was taken away – just as Ezekiel had suffered such a loss when his wife died (24:25–27).

The news of the disaster is terrible, but suddenly Ezekiel is popular. He is a prophet whose word has come true!

The Lord speaks to Ezekiel about the survivors in Judah. Although they are poor and living in the ruins, they are claiming the land of Israel as their inheritance. If Abraham could claim it and he was only one person, how much more do they have the right to it, as they number so many?

The question is whether the land belongs to the people who are in exile (who were the leaders of Judah when they were deported) or to the poor and ignorant survivors who are squatting in the ruins and hiding in caves.

Ezekiel declares that the survivors have no right to the land, because they continue to worship idols, ignore the food laws and commit murder, violence and adultery. They will suffer further judgment. Jeremiah's vision of the two baskets of figs deals with the same issue – and comes to the same conclusion: it is the exiles who are the 'good figs' (Jeremiah 24:1–10)!

But Ezekiel also has a warning for the exiles. They are eager to hear his messages (now that they know his words are from the Lord), but they treat his words like a beautiful tune rather than a call to change their lives. They listen and enthuse – but go away and do nothing.

From now on, Ezekiel will have messages of renewal and restoration. He will prepare the exiles for their return home.

God will be the shepherd (34:1–31)

Ezekiel looks forward to Israel being restored. If the failings of the past are to be avoided, there must be a new standard of leadership.

In the ancient Near East, a common description of a leader is the shepherd. He walks ahead of his sheep, leads them to pasture and defends them from wild animals. Both Moses and David are described as 'shepherds' to their people – and both served their apprenticeship looking after real sheep.

Ezekiel delivers the Lord's judgment on the kings who have been Israel's shepherds in the recent past. They have behaved scandalously: exploiting their people, neglecting the weak and allowing the nation to be scattered. They have used and abused the flock as their own, when in truth it was God's.

Now the Lord himself will rescue his people. He will search for them and bring them back from the nations to which they have been scattered. 'Scattering' is one of Ezekiel's favourite terms for the exile. God is to bring his people home, not only from Babylonia but also from Egypt, Phoenicia and Arabia.

When the Lord restores his flock, it will be a day of both rescue and judgment. He will tend the injured and weak, but the sleek and strong he will destroy. This will be the fate of those ruthless and greedy members of society who grow fat at the expense of the rest. Ezekiel hints at the social justice and freedom from oppression which are such an important theme in the prophecy of Amos.

Here is the just and gentle rule of God. He is the good shepherd. God's longing to search for the lost must be the seed thought for a famous parable of Jesus (Luke 15:4–6), and the source of his deep compassion (Matthew 9:36).

Finally, God will place his people in the care of David, who will be a 'prince' among them. The actual descendants of David have failed in their kingship; but now God promises to appoint a ruler with David's qualities who will shepherd Israel for ever. This will be the Messiah – the perfect ruler of the restored community.

A judgment on Edom (35:1–15)

God tells Ezekiel to prophesy against Mount Seir, which is the home of the Edomites.

The Edomites nurse an ancient enmity with Israel. This enmity dates back to the rivalry between Esau and Jacob. The Edomites are descended from Esau and the Israelites from Jacob.

The Edomites have failed to help when Judah was invaded and Jerusalem besieged by the Babylonians. They hoped to take possession of the 'two countries' of Israel and Judah (35:10) once the Babylonians had withdrawn.

Now God is going to judge Edom. Just as Edom has rejoiced over the destruction of Israel, so God will make all nations rejoice over the destruction of Edom (35:14–15).

Israel's coming home! (36:1–38)

Ezekiel is to prophesy to the mountains of Israel: the peaks that have been abused by fertility rites and trampled by pagan armies. God has seen enough of their suffering. He is angry at the derision of other nations, who laugh at Israel's defeat and say her God doesn't care (36:1–3).

God now declares to the whole landscape of Israel that she will flourish once again. Her people are coming home (36:6–8)!

God is concerned to put the record straight. He is not restoring Israel because her goodness has earned it. He is restoring Israel because his holy name has been insulted. Now he is going to gather his people and cleanse them from idolatry (36:22–25).

New heart, new start

God is going to work a miracle of his grace. He will change Israel's heart from stone to flesh, from hardness to softness, from death to life (36:26). The law which was engraved on stone and so always 'outside' people will now be planted within them (36:27). Israel will become a renewed people in a restored land, replanting and rebuilding to the glory of God (36:28–38).

'Prophesy to these bones' (37:1–28)

Ezekiel is in a valley – either literally or in a vision. The valley floor is covered with a deep layer of bones – as though an army has been massacred there. It is a picture of Israel – dead and dismembered by defeat and dispersion.

The Lord puts the question to Ezekiel: 'Son of man, can these bones live?' He replies, 'O Sovereign Lord, you alone know.'

Israel's survival and revival is in God's hands. The situation is beyond human help. Only God can make these bleached and crumbling bones rise to form an army again. Only God can resurrect his people Israel and restore to them their land and temple.

The Lord commands Ezekiel to prophesy to the bones: to tell them that God will reconstitute them into skeletons, clothe them with muscles and flesh, put breath in them and bring them to life! Ezekiel does so. As he watches, the bones come together and are formed into corpses, but the army is still lifeless.

God commands Ezekiel to prophesy to the breath. 'Breath' means 'wind' as well as 'spirit': invisible, powerful and life-giving. In Hebrew it is 'ruach' – the wilderness wind; the image of the Spirit of God.

Ezekiel summons the breath to inspire the dead – and the mighty army springs to life! This is the power of God's word and Spirit, in partnership with the faith and obedience of his prophet.

Israel will rise again, at the word of the Lord. The God who brought creation into being by his powerful word will restore his people to their life and land.

Prophecy against Gog (38:1–39:29)

Ezekiel's prophecies of the restoration and renewal of Israel are interrupted by oracles about a great battle in the far future. We don't know why the compiler has inserted them here.

These two chapters are unique. They describe an invasion of foreign powers against the people of God, even after the Messiah's reign of peace has begun. Ezekiel prophesies defeat and destruction for these pagan hordes – the massed armies of Gog.

Gog is the commander of an alliance which is bent on the destruction of Israel. His name may come from 'Gygyes', king of Lydia, or the place name Gagaia, a land of barbarians. Gog is described as prince of Meshech and Tubal (probably Phrygia and Cappadocia, to the east of Asia Minor). Some scholars have tried to identify Gog as a historical conqueror such as Alexander the Great.

The nations attacking Israel are from Persia, Cush (Ethiopia), Put (North Africa), Gomer (north of the Black Sea) and Beth Togarmah ('the uttermost north' – perhaps Armenia). They will sweep in like a storm and cover the land like locusts. But God himself will curb them with hooks through their jaws, as he tamed the chaos monster.

Israel is living in quiet prosperity at this future time, enjoying the peace of the Messiah's kingdom. When the invasion takes place, God will defend her with an earthquake, confusion, plague, bloodshed, storm and burning sulphur. His victory will show the world that he is the great and holy God (38:16).

Israel's triumph will be complete. It will take seven months to bury the bodies of the enemy (outside God's land, in the valley of Hamon Gog) and the captured weapons will provide firewood for seven years.

Other prophets predict an end-time battle between the forces of evil and the people of God. Joel speaks of God's defeat of 'the northern army' (Joel 2:20) and Jeremiah of 'a besieging army... coming from a distant land' (Jeremiah 4:16). Amos and Zephaniah both describe a 'Day of the Lord' which features darkness and destruction (Amos 5:18–20; Zephaniah 1:14–18).

These prophecies are 'apocalyptic' in style. They reveal the true state of things in cosmic images of God's judgment and victory. They assure God's people of his purpose and power to bring all things to a glorious and successful conclusion. This enables believers to live confidently through many terrible trials.

The book of Revelation, at the close of the whole Bible, describes a final invasion by the forces of Satan against God's people and city. The writer identifies Satan's allies as Gog and Magog (Revelation 20:7–9)! Their reputation has travelled a long way from the oracles of Ezekiel.

A vision of the perfect temple (40:1–43:27)

It is now twenty-five years since Ezekiel was taken from Jerusalem to exile in Babylon, and fourteen years since the news arrived that Jerusalem and her temple were destroyed.

Since that dreadful day, Ezekiel's fellow exiles have recognized him as a true prophet. God has given him many visions and messages of restoration and renewal. Israel will be gathered and cared for by God himself. He will raise her to new life, like a living army from a pile of bones.

Ezekiel's final visions are of a new temple, beautifully and perfectly built; and of the Lord returning to dwell among his people. As Ezekiel is both priest and prophet, this is a fitting climax for his book.

In a vision, Ezekiel is taken to Israel and set on a 'very high mountain'. Immediately we think of Mount Zion, with Jerusalem 'lifted up' to her heavenly status as God's holy city.

Ezekiel is met by a man whose appearance is 'like bronze' – an angelic messenger, equipped with a linen cord and measuring rod. He tells Ezekiel to take in every detail of the new temple's design. Together

> ### The temple building
>
> Ezekiel's angel guide measures out the temple building in cubits. This is the 'long' cubit, which is about twenty-one inches. The measuring rod is about ten feet and three inches long, which is the thickness and height of the wall surrounding the temple area.
>
> This outer wall is the 'dividing partition' which separates the sacred space from the secular. There was no such wall in Solomon's temple, but it is now introduced to emphasize the separation of holy things.

they tour the temple complex, viewing and measuring the walls, gates, porticoes, courts and rooms.

They come to the centre of the temple area and measure the outer and inner sanctuaries. The Most Holy Place is twenty cubits square, while the temple building is 100 cubits square. Everything is square and symmetrical – the perfect proportions expressing the holiness of God.

Ezekiel notes that some of the walls are decorated with palm trees, while the walls and floors of the sanctuaries are finished in wood. The walls around the outer and inner sanctuaries are decorated with palm trees and cherubim.

Ezekiel is shown the wooden altar for the bread of the Presence, the accommodation for the priests and the rooms for the washing and preparation of sacrifices.

When they come to the east gate, Ezekiel has a vision of the glory of the God of Israel. The Lord returns to his temple from the east, the direction of the sunrise, and enters through the east gate. He is awesome in appearance, as when Ezekiel first saw him by the River Kebar. Ezekiel falls on his face before him.

Nineteen years after Ezekiel's vision of the Lord departing from his temple, the prophet witnesses the glorious return. The glory of the Lord fills his temple.

The Lord tells Ezekiel that this temple is to be holy – the place where he will live among his people. There is to be no repetition of the pagan practices which brought judgment and disaster before.

Ezekiel is to describe the temple to the Israelites, so that they may catch the vision of its holiness and perfection.

Next, Ezekiel is introduced to the laws which will govern the worship of the temple and its administration. He is shown the altar of burnt offering and told of the week-long sequence of sacrifices by which it is to be consecrated.

Regulations for the restored community (44:1–46:24)

The prince, the levites and the priests

The east gate

The man (the angel guide) brings Ezekiel to the outer gate of the sanctuary, facing east. This gate is to remain shut, because it is the one through which the Lord God returned to his temple. It is sacred to him and is not to be used by humans. Is it shut because the Lord will never leave his temple again?

The prince

The prince is the only person who will be allowed to sit inside this east gate within the sanctuary – but he must enter and leave by the portico. The human ruler of Israel is to have a privileged but much more humble role than the kings of the past. He is not to be seen as God's representative in the way that David or Solomon were.

Once again, Ezekiel sees the glory of the Lord filling the temple, and falls on his face in awe of his presence.

Reforms

Ezekiel is given detailed instructions about the way the new temple is to be used. There are to be some important changes to avoid the mistakes and abuses of the past.

Access to the temple is to be restricted to members of the community of Israel.

In the past, foreigners have been allowed in – people who didn't share the race and faith of Israel ('uncircumcised in heart and flesh'). Sometimes such people have even been put in charge of the sanctuary. This must change.

In future, the people who come to the sanctuary must be members of the true Israel, the community of faith in the Lord. This isn't a racist ban. It is an attempt to keep the use and care of the sanctuary holy. Only those who know and mean what they're doing are to be allowed in.

These rules may have been drawn up after the time of Ezekiel. His 'perfect temple' was never built, and perhaps some of the old abuses began to occur again. If so, these regulations may have been introduced to guard Ezekiel's vision and protect the temple and its worship from defilement.

Levites and Zadokites

The Levites are not allowed to serve in the temple as priests. Instead, they must do the work which was previously done by foreign slaves. The slaves cannot now enter the sanctuary because they are not circumcised and don't share Israel's faith.

The Levites are to lose their priesthood because they worshipped pagan idols in the years leading up to the exile. Now they are to look after the temple in practical ways. They are the 'lay' administrators and gatekeepers.

God chooses the descendants of Zadok to be his priests. Zadok was the high priest who was appointed by David to serve alongside Abiathar. When Solomon became king, Abiathar was banished and Zadok became the sole high priest. Through Zadok, the priests trace their family line back to Aaron. They will be the priestly group throughout the time of the second temple – the one that will be built after the exile.

The Zadokite priests are given rules about their robes, hair length, wine, marriage and contact with dead bodies. All these rules are designed to show a difference between things that are holy and things that are common.

The priestly robes are to be made of linen, which is lighter than wool. Linen will help to prevent them perspiring. They must change out of these robes before mixing with ordinary people after the services.

The priests must keep their hair trimmed (neither shaven too close nor worn too long); and they are not to drink wine before entering the inner court (the sanctuary). They are to be clean, cool, tidy and sober for their sacred work. Cleanliness and godliness go together. Their outward behaviour should express a pure heart and dedicated life.

The rules for priests cover the same aspects of life as the vows of the Nazirites. The Nazirites (of whom Samson was one in the days of the judges) were to wear their hair long, abstain from strong drink and avoid contact with dead bodies (Numbers 6:1–21).

Ezekiel is seeing a vision of a reformed, holy and disciplined priesthood. When the exiles start to return to Judah and Jerusalem, their leaders will emphasize certain ways to express holiness. These will include circumcision, keeping the law and avoiding intermarriage with non-Jews. The prophet Haggai, the priest Ezra and the governor Nehemiah will commend and pursue these policies.

A priest is not to go near a dead body, unless it is that of a close relative. A corpse is dead and decaying, but priests are to be symbols of health and wholeness.

The priests are not to own any land. God himself is their inheritance – all they have and all they need. The grain and meat that are brought for sacrifices will supply the priests with food.

Division of the land

God has just told Ezekiel how the priests are to be provided with food. Now he describes how the land is to be divided when Israel returns from exile (45:1–12).

First of all, an area of land is to be set aside and devoted to God. On this land the temple will be built, together with accommodation for the priests. On the surrounding plots, the Levites, the prince and 'the city' (the state) will have allocations. In this way, the temple will be protected by a sacred buffer zone.

After the exile, the prince is to have a set and limited allocation of land. There is to be no more seizing of other people's property, as there was when King Ahab took Naboth's vineyard (1 Kings 21).

All the rest of the land is to be divided between the tribes for their towns, families and farms.

The Lord commands Israel's princes to act fairly. They are not to use their powers and privileges to bully and cheat. In particular, the weights and measures are to be set at an agreed standard. The ephah (for dry goods) and the bath (for liquids) are both to be 'a tenth of a homer'. An ephah is a little less than five gallons. Ten ephahs make a 'homer', which is six bushels of dry goods or 48.4 gallons of liquid. The word 'homer' means 'donkey-load'.

Offerings and holy days

The people are to allocate a proportion of their grain, oil and sheep to the prince (45:13-25). These are 'special gifts', like a tithe: a sixtieth of their wheat and barley, a hundredth of their oil, and one out of every 200 sheep.

There is no mention of wine. In the days before the exile, wine was poured out as an offering and also drunk at the festivals. Perhaps it has been abused and the custom is discontinued. The priests are forbidden to drink when they are on duty (44:21).

The prince, in turn, is to provide the sacrifices which will be offered in the temple on behalf of all the people.

The holy days in the new regime are to be New Year's Day, Passover and the Feast of Tabernacles. There is no mention of the Feast of Weeks or the Day of Atonement – although the latter may be suggested by the extra sacrifice which is to be offered a week after the New Year (45:20).

The prince's place

Ezekiel understands that the prince's status is to be strictly limited in the future kingdom (46:1-2).

The prince will be responsible for providing the offerings and sacrifices for the new temple. He will also be permitted to enter the inner court through the east gate – but only on the sabbath and at the New Moon (the first day of each month).

The prince will have a clear view of the worship being offered in the sanctuary, but he himself must not go further than the threshold. This regulation prevents Israel's human ruler from taking on the role of priest, as has happened sometimes in the past.

Offerings on various occasions

Ezekiel is given details of the sacrifices which are to be offered on the sabbath (every seventh day) and at the New Moon (the first day of the month) (46:3-15).

The burnt offerings are the same on each occasion: six male lambs and a ram. With the ram is offered a grain offering of an ephah (twenty-

The significance of the new temple

Ezekiel was a priest before he was called to be a prophet. He looks forward to the return of Israel to Jerusalem and the rebuilding of the temple. But the temple he visits in his vision will never be built.

This is a temple with supernatural features. It is situated on a 'very high mountain'. It has a 'river of life' flowing from its sanctuary. The vision is for inspiration rather than reality.

The Christian understanding is that Christ has fulfilled the Old Testament institutions of temple, priesthood and sacrifice. Jesus Christ is the true temple, where God dwells among his people. He is the great high priest and perfect sacrifice (Hebrews 10:19–21).

So what does this vision mean for Ezekiel? It is an inspiration to return, to rebuild and to hold high the holiness of God. Ezekiel is expressing the centrality and glory of God among his people, in the very best way he can imagine.

John, the writer of the book of Revelation, does not see Ezekiel's temple in the heavenly city, because 'the Lord God Almighty and the Lamb [Jesus Christ] are its temple' (Revelation 21:22).

---

two litres) of flour. With the lambs, the prince may offer as much grain offering as he pleases, together with a hin of oil (six pints) for each ephah of flour.

At New Moon there is an additional sacrifice of a young bull, together with an ephah of flour. All these sacrifices are similar to those offered in the years before the exile.

Ezekiel is also given instructions for annual festivals, daily sacrifices and any occasion when the prince may wish to make an extra (freewill) offering.

The royal land

If the prince wants to give land to his sons, he may do so. He must allocate the land out of his own share and not seize land from other people. The land transferred to a son will continue to belong to that branch of the family (46:16–18).

If the prince gives land to one of his servants, that land will revert to royal ownership at 'the year of freedom'. The 'year of freedom' is probably the Jubilee, every fiftieth year, when debts are cancelled and land restored to its original owner or family (Leviticus 25:13).

A visit to the kitchens

The man (Ezekiel's angel guide) shows Ezekiel the temple kitchens (4:19-24). These are situated in the rooms at the four corners of the outer court – which is all part of the symmetry and perfection of the temple.

The kitchens have ledges for fires, where meat can be boiled and bread baked. The sacrifices and offerings are to be cooked by the priests and eaten by the worshippers.

It is important to keep the food preparation separate from the crowd of worshippers in the outer court. The offerings are sacred and might become defiled. Equally, some unclean people might contract holiness!

The river from the temple (47:1-12)

The man (the angel guide) brings Ezekiel back to the entrance of the temple. This is the east gate, the main entrance, through which the glory of the Lord had entered. Here Ezekiel sees water welling out from under the threshold, flowing from the south side of the temple.

Because the east door is kept closed, the guide takes Ezekiel out of the temple by the north door and round the building on the outside. Arriving at the front of the east gate, Ezekiel sees the water emerging and flowing away.

The guide takes Ezekiel along the course of the river, measuring off distances of a 1,000 cubits (500 yards). At first the water is only ankle-deep, but at the next sounding it is up to their knees. Another 1,000 cubits and the water is waist-deep – after which it becomes impossible to cross on foot. Ezekiel notices a great number of trees growing on the banks.

This is no ordinary river. It is not fed by other streams in the usual way. All the water flows from a single source, which is God's sanctuary. The river is a picture of the blessings which flow from God and give life, fruitfulness and healing to the desert of this world.

The guide tells Ezekiel that this river flows eastwards through the mountains to the Arabah ('the depression'). This is the Jordan Valley which runs down to the Dead Sea.

The Dead Sea is the lowest point on the earth's surface. Normally there is no way of escape for the fresh water which flows into it. The water evaporates in the desert heat, leaving an ever-increasing deposit of salt. But the guide tells Ezekiel that this supernatural river will turn the salt water fresh and make the Dead Sea teem with fish.

The guide describes the paradise which the water from the temple will create. People will stand fishing along the shores of the Dead Sea 'from En Gedi to En Eglaim' – a distance of eighteen miles. All kinds of trees will grow along the river's banks – bearing fruit continually and producing leaves for use in healing.

The water which flows from the temple reminds us of the river which flowed from the Garden of Eden to give life to the world (Genesis 2:10). The writer of Revelation will also remember Ezekiel's vision, in the description of 'the river of the water of life' (Revelation 22:1-2). This is the same supernatural river, but now flowing from the throne of God to make his people fruitful and to give the nations peace.

Boundaries and divisions (47:13–48:29)

Ezekiel has been given a vision of a new temple. This temple is blessed with the presence of the glory of the Lord, and from it flows life for the world. This is the prospect for the people of Israel when they return home from exile. It will be like a new exodus – and a new Promised Land.

The Lord gives instructions for the setting of the boundaries of the land and its division between the tribes. The first exodus was completed by Joshua's allocation of the territory (Joshua 13–21). Now Ezekiel's book closes with a more stylized ('perfect') version.

The boundaries of the land

Israel's northern boundary is to run to the north of Damascus, near Riblah, to the Great Sea (the Mediterranean) just north of Tyre. This is an extension of Israel's historic boundary and includes an area won by David in his conquest of the Arameans. Although it has a natural line of defence, it will prove impossible to retain (47:13-23).

The eastern boundary is to run along the line of the Jordan river, from Hauran in the south to Damascus in the north.

The southern boundary will be on a line with the 'brook of Egypt', the Wadi el-Arish, from a little below the Dead Sea to the Great Sea (the Mediterranean).

The distribution of the tribes

When Joshua divided up the Promised Land between the tribes of Israel, he did so by casting lots (Joshua 18:6). Now the allocation of land is made by God's command, although the details are left to the tribes to agree between themselves (48:1–29).

The land is to be divided by a series of boundaries running from east to west. Each tribal territory is to be the same size, so that the allocation is fairer than before.

The tribes which were previously settled to the east of the River Jordan are now relocated to the west. Israel's territory is consolidated and no land is retained on the far side of the Jordan.

In the centre of the land is the special section reserved for the temple and the priests, the Levites and the prince. Seven tribes will have lands north of the central area and five will have lands to the south.

The tribe of Judah's plot is to be the closest to the temple to the north, while the tribe of Benjamin is to be closest to the south. This is a reversal of the arrangement before the exile, when Judah's land was to the south of Benjamin.

The tribe of Levi has no land, except the area adjacent to the temple. The Lord himself is their portion and inheritance. The tribe of Joseph is represented by two tribes which are named after his sons, Ephraim and Manasseh (Genesis 48).

The foreigners (aliens) who live in Israel are to be treated as part of the community and allocated land by the tribes among which they live. This is the most generous treatment of foreigners in the Old Testament. It is a glimpse of the blessing and inclusion which is always God's will for them.

The central portion of land, which includes the temple, is to be an offering to the Lord. It is 25,000 cubits (seven miles) square – exactly ten times the size of the temple square. The vision of the holy city in the book of Revelation will add the same height, so that the whole place is a perfect cube – a heavenly 'holy of holies' (Revelation 21:16).

The 'new Jerusalem' (48:30–35)

Ezekiel's vision ends with a description of the holy city. It is built on a square, with four walls and twelve gates.

Each gate is named after one of the tribes of Israel. The tribes are those which are descended from the original sons of Jacob (Genesis 29–30). Ephraim and Manasseh are assumed into their father Joseph, and Levi takes his rightful place to make the twelve.

In a vision in the book of Revelation, John will see the heavenly city with twelve gates named after the tribes of Israel, but also with twelve foundations named after the apostles of the Lamb (Revelation 21:12–14). He gives Christian completion to Ezekiel's Jewish vision. One of the names of Jesus Christ is 'Immanuel', which means 'God With Us' (Revelation 21:3).

The name of the city will be 'the Lord is there'. In Hebrew this is 'Yahweh Shammah' – words which sound like 'Jerusalem'. Ezekiel has not mentioned Jerusalem until now. It is the final glory of the holy city that God is present in her.

So Ezekiel concludes his book. For twenty-five years, Ezekiel has served as prophet and priest-in-exile to the people of Israel in Babylon.

He began with a vision of the Lord's chariot-throne, which revealed the God of Israel as supremely glorious and everywhere active.

He saw the Lord withdraw from the temple and predicted the fall and destruction of Jerusalem.

He promised the exiles that God would make a new covenant with his people, to give them a new heart and dwell with them for ever.

He received a vision of the future, with a new temple, priesthood, land and city, all reflecting and expressing God's perfect holiness.

In the dark days of exile, Ezekiel is realistic about God's judgment and certain of a future restoration for Israel. His awareness and portrayal of the glory of God is unsurpassed in the Old Testament. His prophecies and visions hold high the hope that God will one day bring all things to completion and make all things new.

DANIEL

Daniel is one of the Bible's holiest and wisest men. He and his friends are Jews living in exile. As young men they are captured during an attack on Jerusalem and taken to live in Babylon. There they are educated in the pagan court of King Nebuchadnezzar, but refuse to compromise their Jewish faith.

This book tells how God protects Daniel and his friends in a series of desperate situations – including the fiery furnace and the den of lions. Just as Joseph became prime minister of Egypt, so Daniel becomes a leading figure in both the Babylonian and Persian empires.

The second part of the book describes Daniel's strange visions. They depict the rise and fall of empires – and the ultimate victory of God.

OUTLINE

Daniel at the royal court (1:1–6:28)
Daniel's dreams and visions (7:1–12:13)

Introduction

Daniel is a strange book – a mixture of history and visions. It is very difficult to know who wrote it and when.

The 'history' part of the book describes the adventures of the young Daniel and his friends. They have been deported from Jerusalem to Babylon in 597 BC and bravely maintain their faith in the God of Israel.

However, the 'visions' in the book concern a much later situation – the revolt of the Jewish Maccabees in the 2nd century BC. The Maccabees rebel against attempts to introduce the Greek culture and gods to Jerusalem.

Daniel's story is inspiring for everyone who wants to stand for God in a pagan society. Was the original account of Daniel's faith retold and applied to later situations? Or was it the persecution of the Jews in the time of the Maccabees which led to the writing of Daniel's story and visions?

By telling of Daniel's faith, courage and influence in the past, the Jews could make connections with their later sufferings. 'Daniel' became a legend for oppressed people in every age.

A great disaster has overtaken the people of Judah. Their capital city, Jerusalem, has been captured, and their king, Jehoiakim, has been deported. Holy treasures have been taken from the Jewish temple and devoted to the pagan gods of Babylon.

All this is devastating for the Jews. They thought their God was all-powerful and would always protect them. It poses an enormous question: is their God in charge or not? Should they persist in worshipping the God of Israel, or should they give up and join in with the Babylonians?

We follow the story of the young man Daniel and his three friends – Hananiah, Mishael and Azariah. They are among the exiled Jews in Babylon. When they are selected for special training and privileges in the pagan court of Nebuchadnezzar, they resolve to keep faith with the God of the Jews.

The story of Daniel came into its own during the time of the Maccabees. The Jews were then back in their own land, but dominated by the emperor Antiochus IV Epiphanes. He was determined to impose a Greek way of life on the Jews.

Between 175 and 163 BC, Antiochus Epiphanes suppressed all Jewish customs, including the circumcising of baby boys, the keeping of the sabbath as a day of rest and the reading of the Jewish law. He took over the Jerusalem temple and installed a statue of Zeus, the king of the Greek gods. In these oppressive conditions, the story of Daniel inspired the Jews to hang onto their faith in the one true God and to trust that he would rescue his people.

Persecution in the time of the Maccabees

When Alexander the Great died, his empire broke up into four main parts. Judah came to be ruled by a Hellenistic (Greek-style) king of Syria called Antiochus. He added the surname 'Epiphanes' because he claimed to be the 'epiphany' or manifestation of Zeus.

Antiochus tried to make the Jews live like Greeks. Some of the priestly class and aristocracy cooperated, but the common people rebelled. Strict Jews suffered terribly as they saw an image of Zeus set up in the temple, and pigs sacrificed on pagan altars around the country. Innocent families, who refused to defend themselves (and would certainly not fight on the Sabbath) were tortured and killed for upholding Jewish traditions.

At last the Jewish resistance found a leader in a priest named Mattathias. He and his five sons fought a guerrilla war in the hills. One of the sons was Judas 'The Hammer' Maccabeus – and their struggle became known as the Maccabean revolt.

But the Jews were divided in their approach. One group trusted solely in God to defend them. They were the Hasideans, the 'holy ones', who tried to avoid conflict by withdrawing to the desert. They were pursued and slaughtered in a sabbath-day massacre. Meanwhile, the Maccabees were more worldly wise. They realized they would have to defend themselves, however much they trusted in God and regardless of the day of the week.

The Maccabeans and the surviving Hasideans joined forces. They forced Antiochus to back down. Jewish society was once again founded on Jewish law, and the temple was restored. The rededication of the temple on 14 December 164 BC became the feast of Hanukkah in the centuries that followed.

Judas Maccabeus and his descendants became the ruling family in Judah. Their line is known as the Hasmonean dynasty. They ruled until the Roman general Pompey captured Jerusalem in 63 BC.

The Hasidean (strict Jewish) tradition continued in various forms. Some may have founded the Essene community, living in the desert by the Dead Sea at Qumran. The traces of their settlement, and their 'Dead Sea Scrolls' which survived in earthenware jars in the caves, were among the exciting finds of the 20th century.

Other Hasideans may have continued to live holy lives in the midst of Jewish society. Perhaps they became the Pharisees of Jesus' day.

Although the Hasmoneans became the ruling class, the memory of Judas Maccabeus must have inspired the Zealots, who were later to plot the overthrow of the Romans.

Discovering Daniel

Daniel at the royal court

Taking a stand over food (1:1–21)

Daniel and his companions are plunged into the Babylonian way of life and given Babylonian names. Daniel becomes Belteshazzar. The other three become Shadrach, Meshach and Abednego. They ask to be excused the rich royal food and drink. Whether this is because the food has been prepared in pagan temples or because they are thinking of their starving compatriots, we don't know. Perhaps they want to stay physically and mentally alert to avoid temptation and compromise. In any case, to eat the royal food is to accept a close and cooperative relationship with the king. Sharing a meal is the sign of making a covenant; and this they are not prepared to do.

At the end of three years of training, and despite living only on vegetables, the young men are the brightest and fittest of their generation. They enter the king's service, where they prove wiser than all the magicians and enchanters of Babylon. Their wisdom isn't painstakingly gathered from ancient proverbs, but received directly from the living God. Daniel is particularly gifted at understanding visions and dreams.

Explaining Nebuchadnezzar's dream (2:1–49)

One day Daniel has the opportunity to interpret King Nebuchadnezzar's dream. He does so with tact and humility towards the king, and complete trust in God to reveal the mystery.

The dream is of an enormous, dazzling statue. It's not clear whether this statue is an image of Nebuchadnezzar himself. The head is gold, the chest and arms are silver, the belly and thighs are bronze, the legs are iron and the feet are a mixture of iron and clay.

While the king watches, the statue is smashed to pieces by a rock. The rock is from God, 'cut out, but not by human hands'. After destroying the statue, the rock grows to become a mountain which fills the whole earth.

Daniel explains the dream to the king. The statue is a model of the Babylonian kingdom and the empires which will follow. The gold head is Nebuchadnezzar. His kingdom is the first and the finest. After him come kings and kingdoms of lesser quality.

It is possible to identify the great empires which followed Babylon. The silver chest and arms are the Medes and Persians; the bronze belly and thighs are the Greeks; the iron legs are the Romans. By this interpretation, the rock is the impact of Christianity on the world – coming from God to establish his everlasting kingdom.

Whatever the details of the dream, the overall message is clear. God is in control of the rise and fall of earthly empires. All kings are under his rule and his kingdom will ultimately reign supreme.

Daniel's friends in the fiery furnace (3:1–30)

King Nebuchadnezzar seeks to unite his people in the worship of a gold statue. The event is heralded by a big band making a mighty crescendo of sound. The penalty for disobedience is to be thrown into a furnace.

Daniel's three companions refuse to worship the statue. They decide they must make their stand against the excessive demands of the state, and they are not afraid:

If we are thrown into the burning furnace, the God we serve is able to deliver us from it, and he will deliver us from Your Majesty's hand. But even if he does not, we want you to know, Your Majesty, that we will not serve your gods or worship the image of gold you have set up. (3:17–18)

Their brave stand brings to mind the witness of Peter and the apostles when the Jewish Council tries to silence them:

We must obey God rather than any human authority. (Acts 5:29 NRSV)

Daniel's friends are condemned to die in the fiery furnace, but they pass through the fire unharmed. Peering into the fierce blaze, Nebuchadnezzar sees a fourth figure walking freely with them. This fourth person 'has the appearance of a god' (3:25 NRSV). The king declares his faith in the God of the Jews, and promotes the friends to high positions in his government.

Who was Daniel?

There are many other stories about Daniel in addition to those we have in the Bible. A legendary figure with the same name is mentioned by Ezekiel – alongside Noah and Job (Ezekiel 14:14). This could not have been the same person, and the Hebrew spelling is different.

Daniel is the great example of the Jew who stands firm in a pagan culture where his faith is frequently under fire. He is a blessing to his kings and an inspiration to his people, without ever compromising his supreme loyalty to God.

The pride and fall of Nebuchadnezzar (4:1–37)

The king has another dream – this time of a great tree. The tree is huge, beautiful and fruitful – but a heavenly messenger declares it must be cut down.

Daniel, after much heart-searching, warns the king that the fate of the tree is a picture of his own future. Nebuchadnezzar's pride stands between himself and God, and he will be humbled for 'seven times' (perhaps seven years).

As the dream is fulfilled, Nebuchadnezzar becomes for a while like an animal, living in the open fields and eating grass. But in the end his sanity is restored, and he praises God.

I... praise and exult and glorify the King of heaven, because everything he does is right and all his ways are just. And those who walk in pride he is able to humble. (4:37)

The persecuted Jews of the 2nd century told this story. As they suffered terrible atrocities at the hands of Antiochus Epiphanes, the memory of Nebuchadnezzar helped to cut their oppressor down to size.

King Belshazzar's feast (5:1–31)

We move on to another story about Daniel, and another king, Belshazzar. Belshazzar abuses the gold and silver cups from the Jerusalem temple. He calls for them to be used at a drunken feast for toasts to the gods of

Babylon. This is not only a frivolous bit of fun. He is seriously mocking the God represented by the goblets, as though God is powerless and defeated.

Suddenly, at the high point of the revel, a finger appears and writes some letters on the wall. When the wise men and enchanters fail to interpret the signs, the king calls for Daniel.

Daniel reads and interprets the markings on the wall:

MENE, MENE, TEKEL, PARSIN

Mene, Tekel and Parsin are three coins: a mina, a shekel and a half-shekel. Each is smaller than the last. This alone tells Belshazzar that his kingdom is counting down to its end.

Daniel explains that each coin has a root meaning:

'Mene' means 'numbered'. The days of Belshazzar's reign are numbered.

'Tekel' means 'weighed'. Belshazzar has been weighed and found to be short in God's judgment.

'Peres' (a single parsin) means 'divided' or 'Persia'. Belshazzar's kingdom is going to be divided between the Medes and the Persians.

So God's judgment falls on Belshazzar's outrageous behaviour. That night the king is killed and Darius the Mede takes over his realm. We know nothing of Darius other than what the Bible tells us. History shows that the Medes and Persians joined forces around 500 BC and took over the old Babylonian empire. Some scholars suggest that 'Darius' may be the throne-name for the first Persian king – Cyrus.

Daniel in the den of lions (6:1–28)

In the reign of Darius, Daniel is arrested for refusing to pray to the king. Again, there would be many parallels for the Jews of the early 2nd century BC. They were being forced to worship the image of Antiochus Epiphanes, who claimed to be Zeus in human form.

Daniel is sentenced to death in the lion's den, but God protects him by shutting the lions' mouths. King Darius, like Nebuchadnezzar before him, realizes the power and majesty of the 'God of Daniel'. Daniel's enemies have gone against the Persian policy of religious freedom by attacking him. He has done nothing wrong.

Daniel's dreams and visions

Daniel is gifted in telling people the meaning of their dreams. He also has visions of his own.

The second half of the book describes some of Daniel's extraordinary visions. This kind of writing is called 'apocalyptic' – which means that it 'reveals' what is going on behind the scenes of history. Some of Ezekiel's book is written in this way, as well as the second part of Zechariah and (in the New Testament) the book of Revelation.

Daniel's dream of four beasts (7:1–28)

Daniel has a fantastic vision of four beasts. They emerge out of a churning sea:

- a lion with wings which walks like a human being and is given a human heart
- a bear with three ribs in its mouth
- a leopard with wings and four heads
- a nightmare creature with iron teeth and ten horns, more terrifying and destructive than the others.

While Daniel watches, a little horn emerges among the horns of the fourth creature. It uproots three of the other horns – and then starts looking around and boasting!

The vision continues with God, the Ancient of Days, taking his throne in heaven and sitting in judgment on the earth. The first three beasts are disarmed and the fourth is killed and destroyed.

Finally, someone 'like a son of man' comes with clouds of glory into the presence of God. He is given authority, glory and sovereign power. He is made king of a realm which embraces all nations and languages. His is a universal kingdom which will last for ever.

Daniel understands the vision. The beasts are kingdoms which will come and go. Perhaps they are easily recognized by their descriptions:

- a winged lion for Babylon and later emperors, Nebuchadnezzar and Belshazzar
- a voracious bear for the Medes and their king, Darius
- a four-headed leopard for the Persians and their emperor, Cyrus
- a ten-horned monster for the Greeks and their emperor, Alexander the Great.

Another theory has the bear for the empire of the Medes and Persians, the leopard for the Greek empire (which split into four, like four heads) and the ten-horned monster for the empire of Rome.

For the Jews of the 2nd century, the outrageous, boasting little horn would represent the insufferable Antiochus Epiphanes!

Daniel views the glory of God's ultimate power and judgment. God disarms the most awesome of earthly empires – and destroys their strutting despots.

Daniel and Joseph

There are many similarities between the story of Daniel and the story of Joseph.

Both Joseph and Daniel find themselves, through no fault of their own, as strangers in a foreign land. Joseph is in Egypt. Daniel is in Babylon.

Both Joseph and Daniel prove their loyalty to God by their personal standards: Daniel refuses the comforts of court; Joseph refuses to sleep with his master's wife.

Both Joseph and Daniel are able, with God's help, to interpret their ruler's dream. Both are promoted to positions of power in their adopted country.

Both Joseph and Daniel suffer unjustly and almost disappear from history – Joseph in Pharaoh's prison and Daniel in the lion's den.

Both are heroes of faith: trusting God despite many setbacks and proving his guidance in all circumstances.

A book of twos

The book of Daniel is a book of two halves. The first half deals with the experiences of Daniel as a Jew living in exile in Babylon. The second half is an account of his extraordinary visions. The stories and visions complement each other.

Daniel is also a book of two languages. The beginning and end (1:1–2:3 and 8:1–12:13) are in Hebrew, while the middle (2:4–7:28) is written in Aramaic.

The vision of 'one like a son of man' is deeply moving for both Jews and Christians. God has a special place for human beings, made in his image. The human race, the crown of his creation, will also be at the heart of his heaven. The beasts won't win!

For Christians, Jesus is the Son of Man. He used the title Son of Man, with Daniel's meaning, to describe himself. He is our perfect representative before the Father's judgment throne. It is his kingdom which will be established everywhere and for ever.

Daniel's vision of a ram and a goat (8:1-27)

Daniel's next vision is of a ram which conquers territory in three directions. This ram is charged and swiftly overthrown by a goat with a prominent horn. But just as the goat is at the height of its power, its horn is broken off – and four other horns grow in its place.

As Daniel watches, a small horn grows from one of the four horns, and extends its power towards the 'Beautiful Land'. It causes damage in heaven and imposes its terrible power on the saints on earth.

By now we are more familiar with the imagery of Daniel's visions. The ram is the Persian empire – suddenly attacked by the Greeks under the brilliant command of their 'large horn', Alexander the Great. But Alexander is 'broken off' when he dies while still a young man. His empire is divided between his four generals – the 'four horns' that grow in the place of the large one.

One of the generals is Seleucus. He has a vast kingdom which he and his descendants (the Seleucids) rule from Antioch in Syria. One of their successors is the evil Antiochus IV Epiphanes – 'the horn which started small' but has sinister designs on the 'Beautiful Land' of Judah.

Antiochus tries to force Hellenism (the Greek way of life) on the Jews. He does so with immense cruelty, including torture and bloodshed. He desecrates the temple with pagan sacrifices and a statue of Zeus.

Daniel is given a detailed description of Antiochus. He is a master of intrigue who prospers by deceit. He has come to power by no effort of his own – that is, he has simply benefited from the victories of others.

Daniel is assured that the time of Judah's suffering is limited. All the same, he is stunned by the sheer power of evil depicted in the vision.

Daniel's prayer (9:1-19)

Daniel may have some Scriptures in mind, and in particular the prophecy of Jeremiah. The Scriptures are a lifeline for the faith of the exiles. Perhaps their meetings for prayer and study (they have no temples or sacrifices in exile) are the origins of the synagogues which Jesus and Paul will know so well.

From Jeremiah's prophecy, Daniel understands that the desolation of Jerusalem will last for seventy years. He devotes himself to pray about this. He confesses the sins of his people. He acknowledges that the Jews have deserved God's judgment. He pleads that God will forgive and restore them. His prayer is a model of intercession, like the great prayers of Moses and Nehemiah (Deuteronomy 9:25-29; Nehemiah 9:5-37).

The seventy 'sevens' (9:20-27)

As Daniel prays about the end of the exile, the angel Gabriel comes to speak with him.

Gabriel reveals that there is a greater plan and a longer timescale than simply the restoration of Jerusalem after seventy years. He speaks of 'seventy sevens' or seventy 'weeks' of years. This means 'a very great length of time' rather than a carefully counted 490 years.

The seventy 'sevens' will give time for the rebuilding of Jerusalem, for people to put their lives in order and to await the Anointed One, their Messiah. But the Anointed One will be 'cut off', and the city and the temple will be destroyed. War and desolations will continue until the end of time. In particular, 'an abomination that causes desolation' will be set up 'on a wing of the temple' – perhaps beside the altar.

Here is a prophecy which provides a pattern for future events. The sequence will repeat in the years to come.

The first sequence will see the suffering of the Jews under Antiochus in the early 2nd century BC.

The second sequence will see the rejection of the Christ and the destruction of Jerusalem in the 1st century AD.

Jesus warns against trying to calculate the particular times and dates when God will act:

It is not for you to know the times or dates the Father has set by his own authority. (Acts 1:7 NRSV)

We must not make this passage a happy hunting ground for cranky theories.

At one level, Gabriel predicts the return of the Jews to their land and the rebuilding of Jerusalem. An invading ruler (Antiochus) will win cooperation from many (the Jewish priests and ruling families) for a 'seven' (seven years?). But he will cause havoc by stopping the temple sacrifices and introducing an abominable idol.

We don't know who the 'Anointed One' is in this scenario, unless it is a high priest, Onias, who is 'cut off' (perhaps murdered) by Antiochus in 170 BC.

At another level, and on a longer timescale, Gabriel makes a prediction which fits the time of Jesus. This makes sense of the 'Anointed One' (the Messiah or Christ) who will be 'cut off' (crucified). The city of Jerusalem and the temple will be destroyed – a judgment carried out by the Roman armies of Titus in AD 70.

When Jesus himself predicts this tragedy, he links it with this part of Daniel:

When you see the 'abomination that causes desolation' standing where it does not belong… then let those who are in Judea flee to the mountains. (Mark 13:14)

Coded messages and magic numbers?

Some of the book of Daniel is strange and difficult for us to understand. We are not familiar with the numbers and images which would have been like a coded message for Jewish readers.

For all we know, the creatures in the dreams may have been as easily recognized as a lion for England, or an eagle for America.

Again, it was common for names to have a number. This number was calculated by adding the values of the different letters. 'Nebuchadnezzar' is spelled differently in Daniel from other places in the Old Testament. This enables the letters to add up to 423 – the same as the total for Antiochus Epiphanes. It could be that some of what is said about Nebuchadnezzar is to encourage hope that God will overrule Antiochus.

The important thing to realize is that the 'code language' is referring to events which were taking place at the time of writing. It is not describing upheavals and cataclysms in the distant future.

Daniel's vision of a man (10:1–11:45)

Daniel meets a heavenly being – an angel who appears like a glorious man. The vision is terrifying, and Daniel is overwhelmed.

The angel has been sent in response to Daniel's earnest prayer. The angel himself is engaged in the spiritual war in heaven. This war is waged in parallel with the battle between good and evil on earth. He has been striving against the king of Persia – helped by Michael, the guardian angel of the Jews. Angels and human beings are involved together in a conflict which spans earth and heaven.

In New Testament times, Paul teaches that we are in a struggle against invisible powers of evil:

For our struggle is not against flesh and blood, but against the rulers, against the authorities, against the powers of this dark world and against the spiritual forces of evil in the heavenly realms. (Ephesians 6:12)

The ultimate battle for both earth and heaven takes place when Jesus dies on the cross. The book of Revelation describes how:

The great dragon was hurled down – that ancient snake called the devil, or Satan, who leads the whole world astray. (Revelation 12:9)

Michael and his angels are involved in this conflict in heaven, as Jesus defeats the powers of darkness by his death and resurrection on earth.

In chapter 11 the angel gives Daniel more details of the history which has already been enacted in the visions of the beasts.

After Alexander's death, his empire is split between four generals. One of them, Ptolemy, becomes the ruler of Egypt. His descendants are the Ptolemies and they are 'the kings of the South'.

Another general, Seleucus, rules Syria and Babylonia. His descendants are the Seleucids, who are 'the kings of the North'.

As the Seleucids rule from Antioch, they start to take the name Antiochus. Antiochus the Great, for example, gives his daughter in marriage to the reigning Ptolemy in 194 BC. This is described in 11:17 and attracts our attention because the daughter is none other than the famous Cleopatra.

The angel's narrative gives an extraordinary impression of human aggression and intrigue. Antiochus IV Epiphanes appears in 11:21 and his unspeakable treatment of the Jews is again foretold. But his time is limited. Those who are faithful to God should resist him, even if it costs them their lives.

The end-times (12:1–13)

As Daniel's final vision draws to a close, he is told of the end of the world. There will be a period of great distress, but God's people will be delivered. Those who have died will be raised to life and judged. The righteous will be vindicated. The wicked will be sentenced.

There is great hope here that God will put all to rights. There will be life beyond death and glory after suffering. But as for the details and the timing, like Daniel, we must wait and see.

HOSEA

Hosea is a prophet in pain. For many years he has struggled with a broken marriage. But, through his agony and anger, he has realized what love is. He has discovered the heart of God.

God tells Hosea to marry a prostitute, which he does – and they have three children. But his wife, Gomer, is never faithful for long. She leaves her husband and commits adultery with other lovers. She is exploited and abused, and eventually falls into slavery. But Hosea never stops loving her. He goes through every stage of grief and desire for revenge, to arrive at a deeply committed love for his wretched wife – and a longing to restore her.

It is through his experience of a broken heart that Hosea realizes how God must feel about his people Israel. After all, God rescued Israel from Egypt and was married to her by covenant at Sinai. But Israel has been appallingly unfaithful – wantonly chasing after other gods. Now judgment is about to fall on Israel, and she will suffer the terrible consequences of her behaviour. But God's love for her is as deep as ever, and he will rescue and restore her.

OUTLINE

The marriages of Hosea to Gomer, and God to Israel (1:1–3:5)
Israel's unfaithfulness to God (4:1–13:16)
A message of hope for the future (14:1–9)

Introduction

The background to Hosea's prophecies

Hosea is a prophet in the northern kingdom of Israel, during the time when the nation is divided from the kingdom of Judah in the south. His name, like Joshua, means 'The Lord Saves'. From the kings mentioned in the opening verse, it seems that he preaches his message for thirty years before Israel's downfall. Only one king of Israel is mentioned (Jeroboam II), but several kings of Judah are named. This is probably because Hosea believes that the kings of Judah are the true royal line descending from the great King David.

We can date Hosea's messages to the 8th century BC, after those of Amos and before the fall of Samaria (the capital of Israel) in 722 BC. This is a period when Israel is prosperous, proud and pagan – and thoughts of God and judgment seem ridiculous. But it is because Hosea's words prove true that his prophecies are remembered and his promises treasured.

The rising superpower is Assyria. Under the command of their emperor, Tiglath-Pileser III (745–727 BC), the armies of Assyria first threaten, and then conquer, Damascus and Samaria. King Pekah of Israel tries to resist Assyria by making an alliance with Syria, but the effort is useless. This episode is described in Isaiah 7. Damascus falls in 732 BC, and part of Israel is overrun. Another of Israel's kings, Hoshea, tries to get help from Egypt, but without success. The Assyrians lay siege to Samaria for three years, and capture it in 722.

Hosea's message

God's message to Israel through Hosea is that his people are committing spiritual adultery. They are worshipping the 'Baals' – the pagan gods of Canaan. 'Baal' means 'Lord', and the gods of that name are thought to have power over rain, crops and fertility. The Baals are worshipped in blood, with animals being sacrificed and people gashing themselves. There are also festivals at which worshippers have sex with the sacred prostitutes at the Baal shrines. Hosea tells Israel (whom he often calls 'Ephraim') that God feels terrible pain and anger at this rejection. He is also exasperated that Israel has looked for help from Egypt and other alliances, instead of turning to him.

DISCOVERING HOSEA

The marriages of Hosea to Gomer, and God to Israel

Hosea's wife and children (1:1–11)

When the Lord began to speak through Hosea, the Lord said to him, 'Go, marry a promiscuous woman and have children with her, for like an adulterous wife, this land is guilty of unfaithfulness to the Lord.' (1:2)

So Hosea marries Gomer, daughter of Diblaim, and she conceives and bears him a son.

God may have called Hosea to marry one of the sacred prostitutes of Baal. Certainly she is a person who has already led an immoral life. They have three children, and each is given a special name. Their first son, Jezreel, is named after the place where Jehu had broken the power of paganism in the reign of King Ahab. This is described in 2 Kings 9 and 10. Their daughter is called 'Lo-Ruhamah' which means 'Not Loved' – because God's love for his unfaithful people is now exhausted. Their third child, another son, is named 'Lo-Ammi', which means 'Not My People', and means that God is disowning Israel altogether. But, even as the Lord gives Hosea such heartless names for his children, a note of hope creeps in. There will come a day when the people of Israel will once again be called 'children of the living God'.

Israel's adultery and restoration (2:1–23)

Now Hosea draws the parallel between his marriage to Gomer and God's marriage to Israel. Israel has enjoyed God's gifts of grain, wine, oil, silver and gold – and claimed they are blessings from Baal! God will punish Israel by blighting the harvest and humiliate her for her unfaithfulness.

But now comes a gentle note of longing. God will take Israel back to the desert days of their first love, and woo and win her all over again. The Valley of Achor (where Achan sinned – this story is told in Joshua 7:24–26) will become a door of hope. The marriage between God and his people will be closer, deeper and richer than ever before, drawing the whole of creation into its truth and harmony.

Hosea's reconciliation with his wife (3:1–5)

Inspired by his vision of God's love for Israel, Hosea goes in search of his wife and brings her back from slavery. He pays the price of a slave – half in silver and half in grain. There is to be a period of waiting before they are intimate again – just as Israel will be without signs of God for a while, when she is defeated and her people dispersed. But eventually there will be a joyful reunion of husband and wife; and the people will return to God and his king. Christians see this fulfilled in the coming reign of Jesus Christ.

Israel's unfaithfulness to God

Hosea's prophecies are all against Israel (4:1–13:16). He condemns the lawlessness of Israelite society, with its widespread deceit, brutality and immorality. The world of nature is also suffering because of human sin. Hosea singles out the priests and condemns their corrupt leadership and influence. He criticizes the rituals at the ancient pilgrim sites of Gilgal and Bethel. The sacrifices and words of faith are just a shallow sham. He sarcastically renames Bethel ('house of God') as 'Beth Aven' ('house of wickedness'). For Hosea, a *real* knowledge of the Lord is everything. He mimics the cheap and cheerful repentance of the people, as they chirrup, 'Come, let us return to the Lord.' In God's sight their devotion is as fleeting as the morning mist. God cares nothing for sacrifices if they don't signal a changed life and a fair society.

God also looks on Israel's politics with contempt. The kings and princes are hot with wine and burning with passion and deceit. They undermine each other with intrigue and assassination. None of them turns to God for guidance or strength; and the nation appears ageing and ridiculous on the international scene. Israel is as weak and brainless as a dove as she appeals first to Egypt, then to Assyria for protection. Meanwhile God, like a mighty eagle, is about to swoop in judgment.

Hosea has a strong sense of Israel's history. He harks back to the time when Israel was newly rescued from Egypt. Then she was an exciting discovery for God – like finding grapes in the desert, or the first figs of the season. Israel was like a dear son whom God could teach to walk, guiding him with reins of love, easing his problems and stooping to feed him. But now all the youthful promise has vanished. The love of God for Israel is blighted by idolatry and made barren by disobedience.

Looking forward, Hosea sees certain disaster. Any hope of safety through military strength or political alliance will be crushed by the invading armies of Assyria. But even as God contemplates a sweeping revenge, he is moved to mercy:

How can I give you up, Ephraim?
How can I hand you over, Israel?...
For I am God and not a man
the Holy One among you. (11:8-9)

Hosea recalls how God had dealt with Jacob, the cheat who became 'Israel'. After all his thrusting ambition and aggressive self-seeking, Jacob had come to terms with God at Bethel. Now Jacob's descendants must do the same. Israel has taken on the values of Canaan, whose traders are notorious cheats. Israelites are getting rich by deceit – and then being deceived by riches.

Hosea sees that God will reduce them again to the simple life of the desert, or the Feast of Tabernacles, when they live in tents. Pagan altars will become like discarded rubble, and Israel will know once more the touch of a God who really cares.

Hosea's style is quite fragmented and some of what he says is hard to understand. The places and episodes to which he refers are outside our own general knowledge. But Hosea's images are powerful and his phrases are pithy. We can at least follow his tremendous mood swings. He shows us God, sometimes burning with anger and resolving to exterminate his people once and for all:

Like a lion I will devour them;
a wild animal will tear them apart. (13:8)

But at other times, God's heart is almost breaking with longing love:

My heart is changed within me;
all my compassion is aroused.
I will not carry out my fierce anger. (11:8-9)

A message of hope for the future

Hosea's prophecy closes with an urgent call to Israel to return to God and seek his forgiveness (14:1-9). She must abandon all hope of help from Egypt or mercy from Assyria – and reject the gods of paganism made by human hands.

For his part, God promises a new start and a new life for Israel. She will grow beautiful and strong, famous and fragrant – a landmark, shelter and blessing to the nations of the world.

JOEL

Joel's book is small, but packed with big ideas. It is a prophecy written down as a poem. It dates from a time when Jerusalem has been all but wiped from the face of the earth, but promises that she will be rescued and renewed. She will fulfil her eternal destiny as Zion, God's city. Chapter 2 contains one of the Old Testament's most precious jewels: the prophecy that one day God's Spirit will be free for all.

OUTLINE

A devastating plague of locusts (1:1–20)
God's judgment and mercy (2:1–32)
The nations judged and Jerusalem saved (3:1–21)

Introduction

We don't know very much about Joel. His name means 'The Lord is God' and he prophesies in Jerusalem around the year 400 BC.

The Jews have returned from exile in Babylon (538 BC). They have no king, but the national life is focused on Jerusalem. They have built a new temple under the leadership of Zerubbabel (515 BC) and rebuilt the walls under the leadership of Nehemiah (444 BC).

Joel seems particularly interested in the temple and concerned for the worship. He may have been a priest or a 'temple prophet' who worked there.

Joel declares that a terrible plague of locusts is in fact the judgment of God. He calls on God's people Israel to repent of their sins. When they do so, he promises that a long drought and dearth of the harvests will end. There will be grain and wine for the offerings in the temple once again.

Joel also has a greater message. The locusts are an image of an enemy army invading from the north. Joel sees in them a picture of the great and terrible 'Day of the Lord'. This is the time when God will judge all the nations and establish his eternal kingdom of peace with Jerusalem at its centre.

Joel's prophecy may originally have been in verse, and sung to the pilgrims in the temple. Many of his ideas and phrases are the same as older prophets, especially Ezekiel, Isaiah and Zephaniah. His phrase 'the Lord roars from Zion' is an echo of the prophecies of Amos before the destruction of Jerusalem.

Discovering Joel

A devastating plague of locusts (1:1–20)

Joel's prophecy begins with the news of a terrible plague of locusts (1:1–20). Wave upon wave of hungry insects have swarmed over the land like a devouring army. Trees have been stripped of leaf and bark. Fields, vineyards and orchards are all ruined. Farmers and vine-growers are in despair, and the priests have nothing to offer to the Lord.

Joel, like a true prophet, calls the priests and people to turn to God. The devastation of the locusts and the effects of the drought are such that only God can help.

God's judgment and mercy (2:1–32)

Joel sees more in this crisis than a cloud of locusts. He sees the gathering clouds of God's judgment on the world. He calls for the trumpet to sound the alarm, for here comes another invasion of locusts, even more thorough and all-consuming than the last. Darkness and fire envelop the land as millions of the horse-like creatures swarm over it, turning paradise to desert. But the most terrifying news of all is that God himself is at the head of this invincible army. This is the Day of the Lord; and he is sending a plague of locusts not on his enemies, but upon his own people!

The Lord appeals to his people through Joel. This terrible Day has not yet arrived. The nightmare has not yet become a reality. There is still time to repent and get right with God. The Lord would love to see his people turn to him, so that he can change his plan from punishment to blessing.

Joel calls for the entire community to gather for fasting and prayer. Even the very old, the very young and the newly married are to come and pray. Fasting (going without food) is a sign of utter concentration on God, and often goes with loss of appetite at times of worry or grief. The priests are to beg God to spare his people, especially as other nations will judge God by whatever happens to Israel.

Joel promises that if the people truly repent (tearing their hearts and not just their clothes), then God will sweep away the armies of locusts and restore the crops. The autumn and spring rains will bring life to pastures, trees and animals, and the joy of harvest will fill hearts and stomachs. The word Joel uses for the autumn rains can also mean 'teacher'. God is going to bless his people by teaching them his truth and guiding them in right living.

The last part of chapter 2 is so important that it forms a separate chapter in the Hebrew Bible.

God's Spirit will be given to everyone – men and women, young and old, rich and poor. The whole community will be alive to God – able to perceive his will in visions and dreams, and speak his word in prophecy. This mighty blessing of God's people will go hand in hand with a tremendous upheaval throughout creation. There will be darkness and fire, blood and smoke. And then the dreadful Day of the Lord will come. At the centre of it all, Jerusalem will be both the focus of judgment and the place of refuge.

The nations judged and Jerusalem saved (3:1–21)

Joel now delivers God's message about the distant future. The nations who have ill-treated Israel will be summoned and judged. Joel sees this taking place in the Valley of Jehoshaphat – perhaps the Kidron Valley where armies have camped when besieging Jerusalem. Joel names some of Israel's enemies – the Phoenician and Philistine traders who have stolen the temple treasures and sold God's people to be slaves in Greece. These words help us to date Joel's prophecy to the early 4th century BC. Joel predicts that the Jews will get their revenge. This will come about when the Persian emperor Alexander captures Sidon in 345 BC and Gaza in 332 BC. The Jews will trade their captured enemies in Arab slave markets.

The outpouring of God's Spirit

In the New Testament, Peter sees Joel's words being fulfilled. On the great Day of Pentecost, God pours out his Spirit on his apostles. This story is told in Acts 2. The writer of the Acts of the Apostles describes the Spirit as sounding like a violent wind and looking like flames of fire. Those who receive the Spirit are able to praise God in languages other than their own. Peter explains to the crowd that the outpouring of God's Spirit is a sign that Jesus is the Christ, and that God will judge the people who killed him.

Joel ends by describing Zion, God's city – high and holy, safe and secure. Just as God's judgment has been described in images of war and devastation, now his blessing is pictured in terms of peace and plenty. The Lord reigns in Zion, and all is well with his people for ever.

AMOS

Amos is a new kind of prophet in his day. He preaches the astounding message that God is about to destroy his own people. It may be because his words are so shocking that they are kept and written down. Amos is the first prophet to have his work recorded in a book. Amos preaches that God is the judge of all nations, including Israel. But the special relationship that exists between God and Israel doesn't mean that Israel will be spared as a favourite. On the contrary, Israel will be judged first of all – and by the highest standards.

OUTLINE

God will judge the surrounding nations (1:1–2:5)
God will judge Israel, his own people (2:6–6:14)
Visions of doom, and a word of hope (7:1–9:15)

Introduction

Who is Amos?

Amos is a shepherd from the southern kingdom of Judah. His home town is Tekoa, about twelve miles south of Jerusalem. He preaches at a time when Israel is divided, with a northern kingdom of Israel and a southern kingdom of Judah, sometime around 760 BC.

Although Amos comes from the south, he does his preaching in the north – probably at the ancient shrine of Bethel. In chapter 7 we read how the priest of Bethel, Amaziah, treats Amos as a traitor and tells him to go back home. But Amos stands his ground. He explains that he never expected to be a prophet, but God called him and gave him his message for Israel.

Amos denounces society

Amos speaks to a society which is both very prosperous and very religious. Israel is wealthy during the rule of Jeroboam II, but her religion is meaningless because she is ignoring God's law.

There is a great gulf between rich and poor. Amos expresses God's anger at those who exploit and crush their fellows:

They sell the righteous for silver,
and the needy for a pair of sandals –
They... trample the... poor into the dust of the earth,
and push the afflicted out of the way. (2:6–7 NRSV)

The rich and powerful enjoy their pilgrimages and offer generous sacrifices. But God does not want offerings from people who are greedy and immoral unless they also mean to change their ways and keep his law:

I hate, I despise your festivals.... (5:21 NRSV)

Hate evil and love good,
and establish justice.... (5:15 NRSV)

Discovering Amos

God will judge the surrounding nations

Amos begins his prophecy with a description of God roaring like a lion about to attack. The Lord is fiercely angry with each of the nations that surround his people – as well as with Judah and Israel themselves (1:1–2:3).

Damascus, the capital of Syria, is criticized for her aggression and cruelty. God's judgment will fall on her when she is conquered by Assyria in 732 BC.

Gaza, a Philistine city, is condemned for her pitiless slave trading. She will fall to Assyria in 734 BC. Other Philistine strongholds, *Ashdod*, *Ashkelon* and *Ekron* are also sentenced. They will be defeated by successive Assyrian emperors.

The port of *Tyre* has also been involved in slave trading, breaking every law of humanity. She will become subject to Assyria, and eventually be captured in 573 BC.

Edom, Judah's neighbour to the south, is found guilty of remorseless and uncontrolled anger. 'Teman' is Edom by another name, and Bozrah its capital.

Amman has been utterly barbaric in its treatment of pregnant women. God will avenge them with fire and storm.

Finally, *Moab* has desecrated the body of the king of Edom. Even though this action is nothing to do with Israel or Judah, it affronts God. God's moral standards apply to everyone, and he will destroy Moab's ruler in return.

All the nations, capitals and kings that Amos has mentioned are pagan. They don't acknowledge the God of Israel or observe his law. But God still holds them responsible for their actions and decides their fates.

God will judge Judah (2:4–5)

Up to this point, the people of Israel are delighted with Amos' message. God is to judge and punish all their enemies. But now comes the shock. Amos declares God's judgment on his own people, Judah and Israel.

Judah's sins are not those of brutality or bloodshed. Her guilt lies in her rejection of God's law and her preference for worshipping pagan gods. For this she will be conquered by Nebuchadnezzar in 586 BC, and led captive to Babylon.

God will judge Israel, his own people

Sins of social injustice and pagan immorality (2:6–16)

Israel's sins are her social injustice and her pagan immorality. Innocent people are cheated of justice when their judges take bribes:

They sell the righteous for silver,
  and the needy for a pair of sandals. (2:6 NRSV)

Fathers and sons have sex with the same girls – possibly as part of the pagan fertility rites. Honour and respect has broken down in a chaos of greed and abuse.

True religion

The challenge of Amos is that our worship of God should come from our hearts and affect both our personal lives and our social structures. Beautiful music and perfect offerings are nothing without the desire to treat all people fairly and the resolve to live moral and generous lives.

If we don't offer our hearts to God when we worship him, and if we aren't determined to change our ways, then our prayers are a pretence and our lives are a lie. Amos teaches that this angers God and provokes his judgment.

Amos reviews Israel's history, telling it from God's point of view. God rescued his people from Egypt, gave them victory over their enemies and taught them what was holy. But Israel has behaved shamefully in return – commanding God's prophets to be quiet, and getting the Nazirites (holy ones) drunk. Now God is going to crush his people with inescapable judgment. The strongest, the fastest and the bravest will all alike be overrun.

Judgment to come (3:1–15)

Amos explains that God's judgment is inevitable. The process has already begun. The lion has roared his rage and is about to attack. For Amos, the lion's roar is God's word of judgment – the message that has become his prophecy.

Amos is able to give some graphic details of the disaster to come. Israel's defences will be destroyed and ransacked. Only a few people will be spared – just as a shepherd might pick up a few remains of a lamb after a lion has mauled it. In particular, the centres of Israel's sin – the altars given to paganism and the luxury homes built on exploitation – will be razed to the ground. The 'horns of the altar' – where people would cling in prayer for help – will be cut off.

'Prepare to meet your God, O Israel' (4:1–13)

Amos is devastating in his judgment of the well-to-do women of Samaria. He calls them cows. Their pampered lives are maintained by other people's suffering; and this offends God. God doesn't excuse their ignorance, make allowance for their feminine frailty or blame their husbands. They themselves are guilty and they will be led off to slavery.

Amos attacks popular religion. He sees the crowds of pilgrims at Bethel and Gilgal. Sacrifices are plentiful, tithes are all in order and freewill offerings are attracting widespread admiration. But Amos sees the pride and boasting that underlie the worship. The shrine is the place to be seen at, and pilgrimages have been taken over by people showing off.

While pilgrims have been pretending to worship, God himself has been attempting to get through to them. He has tried to attract their attention and prayer by sending bouts of famine and drought, crop disease and locusts, sickness and war. But, despite all their hardships, the people never search their hearts or turn to God. Now they will have to reckon with him whether they like it or not: 'Prepare to meet your God, O Israel!' (4:12 NRSV).

A lament for Israel (5:1–27)

Amos howls a lament for the death of Israel. He forecasts that she will lose her life in battle. Her towns and villages will be decimated. But still the Lord urges her to turn to him for rescue. There is no safety in the pilgrim centres of Bethel or Gilgal – those places are defenceless and unable to help themselves. They will be ruined and their populations exiled.

Israel has destroyed God's standards – turning sweet justice sour, and throwing lofty righteousness to the ground. Now the Lord of the universe, who turns darkness to light and summons mighty floods, is going to bring down change on Israel. Again, Amos recites Israel's sins: that she has trampled the poor so that a few may live in luxury, and allowed corrupt judges to rule the law courts. Everything is fixed by bribery. And yet, if only Israel would turn to God and step into his light, it may not be too late for God to change his mind.

As for those who look forward to the Day of the Lord – they are in for a shock. They assume the Day of the Lord will be a day of glory for Israel. In fact it will be a day of darkness and dismay. God tells Israel how much he hates her phoney religion with its sham sacrifices. Her songs of praise are just a din. God wants to see justice flowing like a great river and righteousness like a stream that never runs dry. In the old days in the wilderness, Israel offered sacrifices with the love of her heart. Now she relies on politics and paganism. God will send her processing off into exile.

The complacency of Israel (6:1–14)

Amos addresses the comfortable and complacent people of Israel. They are enjoying peace and prosperity. Their borders have been made secure by the victories of Jeroboam II, and vigorous trade has brought great wealth. But God sees only pride. Those who think they are the top nation will find themselves top of the list to be judged – and first to be sent into exile. Israel has abused God's standards – like trying to haul a plough over rocks. She has claimed God-given victories as though she had won them by her own efforts. Now God is raising up an enemy who will demolish Jeroboam's little achievements.

Visions of doom, and a word of hope

Visions of destruction (7:1–17)

God shows Amos three terrible pictures of Israel's destruction. In the first, a plague of locusts strips the land bare. In the second, the land is entirely engulfed in flames. Amos cries for mercy. Like Moses before him, he begs God not to destroy his people beyond all hope of survival. The Lord hears and accepts his prayer.

But there is to be a certain judgment. In the third picture, Amos sees God holding a plumb line against Israel. The plumb line is the true standard of God's law, and it shows that Israel should be pulled down and demolished. Amos has no answer to this third vision, for the Lord is doing only what Israel deserves and has brought on herself.

The priest of Bethel, Amaziah, complains to the king that Amos is a traitor. He objects to the forecasts that Jeroboam will be killed and Israel sentenced to exile. He tells Amos to go back to Judah and get the people there to pay for prophecies against Israel. Amos replies that he isn't a professional prophet. He was a shepherd and fruit-farmer, until God called him to prophesy. The message God gave him was specifically for Israel. If he was to obey God, he had no choice but to journey north and deliver it. Amos goes on to give Amaziah a terrible description of the fate awaiting him and his family.

Israel is ripe for judgment (8:1-14)

The 'Sovereign Lord' (Amos' majestic, distinctive title for God) shows Amos that Israel is ripe for judgment. Just as the right time comes for harvest, so has the moment arrived when Israel's sins must be punished. She has been obsessed with materialism – squeezing trade into every possible minute, manipulating quantities and prices, and treating the poor as slaves.

But, in God's universe, everything belongs together. The land is going to rebel against the behaviour of its inhabitants. There will be a major earthquake and the sun will go into eclipse. The joy of Israel's religious celebrations will be plunged into the grief of a family funeral. Most terrible of all, there will be no word from God. When people look for guidance, they will find only silence. The dearth of the Spirit will be more dreadful and complete than any physical famine or drought.

Destruction... and restoration (9:1-15)

The shrine is to be destroyed. Amos sees God directing the work of demolition. The people will find no escape from his anger. There is nowhere to hide from God's judgment, because he is always ahead and in complete control. He is not a local, limited god, or one of merely human origin. He is the all-powerful, ever-present, Sovereign Lord, who governs heaven and earth and directs the history of nations. Israel is to be sifted and sorted along with the rest – because she has behaved no better than they have.

But God has agreed with Amos that Israel's destruction will not be a total annihilation. One day the Lord will restore his people and renew the kingdom of David. Israel will fulfil her calling as God's first nation and other nations will join her in acknowledging the Lord. In the early years of the Christian mission, Amos' prophecy will be quoted by James at the

Council of Jerusalem. It is a mandate for including Gentiles (non-Jews) in the Christian church (Acts 15:13–19).

When God brings Israel back from exile, the whole of creation will celebrate. God will set his people in a land of peace and plenty. The God who has sworn and delivered destruction now promises a perfect future.

OBADIAH

The book of Obadiah is the smallest in the Old Testament, but it packs a very big punch. Its impact is that God will punish the nation of Edom for the part she played at the downfall of Jerusalem. Indeed, a day is coming when *all* the nations of the earth will be judged.

OUTLINE

Judgment on Edom (vv. 1–14)
The Day of the Lord (vv. 15–21)

Introduction

The country of Edom lies south of the Dead Sea, and to the south-east of Judah. Its people are descended from Esau, just as the Israelites are descendants of Jacob. Esau and Jacob were twins. Esau was the elder brother and the rightful heir of the promises God made to his father Isaac and his grandfather Abraham. However, Esau never took God seriously. Jacob, on the other hand, was determined to supplant Esau, and succeeded in cheating him of his inheritance. The story of Esau and Jacob is told in Genesis 25–36.

Centuries later, when the Israelites asked Edom's permission to use the 'King's Highway' (the most direct route from Egypt to Canaan), they were refused. A long-running enmity was established between Israel and Edom, which features frequently in the Old Testament story. Edom becomes a typical example of people who are insensitive to God and oppose his plans.

We don't know who Obadiah was, but his name means 'Servant of the Lord'. There are other people with the same name in the Old Testament, but none of them is the author of this book.

Discovering Obadiah

Judgment on Edom (vv. 1–14)

At the time of Obadiah's prophecy, Edom sits proud and strong in her high mountain setting. Her main cities are Bozrah and Sela (which means 'rocks'). Petra is just such a city (although built later, in the 4th century BC) and is a favourite with tourists today. Obadiah warns Edom that nowhere is too high for God to reach. In fact Edom is about to be brought down to earth very decisively indeed. Her treasures will be ransacked, her allies will betray her, her wise people will be powerless and her warriors will be destroyed.

This catastrophe is to overtake Edom because she looked on and cheered when Jerusalem was sacked by Nebuchadnezzar in 587 BC. Family ties should have drawn Edom to help Judah, but in the event she sided with Babylon. Psalm 137 records the appalling betrayal:

Remember, Lord, what the Edomites did
  on the day Jerusalem fell.
'Tear it down,' they cried,
  'tear it down to its foundations!' (Psalm 137:7)

Obadiah condemns Edom for watching while Jerusalem was looted by foreigners – the Chaldeans from Babylon. He recalls vividly Edom's shameful behaviour towards 'your brother Jacob'. Worse still, the Edomites joined in the looting, ambushed the refugees and handed over survivors to the enemy.

The Day of the Lord (vv. 15–21)

Obadiah has a far greater vision than revenge on Edom. He opens up a vista of all that God will do, for all the nations and for the whole of time.

The day of the Lord is near
  for all nations.
As you have done, it will be done to you;
  your deeds will return upon your own head. (v. 15)

Judgment... and salvation

Obadiah's message of judgment on Israel's enemies is only one aspect of Old Testament prophecy. There are several occasions when the prophets speak of Israel's enemies turning to God and receiving salvation. This is true of Egypt and Assyria in Isaiah's prophecy (Isaiah 19:19–25), and of Nineveh, the Assyrian capital, in the story of Jonah, the next book of the Bible.

Just as the Edomites drank themselves to a stupor when they joined in the sacking of Jerusalem, so will the nations drink God's judgment until they fall into oblivion. But at the centre, safe and strong, will be Mount Zion, God's holy city and refuge. The house of Jacob (God's people) will be fully reinstated; 'the house of Joseph' (the northern kingdom of Israel) will also be restored.

God's people will not be passive when the Day of the Lord comes. They will be like the field fires after the harvest, sweeping across the stubble of God's enemies. The godless 'house of Esau' (Edom and all who oppose God) will be utterly destroyed.

Obadiah ends his message with a description of lands being shared out and possessed as the Jewish exiles return, and other peoples move into Edom's space. Mount Zion herself will become the centre of government and justice, from which 'deliverers' (saviours) will administer God's perfect kingdom.

JONAH

The story of 'Jonah and the whale' is one of the favourites of the Old Testament. Certainly Jonah is the most famous of the twelve little books known as the 'Minor Prophets'. It is most likely that this is a story with a meaning (like a parable) rather than something which actually happened. Listen to it as though it is being told to you by a wonderful storyteller!

OUTLINE

Jonah runs away from God's call (1:1–17)
Jonah's song of praise for his rescue (2:1–10)
Jonah preaches – and Nineveh repents (3:1–10)
Jonah's anger and God's mercy (4:1–11)

Introduction

God tells Jonah to go and preach to Nineveh – the capital of Israel's enemy, Assyria. Jonah refuses and takes a ship in the opposite direction. When God sends a storm, Jonah admits to the sailors that it is all his fault. To save themselves, the sailors throw him overboard. God then sends a great fish to swallow Jonah and bring him safely to land.

God repeats his command to Jonah to go and preach to Nineveh. This time Jonah obeys. The entire community repents, from king to cattle, and God spares the city. Jonah is furious! While Jonah sulks, God uses the short life and death of a plant to show how much he cares for the whole of his creation.

Is this a true story?

We know a little about Jonah from 2 Kings 14. He came from Gath Hepher in Galilee, and prophesied in the northern kingdom of Israel during the reign of Jeroboam. In the book of Jonah, he comes across as someone who understands God's mercy, but doesn't see why the heathen should be let off lightly.

Death and resurrection

Jonah gives us one of the Bible's great images of God's power to save. Just as Joseph was rescued from prison to become prime minister, and Daniel was kept safe among lions, so Jonah is preserved in the belly of a great fish.

These episodes prepare us for their greatest sequel – the resurrection of Jesus from the tomb. Jesus went down into the depths of death and experienced utter loss of God – but was raised as the ultimate proof of salvation.

It seems most likely that the story of Jonah uses this prophet as a character. It's a tall story – and a very funny one. God sends a storm, a huge fish, a fast-growing vine, a very hungry worm and a scorching wind – all to persuade Jonah first to pursue the right action and then to have the right attitude. The story is great fun and makes one of the Bible's most important points: that God loves non-Jews, and even his enemies.

God's love for everyone

It took wind and whale, vine, worm and sunstroke to persuade Jonah of God's care for Nineveh. But the message of God's love for all is one of the Bible's greatest themes. God called Abraham with a view to blessing all the nations of the world (Genesis 12:3). Elijah helped a pagan woman (1 Kings 17) and Elisha healed a foreign commander (2 Kings 5). God's people were always intended to bless others – not withdraw into a life of religious pride and exclusiveness.

In the days of the early church, Peter will have to learn the lesson of Jonah all over again. He will be called to put aside his Jewish prejudice and cross the threshold of a Gentile home. It is interesting that he has a vision of God's care for all sorts of people while he is in Joppa – the very port from which Jonah set sail. Jonah and Peter, centuries apart, were drawn to the same conclusion:

I truly understand that God shows no partiality, but in every nation anyone who fears him and does what is right is acceptable to him.
(Acts 10:35 NRSV)

DISCOVERING JONAH

Jonah runs away from God's call (1:1–17)

This is a story of God's love and human prejudice. God wants Israel's enemies, the Assyrians of Nineveh, to hear his word. He calls his prophet Jonah to go and preach to them, but Jonah runs away. He boards a ship at Joppa – the nearest port to Jerusalem – and sails for Tarshish, which was probably in Spain.

God sends a great wind to blow up a storm, so that the sailors are in fear of their lives. The captain wakes Jonah (who is soundly asleep!) and urges him to add his god to their desperate prayers. Jonah tells the crew that there is only one God, and that the storm is overwhelming them because of Jonah's disobedience. In the end, the sailors agree to throw Jonah into the sea – and the storm abates. As the relieved sailors set about their prayers of gratitude, God sends a great fish to swallow Jonah.

Jonah's song of praise for his rescue (2:1–10)

The fish (called a whale in some translations of the Bible) is Jonah's home for three days and nights. During this time he praises God in a psalm. God has heard his cry for help from the very depths of the sea – and

Jesus and Jonah

Jesus mentions Jonah and the meaning of his story. For Jesus, Jonah was a local hero – Gath Hepher being only an hour's walk from Nazareth. If Jonah's message was that God loved everyone and not just Jews, then this was something for which Jesus himself lived and died.

For Jesus, Jonah's experience was a vital sign. Here was someone who was buried for three days and nights, but God rescued him. Matthew's Gospel sees this as a foreshadowing of Jesus' burial in the tomb, before being raised on the third day. Jesus announced himself as 'one greater than Jonah' (Matthew 12:41). In Luke's Gospel, the 'sign of Jonah' is that Jesus, like Jonah, is calling a whole generation to repent (Luke 11:29–30).

saved him! At the end of his unusual voyage, Jonah is unceremoniously thrown up on a beach.

Jonah preaches – and Nineveh repents (3:1–10)

Again, God tells Jonah to go and preach to Nineveh, and this time Jonah obeys. Nineveh is a huge place, which takes three days to walk around. It seems that Jonah has an impossible task, but no sooner does he start to preach than the whole city starts to repent! The king himself leads the way by wearing sackcloth, sitting in the dust and ordering a total fast. The whole community, including the animals, begs God to have mercy. God sees them and answers their prayer by sparing them from disaster.

Jonah's anger and God's mercy (4:1–11)

Jonah is thoroughly angry at this turn of events. He tells God that he knew all along this would happen. That was why he ran away in the first place. It was so like God to forgive – but what about the embarrassment to his prophet who has announced destruction? Jonah is so ashamed, he wants to crawl away and die.

God asks Jonah if it is right to be so angry. Is God wrong to show mercy? Isn't it wonderful that Nineveh has repented? But Jonah sits down at a high point overlooking the city, and wills the judgment to fall.

The sun's heat is fierce. God makes a vine grow over Jonah's shelter to make him more comfortable. Jonah is pleased – until God sends a worm to destroy the vine, and steps up the heat with a scorching east wind. Jonah, who has been rescued from a watery grave, is now in danger of death by sunstroke. He is indignant that the innocent vine has died.

Gently, God speaks to Jonah. If Jonah can care so passionately for a plant – which he hasn't sown, and which has come and gone in a day – how must God feel about Nineveh? There are thousands of people in the city who are deeply ignorant of God – to say nothing of their cattle. Isn't God entirely within his rights to want to reach them – and spare them?

MICAH

Micah is one of the most far-sighted prophets. Living in Judah at the same time as Isaiah, Micah foresees the destruction of both the northern kingdom of Israel and the southern kingdom of Judah. But, beyond the judgment and suffering that is coming to God's people, Micah predicts a new and everlasting kingdom of peace. This will be the universal reign of God's Messiah.

OUTLINE

God will punish Judah as well as Israel (1:1–16)
God condemns Judah's leaders (2:1–3:12)
God's future plans (4:1–13)
The Messiah will come to rule (5:1–15)
God states his case against Israel (6:1–16)
Present darkness and future glory (7:1–20)

Introduction

Who is Micah?

Micah comes from Moresheth, in the rural lowlands of Judah. Although younger than Isaiah, he prophesies during the same period – the reigns of Jotham (751–736 BC), Ahaz (743–728 BC) and Hezekiah (728–696 BC).

Micah foresees a terrible judgment falling on Israel and Judah. God is going to judge his people because of their idolatry and injustice. Micah sees how powerful people oppress and rob the poor (2:1–2). He also condemns the corruption of the rulers, priests and prophets in Jerusalem (3:9–11).

Micah and Isaiah are both prophesying at about the same time, and they have a similar message. However, they live in very different circumstances and speak from different backgrounds. Isaiah lives in Jerusalem and mixes with the upper class, while Micah lives in a tiny village and sees the plight of the poor in the countryside.

Micah's prophecy begins around 725 BC, when he sees that the religion and identity of God's people are collapsing. The northern kingdom of Israel will be captured and overrun by the Assyrian empire. The southern kingdom of Judah will survive for some years, but will also be judged by conquest – this time by the Babylonians. All this will be God's doing, as a punishment for worshipping other gods and abandoning the covenant promises.

But Micah, like all the great prophets, also sees beyond God's judgment. He looks forward to a future when God will restore Israel. God will make Jerusalem a centre of justice and peace which will attract the whole world to his gentle rule.

DISCOVERING MICAH

God will punish Judah as well as Israel (1:1–16)

Micah declares that God is about to destroy both Samaria (the capital of Israel) and Jerusalem (the capital of Judah). Samaria's pagan idols and images will be smashed. The wealth which has been made from sacred prostitutes will be seized by foreign soldiers, who will in turn spend it on debauchery. All this will be fulfilled when the Assyrian armies, led by Sargon, conquer Israel in 722 BC.

Micah goes into mourning. He sees that the disastrous events will spread south to Judah and Jerusalem as well. He lists twelve towns which will be besieged and captured – and shows how their names spell out destruction. Beth Ophrah, for example, which means 'house of dust', will see her inhabitants rolling in the dust of death or grief.

Jerusalem and the southern kingdom of Judah will not in fact fall for another 150 years. Then the Assyrians under Shalmaneser V and the Chaldeans under Nebuchadnezzar will seal their fate.

God condemns Judah's leaders (2:1–3:12)

Corruption in society

Micah launches a detailed attack on people who have been seizing land, especially by deceitful means (2:1–13). This is an abuse of the Promised Land, which was carefully allocated so that everyone could share it.

Now God is planning to outwit the land-grabbers and give away all their gains.

Micah also tackles the false prophets, who are assuring people that God can never be angry with them. What about the bullying of defenceless travellers, women and children? He accuses the people of listening to anyone who will make easy promises. A prophet of 'free-drinks-all-round' would suit them fine!

But God won't leave his people leaderless and defenceless. He himself will be the shepherd who gathers the survivors after the years of destruction. He will break open the gates of their Babylonian prison, and lead them out to freedom.

Condemnation of the leaders

Micah accuses those in government of behaving like cannibals (3:1–12). The very leaders who should be establishing a good and just society are attacking it and tearing it apart. There will be no help for them when they need it.

The prophets have also abused their position. Instead of preaching God's message without fear or favour, they give words of comfort to people who pay – and threaten those who don't! God is going to plunge the false prophets into darkness. They will be utterly discredited, because they will neither see God nor hear from him.

Micah, by contrast, is in a strong position – full of the Spirit of God, and able to deliver a true and clear message. To be filled with the Spirit is to be passionate for justice. Micah exposes the nation's rulers, judges, priests and prophets for what they are: violent, cruel, greedy and false. They assume God won't depose them because they are custodians of his capital city and his temple. How wrong they are! It is because of them that all will be destroyed.

God's future plans (4:1–13)

Now Micah looks ahead to 'the last days': a golden age for Jerusalem. The terrors of the siege and destruction are long past. The Lord's temple is rebuilt, and God's mountain is raised high above all the mountains of the world.

The nations of the world will come to this mountain in a never-ending stream – knowing they will be taught God's true way of life. Zion (the name for Jerusalem as God's holy city) will be a centre of justice worldwide. Weapons of war will be converted for peaceful purposes (for too long it has been the other way round), and all military activity will cease. Everyone will have their own home, livelihood, space for prayer and peace of mind.

God promises to gather the disabled and scattered remains of his people to Mount Zion, where he will be their king for ever. The watchtower of King Jotham's day will again become a lookout point for the protection of God's people.

Meanwhile, there is terrible suffering in store for Jerusalem. She will find herself without king or counsellors and be thrown into exile in Babylon. But God will rescue her in due time. The nations which gloat over her disgrace will find themselves having to reckon with God. Israel, rescued and renewed, will be God's agent in the threshing (judgment) of the nations.

The Messiah will come to rule (5:1–15)

Micah calls Jerusalem to prepare for a siege. This will be the arrival of Nebuchadnezzar's armies in 587 BC, which will end in the defeat and captivity of King Zedekiah.

But with the downfall of the capital comes a promise of hope. God's plan won't be ruined by the desolation of his people. At some time in the future, the greatest of all kings will be born in the small family town of Bethlehem. God will use the little and the unlikely to change the world.

O little town of Bethlehem

Bethlehem is given her ancient name, Ephrathah. The one to be born in her will spring from a most ancient line: the great King David had come from Bethlehem. Now an even greater ruler will arise, in the same tradition of godly shepherd-kingship. People throughout the world will be safe in his oversight and protection to the end of time.

When the Messiah comes, God will defend his people against enemies such as Assyria, and provide the leaders and weapons to do so. The survivors of God's people will be a great blessing to the world – like refreshing dew on parched grass. They will live among the nations – strong, vigorous and terrifying, like a young lion among sheep. They will overcome all their enemies purely in the strength of God, and without the help of military might, magic powers or pagan gods.

God states his case against Israel (6:1–16)

God lays it on the line with his people. He rescued them from Egypt. He kept them safe on their dangerous journey through the desert. Do they still not know the kind of God he is? Do they really think he needs thousands of dead animals to keep him happy? Or child sacrifice? No! God has made himself quite clear. What he wants is simply this:

To act justly and to love mercy
and to walk humbly with your God. (6:8)

So Micah summarizes the godly life: keeping God's law, sharing God's love and going God's way.

God speaks particularly to the northern kingdom. He has seen them getting rich by cheating – and will bring all their greedy efforts to nothing.

Present darkness and future glory (7:1–20)

Micah weeps for Israel. She feels utterly unloved. Violence, greed and betrayal have damaged every relationship – even in the closest families and between the closest friends. The only reliable person is God. She waits for God to hear and save. Even in deep darkness, she believes her God will bring her out into the light – and wipe the sneer from the face of her enemy.

Micah looks forward to the ultimate reign of God. One day God will turn the whole situation around, and set his people at the centre of the nations and at the summit of creation. Everyone will realize the perfect character and purpose of God – that he is both angry with sin and tender with sinners. The best is yet to be!

NAHUM

Nahum declares that Nineveh is to be destroyed. Nineveh is the mighty capital of the Assyrian empire – an empire which has crushed Judah and struck terror in the heart of all the nations. Now God is going to judge Nineveh for her cruelty and bring an alliance of armies to overwhelm her. She will be wiped from the face of the earth. This is a great contrast to the message of Jonah. Both books show an important truth about God.

OUTLINE

The Lord's anger against Nineveh (1:1-15)
The downfall of Nineveh (2:1-13)
A battle-song against Nineveh (3:1-19)

Introduction

The book of Nahum is an account of a vision. God has shown Nahum the fate that is about to befall Nineveh. We learn that Nahum is from

Nineveh

Nineveh is the capital city of Assyria and the centre of a great empire. As Nineveh dominates the region, she represents all that Israel dreads. She is powerful and impregnable, wealthy, pagan and cruel.

Nineveh rules supreme in the late 8th century BC. Historians have found the remains of the emperors' palaces (one with a famous library), the fine temple to Ishtar (goddess of love and war) and massive fortifications.

There are two different approaches to Nineveh in the prophecies of Israel. Nahum declares God's judgment on her tyranny, but Jonah realizes God's mercy towards her people (and animals). In fact the two views don't conflict. What we are discovering is that God cares deeply about the behaviour of all nations, and longs that all should repent and turn to him (Jonah 4:11).

Elkosh, which is probably a village in Judah. He writes sometime after the destruction of Thebes – the strong and beautiful city on the Nile in Egypt. This had taken place in 664–663 BC. Nineveh itself will be destroyed in 612 BC. This means that Nahum is prophesying at the same time as Jeremiah, Habakkuk and Zephaniah. Unlike the other prophets, Nahum has no charges to bring against Israel or Judah. His fire is entirely concentrated on Nineveh.

DISCOVERING NAHUM

The Lord's anger against Nineveh (1:1–15)

Nahum begins with a poem (1:2–8). The first letters of each line spell out the Hebrew alphabet. The prophet sings of the passion and power of God. The Lord may be patient and slow to lose his temper, but once his anger is aroused, all the destructive forces of nature are at his command.

God's great wrath is to be poured out on Nineveh. She is to be judged for her deep hostility to God, and her thoroughgoing wickedness. Her allies will be rendered helpless. Her power over Judah will be broken. Her idols will be destroyed. Nahum urges Judah to praise God, as though the runner has already arrived with the news that Nineveh is no more.

The downfall of Nineveh (2:1–13)

Nahum tells Nineveh to defend herself. We know with hindsight that her attackers were an alliance of Medes, Scythians and Chaldeans. Nahum sees in vivid detail the red shields and cloaks of the Medes, the flashing armour and the forest of spears. Although Nineveh's commander tries to deploy his defenders, the invaders open the sluices controlling the river, and flood the city. Great buildings have their foundations swept away. The palace collapses.

Nahum sees Nineveh, too, as a pool being drained. Her pride, strength and wealth are ebbing away in the slaughter of her people and the plunder of her treasures. Nineveh which had been like a lion's den – secure in its strength and a breeding place of violence – now lies destroyed. And it is the Lord who has brought about her downfall.

A battle-song against Nineveh (3:1–19)

Nahum chants a battle-song against Nineveh. She is a 'city of blood' – built on slaughter and maintained by stolen wealth. Now she will get the treatment she has handed out to others. The prophet describes her as a prostitute, devoted to paganism and witchcraft, now exposed, stripped and humiliated before the eyes of the world.

If Nineveh doubts that all this can happen, she has only to remember the fate of Thebes. Thebes had been the pride of Upper Egypt. Today the sites of Karnak and Luxor show something of her beauty and power. She was particularly well protected, by the water surrounding her and the political alliances she had forged with her neighbours (to us, Libya and Somalia). Yet she fell to the forces of Ashurbanipal in 663 BC, as the people of Nineveh knew only too well. Some of them had been serving in the victorious Assyrian forces. Now it is Nineveh's turn. Her defences are weak. Her troops are soft. She is ripe for picking. The merchants and administrators who have swarmed in Nineveh like locusts in winter are about to vanish in a moment.

Nahum keeps his final word for the king of Assyria. His leaders are asleep. They no longer care. His people are dispersed. The damage is final and irreversible. Nineveh has at last suffered the fate she so richly deserved.

HABAKKUK

Habakkuk dares to ask God some blunt questions. If God is completely good and totally powerful, why isn't he answering all the cries for help? How can God use evil to carry out his judgments?

Habakkuk sees the corruption and lawlessness of Israel's society, and longs that God will establish his reign of justice. However, the prophet realizes that God is going to use a Babylonian (Chaldean) invasion to discipline Israel. This is a strange and awesome development, because the Babylonians are even worse than the Israelites!

Habakkuk's questions are resolved when he has a vision of God as a warrior of overwhelming glory, conquering all before him. The Lord is king of all the nations, and his judgments will bring about salvation. Like Job, Habakkuk comes to see his little situation in the vast context of God's majesty and purpose.

OUTLINE

Habakkuk questions God (1:1–17)
Babylon is doomed (2:1–20)
God is supreme (3:1–19)

Introduction

Habakkuk is a prophet who is probably based in Jerusalem at the same time as Jeremiah. Part of his message (chapter 3) is set out as a song, with instructions for the way it is to be sung in the temple. The name Habakkuk may come from the Hebrew for 'hug' or 'hang on tightly'. Certainly, he hangs onto God in this prophecy.

Habakkuk prophesies at a time when the armies of Babylon are invading Palestine. His work is different from that of the other prophets, in that it is entirely addressed to God. When will God intervene to punish oppression and expose idolatry? Why is he delaying his promised kingdom?

God reveals to Habakkuk that he is rousing the Babylonians to wreak his judgment on Judah. It is an astonishing turn of events.

Habakkuk stations himself before God like a watchman (2:1), to await his word. He is rewarded with the assurance that God is working out his purpose. It may seem slow from a human point of view, but it will surely come about.

Habakkuk arrives at a position of settled faith. Whatever happens, God is Lord. There may be total destruction in earthly terms, but with God there is perfect salvation. This realization gives Habakkuk a surge of confidence and praise.

DISCOVERING HABAKKUK

Habakkuk questions God (1:1–17)

Habakkuk asks God his first big question: 'How long must I call for help but you don't listen?' There is so much evil going on, with no one able to do anything to stop it. So why doesn't God get involved?

God replies that he is about to do something quite extraordinary. He is bringing in the armies of Babylon – the strongest, cruellest and most unscrupulous force on earth. A self-made people who worship their creator.

Judah is a little nation, tossed on the waves of great empires. The empires rising and falling at this time are Assyria, Babylon and Egypt. As Habakkuk writes, Babylon is rising. Her armies are on the march. She has defeated the Assyrians – destroying Nineveh in 612 BC. A few years after this, in 608 BC, Judah is defeated by Egypt at the battle of Megiddo. Pharaoh Neco, the Egyptian king, kills Josiah the king of Judah and appoints his own rulers.

But Babylon is far stronger than Egypt. Nebuchadnezzar defeats Pharaoh Neco at the battle of Carchemish in 605 BC. After twenty years of threat and fear, Babylon will also defeat Judah – and carry her population into captivity in 586 BC.

Habakkuk asks a second question. How can God possibly use the forces of evil to carry out his holy judgments? How can he watch people being treated like fish in a net? Especially when those who gleefully catch the fish not only live in luxury, but worship the net that gives them success.

Babylon is doomed (2:1-20)

Habakkuk insists on waiting for God's reply. God doesn't give him a straight answer, but tells him to write down a revelation on tablets of clay. This is a message which is to be kept and passed on – which will prove to be right in the end.

God reveals the truth about the Babylonians. They are proud, misguided – and doomed. They will get rich for a while by plundering other nations – but the time will come when they themselves will be ransacked. Crime and bloodshed are no way to establish a society, and God will bring their achievements to nothing.

Meanwhile, the right way to live is by faith in God.

The earth will be filled with the knowledge of the glory of the Lord, as the waters cover the sea. (2:14)

Judah is to be destroyed by the Babylonians, a people far more vile and violent than Israel has become. But God will ensure that the Babylonians will themselves be judged and their conquests and achievements brought to nothing. In the end, the world will not be the domain of any human empire, but of the glorious kingdom of God.

Habakkuk chants five warnings against those who steal and murder. God will see to it that they get exactly what they deserve. The warnings seem to apply to individuals as well as nations. They seem to apply especially to Babylon:

- Those who have got rich by plunder will be plundered themselves.
- Those who have built on the profits of crime will find their very houses giving evidence against them.
- Nothing will last which is built by violence. God will use it for matchwood – and put a sea of justice in its place.
- Those who have brought about the shame of others will find that it's their own turn to be disgraced.
- Those who make idols are trusting in objects of wood and stone which are powerless to give teaching or guidance.

'The righteous will live by their faith'

The message of Habakkuk is that the right way to live is by faith in God (2:4). The future doesn't lie with the passing empires of this world, but with the glory of God. Lasting victory isn't won by armed strength – or even by religion. The victory is God's, and he will share it with his faithful people. Those who serve God now are on the right track, because knowing God is the only thing that will survive in the end. In centuries to come, Paul will quote this saying, 'The righteous will live by their faith,' in two of his letters – to the Romans and the Galatians.

Talking of the silence of dumb idols, Habakkuk urges the whole earth to keep silence in the holy presence of God.

God is supreme (3:1–19)

Habakkuk offers a prayer, which is a poem or psalm of great power and beauty. The word 'shigionoth' may come from a Hebrew word meaning 'to wander' – so perhaps he hopes the musicians will improvise.

Like Job before him, Habakkuk's questions have led him to a new view of God. He praises the Lord who brought Israel from the south (Teman is Edom) and gave them the law in Sinai (the region of Mount Paran). God's majesty covers both heaven and earth. He can use all the forces of nature to deliver his judgments, making the sea roar or the sun stand still. He is ready, willing and able to defeat his enemies and deliver his people.

Habakkuk is left shaken and speechless by this awesome revelation of God. God is God and he will save! When and where and how he does it is entirely up to him. Habakkuk realizes he can wait for God. He isn't anxious any more. Food and wine don't matter now that his gladness comes from God.

With this glorious perspective, Habakkuk feels totally renewed and refreshed. He could jump a mountain for joy!

ZEPHANIAH

Like the other prophets, Zephaniah preaches both judgment and hope. Most of his book declares God's certain punishment. But he also promises that God's people will emerge from their days of darkness and scattering.

Zephaniah foresees that God is going to judge not only Judah but all the nations of the world. This is 'the Day of the Lord', and it is approaching fast (1:14). But Zephaniah calls on those who are humble to do what is right and so escape destruction (2:3). In fact, there is the hope that God's judgment will lead to a change and transformation for many peoples (3:9).

Zephaniah's insights link the messages of all the prophets, before, during and after the destruction of Jerusalem and the exile in Babylon. He sees that God's judgment, though terrible, is part of his great salvation.

OUTLINE

God's judgment of the whole world, especially Judah and Jerusalem (1:1–18)
God's judgment of the nations around Judah (2:1–15)
The fate of the present Jerusalem and the vision of a delightful future (3:1–20)

Introduction

Zephaniah is a young prophet who preaches during the reign of a young king, Josiah. Josiah came to the throne of Judah in 640 BC and reigned for thirty-one years.

The voice of prophecy has been silent for some seventy years – since the days of Isaiah and Micah. Despite the terrible fate of Samaria in 722 BC, the people of Judah have steeped themselves in paganism. King Manasseh has ignored his father Hezekiah's godly example and reverted to the Baal-worship of his grandfather Ahaz. Manasseh's long, evil and violent reign (696–642 BC) has seen Judah following Assyrian practices of nature-worship and astrology. Nature-worship has involved the gross immorality of fertility rites and bloodshed. Astrology has bred widespread superstition and fear.

Now Zephaniah steps forward to be the herald of the new age of King Josiah's reforms. These reforms take place in 621 BC. Josiah's reforms are described in 2 Kings 22–23. Unfortunately they are too little and too late to avert God's judgment.

Zephaniah is the first of the generation of prophets which will include Jeremiah, Habakkuk, Obadiah and Ezekiel. These are the men who will not only proclaim God's judgment on Judah and Jerusalem, but also be caught up in it themselves. Some of them will live right through the disaster as God's representatives and commentators, announcing and interpreting events.

We are told more than usual about Zephaniah's family line. If his father Cushi was a Cushite (Ethiopian), it may have been important to emphasize his true Jewish pedigree. On the other hand, his great-great-grandfather may have been Hezekiah the king.

DISCOVERING ZEPHANIAH

God's judgment of the whole world, especially Judah and Jerusalem (1:1–18)

Zephaniah, speaking for God, proclaims a great and worldwide destruction. This will be focused particularly on Judah and her capital Jerusalem.

God will destroy the priests and people who are worshipping the Canaanite god Baal, the god Molech (the Ammonite god Milcom, favoured by some of King Solomon's wives) and the sun, moon and stars. The priests have been mixing pagan worship with the worship of the Lord. The royal court has been mixing the Hebrew way of life with foreign dress and superstitions. All this has obscured the truth about God and muddied the purity of his people. Zephaniah calls for absolute silence, as God approaches the very moment of judgment.

Zephaniah shows his local knowledge as he describes God striking the areas of Jerusalem where the traders operate and where the smart people live. The self-sufficient merchants and self-satisfied homeowners will find their wealth swept away. Those who think God won't touch them will be forced to think again.

Zephaniah describes the Day of the Lord. It is approaching rapidly, plunging the world into darkness and war. People will wander in a state of shock, until they are cut down and destroyed. No amount of wealth will protect them when God's jealous rage sweeps in like fire.

'The Day of the Lord' is the day when God will be roused thoroughly and finally to judge the world. The prophets are convinced that the day will come when God can no longer endure the wickedness of the nations or the unfaithfulness of his own people. On that day his love, hatred of evil, and zeal for justice will boil over in wrath. It will be a day of cosmic upheaval, natural disasters, darkness, despair and death.

God's judgment of the nations around Judah (2:1–15)

Zephaniah calls everyone to gather together and surrender to God. The only glimmer of hope is that God will see their humility and obedience and have mercy.

Zephaniah predicts the fate of the nearby nations. To the west, towards the coast, are the cities of the Philistines – Gaza, Ashkelon, Ashdod and Ekron. They are strong communities, thriving on trade. But Zephaniah warns that God will destroy them, leaving them deserted and

Lightning strikes

Zephaniah may have the image of a Scythian raid in his mind as he describes the swift, merciless attack of God's Judgment Day. The Scythians were warlike nomads who fought with the Assyrians against the Medes. With their swift horses they could make lightning strikes even as far south as Egypt. Although the Scythians never attacked Jerusalem, the idea of their ruthless power and surprising speed colours Zephaniah's description of God's judgment. The actual destruction of Jerusalem, when it came, was by the Babylonians in 587 BC.

in ruins. The coastal plain will become pasture for the sheep of Judah – a glimpse of a future for God's people after the coming crisis.

Moab and Ammon lie to the east of Judah. They are twin nations descended from Lot. They have long despised Judah, and God has been particularly offended by their arrogance and paganism. Now God solemnly declares that he will treat them like Sodom and Gomorrah – inflicting on them the judgment Lot escaped.

Cush is the name for Ethiopia, which is to the far south of Judah. It may be Zephaniah's way of referring to Egypt, which had Ethiopian kings between 715 and 663 BC. He forecasts that God will destroy this southern power – a prediction which may have been fulfilled by Nebuchadnezzar's invasion of Egypt in 568 BC.

Lastly, Zephaniah declares the fate of Assyria and her capital Nineveh. As he speaks, she dominates the international scene with invincible power and legendary cruelty. For half a century she has demanded and received tribute from Judah as the price of peace. She thinks she is God, but Zephaniah proclaims her destruction. Ninevah will become a rubble-strewn ruin, inhabited only by wildlife.

The fate of the present Jerusalem and the vision of a delightful future (3:1–20)

Zephaniah proclaims, 'Woe to the city of oppressors' (3:1). This is almost certainly Jerusalem. He sees that she has no relationship with God, except to resist him. Officials, rulers, prophets and priests are all unworthy of their high calling. But God hasn't changed. His presence and standards have remained steadfast. His judgments of other nations have been intended as a warning to his own people; but Judah has taken no notice.

God declares that time is running out. The day is coming when he will gather the nations and destroy them. Here Zephaniah looks beyond the events of history to the Judgment Day of God.

Zephaniah goes on to describe the world that God will bring in after the fires of judgment. There will be a new unity in God's service, with people coming from as far away as Egypt to worship him. Those who were proud and hostile to God will have been weeded out. The people who remain will be those who are humble and truthful; and they will be able to live in peace.

Zephaniah calls God's people to sing for joy at the prospect of God's reign. Punishment and fear will become things of the past, as God rescues his people from shame, handicap and exile. Israel will know herself truly secure and loved by God, and honoured by all the nations of the world.

HAGGAI

Haggai is a prophet who urges Judah's leaders to rebuild the temple. The people have returned to Jerusalem after the years of exile in Babylon. They have restored their own houses, but the temple is still a ruin. Haggai explains to them that their failure to put God first is resulting in famine and poverty. His message is well received, and a temple is quickly built. Haggai is one of the few prophets who lives to see his words fulfilled.

OUTLINE

God calls his people to build the temple and they obey (1:1–15)
Words of encouragement, teaching and promise (2:1–23)

Introduction

A call to build the house of the Lord

Haggai dates his messages quite specifically. They are given to him by God between 29 August and 19 November 520 BC. As he calculates his dates by the reign of King Darius I, we realize that Judah is now just a small province in the great Persian empire.

Persia has replaced Babylon as the superpower. Darius I is Emperor Hystaspes of Persia, who reigned from 522–486 BC. It was one of his predecessors, Cyrus, who had given permission for the Jews to return to their land, in 536 BC, and allowed them to govern themselves once more.

In Cyrus' time there had been plans to rebuild the temple, but the work had lapsed. Persia was distracted by its own leadership struggle, which was eventually won by Darius. The Jews were harassed by their Samaritan neighbours and impoverished by poor harvests. People decided to look after themselves and establish their own homes, rather than face the task of rebuilding the temple.

Discovering Haggai

God calls his people to build the temple and they obey (1:1–15)

Haggai's first message is for Zerubbabel and Joshua. Zerubbabel is the governor of Judah, and Joshua is the high priest's son.

Zerubbabel is a descendant of King David, grandson of Jehoiachin (the last king of Judah) and heir of the royal line. His name means 'seed of Babylon'. He and Joshua had returned from exile with the first group, led by Sheshbazzar, in 537 BC. It was Zerubbabel and Joshua who had organized the laying of the temple foundations, but the work has been at a standstill for sixteen years. (This episode is narrated in Ezra 3.)

Haggai's message contrasts the fine new houses with the state of the temple. People have proudly panelled the walls of their homes, but have neglected to bring timber for the Lord's house. They have excused themselves by saying it isn't the right time.

Haggai calls them to review their way of life. Times are hard. People don't have enough to eat and drink. Their clothes don't keep them warm. Their money goes nowhere… He explains that all this is happening because they have neglected God's house. Worship and lifestyle go together. It *is* the time to build the temple!

Zerubbabel, Joshua and all the people are inspired by God's word to them through Haggai. The work on the temple begins.

Three months in the light of eternity

Haggai's recorded ministry spans only three months of 520 BC, but his words break a lethargy which has lasted sixteen years. The prophet has a remarkable ministry of challenge and encouragement.

Haggai urges the people building the temple to see its long-term significance. It isn't just for the prestige of the nation, but for the glory of God. It won't matter that the new temple isn't as impressive as Solomon's. The important thing is that God himself will bring splendour to the building, because it is his house (2:6–9).

Words of encouragement, teaching and promise (2:1–23)

God will glorify the new temple

The work has been going on for a month, when God's word comes to Haggai again. This time it is to encourage the builders. They may feel that their effort is poor when compared with the splendid temple of Solomon. But God is with them. The point of the temple is not human fame, but God's glory. God intends to make this house a focus of his glory for all nations. He will fill it with his presence and peace (2:1–9).

A new start

Two months later, Haggai has a particular question for the priests. Does touching something holy make a person holy? Obviously the answer is, 'No.' In the same way, building the temple won't in itself change the people's lives. If they don't mend their ways, they will still be diseased by sin.

Haggai reminds the people of the shortages which prompted them to listen to the Lord, and resulted in the new work on the temple. From this point on, God promises to bless them (2:10–19).

A message for Zerubbabel

On the same day, Haggai has a special word for Zerubbabel (2:20–23). God is going to cause havoc among nations and between peoples. In this upheaval, Zerubbabel will emerge as God's chosen servant and leader.

History doesn't tell us Zerubbabel's fate, but here is God's endorsement of the royal line which will lead on down the centuries – to Jesus Christ.

ZECHARIAH

Zechariah serves us a spicy mixture of visions and prophecies. Some of his messages are flavoured with the work and words of earlier prophets. Some of his images are new – unique and vivid. They will take their place in the prophetic tradition until the end of time. Jesus and the Gospels will draw on his insights, and his visions will become the mighty vistas of the book of Revelation.

We know very little about Zechariah. His name is a common one, meaning 'The Lord Remembers'. He prophesies in Jerusalem at about the same time as Haggai – both of them urging the national leaders to complete the rebuilding of the temple.

OUTLINE

Visions to challenge and encourage (1:1–8:23)
Prophecies of judgment and restoration (9:1–14:21)

Introduction

The setting of Zechariah's prophecies

The Persian emperor, Cyrus the Great, has conquered Babylon. He has passed a decree in the very first year of his reign, allowing all Babylon's captives to return home. He has even encouraged nations to rebuild their temples and restore their gods. No returning group can have been more delighted with their new-found political and religious freedom than the Jews.

Zerubbabel, the living heir of David, has led the return. The foundations of the temple have been laid, but the work has come to a standstill. Perhaps people can already see that the new temple will never compare with the glory of the one built by Solomon. But Zechariah prophesies that God will be the glory of his restored temple.

We know little about Zechariah, but his prophecies are dated around the same time as those of Haggai. He begins in 'the second year of

Darius of Persia' (520 BC) and continues for four years. Like Haggai, he encourages the community of returned exiles as they try to rebuild their ruined lives. He draws on the themes of David's kingship and the divine purpose for Jerusalem (to become the heavenly Zion) from before the days of the exile in Babylon.

Some people think that Zechariah's later prophecies (9:1–14:21) have been developed by other people. They continue his themes but have material which could refer to a later time, personalities or situations.

A book of two parts

Zechariah's book is in two parts. Chapters 1–8 are an account of the 'night visions' he received between 520 and 518 BC. Chapters 9–14 are prophecies of God's judgment and his coming kingdom. Although the book of Zechariah is in two distinct halves, it has always been treated as a whole. Although the style changes, the messages belong together and match each other. All the same, some of the ideas are very jumbled and obscure. It is quite possible that Zechariah didn't understand them all himself. Many of them make better sense once Jesus appears on the scene; and who knows what others will become clear in due course?

DISCOVERING ZECHARIAH

Visions to challenge and encourage

A call to return to the Lord (1:1–6)

Zechariah dates his prophecy in 'the eighth month of the second year of Darius'. Darius I is the Persian emperor who reigned from 522 to 486 BC. In our terms, Zechariah is receiving God's word in October or November 520 BC. His message fits between two of Haggai's prophecies (Haggai 2), both in date and content.

Zechariah and Haggai are prophesying in the same place and at the same time. They also strike the same note of urgency. It is now eighteen years since the Jews returned from their exile in Babylon, and time to press on and complete the rebuilding of the temple.

Zechariah begins by calling the people to return to the Lord. They must learn from the mistakes of the past and not repeat the damaging disobedience of their ancestors.

Eight visions (1:7–6:8)

Zechariah has visions of Zion being restored and the king who is to come. He has eight 'night visions'. The first three are about the renewal of Jerusalem. The next five are about the Messiah. Zechariah is wide awake and able to ask questions. An angel acts as his guide and interpreter.

The first vision: The man among the myrtle trees

Zechariah sees a man on a red horse, standing among myrtle trees in a ravine (1:7–17). Behind him are other horses of various colours. Coloured horses appear again in Revelation 6. Red stands for the blood of war; white is for victory and peace; brown, like churned-up mud, is the colour of unsettled times.

The rider of the horse reports to an angel that they have completed a survey of the world and found everywhere at peace. God is now extending this peace to Jerusalem, giving time and opportunity for the city to be restored and the temple rebuilt.

The temple is completed quickly, over a period of four years. It doesn't compare well with Solomon's temple which it replaces. The walls of Jerusalem will be rebuilt by Nehemiah in 445 BC. Zechariah proclaims an age of prosperity, which will come about in the reigns of the Maccabean princes in 165 BC. The ultimate peace and glory of Zion is still in the future.

The second vision: Four horns and four skilled workers

Zechariah sees four horns and four skilled workers (1:18–21). The four horns are the powers which destroyed Israel, Judah and Jerusalem. They could stand for Assyria, Babylon, Medo-Persia and Greece; or they may symbolize the four directions from which an attack might come. The four skilled workers are God's workers (perhaps temple builders) who will now overcome the forces of ruin with the power of peaceful construction.

The third vision: A man with a measuring line

Zechariah sees an angel tell a young man not to measure Jerusalem for rebuilding (2:1-13). The new city is to be far greater than the old, and God himself will be its protector and its glory. The Lord calls any stragglers to escape from Babylon and come into the safety of Zion. The vision breaks into a song of joy as God declares that he will draw many nations to be his people, and will himself live among them. God through his Messiah is going to make Jerusalem his centre and Judah his holy land.

The fourth vision: Clean garments for the high priest

Zechariah sees Joshua, the high priest (3:1-10) He is standing, grimy and guilty, before God. Satan, whose name means 'accuser', is about to present the case for the prosecution, but God interrupts. God declares that he has rescued Joshua from the fires of judgment and is now restoring him as high priest. He forgives Joshua's sin and commands that he be dressed in clean and splendid robes. God tells Joshua that he and his fellow priests are signs of the Messiah, who is the great priest-king to come. The Messiah is 'the branch' of King David's family tree. He is like a jewel that shines in every direction, with seven eyes which see everywhere. Through his Messiah, God will achieve a perfect cleansing of his people, to bring in an age of human dignity, social harmony and universal peace. The name 'Joshua' is the Hebrew for 'Jesus' and means 'God Rescues'.

The fifth vision: The gold lampstand and the two olive trees

Zechariah is woken up to see a gold lampstand with seven lights on it (4:1-14). The lampstand is a symbol of God's people, holding high his light to the world. There was a lampstand in the tabernacle in the days of Moses, and there were ten lampstands in the temple of Solomon. In the rebuilt temple of Zechariah's day there will be only one.

Zechariah sees that the lampstand is fuelled by oil from two olive trees, one on each side. God is supplying power without the help of either priest or manufacturer. Zechariah is to encourage Zerubbabel to complete the rebuilding of the temple which he began several years ago, and to do so with God's help. The two trees are symbols of Joshua and Zerubbabel, priest and king. They are 'the two who are anointed'. Together they are a sign of the Messiah (the Anointed One) whom God will one day introduce as his supreme priest-king.

The sixth vision: The flying scroll

Zechariah sees God's missile – his powerful word, like a huge flying scroll (5:1-4). This is God's notice, served on every thief and liar. It has power to lodge in the house of an offender and completely destroy it.

The seventh vision: The woman in a basket

Zechariah sees a woman being kept in a large basket (5:5-11). She is wickedness. The prophet watches as she is airlifted off to Babylon. So evil is to be expelled from Israel, and sent where all rebels against God belong. Babylon is called Shinar in Genesis 11. It is where the people so proudly erected the tower of Babel. Wickedness is honoured there, and they will build the woman a house.

The eighth vision: Four chariots

Zechariah sees four chariots emerging from between two bronze mountains (6:1-8). The chariots are drawn by powerful horses – red, black, white and dappled. The angel explains that they are God's horses, going north, west and south. There is no mention of the white horse going east as we might expect. The mission of the chariots is to establish God's peace throughout the world. A particular triumph is that God's Spirit is now satisfied in 'the north country' – the lands of the great invading empires are now brought under God's control.

A crown for Joshua (6:9-15)

Zechariah is told to crown the high priest, Joshua. He is to do this in a private house, in the presence of three witnesses. The witnesses are all returned exiles. Their wealth is to be used to make the crown.

Joshua is to be told that he is the branch – the one who is to branch out, build the temple and be enthroned as a royal priest. Isaiah and Jeremiah have already used 'the branch' as a prophetic code name for the expected Messiah.

Joshua is to be a symbol of the Messiah. His crown is to be entrusted to the witnesses and placed in the temple. So Zechariah understands that the returning exiles have a key role in the unfolding of God's plans. We don't know why it isn't Zerubbabel, the rightful descendant of David, who is to be crowned. Perhaps the emphasis is on God's appointment rather than on human succession.

The 'branch'

Zechariah sees that God is preparing the world for the coming Messiah. One day the Messiah's kingdom will extend to all nations and to the whole of creation. God is preparing Jerusalem and her people to be the focal point of this earthly rule – a kingdom of justice and peace.

The Messiah will emerge from the family tree of David. For this reason, Zechariah calls him the 'branch' (6:12). He will be the perfect combination of priest and king, and will care for God's people as an ideal shepherd. The early Christians found many images of Jesus in Zechariah's words: his birth, ministry, lifestyle, kingship and death are all foreshadowed here. Jesus himself will take up the strange, vivid pictures which Zechariah uses to describe the awesome and awful events at the end of the age.

Motives behind fasting (7:1-14)

The next part of the book of Zechariah is a record of encounters and teaching which take place two years after the night visions. The date is December to January 518 BC.

A deputation comes from Bethel to ask about fasting. They ask if they should still keep the fast of the fifth month, which remembers the destruction of the temple in 586 BC.

The Lord urges Zechariah to probe the motives behind fasting and feasting. Are fasts and feasts held in honour of God, or have they become an occasion for people to show off? Zechariah must think again about the reasons for God's judgment on his people, which led to the destruction of the temple. If people refuse to listen to God, then they must realize that one day he will refuse to listen to them.

God promises peace for Jerusalem (8:1-23)

God promises peace for Jerusalem. The scattered exiles will come to live there in great contentment. Meanwhile, the temple must be rebuilt, and people must start to deal truthfully and fairly with each other. The old fasts are to be turned into joyful feasts. People from other nations will come to Jerusalem to find God, because they have heard he is there. The earthly Jerusalem is being transformed into the heavenly Zion.

In 8:23 Christians have glimpsed the Greeks who came and asked the disciple Philip if they could be introduced to Jesus (John 12:20-21). Zechariah prophesies that one day large numbers of Gentiles will ask the Jews to lead them in God's ways.

Prophecies of judgment and restoration

Destruction of Israel's enemies and the arrival of Zion's king (9:1-17)

God declares that he will overthrow the cities of the Philistines, which have so long been Israel's enemies. Alexander the Great will conquer this area in 332 BC, and the Philistines will disappear from history. In fact they will merge with the Jews, and Palestine will be named after them.

Zechariah proclaims the arrival of Zion's king. He echoes the joy of Zephaniah's prophecy in 630 BC. The true heir of David approaches in peace. Instead of a mighty warhorse, he rides a gentle donkey. God will do away with the weapons of war and establish a worldwide kingdom of peace. Some scholars think this is a description of the great Jewish champion, Judas Maccabeus. Christians follow John's Gospel in seeing here Jesus the Messiah, riding humbly into Jerusalem as its true king (John 12:14-15). The chapter closes with God giving his people victory over all their enemies, making them as safe as his flock and as delightful as his jewels.

Restoration of Judah (10:1-12)

Zechariah turns again to the present plight of the Jews. They are defeated and demoralized – the victims of strong enemies and weak leaders. But God is going to rescue them. He will take over as their leader and transform their morale. He will gather them in from their places of exile – Egypt, Assyria, Gilead and Lebanon. It will be like the exodus from Egypt all over again, as Israel and Judah are reunited and brought triumphantly home.

The rejection of the shepherd (11:1-17)

Zechariah announces a coming judgment. It will sweep in like fire. It will destroy like an axe. He hears the shepherds wailing. They are the corrupt rulers who now see their power and privilege vanishing.

God gives Zechariah a heartbreaking task. He is to care for a flock which is not only doomed to die, but is resentful of his control. He calls his shepherd's staffs Favour and Union – but snaps them to demonstrate God's frustration. Favour (the covenant between God and his people) is broken. Union (the family bond between Israel and Judah) is destroyed. Zechariah is paid thirty pieces of silver for his pains – which he throws down in the temple.

There is a medley of gospel themes here. One day Jesus will come as the good shepherd, challenging all phoney, careless and oppressive leaders. Tragically, he will be rejected by the very people he has come to save. When Judas betrays Jesus to his enemies, he will be paid a familiar sum: thirty pieces of silver.

God tells Zechariah to act out the part of a selfish and lazy shepherd – and to feel God's fury that his people are so exploited and neglected.

Military triumph and spiritual renewal (12:1–14)

After the searing warnings of judgment come further words of hope. God declares that when the nations of the world are finally gathered to attack Jerusalem, he will confuse and break them. He will make Jerusalem impregnable, and her leaders unbeatable. Every citizen will be at least as great as David.

Spiritual renewal will go hand in hand with military triumph. God will give his people a new desire and ability to pray. They will grieve deeply for the hurt they have caused, especially to God or his servant. Zechariah sees them looking at someone they have killed unjustly – an echo of Isaiah's suffering servant, and a prediction of the crucifixion of Jesus. Everyone will be united in mourning: families, clans and individuals; royalty, prophets and priests. We read of the suffering servant in Isaiah 52–53.

Cleansing from sin (13:1–9)

After victory and repentance, God will enable his people to stay pure. Zechariah says they will be given a fountain which will wash away sin. Idols will be abolished and false prophets will be disciplined and reformed. When former prophets are asked about the scars where they once cut themselves, they are to say they are the marks of childhood accidents.

The idea of being hurt by friends leads on to the next prophecy. God's shepherd is to be killed by someone close to him. The flock will be scattered, and two-thirds of it lost. But God will gather the part of the flock that remains, and make it supremely valuable. God and his people will be proud of each other.

God comes and reigns (14:1–21)

Zechariah has more to say about Jerusalem's victory over her enemies. At first the other nations will crush her, halving her population and wrecking her property. But God will arrive to defend his people, and open up a valley for their escape. This is a new exodus – this time through solid rock!

Zechariah describes a new, unique and everlasting day: a mode of existence in which God is king. The light and the climate will be perfect. Jerusalem will be a source of life for the world, as fresh water flows from her to east and west. God will reign over a perfect world – a world in which he is acknowledged as the only God. Jerusalem will be raised high above the surrounding plain, and her people will live in safety.

Zechariah closes by seeing the Feast of Tabernacles as a harvest festival of nations. God's enemies will be left to their fate like rotting crops. Those who gather to God will find themselves at peace with his creation. Every detail of every day, from the bells on the horses to the pots on the hearth, will express the holiness of God.

MALACHI

Malachi stands like a beacon at the end of the Old Testament. He shines for God's truth at a dreary and dispirited time in Israel's history. Although the Jews have returned from exile and the temple has been rebuilt, there is a strong drift away from God.

OUTLINE

God's love for his people (1:1–5)
Israel's indifference to God (1:6–14)
A last warning for the priests (2:1–9)
God cannot bear unfaithfulness (2:10–16)
Judgment will be hot for the wicked! (3:1–5)
Test God by tithing (3:6–12)
The fickle and the faithful (3:13–18)
The Day of the Lord (4:1–6)

Introduction

'My messenger'

'Malachi' means simply 'my messenger'. We don't know for sure if Malachi is the name of the prophet who delivered these messages. We have no other example of Malachi being used as a person's name.

Half-hearted worship

The temple has been rebuilt for some time and the worship has become half-hearted. The priests are setting a bad example by offering second-rate sacrifices. The Jewish men are marrying outside the faith – mixing their pure religion with the more exciting aspects of paganism. There is a rising divorce rate, as first marriages are abandoned. God's people have lost their enthusiasm and their nerve. They are not sure that serving God is worthwhile, as proud, ungodly people seem to get on much better without him. As this was the situation in the 5th century

BC, at about the time of Nehemiah's reforms, we may date Malachi at about 460 BC.

Discovering Malachi

God's love for his people (1:1–5)

Malachi begins by telling people that God loves them. If they doubt it, they have only to look at the fate of Edom. The Edomites are Israel's neighbours to the south. They are the descendants of Esau. The enmity between the two peoples dates back to the rift between Esau and Jacob in the distant past.

The Edomites were obstructive to the children of Israel when they were making their desert journey from Egypt to Canaan. Most recently, the Edomites have taken advantage of Israel's weakness and joined in the looting when Jerusalem and Judah were overthrown. Now Edom has herself been finally defeated, and her towns will never be rebuilt. Israel, on the other hand, has been amazingly restored – brought back from exile in Babylon, and encouraged to occupy her land again and rebuild her temple. This, says Malachi, is the clearest possible proof of God's love.

Israel's indifference to God (1:6–14)

But if God is proving his fatherly love for Israel, Israel isn't showing anything like a child's love for God. The priests are bringing disabled and diseased animals to the altar. They wouldn't dream of offering such gifts to an earthly governor. Some people are promising a good animal and then swapping it for a reject. The prophet says it would be more honouring to God to close the temple altogether. The Lord will look to other nations and other places for pure and wholehearted worship.

A last warning for the priests (2:1–9)

Malachi has a direct warning for the priests. God will embarrass them by withdrawing his support from their work. He will turn their blessings to curses. He will humiliate them by smearing their faces with offal. They must return to God's standard – the standard set by their ancestor Levi.

Levi was the son of Jacob whose descendants were set aside to be a tribe of priests. Levi not only had great reverence for God, but he taught God's truth faithfully, and set an example by his own way of life.

Malachi outlines a high standard for what the priest is to be and do. He is far more than a caretaker for the temple or an expert in sacrifices. He is to be nothing less than God's messenger.

God cannot bear unfaithfulness (2:10–16)

It isn't just the priests who are at fault. The people, too, have betrayed God. Men are rejecting wives of the same race and faith, and marrying pagan women – no doubt hoping to combine the best of the different religions. They still make sacrifices to the Lord and swear their devotion to him. This is an awful confusion of God's standards. God himself is unswervingly faithful to his covenant. He wants his people to live to the same high level of commitment in their marriages, and to raise godly children. He states clearly: 'I hate divorce.' To tear a marriage apart is an act of violence.

Malachi tells people that they have tired the Lord with their special pleading – their arguments by which they turn truth on its head to justify their actions.

'Put me to the test!'

God calls on his people to pay their full tithes, to provide for the work of the temple and the support of the priests. The tithe is an ancient tax, based on the idea that everything comes from God and a tenth is offered back to him.

Now the tithe has become neglected, because people feel they are poor and need the money for themselves. But God challenges them to 'put him to the test' – that is, to take the risk of giving a tenth of income or produce to him (3:10). He promises that he will respond with an overflowing blessing. It is impossible to out-give God!

When Jesus is tempted by Satan, he reminds the devil that we should not put God to the test (Luke 4:12). In saying this he is quoting from the law of Moses (Deuteronomy 6:16). Satan challenges Jesus to test God for reasons of doubt; but God invites his people to test him out of faith.

Judgment will be hot for the wicked! (3:1–5)

Those who long for the Lord to appear in his temple are in for a surprise. He will indeed arrive – suddenly – and they will feel the heat of his holiness. He will be like a furnace, or like a caustic cleanser. He will begin with the priests and make them pure for their holy tasks. Witchcraft and adultery, lying, bullying and injustice will all be purged.

But God will not destroy his people. He never has done and he never will. His way is to cleanse them with the utmost care and at whatever cost to himself.

Test God by tithing (3:6–12)

At present, people are robbing God. They are failing to offer their tithes. A tithe is 10 per cent of a harvest or a wage which is given to God, to provide for the priests and the upkeep of the temple. Through Malachi, God invites people to test him – to bring in their tithes, and to discover that God will deluge them with blessings. In particular, God will protect their crops from disease and give them abundant harvests.

The fickle and the faithful (3:13–18)

But people have lost heart. They can't see God, and they can't see the point of taking him seriously. God's law seems to crush all joy out of life, while the proud and assertive go from strength to strength.

But a group of faithful people get together. They compare notes. They resolve to commit themselves wholeheartedly to God. God records their names and their resolutions on a scroll and swears he will stand by them and prove them to be true.

The Day of the Lord (4:1–6)

Malachi warns that a day is coming, when evil will be destroyed like stubble in a field fire after the harvest has been gathered in. But for those who are faithful to God, there will be the warm sunshine of his deliverance. They will be like calves let out of their cramping stalls to leap in the open pasture in spring. The wicked will be like ash under their feet.

Finally, Israel will do well to remember God's law – the law he gave to Moses. In due course, a prophet like Elijah will come – calling future generations to respect and love each other. If they fail to do this, the land will fall under God's curse.

Many Jews expect Elijah to return before the Messiah himself will appear. Jesus explains that this is fulfilled in John the Baptist, who faithfully announces the kingdom of God and prepares the way for the king (Matthew 11:14). If John is 'Elijah', then who is Jesus?

THE DEUTEROCANONICAL BOOKS

There are fifteen books or parts of books in the Deuterocanonical Books or 'Apocrypha'. They form a separate section in Protestant Bibles (usually between the Old and New Testaments) and take their place among the Old Testament books in Roman Catholic Bibles.

In AD 382, the great scholar Jerome started work on a complete Latin translation of the Bible – the 'Vulgate'. In doing so, he decided to reject the Old Testament books whose original texts were only found in Greek. He described such books as 'apocryphal' (from a Greek word meaning 'hidden things'), although they had never in fact been hidden or secret.

The books of the Apocrypha are also known as the 'Deuterocanonical Books'. They form a 'second division' of sacred texts in the Bible, being written later than the 'canonical' books of the Old Testament and before the books of the New Testament. They give valuable information about politics and religion at a time when the Jews were under extreme pressure to conform to Hellenistic (Greek) culture. These years shaped the nation of Israel into which Jesus was born.

Martin Luther (from about 1520) decided that 'apocryphal' books should be published as a separate section in Protestant Bibles. The Church of England today accepts them for public reading, but does not draw on them in formulating the church's official teaching.

Tobit is a romantic adventure story about faithful Jews living in the 'Diaspora'. When Jewish communities were 'dispersed' around the ancient world (after the Assyrian and Babylonian conquests) they began to think seriously about their distinctive religion, laws and moral values.

Tobit lives in exile in Nineveh – although the historical and geographical 'facts' are for effect rather than information! He becomes blind and sinks into poverty because he kindly buries the corpse of an executed Jew. Thanks to his brave son Tobias (who is helped by the angel Raphael, disguised as Azariah), Tobit eventually recovers both his sight and his fortune.

The Books of the Apocrypha

Tobit
Judith
The Greek Additions to the Book of Esther
The Wisdom of Solomon
Ecclesiasticus (Wisdom of Jesus Son of Sirach)
Baruch
    The Letter of Jeremiah
1 Esdras
2 Esdras
The Additions to the Book of Daniel
    The Prayer of Azariah and the Song of the Three Young Men
    Susanna
    Bel and the Dragon
1 Maccabees
2 Maccabees
3 Maccabees
4 Maccabees
The Prayer of Manasseh
Psalm 151

Tobit's relative, Sarah, is a virtuous and prayerful young woman. She has married seven times, but each husband has been killed by a jealous demon called Asmodeus. Tobias is again the hero as he overcomes the demon and marries Sarah.

Tobit reminds us of the suffering and vindication of Job. Suffering is a test and righteousness will result in prosperity. The Jews are encouraged to trust God and their own best efforts for a good and successful life.

Judith is a beautiful and devout Jewish widow, who delivers her people from invasion by seducing and assassinating an enemy commander. The historical and geographical details are wildly inaccurate, and Judith's behaviour is sensational. She becomes a liar and a murderer in the just cause of defending her people.

The Greek Additions to the Book of Esther seem to have been introduced to make the Hebrew original more 'religious'. After all, the book of Esther in Hebrew, which may date from the 5th century BC, doesn't mention God at all! The later material portrays God as more active – and the Jews as more racist.

The Wisdom of Solomon was probably written by a Greek-speaking Jewish scholar in Alexandria. It is certainly not the work of the wise King Solomon, but a much later work which attempts to relate Greek and Jewish lines of thought. The book shows that the Jews have an attractive and coherent alternative to the learned and secular culture in which they have to live. The great questions of 'wisdom' literature are explored: why do the godless prosper and the righteous suffer; will those who are faithful receive justice; and is there a hope of life after death?

The souls of the righteous are in the hands of God,
and no torment will ever touch them.
In the eyes of the foolish they seemed to have died,
and their departure was thought to be a disaster,
and their going from us to be their destruction;
but they are at peace. (Wisdom of Solomon 3:1–3)

The Maccabean rebellion

From 200 BC onwards, Judah was dominated by the Seleucid empire, whose emperors raided the temple for money and accepted bribes from those Jews who wanted to become high priests. Two such candidates, Jason and his rival Menelaus, set out to turn Jerusalem into a Hellenistic (Greek-style) city-state.

In 167 BC the emperor Antiochus 'Epiphanes' 'tried to compel the Jews to forsake the laws of their ancestors and no longer live by the laws of God, and also to pollute the temple in Jerusalem and call it the temple of Olympian Zeus' (2 Maccabees 6:1–2). The statue of Zeus was the 'desolating sacrilege' which he commanded to be erected on the temple altar (1 Maccabees 1:54).

The rebellion against these attempts to erase the Jewish culture and nationhood was led by Judas, called 'Maccabeus' ('the Hammer'), and his son Jonathan. After several victories in Judah, Judas occupied the temple area, purged it of non-Jewish worship and rededicated it in December of 164 BC. This was the institution of the Jewish festival of Hanukkah.

Ecclesiasticus or the **Wisdom of Jesus Son of Sirach** is the longest portion of 'wisdom' literature in the Bible. It is very like the book of Proverbs and is written by the person named in the title. His grandson translated the work into Greek, and its Latin title Ecclesiasticus may indicate that it was used in churches but not synagogues.

Baruch is a collection of several short pieces, all on the theme of the fall of Jerusalem in 587 BC.

The Letter of Jeremiah (Baruch 6:1–73) denounces the foolishness of idolatry.

1 Esdras is an alternative version of the Hebrew book of Ezra. It includes a short extract from 2 Chronicles at the beginning and from Nehemiah at the end.

2 Esdras is an 'apocalyptic' work featuring supernatural revelations. It is different from the other books of the Apocrypha in that it was written later and includes Christian material.

The Additions to the Book of Daniel include **The Prayer of Azariah and the Song of the Three Young Men**, and the stories of **Susanna** and **Bel and the Dragon** (or snake). They are all additions that appear in the Greek text of the book of Daniel. The Prayer and the Song are liturgical hymns, while the stories are popular tales in which Daniel is the hero.

These writings encourage the Jews to remain faithful to their religion, despite the pressures and attractions of the Greek (Hellenistic) culture which is being imposed upon them by Antiochus IV Epiphanes.

The Books of the Maccabees are all independent of each other. 1 and 2 Maccabees record the Maccabean rebellion, while 3 Maccabees is a historical novel about it, and 4 Maccabees is a discussion of reason, which arises out of the martyrdom of the Maccabean rebels.

The Prayer of Manasseh is a short and beautiful confession. It has been composed by someone to supply the words of the prayer of King Manasseh which is mentioned in 2 Chronicles 33:11–13.

Psalm 151 celebrates the young shepherd David's victory over the Philistine giant Goliath. It is included at the end of the Psalms in the Greek Bible.

INDEX

A

Aaron 68, 69, 86, 94, 103, 104, 129, 133, 136, 137, 138
Abel 34
Abijah 231, 285
Abimelech 46, 189
Abner 212
abomination that causes desolation 547
Abraham 41, 47, 265
Absalom 218
Achan 171
Adam 23, 31, 33, 34, 35, 265
adultery 216, 387, 388, 552
Agur 385, 396
Ahab 223, 237, 239
Ahasuerus 310
Ahaz 249, 294, 295, 423, 424, 425
Ahaziah 239, 290
Ahijah 229, 231, 282, 283
Ai 170, 173
alleluia *see* hallelujah
Amalekites 77, 205, 211
Amaziah 246, 291–292
ambition 334
Amman 562
Ammon 590
Amnon 218
Amon 255, 299
Amos 560
Amos, book of 560
Anathoth 463
Ancient of Days 543

angels 25, 45, 52, 117, 188, 526, 527, 548, 597
anger 551, 574, 581
animals 28, 36, 97, 105, 106, 110, 135, 153, 385, 605
anointing 86, 88, 103, 207, 208, 226, 276, 366, 364, 447, 456, 546, 547, 598
ant 387
Antiochus Epiphanes 537, 538, 544, 612
anti-Semitism 331
apocalyptic 525, 543
Apocrypha 609
Aram 237, 238, 425
Aramaic 313, 545
Ararat 36
Araunah 222, 226
ark 36
ark of the covenant 83, 203, 204, 213, 270, 271
Artaxerxes I 306, 310
Artaxerxes II 306, 310
Asa 231, 232, 285, 286
Asaph 357, 359, 371
Ashdod 166, 325, 435–436, 561, 589
Asherah 150, 186, 188, 257, 286
Ashkelon 184, 561, 589
Ashtoreth 187
Ashurbanipal 461
assurance 38, 132, 340, 366, 408, 431, 475, 480, 501, 544

Assyria and Assyrians 223, 238, 248, 252, 424, 430, 431, 434, 435, 571, 580, 590
Athaliah 245, 290
atonement 96, 97
Atonement, Day of *see* Day of Atonement
Azariah 246, 286

B

Baal 187, 190, 233, 234, 235
Baasha 232
Babel, tower of *see* tower of Babel
Babylon 40, 254, 307, 308, 426, 435, 441, 442, 461, 487, 493, 494, 504, 505, 511, 512, 513, 536, 583, 584
Babylonians 426, 441, 442, 497, 498
Balaam 139, 140
Barak 186, 188
Baruch 464, 490, 493, 494
Bathsheba 216, 369
beasts 543
behemoth 353
believer 371, 525
Belshazzar 541
Ben Hinnom 257, 470
Ben-Hadad 237, 238, 245
Benjamin 52, 193, 194, 267

bereavement 340, 350, 351, 458, 517
Bethel 51, 183, 184, 564
Bethlehem 196, 197, 270, 578
Bezalel 93
Bible 418 *see also* scripture
what is the Bible? 8
Bildad 343, 345–346
blasphemy 121, 238, 381
blessings 130, 152, 160, 163
blood 109, 110
bloodshed 157
boasting 564
Boaz 198, 227
body 31, 64, 107, 108, 129, 130, 343, 414, 417
boldness 273
Book of the Law 256, 321
Booths, Feast of *see* Feast of Booths
Branch 599, 600
bread 120, 121
bread of the Presence 83, 85
broken jar 478
bronze snake 138
burning bush 67
burnt offering 102

C

Cain 34
Caleb 134, 135, 141
calf, golden *see* golden calf
Canaan 134, 144, 165, 165, 166 *see also* Israel; Palestine
Canaanite 48, 111, 125, 183, 184, 189
captivity *see* exile
caring 407, 457
Carmel, Mount 234, 235
child sacrifice 111, 470
children 92, 149, 150, 342 *see also* relationships
choice 235
chosen people 140, 429, 496
Christ *see* Jesus Christ; Messiah
1 & 2 Chronicles, books of 261
circumcision 45, 170
cities of refuge 145, 156, 177
city of David 213, 270
clean 105, 106, 108, 126, 153, 602
cloud 62, 63, 83, 94
comfort 442, 456
commandments 367, 377 *see also* Ten Commandments
commitment 47, 125 *see also* covenant
common 104, 105, 106
Communion *see* Lord's Supper
complacency 565
compromise 150
conscience 34, 57, 351, 367
covenant 43, 45, 82, 146, 161, 173, 498
creation 27, 28, 352
cross 368
cupbearer 316
curses 160, 161, 192, 212, 605
curtain 84, 85
Cush 590
Cyrus 302, 307, 309, 330, 426, 447, 448, 449

D

Dagon 204
Damascus 561
Dan 176, 193, 230, 250, 275, 297
Daniel 536, 540, 544
Daniel, book of 536
Darius 310, 311, 312, 330, 542, 592, 596
darkness 27, 71, 149, 380, 432, 455, 456, 564, 579, 589
David 202, 208, 209, 262, 269, 270, 272, 356, 358, 368, 369, 599
Day of Atonement 108, 119, 142
Day of Pentecost 559
Day of the Lord 519, 525, 556, 557, 564, 569, 589, 607
Dead Sea 42, 55, 140, 144, 176, 532, 538
Dead Sea Scrolls 538
death 386, 387, 390, 414, 571, 572, 574
Deborah 186, 188
debts, cancelling of 154
deceit and deceivers 54, 216, 447, 553, 576
delight 365, 378, 379
Delilah 191
deliverance 358
desert *see* wilderness
despair 349

deuterocanonical books 609
Deutero-Isaiah 426, 443
Deuteronomy, book of 146
devil *see* Satan
devotion 358
Dinah 54
director of music 357
dirt 105
discipline 106, 128, 129, 374, 394
disease and illness 107, 108, 374, 434
disobedience 24, 33, 125, 148, 160, 165, 207, 376, 573
doubt 77, 340, 606
dream 51, 54, 56, 314, 408, 539, 540, 541, 544
drunkenness 438, 439

E

earthquake 236, 566
Ecclesiastes, book of 399
Eden, Garden of
 see Garden of Eden
Edom 55, 138, 522, 562, 568, 569, 570, 605
Egypt 42, 55, 60, 67, 68, 69, 70, 511, 512, 518, 519
Ehud 186, 187
Ekron 184, 561, 589
Elah 232, 233
Eli 203, 473
Elihu 352
Elijah 225, 233, 234, 239, 608
Elim 75

Elimelech 197
Eliphaz 344
Elisha 225, 236, 237, 240, 241, 246
Emmanuel
 see Immanuel
encouragement 163, 234, 425, 594
end-times 549
Endor, witch of
 see witch of Endor
enemies 63, 82, 125, 181, 200, 216, 247, 277, 303, 318, 324, 334, 358, 359, 360, 395, 450, 451
Enoch 35
ephod 104
Ephraim 57, 58, 176, 177, 180, 184, 190, 191, 193, 230, 267, 268, 292, 425, 431, 441, 551
Esau 49, 55, 265
Esther 327, 328, 330
Esther, book of 327
Ethiopia 590
Eucharist *see* Lord's Supper
Euphrates, River 37, 44, 140, 148, 474, 495, 504
Eve 23, 31, 34
evil 584
exile 301, 360, 426, 427, 460, 481, 486, 487, 504
exile, return from 303, 304, 305, 307, 314
exodus 61, 73, 446, 451
Exodus, book of 60
Ezekiel 504, 505, 530
Ezekiel, book of 504
Ezra 261, 303, 313, 314, 321
Ezra, book of 303

F

failure 82, 216, 263, 438
fair trial 155
faith 43, 185, 585, 586
faithfulness 47, 48, 498
fall, the 32
false prophets 500, 577
fasting 215, 334, 454, 600
Feast of Booths 321
Feast of Harvest 81
Feast of Ingathering 81
Feast of Tabernacles 120, 142, 309
Feast of Trumpets 119, 142
Feast of Unleavened Bread 81, 117
Feast of Weeks 81, 118
feasts 119, 154, 541
fellowship 99, 350, 370
fellowship meal 44, 99, 103
fellowship offering 103
female 29
Festival of Hanukkah 611
fiery furnace 540
figs 481
first-born 51, 58, 72, 157, 322, 391
firstfruits 118, 159, 386
fish and fishing 571, 572
flood 36, 37
food 105
fool and folly 382, 388, 395, 405, 413
forgiveness 215, 358, 369, 374, 501
freedom 378

freeing slaves 154
friends and friendship
   394, 395
futility 405

G
Gad 266
Galilee 248, 571
Garden of Eden 23, 451
Gaza 561, 589
Gedaliah 259
Gehazi 242
Gehenna 470
Genesis, book of 21
gentleness 444, 576, 601
Geshem 319
Gibeonites 174, 220
Gideon 186, 188
gifts, spiritual
   see spiritual gifts
Gihon spring 255
Gilead 248
Gilgal 169, 170, 564
giving 79, 392, 606
glory 91, 94, 366, 367,
   372, 506, 526
God *see also* Holy
   Spirit; Jesus Christ
   Creator 472
   faithfulness of 273,
      274, 375, 452
   glory of 91, 438, 455,
      456, 523, 586, 594
   grace and mercy of
      21, 24, 127, 370, 374,
      453, 574 *see also* God,
      love of
   greatness of 357, 358
   holiness of 67, 95,
      226, 314, 315, 430, 432,
      440, 516
   Lord 31, 45, 69, 70,
      71, 72, 73, 78, 79, 82,

83, 112, 130, 150, 162,
174, 221, 281, 291, 292,
352, 358, 367, 368, 369,
374, 375, 430, 447, 456,
465, 481, 525, 534, 535,
551, 556, 589, 592, 596,
597, 607
   love of 31, 105, 151,
      160, 369, 374–375, 417,
      418, 572, 605
   mercy of *see* God,
      grace and mercy of;
      God, love of
   name of 68
   power of 22, 93, 170,
      185, 333, 524, 573, 581
   throne of 109, 506,
      533
   will of 162, 164, 167,
      171, 172, 366–367, 434
Gog 524
golden calf 62
Goliath 208
Gomer 551, 552
Gomorrah 45
goodness 116, 322, 342,
   369, 374, 375
government 205, 210,
   213, 277, 285, 288, 382,
   395, 434, 456, 570
grace 374
grain offering 102
Greeks 330, 366, 431,
   536, 537, 545
grief 497, 500
guidance 104, 152, 194,
   212, 308, 359, 379
guilt offering 103

H
Habakkuk 583, 584
Habakkuk, book of 583
Hagar 45

Haggai 306, 593
Haggai, book of 592
hallelujah 360, 381
Ham 39
Haman 327, 328, 332,
   333
Hannah 203
Haran 52
Harvest, Feast of
   see Feast of Harvest
Hazael 237, 243
Hazor 175
heaven 52, 239, 240,
   241, 342, 366, 367, 374,
   543
Hebrew 61, 68, 69, 150,
   217, 313, 340, 377, 403,
   581 *see also* Jews
Hebron 47, 177, 212
hell 257, 299, 478
Hezekiah 252, 254, 295,
   394, 423, 426
Hezekiah's Tunnel 255
high priest 104 *see also*
   Jesus Christ, high
   priest
Hiram 226
holiness 67, 96, 103,
   104, 105, 106
Holy Communion
   see Lord's Supper
Holy One of Israel 427
Holy Place 85
Holy Spirit 118, 506,
   558
holy war 143, 169
hope 349, 429, 431, 442,
   496, 552, 587, 602
Hophni 203
Horeb, Mount 235
Hosea 550, 551
Hosea, book of 550
Hoshea 250, 551

humanity 25, 29, 31, 32, 33, 35, 358, 366, 370
Huram 227

I
idols 79, 461
illness *see* disease and illness
image of God 29, 38
Immanuel 425, 431, 432
immorality 562
imprisonments 490
in Christ 33
incarnation *see* Jesus Christ
incense 84, 87, 88, 136, 248, 440
indifference 605
Ingathering, Feast of *see* Feast of Ingathering
injustice 195, 247, 329, 407, 430, 453, 455, 456, 501, 562, 575, 607
integrity 337, 347, 351, 410
intermarriage 315, 322, 326
Isaac 45, 46, 265
Isaiah 248, 253, 254, 423, 424, 425, 443
Isaiah, book of 423
Ishmael 49, 265
Israel 50, 61, 62, 148, 223, 284, 424, 441, 442, 487, 550, 551, 560, 562, 563, 573, 575 *see also* Canaan; Palestine
fall of 249
in Old Testament times 178
Issachar 267, 297

J
Jacob 49, 50, 58, 265
Jair 190
Jakin 227, 279
Japheth 38, 39
jealousy 34, 334, 358, 359, 394
Jehoahaz 258, 301, 460, 462, 479
Jehoash 246
Jehoiachin 258, 301, 460, 462, 495
Jehoiakim 301, 460, 462, 480, 488, 489
Jehoram 243, 289
Jehoshaphat 239, 287
Jehovah *see* God, Lord
Jehu 237, 244
Jephthah 186, 190
Jeremiah 460, 466
Jeremiah, book of 460
Jericho 169
Jeroboam I 229, 230
Jeroboam II 246
Jerusalem 213, 214, 307, 308, 309, 310, 323, 360, 424, 439, 450, 459, 496, 497, 499, 508, 514, 516, 578, 588, 589, 590, 592, 600, 601, 612
fall of 258, 301, 493, 495
siege of 259
walls of 316, 317, 319, 323
Jesus Christ *see also* Messiah
bridegroom 420
death of 574
high priest 64, 96, 109, 110, 364, 531
king 361, 364, 366, 600, 601
Lamb of God 117
priest 599
resurrection of 572
servant 445, 451, 452
Son of God 364
Jethro 78
Jews 335 *see also* Hebrew
Jezebel 233, 234, 238, 244
Joab 213, 216
Joash 245, 290, 291
Job 338, 342
Job, book of 337
Job's friends 338, 343
Joel 556, 557
Joel, book of 556
John the Baptist 608
Jonah 571, 573, 574 *see also* sign of Jonah
Jonah, book of 571
Jonathan 209, 211, 212
Joppa 226, 278, 309
Joram 243
Jordan, River 169
Joseph, son of Jacob 56, 58, 59, 180, 544
Joshua 77, 133, 134, 142, 162, 165, 185
Joshua, book of 165
Joshua, high priest 593, 599, 600
Josiah 256, 299–300, 460, 461–462, 587
Jotham 249, 294
joy 214, 357, 359, 412, 591
Jubilee 122, 123, 124
Judah 212, 223, 243, 244, 251, 252, 256, 257, 264, 266, 283, 423, 424, 427, 438, 441, 460, 461,

Judah (*cont.*)
487, 560, 561, 575, 576, 584, 587, 601
fall of 257
judges 154, 185, 186, 187, 188, 189, 190, 200
Judges, book of 181
judgment 162, 433, 435, 437, 458, 480, 482, 514, 557, 563, 588, 589, 601, 602, 607
Judgment Day 590
justice 157, 455, 456, 562, 564
justification 43

K
Kadesh, Kadesh Barnea 73, 134, 137, 144, 163
Kerith 234
Kidron Valley 219, 222, 296, 317, 558
kindness 158, 198, 295, 351, 395
kingdom, division of 229
1 & 2 Kings, books of 223
kinsman-redeemer 198, 349
Kiriath Jearim 204, 270
knowledge 360, 372, 381
Korahites 358

L
Laban 51
Lamentations, book of 496
lampstand 84
last days 577 *see also* end-times

Last Supper 118
last things *see* end-times
law 78, 79, 80, 81, 149, 158, 159, 162, 164, 320, 321, 322, 358, 360, 361, 365, 367, 368, 374, 376, 377, 378, 606, 607, 608
laziness 387
leaders and leadership 210, 211, 577
Leah 52, 111, 160, 173
leaven 117, 118
Lebanon 226, 278, 309, 385, 428, 442, 519
legalism 117
Lemuel 385, 397
leprosy 107, 108, 242
Levi 52, 54, 152, 177, 267, 534, 535, 605, 606
Leviathan 353
Levites 123, 129, 131, 137, 144, 177, 193, 194, 273, 308, 323, 527
Leviticus, book of 95
lies 32, 46, 80, 238, 484
life 382, 400, 404, 408
lions 191, 221, 506, 542, 561
locusts 70, 71, 556, 557, 565
longing 358, 359, 363
Lord's Supper 102
Lot 41, 42
love 105, 358, 417, 420, 498, 552, 553, 572, 605

M
Maccabean rebellion 612
Maccabees 536, 537 *see also* deuterocanonical books

Malachi 604
Malachi, book of 604
male 29
man 31
Manasseh 58, 143, 145, 176, 177, 184, 255, 266, 267, 268, 298, 299, 461 *see also* deuterocanonical books
manna 76, 132
maps
   Israel in Old Testament times 178
Marah 75
marriage 158, 387, 398, 417, 418, 422, 551
maturity 413
meaninglessness 399, 404, 409
Megiddo 249
Melchizedek 42
Menahem 248
mercy 370, 374, 496, 557, 574
Mesopotamia 37, 41, 167, 179, 448
messenger 234, 291, 451, 507, 541, 604
Messiah 364, 487, 578, 598, 599, 600 *see also* Jesus Christ
Methuselah 35
Micah 575
Micah, book of 575
Micaiah 238, 287
Michal 209, 214
Midianite 188
ministry *see* service
miracles 237, 240
Miriam 74, 133
Mizpah 53, 194, 204, 492

Moab 132, 140, 197, 562, 590
money 392, 408
Mordecai 327, 328, 331, 333
Moriah, Mount 47, 279
Moses 26, 66, 67, 74, 89, 127, 128, 132, 143, 144, 146, 148, 149, 162, 163, 168
Most Holy Place 64, 85, 108
murder 35, 66, 216
music 271, 280, 323, 324, 357, 362, 372, 405, 429, 503, 563

N
Naaman 242
Naboth's vineyard 238
Nadab 232
Nahum 580, 581
Nahum, book of 580
Naomi 196, 197
Naphtali 267
Nathan 214, 216
Nazirite 130, 191, 529
Nebuchadnezzar 258, 259, 460, 490, 491, 493, 539, 540
Nehemiah 304, 305, 316, 323, 324
Nehemiah, book of 303, 316
new covenant 44, 487
new creation 427, 440, 453, 458
New Jerusalem 40, 375, 535
Nile, River 66, 68, 70, 71, 152, 330, 493, 519, 581
Nineveh 571, 574, 580, 581, 582, 590
Noah 35, 36
numbers 548
Numbers, book of 127

O
Obadiah 568, 569
Obadiah, book of 568
Obed 199
obedience 125, 152, 160, 167
offerings 100, 101, 131, 446, 458, 459, 470, 471, 534
oil 86, 87, 88, 103, 104, 120, 208, 234, 241, 313
Old Testament 11
Omri 233
opportunities 387, 406, 478
Othniel 186

P
paganism 37, 81, 90, 97, 110, 111, 140, 147, 150, 185, 209, 223, 252, 256, 461, 463, 511, 512, 551, 582, 587, 588
pain 350, 368, 445
Palestine 39, 41, 42, 176, 189, 313, 387, 583, 601 *see also* Canaan; Israel
Passover 64, 71, 72, 73, 117, 131, 312, 360
Passover lamb 64, 117, 312
pastoral care 369
patience 67, 410
patriarchs 41, 212
Paul 118
peace 31, 359, 392, 453
pearls 393
Pekah 248, 551
Pekahiah 248
Pentecost, Day of *see* Day of Pentecost
perfect 23, 115, 367, 525
perfume 403
persecution 537
Persia 443, 592
Persian empire 329
  kings of 310
Pharaoh 42, 62, 69
Philistia 205, 489, 494, 517
Philistines 190, 203, 204, 205
Phinehas 203
plagues 70
pleasure 31, 34, 137, 339, 341, 399, 404, 405, 409, 417
plot 332, 365, 473, 483, 501, 509, 538
poetry 212, 253, 338, 356, 357, 417, 418, 445, 496, 497, 498, 500, 501, 502, 503, 556, 581, 586
Pool of Siloam 120, 317
poor 81, 101, 112, 119, 123, 124, 154, 159, 160, 247, 319, 392, 407, 408, 409, 427, 433, 444, 469, 479, 480, 561, 575 *see also* poverty
Potiphar 56
potter and pottery 477, 478
poverty 123, 154, 161, 304, 319, 350, 388, 408, 500, 592 *see also* poor

power 408, 586
praise 356, 357, 359, 360, 368, 372, 374, 375, 573
prayer 215, 334, 500, 546
prejudice 572, 573
pride 24, 38, 209, 249, 268, 298, 383, 410, 435, 474, 518, 541, 564
priests and priesthood 85, 86, 103, 114, 360, 605
priorities 394
Promised Land 47, 48, 146, 148, 159, 168
property 123
prophecy and prophets 133, 156, 208, 244, 274, 304, 305, 309, 423, 434, 435, 460, 461, 474, 475, 481, 504, 535, 550, 556, 560, 566, 571, 575, 581, 583, 587, 592, 595, 604
prostitutes 168, 388, 390, 394, 439, 551, 582
protection 81, 97, 243, 314, 342, 358, 360, 378, 380, 435, 438
Proverbs 382, 383, 386, 393, 394
Proverbs, book of 382
psalms 355, 356, 361, 362, 364, 365
Psalms, book of 355
punishment 23, 37, 102, 113, 114, 124, 159, 295, 338, 354, 406, 452, 471, 477, 478, 496, 562
Purim 329, 332, 335
purity 105, 114, 153, 304, 383

Q
quail 76
queen of Sheba 228
questions 584

R
Rachel 52, 55, 160, 173
Rahab 168
rainbow 38
Rebekah 48
rebellion 33, 134, 136
Recabites 488
reconciliation 552
Red Sea 73
redeemer 346, 349
Rehoboam 229, 230, 283
rejection 291, 445, 452, 463, 547, 601
relationships 55, 406
reliance 358
religion 424, 563
remnant 433, 437, 458
renewal 161, 173, 179, 245, 256, 300, 311, 452, 521, 523, 524, 525, 556, 602
repentance 215, 217, 321, 359, 370, 574
rescue 358, 359, 360
resettlement 323
responsibility 30, 34, 147, 480, 520
rest 29, 30, 79, 81, 116, 117, 149, 325, 373, 458, 477
restoration 359, 503, 552, 566
resurrection 572
Reuben 136, 143, 266
revival 358, 523

rich and riches 372, 392, 408
righteousness 359, 453, 564, 565, 586
river of life 532
Ruth 197
Ruth, book of 196

S
sabbath 30, 79, 116, 135, 322, 325
sabbath year 122, 302
sacrifice 96, 97, 100, 101, 115, 564
salt 46, 88, 102, 313, 533
salvation 373, 378
Samaritans 251, 310, 311
Samson 186, 191
Samuel 201, 202, 203, 204, 207
1 & 2 Samuel, books of 200
Sanballat 317, 318, 319, 320
Sarah 41, 47
Satan 32, 339, 340, 341
Saul *see* Paul
Saul, king 201, 206, 207, 210, 211, 212, 263, 267, 269
science 28, 349
scoundrel 388
scripture 357, 418
  see also Bible
self-control 80, 392
Sennacherib 252
Septuagint 39, 201, 262, 494
servant 443, 444, 445, 450, 451, 452

service 105
sex 111, 112, 158, 416
Shadrach, Meshach and Abednego 539
Shallum 248
Shalmaneser 245, 250
Shamgar 187
Sheba 220
Shechem 173, 179
Shem 39
Shema 150
shepherd 369, 480, 521, 522, 601
Shiloh 203
sickness *see* disease and illness
Sidon 309, 518
sign of Jonah 573
Simeon, son of Jacob 54, 57, 266
sin 33, 119, 476
sin offering 101
Sinai Desert 132
Sinai, Mount 61, 78
sluggard 387, 395
snake, bronze *see* bronze snake
social injustice 522, 562
Sodom 45–46
Solomon 202, 217, 225, 226, 227, 228, 262, 263, 275–276, 385, 417
Solomon's temple 278, 279
son of man 543
Song of Solomon 417
Song of Songs, book of 416
sons of Korah 357
Spirit *see* Holy Spirit
spiritual gifts 93
statutes 378

strength 113, 143, 146, 149, 150, 165, 182, 185, 191, 292, 363, 438, 579
submission 216, 345, 353, 367
suffering 338, 353
suffering servant 445, 452
Susa 330, 331
synagogue 357, 546
Syria 237, 242, 424

T
tabernacle 62, 63, 84, 92, 93, 129, 131
Tabernacles, Feast of *see* Feast of Tabernacles
table 83
Tamar 218
tax 313, 606
Teacher 400, 401, 403, 404
teaching 400, 401, 403, 404
temple 214, 226, 227, 245, 259, 272, 278, 279, 280, 307, 312, 360, 470, 496, 497, 525, 526, 527, 531, 532, 593, 594, 604, 611
temptation 150, 167, 272, 388, 417
Ten Commandments 78, 149, 215
tent of meeting 91, 108–109, 120, 131, 134
Thebes 582
Tiglath-Pileser II 249
Tiglath-Pileser III 248, 551
Tigris, River 37
time 402, 406

timeline 16
tithe 126, 137, 154, 323, 607
Tobiah 305, 317, 324–325
Tola 190
tomb 49, 452, 573
tongue 69, 381, 392
Topheth 257, 470
Torah 75
tower of Babel 40, 41
Trans-Euphrates 310, 311
Trans-Jordan 143, 248
treasure *see* rich and riches
tribes of Israel 268
Trinity 30 *see also* God; Holy Spirit; Jesus Christ
trumpets 78, 116, 119, 132, 171, 189, 280, 381, 557
Trumpets, Feast of *see* Feast of Trumpets
trust 21, 32, 43, 63, 148, 202, 368, 386, 399, 477
truth 100, 117, 253, 365, 382, 453, 455, 604
Tyre 309, 518, 519, 561

U
unbelief and unbelievers 117, 371
unclean 103, 105, 106, 107, 126, 153
unfaithfulness 552, 553, 606
universe 22, 23, 27, 28, 341, 371, 381, 472
Unleavened Bread, Feast of *see* Feast of Unleavened Bread

Upper Pool 254, 255
Uriah 216
Urim and Thummim 104
Uzziah 247, 248, 292, 293, 425, 430

V
vine 511, 513, 574
visions 430, 469, 506, 531, 543, 545, 548, 565, 580, 596, 597
vows 36, 48, 79, 101, 125, 126, 130, 143, 408, 529

W
war 157
watchfulness 467
watchman 507, 520, 584
water 36, 77, 204, 227, 234, 255, 363, 375, 376, 377, 432, 446, 532, 585
weakness 62, 70, 216
wealth *see* rich and riches
wedding *see also* marriage

weeds 474
Weeks, Feast of *see* Feast of Weeks
wilderness 73, 97, 116, 120, 127, 142, 148, 170, 227, 271, 429, 446, 451
will of God *see* God, will of
wisdom 185, 349, 382, 384, 390–391, 395, 401, 405, 409, 410
witch of Endor 210
witnesses 65, 155, 156, 162, 228, 367, 526, 540, 599
wives 386 *see also* relationships
woman 31, 32
words 356, 372, 376, 377, 385, 386, 392
worry 408, 414
worship 79, 357, 359, 372, 407, 562, 563, 604

X
Xerxes 310, 327, 328, 330, 334

Y
Yahweh *see* God, Lord
Year of Jubilee 122
yeast 117
yoke 465, 483

Z
Zadok 271
Zadokites 528
Zarephath 234
Zechariah, book of 595
Zechariah, king 248
Zechariah, prophet 306, 595, 599
Zedekiah, king 258–259, 301, 461, 464, 465, 479, 488
Zedekiah, prophet 287
Zephaniah 587, 588, 601
Zephaniah, book of 587
Zerubbabel 303, 304, 308, 593, 594, 595, 598
Zimri 232
Zion 227, 428, 455, 512, 559, 578, 600
Zophar 343, 347

www.ingramcontent.com/pod-product-compliance
Lightning Source LLC
Chambersburg PA
CBHW050522300426
44113CB00012B/1926